Cooking Around the World All-in-One For Dummies®

Common Abbreviations

Abbreviation(s)	What It Stands For
C, c	cup
g	gram
kg	kilogram
L, l	liter
lb	pound
mL, ml	milliliter
oz	ounce
pt	pint
t, tsp	teaspoon
T, TB, Tbl, Tbsp	tablespoon

The recipes in this cookbook were not developed or tested using metric measures. There may be some variation in quality when converting to metric units.

Volume

U.S Units	Canadian Metric	Australian Metric
¼ teaspoon	1 mL	1 ml
½ teaspoon	2 mL	2 ml
1 teaspoon	5 mL	5 ml
1 tablespoon	15 mL	20 ml
¼ cup	50 mL	60 ml
⅓ cup	75 mL	80 ml
½ cup	125 mL	125 ml
⅔ cup	150 mL	170 ml
¾ cup	175 mL	190 ml
1 cup	250 mL	250 ml
1 quart	1 liter	1 liter
1½ quarts	1.5 liters	1.5 liters
2 quarts	2 liters	2 liters
2½ quarts	2.5 liters	2.5 liters
3 quarts	3 liters	3 liters
4 quarts	4 liters	4 liters

For Dummies: Bestselling Book Series for Beginners

Cooking Around the World All-in-One For Dummies®

Weight

U.S Units	Canadian Metric	Australian Metric
1 ounce	30 grams	30 grams
2 ounces	55 grams	60 grams
3 ounces	85 grams	90 grams
4 ounces (¼ pound)	115 grams	125 grams
8 ounces (½ pound)	225 grams	225 grams
16 ounces (1 pound)	455 grams	500 grams
1 pound	455 grams	½ kilogram

Measurements

Inches	Centimeters
½	1.5
1	2.5
2	5.0
3	7.5
4	10.0
5	12.5
6	15.0
7	17.5
8	20.5
9	23.0
10	25.5
11	28.0
12	30.5
13	33.0

Temperature (Degrees)

Fahrenheit	Celsius
32	0
212	100
250	120
275	140
300	150
325	160
350	180
375	190
400	200
425	220
450	230
475	240
500	260

Copyright © 2003 Wiley Publishing, Inc.
All rights reserved.

Item 5502-2.

For more information about Wiley Publishing,
call 1-800-762-2974.

For Dummies: Bestselling Book Series for Beginners

Cooking Around the World

the World
ALL-IN-ONE

FOR

DUMMIES®

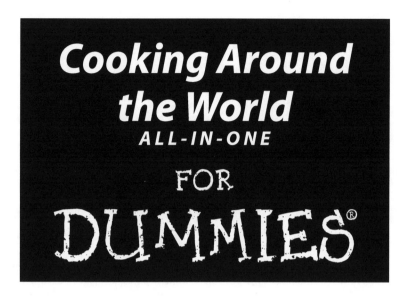

Cooking Around the World
ALL-IN-ONE
FOR DUMMIES®

by Jack Bishop, Cesare Casella, Heather Dismore,
Kristin Eddy, Susan Feniger, Tom Lacalamita,
Mary Sue Milliken, Joan H. Moravek, Helene Siegel,
Dede Wilson, and Martin Yan

WILEY

Wiley Publishing, Inc.

Cooking Around the World All-in-One For Dummies®

Published by
Wiley Publishing, Inc.
111 River Street
Hoboken, NJ 07030
www.wiley.com

Copyright © 2003 by Wiley Publishing, Inc., Indianapolis, Indiana

Published by Wiley Publishing, Inc., Indianapolis, Indiana

Published simultaneously in Canada

For general information on our other products and services or to obtain technical support, please contact our Customer Care Department within the U.S. at 800-762-2974, outside the U.S. at 317-572-3993, or fax 317-572-4002.

Wiley also publishes its books in a variety of electronic formats. Some content that appears in print may not be available in electronic books.

Library of Congress Cataloging-in-Publication Data:

ISBN: 0-7645-5502-2

10 9 8 7 6 5 4
1B/SR/QS/QT/IN

About the Authors

Mexican Cooking

Mary Sue Milliken and **Susan Feniger** may be "two gringas from the Midwest," but they fell deeply in love with Mexican food when first introduced to it more than 20 years ago. The two chefs became friends in the late '70s while working in the otherwise all-male kitchen of a prestigious French restaurant in Chicago called Le Perroquet. After honing their skills in fine restaurants in France and America, they opened their first restaurant, the highly celebrated City Café, in Los Angeles in 1981. These days, they divide their time between their three restaurants, Border Grills in Santa Monica and Las Vegas, and the upscale Ciudad in downtown Los Angeles. They also have authored five previous cookbooks, including *Mexican Cooking For Dummies,* host the popular Television Food Network series, *Too Hot Tamales,* and are heard regularly on Southern California radio.

Helene Siegel is the co-author with Mary Sue and Susan of *City Cuisine, Mesa Mexicana, Cooking with the Too Hot Tamales,* and *Mexican Cooking For Dummies.* She also is the author of *The Ethnic Kitchen* series and 32 single-subject cookbooks in the best-selling *Totally Cookbook* series. Her articles have appeared in the *Los Angeles Times,* the *Times Syndicate, Fine Cooking,* and on the Web at cuisinenet.com.

Italian Cooking

Cesare Casella was born in a small town outside Lucca, Italy. He grew up in and around his family's restaurant, called Il Vipore. As a young chef, he transformed Il Vipore into a world-class establishment, earning a well-deserved Michelin star. Since 1993, Casella has been working as a chef at several leading Italian restaurants in New York. He is the coauthor of *Diary of a Tuscan Chef* and *Italian Cooking For Dummies.*

Jack Bishop is the author or coauthor of several books on Italian food, including *The Complete Italian Vegetarian Cookbook, Pasta e Verdura, Lasagna,* and *Italian Cooking For Dummies.* He is the senior writer for *Cook's Illustrated* and writes for various national magazines and newspapers. He has studied cooking in Italy.

French Cooking and Greek and Middle Eastern Cooking

Tom Lacalamita (Long Island, New York) is a best-selling author of five appliance-related cookbooks. Nominated for a James Beard cookbook award, Tom is considered a national authority on housewares and has appeared on hundreds of television and radio shows across the country. With a passion for food, cooking, and all sorts of kitchen gadgets, Tom is a spokesperson for various food and housewares manufacturers. He is the author of *Slow Cookers For Dummies* and *Pressure Cookers For Dummies.*

Indian Cooking

Heather Dismore began her career as a well-traveled, highly productive restaurant manager. She left the industry to devote time to her family and her love of writing. In a publishing career spanning over a decade, her work has impacted some 400 titles. Dismore resides in Naperville, Illinois, with her husband, who is a professional chef, and their two daughters. She is the owner of PageOne Publishing, a freelance Web content development company with a focus on the hospitality industry.

Chinese Cooking

Martin Yan, celebrated host of more than 1,500 cooking shows, highly respected food and restaurant consultant, and certified master chef, enjoys distinction as both teacher and author. His many talents are showcased in over two dozen best-selling cookbooks, including *Martin Yan's Feast: The Best of Yan Can Cook, Martin Yan's Invitation to Chinese Cooking,* and *Chinese Cooking For Dummies.* Yan is the founder of the Yan Can International Cooking School in the San Francisco Bay Area. *Yan Can Cook* has received national and international recognition, including a 1998 Daytime Emmy Award, a 1996 James Beard Award for Best TV Food Journalism, and a 1994 James Beard Award for Best TV Cooking Show.

Japanese Cooking

Dede Wilson, CCP (Certified Culinary Professional), is a self-taught chef who loves making appetizers and organizing parties. She has worked professionally for more than 17 years as a restaurant chef, bakery owner, caterer, recipe developer, radio talk-show host, and frequent television guest. Dede is also a frequent contributor to *Bon Appétit* magazine and a contributing editor to *Pastry Art and Design* magazine and is the food and entertainment expert for CanDoWoman.com. Dede has written three other cookbooks, including *The Wedding Cake Book* (Wiley, 1997), which was nominated for an IACP Julia Child Cookbook Award. She also authored *Christmas Cooking For Dummies* and *Appetizers For Dummies.*

Thai Cooking

Joan H. Moravek left the Securities Industry in 1990 and decided to pursue a career in the food service industry. The last 12 years have led her to explore some of the many facets of the culinary profession. A lifelong resident of Chicago, Joan has traveled extensively and continues to educate herself by researching, cooking, and "eating her way" through the cuisines of many countries.

Kristin Eddy is the Food Writer for the *Chicago Tribune* and also covers Travel and Health stories for the paper. During 17 years as an award-winning writer, Eddy has worked for the *Washington Post, Atlanta Journal-Constitution* and the *Cleveland Plain Dealer,* covering everything from news and health stories to restaurant reviews and the 1996 Olympic Games. As the daughter of a diplomat, Eddy was born in Beirut, Lebanon, and lived in Aleppo and Damascus, Syria; Istanbul, London, and Paris. She has traveled widely on assignment for the *Tribune,* reporting food stories from around the U.S. as well as Istanbul, Thailand, Vietnam, Indonesia, India, and Jamaica. Eddy has had 14 years of experience in writing about food, developing, testing, and editing recipes for various newspapers.

Publisher's Acknowledgments

We're proud of this book; please send us your comments through our Dummies online registration form located at www.dummies.com/register/.

Some of the people who helped bring this book to market include the following:

Acquisitions, Editorial, and Media Development

Compilation Editor: Elizabeth Netedu Kuball

Senior Project Editor: Tim Gallan

Acquisitions Editor: Pam Mourouzis

Copy Editor: Tina Sims

Acquisitions Coordinator: Holly Grimes

Recipe Testers: Keith and Kate Brown, Heather Dismore, Emily Nolan, Mike Tully

Editorial Manager: Christine Meloy Beck

Editorial Assistants: Melissa Bennett, Elizabeth Rea

Illustrator: Liz Kurtzman

Cartoons: Rich Tennant, www.the5thwave.com

Production

Project Coordinator: Erin Smith

Layout and Graphics: Carrie Foster, Kristin McMullan, Barry Offringa, Jacque Schneider, Julie Trippetti, Scott Tullis, Erin Zeltner

Proofreaders: Andy Hollandbeck, Susan Moritz, Angel Perez, Linda Quigley, Dwight Ramsey, Charles Spencer

Indexer: Sherry Massey

Special Help: Jennifer Bingham, Greg Pearson, Laura Peterson, Chad Sievers

---

Publishing and Editorial for Consumer Dummies

    Diane Graves Steele, Vice President and Publisher, Consumer Dummies

    Joyce Pepple, Acquisitions Director, Consumer Dummies

    Kristin A. Cocks, Product Development Director, Consumer Dummies

    Michael Spring, Vice President and Publisher, Travel

    Brice Gosnell, Publishing Director, Travel

    Suzanne Jannetta, Editorial Director, Travel

Publishing for Technology Dummies

    Andy Cummings, Vice President and Publisher, Dummies Technology/General User

Composition Services

    Gerry Fahey, Vice President of Production Services

    Debbie Stailey, Director of Composition Services

Contents at a Glance

Table of Contents

Recipes at a Glance

Book II: Italian Cooking

Book III: French Cooking

Book IV: Greek and Middle Eastern Cooking

Book VI: Chinese Cooking

Book VII: Japanese Cooking

Introduction

Climb aboard for a tour of some of the most fascinating, tantalizing, and beloved cuisines on earth. And don't worry if you don't have anything packed because the only bags you'll need are the ones you find at the grocery store. Just rustle up some down-to-earth ingredients, basic pieces of equipment, and an adventuresome spirit, and you're ready to go.

This book includes eight smaller books about eight of the world's best-loved cuisines: Mexican, Italian, French, Greek and Middle Eastern, Indian, Chinese, Japanese, and Thai. For each cuisine, you'll find information about the way of eating in that region, common ingredients and techniques, and special tools and how to use them. You'll also find an array of mouthwatering recipes, from soups to entrees to desserts, that enable you to make your favorite restaurant dishes at home and maybe even try a few new things.

About This Book

Lots of cookbooks on the market cover one specific cuisine, be it Japanese or Portuguese or Russian. But we figure that not all cooks want to get that in-depth about one particular type of food. This book gives you the best-loved recipes from many different regions — those that you are likely to be familiar with from dining out in restaurants, but may not know much about preparing at home.

Conventions Used in This Book

You've probably heard this advice a million times, but trust us: Read the recipes all the way through before you get started, and pay attention to the stuff in the notes at the beginning and end of the recipes. You'll know whether you need any special equipment, how much time to allow, and whether you need another recipe from a different part of the book to complete the dish.

To keep the ingredient lists in this book concise, we follow certain conventions (exceptions are noted in the recipes):

- Milk is whole.
- Butter is unsalted.
- Salt is coarse kosher salt.

✔ Pepper is freshly ground black pepper.

✔ Eggs are large.

✔ Flour is all-purpose.

✔ Olive oil is extra-virgin.

✔ Herbs are fresh.

✔ Citrus juices are freshly squeezed.

Foolish Assumptions

We certainly don't expect you, the reader, to be an experienced chef in order to follow the recipes in this book. In fact, even novice cooks should have no trouble creating the culinary treats presented throughout this book. None of the cooking techniques require much more than a little practice to perfect. Every recipe tells you how long it's going to take to prepare and cook.

How This Book Is Organized

You can tackle this book from many angles, but knowing how it's set up gets you where you want to go more efficiently.

Book 1: Mexican Cooking

If you like to eat Mexican food, you're going to love cooking it. This casual style of cooking relies on the same few easy-to-find ingredients — tomatoes, limes, onions, cilantro, and chile peppers — simple home-based techniques like roasting and frying, and nothing more complicated than a blender in terms of equipment. This book, an abridgement of *Mexican Cooking For Dummies,* gives you a short tour through the Mexican kitchen and shows you how to make favorite south-of-the-border dishes.

Book 11: Italian Cooking

If you've ever eaten pasta or pizza (and who hasn't?), you already know something about Italian cooking. But real Italian cooking, as prepared by home cooks in Italy, is often quite different from the dishes you may enjoy at your local pizza parlor or pasta joint. This book, excerpted from *Italian Cooking For Dummies,* explains the philosophy behind great Italian cooking and discusses the ingredients that make Italian cooking so distinctive.

Book III: French Cooking

People have all sorts of strange notions about French cooking: It's difficult, it's time-consuming, and it's too high-brow. Well, to be honest, those notions are just plain wrong. Sure, French cuisine features intimidating dishes such as paté and bouillabaisse, but it also offers simple, elegant dishes that a cook of any experience level can prepare, from sauces to stews to sweets. This book presents a general overview of French cuisine, offering you a variety of impressive recipes for all occasions.

Book IV: Greek and Middle Eastern Cooking

So many people love to visit Greek and Middle Eastern restaurants, but they never think of trying to cook the food themselves. It's mostly a matter of familiarizing yourself with some unfamiliar spices and picking up some new ingredients and techniques. You'll be surprised at how easy it is to whip up a dish of hummus or make a delicious entrée of stuffed grape leaves. The only hard part is pronouncing the names of all the new spices and ingredients you'll be using!

Book V: Indian Cooking

Don't kid yourself: Indian food isn't the easiest cuisine to get a handle on. You need to work with all kinds of strange and wonderful spices that you just don't see in most kitchens in the Western world. But once you get past the initial hesitation and try a few recipes, you'll be rewarded by experiencing one of the most enticing cuisines on the planet. This book, which features recipes from *1,000 Indian Recipes* by Neelam Batra (Wiley Publishing, Inc.) gives you a glimpse of what Indian food has to offer, from the basics such as breads and rice to grilled meats, deep-fried vegetables, curried stews, spiced fruits, and so much more.

Book VI: Chinese Cooking

Chinese cuisine offers so much more than the run-of-the-mill dishes served at the nearby Chinese carry-out. It's a celebration of diverse cooking styles from the four corners of China. This book, a shortened version of *Chinese Cooking For Dummies,* shows you the techniques and explains the ingredients so that you'll be reaching for your own wok rather than the telephone the next time you get a craving for Chinese food.

Book VII: Japanese Cooking

Japanese cooking has a lot more to offer than sake and sushi, not that there's anything wrong with sake or sushi. From soups to tempura to main dishes and even sushi of all types, this book shows you the flavors, colors, and textures that make Japanese cuisine a joy to both prepare and eat.

Book VIII: Thai Cooking

Thai food entices with exotic spices, delectable sauces, and unusual preparations. If you want to prepare Thai at home, this book guides you through the surprisingly easy process. After some background information on Thai ingredients and preparation methods, you'll find out how to prepare a number of traditional dishes from Chicken Satay to Red Curry Beef.

Icons Used in This Book

To make this book easier to use, we've included icons in the margins to draw your attention to especially noteworthy material. Here's what the icons stand for:

This icon highlights inside information, expert techniques, and time-saving shortcuts.

This icon points to food or cooking concepts that you shouldn't forget.

This icon steers you clear of potentially dangerous mishaps.

Where to Go from Here

You can start your world tour of cuisine anywhere you like. Pick a country and try a dish or two, or prepare a meal made up of dishes from all over the globe. Be adventurous and have fun!

Book I
Mexican Cooking

The 5th Wave   By Rich Tennant

"Let me know when you've got enough lettuce on that taco."

In this book . . .

*¡*Aye caramba! Americans tend to think that Mexican food is too spicy, too heavy, and too hard to prepare at home. Nothing could be farther from the truth. If you're ready to put your preconceived notions aside and cook some flavorful, healthy, easy-to-fix Mexican meals, then you've turned to the right section of this book. We give you an overview of what *really* goes into a delicious Mexican meal, help you to master Mexican cooking techniques, and then dive right in to the recipes. From great guacamole to an amazing Margarita Sorbet, we help you plan the perfect Mexican feast!

Contents at a glance

Chapter 1

Understanding Mexican Cooking

In This Chapter

▷ Debunking common Mexican food myths

▷ Getting a taste for Mexican cooking

Experiencing pasta overload? Burnt out on grilled chicken breasts and left cold by one more turkey burger? Ready to take a culinary adventure full of sizzle and spunk, exciting seasonings, terrific party foods, and world-class cocktails? Open your heart, mind, and kitchen to Mexican food, and your guests and family will thank you a thousand times.

Forget about those cheesy restaurant combination platters of yesterday, with their heaping portions of rice, beans, and fried foods. Our style of Mexican cooking is much lighter than that, and it can be as hot and spicy as you like. Big flavors, inexpensive ingredients, easy preparation, and casual presentation are what our kind of Mexican cooking is all about.

Before you begin your journey into Mexican cooking, we want to fill you in on a couple of things to get you started out right, including blasting a few myths about Mexican cooking and giving you a few hints about how to approach this great cuisine.

Dispelling Mexican-Cooking Myths

Although it's one of the world's most beloved cuisines, Mexican food has been severely misunderstood and sloppily translated north of the border. Here are a few myths you can toss aside when you start cooking with us.

✔ **Myth #1: Mexican food is too spicy.** To think of Mexican food as merely hot and spicy is to oversimplify a complicated set of sensations. The great traditional foods of Mexico are a complex blend of savory and earthy flavors, with chopped condiments and spicy salsas generally served on the side as a seasoning and for textural contrast.

For some reason, perhaps because it was a hot concept that could be easily communicated, spiciness became the defining characteristic of all things Mexican in the United States. It just ain't so.

✔ **Myth #2: Mexican food is too heavy.** Old-fashioned Mexican-American restaurant food is heavy. Real Mexican food and the modern updates we favor feature lots of fresh fruits and vegetables, herb garnishes, fresh chopped salsas, rice, beans, tortillas, and a small serving of meat or chicken. Modern Mexican cuisine is light and healthful, with a large dose of flavor.

All that sour cream and melted cheese associated with Mexican food is actually an American restaurant innovation. Typical corn and tortilla snacks, such as enchiladas, tacos, and quesadillas, are meant to be delicate, nutrient-dense morsels, not leaden doorstops.

✔ **Myth #3: Mexican food is hard to cook.** It's ironic that such a rustic, family style of cooking is intimidating to American home cooks. For many, it remains a food to go out to restaurants for rather than something to cook at home. One reason may be the exacting authenticity demanded by stern cookbook authors who shall remain nameless.

When you gain experience handling a few unfamiliar ingredients and start keeping them on hand, Mexican cooking should fit right into your already overflowing schedule. The Mexican food we love has its roots in the home kitchen and the market, with no fancy last-minute techniques or special equipment necessary to create great soul-satisfying dishes.

Getting Started with Mexican Cooking

Cooking a new cuisine, like speaking a new language, can be intimidating. Here are some pointers for taking those first few tentative steps.

✔ **Keep the food manageable.** Start small, with familiar, accessible foods like tacos or marinated and grilled meats with salsas. (Look in Chapter 4 of Book I for salsas and tacos and Chapter 5 for meaty recipes.) Save the more technique-intensive recipes for later when you have a weekend to tool around the kitchen and linger over a pot of stew.

✔ **Experiment with chiles.** Get to know one or two chiles well — serranos and poblanos are a good place to start. After you feel comfortable with your "starter chiles," branch out to other, more exotic chiles. The techniques for roasting, peeling, and seeding are the same no matter what kind of chile you cook with. Chapter 3 of Book I gives you all kinds of helpful hints on working with chiles.

✔ **Entertain Mexican style.** If you're a weekend cook, increase your popularity by entertaining Mexican style. You can't go wrong with chips, salsas, guacamole, two or three kinds of tacos, and a pitcher full of margaritas in the house.

✔ **Keep your mind (and mouth) open to new experiences.** Be daring: Taste that goat taco at the ethnic food stand, mix up a drink with dried hibiscus flowers, and surprise your friends with homemade tamales or salsas during the holidays. Mexican food is all about expanding your horizons and breaking out of familiar food habits — for the fun of it!

Seeking out great tastes in Mexico

You may be lucky enough to travel to Mexico and experience the great flavors of the country firsthand. If so, we have a few tips to help you find wonderful, authentic foods.

Tourism plays such a large part in the Mexican economy that certain places have been developed specifically to make tourists feel at home, or not quite in Mexico. Destinations like Acapulco, Puerto Vallarta, Baja, Cancun, and Cozumel may be great for kicking back and sipping margaritas by the pool; but if it's a culinary adventure you're after, you're unlikely to find it in those sanitized, prepackaged locales. Twenty minutes outside of town, however, it's another story.

The best way to sniff out real regional foods is to visit the main marketplace, usually located near the center of town, or *zocalo* (*zoh*-ka-low). Inside the market, and along the streets surrounding it, you can find vendors at stands, pushing carts, or stationed on blankets on the street, who sell the very best, homemade regional specialties. The cart may be tattered and worn, but as long as it looks clean, we don't hesitate to order up whatever may be offered. Chances are it's delicious.

For scrumptious street snacking, you can't go wrong with roasted corn slathered with mayonnaise, lime juice, and cayenne; cold mango on a stick; any fruit juice or liquado; salted tamarind seeds; garbanzos roasted in the shell; and beautifully sliced and seasoned fruit.

We recommend *A Cook's Tour of Mexico*, by Nancy Zaslavsky (published by St. Martin's Press), to the seriously food-possessed. This Angeleno has traveled extensively over a 20-year period to complete her research. She can tell you where to go in each region for the best marketplaces, vendors, snack stands, and informal restaurants for a truly authentic dining experience in Mexico.

Our favorite regions for authentic food are the southern state of Oaxaca, with its ancient mole (*mo*-lay) recipes and active Zapotec culture, and the Yucatán, along the Caribbean coast, with its super citrus-marinated seafood and lightly grilled foods.

Chapter 2

Ingredients for Mexican Cooking

Mexican cooking doesn't call for a wide array of esoteric ingredients. In Mexican cooking, you use common fruits and vegetables, such as chiles and tomatoes; easy-to-find cuts of meat; inexpensive cooking oils and vinegars; and a few seeds and spices. The secret to successful Mexican cooking lies in the care and time you take transforming these simple ingredients into exotic dishes. To us, the end result of working with the ingredients of the Mexican kitchen is always magic.

Fruits and Vegetables

Fresh fruits and vegetables are an integral part of everyday eating in Mexico. Tropical fruits like mango, pineapple, guava, and watermelon — beautifully sliced and seasoned — are sold on the street as snacks and pureed into mouthwatering drinks at juice stands all over Mexico.

And vegetables aren't sad little afterthoughts that appear alongside a big serving of meat. They're sliced, diced, and pureed into sauces, stews, and garnishes that make any vegetarian smile. Mexicans also eat vegetables such as cucumbers and jícama as snacks throughout the day.

Avocado

Pebbly-skinned greenish brown Hass (rhymes with pass) avocados are our first choice for Mexican cooking. Their rich, nutty flesh strikes the perfect balance with fiery Mexican foods, and this avocado is irreplaceable for gua-camole, salads, sandwiches, tacos, and soups.

If you can't find high-quality Hass avocados, our second favorite type is the leaner, smooth-skinned Fuerte. Its flesh is more watery and its seed is bigger.

When shopping for avocados, remember to not judge this fruit by its cover. The condition of the skin isn't necessarily an indication of what lies within. Sometimes scaly, blemished skin covers luxurious flesh.

For judging ripeness, we rely on the squeeze test. If the flesh has a little give when you press it with a finger, plan on using the avocado within a day. However, if it puts up no resistance and squishes beneath your thumb, put it back. The flesh inside is probably already turning brown and losing its flavor.

Rock-hard fruit takes about a week to ripen. To ripen avocados, store them in a sealed brown bag on the counter for about a week. Placing an apple in the bag speeds up the process.

To remove the pit from an avocado and extract the meat, follow these steps (see Figure 2-1):

1. **Cut the avocado in half lengthwise and pull the halves apart.**

2. **Place the half with the pit in it on a counter and hit the pit with the sharp edge of a heavy knife until it plunges in.**

3. **Twist the blade to remove the pit.**

4. **Scoop out the meat with a spoon.**

How to Pit and Peel an Avocado

Figure 2-1: Pitting and extracting the meat from an avocado.

Slice avocado in half lengthwise and pull apart.

Firmly strike the pit with a chef's knife.

Lift the pit out with a gentle twist of the knife.

GENTLY scoop out the meat with a spoon.

Chop or slice according to your recipe.

After you cut an avocado, the flesh spoils quickly. To slow the aging process, you can sprinkle the flesh with lemon or lime juice or cover the avocado skin-tight with plastic wrap and store the fruit in the fridge.

Banana leaves

Large, green banana leaves are available year-round in the freezer section of Latin American markets. Banana leaves are popular in the southern and Gulf coast states for wrapping fish, tamales, pork, and chicken. In addition to keeping foods moist, these fragrant green leaves impart a delicious fruity flavor. You can also use them to line and cover pans for roasting meats.

To soften banana leaves for folding, use a knife to trim out and discard the tough stalk in the center. Then pass the leaf over a low gas or electric burner for less than a minute until it becomes pliable. Because the leaves are huge, trim them into 9-inch squares for wrapping. Unused leaves can be tightly wrapped and stored in the freezer for several months.

If you can't find banana leaves, briefly blanched collard greens are a good substitute. Trim and discard any tough stems so that the leaves are pliable.

Cactus paddles

The type of cactus most often eaten in Mexico is the prickly pear, the one traditionally pictured in movies about the Old West. Mexican cooks simply go into their front or backyards and cut off the tender, young paddles, no larger than about 6 × 8 inches, as needed.

Look for cactus paddles, or *nopales* (noh-*pahl*-es), also from the prickly pear, at farmers markets or ethnic grocers. They're usually sold already cleaned (with their needles removed), in plastic bags. The best, freshest paddles are bright green and firm and reverberate when flicked with a finger.

You may have to buy your cactus paddles au naturel and clean them yourself. The best way to remove the needles is to shave across the paddle with a sharp paring knife. Store the cleaned paddles in plastic bags in your refrigerator's vegetable bin.

Our favorite way to cook 'em is grilled. Boiling, which some cookbooks recommend, enhances their okralike quality, but we don't recommend it.

Chayote

This pale green, pear-shaped squash was one of the principal foods of Central America's Aztec and Mayan people. We admire the bland little vegetable for its versatility, easy preparation, and low cost. Also known as the *mirliton* in Louisiana, the chayote mixes the mild taste of zucchini with the firmer texture of kohlrabi. It's low in calories and an excellent source of potassium.

You can use chayote in any recipe calling for a summer squash such as zucchini; everything, including the large seed in the center, is edible. You can also eat it raw in salads.

Look for chayote year-round in Latin and Asian markets. Choose small, unblemished squashes and store them in your refrigerator's vegetable bin for as long as a month.

Corn husks

Supermarkets sell packaged dried cornhusks year-round. They're the traditional wrappers for tamales, but you can use them to wrap other foods for steaming or grilling. (Achiote-marinated fish strips for the steamer and slices of lime-marinated pork loin for the grill are two mouthwatering examples.) Corn husks protect tender foods as they cook while infusing them with corn essence.

One package of husks is usually enough to wrap about a dozen tamales. Store dry husks in an airtight package in the pantry for as long as a year.

Always soak dried husks in hot water before using them — they need to soak for at least two hours. Choose the largest pieces for wrapping and shred thin strings from the edges for tying tamale packages closed.

Jícama

Jícama (*hee*-ka-ma) is one root vegetable it pays to know. This plain, round, brown-skinned root yields crisp, white flesh that's terrific for adding sparkle to salads and raw vegetable platters.

Like water chestnuts in Chinese cooking, jícama is primarily a texture food. In Mexico, jícama is cut into sticks; sprinkled with salt, cayenne, and lime juice; and sold on the street as a snack. Because its flavor is rather bland (it's mildly sweet like a water chestnut), it needs at least some salt and lemon or lime to perk it up.

Look for jícama in your supermarket's produce section. Always remove the fibrous brown skin with a knife and, after you cut it, cover the flesh with plastic wrap to avoid drying. You can store jícama in your refrigerator's vegetable bin for a few days.

Lime

Mexican cooks use the yellow-skinned key lime, or *limón,* because it tastes sweeter than the limes typically eaten elsewhere. They use limes for marinating fish and chicken, perking up salsas, garnishing soups, and balancing margaritas, among other uses.

If you can't find key limes in your local supermarket, you can create a similar taste at home. Just mix half lemon juice and half lime juice anytime a recipe calls for lime juice to get closer to the true Mexican flavor.

In the United States, the green Persian lime is the most widely available lime. Persian limes can be disappointingly hard, juiceless, and expensive to boot. Choose them wisely: Look for small, soft, thin-skinned fruit, with a yellowish tint in the supermarket or farmers market.

Store limes in a bowl or basket on the countertop. Don't put them in the refrigerator — they go bad faster in there!

We prefer to juice limes by hand (see Figure 2-2). Roll them on the counter first, bearing down to break up the juice sacs. Then cut the lime in half across its width, and holding a half in one hand, plunge the tines of a fork into the pulp. Twist the fork to loosen the juice, and pour into a bowl.

How to Juice a Lime

Cut a lime in half, across the middle.

Hold a half in one hand at an angle. Use a fork to apply pressure and squeeze out the juice!

Figure 2-2:
Juicing a
lime.

If juicing a quantity of limes in advance, you can store the juice in a sealed jar in the refrigerator up to two days. Or, if your quantity is really large, transfer the juice to freezer bags and freeze it. For smaller portions, freeze the juice in ice cube trays. You never want to be caught without lime juice.

Plantains

These large, thick, cooking bananas are a staple food in the Caribbean, where they're fried, mashed, boiled, simmered, pureed, and baked into soups, stews, breads, and side dishes. Although the plantain is classified as a fruit, like the banana, Caribbean cooks, including those of Mexico's Yucatán peninsula, use plantains more as a starchy root vegetable, like a yam.

The trick to handling plantains is knowing their stages of ripeness. Their color ranges from green when picked to black when thoroughly ripe, and although you can cook them at every stage, they only turn sweet when their skin has entirely blackened and their starch has turned to sugar. A cooked green plantain more closely resembles a potato than a banana.

If you plan to enjoy them sweet, purchase plantains that are yellow to black rather than entirely green because green fruit may be difficult to ripen. To speed up the ripening process, store fruit wrapped in newspapers or a brown paper bag out of sunlight, and add an apple if you want to speed up the ripening process. Look for plantains in the supermarket or Latin markets.

Tomatillos

These small, pale green fruits are the key to most green salsas. Though they resemble green tomatoes when out of the husk, tomatillos are acidic, pale-green members of the Cape Gooseberry family, and bear no relation to tomatoes.

Look for tomatillos that are small, not rock hard, and still in the husk in your supermarket's produce section. Store tomatillos, in the husk, in your refrigerator's vegetable bin. When you're ready to use them, just pull off the papery husks with your fingers and rinse off the fruit's naturally sticky coating with cold water.

Our favorite way to eat tomatillos is raw or very briefly cooked in order to retain their crunch and spunky bright flavor. Try them chopped in place of the tomatoes in Fresh Salsa (Chapter 4 of Book I) or diced and marinated in some lime juice and olive oil and spooned over raw oysters.

Revisiting Chiles 101

Though chile peppers are enjoyed all over the world (China, Thailand, India, and Korea are big chile-growing and -eating countries), no other country matches Mexico's passion for them. Mexican farmers grow more than

140 varieties, and Mexican cooks are legendary for their skilled appreciation of every facet (not just the heat) of this complex vegetable that's technically a fruit.

Chiles have been misunderstood as an ingredient, perhaps because of their striking heat. If you stop to appreciate chiles, you start to notice a wide range of exotic flavors. From snappy, sparkly jalapeños to smoky chipotles and earthy poblanos, chiles are a light, healthful way to bring a wide range of strong, new flavors to your cooking. Just start with a little at a time, find out what you like, and don't let all the macho hype about the heat deter you.

If you're totally new to chiles and you're the type who likes to dip a toe in the water before diving in, start out gently. Try adding a dried chile or two to a pot of your favorite soup or stew and let it steep until it plumps up. Then remove the chile before serving. The flavor of the chile infuses the broth, but doesn't scorch anyone with a mouthful of heat.

Shopping for chiles

The names of chiles aren't consistent all over the United States, so study the chart in the upcoming "Identifying the types of chiles" section, and judge chiles by their appearance and taste, not only their name.

A general rule for predicting the flavor and heat of a chile is the smaller the chile, the hotter the heat. Red indicates a ripe, and probably sweeter, chile than green. Cutting off and tasting a tiny piece of a slice of fresh chile is really the best way to predict its heat and flavor when cooked.

When purchasing fresh chiles, look for bright, smooth, shiny skin and buy about a week's supply. Store the chiles in your refrigerator's vegetable bin and rinse them before using.

Dried chiles should be fragrant and flexible enough to bend without breaking. Look for unbroken chiles that aren't too dusty. (Because chiles are dried out-doors, they can become dirty and dusty, and you need to wipe them off before using them.) Store dried chiles in airtight bags in the freezer and let them soften a minute or two at room temperature before using. (See "Plumping up dried chiles" on the following page for more information.)

Handling fresh chiles

After chopping or otherwise handling chiles, you want to be mindful of the other surfaces that have come in contact with cut chiles. The hot oils from the cut chiles spread like, you guessed it, wildfire.

Immediately after handling chiles, wash off your cutting boards, knives, and hands with hot, soapy water. Be careful not to touch your face or eyes before hand washing because chile oil in the eye isn't fun.

Some cooks like to wear gloves when handling chiles, and other cooks coat their hands with a layer of cooking oil to protect them. Just wash with soap and water to remove the oil.

Plumping up dried chiles

Dried chiles are often rehydrated by taking a long soak in hot water or stock before joining the dish. Softening a not-too-hard chile takes about 20 minutes. Read the recipe thoroughly before tossing out the soaking liquid because this chile-infused liquid is often called for later in the recipe.

Dried chiles have a whole other texture and taste. Don't use dried chiles as a substitute for fresh chiles. You can toast dried chiles to improve flavor just like fresh chiles (see Chapter 3 of Book I), and you can remove the seeds to reduce heat.

Identifying the types of chiles

In our cooking, we rely on the nine types of chiles described in the following list and shown in Figure 2-3:

- **Ancho:** Anchos are the dried version of our favorite green chile, the poblano. This wrinkled, red-brown, wide-shouldered chile has a mellow, sweet flavor, similar to a bell pepper, with just a touch of heat. We like to add it, julienned, to sauces for its chewy texture or pureed at the beginning of a sauce to add body and pure chile flavor.

- **Chile de arbol:** Arbols, also known as dried red chiles, are the papery thin, long, dried chiles sold by the bag in the supermarket. Used extensively in Chinese and Mexican cooking (they put the pow in Kung Pau chicken), these inexpensive little chiles pack a powerful punch of heat, especially after they're chopped and cooked. To tame their heat, you can add them whole to stews and soups and remove them before serving.

- **Chile negro or dried pasilla:** This long, narrow, dark brown chile is a dried chilaca chile. Similar in flavor to the more popular ancho, pasillas are often used in combination with other dried chiles in traditional moles. Look for them via mail order or in ethnic markets.

- **Chipotle:** Chipotles, or dried, smoked, red jalapeños, are one of those life-changing ingredients. When we tasted chipotle salsa, on our first tasting expedition to Mexico back in 1984, we never looked back. We've been using these wrinkled, reddish-brown chiles to add a mysterious, smoky, sweet flavor to everything from salad dressings to grilled chicken and salsas ever since.

  Though usable as a substitute, canned chipotles en adobo (dried chiles packed in a sweet, sour, spicy sauce) are quite different. They're actually hotter and their texture is softer. If you use chipotles en adobo, wipe them off to remove excess sauce and reduce by half the quantity called for in the recipe.

- **Habañero:** This chile lives up to its reputation. It's pure heat. Along with the Scotch Bonnet, the habañero is considered the world's hottest chile. These small, lantern-shaped (usually) chiles are most often used in the Yucatán. You can shop for them at Latin and farmers markets where their color can range from dark green to orange and even red. We prefer the taste of fresh rather than dried habañeros and recommend substituting a larger quantity of serranos (seeds and all) in a pinch.

- **Jalapeño, red and green:** The jalapeño, America's favorite chile, is thick-fleshed, small (about 3-inch long), and bright green or red. With its sweet, fresh, garden flavor and medium heat, this versatile chile is great for garnishing just about anything. In Mexico, we've even seen jalapeños eaten as an accompaniment to rich stews and tacos. They're easy to find at the market, but you can substitute serranos if you prefer.

  Canned jalapeños aren't a good substitute for fresh peppers because their taste and texture are quite different.

- **Morita:** These small, brown, dried chiles look like thin chipotles but are less smoky with a spicier taste. They're a variety of dried, smoked jalapeños. Use fewer moritas to replace chipotles in a recipe.

- **Poblano:** These dark green, medium-sized, thick-fleshed chiles are our favorite fresh green peppers for cooking. We feature them in soups, sauces, and chilis; and they're always our first choice for stuffing because of their wide shoulders, thick skin, and smoldering flesh. They're superb as *rajas* (roasted pepper strips) because of their meatiness.

  Look for smooth-skinned poblano chiles with nice wide shoulders for stuffing. You can substitute less spicy, skinnier Anaheims for stuffing, but you can easily find poblanos in a well-stocked supermarket.

- **Serrano:** Small, thin serranos are similar to jalapeños but pack a little more punch. We mostly use the green variety (the reds are a bit sweeter) in salsas and as a raw garnish in salads and soups. They're easy to find at the supermarket, and you can use them interchangeably with jalapeños.

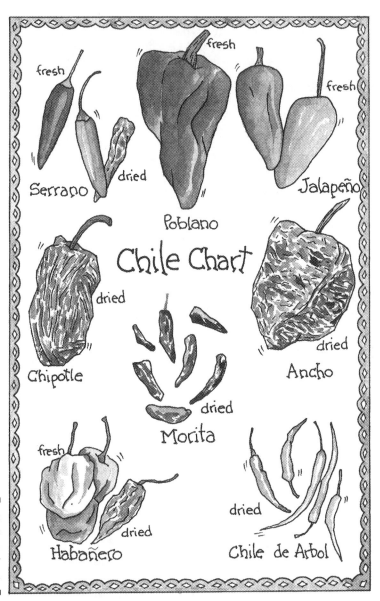

Chile Chart

fresh — fresh — fresh

Serrano — dried

Poblano

Jalapeño

dried

Chipotle

dried

Ancho

dried

Morita

fresh

Habañero — dried

dried

Chile de Arbol

Figure 2-3:
Consult this chart when shopping for chiles.

Herbs and Spices

If the variety of herbs on the market makes you feel insecure, you can relax. The Mexican kitchen uses the same three herbs over and over again: cilantro, oregano (fresh and dried), and epazote. If you start cooking Mexican often, you may want to buy a few of these easy-to-grow plants for the garden and save last-minute shopping trips.

The Mexican spice shelf is reassuringly short: cumin for savor and cinnamon for sweetness. The magic lies in how these spices are combined with chiles, salt, pepper, assorted seeds, and other flavorings to make this simple soul-satisfying cuisine.

Cilantro

Cilantro is one of those ingredients that arouses emotions. People either love it or hate it, and it's not easy to change a hater's taste. Still, we recommend that you give this unique flavor a few chances if you don't immediately care for it. It just may grow on you.

On the other hand, if the thought of a cilantro leaf passing your lips still makes you quiver after a few tastes, please don't give up on Mexican (or Thai or Chinese) food. Simply replace it with flat-leaf parsley or an herb that you love, and, if anybody asks, tell him or her that two highly trained chefs gave you permission.

Because cilantro is so delicate, it's best not to chop it in advance. Likewise, don't stress about removing the thin stems; they're entirely edible. Don't ever use dried cilantro to replace fresh. This herb doesn't dry well.

Epazote

Stronger tasting than most herbs, epazote grows like the weed that it is all over North America. You may have a difficult time finding it in the supermarket (though you're liable to find it in the weeds growing alongside the highway in Los Angeles), but you can easily grow it from seed in the garden or a pot. We've tried the dried variety and don't recommend it because it's virtually flavorless.

The flavor of fresh epazote is so dominant that you should use it alone, not in combination with other herbs, when flavoring a dish. In Mexico, cooks often use it to complement mushrooms, black beans, squash, and even quesadillas.

When cooking with epazote, always trim off the tough stem.

Oregano

Oregano, familiar from Italian-American cooking, is the most popular herb in the Mexican kitchen. Thirteen varieties of this small, soft, green-leafed plant grow in Mexico. Look for it in your supermarket's produce section, and always remove the leaves from the tough stems.

Mexican cooks also use dried oregano. You can purchase cellophane bags of Mexican dried oregano, containing larger pieces of leaves and stems, and crumble the large pieces by hand before adding or just use common dried oregano. We sometimes add a smoky edge by toasting the dried herb first in a dry skillet over low heat.

Cumin

If we had to pick the one fragrance that instantly identifies Mexican food, it would be cumin. We recommend using this spice liberally in your Mexican cooking, combined with cinnamon, nutmeg, cayenne, and arbol chiles for a sweet, spicy kick, or combined with onion, garlic, ground ancho, paprika, and cayenne for a full, earthy, chile flavor.

Use it ground, if you want its flavor to pervade the dish, and always develop the flavor by cooking it first in fat. Use about 1 teaspoon of whatever fat is in the dish to each teaspoon of spice. If it's just dropped into a bubbling soup or stew, the flavor never goes as deep. Use cumin seeds whole when you're looking for an assertive pop of flavor when you take a bite.

As with all dried spices, you can purchase cumin in small enough quantities to last on your shelf no longer than six months. Store out of sunlight and check expiration dates in the store before purchasing. You're likely to find fresher cumin in an Indian or Mexican market where cooks purchase it a lot.

Cinnamon

Mexican cooks use cinnamon, known as *canela* in Spanish, to flavor both savories and sweets. The thin, papery, brown bark known as Mexican cinnamon has a rougher edge and is less expensive than the tightly wound variety commonly found in the supermarket. Look for the Mexican variety (actually from Sri Lanka), packed in hanging cellophane bags, in the ethnic section of the market. Use the bark to infuse drinks, stews, moles, and sauces and then discard it. Ground cinnamon can always be used in its place.

Store cinnamon in airtight containers away from the sun, and replenish after about six months because the bark dries out.

Nuts, Seeds, and Seasoning Pastes

Nuts and seeds are much more than a snack food or dessert ingredient in the Mexican kitchen. Since pre-Columbian times, cooks have used peanuts, pecans, and pumpkin seeds to thicken sauces and moles. And the Spanish influence can be seen in the use of almonds and walnuts in rich ground-nut sauces and stuffings.

Annatto seed and achiote paste

These tiny, rock hard, brick red seeds from the South American annatto tree give Mexican food its characteristic orange tint. The seeds alone have a slightly musky flavor, but when ground and combined with garlic, oregano, cumin, cinnamon, pepper, and cloves, they make fragrant achiote paste, a seasoning mixture popular in the Yucatán for marinades and sauces.

Annatto seed, available in ethnic markets and by mail order, is used by U.S. food producers to add an orange tint to butter and cheddar cheese. You can use the seeds to flavor oil by simply heating them in the oil and then straining out the seeds, or you can grind them in a coffee or spice grinder and use them to color masa for tamales. Always cook annatto or achiote in fat to remove any chalkiness.

Achiote paste, sold in bricks in Mexican markets, is an easy-to-use spice rub for fish and meats. When the paste is thinned with vinegar or citrus juices, the spices develop a wonderful tropical fruitiness. Achiote paste can be kept, well wrapped, in the refrigerator for a long time.

Be sure to wash off any utensils or cutting boards that come into contact with annatto or achiote right away. There's a reason this is an industrial-strength dye. A little goes a long way.

Tamarind seeds and paste

Tamarind is a leathery, dried brown seed pod that produces a deliciously sticky, sweet-sour paste when cooked. One of the key ingredients in Worcestershire sauce, it's popular in Indian, Mexican, Indonesian, and Thai cuisines as a tart balance to fatty foods. You can find it in brick and pod form in ethnic markets.

To reconstitute dried tamarind pods, first remove the hard outer pods by hand and discard them. Place the fruit in a pan, generously cover with water, and cook at a boil about 15 minutes, until soft. Strain before using. The finished paste should be the consistency of ketchup.

Soak bricks of tamarind pulp in hot water to soften about 30 minutes and then press through a strainer to separate any solids from the thick puree.

A good substitute for tamarind paste is pureed, dried apricots, enhanced with some lemon juice.

Coconut

Coconuts are available year-round in the supermarket. The best ones feel heavy in your hand and sound full of liquid when shaken. If the eyes are soft and the coconut smells spoiled when you sniff it, chances are that it's rotten inside.

In some Latin markets, coconuts are sold already husked and wrapped to go in plastic. But if you can't get to a Latin market, here's how to get to that sweet, white meat: Poke a hole in two or three eyes with a screwdriver or ice pick and drain the liquid. Place the coconut on a baking tray in a 350-degree oven for about 10 minutes, and then remove it and crack it open with a hammer on the floor (to avoid damage to your kitchen counters).

For delicious, large shards of coconut meat ready-to-go, shop for unsweetened, shaved (not shredded) coconut in health-food markets. Store the coconut in plastic bags in the freezer.

Pepitas

Pumpkin seeds, or pepitas, are native to Mexico and show up in sauces, salads, moles, and, of course, snack foods. The seeds sold in Mexico, often with the thin, white husks still on, have much more flavor than those sold in the United States. The thin husks are edible.

Like all seeds and nuts, pepitas should be stored in airtight containers in the freezer. They need not be defrosted before using.

Beans and Starches

These beans and starches are the simple and substantial backbones of every Mexican meal. No good Mexican cook is ever without them.

Beans

The two beans Americans most often associate with Mexican cooking are black beans and larger mottled pink pintos, but in Mexico, people enjoy a wider variety. Beans and rice are served at virtually every meal to ensure a daily dose of protein in diets that don't depend upon a large portion of meat.

Most important when shopping for beans is to purchase from a store that does a brisk business. Beans can age, which makes them impossible to ever cook up soft — and you can't spot these little scoundrels before they're cooked.

If you don't have time for all the boiling dried beans require, you can always substitute a good canned bean. A good way to enhance the flavor of canned beans is to sauté a clove or two of garlic with a chopped onion in some oil until they're soft and nearly brown. Add this mixture to the beans with their cooking liquid and warm through.

Tortillas

You can't eat Mexican food without tortillas. Would you ask a Frenchman to sit down to a meal without his baguette? Not only are tortillas the sustaining bread of the Mexican people, but they also make a darn good fork in a pinch. Just hold the tortilla in your hand and pinch the food in between for instant taco transport.

If you do much cooking, you should stock up on large packs of 6-inch taco-sized corn tortillas (which are widely available in stores) because they're so versatile. Deep yellow corn tortillas are our favorite, but white can be good too, depending on your preference. You can use corn tortillas for making chips, enchiladas, chilaquiles, and tostadas, to name a few dishes, and they keep a long time in their sealed package in the fridge. (In Chapter 4 of Book I, you can find out how to make your own corn tortillas at home.)

Flour tortillas, with or without lard, are also available in various sizes and packs in the supermarket. You may want to stock these tortillas if you like making burritos and quesadillas. Also, search for uncooked tortilla dough in the supermarket freezer next to the cookie dough. (Chapter 4 of Book I tells you how to make flour tortillas.)

Masa harina

Masa harina is flour made from corn dough that has been dried and then ground into a powder. Quaker Oats sells it in the supermarket baking section. Ordinary yellow cornmeal for making cornbread isn't a good substitute.

Dairy Products

You can find authentic Mexican cheeses in most supermarkets. With the three basic cooking cheeses — panela, añejo, and manchego — or their substitutes, you have all the cheeses you ever need to cook authentic quesadillas or queso fundido, or to just add a bite of richness to salads, soups, and enchiladas. Remember, as a general culinary principle, just say no to orange cheese.

Añejo

Also known as Cotija (koh-*tee*-jah), for the town where it was first made, añejo (ah-*nyeh*-hoh) is a dry, aged cow's milk cheese prized for its salty bite. Because añejo isn't a good melter, you should combine it with other cheeses in cooked dishes. For sprinkling over beans, soups, and salads, it's perfect alone. Use it as you would grated Parmesan in your Italian cooking. Either Parmesan or Romano makes a good substitute.

Panela

Panela, a semi-soft, white cow's milk cheese, has a delightfully fresh milky flavor. In the freshest panela, the curds are still visible, as well as the circular pattern imprinted from the basket in which the curds were set to drain. We like it diced, as a garnish for soup or posole, and in cubes in a salad because it holds its shape so well.

Contrary to its mozzarella-like appearance, panela isn't a good melter and always needs to be teamed with a Jack-like cheese for quesadillas. We recommend dry curd farmer's cheese, dry cottage, or dry ricotta as substitutes.

Mexican manchego

Don't confuse this inexpensive semi-soft cheese with Spanish manchego, a stronger aged eating cheese. Soft, mild Mexican manchego is the melter in the group. You can substitute Monterey Jack cheese for manchego.

Crema

Mexican crema, sold in jars in your supermarket's refrigerator case, is a soured milk product similar to buttermilk and sour cream. This salty, white drizzling cream is thinner and less sour than sour cream and used most often as a garnish or dressing.

We're not big fans of commercially produced crema because of the additives. The best substitute is crème fraîche, but sour cream thinned with a bit of lime juice or buttermilk to the consistency of a creamy salad dressing works in a pinch. Chapter 6 of Book I contains a recipe so that you can make your own crema at home.

Our cheese mix

We like to use a grated mixture of one part manchego, one part panela, and one part añejo rather than one cheese in our cooked dishes. The mix results in a more complex texture and flavor. Manchego lends its texture, añejo its salt, and panela its milkiness.

Of course, if you can't get your hands on all three, feel free to improvise with substitutes or use two rather than three types of cheese. The basic idea is that a variety of cheeses is always preferable to one in any melted cheese dish.

Book I

Mexican Cooking

Chapter 3

Mastering a Few Simple Techniques

In This Chapter
▶ Discovering the techniques used in Mexican cooking
▶ Cooking the perfect beans

The techniques of the Mexican kitchen don't call for split-second timing or finicky, precise movements. Just roll up your sleeves and get ready to chop, dice, slice, and occasionally whir the blender or sizzle foods in hot oil. Mexican cooking methods, based on techniques honed by home cooks over the years, depend only on your willingness to dive in and do the work.

Toasting and Seeding Vegetables and Seeds

If, in your previous attempts at cooking, you've taken heat for burning the food, you're in luck now. Good Mexican cooking calls for lots of roasting, toasting, and charring to give the food that mysterious deep, smoky, rustic edge. This may be the only time in your cooking career where to blacken is not only okay but preferred. Here's how to roast and toast some ingredients typically found in Mexican foods.

Fresh chiles and bell peppers

You can roast fresh chiles and bell peppers directly over a gas flame or on a tray under the broiler. Keep turning until the skin is evenly charred, without burning the flesh. Transfer the charred peppers to a plastic bag, tie the top closed, and let the peppers sit until they're cool to the touch, about 15 minutes. (To speed things up, you can place the bag in a bowl of iced water.) Remove the blackened skin by pulling it off by hand, and then dip your fingers in a bowl of water to remove any blackened bits. After they're peeled, cut away the stems, seeds, and veins with a paring knife.

Don't peel roasted peppers under running tap water or you'll wash away the tasty, precious juices.

Figure 3-1 shows how to roast, peel, seed, and julienne a chile.

How to Roast, Peel, Seed, and Julienne a Chile

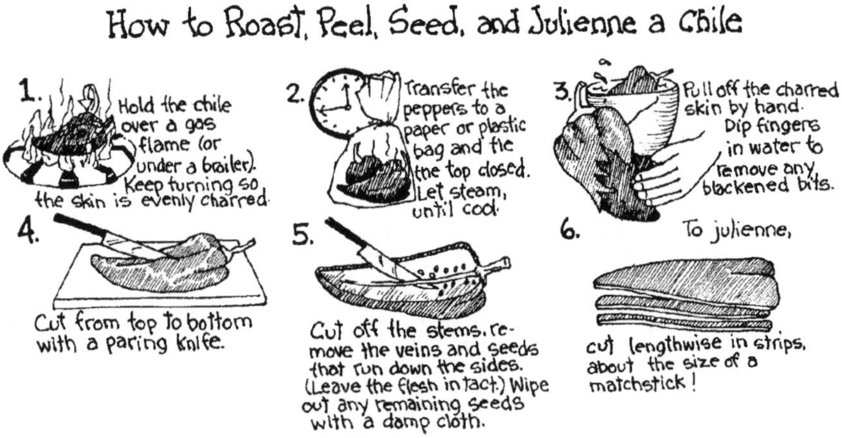

Figure 3-1:
Preparing
a chile.

1. Hold the chile over a gas flame (or under a broiler). Keep turning so the skin is evenly charred.

2. Transfer the peppers to a paper or plastic bag and tie the top closed. Let steam, until cool.

3. Pull off the charred skin by hand. Dip fingers in water to remove any blackened bits.

4. Cut from top to bottom with a paring knife.

5. Cut off the stems, remove the veins and seeds that run down the sides. (Leave the flesh intact.) Wipe out any remaining seeds with a damp cloth.

6. To julienne, cut lengthwise in strips, about the size of a matchstick!

Dried chiles

Dried chiles, like anchos, develop more flavor if lightly toasted. Just place them directly over a low gas flame or in a dry skillet over low flame and warm a few seconds on each side, until the flesh is bubbly and lightly toasted.

Vegetables

Tomatoes, tomatillos, onions, and garlic are often roasted on a tray under the broiler when making salsas, soups, and stews. Simply arrange all the vegetables to be roasted on a large baking sheet, protecting small garlic cloves by tucking them under larger vegetables. Stay nearby and keep turning the vegetables with tongs until everything is evenly blackened. Be careful to transfer the juices that collect on the baking sheet to the blender because they carry lots of delicious flavor.

You can also roast vegetables in a heavy, dry cast-iron skillet over a medium flame. Cook, turning frequently, until blackened.

Seeds

You can toast whole coriander, cumin, and fennel seeds on the stovetop. Place the seeds in a dry skillet over medium heat and keep shaking and tossing the pan until their aroma is released, less than a minute.

Ready, Set, Puree

We're huge fans of the humble blender that you can purchase for about $40 at your local hardware, discount, or department store. Nothing beats it for a uniform puree. If we had to live without it, our next best choices for grinding would be a hand-cranked food mill or sieve.

When using the blender to puree hot liquids for soups or stews, follow these tips:

- ✔ **Never fill a blender more than halfway.** Always leave a crack open at the top for steam to escape.

- ✔ **Control the proportion of liquids to solids in the container by lifting solids from the pot with a spoon and then pouring a small amount of liquid from the pot to the blender.** A combination of about half liquid and half solids is good.

- ✔ **Always cover the top of the blender with a towel to protect yourself from escaping liquids.** You don't want more of a mess to clean up, do you?

- ✔ **Begin the action by briefly pulsing a few times to start liquefying.** When the blades are moving freely, you can let it rip.

To puree garlic in quantity, first break the bulbs apart. Peel them by first flattening the cloves with the flat side of a heavy knife or cleaver and then removing the skin. Puree with a small amount of olive oil in a blender or food processor fitted with a metal blade. Store in the refrigerator for as long as a week. You can always use pureed garlic in place of minced garlic. One tablespoon pureed equals about three cloves, minced.

Cooking Perfect Beans

Here are some suggestions to help assure perfectly cooked beans every time:

- **Never salt the water.** Salt toughens the beans' skins. Add salt to flavor after the beans are done.

- **For maximum creaminess, always cook over low heat, with the cover on, to prevent drying.** You don't want to serve dried-up, tasteless beans, do you?

- **To prevent scorching, stir with a wooden spoon several times during cooking, always reaching down to the bottom of the pot.** Burnt beans on the bottom of the pot infuse the whole pot with their unlovely aroma.

- **To test for doneness, taste a few of the smallest beans because they take the longest to cook through.** If their centers are smooth and creamy, the batch is done.

- **Use cool water in your sink to cool beans in a hurry, as shown in Figure 3-2.**

- **Use a pressure cooker for cooking beans.** Just follow the machine's instructions.

Cool Your Beans!!

Fill the sink with COLD water... Submerge the pot of beans into the water. Don't get the beans wet!! Stir up from the bottom! Repeat, until cool.

Figure 3-2:
Cooling beans quickly.

Popping Peppercorns

To crack peppercorns, place the whole peppercorn in the middle of a cutting board. To keep the peppercorns from flying away when you crack them, roll up a towel and use it to surround the corns. Place the heel of a skillet or saucepan on top and push down and away from you several times (see Figure 3-3).

How to Crush Peppercorns

Figure 3-3:
Cracking
peppercorns
down to
size.

gather whole peppercorns in the middle of a cutting board.

Roll up a towel and... use it to surround the peppercorns so they don't fly off the cutting board.

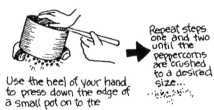

Use the heel of your hand to press down the edge of a small pot on to the peppercorns.

Repeat steps one and two until the peppercorns are crushed to a desired size...

Chapter 4

Starters, Snacks, and Sides

In This Chapter

▶ Stirring up salsas and dips

▶ Creating great-tasting flour tortillas

▶ Making a well-balanced quesadilla

▶ Tantalizing your guests with tacos

▶ Assembling the real enchilada

▶ Tempting your taste buds with tortas, empanadas, and tamales

▶ Stuffing chiles with success

▶ Making soups and salads, Mexican style

▶ Frying rice

▶ Enjoying beans for all seasons

▶ Varying the menu with veggie sides

*W*e love to get a party rolling by serving large bowls of Mexican finger foods. When everyone crowds around and starts reaching into the same bowl, inevitably conversations start flowing. All the finger foods in this chapter are terrific for a party or a buffet. They're easy to prepare and interesting to eat, and most fit well on a chip. So encourage your guests to dig in, dip their chips, and accompany their drinks with any of these enticing salsas and dips.

In this chapter, you also find great recipes for quick snacks — to satisfy those Mexican-food cravings that just can't wait. We fill you in on how to make some more time-consuming Mexican treats as well — for when you have some time to spend. And we get your Mexican meal off to a great start with soups, salads, and side dishes.

Salsas and Dips

Salsas are the heart and soul of the Mexican kitchen. We use them in hundreds of recipes, from soups and stews to casseroles.

With a handful of simple ingredients and no tricky techniques or precise timing, Mexican cooks can toss together sauces as diverse as chunky fresh tomato and onion salsa; smooth, tart green tomatillo sauce; and mysteriously complex dried chile salsa in minutes. In fact, the speed with which delicious salsas are thrown together was the first thing that fascinated us about Mexican cooking.

Since Americans have discovered salsa, making it second only to ketchup in the condiment sweepstakes, hundreds of salsa recipes have been created, featuring everything from strawberries to sun-dried tomatoes. But don't be fooled! The basic Mexican salsas — perfect as chip dips, marinades for grilled foods, bases for stews and soups, and toppings for just about anything — are still the best.

Keep a stock of salsas in your refrigerator for maximum flexibility with your recipes. If you're counting calories, remember that salsas are exceptionally lowfat sauces to use in all your cooking.

The smooth, rich dips are the opposite end of the spectrum from sprightly salsas. They soothe the nerves and balance the typical fiery flavors of the Mexican kitchen.

All the dips in this section can be scooped up with tortilla chips for a tasty treat, and many of the dips can accompany a wide variety of dishes.

Fresh Salsa

This uncooked table sauce, also known as pico de gallo, salsa cruda, or plain old tomato salsa, is probably Mexico's best-known salsa. With its chunks of tomato, chiles, and onion, it's the model for most bottled salsas; but let's face it, how fresh can a sauce from a bottle be?

Preparation time: *15 minutes*

Yield: *2 cups*

4 medium-size ripe tomatoes, cored, seeded, and finely diced

¼ red onion, minced (¼ cup)

2 jalapeño chiles, stemmed, seeded, and minced

1 bunch cilantro, leaves only, chopped (about ½ cup)

2 tablespoons freshly squeezed lime juice

¾ teaspoon salt

Pinch of pepper

Combine all the ingredients in a mixing bowl. Stir, toss well, and serve. Store in a covered container in the refrigerator for up to 1 day.

Tip: *Freshness makes all the difference in this salsa. Use only the freshest ingredients, and don't make the salsa in advance. After a day, the fresh flavors fade, and the salsa becomes mushy. Avoid the temptation to reach for the food processor to do all this chopping. You want uneven, chunky bits here, not a pureed mush.*

Green Tomatillo Salsa

We love the acid bite of raw tomatillos in this quick, uncooked sauce. Use it to counter rich, creamy dishes like tamales, or with any simply grilled fish. (See Chapter 2 of Book I for information about tomatillos, the green fruit that resembles a tomato.)

Special tool: *Blender or food processor*

Preparation time: *10 minutes*

Yield: *2 cups*

¾ pound tomatillos, stemmed, husked, the stem scar cut out, and cut into quarters

3 serrano chiles, stemmed, seeded, and coarsely chopped

⅓ cup cold water

1 bunch scallions, white and light green parts, coarsely chopped (about 1 cup)

1 large bunch cilantro leaves and tender stems, roughly chopped (about ½ cup)

1½ teaspoons salt

Place the tomatillos, chiles, and water in a blender or food processor. Puree just until chunky. Add the scallions, cilantro, and salt and puree about 2 minutes longer, or until no large chunks remain. Store in the refrigerator, in a covered container, for up to about 3 days.

Vary It! For a mellower version of tomatillo salsa, try roasting the tomatillos, chiles, and scallions under the broiler until blackened, about 5 minutes. Then place the roasted items in a blender or food processor with the remaining ingredients and puree.

Red Roasted Tomato Salsa

Roasting the tomatoes until blackened gives this smooth red sauce its distinctive
Mexican flavor.

Special tool: *Blender or food processor*

Preparation time: *10 minutes*

Cooking time: *25 minutes*

Yield: *1 quart*

1 pound Roma tomatoes, cored	*2 tablespoons olive oil*
6 garlic cloves, peeled	*1 cup tomato juice*
2 serrano chiles, stemmed and seeded	*1 teaspoon salt*
1 medium onion, cut into ½-inch slices	*Pepper to taste*

1 Preheat the broiler.

2 Place the tomatoes, garlic, chiles, and onion on a foil-lined baking tray. Drizzle with the
olive oil. Broil 6 to 8 inches from the flame for about 12 minutes, turning frequently with
tongs, until evenly charred.

3 Transfer the vegetables and any accumulated juices to the blender or food processor.
Add the tomato juice, salt, and pepper. Puree, in batches if necessary, until smooth.

4 Pour into a medium saucepan. Bring to a boil, reduce to a simmer, and cook, uncovered,
for about 5 minutes. Season with salt and pepper. Cool to room temperature for table
salsa, or use warm as an ingredient in rice or chilaquiles. Store in the refrigerator for
2 to 3 days, or in the freezer for 2 weeks.

Vary It! *For the lazy cook's version of this salsa, you can use canned Roma tomatoes and
totally skip the broiling part. The salsa still tastes delicious, though definitely not roasted.*

Roasted Green Chile Salsa

A chile-intensive sauce, such as this one, is a terrific complement to any red meat — grilled steaks, lamb chops, or burgers are great. If all three types of chiles aren't available, improvise according to your taste. (See Chapter 2 of Book I for details on choosing chiles.)

Special tools: *Food processor*

Preparation time: *15 minutes*

Cooking time: *10 minutes*

Yield: *3 cups*

2 slices red onion, sliced ½-inch thin	*3 poblano chiles, halved and seeded*
4 garlic cloves	*2 tablespoons olive oil*
1 pound medium tomatillos	*Juice of 2 limes*
4 serrano chiles, halved and seeded	*2 teaspoons dried oregano*
12 jalapeño chiles, halved and seeded	*1½ teaspoons coarse salt*

1 Preheat the broiler.

2 Arrange the onion, garlic, tomatillos, and chiles on a baking sheet. Drizzle evenly with the olive oil. Broil 6 to 8 inches from the flame, turning frequently with tongs, until evenly charred, about 12 minutes.

3 Transfer to a food processor and pulse until finely chopped. Add the lime juice, oregano, and salt and process until smooth. Serve at room temperature or chilled. Store in the refrigerator for up to 4 days.

Salsas from a bottle

Our hands-down favorites of the prepared salsas we tasted are from restaurant chef Rick Bayless of Chicago. His salsas have a good homemade quality, with charred bits left in for smokiness and no additives or weird ingredients. Two of our favorites are Frontera Chipotle Salsa and Frontera Tomatillo Salsa.

Most of the commercial tomato salsas are too chunky for our tastes. We recommend pureeing them in the blender before using them in cooking. After giving several a critical tasting, here are our recommendations:

✔ Jardine's Cilantro Texasalsa

✔ Tostitos Restaurant Style

✔ Pace Hot

✔ Newman's Own

Guacamole

This mashed avocado dip is great for cooling down hot foods or just adding richness to anything it touches. Guacamole is terrific spread on turkey or pork sandwiches, as well as spooned over tacos, burritos, and tostadas.

Preparation time: *15 minutes*

Yield: *2 cups*

3 ripe avocados, preferably Hass (see Chapter 2 of Book I)

½ bunch fresh cilantro leaves, chopped (about ¼ cup)

½ medium red onion, diced

3 jalapeño chiles, stemmed, seeded, and finely diced

3 tablespoons freshly squeezed lime juice

1½ teaspoons salt

½ teaspoon pepper

Cut the avocados into quarters. Remove the seeds, peel, and place in a mixing bowl. Mash with a potato masher or fork until chunky. Add the cilantro, onion, chiles, lime juice, salt, and pepper and combine with a fork. Store in the refrigerator up to 1 day.

Even though guacamole is such a simple dish, people often prepare it incorrectly. Here are some secrets to making great guacamole. Follow these tips, and you can create guacamole that people can't wait to dip with a chip:

- ✔ **Do not overmash your avocados.** The proper texture is slightly chunky, not liquefied into a paste or filled with air.

- ✔ **Absolutely no tomatoes are permitted in the land of the perfect guacamole.** They add too much liquid.

- ✔ **Nix on the garlic as well.** We don't care what other cookbooks may advise. This luscious green dip is meant to be garlic-free.

Queso Fundido

Queso Fundido (*keh*-soh fuhn-*dee*-thoh), which means "melted cheese," is a traditional dish from northern Mexico. The gooey richness of the melted cheese in this dip is irresistible. We add interest to this recipe by combining three cheeses: Mexican manchego for texture, añejo for salt, and panela for milkiness.

Special tool: *Six 4-ounce ceramic or glass ovenproof dishes or one 1½-quart casserole*

Preparation time: *15 minutes, plus 10 minutes to make the Green Tomatillo Salsa*

Cooking time: *25 minutes*

Yield: *6 servings as an appetizer*

1½ cups (6 ounces) grated Mexican manchego or Monterey Jack cheese

½ cup (2 ounces) grated añejo cheese

½ cup (2 ounces) grated panela cheese

2 poblano chiles, roasted, peeled, seeded, and julienned (see Chapter 3 of Book I)

½ small red onion, diced (⅓ cup)

Pepper to taste

12 flour or corn tortillas, warmed

Green Tomatillo Salsa for garnish (see the recipe earlier in this chapter)

1 Preheat the oven to 375 degrees.

2 Set six 4-ounce ceramic or glass ovenproof dishes, or one 1½-quart casserole, in the oven for 10 minutes to warm.

3 Mix the manchego, añejo, and panela cheeses in a bowl. Divide the cheese evenly among the warm dishes. Bake for 5 minutes. Arrange the chiles and onion over the warm cheese and return to the oven, until the cheese is completely melted and bubbly, about 6 minutes. Season with pepper and serve immediately with warmed tortillas for dipping and Green Tomatillo Salsa according to taste.

Vary It! *For a crunchy dollop of protein, add 6 ounces of thinly sliced uncooked Spanish chorizo sausage along with the chiles and onion to the melted cheese. Or, if your grill is heated up, you can melt the cheese in aluminum foil packets on the covered grill for an authentic smoky flavor.*

These chips are made for dipping

You should notice a world of difference between a warm, recently fried corn tortilla chip and one that comes from a bag. But sometimes chefs have to be realists. If you're going to buy chips for dipping or including in other dishes, look for corn chips without any added flavor or too much salt to overpower other flavors.

Here are the brands we recommend, as a result of a blind taste test:

✔ Santitas are a thin, white or yellow corn chip with just the right balance of salt and corn, and no other flavors to distract.

✔ Tostitos are a thicker, exceptionally crunchy white corn chip.

✔ Garden of Eatin' is an organic corn chip with a deep-yellow color and strong corn flavor. The perfectly round shape feels too machine-made for our tastes, but the flavor is tops of those we tasted.

✔ Padrino, Restaurant Style, a regional California brand, packs lots of corn flavor into a not-too-salty chip.

Quick Snacks

The foods in this section are sold and eaten at the local markets or informal stands scattered all over Mexico. People usually eat them as small snacks, sometimes even for breakfast, while they're out conducting their business. But in our homes, they fit in perfectly with the way we try to eat and feed our families. They make excellent use of leftovers, offer well-balanced servings of small portions of meat combined with vegetables and grains, and taste terrific.

As an added benefit, tacos and tortas make excellent, informal party foods. You can arrange all the fixings on a buffet table, along with chips and salsas, cold drinks, and maybe something easy for dessert, like cookies, so that everyone can just dig in, relax, and have fun.

Getting stuffed on quesadillas

Quesadillas (keh-sah-*dee*-yahz) are the Mexican answer to the grilled cheese sandwich or pizza. They're a versatile dish of flour tortillas, usually stuffed with cheeses and one or two other ingredients, cooked quickly enough to just melt the cheese and marry all the flavors. What makes a quesadilla rise to greatness, however, is the quality of those few simple ingredients and the care taken in cooking them.

Paying attention to your ingredients

Quesadillas contain very few ingredients; however, they can literally fall apart on you if the ingredients aren't brought together in the right proportions and handled properly. Here are some pitfalls to avoid when creating your own melted cheese creations:

- ✔ **Too much cheese:** Strive for a balance between tortilla and cheese so that one ingredient doesn't overwhelm the other. A quesadilla should taste of more than cheese.

- ✔ **Raw vegetables:** Each component of the quesadilla should be seasoned and cooked before being added. If you want to add a vegetable (or meat), remember that after a quesadilla is tossed into the oven or pan, you're cooking it quickly, just long enough to melt the cheese. Uncooked ingredients in the center will remain uncooked, and they won't be nearly as delicious as cooked and seasoned vegetables.

Making your own flour tortillas

In Mexico, people make tortillas by hand and eat them at almost every meal in some form or another. People in northern Mexico eat flour tortillas, while those in the south favor corn tortillas. The taste of a good homemade flour tortilla adds an extra dimension to any dish; however, if you're pressed for time, you can substitute good store-bought tortillas.

Flour Tortillas

Ever wonder what to do on one of those afternoons when it seems like there's nothing going on? Why not gather the kids together and roll out a batch of unbelievably delicious homemade tortillas? They're easier to make than bread (see Figure 4-1), and the rewards are immediate. Children love them slathered with butter and honey for breakfast.

Preparation time: *25 minutes, plus 15 minutes resting time for dough*

Cooking time: *15 minutes*

Yield: *Twelve 8-inch tortillas*

3½ cups flour plus extra for dusting	*1½ teaspoons salt*
½ cup plus 1 tablespoon vegetable shortening	*1 cup plus 2 tablespoons lukewarm water*

1 Place the flour, shortening, and salt in a bowl and lightly rub the ingredients together with your fingers until evenly mixed. Pour in the warm water and stir with a wooden spoon. Then gather the dough together and knead a few times by hand until a smooth dough is formed.

2 Divide the dough into 12 equal-sized pieces. Roll each piece into a ball and place on a baking tray or cutting board. Cover with a tea towel and let rest at room temperature for at least 15 minutes, or up to 1 hour.

3 Cut out twelve 10-inch squares of waxed or parchment paper for stacking the tortillas. On a lightly floured board, roll each ball into an 8-inch circle and transfer to a paper square. Stack the tortillas on a baking tray or platter and refrigerate until cooking time. You can keep uncooked tortillas in the refrigerator for up to 2 days if they're well wrapped with paper squares between the layers.

4 To cook, heat a dry griddle or 12-inch nonstick skillet over medium heat. Carefully peel the paper from the tortillas and cook them, one at a time, until they're puffy and slightly brown, about 40 seconds per side. Set aside to cool slightly on a paper towel-lined platter. Bring them to the table wrapped in a towel for warmth, or wrap well and store in the refrigerator for a few days or in the freezer for up to a month.

Vary It! *You can crisp flour tortillas in the oven for a delicious, nutritious treat. Brush the tortillas with melted butter, sprinkle with a mixture of cinnamon and sugar, and arrange them in a single layer on an uncoated baking sheet. Bake in a 350-degree oven until crisp, about 10 minutes. For a savory version, brush with olive oil, sprinkle with savory seeds and spices like cumin, sesame, and chiles, and bake until crisp, about 10 minutes.*

Cooking up quesadillas

In the following recipes, we have you put the quesadillas in the oven for the final bring-it-all-together stage. However, you can cook a quesadilla in more than one way, especially if you're cooking at home for just one or two people. You can prepare quesadillas quickly on the stovetop, using our quick and easy method: Heat the tortilla on both sides in a lightly oiled or buttered skillet over low heat. Then sprinkle on and lightly melt the cheese, scatter on the toppings, and fold. Cook, turning once or twice, until the cheese is completely melted.

How to Make Your Own Flour Tortillas

1.

Place flour, shortening and salt in a bowl. Lightly rub together with fingers until evenly mixed.

Pour in warm water. Stir with a wooden spoon until a smooth dough has formed.

2. Divide the dough into 12 pieces. Roll each piece into a ball and place on a baking tray. Cover with a towel. Let rest at room temperature, 15 minutes to 1 hour.

3. Cut out parchment paper squares for stacking the tortillas. On a lightly floured board, roll each ball into an 8 circle. Transfer to a paper square.

Stack on a baking tray or platter. Refrigerate till cooking time.

4. To cook, heat a dry griddle or skillet over medium heat....

Carefully, peel off paper. Cook tortillas one at a time till puffy, slightly brown, about 40 seconds per side. Set aside to cool on towel lined platter.

Figure 4-1:
Making flour
tortillas.

Grilled Vegetable Quesadillas

Here is a great use for leftover grilled or roasted vegetables. You need to start out with about 2½ cups of whatever veggie mix you choose to use.

Preparation time: *20 minutes*

Cooking time: *15 minutes*

Yield: *6 servings*

¼ cup olive oil	*2 small yellow crookneck squash, trimmed*
2 tablespoons red wine vinegar	*1 large red bell pepper, stemmed and seeded*
1 teaspoon salt	*1 medium red onion*
½ teaspoon pepper	*3 jalapeños, stemmed and seeded*
2 cloves garlic, minced	*Butter for greasing baking sheets*
½ bunch fresh oregano or marjoram leaves, coarsely chopped (¼ cup), or ½ tablespoon dried oregano or marjoram leaves	*Six 8-inch flour tortillas*
2 small zucchini, ends trimmed	*2 cups (8 ounces) grated Mexican cheeses, such as Mexican manchego, panela, and añejo*

1 Prepare a medium fire in a grill or preheat the broiler.

2 In a large bowl, whisk together the olive oil, vinegar, salt, pepper, garlic, and oregano or marjoram.

3 Cut the zucchini, squash, red pepper, onion, and chiles into quarters lengthwise. Place them in the bowl with the olive oil mixture and mix to evenly coat. Grill or broil slowly, turning frequently, until lightly golden and soft, about 10 minutes. Cool slightly and cut all the vegetables into 2-inch pieces. Transfer to a bowl and set aside.

4 Adjust the oven temperature to 350 degrees. Lightly butter 2 baking sheets and arrange the tortillas in a single layer. Spread equal amounts of the grated cheese mix over each tortilla and bake for 5 minutes, until melted. Spoon equal amounts of the grilled vegetable mixture over the cheese, fold over to enclose, and return the tortillas to the oven just to heat through, about 4 minutes. Serve hot, whole or cut in wedges.

Vary It! *If you're firing up the gas grill for the veggies, you can make your quesadillas on the grill as well. Turn the heat down to medium-low and place a cookie sheet, or sheet of foil, over the grate to avoid messy cheese drops.*

Quesadilla riffs

Like other great melted cheese dishes, quesadillas lend themselves to improvisation. Here are a few alternative ideas for topping our standard cheese mix (see in Chapter 2 of Book I for more about our cheese mix). Regardless of what kind of cheese you use, the technique remains the same: First top the tortilla with grated cheese, melt slightly, scatter on toppings, and bake until melted through.

✔ Mashed, roasted garlic and shredded, roasted, or barbecued pork

✔ Sautéed whole zucchini blossoms, seasoned with salt and pepper

✔ Sautéed, sliced mushrooms (the wilder the better), with garlic and herbs

✔ Fresh Salsa (see the recipe earlier in this chapter) over cheese

✔ Sautéed small shrimp and Green Tomatillo Salsa (see the recipe earlier in this chapter)

✔ Sautéed corn kernels, avocado slices, and Fresh Salsa (see the recipe earlier in this chapter)

✔ Crumbled blue cheese or cream cheese (instead of the cheese mix) with guava jelly or plum jelly

Transforming tortillas into tacos

Ever since we started hanging out at Los Angeles's taco stands in search of authentic snack foods, we've been taken with the taco's ability to satisfy like very few fast foods.

The foundation of a taco is two warmed, soft corn tortillas, stacked. These tortillas are topped with a savory filling like meat or fish and then sprinkled with spicy, crunchy garnishes and salsas to taste. The resulting package is tender and juicy. Our mouths water at the thought of those little bits of grilled or stewed meats; chunks of crunchy onion, cabbage, or lettuce; and soothing avocado, all doused with spicy salsa and sloppily tucked into fragrant, soft, corn tortillas. Yum! Sure beats a hot dog on a stick and those crisp tacos sold at fast-food joints.

If you don't have all the suggested toppings in the house, don't let that come between you and a good taco. After all, tacos were created to make good use of leftovers. Almost anything that you can wrap in a tortilla and bring to your mouth qualifies as a taco. Chopped fresh onion, cilantro leaves, lime wedges, sour cream, and bottled salsa make great authentic toppings for most fillings. And tacos are terrific interactive party foods. Just place some grilled, sliced meats out on a buffet table with an assortment of salsas and toppings and watch your guests improvise.

Making your own corn tortillas

Handmade corn tortillas have a pebbly texture and a definitive, earthy corn flavor. They're a wonderful addition to a Mexican-themed party, where their heavenly aroma is sure to draw guests into the kitchen to start the nibbling. In the Mexican home, fresh tortillas are bought daily, as the French buy baguettes.

Corn Tortillas

The Quaker Oats brand of masa harina or the Aztec Milling Company's deep yellow masa harina works well in this recipe. (See Chapter 2 of Book I for more about masa harina.)

Special tool: *Tortilla press*

Preparation time: *15 minutes*

Cooking time: *20 minutes*

Yield: *Twelve to eighteen 6-inch tortillas*

2 cups masa harina

Pinch of salt

1 to 1½ cups lukewarm water

1 Combine the masa harina and salt in a large mixing bowl and add the lukewarm water while stirring, until smooth. The dough should be slightly sticky and form a ball when pressed together. To test, flatten a small ball of dough between your palms or 2 sheets of plastic wrap. If the edges crack, add more water a little at a time until a test piece doesn't crack.

2 Divide the dough into 12 to 18 pieces, depending upon the size you prefer for your tortillas. Roll each piece into a ball and place the ball on a plate covered with a damp cloth towel.

3 Heat a dry cast-iron or nonstick frying pan or a stovetop griddle over medium heat. Flatten each ball of dough between 2 sheets of heavy plastic wrap either in a tortilla press (see Figure 4-2) or on a counter by using your hands or with a rolling pin. Remove the plastic from the top and, holding the tortilla with your fingertips, peel off the bottom sheet of plastic. Lay the tortillas, one by one, on the griddle and cook for about 1 minute and 15 seconds per side, gently pressing the top of the second side with your fingertips to encourage the tortilla to puff. Use tongs or a spatula to turn.

4 Cool the hot tortillas in a single layer on a towel. When they are still warm, but not hot, stack and wrap in the towel. Serve immediately or let cool, wrap well in plastic, and store in the refrigerator up to 1 week. Corn tortillas can be frozen for 2 weeks.

Reheating tortillas

To reheat refrigerated corn or flour tortillas, just follow these steps:

1. **Heat the oven to 200 degrees.**

2. **Warm a tea towel by placing it on a baking sheet and putting it in the oven briefly.**

3. **Place a dry skillet over medium heat. Warm the tortillas in the skillet, one at a time, about 30 seconds per side, and stack them,** **covering them with the warm towel between additions.**

   If the tortillas are dry, sprinkle them with water before reheating.

4. **Wrap stacked tortillas in the towel, wrap the towel with foil, and place in the oven until ready to serve.**

Using a Tortilla Press

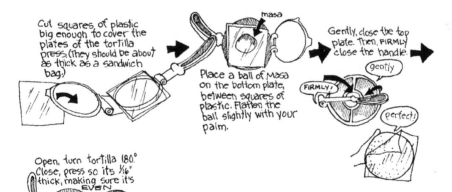

Cut squares of plastic big enough to cover the plates of the tortilla press. (They should be about as thick as a sandwich bag.)

masa

Place a ball of masa on the bottom plate, between squares of plastic. Flatten the ball slightly with your palm.

Gently, close the top plate. Then, FIRMLY close the handle.

gently

FIRMLY!

perfect!

Open, turn tortilla 180°. Close, press so it's ⅛" thick, making sure it's EVEN

Open and carefully lift off the top plastic. Turn the bare tortilla on to your hand and lift off the second sheet.

Figure 4-2:
Shaping a tortilla by using a tortilla press.

Building a taco

A good taco is a well-balanced meal in a package. It can be as simple or as complex as you like, but here are some blueprints:

1 **Warm the tortillas by quickly dipping each in a shallow pan of water and placing them on a grill or hot dry sauté pan for 30 seconds on each side to soften.**

   Stack and wrap in a damp tea towel and then in aluminum foil. Set the tortillas aside in a warm place for up to 30 minutes.

2. **Stack two warm, soft corn tortillas together.**

3. **Top with warm, well-seasoned meat, either chopped or shredded.**

4. **Add some spicy salsa.**

5. **Sprinkle with a variety of garnishes.**

   For crunch, add chopped onion, shredded cabbage, sliced radish, or Fresh Salsa (see the recipe earlier in this chapter). For creaminess, add Crema (see Chapter 6 of Book I), Guacamole (earlier in this chapter), chopped avocado, sour cream, or shredded cheese.

6. **Fold to enclose and carry to your mouth quickly for instant ingestion.**

Making tasty tacos

The best tacos probably don't start with a recipe at all. They spring from surprising sources — like the leftovers in the back of your refrigerator. Here are some likely inspirations:

- Holiday turkey
- Roasted chicken or last night's Mexican take-out chicken
- Leg of lamb
- Steak
- Pork, roasted or barbecued
- Brisket
- Fish fillets
- Cold, poached shrimp, lobster, or crabmeat

The following recipes aren't quite as adventurous as the previous suggestions, but they give you a great place to start experiencing the taco.

Grilled Steak Tacos

Mexican street vendors, pushing charcoal-burning pushcarts, sell fabulous *tacos al carbon*, or grilled tacos.

Preparation time: *10 minutes, plus 15 minutes for Fresh Salsa*

Cooking time: *15 minutes*

Yield: *4 to 6 servings*

1 pound, skirt or tri-tip steak, trimmed of fat and silverskin	*1 bunch coarsely chopped cilantro leaves (about ½ cup)*
Salt and pepper to taste	*2 peeled, seeded, and sliced avocados*
2 cloves garlic, minced	*1 bunch diagonally sliced scallions*
1 teaspoon dried oregano	*Garnishes: Lime wedges, ¼ head shredded white cabbage or lettuce, Fresh Salsa (see the recipe earlier in this chapter)*
1 tablespoon olive oil	
Juice of ½ lime (1 tablespoon)	
Twelve 4½-inch or eight 6-inch corn tortillas	

1 Prepare a hot fire in a gas or charcoal grill.

2 Half an hour before grilling, season the steak evenly with salt and pepper. Rub with the garlic and oregano and evenly drizzle with the olive oil and lime juice. Turn to evenly coat steak and refrigerate.

3 Grill the steak over high heat for 1½ minutes per side, or until it's caramelized on the outside and pink in the center. Let sit for 5 minutes before slicing into ¼-inch strips across the grain (at a right angle to the way the meat's fibers are running). Serve immediately with warmed tortillas, garnishes, and plenty of Fresh Salsa.

Vary It! For grilled chicken tacos, season the meat with plenty of salt and pepper or marinate in your favorite marinade. Grill about 1¼ pounds of chicken thighs or breasts, on the bone, for 30 minutes over medium heat, turning frequently. Remove the meat from the bones, cut into ¼-inch strips, and use as a filling with the same garnishes suggested in the Grilled Steak Tacos recipe.

Fish Tacos

We like our fish tacos soft, juicy, and overflowing with luscious chunks of fish and bits of vegetables. If you don't have time to make the special Cucumber Salsa that we suggest to go along with these tacos, you can just add chopped cucumbers, chiles, and tomatoes, along with a squirt of lemon or lime juice and some olive oil.

Preparation time: *10 minutes, plus 50 minutes for the Cucumber Salsa*

Yield: *3 servings*

1½ pounds salmon, snapper, bass, or halibut fillet	6 lettuce leaves
Extra-virgin olive oil for drizzling	Cucumber Salsa (see the following recipe)
Salt and pepper to taste	Lime wedges for squeezing
Twelve 6-inch corn tortillas, warmed	Garnishes: Avocado, radish slices

1 Prepare a medium-hot fire in a charcoal or gas grill.

2 Drizzle the fish with olive oil, season with salt and pepper, and grill until barely done, for 2 to 5 minutes per side, depending on the thickness. Remove the fish from the grill, let cool slightly, and then pull apart into large flakes.

3 Place the tortillas on a work surface. Line each with a piece of lettuce and top with chunks of fish. Top each with a generous spoonful of Cucumber Salsa, a squirt of lime, and a drizzle of olive oil. Garnish with avocado and radishes and serve.

Cucumber Salsa

Preparation time: *20 minutes, plus 30 minutes marination*

Yield: *3 cups*

4 pickling cucumbers, diced	3 tablespoons freshly squeezed orange juice
½ small red onion, diced	2 teaspoons salt
½ bunch cilantro, chopped (½ cup)	½ teaspoon pepper
1 small tomato, seeded and diced	2 serrano chiles, stemmed and sliced in thin rounds
3 tablespoons freshly squeezed lime juice	

Place all the ingredients in a bowl, combine well, and let stand, covered, for at least 30 minutes. Store in the refrigerator for up to 48 hours.

Vary It! *You don't have to start this recipe with uncooked fish. Tacos are a terrific way to use leftover fish. Just warm the fish first and then pull the flesh apart into large flakes.*

Entertaining with enchiladas

Authentic enchiladas aren't at all like the heavy, goopy concoctions, over-burdened with cheese and swimming in sauce, found on most combination plates in Mexican restaurants in the United States. In Mexico, enchiladas are a dish of day-old tortillas, lightly coated with sauce, filled with small bits of meat or vegetables, rolled up, and then baked to meld the flavors. At home, they make a terrific inexpensive, healthy, small meal to serve at informal gatherings.

The rolling involved in assembling enchiladas can sometimes frustrate beginning cooks. For perfectly rolled enchiladas every time, make sure that your tortillas are properly soaked and soft (see the following recipe for the details on what to soak them in) and then follow these steps (see Figure 4-3):

1. **Place 1 tortilla flat on your work surface. Place the enchilada filling in the center of each tortilla, spreading it evenly from edge to edge.**

2. **Fold one-third of the tortilla over the center.**

3. **Fold the other one-third of the tortilla over to enclose the filling.**

4. **Place the enchilada in a casserole dish with the seam side down.**

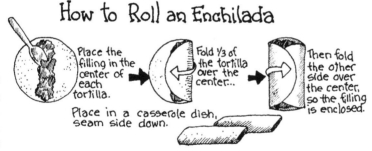

Figure 4-3:
Rolling an
enchilada.

Enchiladas are great for weeknight entertaining. Just assemble the casserole in the morning and store it in the refrigerator. When you get home at night, pop the enchiladas in the oven to heat through and serve. Tortillas, by the way, last in the refrigerator for as long as a week.

Green Enchiladas with Pork

Rich pork and tangy light green salsa are a natural combination in the Mexican kitchen. Add the earthiness of toasted corn from the tortillas, and you've got a winning dish.

Preparation time: *5 minutes, plus 15 minutes for Green Tomatillo Salsa*

Cooking time: *1 hour and 30 minutes*

Yield: *6 servings as an appetizer, 4 as an entrée*

1¼ pounds boneless stewing pork butt or shoulder, cut into 2-inch chunks

Salt and pepper to taste

3 cups Green Tomatillo Salsa (see the recipe earlier in this chapter)

1 cup vegetable oil

Twelve 6-inch corn tortillas

4 ounces panela cheese, crumbled

½ red onion, cut into rings

1 Preheat the oven to 350 degrees.

2 Season the pork all over with salt and pepper and place in a small ovenproof casserole dish. Pour on 1 cup of the Green Tomatillo Salsa. Cover with foil and bake for 1 hour, until tender. Let the pork cool and then shred it, reserving it in the sauce.

3 Pour the vegetable oil into a large skillet and place over medium heat. One at a time, dip the tortillas in the hot oil, and fry for about 10 seconds on each side. Drain on a rack.

4 Pour the remaining 2 cups of salsa into a shallow bowl or pie dish. Dip each tortilla into the salsa to lightly coat and place them on your work surface. (Reserve the remaining salsa for the next step.)

5 Divide the meat into 12 servings, and spoon into the center of each tortilla. Roll to enclose the meat in the tortilla.

6 Arrange the enchiladas in a single layer in a medium casserole dish, seam side down, and pour the remaining salsa over the top, discarding the fatty juices in the bowl. Bake for 15 minutes, until heated through. Sprinkle with the cheese and onions and serve.

Snacking on tortas

In addition to fabulous tacos for snacking anywhere, Mexican cooks also make delectable sandwiches called *tortas*. These small, overstuffed sandwiches, served on hollowed-out crusty rolls called *bolillos* (boh-*lee*-yohs), are generally found at small stands specializing in tortas.

We first tasted a torta after waiting in line outside a small shack in Mexico City. Sampling one of these well-packed, warm little bundles, served with its requisite selection of pickled vegetables, was well worth the wait.

Bolillos

Bolillos are a plain, crisp, white roll that you can use to make sandwiches or to eat with butter and jam at breakfast. They're a delight to have in the house, but if you don't have the time, a good substitute is a small, crisp French roll or a light sourdough roll.

Always pull out the doughy filling of these rolls with your fingers before making tortas.

Preparation time: *25 minutes mixing, plus 30 minutes sitting and 1 hour and 30 minutes rising*

Cooking time: *25 minutes*

Yield: *Twelve 6-inch rolls*

2 cups lukewarm water	*1 tablespoon salt*
Two ¼-ounce packages dry yeast	*½ cup milk*
1 tablespoon sugar	*2 tablespoons vegetable oil for coating the bowl*
¼ cup vegetable shortening	
7 cups flour plus flour for coating work surface	*1 tablespoon salt dissolved in ½ cup water for brushing*

1 Preheat the oven to 375 degrees.

2 In a large mixing bowl or bowl of an electric mixer with a paddle, combine the water, yeast, and sugar. Stir to dissolve the yeast. Add the shortening and 2 cups of the flour and mix until smooth. Set aside at room temperature for 30 minutes.

3 Stir the salt into the milk and add to the flour mixture. With the machine running, gradually add the remaining 5 cups of flour until the dough pulls away from the sides of the bowl. Switch to the dough hook and knead at low speed for an additional 15 minutes. Transfer the dough to a lightly oiled bowl and turn to coat all sides of the dough. Cover with a damp towel and set aside to rise in a warm place until doubled in bulk, about 1 hour.

4 Punch down the dough and briefly knead on a lightly floured surface. Divide the dough into 12 portions. Roll each portion into a ball, or shape into a flat oval and pinch the ends. Place the balls on baking sheets with 2 inches between each, cover with a damp towel, and let rise, about 30 minutes, or until the dough holds a fingerprint when poked.

5 Brush the salt water over the rolls and bake for 20 to 30 minutes, until the crusts are golden brown. Cool and serve, or wrap well and freeze.

Chicken Black Bean Torta

A warm chicken sandwich such as this torta, served with interesting garnishes, is so much more satisfying than an ordinary cold meat sandwich.

Preparation time: *5 minutes*

Cooking time: *5 minutes*

Yield: *4 sandwiches*

2 tablespoons butter for spreading

4 Bolillos (see the recipe earlier in this chapter), cut in half lengthwise and excess dough removed from both halves

1 cup Refried Black Beans (see the recipe later in this chapter), or good-quality canned refried black beans

8 tablespoons (2 ounces) grated añejo cheese

1 chicken breast, cut into 4 thin slices crosswise and pounded to ⅛-inch thickness

Salt and pepper to taste

Olive oil for coating

1 cup Pickled Red Onions (see the following recipe)

Freshly cracked black pepper

1 Preheat the broiler or prepare a medium-hot fire in a charcoal or gas grill.

2 Lightly butter both halves of the Bolillos. Toast on the hot grill or under the broiler until golden, about 3 minutes. Spread the bottom halves with the black beans, sprinkle with cheese, and warm on a tray in the oven for about 5 minutes.

3 Season the chicken all over with salt and pepper. Lightly coat a skillet with the olive oil and place over high heat. Sauté the chicken for about 30 to 45 seconds per side, until cooked through. Place the chicken on the top halves of bread. Top with Pickled Red Onions and plenty of fresh cracked pepper. Close with the bean-lined halves of the bolillos and serve.

Pickled Red Onions

1 red onion, sliced into thin rings

1 teaspoon salt

½ teaspoon dried oregano

1 habañero chile, seeded and sliced

½ cup freshly squeezed orange juice

¼ cup freshly squeezed lime juice

Place the onion rings in a bowl and pour on enough boiling water to cover them. Let sit for 2 minutes. Drain, add the salt, oregano, chile, orange juice, and lime juice, and store in the refrigerator for 4 hours or up to 2 days.

Vary It! *For a turkey torta, purchase thinly sliced, uncooked turkey breast slices and substitute for the chicken.*

Stuffed Treats

The foods in this section are among the most traditional and beloved in Mexico. All the recipes take some extra time to prepare because of the many steps and the handwork involved in wrapping the foods. But just like any carefully chosen gift, they're more special because of all that work.

Empanadas: Little pies full of flavor

If you explore your local Spanish-speaking neighborhood and wander into a few small grocery stores or bakeries, you're sure to spot a fragrant stack of *empanadas* behind the counter. Sometimes they're big overstuffed half moons, and sometimes they're delicate miniature pastries, but whatever shape they take, a local cook usually made them at home.

With their irresistible savory fillings and neat handheld size, these little pastries are a popular snack food in most Latin American communities. In addition to making wonderful, interesting appetizers for a party at home, empanadas make a terrific lunch and are naturals for packing into picnic baskets and lunch boxes.

Empanadas de Picadillo

Picadillo is a dish from Spain. It contains highly seasoned, slightly sweetened, ground fried meat. In addition to making an excellent stuffing for these little turnovers, you also can use picadillo to stuff chiles for baking, to fill tacos, or to simply serve alongside rice and beans. You can make the dough recipe a few days ahead and refrigerate it.

Preparation time: *20 minutes, plus 30 minutes chilling and 1 hour to make the salsas*

Cooking time: *35 minutes*

Yield: *15 empanadas*

1 pound lean ground beef

1 medium yellow onion, chopped

2 cloves garlic, peeled and chopped

½ cup raisins, chopped

½ cup green olives, chopped

1 teaspoon salt

1 teaspoon pepper

2 teaspoons ground cumin

¼ teaspoon ground cloves

1 tablespoon brown sugar (optional)

½ cup Red Roasted Tomato Salsa (see the recipe earlier in this chapter) or store-bought salsa

Empanada Dough (see the following recipe) or 1 pound frozen pie dough

1 egg combined with 2 tablespoons milk, lightly beaten for brushing on dough

Garnish: Roasted Green Chile Salsa (see the recipe earlier in this chapter)

1 Brown the ground beef in a large heavy skillet over medium-high heat, stirring frequently, about 7 minutes. Drain off and discard the excess fat. Add the onion and sauté for 5 minutes. Then add the garlic, raisins, olives, salt, pepper, cumin, cloves, and brown sugar, if desired. Cook until their aromas are released, about 2½ minutes. Stir in the Red Roasted Tomato Salsa, bring to a boil, and set aside to cool.

2 Roll out the dough and cut into circles as described in the following recipe.

3 Place a generous tablespoon of the beef filling in the center of each pastry round. Fold over and press the edges together to seal. Transfer to a baking sheet and chill for a half hour, or wrap and freeze. (You don't have to defrost frozen empanadas before baking.)

4 Preheat the oven to 400 degrees.

5 Brush the pastries all over with the egg wash and arrange in a single layer on a baking sheet. Bake until golden, about 15 minutes. Serve hot with the Roasted Green Chile Salsa.

Empanada Dough

Book I

Mexican
Cooking

Preparation time: *20 minutes, plus 1 hour chilling*

2 cups flour plus additional for dusting

12 tablespoons cold butter

½ teaspoon salt

1 teaspoon sugar

¼ cup water

1 Combine the flour and butter in a large bowl. Lightly blend with your fingertips until the butter is evenly distributed in chunks. Dissolve the salt and sugar in the water and stir into the flour mixture.

2 On a lightly floured surface, turn out the mixture and lightly knead the dough until it forms a ball, adding a bit more water if necessary. Knead by pushing the ball of dough away from you with the heel of your hand, and then gathering it up, and making a quarter turn before repeating. Wrap in plastic and refrigerate for at least 1 hour or freeze as long as a week. Return to room temperature before rolling.

3 Divide the dough in half. On a floured board, roll out half the dough to a thickness of ⅛ inch. With a cookie cutter or a drinking glass, cut out 4-inch circles. Gather the scraps, add to the remaining dough, and reroll and cut out circles until all the dough is used.

Vary It! *For cocktail-sized servings, we sometimes make empanadas into tiny bite-sized pieces. When cutting out the dough, make sure that each circle is large enough to stuff. You want each bite to contain both meat and pastry. We find a 3-inch circle is just the right size.*

Tamales: Feast-day treats

Making tamales, like eating tamales, is an activity meant to be shared. In Mexico, where tamales have been a fiesta food since the Indians first offered them to the gods, groups traditionally prepare these labor-intensive stuffed and steamed packages in a sort of pre-party party. The holiday they are most closely associated with in Mexico is All Saints' Day, while in the United States, tamales are a Christmas tradition.

Wrapping a tamale

Before you can unwrap and enjoy the delicious filling of a tamale, you first need to create the tidy corn-husk packages. Just follow these steps (and have a look at Figure 4-4):

1. **Soak the dried corn husks in hot water for 2 hours or overnight.**

2. **Drain the corn husks on paper towels.**

3. **Cut out 9-inch squares of aluminum foil.**

   You need one for each tamale.

4. **Spread 1 or 2 husks lengthwise on the counter with the narrow end pointing away from you.**

5. **Spread about 2½ tablespoons of filling down the center, leaving about 2 inches bare at the top of the husk.**

6. **Fold over the sides and then the ends to enclose the filling.**

7. **Place the folded tamale on a square of foil and fold over the foil to enclose the package.**

   Repeat with the remaining filling and additional corn husks.

Banana leaves also make excellent wrappers for tamales. To use, holding them in your hands, run the leaves directly over a stovetop gas or electric burner on low heat or place in a dry skillet for a few seconds. This process softens the leaves, makes them fragrant, and brightens the green color. Cut them into 9-inch squares, trimming out the tough center stem, and wrap the stuffed banana leaf in foil to enclose.

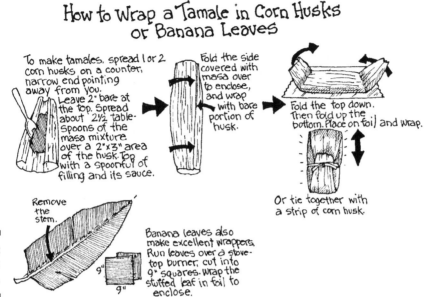

Figure 4-4:
Wrapping a
tamale.

Steaming the tamales

Small batches of tamales can fit into a vegetable steamer basket, but for larger quantities, you need a steamer, which is a large pot with a perforated portion on top for the tamales.

If you don't have a steamer, you can improvise by balancing a rack or colander on top of one or two empty cans or inverted coffee cups that are set in a large pasta or soup pot. Make sure that the water doesn't touch the rack's bottom.

Always keep an eye on the pot while the tamales are steaming so that the water doesn't get too low or entirely evaporate. And always line the steamer tray with extra husks to cushion the cooking process.

Tamales for every occasion

Mastering tamale making is really just a matter of getting organized and setting aside the time, preferably with a group of friends, to dig in and cook.

Basic Masa Tamales with Fillings

Our basic masa tamale recipe is built for flexibility. First, we explain the technique for beating the masa, filling the corn husks, and then steaming. We follow that recipe with three options for savory fillings to flavor the masa — chiles and cheese, chicken and salsa, and pork in adobado sauce. You can use the salsas or sauces that go with the fillings in three ways: ½ cup gets beaten into the masa, ½ cup gets mixed into the filling, and the remaining ½ cup is served with the finished tamales.

Tamales as delicious as these deserve to be the main focus of a meal. The traditional accompaniments are rice and beans, but we prefer to serve them with something lighter, like a big green salad.

Preparation time: *30 minutes (not including the preparation time for the filling and sauce and softening time for corn husks)*

Cooking time: *1 hour and 15 minutes (not including the preparation time for the filling and sauce)*

Yield: *12 to 14 tamales*

½ cup sauce from one of the filling recipes that follow this recipe	1 pound cold prepared ground masa for tamales, or 1¾ cups dry masa harina, moistened with 1 cup warm water and then chilled
1 cup chicken stock (later in this chapter), at room temperature	
1 teaspoon baking soda	8-ounce package dried corn husks, softened
1½ teaspoons salt	Fillings and sauces (see the following recipes)
½ cup vegetable shortening or cold lard	Garnish: Sour cream

1 Mix together ½ cup of the salsa or sauce from one of the fillings, the chicken stock, baking soda, and salt, and set aside.

2 Place the masa in the bowl of an electric mixer and beat at medium speed until light in texture, about 6 minutes. Slowly add the chicken stock mixture while beating continuously at medium-high speed. Turn the mixer speed up to high and add the shortening or lard, a tablespoon at a time, beating well after each addition. Continue beating and scraping down the bowl until the mixture is light and fluffy, about 15 minutes total. Test for lightness by dropping 1 tablespoon of masa into cold water: If it floats, the mixture is light enough. If not, continue beating at high speed a few minutes longer.

3 Wrap the tamales according to the instructions in "Wrapping a tamale" earlier in this chapter, spreading about 2½ tablespoons of the masa mixture over a 2-x-3-inch area of husk. Top with a spoonful of filling and its sauce.

4 To cook, line a steamer with corn husks and fill with tamales, upright in layers. Cook over simmering water for 1 hour and 15 minutes, until the husks just pull away from the masa without sticking. Serve hot with the remaining sauce and sour cream. (You can reheat cold tamales in a steamer over simmering water for 30 minutes.) Store leftover tamales in the refrigerator as long as 4 days, or you can freeze them. Reheat for about 30 minutes in the steamer.

Green Chile Cheese Filling

If you like chile rellenos, you'll love this recipe.

Preparation time: *15 minutes, plus 15 minutes to make the Green Tomatillo Salsa*

Yield: *12 to 14 tamales*

*1½ cups Green Tomatillo Salsa (see the
recipe earlier in this chapter)*

*4 poblano chiles, roasted, peeled, seeded,
and cut into ½-inch strips*

*1 pound Mexican cheese, such as Ranchero,
queso fresco, panela, or manchego, cut into
½-inch cubes (about 3 cups)*

In a large mixing bowl, combine ½ cup of the salsa, the chiles, and the cheese. (Reserve ½ cup of the salsa to incorporate into the masa.) Serve the remaining ½ cup of salsa alongside the finished tamales.

Roasted Tomato Chicken Filling

Olives and raisins add sweet and salty accents to this easy chicken filling.

Preparation time: *5 minutes, plus 35 minutes to make the Red Roasted Tomato Salsa*

Cooking time: *15 minutes*

Yield: *12 to 14 tamales*

*1½ cups Red Roasted Tomato Salsa (see the
recipe earlier in this chapter)*

2 cups shredded cooked chicken

½ cup green olives, pitted

½ cup golden raisins

In a medium saucepan over medium heat, combine ½ cup of the salsa, the chicken, olives, and raisins. Simmer for about 15 minutes, until heated through. (Reserve ½ cup of the salsa to incorporate into the masa.) Serve the remaining ½ cup salsa alongside the finished tamales.

Pork and Green Chile Adobo Filling

Rich pork and spicy green chiles are a tough combination to beat.

Preparation time: *5 minutes, plus 1 hour 20 minutes to make the Adobado Sauce*

Cooking time: *15 minutes*

Yield: *12 to 14 tamales*

*1½ cups Adobado Sauce (see Chapter 5 of
Book I)*

2 cups shredded, cooked pork

*1 poblano chile, roasted, peeled, seeded and
cut into ½-inch-wide strips*

In a medium saucepan over medium heat, combine ½ cup of the Adobado Sauce, the pork, and the chile. Simmer for about 15 minutes, until heated through. (Reserve ½ cup of the sauce to incorporate into the masa.) Serve the remaining ½ cup sauce alongside the finished tamales.

Soups and Salads

Making Mexican soups is very easy. No silky smooth bisques require multiple strainings, no expensive ingredients like lobster or crab make you check your credit card balance, and no delicate techniques set your teeth on edge. With just a few simple ingredients and the push of a blender button, you can make the kind of flavorful, satisfying soups that mean pleasure in any language.

Salad doesn't play the same part in the Mexican meal plan as it does in other parts of the world. Mexican cooks use so many fresh vegetables in their garnishes and salsas that serving a bowl full of chopped lettuce and tomato as an accompaniment just doesn't make sense. Instead, they top tacos with chopped onion, cilantro, and tomato; generously garnish posoles with shredded cabbage, radishes, and avocado; and sell sliced cucumbers, roasted corn, and fresh fruit on the street as snack foods.

Setting your sights on Mexican soups

Mexican soups are a snap to prepare, once you have the right tools and a few tips under your cooking belt.

Mexican cooks make several types of brothy dishes, but the most popular are the thinner broths referred to as *sopas* (Spanish for "soups"). They run the gamut from rich creamed vegetable soups, to cold gazpacho, to the thin and familiar tortilla soup, but the unifying thread is that all are light enough to be eaten as a first course.

Sopa secas are leftover sopas in which the liquid has been absorbed enough for the dish to be eaten as a side dish or starter, with a fork.

Gazpacho

Gazpacho is a perfect first course for just about anything you choose to serve in the heat of the summer — except for a tomato-based entree. It's one of those simple uncooked dishes in which a quality olive oil makes a great deal of difference. So haul out that expensive extra-virgin olive oil you got as a present for your last birthday and let it pour. You won't regret it.

Preparation time: *20 minutes, plus 2 hours chilling time*

Yield: *4 to 6 servings*

1 slice white bread, crusts removed	*2 cloves garlic, peeled*
2 tablespoons red wine vinegar	*½ cup extra-virgin olive oil*
3 cups tomato juice, plus more if needed to thin the soup	*3 jalapeños, stemmed, seeded, and chopped*
6 pickling cucumbers, peeled, seeded, and diced	*1 teaspoon sugar*
	¾ teaspoon salt
4 scallions, thinly sliced	*½ teaspoon black pepper*
1 red bell pepper, seeded and diced	*Sliced chives for garnish*

1 Place the bread on a plate, sprinkle it with the vinegar, and let sit until thoroughly moistened, 5 minutes.

2 Combine the tomato juice, cucumbers, scallions, and red pepper in a large bowl.

3 Transfer about one-fourth of the vegetable mixture to a blender or food processor. Add the moistened bread, garlic, olive oil, jalapeños, sugar, salt, and pepper. Puree until smooth.

4 Pour the puree into the bowl with the vegetables. Stir to combine. Thin with more tomato juice if desired and adjust seasonings. Chill for at least 2 hours. Serve cold and garnish with chives. Store in the refrigerator for up to 2 days.

Remember: *Because the taste of tomato juice is so dominant in gazpacho, the juice you choose is important. Read the labels carefully before purchasing a juice. Reject any juices with weird ancillary ingredients. If Mother Nature had intended bisulfates to be in tomato juice, she would have put them in tomatoes. Don't even think about buying tomato juices containing sugar or Bloody Mary spices. Tomatoes and salt are all you really want to see on that label.*

Corn and Chile Chowder

You can make this lovely corn soup year-round if you use an excellent canned or frozen corn. It makes a nice first course for a dinner party with a grilled meat entree. To make the Corn and Chile Chowder or any milk-based soup in advance and freeze, cook until the end of Step 1. Then freeze. To defrost and finish, warm the corn mixture in a soup pot and continue the recipe at Step 2.

Preparation time: *20 minutes*

Cooking time: *40 minutes*

Yield: *4 to 6 servings (6 cups)*

2 tablespoons olive oil

1 medium yellow onion, diced

1 teaspoon salt

4 cups fresh or canned corn kernels, drained (8 ears fresh corn, two and a half 12-ounce cans, or three 10-ounce packages, frozen)

2 to 3 cloves garlic, peeled and minced

1 teaspoon ground cumin

3 poblano or Anaheim chiles, roasted, peeled, seeded, and diced (see Chapter 3 of Book I)

2 cups milk or half-and-half

2 cups chicken stock

Garnish: ½ bunch chives, thinly sliced diagonally (¼ cup)

1 Heat the olive oil in a large stockpot over medium heat. Sauté the onion with the salt until golden brown, about 15 minutes. Add the corn, turn the heat to high, and cook for 5 to 7 minutes, until slightly browned. Stir in the garlic and cumin and cook, stirring frequently, 2 minutes longer. Reduce the heat to low, stir in the chiles, and cook for 2 to 3 more minutes.

2 Pour in the milk and chicken stock. Bring to a simmer over low heat, being careful not to boil. Gently simmer, uncovered, for 15 minutes.

3 Pour one-third of the soup into a food processor or blender and puree. Stir back into the stockpot and simmer for 5 minutes longer. Serve hot, garnished with chives.

Vary It! *If you can't get your hands on the more exotic chiles, substitute 2 green bell peppers and 2 jalapeños, both roasted and diced.*

Tortilla Soup

Tortilla soup, probably the best known of the Mexican soups, is a brilliant use of two common Mexican leftovers — tortillas and salsa. If you don't feel like making the Red Roasted Tomato Salsa first, you can substitute a favorite bottled smooth red salsa. You can also simply puree the following ingredients in the blender: 1½ pounds of Roma tomatoes, 6 cloves garlic, 1 small yellow onion, and ½ cup water and add to the pot along with the stock.

Preparation time: *15 minutes, plus 15 minutes for Red Roasted Tomato Salsa*

Cooking time: *1 hour*

Yield: *6 servings*

3 tablespoons olive oil	*1 teaspoon salt*
1 large yellow onion, diced	*¾ pound fried tortilla chips*
3 cloves garlic, peeled and minced	*Garnishes: 1 bunch cilantro leaves (½ cup);*
2 cups Red Roasted Tomato Salsa (see the recipe earlier in this chapter)	*1 avocado, peeled, seeded, and coarsely chopped; ½ cup Crema (see Chapter 6 of Book I); 2 limes, cut in wedges*
5 cups chicken stock	
1 dried chipotle chile, stemmed and seeded (optional)	

1 Heat the olive oil in a large stockpot over low heat. Add the onion and cook, stirring frequently, until pale brown and caramelized, 10 to 15 minutes. Stir in the garlic and cook 10 minutes longer.

2 Pour in the tomato salsa, chicken stock, chipotle chile (if desired), and salt. Bring to a boil, reduce to a simmer, and cook, uncovered, for 20 minutes. Stir in the fried tortilla chips and cook 10 minutes longer, until the chips soften. Remove and discard the chile. Serve hot, topped with cilantro, avocado, Crema, and lime wedges.

Border salads

Tostadas are wonderful, healthy salads served on edible fried tortilla plates. With their small meat portions, they make terrific all-in-one suppers. You also can think of them as healthy sandwiches because they combine carbohydrates (corn), veggies, and a little bit of meat.

The key to a terrific tostada is to season each part separately and well. The chicken or meat, as well as the salad, should be moistened and seasoned with dressing so that every bite is moist and flavorful. You almost force people to eat the perfect balance of foods by putting something with acidity and texture on top of something rich like the beans. If you serve salad on the side, people tend to eat it separately.

Making the bean salad in this section is a snap if you keep these tips in mind:

- ✔ As much as we love our beans, nothing is worse than undercooked or overcooked beans in a salad. Always test beans for doneness by biting into the smallest, densest one. The center should be creamy, and all the beans should hold their shape.

- ✔ Anytime you're dressing beans or lentils for a salad, they absorb the dressing better if you coat them while they're still slightly warm.

Chicken Tostada Salad

In a tostada, spread the beans out to all the edges and scatter the other components evenly. Each bite should deliver a combination of flavors. Who wants a mouthful of plain tortilla with those wonderful tastes congregating in the middle?

Preparation time: *25 minutes*

Cooking time: *15 minutes*

Yield: *4 servings (8 tostadas)*

¾ pound cooked, shredded chicken	*Salt and pepper to taste*
1 small red onion, diced	*¾ cup vegetable oil for frying*
1 bunch cilantro leaves, chopped (about ½ cup)	*8 large (6-inch) corn tortillas or 8 prepared tostada shells*
1 small or ½ large head romaine lettuce, finely shredded	*1 cup Refried Black Beans (see the recipe later in this chapter) or good-quality canned refried beans*
1 medium tomato, cored, seeded, and diced	
½ cup (2 ounces) grated añejo cheese	*Garnishes: 3 tablespoons Crema (see Chapter 6 of Book I) and 1 large avocado or 2 medium avocados, peeled, seeded, and thinly sliced*
½ cup red wine vinegar	
¾ cup olive oil	

1 Combine the chicken, onion, and cilantro in a medium bowl.

2 In another bowl, combine the lettuce, tomato, and cheese.

3 To make the dressing, combine the red wine vinegar, olive oil, and salt and pepper in a small jar or bottle. Cover and shake vigorously to combine, or whisk the ingredients together.

4 Pour the vegetable oil to a depth of ½ inch in a small frying pan. Heat the oil over moderate heat. Fry the tortillas, using tongs to turn them over so that the tortillas are crisp on both sides. Drain on paper towels.

5 Heat the beans through in a small pot over low heat, stirring often to prevent sticking. Add some water if the beans are dry.

6 To assemble, spread a thin layer of beans on each crisp tortilla. Drizzle with about 1 teaspoon Crema and top with a few avocado slices. Pour enough dressing on the reserved chicken mixture to coat generously and toss well. Scatter over the tortillas. Toss the remaining dressing with the lettuce mixture and generously cover each tostada with it.

Fiesta Bean Salad

We jazz up a typical American-style bean salad with three different beans and a colorful confetti of diced peppers. This versatile salad is a great choice for a buffet table or picnic because it can remain out without wilting. Or serve it as an accompaniment to a full-flavored entrée like ribs or fried chicken.

Preparation time: *10 minutes, plus 2 hours chilling*

Yield: *4 to 6 servings*

1 red bell pepper	*1 small red onion, finely diced*
1 yellow bell pepper	*1 cup canned, drained black beans*
1 poblano chile	*1 cup canned, drained pinto beans*
½ cup olive oil	*1 cup canned, drained red beans or kidney beans*
¼ cup red wine vinegar	
1 teaspoon salt	*½ bunch cilantro leaves, coarsely chopped (¼ cup)*
½ teaspoon pepper	

1 Core and seed the bell peppers and poblano and cut them into ¼-inch cubes. The pepper and chile cubes should be similar to the size of the cooked beans.

2 To make the dressing, in a large bowl whisk together the olive oil, vinegar, salt, and pepper. Toss in the diced peppers, chile, onion, beans, and cilantro, and mix well. Refrigerate for 2 hours or overnight before serving.

Vary It! *If you have a smoker, try smoking the beans for Fiesta Bean Salad. A chipotle chile pureed into the dressing emphasizes the smokiness of the beans, giving the whole salad a heartier taste.*

Side Dishes

No matter how much time we spend in the professional kitchen, we're always awed by the inventiveness of Mexican cooks, who create a healthy and exciting cuisine with such a simple handful of ingredients. Thanks to the creativity of Mexican cooks, meager ingredients like rice and beans are elevated to complex, sensual foods.

In these delicious side dishes, salsa, chiles, and herbs bring rice to a whole new level of interest. Beans are mashed and enriched with fat to make luxuriously creamy refried beans. Old tortillas never die or get thrown out; instead, they are reborn as crispy, scrumptious tortilla chips and tostadas.

In addition to their ability to breathe new life into simple ingredients, some of these side dishes are also very healthy. Remember that combining beans (without lard, of course) and rice forms a full protein.

This section focuses on the simple, inexpensive side dishes that most Mexican meals are built around. In most Mexican homes, a pot of beans is always bubbling on a burner, some rice is in the fridge for reheating, and tortillas are always present.

Getting the rice spirit

The Mexican method for cooking rice is a great example of how the simplest foods can become a special occasion in the hands of gifted cooks. Frying the rice to develop a toasty flavor and then infusing it with salsa to give it color, flavor, and pizzazz is one of the most exciting techniques we've learned from the Mexican kitchen. Although cooking rice the Mexican way takes more time than the ways you may be used to cooking rice, these special rice dishes are well worth the extra effort.

To get the most from your Mexican rice, you need to start with the right ingredients and treat them right during preparation. Follow these tips to increase your success:

- Start with well-rinsed long-grain rice. We always rinse rice before cooking to remove the excess starch that causes gumminess. To rinse the rice, place it in a large bowl, not a colander, and rinse under cold running water for 5 minutes, or until the water runs clear. Keep stirring the grains with your hand to loosen starch particles.

- If your recipe calls for you to toast the rice (which is done on the stove top in a skillet, rather than in the oven), go for a full golden color and roasted aroma.

- Always let your rice rest before serving it. Doing so allows the rice to finish cooking and cool slightly.

✔ Stirring rice with a spoon to cool it down can break delicate grains. Instead, use a fork to gently separate the rice and cool it down before serving it. Cool overcooked or mushy rice by emptying it out onto a baking sheet and spreading it thinly so that air can circulate.

✔ For an interesting twist, try tossing some broken, dry spaghetti or tiny, whole orzo (tiny, rice-shaped pasta) into the pot along with the rice and fry until golden. If you want to add the spaghetti, use the thin-style spaghetti and break it into small pieces of about ¼ inch.

✔ More is always better than less when adding chiles and salsas to these rice dishes. Creating a full-flavored rice takes a gutsy dose of spice and salsa. (Chapter 2 of Book I tells you all about chiles. We discuss salsa earlier in this chapter.)

Red Rice

This basic tomato-tinged rice accompanies many Mexican dishes. You can make the Red Roasted Tomato Salsa, which gives the rice its color, as long as a week in advance.

Preparation time: 5 minutes, plus 35 minutes for the Red Roasted Tomato Salsa

Cooking time: 45 minutes

Yield: 6 to 8 servings

3 tablespoons vegetable oil

1½ cups long-grain rice, rinsed

½ medium yellow onion, chopped

2 cloves garlic, peeled and chopped

Salt and pepper to taste

5 serrano chiles, or to taste, stemmed, seeded if desired

2 cups chicken stock, vegetable stock, or water (see the stock recipes earlier in this chapter)

1½ cups Red Roasted Tomato Salsa (see the recipe earlier in this chapter)

1 Heat the oil in a medium-size heavy saucepan or skillet over medium-low heat. Sauté the rice, stirring constantly, until golden brown and crackling, about 5 minutes. Add the onion and sauté just until soft. Stir in the garlic, salt and pepper, and chiles and sauté until the aroma is released.

2 Pour in the stock or water and the salsa, mixing well to combine. Bring to a boil, reduce to a simmer, cover, and cook for 20 minutes. Let rest 10 minutes. Fluff with a fork and serve hot.

Beautiful, beautiful refried beans!

With their dollop of richness from lard or other fat, refried beans are an inexpensive way to satisfy the universal need to feel full and happy. Refrieds are a little more special than ordinary beans, and they're typically served alongside small snacks like tacos or enchiladas to round out the meal.

Wash and pick over your beans before cooking. Wash them in a colander with cold water and then spread the beans out on a cookie sheet or counter. Pull out and discard any stray dirt, stones, or shriveled beans.

The following recipe calls for lard because that is the most typical Mexican fat for beans and it adds a hint of pork flavor that makes the dish delicious. You can't fry beans without fat, but you can use different fats if lard isn't to your liking. In place of the lard, you can substitute bacon drippings, vegetable oil, or half butter and half olive oil in the same quantity as specified.

Chapter 3 of Book I offers additional tips for working with beans.

Refried Black Beans

Frying beans with a bit of fat and onion accentuates their rich, creamy quality. Our own tastes tend toward even more lard than the following recipes calls for, but we don't want to scare away the faint-hearted. Feel free to increase the lard for a richer, more authentic refried bean. Remember that if you don't eat refried beans with lots of meat or protein, the overall proportion of fat in the meal isn't unhealthy.

Preparation time: *10 minutes*

Cooking time: *1 hour and 30 minutes*

Yield: *4 to 6 servings*

2 cups dried black beans, washed and picked over	1 large onion, diced
8 cups water	1½ teaspoons salt
⅓ cup lard or vegetable oil	½ teaspoon freshly ground black pepper

1 Place the beans and water in a large pot and bring to a boil. Cover, reduce to a simmer, and cook for 1 hour and 15 minutes, or until the beans are tender and creamy in the center. (To test for doneness, taste 3 or 4 of the smaller beans.) Crush the beans in their liquid with a potato masher or the back of a wooden spoon.

2 Heat the lard or vegetable oil in a large saucepan over medium heat. Sauté the onion with the salt and pepper until golden, about 10 minutes. Add the beans and their liquid and continue cooking over medium heat, stirring frequently, until the liquid evaporates and the beans form a creamy mass that pulls away from the bottom and sides of the pan, about 15 minutes. Serve immediately.

Vary It! *If you're lucky enough to find epazote (see Chapter 2 of Book I), add a sprig or two to the pot of the refried beans for the last 15 minutes to give the beans an authentic flavor. Epazote has also been known to counteract the unpleasant side effect of beans on the digestive system!*

Spicing things up with veggie sides

We love to eat our veggies. In fact, if we weren't chefs, we just may cross the line and become vegetarians.

So many of our customers in Los Angeles want to eat light and healthy that we always take special care with our vegetable dishes so that they're as special as everything else on the menu. These Mexican sides are so rich tasting and flavorful that you may wonder how you ever settled for steamed vegetables.

Poblano Mashed Potatoes

These spicy, rich potatoes are one of the most frequently requested recipes at our restaurants. Serve with an entree of equal heft.

Preparation time: *15 minutes*

Cooking time: *35 minutes*

Yield: *6 servings*

2½ pounds baking potatoes, peeled and quartered

1½ tablespoons salt

1 cup sour cream

½ cup olive oil

5 poblano chiles, roasted, peeled, seeded, and diced (see Chapter 3 of Book I for more information on working with chiles)

Salt and pepper to taste

1 Place the potatoes in a large saucepan. Pour in enough water to cover and add the 1½ tablespoons salt. Bring to a boil, reduce to a simmer, and cook, uncovered, until soft, about 25 minutes. Drain well, return the potatoes to the pan, and, while still warm, mash with a potato masher or food mill until slightly chunky.

2 In a small pot, combine the sour cream, olive oil, and chiles and warm over low heat just until warm to the touch. Too much heat causes the sour cream to separate.

3 Add the sour cream mixture to the potatoes and gently stir just to combine. Season with salt and pepper and serve immediately.

Warning: *The worst thing you can do to these mashed potatoes is overmix them, which leads to gummy, starchy potatoes. Gently combine them with the sour cream mixture just until mixed.*

Spicy Grilled Corn

Here is a refined version of a popular Mexican street snack. Just one bite leaves you wondering how you could ever go back to plain old buttered corn.

Preparation time: *15 minutes, plus 10 minutes soaking*

Cooking time: *15 minutes*

Yield: *6 servings*

6 ears fresh sweet corn, in the husk	*2 tablespoons chopped fresh cilantro*
4 tablespoons butter, softened	*1 tablespoon freshly squeezed lime juice*
Salt and pepper to taste	
2 arbol chiles, seeded, stemmed, and coarsely chopped	

1 Preheat the grill to medium-hot.

2 Carefully remove the corn silks, leaving the husks attached. Soak the ears of corn in their husks in a large bowl or sink of cold water for 10 minutes.

3 In a small bowl, mix together the softened butter, salt and pepper, chiles, cilantro, and lime juice until smooth. Set aside.

4 Drain the corn well and place each husk-enclosed ear on the hot grill. Cook for about 12 minutes, turning frequently. The corn is steamed when it loses its raw crunch. Remove each cob from the grill and, when cool enough to handle, strip off and discard the husks.

5 Brush each cob with the seasoned butter mixture and return to the grill for a minute or two just to heat. Serve immediately.

Chapter 5

The Main Event

In This Chapter

▶ Cooking delicious fish, Mexican style

▶ Marinating chicken for maximum effect

▶ Cooking Mexico's native bird, the turkey

▶ Trying your hand at traditional pork and beef dishes

*T*his chapter is the meat of the book. Here you find a whole host of tried and true recipes that serve as wonderful main courses for your Mexican meal. Combine these with the starters and side dishes in Chapter 4 of Book I and the desserts in Chapter 6 of Book I, and you'll be eating Mexican from beginning to end — our idea of the perfect meal!

Fish and Seafood Dishes

With Mexico's 6,000 miles of coastline along the Pacific Ocean, Gulf of Mexico, Sea of Cortez, and the Caribbean, it's not surprising that fresh fish plays such an important part in the Mexican diet. Mexicans eat fresh fish in sparkling ceviches, rustic seafood stews, impressive whole fish entrées, and quick tacos and enchiladas.

Shrimp in a Garlic Bath

In this traditional dish, called *al mojo de ajo* in Mexico, a quick, rustic sauce of garlic and dried chile slivers is cooked in the same pan as juicy rock shrimp.

Preparation time: *10 minutes*

Cooking time: *20 minutes*

Yield: *2 servings*

¼ cup olive oil

10 cloves garlic, peeled and thinly sliced

¾ pound rock or medium shrimp, peeled, deveined, washed, and dried

Salt and pepper to taste

1 large ancho chile, wiped clean, stemmed, seeded, and finely julienned (see Chapter 3 of Book I for more information on working with chiles)

3 tablespoons chicken stock or clam juice

1 tablespoon freshly squeezed lime juice

2 tablespoons chopped fresh Italian parsley

2 cups cooked white rice

1 Heat the olive oil in a large skillet over medium-low heat. Cook the garlic slices until tender but not brown, 2 to 3 minutes. Transfer with a slotted spoon to paper towels and reserve.

2 Turn the heat under the pan up to high. Quickly toss the shrimp with the salt and pepper in a bowl. When the oil is nearly smoking, add the shrimp. Sauté, stirring and shaking the pan to prevent sticking, 3 to 4 minutes or just until the shrimp are still slightly undercooked. Remove from the heat. With a slotted spoon, transfer the shrimp to a platter, leaving as much liquid as possible in the pan.

3 Return the pan to the burner and reduce the heat to medium. Add the garlic slices and chile and sauté, stirring frequently, until the oil begins to turn orange from the chile. Stir in the chicken stock or clam juice, along with the shrimp and any juice that has collected on the platter. Add the lime juice and parsley, bring to a boil, and remove from the heat. Serve immediately over white rice.

Tip: *Whatever you do, don't reduce the quantity of garlic called for in this recipe. What's the point of a mild-mannered garlic bath? The trick is to cook the garlic slowly and carefully, without browning, for a delicious sauce that doesn't overpower the fish.*

Grilled Swordfish with Fresh Tomato and Herb Salsa

Our favorite fish preparations are often the simplest, and things don't get much simpler than this recipe. A fresh tomato and herb salsa supplies just enough bright acidity, color, and texture to highlight the fish, without overpowering it like a cooked sauce might.

Preparation time: *15 minutes, plus 15 minutes chilling time*

Cooking time: *15 minutes*

Yield: *6 servings*

½ cup extra-virgin olive oil

1 teaspoon salt

½ teaspoon pepper

6 ripe tomatoes, seeded and diced

½ bunch oregano leaves, chopped (¼ cup)

½ bunch Italian parsley leaves, chopped (¼ cup)

½ bunch cilantro leaves, chopped (¼ cup)

3 tablespoons capers, chopped with juice

3 scallions, light green and white parts, thinly sliced

6 skinless swordfish fillets, 6 ounces each

Sea salt and black pepper to taste

1 To make the salsa, combine the olive oil, salt, pepper, tomatoes, oregano, cilantro, parsley, capers, and scallions in a bowl. Reserve in the refrigerator.

2 Season the fish all over with the sea salt and pepper. Cook on a very hot, clean grill, about 3 minutes per side. The inside should be bright pink. Transfer to a platter and chill 15 minutes.

3 Arrange the fillets on individual plates. Spoon the salsa over the fish and serve cold.

Vary It! *Sure, oregano, cilantro, and parsley are good choices for the Fresh Tomato and Herb Salsa. But a fresh salsa such as this one is no time to be fussy. Substitute other herbs, such as tarragon, chervil, basil, or chives, as the spirit (or the marketplace) moves you.*

Cooking fish to perfection

The trickiest part about cooking fish properly is judging when it's done. An additional minute or two of high heat can make a big difference with such tender flesh.

We're big believers in slightly undercooking fish because it continues to cook even after you remove it from the heat. If you cook fish all the way through, it will probably taste dry by the time it's served. At our restaurants, we cook our fillets until opaque on either side but still slightly translucent in the middle.

To judge doneness, trust your senses rather than the clock because too many variables come into play when you're cooking delicate fish. Toss out those old-fashioned cooking charts and use the tip of a knife to pull aside the flesh and peek at the center to judge for yourself.

Pan-Seared Bass with Chile Lime Broth

Popular sea bass is a great choice for home entertaining. You can't easily overcook it, and it holds its own with assertive flavors like olives, garlic, chiles, and lime. For a complete meal, serve with wedges of roasted potatoes and seared greens.

Preparation time: *15 minutes*

Cooking time: *20 minutes*

Yield: *4 servings*

1½ pounds skinless, boneless fillet of sea bass, or other firm-fleshed fish, cut in 4 portions

Salt and pepper to taste

3 tablespoons olive oil

1 small yellow onion, thinly sliced

4 cloves garlic, peeled and minced

2 serrano chiles, stemmed and sliced in ¼-inch disks

1 lime, cut in 8 wedges

1 tomato, cored, seeded, and cut in strips

½ bunch fresh oregano leaves, coarsely chopped (¼ cup)

½ cup Spanish green olives, sliced

½ cup white wine

¾ cup fish stock or clam juice

1 Season the fish fillets evenly with salt and pepper. Heat one very large skillet or two medium skillets over medium-high heat for a minute and then coat the pans with the olive oil. Add the fillets and turn the heat to very high. Sear until golden brown, about 2 minutes, then flip to sear the other side, about 1 minute. Transfer the fillets to a rack over a plate to catch the juices, and reserve.

2 Return the pan (or pans) to high heat. Add the onion slices and sauté, stirring frequently, for 1 minute or until they start to brown. Add the garlic, chile slices, lime wedges, tomatoes, oregano, and olives and sauté briskly for 1 minute. Add the wine and boil until reduced by half.

3 Pour in the fish stock or clam juice, bring to a boil, and then reduce to a simmer. Return the fish fillets, along with their juices, to the pan. Cover and cook gently for 2 minutes or longer, depending on the thickness of fillets. Taste the broth and adjust the seasoning with salt and pepper. Serve immediately in soup plates with a generous puddle of broth and garnish of vegetables.

Tip: If you've ever considered preparing fish for a crowd but ruled it out as too scary, this light, healthy, one-skillet dish is a great choice. We've prepared it for 500 guests at a time without a hitch. To serve a large group, just pan-sear all the fish, transfer to a casserole, cover with foil, and reserve. Then, when it's time to serve, cook the sauce in a few pans, pour over the fish, and finish cooking in a 350-degree oven for about 5 minutes. What a great party dish!

Chicken and Turkey Dishes

If you've been stuck in the same old lemon, parsley, and garlic rut with your poultry, take a walk on the wild side and try cooking your next chicken or turkey Mexican style. Doing so is bound to give you a tangier, spicier perspective on meats that you don't often look to for new taste sensations.

Citrus Chicken with Orange Cilantro Salsa

As flavor mavens, we've developed a special method for cooking chicken breast, one of the least flavorful cuts of meat. First we boost flavor with a strong marinade, and then we moisten the grilled meat some more with a sprightly salsa. The natural sugar in the orange juice caramelizes and adds the perfect sweetness. This choice is great for your summer barbecues.

Preparation time: *15 minutes, plus 35 minutes for Red Roasted Tomato Salsa, plus 6 hours marination*

Cooking time: *25 minutes*

Yield: *6 servings*

½ cup freshly squeezed orange juice	*2 tablespoons vegetable oil*
2 tablespoons freshly squeezed lime juice	*½ teaspoon salt*
1 morita chile or 3 arbol chiles or 1 chipotle	*6 whole chicken breasts, boneless with skin on*
¾ cup Red Roasted Tomato Salsa (see Chapter 4 of Book I)	*Orange Cilantro Salsa (see the following recipe)*

1 To make the marinade, combine the orange juice, lime juice, and chile in a small saucepan and bring to a boil. Reduce to a simmer and cook, uncovered, until the chile is plump, about 5 minutes. Set aside to cool and pour into a blender. Add the Red Roasted Tomato Salsa, oil, and salt and puree until smooth.

2 Wash the chicken breasts and place them in a large stainless steel or plastic container. Pour on the marinade, cover, and refrigerate for at least 6 hours.

3 Preheat the grill or broiler until medium-hot.

4 Grill the chicken breasts, skin side down on the grill, or skin side up in the broiler, about 3 minutes. Then turn and cook the other side, moving away from direct heat. Keep turning the chicken every minute or two to prevent it from blackening or sticking. Total cooking time is about 12 minutes for small breasts and about 20 minutes for larger breasts. If checking meat with a thermometer, the internal temperature should be 175 degrees. Remove breasts from the heat for about 5 minutes. Serve over Red Rice and Refried Black Beans (see Chapter 4 of Book I) and top with the Orange Cilantro Salsa.

Tip: Grilling chicken breasts calls for careful technique. With any citrus marinade, you need to be watchful not to burn the meat because the sugars in the juice caramelize quickly on the grill. The trick is to stay nearby and keep turning the chicken frequently, never blackening the skin or meat. We always keep the skin on for flavor, moisture, and a little insurance against charring. If guests prefer skinless chicken, we just remove it before serving.

Vary It! Leftover Citrus Chicken is delicious served at room temperature the next day. For a quick main-course salad, slice the chicken and serve over mixed bitter greens, using the salsa as part of the dressing.

Orange Cilantro Salsa

A refreshing fruit and herb salsa, such as this one, is also great over grilled salmon. Make the salsa no more than a day ahead to really enjoy the freshness.

Preparation time: 10 minutes

Yield: 1½ to 2 cups

4 oranges or other citrus fruit, peeled and sectioned

1 bunch cilantro, leaves and stems, coarsely chopped (½ cup)

2 serrano chiles, stemmed and thinly sliced

1 small red onion, freshly julienned

¼ cup olive oil

¼ cup red wine vinegar

1 teaspoon salt

½ teaspoon cracked black pepper

Combine the oranges, cilantro, chiles, onion, olive oil, vinegar, salt, and pepper. Mix well and set aside or chill until serving time.

Chipotle Glazed Chicken

When roasting chicken, all anyone seems to know is the Italian method — a combination of lemon, olive oil, and herbs. It's delicious, but why not break out and try roasting a Mexican-style chicken for a change? Smoky, brown chipotles add a unique, complex touch to the sweet and sour glaze.

Preparation time: *15 minutes, plus 1 hour marination*

Cooking time: *1 hour and 15 minutes*

Yield: *4 servings*

3-pound roasting chicken	1 cup freshly squeezed orange juice
3 cloves garlic, peeled and finely chopped	½ cup honey
Salt and pepper to taste	⅔ cup red wine vinegar
2 tablespoons paprika	3 canned chipotle chiles
3 tablespoons red wine vinegar	Garnish: ½ bunch parsley leaves, coarsely chopped (¼ cup)
3 tablespoons olive oil	

1 Rinse the chicken, remove any excess fat, and pat dry with paper towels. In a small bowl, mix together the garlic, salt and pepper, paprika, 3 tablespoons vinegar, and olive oil. Rub the vinegar mixture all over the chicken, including the cavity. Cover with plastic wrap and marinate, at room temperature, for 1 hour.

2 Preheat the oven to 450 degrees.

3 To make the glaze, combine the orange juice, honey, ⅔ cup vinegar, and chiles in a small saucepan. Cook over medium heat until the liquid is reduced by half. Strain, pushing the chiles through a sieve, and reserve.

4 Unwrap the chicken and place in a roasting pan. Roast for 15 minutes. Then reduce the heat to 375 degrees and continue roasting for another 45 minutes. Begin brushing glaze generously all over the chicken, every 5 minutes until done, about another 20 minutes. When a leg can be loosely twisted, the chicken is done. Sprinkle with parsley, let rest 10 minutes, and serve.

Chipotle Black Bean Turkey Chili

This updated, reduced-fat chili features three of our favorite ingredients: smoky chipotle chiles, creamy beans, and rich, meaty turkey. A chili this satisfying doesn't need a lot of garnishes — a dab of sour cream and a moist square of corn bread are all it takes to round out the meal.

Preparation time: *10 minutes*

Cooking time: *2 hours*

Yield: *4 servings*

2 cups dry black beans	*3 cloves garlic, peeled and minced*
8 cups water	*2 green bell peppers, stemmed, seeded, and diced*
2 arbol chiles	*1 tablespoon chili powder*
3 bay leaves	*1 tablespoon ground cumin*
2 tablespoons vegetable oil	*4 canned chipotle chiles, stemmed and minced*
1 pound coarsely ground turkey, dark meat	
1 large yellow onion, diced	*2½ cups chicken stock*
1½ teaspoons salt	*Garnish: Sour cream*
½ teaspoon pepper	

1 Place the beans in a large pot with 8 cups water, arbol chiles, and bay leaves. Bring to a boil, reduce to a simmer, and cover. Cook until tender, about 1 hour. Remove the chiles and bay leaves and discard. Don't drain the beans.

2 Heat the vegetable oil in a large heavy pot over medium-high heat. Fry the turkey, stirring often and breaking up with a spoon, until evenly browned. Add the onion, salt, and pepper and sauté over moderate heat, stirring occasionally, until lightly golden, about 10 minutes. Stir in the garlic, green peppers, chili powder, cumin, and chipotles. Cook, stirring frequently, for 3 minutes, or until aromas are released.

3 Stir in the black beans, their liquid, and the chicken stock and cook, uncovered, for 40 minutes or until the flavors have blended and the chili has thickened. Serve in bowls with a dollop of sour cream on top.

Tip: *Like all good chilis, Chipotle Black Bean Turkey Chili is a great dish to make ahead and freeze for a party. You can store it in the refrigerator a few days or freeze as long as 4 weeks.*

Beef and Pork Dishes

Although beef and pork are beloved in Mexico, they aren't often featured as a meal's centerpiece. In traditional foods like posole or mole, Mexicans eat a small amount of meat along with a healthful array of fresh vegetables and spices so that the focus is on the artfulness of the whole dish rather than on the quality of a lone slice of beef. And although Mexicans greatly enjoy beef and pork, they don't eat those meats every day, but a few times a week, as one small part of a larger meal.

Mexican cooks are legendary for cooking inexpensive cuts of beef and pork to perfection. Nothing goes to waste. Stomachs, intestines, hooves, ears, tongues, and butts are slowly cooked with just the right amount of lime and chiles to enhance their natural flavors without overwhelming their essential meatiness.

Baby Back Ribs Adobado

Ribs need special attention to cook up tender, juicy, and falling off the bone. We like to first give ours a strong spice rub for flavor, followed by a steamy bake for tenderness, and then a quick turn on the grill or in a high oven for a crisp edge and some smoke.

Because undercooked ribs are so awful, steaming a little longer can never hurt.

Preparation time: *20 minutes, plus 2 hours refrigeration, plus 1 hour and 25 minutes to make the Adobado*

Cooking time: *1 hour and 35 minutes*

Yield: *4 servings*

¼ cup paprika	2 tablespoons salt
¼ cup ground ancho chiles or chili powder	4½ pounds pork baby back ribs
¼ cup cumin	3 cups Adobado (see following recipe)

1 Combine the paprika, chiles, cumin, and salt in a small bowl. Pat the spice mixture all over the ribs. Place in a pan, cover with plastic wrap, and refrigerate for at least 2 hours or overnight.

2 Preheat the oven to 350 degrees.

3 Place the ribs in a single layer in a baking pan and pour in water to a depth of about ¾ inch. Bake, uncovered, for 45 minutes. Cover with foil and return to the oven for an additional 30 minutes.

4 Meanwhile, make the Adobado.

5 Turn up the oven heat to 450 degrees or heat the grill to medium-high.

6 If finishing the ribs in the oven, brush generously with the Adobado and bake for another 10 minutes per side, basting every 5 minutes. To grill, generously glaze the ribs and grill for 5 minutes per side, frequently brushing with additional Adobado sauce. Cut the ribs apart and serve hot.

Tip: Inexpensive country-style ribs, available at the supermarket, are a meaty, tasty alternative to baby back ribs. After applying the spice rub, steam in a sealed heavy-duty plastic bag in the top of a double boiler over simmering water for 45 minutes. Then finish in a hot oven as we describe in Step 6.

Adobado

Adobado is a very traditional, sweet, tart Mexican barbecue sauce. It's great to have on hand for heating up with leftover bits of chicken, pork, or lamb and for serving on rolls for delicious barbecue sandwiches.

Preparation time: *20 minutes*

Cooking time: *1 hour and 5 minutes*

Yield: *3 cups*

6 ancho chiles, wiped clean	*2 cups chicken stock*
¼ cup white vinegar	*1 tablespoon brown sugar*
1 cup water	*2 tablespoons freshly squeezed orange juice*
2 tablespoons olive oil	*2 tablespoons freshly squeezed lemon juice*
1 medium yellow onion, thinly sliced	*1 tablespoon tomato paste*
3 garlic cloves, peeled and sliced	*½ tablespoon salt*
½ tablespoon ground cumin	*⅛ teaspoon pepper*

1 Briefly toast the chiles directly over a medium gas flame or in a cast-iron skillet until soft and brown, turning frequently to avoid scorching (see Chapter 3 of Book I). Transfer the toasted chiles to a saucepan and add the vinegar and water. Bring to a boil, reduce to a simmer, and cook for 10 minutes to soften.

2 Transfer the chiles and liquid to a blender or food processor. Puree until a smooth paste the consistency of barbecue sauce or ketchup is formed, adding 1 or 2 tablespoons of water if necessary to thin. Set aside.

3 Heat the olive oil in a medium saucepan over medium-high heat. Sauté the onion until golden brown, about 10 minutes. Stir in the garlic and cook briefly just to release the aroma. Then stir in the cumin and cook for another minute. Add the chicken stock and reserved chile paste. Bring to a boil, reduce to a simmer, and cook for 20 minutes.

4 Meanwhile, mix together the brown sugar, orange juice, lemon juice, tomato paste, salt, and pepper to form a paste. Add to the simmering stock mixture and cook for 15 minutes longer. You can store Adobado in the refrigerator for 1 week or frozen indefinitely.

Pork Chile Verde

Tart, green tomatillos are perfect for cutting the richness of pork — our favorite stewing meat and a popular meat in Mexico. What makes this dish typically Mexican is its focus on chiles rather than beans. To round out the meal, serve with warm tortillas and Red Rice (see Chapter 4 of Book I), which provides a delightful contrast.

Preparation time: *20 minutes*

Cooking time: *2 hours and 30 minutes, plus 50 minutes for Red Rice*

Yield: *6 to 8 servings*

2½ pounds boneless pork butt or shoulder, trimmed of fat and cut into 2-inch cubes

Salt and pepper to taste

Flour for dredging

¼ cup vegetable oil

2 small yellow onions, cut into 1-inch chunks

3 poblano chiles, cut into 1-inch chunks

4 jalapeños, seeded and finely chopped

3 cloves garlic, minced

1½ pounds tomatillos, roasted, peeled, and chopped (see Chapter 3 of Book I for tips on roasting)

2 teaspoons dried oregano

1 teaspoon ground cumin

1 bunch cilantro leaves, chopped (½ cup)

3 cups chicken stock

1 Generously season the pork with salt and pepper. Lightly coat with the flour. Heat the oil in a large, heavy skillet over medium-high heat. Fry the pork in small batches until well browned on all sides. With a slotted spoon or tongs, transfer the pork to a wide, heavy soup pot.

2 Drain the fat from the pan. Place the onions in the same skillet and cook over moderate heat, stirring occasionally, until limp, about 5 minutes. Add the poblano chiles and jalapeños and cook for 4 minutes longer. Stir in the garlic and cook for about 2 minutes longer.

3 Transfer the onion-chile mixture to the pot with the pork. Add the tomatillos, oregano, cumin, and cilantro. Pour in the chicken stock and bring to a boil. Reduce to a simmer and cook, uncovered, for 2 hours, or until the pork is fork tender. Adjust the seasonings with salt and pepper.

Vary It! *To turn our green chile red, substitute 2 red bell peppers for the poblanos, 1½ pounds tomatoes for the tomatillos, and 3 tablespoons ground red chile for the jalapeños and eliminate the cilantro.*

Cumin and Chile Marinated Skirt Steak

This marinated skirt steak is so flavorful that all it needs is some rice and beans (see Chapter 4 of Book I for ideas).

Preparation time: *20 minutes, plus 4 hours marination*

Cooking time: *15 minutes*

Yield: *6 servings*

⅓ cup cumin seeds

6 serrano chiles, stemmed, cut in half, and seeded, if desired

6 cloves garlic, peeled

½ cup freshly squeezed lime juice

2 bunches cilantro, including stems and leaves (1 cup)

½ cup olive oil

Salt and pepper to taste

3 pounds skirt steak, trimmed of excess fat and cut into 6 serving pieces

1 Lightly toast the cumin seeds in a dry medium skillet over low heat just until their aroma is released, about 5 minutes. Transfer the seeds to a blender.

2 Add the serranos, garlic, and lime juice and puree until the cumin seeds are finely ground. Then add the cilantro, olive oil, and salt and pepper and puree until smooth.

3 Generously sprinkle the steak all over with salt and pepper. Generously brush all over with the cumin seed marinade and roll each piece up into a cylinder. Arrange the rolled steaks in a shallow pan and pour on the remaining marinade. Cover and marinate in the refrigerator for at least 4 hours or as long as a day.

4 About 30 minutes before cooking, remove the meat from the refrigerator. Unroll the steaks and place on a platter.

5 Preheat the grill or broiler to very hot.

6 Cook the steaks just until seared on both sides, about 4 minutes per side for medium rare (or pan-fry in a hot cast-iron skillet lightly coated with oil). Transfer to a cutting board and slice across the grain into diagonal strips. Serve hot with warm flour tortillas.

Chapter 6

Sweet Endings

*J*ust as Mexicans prefer extremes at the spicy end of the spectrum, they also like their sweets extra sugary. Street vendors sell sticky, gooey candies, candy stores stock the candies to be nibbled throughout the day, and hardly a meal ends without its requisite flan, rice pudding, or some more elaborate dessert.

Our own tastes, on the other hand, veer toward simplicity — an ice-cold mango with a wedge of lime or a refreshing fruity ice cream sounds just fine at the end of a long, satisfying meal. And though we do offer a spectacular chocolate cake at the restaurant, we can't resist sneaking in something sour, like a topping of crème fraîche, to take the edge off all that sweetness.

The selections that follow reflect our respect for what's traditional in Mexico, our own acid-craving appetites, and the American hunger for a deliciously sweet reward for finishing dinner.

Old-Fashioned Desserts

Restaurants all over Mexico offer these unfussy puddings, the most traditional Mexican desserts. They're easy to prepare, taste just as good after a day in the refrigerator, and offer tummy-coating comfort after the excitement of a savory Mexican meal.

Mexican Bread Pudding

More like a soft and crunchy bread casserole than an eggy pudding, this sweet and savory dessert, known as *capirotada* (kah-pee-*roh*-tah-dah) in Mexico, is bound to appeal to those who don't usually like custards. It doesn't contain any eggs or milk.

Preparation time: *25 minutes*

Cooking time: *20 minutes*

Yield: *8 to 10 servings*

8 tablespoons (1 stick) butter

½ loaf crusty Italian or French bread, crust on, cut into small cubes (about 6 cups)

1½ cups brown sugar

1½ cups water

1½ teaspoons ground cinnamon

½ cup golden raisins

1 large Granny Smith apple, peeled, cored and chopped

½ cup walnuts, chopped

½ pound crumbled añejo cheese

1 cup Crema (see the following recipe), heavy cream, or crème fraîche

1 Preheat the oven to 350 degrees. Butter a glass casserole or lasagna pan.

2 Melt the butter in a medium saucepan, add the bread cubes, and stir them to coat evenly. Spread the cubes on a baking sheet and bake for 15 minutes, stirring once, or until lightly brown and crisp. Remove the bread and turn up the oven temperature to 400 degrees.

3 Combine the sugar and water in a small saucepan and bring to a boil. Remove the syrup from the heat. Stir in the cinnamon and the raisins and set aside.

4 In a large mixing bowl, combine the chopped apples, walnuts, cheese, and toasted bread cubes. Drizzle with the reserved sugar syrup and mix ingredients to evenly distribute the syrup. Transfer the mixture to the prepared pan.

5 Bake, uncovered, stirring occasionally, for 15 minutes. Then bake an additional 5 minutes, without stirring, until the top is golden brown and crusty and the liquid is absorbed. Serve the bread pudding warm in bowls, with pitchers of Crema or heavy cream for adding at the table.

Crema

A drizzle of Crema adds that sour tang we crave with our sweets.

Preparation time: *5 minutes, plus 8 hours setting*

Yield: *2 cups*

2 cups heavy cream   ¼ cup buttermilk

Whisk the cream and buttermilk together in a bowl. Cover and set the bowl in a warm place (a gas oven with just the heat from the pilot light is fine) for 8 hours until thick as custard. Store in the refrigerator for as long as a week.

The many faces of flan

For Coconut Flan: Substitute one 14-ounce can unsweetened coconut milk plus enough milk to make 2 cups for the 2 cups milk. (Make sure that you purchase unsweetened canned coconut milk. You can find it in the ethnic section of the market near the Thai ingredients. Don't buy the canned coconut milk in the beverage section because it's probably sweetened for cocktails like piña coladas and smoothies.) Sprinkle 1 cup of grated unsweetened coconut over the uncooked flan in the pan. When the flan is served, the coconut will be scattered on the bottom.

For Chocolate Flan: Use 5 rather than 6 whole eggs and stir 3 ounces chopped bittersweet chocolate into the milk mixture just before it boils.

For Red Yam Flan: In a large bowl, combine all the ingredients in the plain flan list with 1 cup cooked pureed yams, sweet potato, or pumpkin, 2 teaspoons ground cinnamon, 1½ teaspoons ground allspice, 1½ teaspoons ground clove, and 3 tablespoons dark rum. Mix well, strain into the caramel-coated pan, and bake.

Flan

One dessert you can count on in most Spanish or Mexican restaurants is this classic caramel-flavored, sweet and silky vanilla custard. The perfect make-in-advance dessert, flan is a soothing, light finale to spicy foods, and, as an added bonus, it keeps for a few days in the refrigerator without losing freshness or flavor.

Preparation time: *25 minutes, plus 4 hours refrigeration, plus 20 minutes for Caramel*

Cooking time: *1 hour and 15 minutes*

Yield: *8 to 10 servings*

1 recipe Caramel (see the following recipe)	*2 teaspoons vanilla extract*
6 large eggs	*2 cups milk*
6 large egg yolks	*2 cups half-and-half*
One 14-ounce can sweetened condensed milk	*1 vanilla bean*

1 Prepare the Caramel and coat a 9-inch round cake pan.

2 Preheat the oven to 325 degrees.

3 In a large mixing bowl, gently whisk together the eggs, yolks, sweetened condensed milk, and vanilla extract. (Avoid incorporating air as happens when you whisk more briskly.)

4 Pour the milk and half-and-half into a medium saucepan. Split the vanilla bean lengthwise and, using the tip of a paring knife, scrape the black seeds into the milk. Add the bean also and bring the milk to a boil. Remove the saucepan from the heat.

5 Gradually pour the hot milk into the egg mixture, whisking constantly. Pass the milk and egg mixture through a strainer into the caramel-coated cake pan. Place the cake pan inside a large roasting pan and carefully pour hot tap water in the larger pan until it reaches halfway up the sides of the flan pan.

6 Bake for 1 hour and 10 minutes, until the center just feels firm when pressed with a finger. Set aside to cool in the pan of water. Then remove from the water bath, cover with plastic wrap, and refrigerate at least 4 hours or overnight.

7 To serve, run a knife along the inside edge of the pan and gently press the center of the bottom to loosen. Cover the pan with a platter, invert, and lift the pan off the flan. Cut the flan in wedges and serve topped with cold Caramel.

Tip: *Vanilla beans, the long, thin, dried, brown pods sold in the supermarket spice section, are the fermented pods of a Mexican or Tahitian yellow orchid. Look for pliability when purchasing. A good vanilla pod should be as flexible as a dried apricot. To release the bean's essential oils and flavor, always split it lengthwise with the tip of a paring knife, and scrape the small brown seeds into whatever you're infusing. Those tiny dark seeds are the speckles in "pure" vanilla ice cream. Their perfume is unmistakable — some even say it's an aphrodisiac.*

Caramel

A truly great flan should have a luxuriously silky consistency and a rich caramel flavor that lingers on the tongue. To make the caramel, you want to cook the sugar slowly, a longer time than you suspect, and watch it carefully. The color should turn from light caramel to dark coffee, and the fragrance should be rich and very caramel-like. You can store leftover sauce in the refrigerator and thin it with some hot water the next day.

Cooking time: *20 minutes, plus 1 hour chilling time*

Yield: *Enough for one 9-inch flan*

2 cups sugar	*1¼ cups water*

1 Have ready a 9-inch round cake pan. Combine the sugar and ½ cup of the water in a medium saucepan. Cook over moderate heat, swirling the pan occasionally, until the color is dark brown and the mixture has a distinctive fragrance of caramel, about 15 minutes. Use a pastry brush dipped in cold water to wash down any sugar granules from the pot's sides. Pour enough of the hot caramel into a 9-inch round cake pan to coat the bottom and sides. Swirl to coat evenly.

2 Slowly and carefully add the remaining ¾ cup water to the caramel in the saucepan. Bring to a boil and cook over moderate heat until the caramel dissolves, about 5 minutes. Occasionally stir and brush down the sides with the pastry brush dipped in cold water to prevent crystallization. Set this caramel sauce aside to cool and then chill until serving time.

New Border Sweets

For these personal favorites, we've taken ingredients that ring true to Mexico and given them an American spin. A luscious cream pie and a refreshing tequila ice end any get-together, Mexican or not, on an upbeat, sugar-induced note. As an added bonus, both of these little gems are easy to prepare.

Creamy Lemon Lime Pie

Here is a delicious unbaked version of Key Lime Pie that you can simplify even more by substituting a baked graham cracker crust. It's one of our best-sellers at the Border Grill.

Special tools: *Food processor, parchment paper*

Preparation time: *10 minutes, plus 4 hours chilling for filling and 1 hour chilling for dough*

Cooking time: *25 minutes*

Yield: *6 to 8 servings*

Empanada Dough (see Chapter 4 of Book I)
½ cup freshly squeezed lime juice
⅓ cup freshly squeezed lemon juice
1 pound cream cheese
14-ounce can sweetened condensed milk

Zest of 1 lime, finely grated, without any bitter white pith
1 cup heavy cream, cold
2 tablespoons powdered sugar
½ lime and ½ lemon

1 Preheat the oven to 350 degrees.

2 On a floured board, roll out the dough into a ¼-inch thick, 12-inch circle. Place in a 9- or 10-inch glass pie plate. Trim the edges with a paring knife, leaving a ½- to ¾-inch overhang. Tuck under and crimp the edges. Chill for 1 hour. Prick the dough all over with a fork. Line the pie shell with parchment paper or foil; fill with raw beans, rice, or weights; and bake about 25 minutes or until very lightly browned. Remove from the oven, immediately remove the weights, and thoroughly cool on a rack.

3 Combine the lime and lemon juices, cream cheese, and sweetened condensed milk in the bowl of a food processor with a metal blade and mix until smooth, scraping down the sides often. Add the lime zest and mix thoroughly. Pour into the chilled pie shell and return to the refrigerator.

4 Meanwhile, whisk the cream and powdered sugar in a bowl until soft peaks form. Spread over the top of the pie. Slice 8 thin circles each of lime and lemon from the center of each fruit and cut each disk once from the center to the edge to make twists. Stand these twists upright, evenly spaced, along the edge of the pie and chill at least 4 hours or overnight. Serve cold.

Tip: *In recipes that call for citrus zest and juice, grate the zest first and then juice the fruit. If your recipe calls for more zest than juice, store the leftover fruit, in its white pith, in the refrigerator.*

Margarita Sorbet

Delicious, fresh fruit ices play such an important role in the Mexican diet that we offered handmade, miniature Popsicles at our first Mexican restaurant. The ingredients for this sparkling, tart, lime and tequila sorbet should be on the shelf of any well-stocked Mexican-style pantry.

Special tool: *Ice-cream maker*

Preparation time: *10 minutes, plus 30 minutes chilling for syrup and 1 hour for tequila mixture*

Yield: *4 servings*

1½ cups tequila

1 cup freshly squeezed lime juice

½ cup Triple Sec

½ cup light corn syrup

2 cups Simple Syrup (see the following recipe)

½ cup water

1 Pour the tequila into a small saucepan and bring to a boil. Cook until the tequila is reduced by half (most of the alcohol boils off). Pour into a bowl and stir in all the remaining ingredients. Refrigerate until cold.

2 Pour the chilled mixture into an ice-cream maker and process according to the manufacturer's instructions for sorbet. Store in the freezer.

Simple Syrup

Cooking time: *5 minutes*

Yield: *2 cups*

1¼ cups sugar

1¼ cups water

Combine the sugar and water in a saucepan and bring to a boil, stirring until the sugar dissolves. Let cool. Store the syrup in the refrigerator.

Book II
Italian Cooking

The 5th Wave   By Rich Tennant

"I'm pretty sure it's pizza dough that gets tossed, not pasta dough."

In this book . . .

*I*n Italy, food is of paramount importance, and each meal is considered a work of art. You may think that you know all about Italian cuisine, but Italian cooking has much to offer beyond pizza and spaghetti. There are many different regional variations, and in this section, we introduce you to several. Italian cooking is perfect if you want to experiment with a cuisine that emphasizes freshness, spontaneity, and seasonal food choices. We explain the basics of Italian food preparation and give you an overview of ingredients key to this cuisine. We cover all sorts of pasta dishes, traditional grilled meats, and a killer tiramisu. From a staggeringly delicious five-course meal, to a much quicker weeknight dinner, we show you how to plan and prepare a *magnifico* Italian meal.

Contents at a glance

Chapter 1

How to Think Like an Italian Chef

In This Chapter

▶ Defining authentic Italian cooking

▶ Structuring a modern-day Italian meal

▶ Understanding the three tenets of Italian cooking

*I*f you think that Italian cooking is nothing more than tomato sauce and tiramisù, think again. Italian cooking is one of the world's great cuisines, with a tremendous diversity of flavors and methods of preparation. Many dishes are hundreds of years old, and some have their roots in the Roman Empire. Although Caesar and friends couldn't phone for takeout, they still enjoyed grilled flatbreads not all that different from modern-day pizzas.

Unfortunately, the quality of Italian food prepared outside Italy often isn't very high. In fact, some so-called Italian food is pretty awful. For many people, Italian food is fast food, akin to burgers and fries. Like anything that becomes overexposed (think Britney Spears), Italian cooking has become a victim of its own success.

In this chapter, we tell you everything you need to know to think like an Italian chef. Don't worry — it's surprisingly simple stuff.

All Cooking Is Local

Ready for your world to come crumbling down? There is no such thing as Italian cooking. Until the late 19th century, Italy wasn't even a unified country, and tremendous regional differences still persist today. Local traditions, coupled with the varying availability of ingredients, have shaped dozens, if not hundreds, of different styles of cooking, or *microcuisines*.

In the 1970s and 1980s, many Italian restaurants in North America and Europe introduced "Northern Italian cuisine" to their patrons. They banished spicy tomato sauces and heavy lasagnas; instead they showcased rice dishes and refined pastas with cream sauces. Although this trend helped break the notion of one single Italian cuisine, it confused a lot of people and left the impression that two Italian cooking traditions exist — one from the South, which is based on tomatoes and olive oil, and another from the North, where butter, cream, rice, homemade pasta, and polenta rule. Although you can find some truth in this generalization, it vastly oversimplifies the true nature of modern Italian cooking.

Italy has 20 regions, each with its own distinct personality and traditions. Sicily, for example, has a warm Mediterranean climate that supports the growth of citrus fruits. The island endured numerous invasions and immigrations of people from Greece and North Africa, so couscous, chiles, olives, and capers became important ingredients in Sicily. In north-central Italy, the state of Tuscany has a very different climate and topography. And even within Tuscany, the area has important distinctions in cooking styles from the coast to the mountainous interior regions. Urban areas, such as Florence and Siena, have their own culinary traditions, many of which date back to the Renaissance.

As former U.S. Speaker of the House Tip O'Neill once said, "All politics is local." The same is true of Italian cooking. Each region has its own distinct tradition. Each is equally Italian, but none is the sole voice of Italian cooking.

So Many Courses, So Little Time

The Italian meal is a celebration. Tradition dictates that the meal should take at least an hour or two to enjoy. The meal is a leisurely process, with several distinct courses. Usually eaten at midday, lunch gives families a chance to talk. Eating becomes a communal activity — a time to share news of the day while enjoying the fruits of the cook's labor.

To some extent, modern life has taken its toll on this tradition. Italians compete in a world economy, which means shorter lunches to keep up with developments in New York, Tokyo, or London. But tradition still remains, especially on weekends and holidays. Even during the week, many people go home for long lunches, and most business comes to a halt in the early afternoon, only to reopen again around 3 or 4 o'clock. (The Italians we know give up an afternoon siesta to compete in the global economy, but they haven't given up their midday bowl of pasta.)

Putting together five easy pieces

So what's the structure of the traditional Italian meal? It actually has five components. Not every meal contains all five, but many do.

- **The antipasto:** A traditional Italian meal starts with something to nibble on, called an *antipasto,* which translates into English as "before the meal." The antipasto may consist of a bowl of marinated olives and some fresh fennel for dipping in extra-virgin olive oil, with a wedge of fine Parmigiano-Reggiano and some bread. You can also serve drinks, such as wine, sparkling water, *prosecco* (the Italian equivalent of champagne), or cocktails (such as Campari and soda). You can serve this part of the meal at the table or, better yet, on the patio or in front of a roaring fire. (For more on antipasti, see Chapter 4 of Book II.)

- **The primo:** We know some non-Italian people who consider a pound of pasta dinner for two. The average American family feeds four from a pound of dried pasta. But in Italy, pasta is a first course, or primo, served as an appetizer, not as the main event. In Italy, a pound of pasta yields six, or even eight, first-course portions. Soup, rice, and polenta are the other main options for the primo. (For first-course ideas, see Chapter 4 of Book II)

- **The secondo:** After the plates for the first course have been cleared, it's time for the main course (called *il secondo,* or "second course"). Chicken, meat, or fish are the usual choices, and portions are generally small. These main courses are usually fairly simple, especially if a rich pasta or rice dish precedes them. Italian cooks usually serve a grilled steak, a roast loin of pork, or maybe some sautéed fish. Sauces are usually light or nonexistent. (For more on the main course, see Chapter 5 of Book II.)

- **The contorno:** A platter of vegetables usually accompanies the main course. This side dish highlights the simple goodness of the vegetable — for example, potatoes roasted with garlic and herbs, peas cooked with bacon and onion, or maybe some oven-roasted asparagus with olive oil and salt. The word *contorno* loosely translates as "contours" and refers to the fact that the vegetable course helps shape and define the meal. The cook uses the corntorno to connect with the season. Asparagus, peas, and artichokes herald the arrival of spring. Peppers, eggplant, and tomatoes celebrate summer. Broccoli, cauliflower, and mushrooms signal the arrival of cooler fall weather. And carrots, winter squash, and Savoy cabbage round out a winter meal.

- **The dolce:** A *dolce,* or "sweet," ends a traditional Italian meal. On most days, the dolce is a bowl of fruit. Some hard Italian cookies, called biscotti, and dessert wine for dunking are another option. Italians serve more elaborate cakes, tortes, and custards on special occasions. (See Chapter 6 of Book II for more information on sweet endings to your meal.)

Book II

Italian Cooking

Assembling a menu

The structure of an Italian meal ensures that the meal is well balanced. No single component dominates. (Italians are aghast at the notion of serving each person a 12-ounce steak.) The pacing is leisurely so that you can fully enjoy and digest your food. The five-course meal also allows for a good balance of flavors, textures, and colors.

Planning a traditional Italian meal is like putting together a jigsaw puzzle. Start with the facts that you can't change, such as your budget, the number of people coming to dinner, the amount of time you can devote to cooking, or the availability of ingredients. These facts are the corner pieces of the puzzle, the ones you should put into place first. Then you can start playing with the other components of the meal, making them fit as necessary. When you've struck the right balance, the result is a culinary mosaic, attractive to both the eye and the palate.

Adapting this tradition for the 21st century

Unfortunately, five-course meals aren't terribly practical, especially if you're pressed for time like most cooks we know. There is that thing called life, with jobs to do and kids to tend. For holidays, the traditional Italian meal structure may help, but day-in and day-out, most cooks need to assemble meals with fewer components. Italian cooking is flexible in this regard.

So how can you make this structure work when you get home from the office at 5:30 p.m. and the kids are screaming for dinner? Here are some lessons for making more with less. All these solutions attempt to accommodate the Italian preference for balance, while keeping your work to a minimum.

- ✔ **Serve a secondo with two contorni, making sure that the vegetables complement each other.** Oven-roasted mushrooms and sautéed spinach work together. However, you don't want to serve broccoli with the spinach — too much green.

- ✔ **Beef up the primo and forget about the secondo.** A double portion of pasta or risotto can make a meal, especially if a vegetable side dish or salad accompanies it.

- ✔ **Serve an antipasto or two and then skip right to the secondo.** This alternative is better for casual entertaining than for weeknight dinners, but it allows you to add some pacing to the meal without a lot of extra cooking or cleanup. You can always buy the antipasto — cheese, marinated olives, and so on — to save even more work.

> ✔ **Choose a few kinds of fruit and place them in an attractive bowl.**
> Italians know that fruit, if well presented, makes a light but impressive
> ending to a meal. You're already in the market to shop for dinner, and
> assembling a fruit bowl at home takes less than five minutes.

The Three Tenets of Italian Cooking

Understanding the structure of an Italian meal is one part of the process. But
how do you capture the style — the poetry — of Italian cooking? How do you
think like an Italian chef? To help, we've devised three simple rules. We call
them the three tenets (not to be confused with the Three Tenors — we're talking philosophical beliefs, not opera singing). These tenets are a way of life.
When you're in the kitchen or at the market and you're trying to make a split-
second decision, keep these points in mind.

Be spontaneous

Accomplished Italian chefs are flexible and creative. They react to the situation at hand and adjust accordingly. To prevent making mistakes, think of a
recipe as an outline. Make a dish once and then feel free to change nonessen-
tial elements as you like to make use of the ingredients on hand or accommodate other constraints, such as time or money.

The trick to successful spontaneous cooking is knowing when to stop and
when one change necessitates another. For example, if you don't have enough
eggs, don't try to make a *frittata* (an Italian open-faced omelet) with less. The
frittata is an egg dish after all, and if the recipe calls for six eggs, four eggs just
won't work.

Spontaneous cooking also requires some common sense. Say you don't have
fresh oregano, but you see a jar of dried oregano in the cupboard. You also
know that for every teaspoon of fresh herb, you generally substitute one-
quarter to one-third of a teaspoon of dried herb. (See Chapter 2 of Book II for
more information on using fresh and dried herbs.) But as you can see from
the following example, a little knowledge can be dangerous.

A salad that calls for several leaves of fresh oregano isn't the place to get
spontaneous and substitute dried oregano. Think ahead. Do you really want to
eat tough, little bits of dried oregano in a salad? Of course not. (Another fresh
herb, such as thyme or basil, would be a better substitute.) But say you're
making a soup that calls for fresh oregano. This dish turns out fine with dried
oregano because the tiny flakes soften and release their flavor into the liquid.

All cooks, even good ones, make mistakes occasionally. If you can learn from your mistakes, they're worth the inconvenience. If you continue to make the same mistakes over and over, then recognize your creative limitations and vow to follow recipes in both spirit and letter.

Act seasonally

Italians approach shopping and menu planning quite differently than Americans do. With large refrigerators and crowded supermarkets, Americans try to shop once a week. They may make quick runs to convenience stores for bread or milk, but they generally purchase vegetables, meats, staples, and other items once a week. This shopping style makes menu planning a challenge, especially toward the end of the week when any "fresh" foods left in the refrigerator are looking old and tired.

Italians keep the kitchen stocked with certain staples — pastas, rices, and cornmeal — but for the most part, they visit the market daily to pick up fresh fruits, vegetables, and meats. Italians have traditionally shopped this way, and because their refrigerators are about the size of a dishwasher, they still keep to this routine.

Because Italian cooks shop daily, they're more likely to plan menus seasonally. The Italian cook reacts to what looks good at the market and often composes a menu at the market, not at home. Shopping without a list may seem impossible (and it is if you expect to pick up a week's worth of groceries at one time), but it doesn't have to be. Shopping without a list (or with a minimal list that you change as you survey what's available) gives you flexibility and allows you to take advantage of the best seasonal produce.

Keep your kitchen filled with basics. If you like pasta, keep an assortment of shapes on hand. If you like risotto, make sure you have some Arborio rice in the cupboard. Use your weekly big marketing trips to stock up on these items, as well as meats and poultry, which can go in the freezer. Make sure that you always keep vegetables that last for weeks (like onions and garlic), as well as oils and vinegars, on hand. Then stop at a natural food store or produce market a couple of times a week and get inspired.

Get fresh

Italian cooking stresses freshness. Why eat a tomato that has been shipped 3,000 miles and gassed along the way to change its color from green to red?

It may look pretty, but how does it taste? And why use dried herbs, which don't have all that much flavor, if the supermarket stocks a dozen fresh herbs? (Italians rarely use dried herbs, and neither do we.)

Good Italian cooking reveals the true essence of ingredients. It's honest and direct. No elaborate sauces mask inferior cuts of meat or tired vegetables. The ingredients should be as fresh as possible and should be presented with a minimum of fuss. Starting with less-than-fresh ingredients makes your work more difficult. Start with really fresh ingredients that taste good, and your work is almost done.

Putting freshness above all else makes your cooking pretty good. Adding some traditional Italian techniques (which we share with you in this book) makes your cooking great. All this sounds easy . . . because it is.

Book II

Italian
Cooking

Chapter 2
Ingredients for Italian Cooking

In This Chapter

▶ Shopping for Italian ingredients

▶ Using fresh herbs

▶ Buying cheeses and olives

*I*talian food relies on a number of key ingredients to give dishes their distinctive flavor, and sometimes the choices can be confusing. Some of these products are imported, and labels aren't always clear. In other cases, the choices are astounding. Decent cheese shops may carry a dozen or more Italian cheeses. Even the most basic supermarket stocks half a dozen or more olive oils, and some gourmet stores may have 20 or 30 different brands.

In this chapter, we show you how to choose quality Italian ingredients. Italian food is so simple that the quality of the ingredients really matters. If you do any Italian cooking, most of the ingredients that we talk about in this chapter quickly become essential.

Pasta

Can you imagine Italian cooking without pasta? Many cooks swear by one particular brand. They never consider using anything other than something imported from Italy. Other cooks buy whatever is on sale, claiming that all pasta is the same. Who's right? We're going to be diplomatic and say that both camps are right. The differences among brands of pasta are fairly slight. After the pasta is sauced, tasting any differences in wheat or water quality is difficult.

All dried pasta may taste the same, but some brands do seem to cook up slightly better than others. (Italian pasta companies say that they slow-dry their pasta for a superior product. Some companies also use higher grades of wheat, which can make a difference in the way the pasta cooks up.) Good pasta remains firm even when slightly overcooked. Some brands seem to go from too firm to too soft in a matter of seconds. But much of this is subjective and has to do with the skill of the cook.

Okay, so the brand you buy isn't all that critical. What about the shape? Do you need to stock your pantry with a hundred shapes? Of course not. Italians are a creative people — think of Michelangelo or Leonardo DaVinci — and many dried pasta shapes are the product of some overactive imaginations. That said, shape does matter. So does size.

Certain sauces work best with certain shapes. If a recipe calls for linguine, you can use spaghetti, but ziti may not work well.

Keeping several shapes in your pantry is a good idea. Include something long and thin like spaghetti or linguine as well as something short and tubular like penne and ziti. Test-cook a variety of shapes to find those that you like. Eventually, you'll probably pick a few that become standard items in your house. Other shapes may make guest appearances when a recipe specifically calls for them. (See Figure 2-1 for illustrations of some particularly common shapes.)

Figure 2-1:
Common
pasta
shapes.

Meats

Many Italian soups, pasta sauces, rice dishes, and stews rely on small amounts of pork to add flavor and richness. *Pancetta* is unsmoked Italian bacon that's salted and spiced and rolled up into a log that looks like salami. When sliced, you can see spirals of pink meat surrounded by milky white fat. You usually slice pancetta thin (like other cold cuts). For most recipes, you want to chop it quite fine as well.

American bacon is an imperfect substitute for pancetta because it's smoked. If you can't find pancetta, try cooking strips of regular bacon in simmering water for a minute or two to remove some of the smoky flavor. More and more supermarkets carry pancetta, as do most gourmet stores and all Italian delis. If you like, you can freeze pancetta in small packages and just pull it out as needed.

Prosciutto is salted and air-cured ham. Like pancetta, you often cook prosciutto along with aromatic vegetables, such as onions and carrots, to establish a flavor base. Of course, you can also serve prosciutto as is for appetizers or use it in pizza toppings. *Prosciutto crudo* is the standard product that has been cured but not cooked. *Prosciutto cotto* has been cooked, like a boiled or Virginia ham. Unless a recipe says otherwise, use prosciutto crudo.

Book II

Italian
Cooking

Cheeses

You have hundreds of Italian cheeses to choose from. Most, however, aren't exported. The following list describes some of the most popular and useful Italian cheeses. Supermarkets sell some, while a good cheese shop or gourmet shop has them all.

- **Fontina:** Real fontina cheese from Valle d'Aosta in the far north is rich and creamy with a buttery, nutty flavor. At room temperature, it becomes soft. Fontina never gets runny like brie, but it shouldn't be firm, either. You can eat fontina as is, or because it melts so well, you can use it in sandwiches or pizzas.

   Avoid fontina from sources other than Italy. Most supermarkets carry a rubbery, bland fontina cheese from Denmark or Sweden with a texture more like cheddar and absolutely no flavor.

- **Gorgonzola:** Italy's prized blue cheese can be made in various styles. Sometimes Gorgonzola is dry and crumbly and has an intense blue cheese flavor similar to Roquefort, a popular blue cheese from France. Although this aged cheese is fine for nibbling, when cooking we generally prefer a milder, creamier type of Gorgonzola called *dolce* or *dolce latte* ("sweet" or "sweet milk"). The texture is creamy, and the distinctive blue cheese flavor isn't overpowering.

If you can't find Italian Gorgonzola dolce, you may want to try Saga Blue, a Danish blue cheese readily available in supermarkets. The flavor isn't as distinctive as Gorgonzola, but Saga Blue is milder and creamier than most supermarket blue cheeses.

✔ **Mascarpone:** This Italian version of cream cheese often appears in desserts. (It's essential in the trendy tiramisù.) You can also use mascarpone to enrich pasta sauces or fillings. The imported and domestic versions of this fresh cheese are all pretty good and are sold in plastic tubs. Mascarpone has a light, creamy texture and buttery flavor. Don't try to substitute American cream cheese. The texture is much stiffer, and the flavor is quite different. Mascarpone has a short shelf life, so pay attention to expiration dates when shopping and try to use the cheese quickly.

✔ **Mozzarella:** You can find so many styles of this important Italian cheese that figuring out where to start may seem hard. Most fresh mozzarella (the fresh cheese is packed in water, not shrink-wrapped) is made from cow's milk and called *fiore di latte.* The flavor is milky and sweet, and the texture is springy, yet yielding. You should eat this cheese as is in a simple mozzarella, tomato, and basil salad (see Chapter 4 of Book II) or perhaps marinated in olive oil and served as an antipasto. When cooked, it loses some of its delicacy.

Fresh mozzarella is made by hand and is usually sold in large balls that weigh between half a pound and one pound. You can also find smaller balls, usually no more than an ounce or two. Look for words that indicate size, such as *bocconcini* ("little mouthfuls") or *ciliegine* ("little cherries"), when shopping. When buying fresh mozzarella, try to get cheese that has been made that day. Mozzarella starts to go downhill after a day or two, and after three or four days, it's usually not worth eating. The cheese should look white and have a fresh, sweet smell. If the cheese smells at all sour or looks dried out, go to another shop. When you get fresh mozzarella home, use it immediately. If you must keep it for a few days, refrigerate the cheese in a container filled with enough very lightly salted water to cover the cheese.

Most of the world relies on shrink-wrapped versions of mozzarella cheese that are rubbery and bland. Never use these cheeses in a dish in which you don't cook the cheese. We prefer fresh mozzarella in pizzas, but you can use supermarket mozzarella in cooked dishes. When the cheese melts, the rubbery texture is less of a problem, and if you include other assertive ingredients (tomato sauce and pizza toppings), you may not notice that the cheese has no flavor.

✔ **Parmesan:** Parmigiano-Reggiano is the king of Italian cheeses. This name is given to the finest aged Parmesan cheese produced in the Parma area in northern Italy. Another Italian Parmesan cheese, called Grana Padano, is quite good, but nothing compares to the real thing. Although you may balk at paying $12 a pound for Parmigiano-Reggiano, most recipes call for very little, and the cheese delivers a large impact. Freshly grated

Parmigiano-Reggiano (don't buy pregrated cheese; it dries out and loses much of its flavor) has a rich, buttery, nutty flavor. Parmigiano-Reggiano is so good that Italians often break off tiny pieces from a hunk and eat the cheese with drinks as an appetizer.

When shopping for Parmigiano-Reggiano, try to buy small wedges (about half a pound is a good size for grating) that have been freshly cut from a whole wheel of the cheese. A whole wheel weighs at least 65 pounds and has the words *Parmigiano-Reggiano* stenciled on the rind. When buying wedges, check the rind to make sure that part of this stenciling appears — this stenciling is the only way to know that you're getting the real thing. You can wrap Parmigiano-Reggiano in wax paper or plastic wrap and keep it in the refrigerator for several weeks, at least.

If Parmigiano-Reggiano is just too expensive for your budget, look for Grana Padano, an Italian cheese made in the same region but usually not aged quite as long. Although not as complex, this cheese is still quite delicious, and it often costs much less (sometimes half as much) than Parmigiano-Reggiano.

We're less impressed with Parmesan cheeses made in the United States and South America. They tend to be much saltier and lack the subtlety and flavor of the real thing. And as for grated Parmesan in a can, we'd rather sprinkle sawdust on our food!

✔ **Pecorino:** Pecorino is traditionally made from sheep's milk, although some manufacturers add some cow's milk to reduce the pungency or to save money. In Italy, stores and restaurants usually sell pecorino fresh or lightly aged and serve it as an eating cheese. Young pecorino isn't widely known elsewhere. Most of the exported pecorino has been aged much longer. Like Parmesan, aged pecorino is designed for grating, but it has a much saltier and more pungent flavor.

Most exported pecorino is from the Rome area, hence the name Pecorino Romano. (Pecorino cheeses are also made in Sardinia, Sicily, and Tuscany.) Pecorino Romano is bone-white cheese that has an intense peppery flavor. Like Parmigiano-Reggiano, the words *Pecorino Romano* appear stenciled on the rind to make shopping for the authentic product easy. Many American-made pecorino cheeses taste of salt and nothing else; avoid these American varieties.

Pecorino is best in dishes with assertive ingredients, such as capers, olives, or hot red pepper flakes. Pecorino also works well with vegetables such as eggplant and zucchini. Pecorino is widely used in Sicilian and Sardinian dishes.

✔ **Ricotta:** Like mozzarella, ricotta should be freshly made and consumed within a few days. It should be creamy and thick, not watery and curdish like so many supermarket brands sold in plastic containers. In Italy, local cheese makers produce fresh ricotta with a dry, firm consistency (akin to goat cheese). The flavor is sweet and milky. This cheese is so perishable that it's rarely exported.

Book II

Italian Cooking

In the United States, you can get fresh, locally made ricotta in and near urban centers with large Italian-American populations. This cheese shares many qualities with the Italian versions. These U.S. versions are especially good in ricotta cheesecakes and pasta sauces or fillings, in which the cheese is the main ingredient.

You can use supermarket ricotta cheese, but it's bland and the texture is mushy and unappealing. You may try draining supermarket ricotta in a fine-mesh strainer for an hour or two to remove some of the water. This method can improve the texture, but you can't really do anything to improve the flavor.

Italians are rightly famous for their cheeses. Cooks worldwide use Parmesan cheese to flavor pasta dishes, as well as egg, rice, and meat dishes. When shopping for cheeses, here are some guidelines to help you:

- **Search for only fresh cheeses.** Shop from a store that handles the cheese properly and does a brisk business so that nothing sits around for very long. A wedge cut to order is fresher than a precut and wrapped wedge.

- **Taste everything before you buy.** Good cheese shops unwrap cheeses and cut off small slices for you to sample.

- **Buy Italian.** Many Parmesan and other Italian cheeses made in the United States, Argentina, Canada, Denmark, and Switzerland lack the full flavor of the original. Read labels, which usually cite the country of origin. If in doubt, ask someone.

Garlic and Onions

Oh, how do we love garlic and onions? Let us count (and sniff) the ways. Well, if you read closely, you can see that more than half the recipes in this book contain one or both of these ingredients — and that makes a lot of ways.

Many Italian recipes begin by sautéing onions or garlic in olive oil. These two *alliums* (a family of vegetables that also includes leeks, chives, and scallions) provide the flavor base for pasta sauces, rice dishes, roasts, vegetable side dishes, and more.

Although many Americans fear that onions and, in particular, garlic give food a harsh, overpowering flavor, this rarely happens in good Italian cooking. Italian cooks use the onions and garlic like salt to help bring out the flavors in other ingredients. They are infrequently the focal point of a dish and should never be so prominent that they're objectionable.

You must use a light hand, especially with the garlic. Two cloves can make a pasta sauce delicious. Use eight cloves only if you're expecting vampires that night. Also, cooking garlic over medium heat (not high heat — the garlic burns and becomes bitter) tames its flame and brings out its sweeter notes. You should finely mince garlic (smaller pieces cook evenly and are less likely to burn that larger pieces) and cook it until golden.

Cooking also changes the flavor of onions. The harshness fades, and the onions become sweeter as they start to color. The darker the onions become, the sweeter and more caramelized their flavor. Only when onions are burned do they become bitter.

When shopping for garlic, look for firm bulbs with no green sprouts or shoots. When shopping for onions, pick up red onions for most recipes. Cooks (especially in the north) use yellow onions, but red onions are the standard in most Italian recipes. Unless otherwise indicated, recipes in this book use red onions, although you can use yellow onions with a slight difference in flavor.

Book II

**Italian
Cooking**

Store garlic and onions at room temperature. They should stay fresh for weeks.

To peel garlic, simply use the side of a chef's knife to crush the cloves and loosen the papery skin, as shown in Figure 2-2.

Figure 2-2:
Peeling
garlic.

Use the side of a large chef's knife to press down on a garlic clove and loosen the papery skin...

To prepare an onion for cooking, follow these steps, as shown in Figure 2-3:

1. **To peel the onion, cut off the stem and cut the onion in half through the ends. Gently lift off the dry outer layers of skin.**

2. **Lay the halves down on a work surface. To chop or mince, make parallel lengthwise cuts, starting just in from the root end.**

   Keep the root end intact to keep the onion layers from separating.

3. **Turn the knife so that it's horizontal to the work surface and slice through the onion, again leaving the root end intact.**

   For small onions, one slice is fine; larger onions require several slices to produce finely minced pieces.

4. **Cut across the onion to turn out pieces of the desired size.**

How to Mince an Onion

1. Cut off stem Cut in half through the root Peel off skin

2.  Make parallel lengthwise cuts don't cut through root end!

3.  Cut horizontal slices from top to bottom not all the way through!

4.  Now cut crosswise

Figure 2-3: Cutting an onion.

Herbs

Dried herbs have almost no place in Italian cooking. Sure, Italian cooks use dried bay leaves to flavor soups and beans as they cook. And some Italian cooks may add a pinch of dried oregano to a tomato sauce as it cooks. But that's it. Otherwise, Italian cooks use fresh herbs. Why? Because fresh herbs taste a lot better than dried herbs do.

Fresh herbs have all their aromatic oils. Dried herbs are weak and often about as tasty as fallen leaves. If you have any doubts, rub a fresh sage leaf between your fingers. The aroma is intoxicating and immediately recalls the woods. Next, open a jar of dried sage. You can detect some aroma, but it's faint and one-dimensional.

Most supermarkets carry a half dozen or more fresh herbs. And if you do any gardening at all, we recommend throwing a few herbs in the ground every spring. Planting takes very little time, the plants require minimal maintenance, and you end up with a steady supply of fresh herbs all summer, at great savings. Put plants into the ground or in clay pots and make sure that they get a lot of sun and some water every day or two.

One final note about herbs: If you can't get the fresh herb specified in a particular recipe, think about using another fresh herb rather than the dried equivalent. A dish may not taste the same, but it can still turn out to be delicious. For example, a fresh tomato sauce with fresh basil is equally good with fresh mint or parsley, but dried basil adds little to the sauce.

Herbs do vary in intensity, so when substituting, try to pick something with a similar punch, or be prepared to adjust the amount of herb. We find that parsley and basil are the mildest herbs, and you can use them in the greatest amount. Mint, chives, and tarragon are more potent; you should use them with a lighter hand. Thyme, oregano, marjoram, and rosemary are the most potent — use them sparingly. Table 2-1 lists the most important herbs used in Italian cooking.

Table 2-1		Favorite Herbs for Italian Cooking
Herb	**Italian Name**	**Description**
Basil	Basilico	Italy's best-known herb, basil has a strong anise flavor. A must in pesto, basil is a natural with tomatoes. (Basil's sweetness works nicely with the acidity in the tomatoes.) Tarragon, which isn't widely used in Italy, has a similar anise flavor, and you can use it as a substitute. You can also use parsley in most recipes calling for basil.
Bay leaf	Alloro	Once sold only dried, this herb is increasingly available fresh as well. Dried leaves are often dropped into a pot of simmering beans or soup to impart their gentle aroma. You can use fresh leaves, which tend to be longer and thinner, in the same fashion.
Marjoram	Maggiorana	This herb is similar to oregano but milder in flavor. Popular in the Riviera, marjoram is good with meats and seafood.
Mint	Menta	You can find hundreds of kinds of mint. Some are mild and sweet; others spicy and hot. Mint is used more in southern Italy and has an intensity and freshness similar to basil, which is perhaps the best substitute.
Oregano	Origano	This herb has a potent aroma and flavor that predominates in much southern-Italian cooking and is used commonly with tomatoes.
Parsley	Prezzemolo	This herb is the unheralded star of Italian cooking. Basil may get all the attention, but parsley is more widely used. Flat-leaf varieties have a stronger flavor than curly-leaf varieties. You can cook parsley with garlic and onions in olive oil to form the flavor base for many dishes.
Rosemary	Rosmarino	With rosemary's strong resinous (or pine) aroma and flavor, you must use it sparingly. The tough needles need time to soften, and you shouldn't add it to dishes that you don't cook. Rosemary is a natural with potatoes, chicken, lamb, and beef.
Sage	Salvia	Sage is especially popular in Tuscany and other parts of central and northern Italy. Sage is pungent with a musty mint taste and has an affinity for butter sauces, as well as pork and chicken.

Book II

Italian Cooking

Anchovies, Capers, and Olives

Italians use anchovies, capers, and olives to make simple dishes taste special. These ingredients are especially popular in southern Italy and add a salty, piquant flavor to dishes. Italian cooks commonly use them with tomatoes, either singly or in combination.

Anchovies are small fish that are especially popular in Sicilian cooking. These fish are often filleted, packed in oil, and canned. The canned form is the most common found in North American markets. Try to pick brands with olive oil as the packing medium. The anchovies taste better, and you can use the oil. For example, in many recipes, you cook the anchovy fillets in oil (either from the can or fresh oil) and mash them until they dissolve. This way, the anchovies impart their briny, fishy flavor to a dish without diners having to encounter large chunks that could otherwise prove overwhelmingly salty.

Capers are the preserved green flower buds of a bush that grows all around the Mediterranean. Capers are usually packed in brine made with white vinegar, salt, and water, which act as a preservative. Capers are also packed in salt, although this variety doesn't keep well (brined capers stay fresh in the refrigerator indefinitely) and is hard to find.

You need to drain brined capers before use and rinse them to remove excess saltiness and the vinegar flavor. You must rinse salted capers thoroughly. Capers come in a variety of sizes — you can add very small whole capers to dishes; you should chop larger capers.

You have dozens of varieties of olives to choose from, each with a different shape, size, and color. Unlike other fruits (olives are like cherries, a pitted fruit that arises from tree blossoms), you must cure olives before eating them. Straight from the tree, they're bitter and inedible.

When olives are picked before they fully ripen, the color is green. As olives ripen on the tree, they turn black or purple. After olives are harvested, all olives (whether they're picked green or black) are soaked in a weak alkali solution to remove some of the bitterness. They're then washed and put in a vinegar, salt, and water solution. (Some black olives are dry-cured in oil and salt. The result is a meaty, very salty olive, better for cooking than eating out of hand.)

Never buy canned olives, which usually come from California. These olives have been boiled and pitted, a process that strips all character from the olives and leaves them bland and mushy. Jarred imported olives are a fine choice, as are olives sold loose in brine at the deli counter. Of course, you must taste to find a variety and brand you like.

To remove olive pits, try using a cherry pitter, or place olives on a cutting board and use the side of a large chef's knife or cleaver to lightly crush the olives. After the olives have split, popping out the pit and chopping the flesh should be easy.

Always keep olives packed in their brine to keep them from drying out. Instead of draining them, we usually use a long spoon to fish out olives from the jar, one at a time. Rinsing brined olives to remove some of the vinegar before using them in recipes is also a good idea.

Olive Oil

Perhaps more than any other ingredient, olive oil gives Italian cooking its distinctive flavor. Italian olive oils are rightly regarded as the world's finest, although excellent oils also come from Spain, Greece, North Africa, the Middle East, and California. But Italian oils set the standard. In fact, many oils with Italian names are actually made from olives grown elsewhere that are shipped to Italy for processing.

Several cooks and "experts" have written a lot about olive oil in the past decade, and some of the information has been quite confusing. Here's what we think you need to know.

When shopping, you're likely to encounter three types of olive oil:

- **Extra virgin:** Refers to a grade. Extra-virgin oils are extracted from olives by cold mechanical pressure and have the best flavor and lowest acidity. Traditionally, the olives were placed between straw mats and ground between heavy stones powered by animals, much the way flour was once milled. Modern equipment has made the process faster, but without heat or solvents, the olives don't give up all their oil.

- **Pure:** Also refers to a grade. When heat or solvents are applied to increase the yield, the oil is called "pure." Pure oils are relatively characterless.

- **Light:** The third kind of olive oil sold in the United States is called light olive oil. Despite the name, it has the same nutritional profile as other olive oils. However, this oil has been stripped of all flavor, hence the name "light." Brilliant marketers thought that the real stuff scared Americans because of its strong flavor. But that's the beauty of olive oil. Unlike corn or vegetable oil, it adds something to dishes besides fat and calories.

If you want bland oil, buy corn oil or canola oil. If you want olive oil, buy the real thing.

Olive oil can be refined and filtered (as are most extra-virgin oils sold in super-markets, as well as all pure oils), or it can be left relatively untouched and sold with lots of sediment. Many premium Italian oils available in gourmet shops come to market this way. In general, the less the oil is processed, the more likely that the oil has captured all the nuances from the olives.

In our kitchens, we use extra-virgin olive oil for almost everything. (We use pure olive oil for deep-frying.) When sautéing, we turn to a relatively inexpensive extra-virgin olive oil from the supermarket. At $10 a liter, these oils aren't cheap, but they have much more character than pure oils. Many of these oils are bottled in Italy but aren't really Italian oils. But they're good enough for everyday use.

When using the oil raw (in salad dressing or to drizzle over a piece of cooked fish or some vegetables), we use an unrefined extra-virgin olive oil from a small Italian producer. Sometimes called estate oils, these oils represent the finest quality. They often cost $20 or $30 a liter or more, but the aroma and flavor are unmatched. Some of these oils are spicy, while others are gentle with the flavor of almonds, artichokes, or even flowers dominating.

When shopping for estate oil, look to see whether the oil is clear or cloudy. A little cloudiness indicates that the oil hasn't been filtered excessively. Note that filtering does prolong shelf life, so make sure that you use unfiltered oils quickly, within six months. Also read the label. Oil made from Italian olives has a label that says "produced and bottled in Italy." If you don't see these words, assume that the manufacturer used some non-Italian olives, even if the label says "imported from Italy."

Color, which ranges from golden to green, indicates the type of olives and their ripeness but isn't a gauge of quality. If you can, try to smell an open bottle of the oil. Oil that smells good probably tastes good. You should also detect nuances when smelling the oil. Some oils smell like grass or herbs; others smell like almonds or flowers. Eventually, you find traits that you enjoy, but the important thing is that the oil has some character.

Vinegar

When it comes to vinegar, you have several choices:

- **Red wine vinegar:** The better the red wine, the better the vinegar. Imported red wine vinegar tends to be slightly more acidic than domestic brands, but either makes a dressing with a strong kick. Like wine, good red wine vinegar is full-bodied and complex.

- **White wine vinegar:** Less full-bodied than vinegar made with red wine, white wine vinegar is still fairly acidic. Don't buy distilled white vinegar, which is made from grains, not wine, and has little flavor.

- **Balsamic vinegar:** Balsamic vinegar has a rich brown color and sweet, woody flavor that comes from aging in casks.

You say you've tried balsamic vinegar and can't figure out what all the fuss is about. Odds are good that you haven't purchased real balsamico. Balsamic vinegar is the trendy condiment of choice for everything from salad dressings to sauces. However, most Americans would be surprised to learn that they have never tasted "real" balsamic vinegar. Even more shocking, balsamic vinegar is more popular in the United States than in Italy, where its culinary uses are actually quite limited. Contrary to what the chef at your local restaurant may think, balsamic vinegar isn't Italy's answer to soy sauce. Balsamic vinegar has very specific uses. One of those is salad dressing.

Many cheap brands of balsamic vinegar are simply red wine vinegar with caramel added for color and sweetness. If a bottle of "balsamic vinegar" costs $2, you can be sure it hasn't been aged and isn't genuine.

Although the real thing can cost upwards of $50 an ounce, a happy middle ground is available. Unaged balsamic vinegar is harsh and unpleasant, but aging for 12 or more years makes the product costly to produce. The solution some companies have adopted is aging for several years in wood. The resulting vinegar has a gentle sweetness combined with a low-to-moderate acidity; a complex, woody bouquet and flavor reminiscent of fruit; and a dense, syrupy consistency — all qualities that are revered in traditional balsamic vinegar. A small bottle costs $5 or $10, but remember that a little goes a long way. When shopping, read labels carefully. Vinegars that are aged usually say so.

Even quality commercial balsamic vinegars aren't used straight in salad dressings in Italy, but are usually combined with red wine vinegar. Other traditional uses — such as sprinkling over steamed asparagus, sliced Parmesan, or vanilla gelato — require very small quantities. Italians don't generally cook with balsamic vinegar because heat destroys its subtle qualities. To use balsamic vinegar in savory foods, add a few drops to a sauce just before serving or drizzle some over a piece of grilled fish.

So why does a 3-ounce bottle of traditional aged balsamic vinegar cost $150? The answer is low yield and high storage fees. A typical vineyard acre may produce enough grape juice to make 800 gallons of wine vinegar. After the juice from those same grapes has been cooked down and aged, during which time massive evaporation occurs, just 20 or 30 gallons of balsamic vinegar remain. High storage costs (just keeping water that long is expensive) add to the final price, which is rarely less than $60 per bottle and can climb to $200.

Is any vinegar worth that much? Traditional balsamic vinegar has a high viscosity, intense but pleasant sweetness, heady aroma, and minimal acidity — all traits that easily distinguish it from commercial vinegars. These characteristics also restrict its uses. Wealthy Italians sip traditional balsamico after dinner or sprinkle a few drops over sliced strawberries. For most other culinary purposes, good commercial balsamic vinegar works just fine. But be prepared. When dining with the Duke and Duchess of Mantua, they may just serve you a spoon of balsamic vinegar after dinner.

Book II

Italian
Cooking

Tomatoes

Imagining Italian cooking without tomatoes is hard. "Red sauce" is almost synonymous with Italian cooking. Many people are surprised to discover that tomatoes originated in the New World and first came to Europe only after Christopher Columbus brought them back from the Americas. Eventually, Italians adopted tomatoes as their own, using them in everything from salads and soups to pasta sauces and pizzas. However, contrary to popular belief, most Italian dishes don't contain tomatoes.

Italians love tomatoes, but they hate bad tomatoes. Unfortunately, the tomato has been much abused in the name of progress. In order to keep our markets stocked with tomatoes 365 days a year, geneticists, farmers, and marketers have engineered tomatoes that look great but taste horrible. Most of the perfectly round, red orbs that fill supermarket bins are picked when green, shipped thousands of miles, and then gassed to turn them red. They're designed for the shopper who selects food based on appearance rather than flavor. Ugh!

We suggest that you buy local, in-season tomatoes for dishes in which you don't cook the tomatoes. If it's January and you live in New York or Toronto, please don't make a tomato salad with mozzarella and basil. Choose another recipe instead of trying to make this dish with tomatoes from Holland, Israel, Mexico, or a hothouse.

When we want the flavor of tomatoes out of season, we rely on canned tomatoes (at least they're picked ripe) or oval plum tomatoes, which are also called *Roma* tomatoes. Plum tomatoes aren't as juicy as round (also called *beefsteak*) tomatoes and don't have as many seeds. Their flesh is usually quite firm (one reason we don't think that most plum tomatoes are worth eating raw), but they do add fresh tomato flavor and texture to cooked dishes.

When preparing tomatoes, remove the *core* — the small brown patch at the stem end. You can then slice or dice the tomatoes as needed. When cooking tomatoes, we often remove the peel first (the skin separates from the flesh and isn't terribly appealing) by submerging the tomatoes in simmering water for ten seconds and then peeling the skin with our fingers. Summer tomatoes are often quite juicy, which can be a problem when adding them to cooked dishes. In some cases, we seed the tomatoes before chopping them.

Chapter 3

Mastering a Few Simple Techniques

You don't need much experience in the kitchen to prepare delicious Italian recipes. But it helps if you're familiar with a few basic techniques. So in this chapter, we fill you in on what you need to know. Flip back to these pages if you need to when you're in the middle of a recipe and you can't remember how to do something.

Making Stock

Many Italian soups use water as their base, while others start with meat, chicken, fish, or vegetable stock. Cooks make stock by simmering bones, scraps of meat, parts with little use (like chicken backs or fish heads), and/or chopped vegetables and herbs in water. The solids flavor the water to create a rich base, called *stock,* which you can use to make soups or sauces.

Some cooks are under the misconception that the stockpot is the place to use limp vegetables, old scraps of meat, and other kitchen leftovers. However, stock tastes only as good as the ingredients used to make it. Meat should be fresh and trimmed of as much fat and gristle as possible. Vegetables should be fresh and clean. Although stock is the perfect place to use up a stray onion or carrot, don't add anything to the stockpot that you don't consider fresh enough to eat.

You can control the intensity of the stock in several ways. At the outset, you can change the ratio of solids to liquid. In general, you want to add enough water to cover the solid ingredients by 1 or 2 inches. Add more water, and the resulting stock will be weak, which may be fine for risotto but isn't appropriate for brothy soup that needs a potent stock. If the solids are just barely covered with water, the stock will be more intense in flavor.

After the solids and water are in the pot, bring everything to a boil and then reduce the heat to a gentle simmer. As the solids cook, they may throw off some impurities in the form of foam. Skim off the foam with a spoon and discard it.

After the solid ingredients have given up their flavor, pour the stockpot's contents through a mesh strainer set over a clean container or pot. (This flavor-finding mission happens quickly — in less than an hour — for vegetables and fish; for chicken and meat, this process can take two or three hours.) The strainer traps the solids. To release as much flavor as possible from the solids, press down on them with the back of a large spoon to squeeze out their juices. A French strainer, called a chinois (see Figure 3-1) has a conical shape that makes extracting every last bit of flavor from the stock ingredients especially easy.

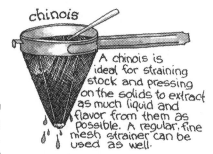

chinois

A chinois is ideal for straining stock and pressing on the solids to extract as much liquid and flavor from them as possible. A regular, fine mesh strainer can be used as well.

Figure 3-1:
A chinois.

To intensify a finished stock's flavor, place the strained liquid back over the heat and cook until reduced to the desired consistency. Because stock is often reduced, you generally don't need to add salt until you're ready to use the stock. When the stock is done, cool it until the fat congeals on top. Remove the fat with a spoon or skimmer and discard it.

Place defatted stock in an airtight container and refrigerate for up to 3 days or freeze for up to several months. When freezing stock, divide a single batch into several smaller containers so that you can pull out just as much as you need when making recipes in the future. Or freeze stock in ice cube trays and store the frozen cubes in plastic bags.

Stock portfolio

Cooks who want to plan strategically for the future should keep chicken, fish, and vegetable stock in the freezer. Stock on hand is the culinary equivalent of owning a diversified portfolio of stocks, bonds, and mutual funds.

✔ **Chicken stock:** Chicken stock is by far the most versatile stock. It's rarely inappropriate (beef stock in fish soup is odd, but chicken stock tastes just fine) and is often the best choice. Use backs, necks, wings, or even drumsticks to make stock. In most cases, the chicken should be balanced with a handful or two of chopped vegetables (onion, carrot, and celery are the usual choices) and perhaps 1 or 2 bay leaves, several peeled garlic cloves, and a dozen or so whole black peppercorns. You can also add some whole parsley sprigs. The chicken is essential; the vegetables are nice but optional.

To make about 2 quarts chicken stock, start with 3 pounds chicken parts (remove any fat and skin first) in a pot and cover with 2½ quarts water. Add vegetables and herbs and simmer for at least 2 hours to extract the full flavor from the chicken.

✔ **Fish stock:** Fish stock has limited uses (for chowders, other fish soups, and seafood risotto), but it can make a good dish great, adding depth of flavor and intensity. Fish stock is usually made from scraps, such as heads, bones, and tails from fish, as well as shells from lobster or shrimp. Avoid oily fish, such as salmon, which makes the stock too fishy. Fish with mild, white, flaky flesh, such as red snapper or flounder, are best for stock. Make sure that innards and gills don't go into the stockpot because they impart an off flavor.

To make about 2 quarts fish stock, place 2 pounds fish heads, bones, tails, and fins in a pot and cover with 2 quarts water. Add aromatics such s bay leaves, parsley, and thyme sprigs, and whole black peppercorns, and simmer for about 30 minutes to extract the flavor from the fish. (Don't cook too long, or the stock will become too fishy.) Many chefs use a little wine along with water as the liquid. The acidity from the wine balances the fish flavor nicely. If you want to use white wine, add 1 cup for every 2 quarts water. You can add a halved lemon as well.

✔ **Vegetable stock:** Some chefs argue that rich chicken broth overwhelms light vegetable dishes, such as an asparagus risotto, and that a milder vegetable stock is the better route. Other chefs find vegetable stocks insipid and prefer to use chicken stock in most every application, other than seafood soups. One camp appreciates the mild sweetness of good vegetable stock, while the other camp wishes vegetable stock were richer and stronger tasting, like chicken stock.

We tend to agree that vegetable stock is nice in certain applications where chicken stock can overwhelm the flavor of vegetables. However, you must use good vegetable stock. Throwing a chicken into a pot with some water produces good stock. Add some aromatic vegetables, such as onions and carrots, and you have great stock. Vegetable stock requires more thought and more work.

To coax flavor from the vegetables, we recommend that you sauté them in a little olive oil before adding the water. Using lots of vegetables (at least a cup of chopped

(continued)

(continued)

vegetables for every cup of water) is imperative. Leeks, onions, carrots, and celery are a must. Typical seasonings include fresh herbs (especially thyme, basil, and parsley sprigs), dried bay leaves, and whole black peppercorns. Add potatoes to give the stock some body, peeled garlic cloves for some intensity, a little dried porcini for some earthy flavor and color, and a chopped tomato or two for color. Finely chop all vegetables so that they release as much flavor as possible.

To make about 2 quarts vegetable stock, place 10 cups finely chopped vegetables in a pot along with 2 tablespoons olive oil. Sauté until the vegetables are golden, 10 to 12 minutes. Add 10 cups water and then simmer until the vegetables have given up their flavor, about 1 hour. When straining the stock, press firmly on the vegetables to extract all their juices.

Cooking Dried Pasta

Cooking dried pasta seems easy enough. Bring water to a boil, add the pasta, and drain when tender. And although cooking pasta is easy, this simple operation has a right way and a wrong way. If your pasta sticks together or seems mushy, you probably are making some simple mistake that you can easily correct. Italian cooking also calls for a lot of improvisation. However, cooking pasta is formulaic. Here are the secrets, spelled out in clear English.

Boil water

Abundant boiling water is key to cooking pasta properly. Dried pasta needs room to swell and rehydrate. If you cook pasta in a small pot or in a small amount of water, the pieces are likely to stick together. Give pasta some room, and it will behave nicely.

Start with cold water. Hot tap water comes to a boil more quickly but usually picks up some odd flavors from your water heater. One pound of pasta requires a minimum of 4 quarts water. In order to leave room for the pasta and prevent boil-overs, start with a 6-quart pot. An 8-quart pot is even better.

If cooking half a pound of pasta, you still need at least 3 quarts of water, and 4 quarts is best. If cooking more than a pound of pasta, use two pots. Even if you own a pot large enough to hold 8 quarts of water and 2 pounds of pasta, we don't recommend cooking pasta in this manner. The water takes forever to boil. After you add the pasta, the water takes too long to come back to a boil, slowing your cooking time.

Add salt

After the water comes to a rolling boil (the surface of the water should be moving, or *rolling,* with large bubbles), you can add salt. Much of the world has become salt-phobic. But Italians know that salt is essential to cooking pasta.

If you simply boil spaghetti in plain water, it cooks up bland. Salting the water makes dried pasta (which doesn't contain any salt) taste better. If you're concerned about your salt intake, go lightly on the salt in the sauce. But whatever you do, don't skimp on the salt in the pasta pot.

So how much salt is enough for 4 quarts water? Some Italian cooks add as much as 3 tablespoons of coarse or kosher salt. Remember that your pot contains a lot of water, and almost all the salt goes down the drain with the cooking water. Adding ¼ teaspoon salt to 4 quarts water is like dropping 1 hot red pepper flake into a pot of tomato sauce. In order to season the pasta properly, you must add at least 1½ tablespoons salt for every 4 quarts water.

Forget the oil

Many pasta cooks outside of Italy add oil to the water to keep the pasta from sticking together. As long as you have started with enough water, adding oil is totally unnecessary. Although oil does keep strands from sticking together, using it has a downside. The oil makes the pasta slick. When you go to sauce the drained pasta, the sauce has a hard time clinging to the noodles. Good dried pasta has a slightly rough surface to which sauce can cling. Oil the pasta, and you've made proper saucing impossible.

Ignore the clock

Many novice cooks read package instructions and watch the clock when cooking pasta. Neither is helpful. Every stove cooks differently, and individuals can have different opinions about how soft they like their pasta. You must taste the pasta in order to figure out when it is ready to hit the colander. Residual heat causes pasta to continue to soften as it sits in the colander and later gets sauced, so take the pot off the flame about 30 seconds before you think that the pasta is perfectly cooked.

You've probably heard that pasta should be cooked *al dente.* Al dente, the Italian term that translates as "to the tooth," is a state of mind as much as a cooking term. When a recipe says "cook until golden brown," most cooks can agree when something looks golden brown. Al dente is another matter. Even within Italy, regional differences abound. Cooks in southern Italy often pull pasta off the heat a minute or two before their brethren in the north. We have eaten pasta in Italy that was so undercooked that it was still a bit crunchy in the center. The chef may think that his pasta is al dente, but we never serve pasta that crunches when chewed.

For us, the pasta should not be chewy or raw tasting. It should be tender throughout, while still possessing some bite or spring. If the pasta is soft or mushy, it's clearly overcooked. The more experience you have cooking pasta, the more you will develop an innate sense of al dente.

Think of al dente this way: When you first got your driver's license, you probably were speeding all the time. You had no way to judge the speed of the car unless you looked down at the speedometer. But the more you drove, the more you knew how fast you were going without having to watch the dashboard. Now you just know what 40 miles per hour feels like. Of course, you can misjudge your speed if you're not paying attention. The same is true of cooking pasta. But if you stay close to the pasta pot and fish out strands occasionally, you will know when the pasta is done.

Drain, don't shake

How you drain your pasta is an often overlooked source of problems. No one likes watery pasta that dilutes the sauce and makes a mess in bowls. However, bone-dry pasta is equally problematic. Thick sauces or sauces based on olive oil have a hard time coating long strands of pasta unless the noodles are moist. Many recipes even call for reserving some of the cooking water and adding it to the pasta and sauce if the mixture looks too dry.

When the pasta is cooked, we fish out some cooking water in a measuring cup and set it aside as an insurance policy. We then pour the pasta and water into a large colander in the sink to let the water drain out. Don't shake the colander — a little water clinging to the noodles is fine. Then toss the pasta and sauce in a warm serving bowl. A bowl that has been warmed in a 200-degree oven for 10 minutes usually works well. The heat of the bowl prevents the pasta from cooling off too quickly. After the sauce evenly coats the noodles, we divide portions among individual bowls.

Serve

In Italy, cooks usually serve pasta in wide, shallow bowls. Flat plates aren't ideal because the pasta can slide onto the floor. You can also use the side of the bowl to help twirl long strands onto a fork.

Pasta is a first course in Italy, eaten in very small portions. The first course is followed by meat, chicken, or fish. Most of the recipes in this book call for 8 ounces of dried pasta, which yields four appetizer portions.

If you like, you can serve pasta as a main course. Eight ounces of dried pasta yields two main-course servings. All the recipes in this book can be doubled to yield four main-course servings.

Making Pasta from Scratch

Some chefs and food writers argue that the only pasta worth eating is fresh pasta. That's like saying you should only eat fresh local tomatoes at their peak of ripeness and then do without any tomatoes (canned or fresh) for the rest of the year. Fresh pasta is wonderful, and everyone should make it a couple of times a year. But can you live off fresh pasta alone? Hardly.

The average Italian cook reserves fresh pasta for very specific uses and special occasions. Grandma makes her noodles for lasagna — she would never dream of using lasagna noodles from a box — or maybe she goes to the local pasta shop and buys fresh tagliatelle to toss with butter, cream, grated cheese, and some shaved fresh porcini mushrooms. In these dishes, fresh pasta makes a world of difference. Its softness and suppleness combined with its mild eggy flavor are divine. Make these recipes once with fresh pasta, and you'll never use dried pasta in these dishes again.

Traditionally, certain dishes require fresh pasta. For example, filled pastas, such as ravioli, must start with fresh pasta.

Although dried lasagna noodles and fettuccine exist, the fresh versions are far superior. Fresh noodles actually absorb some of the creamy sauces that are usually served with these pasta shapes. In contrast, butter, cheese, and cream sauces slide right off dried pasta. The delicate egg flavor of fresh pasta also complements these kinds of delicate, creamy sauces.

Making pasta at home was once a challenge. You had to knead the dough by hand and then roll it out with much finesse into thin sheets that you then cut into the appropriate shape. You can still make pasta this way, but two modern inventions (the food processor and the pasta machine) have made fresh pasta much more accessible, even for novices. Here's what you need to know.

Choosing the ingredients

Fresh pasta requires only four ingredients:

- ✔ **Flour:** Flour produces fresh noodles that are delicate yet elastic enough to stretch and roll out. Unbleached flour is the closest thing to the flour used to make fresh pasta in Italy, although bleached flour, which has been treated with chemicals to make it whiter, also works.

- ✔ **Eggs:** Use the freshest eggs possible because they provide pasta with most of its flavor.

- ✔ **Olive oil:** You can add a tiny bit of olive oil to make the dough more supple and flavorful.

- ✔ **Salt:** A pinch of salt adds flavor as well.

The flour and eggs are essential, but you can consider the oil and salt optional (but recommended).

You can flavor egg pasta in numerous ways. However, many of these flavorings are for cosmetic rather than flavor reasons. For example, tomato paste can dye fresh egg pasta a beautiful orange-red color. But close your eyes, and you won't be able to taste the difference between plain and tomato pasta.

Some flavorings do provide subtle flavors that you can detect if the sauce is especially delicate. However, after you put a spicy tomato sauce on any flavored pasta, you taste the sauce, not the pasta. Flavor fresh pasta if you like, but realize that flavoring is mostly an aesthetic decision.

Making the dough

Before the invention of the food processor, making the dough for fresh pasta took about 20 minutes. With the food processor, it takes about 1 minute. For history buffs, here's how to make it the old-fashioned way (see Figure 3-2):

1. **Place the flour in a pile on the counter.**

2. **Hollow out the center of the pile so that the flour is shaped into a ring.**

   The flour looks like the top of a volcano.

3. **Crack the eggs and place them in the center of the ring. Add the oil and salt to the eggs.**

4. **With a fork, slowly incorporate some of the flour into the eggs.**

   Don't break through the wall of flour and let the eggs run all over the counter!

5. **When you've worked enough flour into the eggs so that they won't run away, start kneading to work in the rest of the flour and then to knead the dough.**

   Pasta dough must be very smooth and well kneaded, so work the dough by hand for at least 10 minutes. When the dough is as smooth as a baby's bottom, you're ready to roll.

The modern method, of course, is much simpler. Just place the flour in a food processor, turn on the machine, add the eggs, and wait about ten seconds. You should still knead the dough by hand after it comes together in the food processor. But this takes only a minute or two, no longer. (See the recipe later in this section.)

After you've kneaded the pasta dough, you can rock and roll. (Well, you can skip the rock part, but you must roll.) Traditionally, Italian home cooks use a rolling pin or even a wine bottle. However, stretching the dough out this way is very hard. The dough is tough and resists your best efforts. In the end, pasta rolled with a rolling pin is usually too thick.

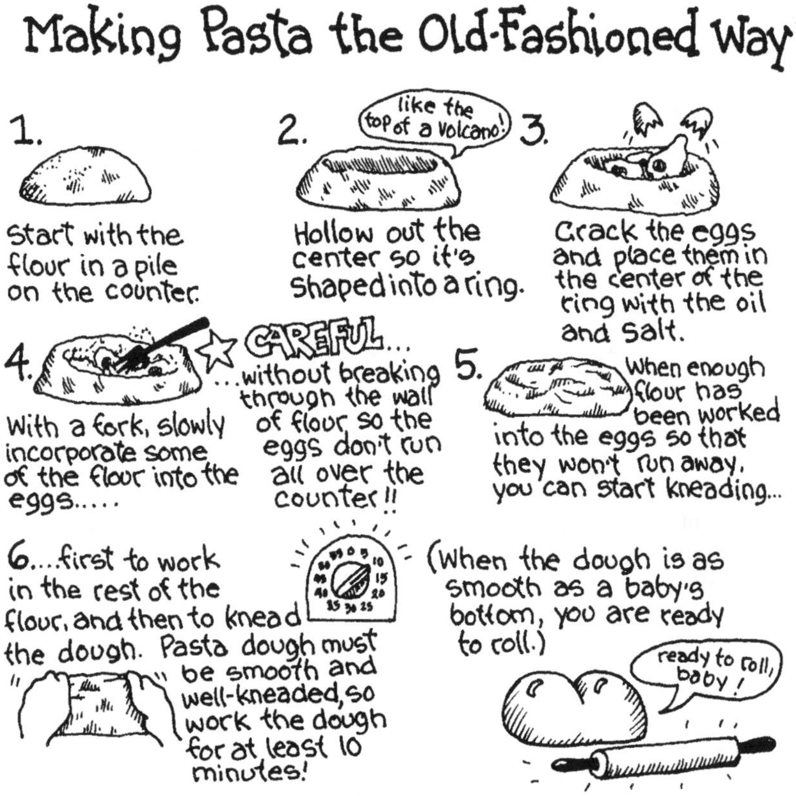

Book II

Italian
Cooking

Making Pasta the Old-Fashioned Way

1. Start with the flour in a pile on the counter.

2. (like the top of a volcano!) Hollow out the center so it's shaped into a ring.

3. Crack the eggs and place them in the center of the ring with the oil and salt.

4. ☆ CAREFUL... With a fork, slowly incorporate some of the flour into the eggs..... ...without breaking through the wall of flour so the eggs don't run all over the counter!!

5. When enough flour has been worked into the eggs so that they won't run away, you can start kneading...

6. ...first to work in the rest of the flour, and then to knead the dough. Pasta dough must be smooth and well-kneaded, so work the dough for at least 10 minutes!

(When the dough is as smooth as a baby's bottom, you are ready to roll.) ready to roll, baby!

Figure 3-2:
Making pasta the old-fashioned way.

We prefer using a manual pasta machine (see Figure 3-3). It rolls the pasta to an even thickness, and you can get the sheets of pasta quite thin. This machine also cuts the pasta. Most models can cut the pasta into fettuccine or spaghetti. The wider fettuccine cutters usually work a little better.

Figure 3-3:
A manually
operated
pasta
machine in
action.

A manual pasta machine produces two shapes — fettuccine or spaghetti. However, you can take the long sheets of dough and cut them to make lasagna noodles. Or take those long sheets and cut them with a knife into long, wide ribbons to make pappardelle or squares for ravioli or tortellini.

After you have cut out the pasta shape, be careful to keep the individual pieces separated. Letting them dry for a half hour or so helps. You can keep fresh pasta on clean kitchen towels at room temperature for several hours before cooking. For longer storage, place the pasta in a resealable plastic bag and freeze it for up to one month. Don't defrost frozen fresh pasta. Simply take the pasta out of the freezer and dump it into a pot of boiling water. The cooking time is a minute or two longer than for fresh pasta.

In addition to pasta machines that you crank by hand, you can find several electric extruders on the market. Unfortunately, most electric pasta machines don't work all that well, and we don't think that they're worth the $200 or so that most companies charge. For that money, you can buy a food processor (for about $150) and a manual pasta machine (for about $40), and the food processor has hundreds of uses. An electric pasta machine is good for only one thing.

Fresh Egg Pasta (Pasta all'Uovo)

Making your own pasta is surprisingly easy, especially if you use a food processor and manual pasta machine.

Preparation time: *50 minutes*

Cooking time: *None*

Special tools: *Food processor, manual pasta machine*

Yield: *6 servings*

2¼ cups flour plus flour for dusting work surface and pasta

3 eggs

Pinch of salt

½ tablespoon olive oil

Book II

Italian Cooking

1 Place the flour in the bowl of a food processor. With the motor running, add the eggs 1 at a time and then add the salt and olive oil. Process for 10 more seconds.

2 Transfer the dough to a flat, flour-dusted surface. Knead it until it forms a smooth, firm ball, about 5 minutes. Place it in a bowl, cover it with a kitchen towel, and set aside for about 30 minutes.

3 Divide the dough into 5 balls. With the palm of your hand, flatten each ball. Set the wheel for the rollers of the pasta machine on the widest setting. Turning the handle, roll the dough through. Lightly dust the pasta with flour and fold it into thirds. Roll it through the machine again. Repeat this 3 more times, folding the dough each time.

4 Continue rolling the pasta through the machine, dusting it with flour, but no longer folding it in between rolling. Make the opening smaller each time, until you have a long sheet of pasta that is about ¹⁄₁₆-inch thick. You can now cut it into different shapes with the pasta machine.

Cooking and saucing fresh noodles

Cooking fresh pasta takes less time than you may think. After the water returns to a boil (it takes a minute or two, depending on how much pasta you've added to the pot and how high the heat is), the pasta may be almost done. Start tasting, and just before you think that the pasta is done (it should be cooked through and tender but still have some chew and elasticity), drain it quickly and get it sauced.

Even more so than dried pasta, fresh pasta goes from perfectly cooked to soggy and overcooked very quickly. After the pasta goes into the pot, stay close (no phone calls, please) and taste the pasta often to make sure that you catch it at just the right moment.

Because fresh pasta cooks so quickly, you must finish the sauce before the pasta goes into the pot.

Making Your Own Pizza Dough

Pizza originated in Naples, but it's now a staple throughout Italy. Students and others on the go may grab a piece of pizza for lunch. Pizza is also popular at night, especially as a light dinner after a traditional multicourse lunch.

Italians generally eat less pizza per sitting than Americans. The pizzas themselves are lighter, without so much cheese and other toppings. Italians recognize that pizza is still a bread dish and that the crust must be good and crisp.

Good crust begins with the right dough. Pizza dough is basically regular bread dough with oil added for suppleness. Keep these points in mind, and we guarantee success:

- ✔ **Yeast likes warm water, but hot water kills the yeast.** Use water that feels a bit warmer than your body temperature; better still, pull out an instant-read thermometer and make sure that the water temperature is between 105 and 115 degrees.

- ✔ **Yeast likes a little sugar.** You can leave this ingredient out, but the yeast takes longer to work its magic — and who wants to wait any longer than is necessary to eat pizza?

- ✔ **You can make pizza dough to work around your schedule.** Cool temperatures slow down the rising process. For example, you can put the dough right into the refrigerator after making it in the morning, let it rise all day in the refrigerator, and then let the dough rise a bit longer on the counter after you get home from work. You can even freeze pizza dough in an airtight container. Just let it rise fully, freeze for up to one month, and then let the dough come to room temperature before stretching.

- ✔ **Mixing dough in a bowl with a wooden spoon is just fine for pizza dough.** If you own a food processor or standing mixer (a handheld mixer is too wimpy to handle bread dough), use it to save time.

- ✔ **To speed rising, tightly cover the bowl containing the dough with plastic wrap and place the bowl in a warm area, away from open windows and other drafts.**

- ✔ **Let the dough rest a bit before stretching it.** Resting allows the gluten in the dough to relax and makes rolling much easier.

Basic Pizza Dough
(Pasta per la Pizza)

You can make pizza dough by hand or with the help of a large food processor or standing mixer. To use a food processor, combine the yeast, water, and oil until smooth; add the flour and salt; and process until the dough comes together in a ball. In a standing mixer, the process is the same as we outline in this recipe, except that the paddle attachment does the mixing and the dough hook does the kneading.

Preparation time: *10 minutes (plus rising time of 1 hour, 15 minutes)*

Cooking time: *None*

Yield: *Two 12-inch pizzas or four 8-inch pizzas*

Book II

Italian
Cooking

1 package active dry yeast	1 teaspoon sugar
1½ cups warm water	2 tablespoons olive oil plus olive oil for greasing bowl
3¾ cups flour, divided, plus flour for dusting work surface	2 teaspoons salt

1 In a large mixing bowl, combine the yeast and water. Wait 2 to 3 minutes for the yeast to rise and then add ½ cup flour and sugar. Mix well. Add the olive oil, salt, and remaining 3¼ cups flour. With your hands or a large wooden spoon, work the ingredients together.

2 Transfer the dough to a smooth flour-dusted surface and knead it until the dough is smooth, about 5 minutes. If the dough becomes sticky when kneading, gradually add up to another ¼ cup flour. Place in a large bowl that's been lightly greased with olive oil. Cover tightly with plastic wrap and allow the dough to double in size, about 1 hour.

3 Divide the dough into 2 pieces (or 4 pieces if making individual pizzas) and roll them into balls. Rest the dough for 15 minutes before using for pizza or calzone.

You have the dough, so now you can turn it into pizza. The process consists of four steps: rolling the dough, transferring the dough to a pizza pan or baking sheet, topping the dough, and baking the pizza.

1. **Place the ball of dough on a floured counter or work surface and flatten it with your hands.**

   Keep stretching and pressing down on the dough until it reaches the desired size. You can use a rolling pin if you like, but this tool isn't essential.

2. **Slide your hands underneath the dough and lift it onto an oiled pizza pan.**

   For large 12-inch pizzas, we recommend using a perforated pizza pan that allows heat to attack the bottom of the crust, ensuring that it becomes crisp in the oven. Cook individual pizzas (about 8 inches each) on flat baking sheets.

3. **Place your toppings on the dough.**

   Toppings on traditional Italian pies are generally light. Italians are aghast at American pizzas with a pound of meat and cheese.

4. **After the dough has been topped, put it in the oven immediately; bake until the cheese turns golden brown in spots and the edge of the crust looks golden brown.**

   If you have any doubts, carefully lift up the crust with a metal spatula (plastic can melt) to see whether the bottom of the crust is lightly browned. You can put two pizza pans or two baking sheets in the oven at the same time, but you may need to reverse their positions in the oven halfway through the baking time to ensure even cooking.

After the pizza comes out of the oven, wait a minute or two to allow the bubbling cheese to solidify again. Then use a pizza wheel to cut the pie into wedges and serve.

Chapter 4

First Impressions

*J*ust as Rome is the cradle of Western civilization, the antipasto marks the birth of civilized dining. No doubt that cavemen and cavewomen ate dinner as quickly as possible — they had fires to build and mastodons to hunt. Eating was something they did to stay alive.

The role of food in human culture has changed over the millennia. For much of the world, cooking is now a recreational activity, something you do when you have the time. Eating has become something pleasurable and even sensual. A leisurely two-hour dinner may be fun, but it's not terribly efficient.

In this chapter, we cover everything you eat before the main entrée, from antipasto to soup to salad. Why limit your Italian cooking to the main course when you can spread it out across several?

Antipasti

The *antipasto,* which translates in Italian as "before the meal," signals a more leisurely approach to eating dinner. If you usually gobble down takeout in the car, this concept may seem alien. But if you prefer to celebrate the communal aspect of eating, the antipasto is essential.

Nibbling on something light as you have a drink and talk with family and friends is the key to unwinding from the stress of the day. Doing so is also a way to connect with others. In culinary terms, the antipasto stimulates your senses so that you're ready to enjoy the meal that follows.

So what exactly is an antipasto? Does anything served before dinner qualify? Technically, yes. If you open up some longnecks and sit around eating peanuts and talking for ten minutes before dinner, that's an antipasto. (Putting the nuts in a bowl is a true mark of civilized behavior.) Italians may laugh at the notion of beer and nuts, but this duo actually meets many of the criteria for a good antipasto. Just check out the list in the following section.

Rules, especially culinary ones, are meant to be broken. But the following guidelines apply to most antipasti:

- **Keep it light.** Remember that dinner is just minutes away. You don't want to fill up now. A few bites for each person is just fine.

- **Keep it portable.** Serve antipasti away from the table. If you want to relax on the sofa or on the porch with drinks, the antipasti should be something small and relatively easy to handle. You can use a plate if you like, but ideally you have the antipasto in one hand and a glass of good wine (champagne is even better) in the other. Toast covered with cheese, tomatoes, or beans is a perfect example of a portable antipasto.

- **Keep it flavorful.** Something salty, something aromatic, or something a bit spicy can take the edge off hunger pangs. Flavorful foods also stimulate the taste buds, readying them for the feast to follow. Avoid mind-numbingly spicy foods. Three-alarm salsa may sound good, but if the antipasto scorches your palate, you may not enjoy the dinner.

- **Keep it brief.** The antipasto course shouldn't last a long time. Otherwise, you may eat too much and drink too much. If you find it hard to get up off the couch, your antipasto course has gone on long enough. Half an hour to an hour is the usual length of time for the antipasto course.

Restaurants tend to put out dozens of antipasti, with platters of marinated vegetables, salamis, cheeses, and grilled seafood. It looks appetizing but intimidating. Surely someone spent all day just making these delicious morsels.

At home, Italians rarely put out such a spread. (Holidays and parties are an exception.) One antipasto, or maybe two for a really fancy meal, is fine. Dinner is still the priority and should receive the lion's share of your attention.

For this reason, most antipasti are simple to prepare. French chefs are wont to make appetizers with several components — tiny pastry shells, a seafood concoction in a rich sauce, and a garnish of caviar. Italians take a simpler approach, one that even the novice cook, working without a chef, can pull off.

Marinated Zucchini
(Zucchine alla Scapece)

In southern Italy, zucchini, eggplant, and even small fish are fried to seal in flavor and then pickled in a vinegar solution. The result is light and refreshing.

Preparation time: *15 minutes*

Cooking time: *15 to 25 minutes (plus 1 hour marination)*

Yield: *6 servings*

4 cups peanut oil	Salt and pepper to taste
6 small zucchinis, cut into strips roughly ⅛-inch thick and 4 inches long	5 cloves garlic, peeled and thinly sliced
1 cup red wine vinegar	3 sprigs fresh mint

Book II

Italian Cooking

1 Heat the peanut oil in a heavy pot over medium-high heat until the oil is hot (about 350 degrees). Add the zucchini in 5 or 6 batches, cooking until the strips are golden — about 3 to 4 minutes for each batch. Sandwich the zucchini slices between paper towels to drain very well and then transfer to a roasting dish or a serving platter with sides.

2 In a small pan over medium heat, combine the vinegar, salt and pepper, and garlic. Bring nearly to a boil and add the mint. Drizzle the vinegar solution over the zucchini. Marinate for 1 to 2 hours. Serve at room temperature.

Sicilian Eggplant Relish (Caponata)

This recipe is one of Sicily's most famous dishes. You cook eggplant with other vegetables (in this case, onions, celery, and an assortment of peppers) in a sweet-and-sour tomato sauce that's flavored with vinegar and sugar. This version is lighter and easier than the traditional recipe, in which you fry the eggplant separately and then add it to the cooked vegetables. You can also mix this sauce into risotto or serve it with pasta.

You can serve this dish with bread or crackers for dipping, or your guests may eat it with a fork.

Preparation time: *15 minutes*

Cooking time: *1 hour, 5 minutes*

Yield: *6 to 8 servings*

¼ cup olive oil

2 medium red onions, diced

6 celery stalks, diced

1 small red bell pepper, seeded and diced

1 small yellow bell pepper, seeded and diced

1 small green bell pepper, seeded and diced

¼ cup sugar

5 tablespoons red wine vinegar

2 medium eggplants, peeled and cut into ½-inch cubes

2 large tomatoes, diced

1½ cups water

1 cup pitted black olives

2 tablespoons chopped capers, drained

2 tablespoons chopped fresh basil, or 2 teaspoons dried basil

2 tablespoons chopped fresh parsley, or 2 teaspoons dried parsley

Salt and pepper to taste

1 In a large skillet, heat the olive oil over medium heat. Add the onion, celery, and peppers and cook for 10 minutes, stirring frequently.

2 Sprinkle the sugar over the vegetables and stir in the vinegar. Cook for 5 minutes, until the vinegar has been almost completely absorbed.

3 Add the eggplant and cook, covered, for another 15 minutes. Add the tomatoes and water and simmer, uncovered, for another 20 minutes.

4 Stir in the olives and capers. Simmer for 10 minutes and then add the basil and parsley. Cook for 2 to 3 minutes more. Adjust the seasoning with salt and pepper. Serve warm or at room temperature.

Bruschetta with Tomatoes
(Bruschetta al Pomodoro)

This dish is a classic summertime favorite. However, it depends on really ripe tomatoes. Give this recipe a try when it's local tomato season; otherwise, you may want to make something else.

Special tool: *Food processor*

Preparation time: *15 minutes*

Cooking time: *5 minutes*

Yield: *4 servings*

Book II

Italian
Cooking

3 medium tomatoes, chopped	3 tablespoons balsamic vinegar
6 cloves garlic, peeled and crushed	3 tablespoons red wine vinegar
12 whole basil leaves	⅔ cup olive oil
Pinch of hot red pepper flakes	8 slices country white bread (Italian or French bread)
Pinch of black pepper	
Salt to taste	

1 Preheat the oven to 350 degrees.

2 Place the tomatoes, garlic, basil, red pepper flakes, black pepper, salt, balsamic vinegar, and red wine vinegar in a food processor.

3 Run the food processor for a few seconds and then shut it off. Repeat this procedure 2 to 3 times. The resulting mixture should be somewhat chunky rather than a smooth puree.

4 Add the olive oil and pulse a few more times. Season with salt as needed and stir.

5 Arrange the bread slices on a baking sheet and place in the oven. Allow the slices to lightly toast for about 5 to 7 minutes and then remove from the oven.

6 Spoon the tomato mixture on the toasted bread and serve.

Cured meats and cheeses are another important category of antipasti. An Italian deli, called a *salumeria,* carries dozens of salamis and cheeses, as well as prosciutto. Although the home cook can embellish these store-bought ingredients, for the most part, meat and cheese antipasti involve little preparation.

Italy produces literally hundreds of cheeses; most varieties never leave Italy. A small handful — no more than a dozen — are available internationally, and of those, only a few are commonly used as antipasti. Here's a list of our favorite cheeses to serve as antipasti. (For more information on buying cheese, see Chapter 2 of Book II.)

- **Mozzarella:** Use only fresh, creamy, homemade mozzarella. You can marinate tiny mozzarella balls, often called *bocconcini* (or "little mouthfuls") in extra-virgin olive oil that has been spiked with hot red pepper flakes.

- **Parmigiano-Reggiano:** A hunk of Parmigiano-Reggiano is perfect for nibbling on with drinks and olives. Use a short, broad-bladed knife with a pointed end to furrow into the cheese and break off irregular chunks. You should eat only the finest Parmigiano-Reggiano this way. You may enjoy good pecorino in the same fashion.

- **Gorgonzola:** This is Italy's famed blue cheese. You can find numerous styles of Gorgonzola — from the creamy, mild *latte dolce,* or "sweet milk," to crumbly, aged versions that are quite potent and usually very salty. We generally prefer the milder, creamier cheeses when planning an antipasto.

- **Other creamy cheeses:** You can serve other creamy cheeses with bread or crackers. Italian fontina has a mild, buttery, even nutty flavor. Taleggio is a buttery, sometimes runny, cheese with a rind — think of this as brie, but with a funkier aftertaste.

In addition to cheeses, your local gourmet shop or Italian market should carry a selection of cured pork products, including salami and prosciutto. A platter of cured meats is a commonly offered antipasto in northern Italy. You may serve these meats singly or in combination, allotting ½ to 1 ounce per person. Here are several possible choices; note that you can find dozens more.

- **Salami** is dry cured sausage made from minced lean meat and pork fat. The meat is usually all pork, but occasionally some beef is added. The meat and fat may be seasoned with garlic, fennel seeds, chiles, or even white wine. Salamis are cured for several months and sometimes up to a year. You can ask the butcher to slice the salami for you or simply cut it yourself into slices or small cubes.

- **Mortadella** is Italy's answer to bologna. Pork is beaten into a smooth puree that is light and airy. This pink puree is seasoned, often with warm spices like cinnamon and nutmeg. Mortadella looks like oversized bologna studded with cracked peppercorns and large cubes of creamy white fat. Mortadella originally hails from the city of Bologna. Although bland bologna takes it name from this city as well, mortadella is much more complex. Never spicy like salami, it nonetheless is richly seasoned and delicious.

- **Coppa** is cured pork shoulder sold in thick, short logs. The meat should be rosy-colored and well marbled with fat. The meat is seasoned with salt and black pepper, as well as with an aromatic spice like cinnamon or nutmeg.

- **Bresaola** is salted, air-dried, and pressed beef that you slice very thin and serve with a drizzle of olive oil and lemon juice. Originally from Lombardy, this cured beef is popular throughout Italy now.

- **Prosciutto** is salted and air-dried fresh ham. Called *prosciutto crudo* in Italian, this product has been cured but not cooked. (The term *prosciutto cotto* refers to cooked ham, not unlike boiled ham.) Prosciutto crudo isn't smoked. The flavor is simply the ham plus the seasonings, usually salt and black pepper. The butcher must slice the prosciutto paper-thin so that pieces melt in your mouth. Italian prosciutto from the Parma region is now available around the globe. It may cost a few dollars more per pound than domestic products, but it's money well spent. You may eat prosciutto as is or with fruit, especially melon and figs. (You don't need a recipe; just serve thinly sliced prosciutto with halved fresh figs or chunks of peeled cantaloupe or honeydew melon.)

Book II

Italian Cooking

Soups

Few dishes capture the essence of Italian cuisine like a bowl of hot soup. Soup in Italy is a humble dish, with its roots in *la cucina povera,* or the cooking of the poor. In not-too-distant times, soup was considered a meal. Historically, Italian cooks cobbled together nourishing, tasty suppers out of a few vegetables and maybe some beans or stale bread. These soups are generally thick, and never pureed. Rich cream soups are a rarity in Italy, at least in traditional home cooking.

Zuppa (zoop-pa) is the Italian word for soup. If you eat in Italian restaurants, you may recognize the term *zuppa di pesce.* With several kinds of seafood, this soup bespeaks of abundance. However, most Italian soups prepared at home are much simpler and less costly to make.

Second-Day Vegetable Soup with Bread (Ribollita)

The Italian name for this Tuscan soup literally translates as "reboiled" or "recooked." Traditionally, this soup is made from leftover vegetable soup. To stretch the leftovers, bread is added. The result is a thick, stewlike vegetable soup. Tuscans have become so enamored of this soup that they often make it from scratch, as we have.

Until this century, most Italians didn't have an oven at home. If they needed to bake something, they took a pot down to the local bakery and used the ovens after the bread for the day was made. We like the idea of baking soup, but you may simmer it on top of the stove if you prefer.

Preparation time: *20 minutes*

Cooking time: *1 hour, 15 minutes*

Yield: *6 servings*

8 slices pancetta or bacon (about 4 ounces), chopped

1 medium red onion, peeled and chopped

1 leek, white part only, rinsed well and chopped

1 cup chopped carrot

1 cup chopped celery

¼ cup plus 2 tablespoons olive oil, divided

2 cups shredded Savoy cabbage

1 bunch (about 8 ounces) kale, rinsed thoroughly and chopped

1 bunch (about 8 ounces) Swiss chard, rinsed thoroughly and chopped

1 zucchini, sliced into ¼-inch rounds

3 medium tomatoes, peeled, seeded, and diced

2 medium potatoes, peeled and diced

1½ cups dried cannellini beans, soaked and cooked (see Chapter 5 of Book II), or one 16-ounce can cannellini beans, drained and rinsed

2 quarts water or homemade vegetable stock

5 slices Tuscan bread, each slice about 1 inch thick, toasted and brushed with garlic

Salt and pepper to taste

6 scallions, chopped

1 cup white wine

1 Preheat the oven to 350 degrees. In a large, oven-safe soup pot or saucepan, combine the pancetta, onion, leek, carrot, celery, and ¼ cup olive oil. Cook over medium-high heat, stirring occasionally, until the vegetables just begin to brown, about 5 minutes.

2 Add the cabbage, kale, Swiss chard, zucchini, tomatoes, potatoes, and cooked cannellini beans. Cook, stirring often, for 5 minutes, and then add water or vegetable stock and the bread. Season with salt and pepper. Stir well, add the wine, cover, and cook for 5 minutes.

3 Transfer the pot to the oven. Bake for 1 hour, stirring occasionally, until the beans and vegetables are soft. Spoon into hot soup bowls and sprinkle with the remaining 2 tablespoons olive oil and the scallions.

Vegetable Soup, Genovese Style (Minestrone alla Genovese)

Minestra is another Italian word for soup. The word *minestrone* translates as "big soup" and refers to the fact that this soup is packed with vegetables. Each region in Italy has its own version of this classic vegetable soup. This version of minestrone comes from Genoa, where pesto or fresh basil is added to the soup. To make this soup heartier, add a handful or two of pasta about 5 minutes before the peas and pesto go into the pot. Small pasta shapes — such as elbows, ditali, or tiny shells — work best.

Preparation time: *30 minutes (plus overnight soaking time for dried beans)*

Cooking time: *1 hour, 15 minutes*

Yield: *6 servings*

Book II

Italian
Cooking

1 cup dried cannellini beans, or one 16-ounce can cannellini beans	3 cups shredded cabbage
2 tablespoons olive oil	1 cup canned Italian plum tomatoes
4 slices pancetta or bacon (about 2 ounces), diced (optional)	Salt and pepper to taste
1 medium red onion, peeled and chopped	2½ quarts cold water
4 cloves garlic, peeled and minced	12 asparagus spears, cut into 1-inch pieces
3 medium carrots, chopped	2 small zucchinis, diced
5 celery stalks, chopped	½ cup frozen peas
1 small fennel bulb, cored and diced	1 cup diced green beans
Pinch of dried red pepper flakes	¼ cup Pesto (see recipe in Chapter 6), or 1 cup finely chopped fresh basil
1 cup white wine	1 cup grated Parmigiano-Reggiano
3 medium potatoes, peeled and diced	

1 Pick over the dried beans to remove broken beans and pebbles and place the beans in a pot or bowl with 5 cups cold water. Soak them for at least 4 hours, preferably overnight. Drain.

2 In a large soup pot, combine the olive oil, pancetta, onion, garlic, carrots, celery, fennel, and red pepper flakes. Cook over medium heat, stirring often, for about 10 minutes. Add the wine and continue cooking until most of it has evaporated, about 5 minutes.

3 Add the potatoes, cabbage, tomatoes, and cannellini beans, stirring to combine. Season with salt and pepper. Add 2½ quarts water. Bring to a boil, reduce the heat, and simmer for 30 minutes. Add the asparagus, zucchinis, and green beans and cook for another 30 to 35 minutes; the cannellini beans should be cooked to the point where they can easily be crushed between two fingers. Add the peas and pesto or basil and cook for 5 more minutes. Adjust the seasoning, if necessary, with salt and pepper. Serve hot or cold sprinkled with Parmigiano-Reggiano cheese.

Pasta and Bean Soup
(Pasta e Fagioli)

If pressed for time, place all the ingredients for the soup in the pot — except the pasta — and simmer until tender. (The beans still should have been soaked overnight.) Cook the pasta in the soup until al dente and serve. Whether making the quick or regular version of this recipe, you can sprinkle each serving of the soup with 1 tablespoon grated Parmigiano-Reggiano cheese.

Special tool: *Food processor*

Preparation time: *20 minutes (plus overnight soaking for dried beans)*

Cooking time: *2 hours*

Yield: *6 to 8 servings*

½ cup dried cranberry beans

½ cup dried kidney beans

½ cup dried pinto beans

2 medium potatoes, peeled and diced

5 cloves garlic (3 cloves peeled and crushed; 2 cloves peeled and minced)

1 sprig fresh rosemary plus 1 tablespoon chopped fresh rosemary

1 sprig fresh sage plus 2 teaspoons chopped fresh sage

4 quarts cold water

1 tablespoon salt

½ cup olive oil, divided

4 ounces (about 8 slices) pancetta or bacon

1 small red onion, peeled and chopped

1 leek, white part only, thoroughly rinsed and chopped

1 small celery stalk, chopped

1 medium carrot, chopped

¼ teaspoon hot red pepper flakes

½ cup white wine

6 tablespoons tomato paste

½ pound dry short-cut pasta, such as pennette

Salt and pepper to taste

1 Rinse the beans, picking through them to remove any pebbles. Soak the beans overnight in a medium bowl with 5 cups cold water. Drain.

2 Put the beans in a large soup pot with the potatoes, crushed garlic, rosemary sprig, and sage sprig. Add the water and bring the mixture to a boil. Add the salt and reduce the heat to a low boil. Cook, covered, until the beans are soft enough to crush easily between 2 fingers, about 40 to 45 minutes.

3 Transfer half of the bean mixture to the bowl of a food processor. Puree until smooth. Return the bean puree to the soup pot.

4 Heat ¼ cup olive oil in a medium skillet. Add the pancetta, minced garlic, chopped rosemary, chopped sage, onion, leek, celery, carrot, and red pepper flakes. Cook over medium heat, stirring occasionally, until the onion is soft and the mixture just starts to brown, about 12 to 15 minutes.

5 Add the wine to the vegetables and cook until the liquid is completely absorbed, about 2 to 3 minutes.

6 Transfer the contents of the skillet to the soup pot with the beans. Add the tomato paste. Stir to combine. Bring the soup mixture to a boil and then reduce the heat to maintain a low boil. Cook for 40 minutes, stirring occasionally.

7 Add the pasta to the soup. Cook for another 8 to 12 minutes (depending on the cooking time of the pasta; check package instructions). Adjust the consistency of the soup as desired, adding up to 2 more cups of water. Adjust seasoning with salt and pepper. Serve the soup hot, drizzled with remaining ¼ cup olive oil.

Book II

Italian Cooking

Salads

Making a good salad should be easy, but not mindless. You may think that preparing salad means opening a bag of prewashed lettuce and tossing it in a large bowl with some bottled dressing. You can make salad this way, but will it taste great? Not likely.

Salad gets a bit more respect in Italy. It's still easy to prepare, but the quality of the ingredients is much higher. You won't find packages of "Italian seasonings for dressing" (which taste too much like grass) or bland greens. Salad shouldn't be something you eat to pass the time, waiting for dinner. It should have its own character and be packed with flavor.

A good salad begins with fresh leafy greens or perhaps some cooked potatoes, sliced fennel and oranges, or steamed mussels. The dressing can be as simple as a drizzle of extra-virgin olive oil and some good vinegar. Of course, you can get fancier by adding herbs, garlic, or other seasonings, but at heart, Italian dressings are ridiculously easy.

Tomato and Mozzarella Salad, Capri Style (Insalata Caprese)

This classic Italian salad works well as a light lunch or as an appetizer. This summer dish depends on ripe tomatoes, fresh basil, and good-quality fresh mozzarella cheese. You can add sliced red onions as well.

Preparation time: *10 minutes*

Cooking time: *None*

Yield: *4 servings*

1 tablespoon red wine vinegar

Salt and pepper to taste

2 tablespoons olive oil

2 cups arugula, washed (optional)

2 large ripe tomatoes, cut into ¼-inch-thick slices

¾ pound mozzarella, cut into ¼-inch-thick slices

8 leaves basil, finely sliced, or 2 tablespoons dried oregano

1 Prepare the dressing, whisking together the vinegar and salt and pepper in a small mixing bowl. Slowly whisk in the oil until the dressing is smooth. Set aside.

2 Line 4 plates with the arugula leaves. Arrange alternating slices of tomato and mozzarella over the arugula to form a circle.

3 Sprinkle the salad with basil and drizzle with the prepared dressing. Serve immediately after the salad is dressed.

Fennel and Orange Salad (Insalata di Finocchi e Aranci)

Fennel, a popular vegetable in Italy, is eaten raw in salads or cooked and served as a side dish. Raw fennel is crunchy like celery but has a sweet licorice flavor. This dish is Sicilian in origin and has the exotic, sweet flavors that are typical of the local cooking.

Preparation time: *15 minutes*

Cooking time: *None (1 hour marination)*

Yield: *4 to 6 servings*

Book II

**Italian
Cooking**

2 small fennel bulbs, stems discarded; bulbs halved, cored, and thinly sliced

3 oranges, peeled and sectioned

2 tablespoons olive oil

2 teaspoons vinegar

1 tablespoon chopped parsley

Salt and pepper to taste

8 or 12 leaves of a colorful lettuce, such as red leaf

1 In a bowl, combine all the ingredients (except the lettuce) and let the mixture marinate for 1 hour.

2 Place 2 lettuce leaves on each salad plate and divide the salad over the top.

Tuscan Bread Salad (Panzanella)

Italian cooks are thrifty by nature. They find uses for everything, including stale bread, which gets used in delicious summer salads. Bread that is too fresh makes the salad soggy, and bread that is too hard doesn't soften up enough. To take the guesswork out of this dish, we suggest toasting slices of fresh Italian bread in a 300-degree oven until dry but not brown, about 5 to 7 minutes. If you have some stale bread on hand, you can use it instead, but be prepared to adjust the marinating time to achieve the right texture. You can add canned tuna and/or anchovies to make this salad more substantial.

Preparation time: *20 minutes*

Marinating time: *1 hour*

Yield: *4 to 6 servings*

6 slices Italian bread, toasted and cut into ½-inch cubes

4 ripe tomatoes, cut into 1-inch cubes

2 stalks celery, cut crosswise into ½-inch pieces

1 medium red onion, peeled and thinly sliced

1 small cucumber, skinned, seeded, halved lengthwise, and cut into ⅛-inch crescents

¾ cup olive oil

½ cup red wine vinegar

1 cup fresh basil, sliced into long ribbons

Salt and pepper to taste

1 Combine all ingredients in a large bowl, toss, and let sit for 1 hour.

2 Serve at room temperature.

Chapter 5

The Main Event

Carbohydrate dishes are what have made Italian cooking so famous, and in this chapter we give them their due. We discuss dried and fresh pasta, along with risotto, *polenta* (a cornmeal-based dish), and dumplings called *gnocchi*. Breads also play an important role in Italian cooking, so we also include recipes for pizza, calzone, and focaccia.

Pasta and pizza are great, but meat still matters. Italians know how to cook meat as well as poultry and seafood. Whether it's chicken cutlets flavored with lemon and white wine or grilled beef with rosemary and garlic, most Italian main courses are simple and delicious. In this chapter, we fill you in on the secrets of cooking chicken, turkey, beef, veal, pork, and seafood, Italian style. So whether you're looking to load up on carbs or you're a protein packer, you can find what you're after in this chapter.

Pizza, Pasta, and Beyond

The recipes in this section cover the staples of Italian cuisine that you've come to know and love. From simple pasta with tomato sauce to ravioli that's to die for, from pizza to calzone, we've got you covered.

Dried pasta

Day in and day out, the average Italian cook uses dried pasta. It's the first choice in Italian homes. And we can find plenty of reasons why dried pasta should be the first choice in yours as well:

- **It's cheap.** A pound of dried pasta feeds four as a main course or eight as an appetizer and costs less than a dollar. Sauces add to the cost, but as long as you avoid pricey ingredients like shellfish, the total cost of a pasta dinner is usually under $5.

- **It's versatile.** Many Italians eat pasta every day and claim to never tire of it. The variety of shapes — you can find literally hundreds — and sauces keep pasta from becoming boring. Because it's relatively bland, pasta takes on many guises — herbaceous and garlicky when served with pesto sauce; spicy and salty when sauced with tomato, anchovies, and capers; and light and fresh when sauced with grilled vegetables and olive oil.

- **It's always available.** Even when the cupboard is quite bare, most cooks are likely to have the ingredients for a pasta dinner on hand. Take some spaghetti, add a little oil and garlic, and you have the makings of a classic Italian dish. For cooks who hate to shop, pasta is a valued ally. It stays "fresh" for years, if stored in its box in a cool, dry pantry. Did you ever throw out spaghetti because it was past its prime? We didn't think so.

- **It's quick.** Depending on the size and shape, dried pasta cooks up in as little as 5 minutes. Even the thickest shapes are done in 12 minutes. Many sauces can be prepared in the time it takes to bring the water to a boil and cook the pasta. Pasta makes the 20-minute meal a reality.

Don't think of dried pasta as something you cook when you don't have the time to make it fresh. Dried and fresh pasta are really two separate animals, each with its own uses. For the vast majority of recipes, dried pasta is actually preferable. Its springy texture is a better foil for all but the most delicate, creamy sauces.

Pasta with Eggs and Bacon (Penne alla Carbonara)

The origins of this very popular pasta dish aren't clear. Some sources indicate that _carbonara_ originated right after World War II, when the egg and bacon rations of American GIs were turned into a pasta sauce. Other sources say that coal miners _(carbonari)_ made this dish. Either way, this dish has become extremely popular throughout Italy. Onions are a delicious addition to the sauce, but they're optional in this recipe.

Preparation time: _15 minutes_

Cooking time: _15 minutes_

Yield: _4 servings_

Book II

Italian
Cooking

¼ cup olive oil	1½ tablespoons kosher salt
1 medium red onion, diced (optional)	½ pound penne
4 slices pancetta or bacon (about 6 ounces), diced	2 eggs
	3 tablespoons heavy cream (optional)
Pinch of hot red pepper flakes	¼ cup plus 2 tablespoons grated Parmigiano-Reggiano, divided
1 cup white wine	
Salt and pepper to taste	2 tablespoons chopped fresh parsley

_1_ Place the olive oil, onion (if using), pancetta, and red pepper flakes in a large skillet and cook over medium heat, stirring occasionally, until the onion is soft — about 10 minutes. Pour the wine into the pan and let it reduce for 3 minutes. Season with salt and pepper. Remove from heat.

_2_ In a large pot, bring 4 quarts water to a boil. Add the kosher salt and the penne, mix well, and cook until the pasta is al dente.

_3_ Drain the pasta and add it to the skillet.

_4_ In a large bowl, mix together the eggs, cream (if using), ¼ cup Parmigiano-Reggiano cheese, and parsley. Slowly add this mixture to the skillet with the onion and pasta. Mix well. Cook over low heat, stirring constantly, for 2 to 3 minutes to heat the eggs through. Don't boil. Sprinkle with the remaining 2 tablespoons Parmigiano-Reggiano cheese and serve immediately.

Spaghetti with Clams
(Spaghetti con Vongole)

Authentic Spaghetti with Clams is made with fresh clams that are served in the shell
with the pasta. Therefore, you need to use the smallest clams possible. In Italy, they
often use clams the size of an adult fingernail. Manila or New Zealand clams are best.
In a pinch, you can use small littlenecks.

Preparation time: *10 minutes*

Cooking time: *15 minutes*

Yield: *4 servings*

¼ cup plus 1 tablespoon olive oil

4 cloves garlic, peeled and chopped

3 tablespoons chopped fresh parsley, divided

Pinch of hot red pepper flakes

¼ cup plus 2 tablespoons white wine

60 Manila or New Zealand small clams, rinsed

Salt to taste

1½ tablespoons kosher salt

½ pound spaghetti

1 Place the olive oil, garlic, 1½ tablespoons parsley, and red pepper flakes in a large skillet. Cook over medium heat, stirring occasionally, until the garlic turns golden, about
3 minutes.

2 Add the wine and clams to the skillet and season with salt. Cook, covered, until the
clams open, about 5 minutes. Discard any clams that haven't opened.

3 In a large pot, bring 4 quarts water to a boil. Add the kosher salt and the spaghetti, mix
well, and cook until al dente.

4 Drain the pasta and add it and the remaining 1½ tablespoons parsley to the saucepan
with the clams. Mix. Serve immediately.

Pasta with Tomato and Basil Sauce (Pasta Pomodoro e Basilico)

With garlic, basil, and canned tomatoes, this slow-simmered sauce is a classic. If you have ripe, fresh tomatoes, this recipe is even better.

Preparation time: *10 minutes*

Cooking time: *1 hour, 5 minutes*

Yield: *8 servings*

⅓ cup plus 2 tablespoons olive oil, divided

4 cloves garlic, peeled and chopped

1 medium red onion, chopped

Pinch of hot red pepper flakes

16 fresh basil leaves, chopped, plus 16 whole leaves, or 1 tablespoon dried basil plus 2 teaspoons dried oregano, divided

⅓ cup white wine

28-ounce can plum tomatoes, not drained

½ cup water

Salt and pepper to taste

1½ tablespoons kosher salt

1 pound pasta, such as spaghetti, fettuccine, or linguine

½ cup grated Parmigiano-Reggiano

1 In a large saucepan, place ⅓ cup olive oil, garlic, onion, red pepper flakes, and half the chopped basil and cook over medium heat for 5 minutes. Add the wine and cook for 2 to 3 minutes, reducing it by half. Add the tomatoes and water, stir, and then simmer for 40 to 45 minutes, stirring occasionally.

2 Season the tomato sauce with salt and pepper and add the remaining chopped basil. Simmer for 10 minutes.

3 In a large pot, bring 4 quarts water to a boil. Add the kosher salt and pasta, mix well, and cook until al dente.

4 Drain the pasta. Add the pasta, 2 tablespoons olive oil, whole basil leaves, and the Parmigiano-Reggiano cheese to the pan with the sauce. Mix well. Cook for 1 minute. Serve immediately.

Penne with Tomatoes, Capers, Anchovies, and Olives (Pasta alla Puttanesca)

This dish comes from Rome, and the name comes from the Italian word *puttana,* or prostitute. Some sources believe that the name refers to the fact that the dish can be thrown together with pantry staples. Other sources mention the strong, salty flavor. In any case, this dish is extremely popular in Italy, especially as a late-night snack.

Preparation time: *15 minutes*

Cooking time: *35 to 40 minutes*

Yield: *4 servings*

¼ cup olive oil

4 cloves garlic, peeled and chopped

1 teaspoon hot red pepper flakes

5 anchovy fillets, chopped

½ cup white wine

16 black olives, pitted

2 tablespoons capers, drained and chopped

2 cups plum tomatoes, fresh or canned, peeled and chopped

½ cup water

½ cup chopped fresh parsley, or 1 tablespoon dried parsley

1½ tablespoons kosher salt

½ pound penne

Salt to taste

1 In a large saucepan, heat the olive oil. Add the garlic and cook over medium heat until golden, about 1 minute. Add the red pepper flakes and anchovies, stir, and cook for another 2 minutes. Pour in the wine. Let it reduce slightly and then add the olives, capers, tomatoes, and water. Cook at a low boil for 25 to 30 minutes, stirring occasionally. During the last 2 minutes of cooking, add the parsley to the sauce.

2 While the sauce cooks, bring 4 quarts water to a boil in a large pot. Add the kosher salt and penne, mix well, and cook until al dente.

3 Drain the pasta and add it to the pan with the sauce. Season with salt and stir. Serve immediately.

Bucatini with Tomatoes, Onions, and Pancetta (Bucatini all'Amatriciana)

This recipe is one of the most popular pasta dishes in Italy. Originally, the dish called for pig's cheek. Because this cut is so fatty, no olive oil was used. Leaner pancetta (or American-style bacon) is now the standard ingredient in this recipe, along with some olive oil to crisp the bacon.

Preparation time: *15 minutes*

Cooking time: *45 minutes*

Yield: *4 servings*

2 tablespoons olive oil

4 cloves garlic, peeled and chopped

1 medium red onion, sliced

Pinch of hot red pepper flakes

1 teaspoon chopped fresh rosemary, or ¼ teaspoon dried rosemary

8 slices pancetta or bacon (about 4 ounces)

1 cup white wine

1½ cups (14-ounce can) plum tomatoes

Salt to taste

1½ tablespoons kosher salt

½ pound bucatini pasta

¼ cup grated pecorino cheese

Book II

Italian Cooking

1 Heat the olive oil in a large skillet or medium saucepan. Add the garlic, onion, red pepper flakes, rosemary, and pancetta and cook over medium heat until the onion is soft, about 10 minutes. Pour the wine into the pan and continue cooking until it has almost completely evaporated. Add the tomatoes, lightly crushing them with a wooden spoon. Season with salt. Simmer for 30 minutes, until the sauce thickens slightly.

2 In a large pot, bring 4 quarts water to a boil. Add the kosher salt and pasta, mix well, and cook until al dente.

3 Drain the pasta and add it to the pan with the sauce. Sprinkle with the pecorino cheese. Stir to coat the pasta evenly with the sauce. Serve immediately.

Fresh pasta

Fresh pasta is a project, but, oh, what fun. If you liked working with Play-Doh as a kid, you'll enjoy turning flour and eggs into thin ribbons of dough for fettuccine or see-through sheets for lasagna. But be warned: Don't plan on serving fresh pasta on a weeknight after a long day at work or taking care of your kids — at least, not if you want to make the pasta yourself.

Most Italian towns, no matter how small, have a shop called a *pastificio* that makes fresh fettuccine, tagliorini, ravioli, and agnolotti. The shops prepare these pastas every day and sell them fresh. If you want to make the recipes in this section but don't have the time to make your own fresh pasta, go to a gourmet store or pasta shop that makes its own pasta every day.

Whatever you do, please, don't buy the so-called "fresh" pasta sold in the refrigerated case at the supermarket. This pasta is expensive and cooks up mushy and tasteless. Fresh pasta was never meant to sit for weeks in the supermarket. It may be edible for weeks or months (at least according to the sell-by dates stamped on most packages), but it's not fresh in the truest sense of the word. Fresh pasta loses its flavor and delicate texture very quickly, so either make it yourself or buy it from someone who makes it fresh every day, like people do in Italy.

If you want to start with something basic, add the following recipe for Meat Sauce to Fresh Egg Pasta (see Chapter 3 of Book II), and you have a fabulous Italian entrée.

Meat Sauce (Ragù di Carne)

This sauce requires very gentle simmering to produce a finely textured, sweet meat sauce that's rich and delicious. You can use the sauce in baked pasta dishes, such as lasagna, or tossed with fresh fettuccine. This sauce stores well, frozen in small containers, for up to 3 weeks.

Preparation time: *25 minutes*

Cooking time: *3 hours*

Yield: *8 servings*

Book II

Italian Cooking

¼ cup olive oil

1 large red onion, peeled and chopped

3 celery stalks, chopped

1 medium carrot, chopped

5 cloves garlic, peeled and minced

¾ pound ground pork

¾ pound ground beef

4 thin slices of pancetta or bacon, minced

4 thin slices of prosciutto, minced

2 cups dry red wine

28-ounce can whole Italian tomatoes, undrained

2 cups water

Salt to taste

½ teaspoon hot red pepper flakes

¼ teaspoon black pepper

Pinch of allspice

Pinch of nutmeg

Pinch of cloves

Pinch of cinnamon

1 In a large pot, heat the olive oil over medium heat. Add the onion, celery, carrot, and garlic and cook, stirring often, until kthe vegetables are tender, about 15 minutes.

2 Add the pork, beef, pancetta or bacon, and prosciutto and cook, stirring frequently, for another 10 minutes.

3 Add the wine and cook for about 5 minutes. Add the tomatoes and water and simmer, covered, for 50 minutes.

4 Season with the salt, red pepper flakes, black pepper, and spices and then stir. Simmer, stirring occasionally, for 90 more minutes, until the sauce is thick and flavorful. Check the sauce during cooking. If it thickens too quickly, add a little bit of water (about ½ cup at a time) and continue cooking. Adjust seasoning with salt, if necessary.

Béchamel Sauce (Bechamela)

You can use this creamy white sauce as a binder in many baked pasta dishes. When making this sauce, you must whisk constantly to prevent the formation of lumps.

Preparation time: *5 minutes*

Cooking time: *9 minutes*

Yield: *1 quart*

8 tablespoons butter

½ cup flour

1 quart warm milk

Pinch of ground nutmeg

Salt and white pepper to taste

1 In a heavy saucepan, melt the butter. Add the flour and cook, stirring, over low heat for 4 minutes. Increase the heat to medium and gradually add the milk, stirring constantly with a whisk.

2 Continue whisking the sauce as it gently boils, about 5 minutes. Add the nutmeg and salt and pepper. Stir well and remove from heat. Use immediately or store in a bowl with plastic wrap touching the surface of the béchamel so that a skin doesn't form on top. Store, refrigerated, for up to 2 days.

Lasagna (Lasagne)

Lasagna is a lot of work, but you can make the Meat Sauce and Béchamel Sauce in advance. You can assemble the entire lasagna, wrap it tightly in foil, and then refrigerate it for up to 1 day before baking.

Preparation time: *25 to 30 minutes (excludes time for preparation of Meat Sauce, Bechamel Sauce, and pasta)*

Cooking time: *35 minutes*

Yield: *12 servings*

2 recipes Fresh Egg Pasta (see the recipe in Chapter 3 of Book II)

2 tablespoons butter, for greasing the baking dish

1½ recipes Meat Sauce (see the recipe earlier in this section)

1 recipe Béchamel Sauce (see the recipe earlier in this section)

1 cup grated Parmigiano-Reggiano

Book II

Italian
Cooking

1 Preheat the oven to 375 degrees.

2 Prepare the pasta. Cut the rolled pasta dough into 8-x-6-inch sheets. Precook the pasta sheets in salted boiling water for 1 minute and then transfer to a large bowl of cold water. After the pasta has cooled, remove the squares and place them on a large platter. Set aside.

3 Butter the bottom and sides of a 9-x-13-inch baking dish. Spread a layer of the meat sauce, about ½ cup, on the bottom of the dish.

4 Line the baking dish with a layer of pasta. Evenly spread a layer of béchamel over the pasta, followed by meat sauce, and then sprinkle with about ¼ cup cheese. Cover with a layer of pasta, béchamel, meat sauce, and cheese. Repeat this process 3 more times. The top layer should have béchamel, meat sauce, and cheese.

5 Bake for 30 to 35 minutes until bubbly and slightly browned on top. Remove from oven, let cool for 10 minutes, and serve.

Spinach Ravioli (Ravioli di Spinaci)

You must squeeze all the moisture out of the cooked spinach or the filling becomes watery. Serve these ravioli with the Meat Sauce or the Tomato and Basil Sauce from earlier in this chapter. Or simply serve the ravioli with some melted butter and grated Parmigiano-Reggiano cheese. If you like, warm several minced sage leaves in the melted butter.

Special tools: *Ravioli cutter, strainer-skimmer*

Preparation time: *45 minutes*

Cooking time: *8 minutes*

Yield: *4 servings*

1 recipe Fresh Egg Pasta (see the recipe in Chapter 3 of Book II)	1 tablespoon chopped fresh parsley, or 1 teaspoon dried parsley
1 cup ricotta	1 tablespoon chopped fresh thyme
½ cup grated Parmigiano-Reggiano	Pinch of ground nutmeg
½ cup cooked spinach, fresh or frozen, water thoroughly squeezed out after cooking	Pepper to taste
1 egg	1½ tablespoons salt
	Flour for dusting work surface

1 Prepare the pasta. Let it rest, wrapped and refrigerated, for 30 minutes.

2 To prepare the filling, combine all ingredients (except salt) in a medium bowl. Mix well and set aside.

3 Lay the pasta sheets out on a flat, flour-dusted surface. Place ½ tablespoon dots of the spinach filling, about 3 inches apart, on the bottom layer and fit a second layer of pasta over the first. With your fingers, press down lightly to seal the sheets together and remove any air. Use a scalloped cutter to cut out the ravioli squares.

4 In a large pot, bring 4 quarts water to a boil. Add the salt and half the ravioli. (You should cook the ravioli in 2 batches.) Gently boil for 2 to 4 minutes, until the ravioli rise to the surface. Place the ravioli in a pan, mix with any sauce that you like, and serve.

Risotto, polenta, and gnocchi

Pasta gets all the attention, at least when it comes to Italian cooking and carbohydrates. But rice is an important starch, especially in northern regions of Italy. Most of this rice is turned into a dish called *risotto* (ree-*zaw*-toh).

Most rice dishes around the world are fairly similar. You take the rice, add a set amount of liquid, bring it to a boil, cover, and simmer until the grains have absorbed all the liquid and are tender. This rice is a side dish.

Italians prepare risotto in a different fashion. They sauté the rice in a bit of fat for several minutes and then stir it constantly as they add hot stock in increments — not all at once. The result is a creamy, hearty rice porridge, not unlike rice pudding in consistency. Of course, you don't make risotto with sugar or milk. However, it does get some dairy creaminess from butter and cheese.

Like pasta, Italians serve risotto in small portions as a first course. You can also serve risotto as a light main course. Like pasta, rice is a blank canvas that you can flavor in countless ways. Risotto has a special affinity for vegetables. For vegetarians, risotto offers a good break from a steady pasta diet. But risotto is so delicious that everyone wants to eat it.

Gorgonzola Risotto (Risotto al Gorgonzola)

A mild or sweet Gorgonzola, usually labeled Gorgonzola dolce, is essential in this rich, creamy risotto. An aged, crumbly blue cheese is too pungent and overwhelms the other flavors.

Preparation time: *10 minutes*

Cooking time: *30 minutes*

Yield: *4 servings*

4 tablespoons olive oil, divided

2 cloves garlic, peeled and finely chopped

¾ cup white wine, divided

6 ounces sweet Gorgonzola cheese

4 cups simmering chicken or vegetable stock or water, divided

1 small red onion, chopped

1¼ cups Italian rice (arborio, carnaroli, or vialone nano)

Salt and pepper to taste

2 tablespoons chopped fresh parsley, or 2 teaspoons dried parsley

5 tablespoons grated Parmigiano-Reggiano

1 In a small saucepan with a heavy bottom, heat 2 tablespoons olive oil. Add the garlic and cook over medium heat for 1 to 2 minutes until limp. Reduce the heat to low and add ¼ cup wine. Cook for 3 to 4 minutes. Add the Gorgonzola and 1 cup simmering stock or water. Simmer, stirring, until the mixture is creamy and smooth, about 5 minutes. Keep the Gorgonzola sauce warm.

2 In a medium saucepan with a heavy bottom, heat the remaining 2 tablespoons olive oil. Sauté the onion over medium heat for 2 to 3 minutes until limp.

3 Add the rice and cook for 1 to 2 minutes, stirring constantly, "toasting" the rice.

4 Add the remaining ½ cup wine and reduce the heat to maintain a low boil. Cook for about 3 minutes until the rice has absorbed almost all the wine.

5 Add 1 cup simmering stock or water and cook, stirring, until the rice absorbs the liquid, another 3 to 5 minutes. Add another cup of stock or water and continue stirring. When this liquid is almost absorbed by the rice, stir in half of the Gorgonzola sauce and another ½ cup stock or water. After 5 minutes, add the remaining Gorgonzola sauce. Add stock or water as needed, until the rice is tender but firm; the total cooking time of the rice shouldn't exceed 15 minutes. The rice should have movement but not excess liquid. If the rice requires more cooking, add a touch more liquid and cook for another 1 to 2 minutes.

6 Season with salt and pepper. Remove from heat and stir in the parsley and Parmigiano-Reggiano cheese. Serve immediately.

Vegetable Risotto (Risotto Primavera)

You use nine vegetables in this attractive and satisfying risotto, each adding a different color, texture, and flavor. The various vegetables go into the saucepan at different times to ensure that you cook each one properly.

Preparation time: *10 minutes*

Cooking time: *25 minutes*

Yield: *6 servings*

Book II

Italian
Cooking

½ cup olive oil

1 medium red onion, chopped

1 medium carrot, chopped

2 celery stalks, diced

4 fresh sage leaves, chopped, or 2 teaspoons dried sage

12 asparagus spears, tough ends snapped off and discarded, spears cut into 1-inch pieces, and tips reserved separately

1 yellow or red bell pepper, seeded and diced

1⅔ cups Italian rice (arborio, carnaroli, or vialone nano)

1 cup white wine

7 cups simmering vegetable stock or water, divided

36 green beans (string beans), trimmed and halved crosswise

½ cup fresh or frozen peas

1 medium tomato, diced (seeds removed before dicing)

1 medium zucchini, diced

12 fresh basil leaves, coarsely chopped, or 2 teaspoons dried basil

2 tablespoons chopped fresh parsley, or 2 teaspoons dried parsley

⅓ cup grated Parmigiano-Reggiano

Salt and pepper to taste

1 In a medium saucepan with a heavy bottom, heat the olive oil. Add the onion, carrot, celery, and sage and cook over medium heat, stirring often, 2 to 3 minutes. Add the asparagus spears and bell pepper pieces and cook for 1 minute. Add the rice and cook for 1 to 2 minutes, stirring constantly, "toasting" the rice.

2 Add the wine and cook, stirring constantly, for 1 to 2 minutes.

3 Stir in 2 cups simmering stock and the green beans. Reduce the heat so that the rice/vegetable mixture remains at a low boil. Stir often. After 3 minutes, add the peas and the asparagus tips, and 2 more cups of stock. Continue cooking for 10 to 11 minutes, stirring frequently and adding more liquid in ¼ cup batches as necessary. Taste a grain of rice; it should be tender but firm. The mixture should have movement but no excess liquid. If the rice requires more cooking, add a touch more liquid and cook for another 1 to 2 minutes.

4 Remove from heat. Stir in the tomato, zucchini, basil, parsley, and Parmigiano-Reggiano cheese. Adjust the seasoning with salt and pepper, if necessary. Serve immediately.

Pasta and risotto are the most common first courses in Italy. Soup is another popular choice. But two other options — neither of which is well known outside of Italy — are also worth discussing. If you like something simple but a bit unusual, then you need to add polenta and gnocchi to your repertoire.

Polenta is cornmeal cooked into a creamy porridge. Think grits, with an Italian name. Polenta may look like a hot breakfast cereal, but polenta is actually a base for savory sauces. You can spoon almost any stewlike mixture of vegetables or meat over creamy polenta.

Gnocchi (*gnoh*-key) are tender, light dumplings made from potatoes, ricotta cheese, or semolina. Unlike many other dumplings, gnocchi are never heavy or leaden. You cook and serve them like ravioli or filled pasta — boiled just until tender, drained, and then sauced with something fairly simple, such as a good tomato sauce or maybe some butter and cheese.

Basic Polenta (Polenta)

You must keep a close eye on the pot, stirring often with a wooden spoon to prevent the polenta from scorching.

Preparation time: *5 minutes*

Cooking time: *45 to 50 minutes*

Yield: *8 servings*

2 quarts cold water	*1 tablespoon salt*
2 cups coarsely ground cornmeal	*2½ tablespoons olive oil*

Combine the water, cornmeal, salt, and olive oil in a large saucepan. Turn the heat to medium and cook, stirring constantly. When the polenta begins to boil, lower the heat to a simmer and continue cooking, stirring often, for 40 to 45 minutes. It should be the consistency of soft ice cream and pull away from the sides of saucepan. If it's too stiff, add a little hot water.

Polenta with Vegetables
(Polenta con Verdure)

Serve a medley of vegetables over a mound of fluffy polenta to make an excellent first course for a spring meal.

Preparation time: *25 minutes*

Cooking time: *45 to 50 minutes*

Yield: *6 to 8 servings*

Book II

Italian
Cooking

1 recipe Basic Polenta (see the recipe earlier in this section)

¼ cup olive oil

2 cloves garlic, peeled and chopped

1 medium red onion, peeled and diced

1 carrot, peeled and diced

2 celery stalks, diced

1 yellow bell pepper, cut into long thin strips

1 teaspoon chopped fresh sage, or 1 teaspoon dried sage

1 teaspoon chopped fresh thyme, or ½ teaspoon dried thyme

Salt and pepper to taste

½ cup white wine

8 asparagus spears, stems cut into 1-inch pieces, tips reserved separately

24 green beans, cut into 1-inch pieces

1 zucchini, diced

2 medium tomatoes, diced

½ cup chopped fresh basil, or 1 tablespoon dried basil

½ cup water

1 Prepare the vegetable sauce before or during the preparation of the polenta: In a medium-sized pan, heat the olive oil over medium heat. Add the garlic, onion, carrot, celery, yellow pepper, sage, and thyme and cook, stirring often, until the vegetables soften, 8 to 10 minutes.

2 Season with salt and pepper and add the wine. Simmer until the wine is reduced by half, about 3 minutes, and then add the asparagus spears and beans. Cook, stirring frequently, for 10 minutes.

3 Add the zucchini, tomatoes, asparagus tips, basil, and water and continue cooking for another 10 minutes. Adjust the seasoning with salt and pepper.

4 Serve the vegetable mixture over a generous mound of polenta.

Potato Gnocchi
(Gnocchi di Patate)

This dish is the most popular type of gnocchi. You can serve potato gnocchi with many of the same sauces you use on pasta, including Tomato and Basil Sauce and Meat Sauce (both earlier in this chapter), as well as Pesto Sauce. Use about ¼ cup sauce per serving of gnocchi. In some regions of Italy, ricotta cheese replaces part or all of the potatoes in this recipe.

Special tool: *Ricer*

Preparation time: *40 minutes*

Cooking time: *25 to 30 minutes*

Yield: *8 servings*

4 medium russet potatoes, unpeeled (2 pounds)

3 eggs, lightly beaten

Salt and pepper to taste

1¾ cups flour plus flour for dusting work surface (you may not need all of it)

11½ tablespoons kosher salt

1 Place the potatoes in a medium pot and cover them with cold water. Add a touch of salt to the water and bring it to a boil. Reduce the heat to a simmer and cook until the potatoes are tender when pierced, but are still firm. Drain.

2 When the potatoes are cool enough to handle, peel them. Using a ricer, squeeze the potato flesh into a mound on a smooth, flat surface. Do this when the potatoes are still hot; otherwise, the gnocchi become gluey when cooked. Allow the riced potatoes to cool.

3 Form a well in the center of the potatoes and add the eggs and salt and pepper. Mix to combine. Sift in 1½ cups flour. Mix until you have a sticky ball. Add more flour if the dough is too wet to knead. Knead the dough until it's smooth and all ingredients are well incorporated. Lightly dust the work surface with flour and then roll out the gnocchi dough so that it forms a 1½-inch-diameter log. Cut into 1-inch pieces. Take each piece and roll it off a fork so that the grid impression remains (see Figure 5-1).

4 In a large pot, bring 4 quarts water to a boil. Add the kosher salt and a fourth of the gnocchi. Using a strainer/skimmer, transfer the gnocchi to a warm plate or serving platter about 1 minute after they float to the surface. Toss with some warmed sauce (see suggestions earlier in this recipe). Repeat 3 times with the remaining gnocchi. Serve immediately.

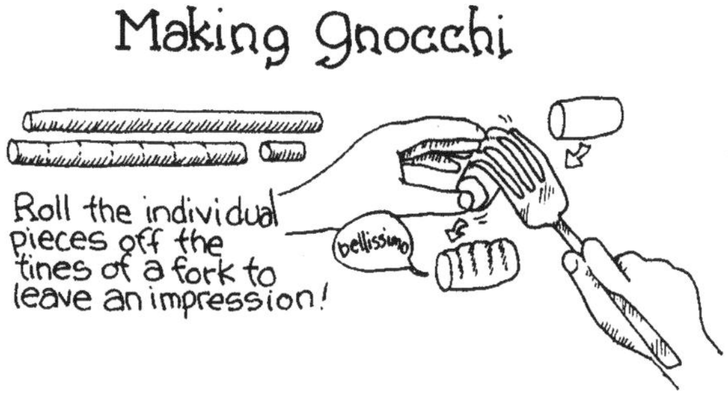

Making Gnocchi

Roll the individual pieces off the tines of a fork to leave an impression!

(bellissimo)

Book II

Italian
Cooking

Figure 5-1: Making gnocchi.

Pizza, calzone, and focaccia: Breads of distinction

Italians love good bread. Even small villages have a bakery that turns out loaves in a variety of shapes, sizes, and flavors. Luckily, the quality of Italian bread has risen dramatically in recent years in the United States. Many artisanal bakers, devoted to small production and high quality, are now working in big cities, as well as in small towns. Buying decent bread is becoming pretty easy. Unless you're a real baking fan, we think it's best to leave bread to the professionals.

Flatbreads, such as pizza and focaccia (foe-*cah*-cha), and their folded and stuffed cousins called calzones, are another matter. You can get pizza almost everywhere by just making a phone call. Calzones are almost as easy to buy, and focaccia is fast becoming a regular item in many markets. However, these breads are rarely made right. At least, they're rarely made as they are in Italy.

Here are some quick definitions to keep in mind.

- **Pizza:** A thin, round disk of dough that's topped fairly generously (often with tomatoes and cheese) and then baked.

- **Calzone:** A thin, round disk of dough that's covered with cheese and other fillings on one half, folded over, sealed tightly, and then baked. The filling is inside the dough, not on top.

- **Focaccia:** A puffier piece of dough (usually rectangular) that's dimpled with fingertips (see Figure 5-2), covered with oil and kosher salt, and then baked. Although pizza and calzone are usually eaten as a meal, focaccia is eaten as a snack. You can top it with vegetables and cheese, and the toppings are usually fairly light. Focaccia bakes up chewier and higher, and you can split the pieces in horizontal halves to make sandwiches.

Figure 5-2:
Dimples, or deep indentations, distinguish focaccia dough from pizza dough.

Use your fingertips to make the dimples, or deep indentations, in the top of the focaccia dough.

Pizza with Tomato and Mozzarella (Pizza Margherita)

This basic recipe is open to countless variations. Feel free to create your own variations. You need 1 prepared recipe of Basic Pizza Dough (see Chapter 3 of Book II).

Preparation time: *10 minutes*

Cooking time: *15 minutes*

Yield: *4 servings*

Olive oil for greasing pizza pans

¼ cup flour

1 recipe Basic Pizza Dough

1½ cups Tomato and Basil Sauce (refer to the recipe earlier in this chapter)

2 cups shredded mozzarella cheese

2 teaspoons dried oregano

Salt and pepper to taste

1 Preheat the oven to 450 degrees.

2 Lightly oil two 12-inch perforated pizza pans or 2 large baking sheets.

3 Spread the flour out on a flat surface. Press each ball of dough out to form a 12-inch circle for 2 large pies or an 8-inch circle for 4 individual pies. Transfer the dough circles to the prepared pans.

4 Evenly spread the sauce over the dough circles. Then top with the mozzarella cheese. Sprinkle the oregano over the top, season with salt and pepper, and place the pans in the oven.

5 Bake for 12 to 15 minutes, turning the pans occasionally, until the cheese is bubbly and the crusts are cooked. Wait 2 to 3 minutes and serve.

Calzone with Prosciutto, Mushrooms, and Mozzarella (Calzone all'Italiana)

This classic calzone has it all — mushrooms, prosciutto, tomatoes, and mozzarella. You need 1 prepared recipe of Basic Pizza Dough. Calzone fillings are open to countless variations.

Preparation time: *15 minutes*

Cooking time: *20 minutes*

Yield: *4 servings*

Book II

Italian Cooking

4 tablespoons olive oil, divided, plus oil for greasing baking sheets	1 recipe Basic Pizza Dough, divided into 4 balls (see the recipe in Chapter 3 of Book II)
3 cups sliced cremini or domestic mushrooms	8 slices prosciutto or ham, julienned
Salt and pepper to taste	½ cup chopped tomatoes or tomato sauce
¼ cup flour (to spread on flat surface)	2 cups shredded mozzarella cheese
	Pinch of dried oregano

1 Preheat the oven to 450 degrees.

2 Lightly oil 2 large baking sheets.

3 Heat 2 tablespoons olive oil in a medium skillet over medium heat. Add the mushrooms and sauté, stirring often, until they've released their liquid and it has evaporated. Season the mushrooms with salt and pepper. Transfer the mushrooms to a medium bowl and let cool.

4 Spread the flour on a flat surface. Press 1 of the balls of dough out to form an 8-inch circle. Transfer the dough to a prepared baking sheet, cover loosely, and set it aside. Repeat with the other 3 pieces of dough.

5 Add the prosciutto, tomatoes, mozzarella cheese, and oregano to the bowl with the mushrooms. Season with salt and pepper and mix well.

6 Spread a fourth of the filling on half of 1 dough circle, keeping it 1½ to 2 inches from the edge. Fold the other side over the filling and pinch the edges together to form a seal. Repeat this procedure with the other 3 calzones.

7 Using a fork, poke a few holes in the top of each calzone. Drizzle with the remaining 2 tablespoons olive oil. Bake until golden brown, 15 to 20 minutes.

Vary It! *Calzone with Eggs and Prosciutto: For the filling, combine 8 quartered hard-boiled eggs, 10 slices of julienned prosciutto or ham, 6 tablespoons grated Parmigiano-Reggiano cheese, and 1 cup shredded mozzarella cheese (optional). Season the mixture with salt and pepper to taste. Serve baked calzones with some of the Tomato and Basil Sauce (see the recipe earlier in this chapter).*

Everyday Focaccia
(Focaccia Tutti I Giorni)

With just olive oil and salt on top, this focaccia is the simplest and most basic. Use it to make sandwiches (just slice squares in half horizontally) or serve it as a snack. It's also great in the breadbasket at a nice meal.

Special tool: *17-×-11-inch jellyroll pan, standing mixer*

Preparation time: *30 minutes (plus rising time of 2¼ to 2¾ hours)*

Cooking time: *30 minutes*

Yield: *8 servings*

1 package dry yeast	3¾ cups flour, divided
1¼ cups warm water	1½ teaspoons table salt
1 teaspoon sugar	Cooking spray
1 cup olive oil, divided	2 teaspoons kosher salt

1 In the mixing bowl of a standing mixer with a dough hook attachment, combine the yeast, water, and sugar. Mix for 3 minutes. Add ½ cup olive oil, 3¼ cups flour, and the table salt. Mix at low speed until it has all come together and is smooth, about 5 minutes. If the dough is very sticky, gradually add up to another ¼ cup flour.

2 Remove the dough and place in a large bowl that's been lightly greased with olive oil. Cover tightly with plastic wrap and allow to double in size, 1½ to 2 hours.

3 Preheat the oven to 425 degrees.

4 Sprinkle the remaining ¼ cup flour over the dough, gently punch it down, and lightly work the added flour into the dough, 1 to 2 minutes. Place the dough in a jellyroll pan that's been sprayed with cooking spray. Roll the dough out evenly, turning the pan as necessary. Cover and allow the dough to rise for 45 minutes.

5 Pour the remaining ½ cup olive oil into a small bowl and dip your fingertips in it. Make fingerprints ¼ inch apart in the focaccia dough. Sprinkle with the kosher salt. Bake for 5 minutes. Then lower the temperature to 375 degrees and bake until golden brown, 25 to 30 minutes.

Vary It! *You can top this basic recipe with fresh herbs, sliced tomatoes, or almost any vegetable. For example, to make Focaccia with Onions, combine 2 thinly sliced medium red onions, 3 tablespoons olive oil, and salt and pepper to taste in a small bowl. After making fingerprints in the dough, sprinkle as directed with kosher salt and then spread the onion mixture evenly over the dough. Bake 25 minutes at 375 degrees.*

Poultry, Meat, and Seafood

Although the first recipes that come to mind when you think of Italian cooking may be pastas and pizzas and other carbohydrate-laden dishes, the Italians definitely recognize the importance of meat and seafood. In the following sections, we prove that point.

Braised Chicken with Tomatoes and Wine (Pollo alla Cacciatora)

The Italian name of this dish, "chicken, hunter's style," refers to the hearty tomato sauce flavored with wine, olives, garlic, rosemary, and hot red pepper flakes. Serve with Basic Polenta (refer to the recipe earlier in this chapter).

Preparation time: *15 minutes*

Cooking time: *1 hour*

Yield: *4 servings*

3- to 4-pound whole chicken, cut into
8 pieces

Salt and pepper to taste

½ cup olive oil

5 cloves garlic, peeled

½ teaspoon hot red pepper flakes

3 sprigs fresh rosemary, or 1 teaspoon
dried rosemary

1 lemon, juiced, with lemon halves reserved
(about 3 tablespoons)

1 cup white wine

3 cups fresh plum tomatoes, peeled and
seeded (or use canned tomatoes)

1 cup black or green olives, pitted

1 Season the chicken with salt and pepper.

2 Heat the olive oil in a large skillet. Add the garlic, red pepper flakes, rosemary, and chicken pieces and cook, turning the pieces occasionally, for 20 minutes.

3 Drain the fat from the skillet and stir in the lemon juice and the wine. Simmer, reducing the liquid by half. Add the lemon halves, tomatoes, and olives and simmer for 30 minutes. If the sauce becomes too dry, add a little chicken stock or water. Adjust the seasoning with salt and pepper and serve.

Chicken Cutlets with Artichokes (Scaloppine di Pollo con Carciofi)

Starting with canned artichokes hearts rather than fresh artichokes saves a tremendous amount of prep time. Serve this dish as is or use the chicken and artichokes as a sandwich filling.

Preparation time: *15 minutes*

Cooking time: *30 minutes*

Yield: *4 servings*

2 cloves garlic, minced, plus 2 cloves garlic, peeled and crushed

2 tablespoons chopped fresh parsley, or 2 teaspoons dried parsley

1 medium tomato, diced

Two 8-ounce cans artichoke hearts, drained

Salt and pepper to taste

¼ cup olive oil

1½ pounds chicken cutlets, pounded (4 cutlets)

¼ cup flour

Juice of 1 lemon (about 3 tablespoons)

1 cup white wine

1 Preheat the oven to 375 degrees.

2 In a medium bowl, combine the minced garlic, parsley, tomato, and artichoke hearts. Season with salt and pepper. Mix. Set aside.

3 In a large oven-safe skillet, heat the olive oil and crushed garlic over medium heat. Cook until the garlic just starts to brown, 2 to 3 minutes. Season the chicken cutlets with salt and pepper and lightly dust them with flour. Place them in the skillet and cook until lightly browned on one side, 2 to 3 minutes. Turn the cutlets over and cook for another 2 minutes. Then drain any fat from the pan. Add the lemon juice and wine and continue cooking until the liquid has reduced by three-fourths, about 5 minutes.

4 Stir in the artichoke mixture and cook for 3 to 4 minutes. Adjust the seasoning with salt and pepper. Cover the skillet and transfer it to the oven. Cook for 10 minutes. Serve the cutlets.

Grilled Steak, Florentine Style (Bistecca alla Fiorentina)

In Tuscany, steaks are generously coated with salt and pepper before grilling. Besides adding flavor, the salt and pepper form a crisp crust that contrasts nicely with the meat's tender interior. T-bone steaks are the most commonly grilled cut in Florence. After the steaks are grilled, the meat is removed from either side of the bone and sliced across the grain into thin pieces. You can serve these steaks this way or choose smaller rib eye or strip steaks and serve 1 to a person.

Preparation time: 5 minutes

Cooking time: 20 minutes

Yield: 4 servings

1 tablespoon salt, divided

Pepper to taste

4 strip or rib eye steaks (about 14 ounces each), or 2 T-bone or porterhouse steaks (about 1½ to 2 pounds each)

1 Preheat the grill to high.

2 When the grill is very hot, generously season the steaks with salt and pepper on 1 side only. Place the seasoned side of the steaks on the grill. Don't move them for 3 minutes; then turn them 90 degrees. When the first side is done, about 8 minutes for medium-rare and 11 minutes for medium (depending on the thickness of the steaks and the heat of the grill), season the top of the steaks and flip them over. Cook the steaks 4 to 6 minutes on the second side to desired doneness. Remove from heat and serve.

Beef Stew (Spezzatino di Manzo)

This recipe demonstrates the Italian cook's ability to turn cheap, tough beef into something delectable. This stew is fairly brothy, so serve it with lots of bread or maybe some mashed potatoes.

Preparation time: *20 minutes*

Cooking time: *4 hours, 10 minutes*

Yield: *6 servings*

½ cup olive oil	2 celery stalks, sliced
3 pounds beef stew meat, trimmed and cut into 2-inch cubes	6 garlic cloves, peeled and roughly chopped
Salt and pepper to taste	2 sprigs fresh rosemary, or 1 teaspoon dried rosemary
2 cups red wine	2 sprigs fresh sage, or 1 teaspoon dried sage
3 medium red onions, sliced	5 cups water or beef stock, divided
3 carrots, sliced	2 cups chopped tomatoes, canned or fresh (optional)

1 Preheat the oven to 350 degrees.

2 In a large ovenproof casserole, heat the olive oil. Season the meat with salt and pepper and then add it to the casserole. Brown over medium heat and then add the wine, stirring to dissolve any bits adhering to the bottom and sides of the pan. Let it reduce for 2 to 3 minutes over high heat.

3 Add the vegetables and herbs, reduce the heat, and simmer, covered, for 10 minutes.

4 Add 2½ cups water or stock, bring it to a simmer, cover, and then place the casserole in the oven. Cook for 1 hour, stirring occasionally. Add 1 cup water and the tomatoes (if using), season with salt and pepper, and cook for another 2 hours. Add the remaining 1½ cups water as necessary to keep the stew moist. The meat is fork tender when done. Adjust the seasoning with salt and pepper, if necessary, and serve.

Braised Veal Shanks (Osso Buco)

This hearty winter dish starts with veal shanks, round pieces of meat about 2 inches thick with a large bone in the center. The shanks are braised for several hours to make them extremely tender. Serve the shanks and their sauce with mashed potatoes or risotto. Many Italians consider the marrow — the gelatinous material inside the bone — to be a delicacy. If you like, give each person a small cocktail fork or demitasse spoon so that they can pull out the cooked marrow when they have eaten all the meat off the bone.

Preparation time: *20 minutes*

Cooking time: *2 hours, 25 minutes*

Yield: *4 servings*

Book II

Italian
Cooking

2 tablespoons chopped fresh rosemary, or 2 teaspoons dried rosemary

2 tablespoons chopped fresh sage, or 2 teaspoons dried sage

4 cloves garlic, peeled and chopped

Salt and pepper to taste

4 meaty veal shanks, each about 2 inches thick

1 cup flour

⅔ cup olive oil

1½ cups white wine, divided

2 medium red onions, chopped

3 medium carrots, cut into 1-inch pieces

3 stalks celery, cut into 1-inch pieces

4 cups water or chicken stock

3 cups canned plum tomatoes, crushed

1 Preheat the oven to 350 degrees.

2 In a medium bowl, mix together the rosemary, sage, garlic, and salt and pepper.

3 Cut 2 to 3 slits in the top of each veal shank and stuff them with the herb/garlic mixture.

4 Season the shanks with salt and pepper and dredge them in flour. Shake off any excess.

5 In a medium, ovenproof saucepan, heat the olive oil over high heat. Add the shanks, browning them well on all sides. Drain and discard any oil remaining in the saucepan. Then add 1 cup wine, stirring to dissolve any bits that have stuck to the bottom of the pan. Add the onions, carrots, and celery. Cover the pan and reduce the heat to medium. Cook, stirring occasionally, for 8 to 10 minutes, and then add the remaining ½ cup wine. Boil the wine for 2 to 3 minutes. Then add the water and tomatoes. Stir well, bring to a simmer, cover, and then transfer to the oven. Cook for 2 hours, stirring occasionally, until the meat is fork tender. Adjust the seasoning with salt and pepper, if necessary, and serve.

Sausage and Beans (Salsiccie e Fagioli)

This recipe is a good example of the Italian cook's ability to stretch a modest amount of meat to feed an entire family. Here, the sausage is cooked with beans and acts more as a flavoring than the focal point of this dish. Serve this stew with good bread to soak up every drop and stretch the meat even further.

Preparation time: *20 minutes*

Cooking time: *35 to 45 minutes*

Yield: *6 servings*

3 tablespoons olive oil

1½ pounds hot Italian sausage, cut into 2-inch pieces

8 cloves garlic, peeled

2 sprigs fresh sage

⅓ cup white wine

1 cup peeled and chopped tomatoes

5 cups cooked cannellini beans (see the sidebar below for the recipe)

Salt and pepper to taste

1 In a large skillet, heat the olive oil over medium-high heat. Add the sausage, garlic, and sage and cook, turning occasionally so that the sausages brown evenly. Lower the heat to medium-low and continue cooking, loosely covered, until the sausages are cooked through, about 10 minutes. Drain and discard the fat from the skillet.

2 Add the wine and let it boil until it completely disappears, about 3 minutes. Add the tomatoes and the beans and season with salt and pepper. Simmer for 10 to 15 minutes, adding a touch of water, if necessary, to keep the mixture moist.

How to cook cannellini beans

Rinse the cannellini beans, removing any stones and shriveled beans. Place the beans in a large bowl and cover with cold water. Soak them for at least four hours (and preferably overnight). Drain the beans and place them in a medium saucepan with a sprig of sage, two celery stalks, and three cloves of crushed garlic. Cover with fresh cold water and bring to a boil. Reduce the heat and simmer until tender, about 1¼ hours. Cool beans and refrigerate them in their cooking liquid until needed, up to four days. Drain the beans and discard the sage, garlic, and celery stalks before using in recipes.

Prepare other dried beans in the same fashion. Cooking times vary depending on the freshness, size, and type of beans. One cup of dried beans yields about 2 cups cooked beans.

Fish with Asparagus
(Pesce con gli Asparagi)

Flouring the fillets helps keep them from falling apart as they cook. The flour also helps to thicken the sauce.

Preparation time: *20 minutes*

Cooking time: *20 to 25 minutes*

Yield: *4 servings*

5 tablespoons white wine vinegar

24 asparagus spears, ends trimmed and discarded

4 fish fillets (such as snapper, Chilean bass, or salmon), 8 ounces each

Salt and pepper to taste

¼ cup flour

¼ cup olive oil

4 cloves garlic, peeled and chopped

2 sprigs fresh thyme, or 1 teaspoon dried thyme

¾ cup white wine

1 cup chopped tomatoes, fresh or canned

2 tablespoons chopped fresh parsley, or 2 teaspoons dried parsley

1 In a medium saucepan, bring 2 quarts salted water to a boil. Add 4 tablespoons vinegar. Cut the tips off the asparagus and slice the spears into ¾-inch pieces. Blanch the asparagus for 3 minutes in the water-vinegar mixture. Drain and set aside.

2 Season the fish with salt and pepper.

3 Spread the flour out on a large plate and coat each fillet with flour, shaking off any excess.

4 Place the olive oil and garlic in a large skillet and cook over medium heat for 2 minutes. Place the fish fillets and thyme in the pan and cook for 3 minutes. Then turn the fish over and cook for another 3 minutes.

5 Pour any excess oil out of the skillet and then add the remaining 1 tablespoon vinegar. Cook for 30 seconds. Add the wine and let it reduce for 2 to 3 minutes. Add the tomatoes and season with salt and pepper. Cook over low-medium heat, partially covered, for 6 to 8 minutes. Add the asparagus and parsley during the last 4 minutes of cooking.

6 Using a spatula, lift the snapper fillets out of the pan and place them on dinner plates. Top each fillet with a large spoonful of the asparagus and tomato sauce.

Salmon with Fresh Tomato Sauce (Salmone con Pomodoro Fresco)

Plum tomatoes are used in this recipe to make a quick pan sauce for seared salmon.

Preparation time: *15 minutes*

Cooking time: *20 minutes*

Yield: *4 servings*

3 tablespoons olive oil	*4 salmon fillets (8 ounces each)*
1 medium red onion, peeled and quartered	*Salt and pepper to taste*
4 cloves garlic, peeled and crushed	*1 cup white wine*
1 sprig fresh thyme, or 1 teaspoon dried thyme	*4 medium tomatoes, cut into 1-inch cubes*
2 sprigs fresh parsley, or 1 teaspoon dried parsley	*8 basil leaves, chopped, or 2 teaspoons dried basil*

1 Heat the olive oil in a large skillet over medium heat. Add the onion, garlic, thyme, and parsley. Sauté for 2 minutes. Drain and discard the oil.

2 Season the salmon with salt and pepper. Add it to the skillet and cook over medium-high heat for 3 to 4 minutes. Then turn the fillets over and cook for 3 minutes.

3 Add the wine, tomatoes, and basil to the skillet and season with salt and pepper. Cook, covered, over low-medium heat for 8 minutes. Serve each salmon fillet topped with a generous spoonful of tomato sauce.

Tuscan Fish Stew (Cacciucco)

Almost every region in Italy makes a hearty fish stew. The version in this recipe comes from Tuscany and contains mussels and clams, as well as shrimp, squid, and fish. Make sure to buy squid that has already been cleaned. Cleaning it yourself is messy and very time-consuming, and cleaned squid is very inexpensive. Fish stock gives this stew an especially rich flavor, but you can use water instead.

Preparation time: *20 minutes*

Cooking time: *50 to 55 minutes*

Yield: *6 servings*

Book II

Italian
Cooking

1 tablespoon chopped fresh rosemary, or 1 teaspoon dried rosemary

1 teaspoon chopped fresh sage, or 1 teaspoon dried sage

1 teaspoon hot red pepper flakes

1 medium red onion, peeled and chopped

8 cloves garlic, peeled and crushed

¼ cup olive oil

½ cup white wine

8 squid, cleaned and cut into 4 pieces each

2 dozen mussels, scrubbed and debearded

2 dozen clams (place in a bowl under cold running water for 5 minutes to remove any sand)

1 pound plum tomatoes (fresh or canned), pureed

3 cups fish stock (see Chapter 3 of Book II) or water

6 large shrimp, peeled and deveined

1 pound boneless fish (any mixture of monkfish, salmon, tuna, grouper, or halibut)

Salt and pepper to taste

4 slices Tuscan or Italian bread, toasted and rubbed with a clove of garlic

1 In a large soup pot, sauté the rosemary, sage, red pepper flakes, onion, and garlic in olive oil over medium heat. When the onion becomes soft, after about 5 minutes, add the wine and cover the pot. Cook until the wine is completely reduced, 5 to 7 minutes.

2 Add the squid and cook, stirring occasionally, for 10 minutes. Add the mussels and clams and cook, stirring occasionally, for 8 minutes. Add the tomatoes and water or fish stock and simmer for 15 minutes, stirring occasionally. Add the shrimp, fish, and salt and pepper to taste and simmer for 8 minutes. Adjust the seasoning with salt and pepper, if necessary. Discard any clams or mussels that don't open. When you're ready to serve, spoon the stew into soup bowls and top with the toasted bread.

Chapter 6

Sweet Endings

*I*talians are rightly famous for their desserts. Some evidence indicates that Italians invented ice cream, or *gelato* as it's called in Italy. Even if ice cream originated elsewhere, the Italians have surely perfected the art and science of making frozen desserts.

There's no doubt that the Italians invented biscotti. These crunchy cookies have become all the rage at coffee bars and restaurants. They're perfect for dipping into a mug of joe, but they also make a great dessert when paired with fruit or ice cream.

Tiramisù, a creamy puddinglike concoction made with ladyfingers and chocolate, was one of the top restaurant desserts of the 1990s. The popularity of tiramisù shows no signs of decreasing. In this section, we show you how to make this dessert at home.

Dessert on a Spoon

A creamy dessert can be so comforting. The texture is smooth and rich, and the flavor of all that cream and eggs is just divine. The following desserts are all meant to be eaten with a spoon.

Tiramisù

This creamy puddinglike concoction starts with ladyfingers (sponge cake) soaked in cold espresso. (Ladyfingers are available in most supermarkets. They're golden brown and shaped like long ovals, or the fingers on a lady's hand.) You layer the soaked cakes in a baking dish and cover them with a mixture of beaten eggs, sugar, and mascarpone cheese. Then, you spoon this mixture over the cakes and dust them with some cocoa powder or grated bittersweet chocolate.

Because you don't cook the eggs in this dish, you may not want to serve this dish to children, the elderly, or people with compromised immune systems.

Special tool: *Stand mixer*

Preparation time: *25 minutes (plus several hours chilling time)*

Cooking time: *None*

Yield: *8 servings*

7 eggs, separated	*¾ cup cold espresso or strong black coffee*
7 tablespoons sugar	*24 ladyfingers*
¼ cup sweet vermouth or liqueur (such as Kahlua)	*3 tablespoons good quality cocoa powder, or 4 ounces bittersweet chocolate, grated*
2½ cups mascarpone cheese	

1 In a large bowl, beat the egg yolks and sugar with a stand mixer until pale and thick, about 5 to 6 minutes. Add the vermouth and mascarpone and beat until the mixture is thick and smooth.

2 Clean the beaters and thoroughly dry them. In another bowl, beat the egg whites until they are stiff and form peaks. Fold the egg whites into the mascarpone mixture.

3 Pour the espresso into a shallow dish. Dip a ladyfinger in, turning it quickly so that it becomes wet but doesn't disintegrate, and place it on the bottom of an 8-×-8-×-2-inch dish. Repeat until the entire bottom of the pan is covered with soaked ladyfingers. Spoon half the mascarpone mixture over the ladyfingers. Repeat with another layer of soaked ladyfingers and cover with the remaining mascarpone mixture. Level the surface with a spatula and then sift the cocoa powder over the top. Cover. Chill for several hours before serving.

Crème Caramel (Crema Caramellata)

For this recipe, you pour rich eggy custard into small ceramic ramekins that have been filled with homemade caramel sauce. The custards are then baked, chilled, and inverted onto individual plates. This dessert is the Italian version of the Spanish dessert called *flan.* (For a flan recipe, see Chapter 6 of Book I.)

You can prepare this recipe fairly quickly, but a number of the steps are tricky. When making the caramel, stay close to the stove. Burning the caramel is easy, and burnt caramel doesn't taste very good. If possible, prepare the caramel in a light-colored pan so that you can easily judge the color of the caramel against a shiny or white background. To keep the custard from curdling in the oven, set the ramekins in a large, deep baking pan, place the pan in the oven, and then add enough hot water to come halfway up the sides of the ramekins. The water moderates the harsh oven heat and keeps the custards from over-cooking. Be careful when adding the water. You don't want to splash any into the ramekins.

Special tools: *Six 4-ounce ramekins or heatproof custard cups, pastry knife or small knife*

Preparation time: *10 minutes*

Cooking time: *40 minutes*

Yield: *6 servings*

Book II

Italian
Cooking

1 teaspoon vegetable oil for greasing the ramekins	*2 cups milk*
1 cup sugar, divided	*¼ vanilla bean, or ¼ teaspoon vanilla extract*
1½ tablespoons water	*3 eggs*
	2 egg yolks

1 Preheat the oven to 350 degrees.

2 Lightly grease the ramekins with the vegetable oil.

3 Prepare the caramel: Combine ½ cup sugar and the water in a small, heavy saucepan and cook over medium heat until the mixture is thick, bubbling, and light brown in color. Don't overcook.

4 Pour the hot caramel into the 6 ramekins. The caramel should be about ⅛-inch deep. Wearing oven mitts, swirl the ramekins to coat the bottom and part of the sides with caramel. Set aside.

5 Prepare the custard: Pour the milk into a small saucepan. Cut the vanilla bean in half lengthwise and scrape the seeds into the pan. Add the bean to the pan. Cook, uncovered, over medium heat, stirring, until mixture is hot. Remove from heat. Whisk the eggs and egg yolks together with the remaining ½ cup sugar just until smooth. While stirring, very gradually pour the hot milk into the egg mixture. Discard the vanilla bean and pass the custard through a fine strainer. Pour the custard into the caramel-coated ramekins.

6 Set the ramekins into a larger baking pan and pour enough hot water into the pan to reach halfway up the sides of the ramekins.

7 Bake for 25 to 30 minutes until the top of the custard is firm to the touch. Let cool at room temperature and then refrigerate for at least 2 hours.

8 To serve, unmold the crème caramel by running a small knife or spatula along the sides of the ramekin to loosen the custard from the sides. Invert each onto a dessert plate.

Chilly Desserts

Frozen desserts have a long history in Italy. Italians love their gelato (gel-*lot*-oh), Italian-style ice cream. Gelato is a lot like American ice cream, with one important difference. Italian gelato is usually much more intensely flavored. Strawberry gelato tastes first and foremost of berries. Many American ice creams are more about the dairy, especially because they contain more heavy cream than gelato. With gelato, the flavor is the thing.

Vanilla Ice Cream (Gelato di Crema)

When making the custard for the ice cream, don't let the mixture come to a boil. To prevent this from happening, cook the custard over medium-low heat and remove from heat as soon as the custard is thick enough to coat the back of a spoon.

Special tool: *Ice-cream machine*

Preparation time: *5 minutes (plus several hours chilling and freezing)*

Cooking time: *10 minutes*

Yield: *6 to 8 servings*

7 egg yolks	*1 cup cream*
⅔ cup sugar	*1 vanilla bean, or 1 teaspoon vanilla extract*
3 tablespoons light corn syrup	*Pinch of salt*
2 cups milk	

1 In a mixing bowl, cream the egg yolks, sugar, and corn syrup together until pale and thick.

2 Combine the milk and cream in a medium saucepan. Cut the vanilla bean in half lengthwise and scrape the seeds into the pan. Add the bean and salt. Cook, uncovered, over medium heat, stirring, until mixture simmers. Remove from heat, discard the vanilla bean, and add about ⅓ cup milk/cream mixture to the mixing bowl. Stir. Slowly add the contents of the mixing bowl to the saucepan, stirring constantly. Place the pan over low-medium heat and cook, whisking, until the custard is thick and coats the back of a spoon, about 3 minutes. Cover the custard directly with plastic wrap (to prevent a skin from forming on the top) and allow it to cool at room temperature. Then refrigerate it, covered, until chilled.

3 Freeze in an ice-cream machine according to manufacturer's directions.

Biscotti

Biscotti (biss-*cot*-tee) translates as "twice-cooked" and refers to the fact that you bake these Italian cookies twice. You usually form the dough into long logs and bake them until firm. You then slice the logs on the diagonal into individual cookies, which are baked again. The finished cookies are dry and hard. You can eat them as is, but they're best when dunked in a mug of coffee or even a glass of milk.

Biscotti make a great afternoon snack. However, you can also serve them as dessert, even at the end of a fairly fancy meal. Biscotti are often served with sweet dessert wine for dunking. (Vin santo is the most common choice, but any good dessert wine is fine.) Biscotti are also a nice way to dress up ice cream or fresh fruit.

Book II

Italian Cooking

Biscotti

This recipe is for the classic almond biscotti that come from Tuscany. Traditionally, a little vin santo is added to the dough. You can use Marsala or white wine if you like.

Special tools: *Parchment paper, serrated knife*

Preparation time: *20 minutes*

Cooking time: *40 to 45 minutes*

Yield: *20 to 28 cookies*

½ cup sweet butter (1 stick)	*½ cup milk*
1 cup sugar	*2 cups flour plus flour for dusting work surface*
2 tablespoons vin santo	*1 teaspoon baking powder*
Grated zest of 1 lemon	*Pinch of salt and pepper*
3 eggs	*2 cups whole almonds, toasted*

1 Preheat the oven to 350 degrees.

2 In a mixer or a large bowl, whip or beat the butter and sugar together until creamy. Add the vin santo and lemon zest and blend well. Add the eggs, 1 at a time, beating with each addition. Mix in the milk. Then slowly work in the flour, baking powder, and salt and pepper. Add the almonds, stirring until they're well dispersed.

3 Divide the dough in half. On a floured surface, shape the dough portions into smooth, baguette-shaped logs (about 3 inches wide). Line a baking pan with parchment paper and then place the dough on top. Bake for 20 to 25 minutes, until light brown, and then remove from the oven and transfer the baked dough to a cutting board. Let cool for 5 minutes.

4 Using a serrated knife, cut slices (cookies) on the bias, about ¾-inch thick. Lower the oven temperature to 300 degrees. Place the cookies back on the lined baking pan in one layer and bake for another 15 to 20 minutes to dry them out slightly. Remove from the oven and cool them on a wire rack.

Book III
French Cooking

In this book . . .

*L*et's face it; French cooking is intimidating. You've seen the fancy cooking shows that showcase this cuisine, and you don't have any intention of spending hours hunting down specialty ingredients, let alone spending even more time cooking up some elaborate concoction your family probably won't even like. Relax. Most people in France don't have time for that either. In this section, I show you some delicious French dishes you can whip up with relative ease. Here you discover simple sauces that will make any meal seem like an elaborate feast. And the French are crazy for eggs — what could be simpler or more elegant than a classic French omelette? Of course, I don't forget what you really turned to this section to find: a variety of delicious French desserts! Bon appétit!

Contents at a glance

Chapter 1

Inside a French Kitchen: Leave Your Fears and Intimidation at the Door

In This Chapter

▶ Defining authentic French cooking

▶ Eating like the French

French cooking is one of the world's most revered, yet feared, cuisines. Because the stereotype of French cooking includes long lists of hard-to-find ingredients and complicated instructions, never has a cuisine been so misunderstood.

The average person in France has a hectic lifestyle and faces the same dilemma that most people do at the end of each day: what to make for dinner. The difference in France is that in general, people don't view food and cooking as necessary evils. People look forward to each meal with great anticipation. They look forward to the daily trip to the greengrocer or bakery and don't dread food shopping the way many people in the United States do, perhaps because their stores aren't so homogenized.

In this chapter, I introduce to you the true cuisine of France and its people. You find out how to think like the French when planning a meal and shopping for the ingredients. I hope that, given this information, you will come to view food as the French do: with joy and respect!

All Cooking Is Local

Classic French cuisine, or *haute cuisine*, is considered to be one of the greatest cuisines in the world. What with pressed duck and succulent *homard à la Pariesiene*, or poached lobsters served in their shells with truffles and artichoke bottoms, this is the food that true gourmands dream of. Consisting of rich and elaborate dishes based on generations of tradition, this type of French cooking, as you can well imagine, is enjoyed by only a small percentage of people and usually in restaurants with star ratings by travel guides. The average person on the street is usually at home enjoying simpler, home-made fare or, as they say in French, *cuisine regionale,* the type of food eaten in a specific region. Both styles of cooking share the French appreciation of quality ingredients, whether it's in a three-star restaurant kitchen or a small galley kitchen in a Parisian apartment.

In order to understand French cooking, you have to know a little something about the history of France. France was originally divided into duchies (small city-states, ruled by minor nobility) and small kingdoms until the 17th century, and each area or region had a distinct language and culture and, in many cases, its own cuisine. Authentic French cooking, therefore, like that of many other countries, is regional fare based on the traditions, geography, and climate of the area. For example, although olive oil is the fat of choice in the Mediterranean region of Provence, the Normandy housewife in northwestern France uses the region's prized butter and cream in her cooking. French cooking can be divided into at least 12 different regions, each with its own distinct personality and traditions.

Over the course of time, especially since the late 1950s and 1960s, culinary boundaries have blurred, with national television and improved and rapid transportation bringing the country closer together for a greater exchange of ideas, lifestyles, and even food. Although maybe France doesn't have what you would call a national cuisine, even the staunchest supporter of traditional, regional cuisine would have to acknowledge some distinct similarities in how people cook today throughout France. For example, people throughout France enjoy crêpes from Brittany and quiche Lorraine from Alsace-Lorraine. Nevertheless, for the most part, the French continue to eat in their small villages, towns, and cities as they have for centuries, entrusting in each new generation of home cooks the culinary traditions of their forefathers.

Considering Important Tenets of French Cooking

To truly understand the intricacies of a cuisine, you have to be willing to learn about the people and culture where it originated. There is always a reason why things are the way they are in the kitchen; if not, Americans would be eating the same food, day in and day out, as our Gallic counterparts. As I have learned, the reasons are quite simple, and I will gladly share with you.

Being spontaneous: The key to good eating

Lately, I find that I need to keep a running list of things to pick up at the supermarket. My list usually includes pantry basics and staples such as milk, butter, sugar, olive oil, pasta, and canned tomatoes. Having lived in Europe for a few years, I've learned to shop elsewhere for perishable things such as produce and meat. I prefer to do as the Europeans do by trying to find a few minutes every day to visit my local vegetable store, butcher, or fish market to see what's available. I base my shopping decisions on what looks best. By going to the same small mom-and-pop stores all the time, I've developed a repertoire with the shop owners. By simply asking, "What's good today?" I know exactly what I should consider cooking that night. Although some people may find this type of shopping time-consuming, I find it a time-saver. Deciding what to cook becomes a collaboration of my preferences and the shopkeepers' recommendations. Cooking also becomes more of an adventure, although you need to be flexible and know how to prepare at least a few simple dishes.

Cooking in season

When you think about it, almost every fresh food has its own season and place in time, as well as in the kitchen. Finger-thin stalks of asparagus, ruby-red strawberries, and tender leaves of baby spinach come to market in the spring. Vine-ripened tomatoes, shiny black eggplants, and bright yellow corn are picked during the hot days of summer. Crisp, sweet, and tart apples and crunchy grapes are harbingers of autumn, while juicy oranges and other citrus fruits signal the arrival of winter. Why is it, then, that so many people insist on eating tasteless peaches in January and mealy apples in April? Granted, new methods of long-term storage and different growing seasons in the Southern Hemisphere mean greater flexibility and availability as to what people can eat year-round, but you often pay a steep price for this. Consider what means more to you: eating whatever you want, whenever you want it, or eating the very best that is available seasonally. I tend to side with the latter. I have to agree with my French counterparts, who welcome the arrival of spring peas at the local market as if they were welcoming an old friend back from a long trip after many months away.

Book III

French Cooking

Getting fresh

Although spontaneity and a focus on seasonal produce and other ingredients are important when grocery shopping, so is the need to use your five senses to make sure that you buy the very best you can find. If your food isn't top quality, what's the sense in buying it in the first place?

The following are some general pointers to getting the very best:

- First and foremost, avoid purchasing any produce or seafood that comes packaged on a plastic tray and wrapped in clear plastic. You can't use any of your senses, except sight, to see whether it's any good.

- Always feel what you're buying. Fruit and vegetables should feel heavy for their size. If not, they're probably dry inside and will be tasteless. In general, avoid very hard or very soft produce, which usually means that it's overripe and perhaps even borderline spoiled.

- See and feel whether fruits and vegetables have any soft spots. They're a sign of bruising or possible spoilage. This also holds true with large things like watermelon.

- Smell it before you buy it. Summer fruits, such as peaches, nectarines, some plums, and melons, should have a pleasant, sweet smell to them. If scentless, they may not be ripe, while a strong smell could mean that they're overripe.

- Seafood should not smell fishy! In fact, if anything, it should have no smell at all.

- Fish should have their heads on them. Their eyes should be clear, bright, and shiny. If you see any mushy spots, put it down and walk away!

- Buy cheese from a reputable store that has a high turnover. Also, never be afraid to ask for a taste. Avoid moldy and smelly cheese unless it's supposed to be that way!

- Loaves of bread such as baguettes and country loaves should have a hard, crisp crust and not be rubbery or soft. Tap on the crust. You should hear a hollow sound; if not, the bread may not be fresh.

Assembling a Menu

In France, as everywhere else in the world, a home cook usually has a collection of tried-and-true recipes that see them through most of the week. Naturally, a special occasion warrants something special, such as a roasted leg of lamb or a chocolate soufflé for dessert. But for the most part, family favorites and treasured recipes make up the bulk of the cooking. The recipes that I have collected and present to you in this book are similar to what a French home cook may have compiled. Balanced and interesting, they represent some of the best of French regional cooking. So that you can better understand how the French actually eat, the following sections describe a typical day of cooking and eating in Anywhere, France.

Breakfast

The French typically aren't big breakfast eaters. A big cup or bowl of sweetened hot milk and strong black coffee usually accompany a length of crusty French bread or a buttery croissant with fruit preserves. This is just enough to hold them over until the early afternoon, when the main meal of the day is traditionally served.

Lunch

Everything used to come to a stop from 1:00 to 2:00 in the afternoon as everyone returned home to sit down and enjoy the main meal of the day. Offices and shopkeepers shut and locked their doors, and children were dismissed from school. But alas, even the French have succumbed to the times, and many workers are unable to follow the old way and must now rely on cafeterias or local mom-and-pop restaurants or bistros. Nevertheless, the American trend of sandwiches or fast food for lunch has been resisted by many. A typical French lunch, depending on the season, might begin with a bowl of soup or some sort of vegetable dish. A meat or fish dish follows, perhaps with a serving of potatoes or some other type of starch. Green salad tossed with vinaigrette follows the main course as a way to help people digest a hearty meal. Fruit is the immediate dessert of choice to accompany lunch or dinner, sometimes with a small selection of cheese, too. Every meal includes bread and usually wine or beer.

Book III

French Cooking

Afternoon coffee or snack

When the mood strikes or on special occasions, the French take time out in the afternoon for a cup of coffee and a piece of cake or pastry, either homemade or from a pastry shop. The favorite snack of schoolchildren continues to be *pain au chocolat,* a piece of crusty bread with a piece of chocolate stuck in the center. Simplicity at its best!

Dinner

The evening meal is usually lighter than the midday one — perhaps some soup or a salad and an egg dish, such as a rolled omelet or a savory tart such as quiche, or *pissaladière.* (You can find all these recipes in Chapter 5 of Book III.)

Chapter 2

Ingredients for French Cooking

In This Chapter

▶ Shopping for French ingredients

▶ Using the best ingredients you can find

▶ Discovering the wonderful world of French cheese

*I*t's been said that a great cuisine can develop only where there are great natural resources. France is a perfect example of this theory. It is blessed with a temperate climate and fertile soil ideal for growing exemplary fruits and vegetables; rolling hills and valleys covered with grapes destined to become France's deservedly famous wines; green fields for grazing cows, sheep, and goats whose milk is used to make some of the best cheese in the world; and over 2,000 miles of Atlantic and Mediterranean coastline full of seafood. As a result of these geographic advantages, France enjoys a variety of high-quality food that you won't find in many other countries.

Fortunately, people in many other parts of the world can purchase imported French cheeses and wines. The renewed interest and appreciation of quality food over the past few years has also motivated many local farmers to produce high-quality fruits and vegetables, as well as to raise grain-fed and free-range meats and poultry.

In this chapter, I discuss how to choose quality French products and locally grown and produced ingredients to use in French dishes that taste as good when made in your kitchen as they would if they were made in France. Remember, everyday food in France is simple fare. The simpler the food, the greater the need for quality ingredients.

Herbs and Spices

In addition to cooking techniques, knowing how to properly combine and use herbs and spices makes a world of difference between a delicious dish and a lackluster one. Seasonings should enhance the natural flavor of food, not overwhelm it. With generations of experience, French home cooks know how to season food expertly. While city dwellers purchase cut herbs at outdoor markets or at their local neighborhood greengrocer, people in small towns and villages usually have small plots of herbs growing in their yards, or pots or window boxes packed full of fresh herbs and edible flowers.

Not too long ago, the only fresh herb found in many U.S. supermarkets was curly-leaf parsley. Today, you can find a broader selection of packaged and even potted fresh herbs, such as rosemary, sage, savory, tarragon, and thyme, in most supermarket produce sections. French cooks regularly use and very much appreciate these types of herbs. Figure 2-1 illustrates many of the most commonly used herbs.

You may see a French recipe call for a *bouquet garni.* Basically, this is a small bunch of fresh herbs — such as a bay leaf and sprigs of parsley, thyme, rosemary, and tarragon — that complement each other tastewise and are tied together and added to a stock, soup, or sauce for flavor. After the flavor has been extracted, you can easily retrieve a bouquet garni by locating the end of the string and then discard the herbs. Cooks sometimes even tie the string to the pot handle.

The following are examples of commonly used herbs in French cooking:

- **Bay leaf** *(laurier):* A member of the evergreen family, this aromatic herb imparts wonderful flavor to almost everything, especially stews and some soups. Bay leaves are oval leaves approximately 2 to 3 inches long. Although fresh bay leaves aren't always readily available, you can find dry leaves sold in jars with the other dry herbs and spices at the supermarket. A leaf or two is usually all you need when cooking. Bay leaf combines well with other traditional Mediterranean herbs, such as oregano, parsley, rosemary, and thyme.

- **Chervil** *(cerfeuil):* This delicate anise-flavored herb should be added to foods like omelets, cream sauces, and soups only right before serving because its flavor dissipates rapidly when heated. It combines well with other herbs such as parsley, chives, and tarragon.

- **Chives** *(ciboulette):* This delicately flavored, spiky herb tastes mildly of onion and should be added to egg dishes, sauces, and soups only right before serving, to retain its flavor and bright green color. Chives are easy to grow in pots and are also available packaged at most supermarkets. The easiest way to cut chives is to take a bunch and snip them into ⅛-inch pieces with a pair of scissors. Chives blend well with most other herbs.

- **Fennel** *(fenouil):* Not to be confused with the fresh, light green bulb, dried fennel seeds taste of anise and licorice. Used traditionally in the Provence region of France, fennel seeds are used in fish and seafood dishes such as *bouillabaisse.* Use judiciously because a little goes a long way!

Book III

French
Cooking

Figure 2-1:
French
cooks rely
on many
herbs
to flavor
their foods.

✔ **Marjoram** *(marjolaine):* Fresh marjoram is a wonderful herb that looks
like thyme but has its own very distinct flavor. It goes especially well
with eggs and vegetables such as zucchini.

✔ **Oregano** *(origan):* It should come as no surprise that oregano, while
underused in most of France, is held in high regard in Provence, which
was originally part of what is today Italy. Oregano is best used dried

because its aroma and flavor are more potent in that form. Just as in Italian cooking, oregano is best when paired with tomatoes and certain roast meats, such as lamb and game birds; and it blends well with other assertive Mediterranean herbs, such as thyme, rosemary, and bay leaf.

✔ **Parsley** *(persil):* Always use fresh parsley, never the dried bottled version, which is tasteless and has a terrible gray color. Available in two varieties, curly-leafed or flat-leafed, the latter is the preferred one to use when cooking because it has more flavor and is easier to chop or mince. Remove the leaves from the stems before chopping or mincing them. Rather than discard the stems, tie them together with other herbs to use as part of a *bouquet* (see the description immediately preceding this bulleted list).

✔ **Rosemary** *(romarin):* A member of the evergreen family, this aromatic herb imparts wonderful flavor, especially to roast meats and fish. Great with pork, lamb, and oily fish, such as sardines and mackerels, rosemary is usually paired with garlic, olive oil, and other Mediterranean herbs to make a fragrant marinade or basting sauce.

✔ **Sage** *(sauge):* Silver green sage leaves have a pungent, almost musty taste and aroma that go exceptionally well with pork and poultry. It's also a fragrant seasoning for sautéed onions.

✔ **Tarragon** *(estragon):* A very popular herb in France, tarragon is best used fresh. Considered to be a bitter herb, it is best used alone and with discretion, or it will overpower a dish. Tarragon is used extensively in preparing things such as chicken and bernaise sauce *(sauce béarnaise).* A couple of tarragon leaves also pair well with some chopped parsley, chives, and chervil. (See Chapter 3 of Book III for a Béarnaise Sauce recipe.)

✔ **Thyme** *(thym):* Probably one of the most popular herbs used in French cooking, thyme is more subtle than oregano, with tones of mint providing well-balanced flavor to most dishes. Fresh thyme leaves should be removed from the woody stems before use in cooking. The fresh leaves have a light, bitter, refreshing taste. Dried thyme blends well in most dishes, holding up well flavorwise without overpowering the food. Use judiciously when roasting and grilling because the dry heat tends to accentuates its flavor.

Shallots and Leeks (Échalotes et Poireaux)

French cooks love to use shallots and leeks for their delicate flavor. Both are members of the allium family, which also includes onions, garlic, chives, and scallions. In addition to slicing and sautéing leeks, you can steam them and treat them like a vegetable, not unlike asparagus. Shallots are used in sauces, soups, and braised and stewed dishes when a mild onion flavor is desired. They look like small teardrop-shaped onions and require a bit of patience to peel and chop, as described in Figure 2-2.

HOW To CHOP A SHALLOT

1. CUT OFF STEM.
CUT IN HALF THROUGH THE ROOT.
PEEL OFF SKIN

2. MAKE PARALLEL LENGTHWISE CUTS
DO NOT CUT THROUGH ROOT END!

3. CUT HORIZONTAL SLICES FROM TOP TO BOTTOM.
NOT ALL THE WAY THROUGH

4. NOW, CUT CROSSWISE!

Figure 2-2:
Chopping a shallot.

Before chopping the shallot, slice off the tip and root part at each end. Lightly score the outer skin lengthwise and peel. Place the flattest side of the shallot on the cutting board and slice from top to bottom into thin slices, without cutting all the way to the root part. Turn the shallot 90 degrees and slice again into thin slices. Now slice the shallot across the slices so that it is now cut into small pieces.

Book III

French Cooking

Salt and Pepper (Sel et Poivre)

I usually like to generously salt and pepper foods as I cook them. Nothing is worse than underseasoned food, especially if it lacks salt. Sure, you can always add more salt when you sit down to eat, but quite honestly, the food doesn't taste the same when you do it that way.

As with everything in life, you do have some options when it comes to salt and pepper.

Salt (sel)

As do most Europeans, the French cook with sea salt, which is collected from salt farms of shallow ponds of seawater, usually located on the northwestern coast of France in Brittany. Coarse and with slightly moist crystals, French sea salt contains not only sodium chloride but also other trace minerals. The two most popular types of salt are the following:

> ✔ ***Fleur de sel*** (or "flower of salt") is a pure white salt that's harvested first off the drying ponds. It has a delicate fragrance and a dramatic flavor.
>
> ✔ **Celtic gray salt** is another popular type. This gray-hued salt has a smooth, milder flavor than *fleur de sel.*

French sea salt is available at most gourmet food stores. However, it averages around $7 to $8 a pound, and I personally find it a very costly import when compared to, say, kosher salt at $1.99 for a 3-pound box. I prefer to use kosher salt over ordinary table salt because it doesn't contain any of the additives found in the latter, which are added to make it flow better. Kosher salt also has a "cleaner" salt flavor and doesn't dissolve as quickly as regular salt, the cause of wilted salad greens.

Pepper (poivre)

Imported primarily from the subcontinent of Asia, pepper should always be in the form of freshly ground peppercorns for maximum flavor. The French sometimes use ground white pepper, which is made from black peppercorns with the outer black skin removed. White pepper is milder in flavor and is used instead of black pepper when the cook doesn't want to see its presence in whatever is being cooked. If you can't find white peppercorns, buy a small container of ground white pepper instead.

Butter (Beurre)

While it's true that the French use quite a bit of butter in cooking and baking, it isn't really as excessive as you may think. In fact, the use of butter is more regional than universal; the fat of choice in the south of France is locally pressed olive oil.

Unlike American butter made with sweet cream, French butter is made from cream that's slightly fermented. Higher in fat than its American counterpart, French butter is a golden yellow and very rich. American unsalted butter is an acceptable substitute when preparing French recipes.

Because butter burns quickly and easily, it is never used for frying and is suitable on no hotter than medium heat for quick sautéing only. To overcome the burning problem, some recipes combine butter and olive oil so that foods can be prepared in butter at a higher temperature.

In France, pieces of butter are also added to sauces at the very end to add body and smoothness. Don't add too much, however — just enough for added richness, which you'll notice on your tongue when you eat it.

Use butter in solid blocks or sticks. Never use tub or whipped butter because it contains water and is therefore unacceptable in cooking and baking.

Olive Oil (Huile d'Olives)

French olive oil, milled in the region of Provence, is enjoyed not only in the south of France but throughout the entire country. It's used in cooking as well as in making vinaigrettes and marinades. In Provence, olive oil is also used instead of butter in making some cakes and cookies.

Olive oil is made in the fall and early winter by cold-pressing the oil from tree-ripened olives by using only mechanical force or pressure. The crème de la crème of olive oil is called extra-virgin or, as they say in France, *extra-vièrge*. To be extra-virgin, the oil must be from the first cold pressing and have an acidity content of less than 1 percent. If the acidity content is greater, the oil is filtered and blended with other olive oil to mellow the flavor. Extra-virgin olive oil is naturally more expensive and of better quality.

Unlike its neighbors Italy and Spain, France is not a major exporter of olive oil. Though unavailable at most U.S. supermarkets, French olive oil is available at some gourmet food stores. A quality Italian or Spanish extra-virgin oil makes for a good substitute.

Other Oils and Fats

Besides using butter and olive oil, the French use nut oils, such as walnut and peanut oils, and solid fats, such as goose fat. Each of these has its own specific use and purpose:

- **Goose fat:** In order to get the biggest livers possible for making *foie gras,* the French force-feed corn to geese, which also produces a lot of fat. Rendered goose fat is used in France for sautéing or flavoring certain dishes, especially in Alsace-Lorraine, where it is popular.

- **Peanut oil:** The oil of choice for deep-frying in France, peanut oil has a smoke point of 410 degrees, which means that it can withstand being heated as high as 410 degrees before it will burst into flames. Because the beloved fried potato, or *pommes frites,* needs to be finished up at 375 degrees, peanut oil can do the job very well, plus it imparts a perfect golden hue to the potato pieces.

✔ **Walnut oil:** Made from cold-pressed walnuts, this subtly flavored oil is used in dressing salads such as Belgian Endive and Walnut Salad (Salade de Chicorée á l'Huile de Noix), a recipe you can find in Chapter 4 of Book III. Because walnut oil turns rancid quickly, buy it in small bottles and store it in the refrigerator.

What would a French cookbook be without a recipe for French fries? Well, believe it or not, French fries should actually be called Belgian fries, named for the country where they were created. Nevertheless, real fried potatoes, or *pommes frites* as the French call them, are as simple and easy to make as they are delicious to eat!

1. **Heat vegetable or peanut oil in an electric deep fryer filled to the maximum level or in a deep skillet, halfway to the top.**

   The oil should be at 325 degrees.

2. **Peel 2 pounds of Idaho or russet potatoes; cut into ¼-inch-thick slices and then cut into ¼-inch square fries.**

   Rinse under cold water to remove most of the surface starch. Dry very well with paper towels.

3. **Place about a quarter of the potatoes in the hot oil and fry for about 4 minutes, or until cooked but not browned.**

4. **Remove the potatoes to a plate lined with paper towels and repeat with the remaining potatoes.**

5. **When all the potatoes have been cooked, raise the heat so that the oil reaches 375 degrees.**

6. **Add the potatoes in small batches and fry until crispy and golden, about 1 to 2 minutes.**

   Drain on paper towels and sprinkle with salt to taste. This recipe serves 4.

Vinegar (Vinaigre)

The French usually choose from one of these three when using vinegar, which is made from fermented wine:

✔ **Red wine vinegar:** The better the red wine, the better the vinegar. Imported red wine vinegar tends to be slightly more acidic than domestic brands, but either makes a dressing with a strong kick. Like wine, good red wine vinegar is full-bodied and complex.

✔ **White wine vinegar:** Less full-bodied than vinegar made with red wine, white wine vinegar is still fairly acidic. Don't buy distilled white vinegar, which is made from grains, not wine, and has little flavor.

✔ **Champagne vinegar:** Champagne vinegar has a straw-yellow color and heady aroma to it. It is best suited for a simple vinaigrette made with a light-tasting olive oil.

You can make wonderful French, fresh-tasting raspberry vinegar at home by simply pouring an equal amount of red or white wine vinegar over fresh red raspberries in a glass or ceramic bowl. Cover and let sit in a cool place for 8 days. Pour through a fine mesh strainer without squeezing the raspberries. Use in vinaigrette.

Dijon Mustard (Moutarde de Dijon)

The most famous of any mustard, true Dijon mustard is made in the French city of Dijon with ground mustard seeds and white wine vinegar. With a certain amount of spiciness, Dijon mustard is used sparingly in vinaigrettes (Chapter 3 of Book III) for a little added zing as well as binding the dressing. French home cooks also rub Dijon mustard on a leg of lamb before roasting it (see the Leg of Lamb recipe in Chapter 5 of Book III) and spread it on slices of country pâté.

Cheese (Fromage)

Book III

French Cooking

France, a country the size of Texas, has hundreds of cheeses to choose from. Most, however, aren't exported and are made to be eaten in the same area where they're made. The following list describes some of the most popular and common cheeses to eat and to cook with (see Figure 2-3). Although some are sold in supermarkets, all should be readily available at a good cheese shop or gourmet food store in your area.

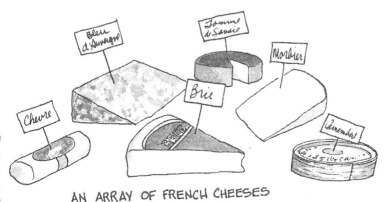

Figure 2-3: French cheeses.

AN ARRAY OF FRENCH CHEESES

✔ **Bleu d'Auvergne:** A gently flavored, blue-veined cheese from central France, this cheese is a true classic. With a rindless, salty exterior, this cow's-milk cheese is white to beige in color, with blue veining throughout. Serve it with all types of fruit and mellow red wines.

✔ **Brie and Camembert:** These are probably two of the best-known French cheeses. Brie is from the Paris area, while Camembert is from the Normandy region to the north. These soft-ripened, round cheeses are approximately 1 inch thick. Although both are made from cow's milk, Brie is made in 1-, 2-, 3-, and 6-pound wheels, while Camembert weighs only 8 ounces. Both cheeses have a thin, white, chalky exterior or rind and a soft, creamy interior. Brie and Camembert both ripen from the inside out, so an underage cheese cut too soon will not continue to ripen. When shopping for Brie or Camembert, look for flat cheeses that have soft, fuzzy white rinds, with no bulges. Both go well with a full-bodied red wine, pears, apples, and walnuts. You can eat the rind on both Brie and Camembert if you wish, as most people do.

✔ **Cantal:** From Auvergne in central France comes this semifirm cow's-milk cheese. Straw yellow in color, it is mild tasting and has a brushed, non-edible rind. Serve it with sweet apples and pears and a fruity white wine.

✔ **Comté:** From the French Alps, this cow's-milk cheese is a world classic. Similar to Gruyère, Comté is made in 80-pound wheels, 4 inches thick and 30 inches round. A great melting cheese, it's used frequently in France to make *au gratin* dishes. A nutty-tasting cheese, Comté is a yellow ivory color and should be served with a full-bodied red wine. Remove the rind before eating or using in cooking. If you can't find Comté, substitute a good Swiss Gruyère.

✔ **Roquefort:** This sheep's-milk cheese is cave-ripened in the limestone caves of Cambalou, near the town of Roquefort-fort-sur-Soulzon in southern France. A soft, crumbly, ivory-colored cheese with green blue veining, Roquefort has an intense, complex, spicy flavor. Because Roquefort doesn't have a rind, it's wrapped in foil. The outer layer, albeit salty, is edible. I especially like to serve this cheese with grapes, ripe pears, and cherries because the sweetness makes for a fabulous contrast.

Cheese is a basic and straightforward food product. Don't let the French names intimidate you! Following are some suggestions for purchasing French cheeses or, for that matter, any cheese:

✔ **Buy French.** Buy imported French cheese whenever possible and not an American-made, French-named cheese.

✔ **Search for only fresh cheeses.** Shop from a store that handles the cheese properly and does a brisk business so that nothing sits around for very long. A wedge cut to order is fresher than a precut and wrapped wedge.

✔ **Taste everything before you buy.** Good cheese shops unwrap cheeses and cut off small slices for you to sample.

Although wine-and-cheese parties are a popular American entertaining creation, serving a plate of cheese with fruit and perhaps nuts for dessert is very French. A selection of three different types of cheeses is a good general rule. For example, from the list of cheeses earlier in this section, Brie, Cantal, and Bleu d'Auvergne go nicely together when paired with muscatel grapes and perfectly ripened pears.

I want to share with you one of my favorite, cheese-inspired winter dishes. If you've ever seen one of the many film versions of *Heidi* or perhaps read the book, you may remember the grandfather scraping melted cheese over bread and potatoes. The name of the cheese he uses is called *raclette,* which comes from the French verb *racler,* meaning "to scrape." Enjoyed in both the French and Swiss Alps, *raclette,* the dish, is quick and easy to prepare when using *raclette,* the cheese. Made from whole cow's milk, *raclette* cheese melts very quickly.

To prepare *raclette* for dinner, follow these steps:

1. **Boil about ½ pound of new baby potatoes in their skins for each adult.**

2. **Remove and discard the rind of the raclette cheese and slice as thinly as possible.**

    Figure on 4 ounces of *raclette* cheese per person.

3. **Place the cheese on heatproof dinner plates and place in a preheated 450-degree oven until the cheese completely melts.**

4. **Place the boiled potatoes on top of the cheese and quarter them.**

5. **Mix together the cheese and potatoes.**

    Serve with small pickled onions and *cornichons* (tiny French pickles).

Friends and family love for me to make and serve them *raclette,* which, by the way, has become more readily available at cheese and specialty food stores over the past few years.

Book III

French
Cooking

Chapter 3

Mastering a Few Simple Techniques

In This Chapter

- Mastering the techniques of French cooking
- Whipping up rich sauces and soufflés
- Flipping for crêpes
- How to turn out delectable tarts, both sweet and savory

Authentic, delicious, home-style French cooking doesn't have to be complicated or difficult to prepare. Like home cooks everywhere, French cooks usually have a handful of tried-and-true favorite recipes that they make week after week, many of which have become international classics. In this chapter, I share with you some of the most popular ones as well as some basic techniques that will assist you in preparing them.

Rich, Smooth Sauces

Well-prepared sauces define French cooking. By using readily available basic ingredients, such as butter, milk, eggs, and lemon juice, and pairing the rich sauce with simply cooked vegetables, meat, poultry, or seafood, you can turn the ordinary into something very special. Serve sparingly because sauces should complement foods and never overwhelm or mask them.

French sauces can be divided into a few basic types: white, brown, egg and butter, oil and vinegar (vinaigrette), and flavored butters. Each one is unique and very different from the others.

White sauces

You make white sauce, or *sauce blanche,* by mixing hot milk or broth with white *roux,* flour cooked in a small amount of butter until foamy (but not allowed to color) and no longer raw tasting. Cooking the flour tames its raw taste and gives the sauce a more complex flavor.

A *sauce blanche* made with milk is called *sauce béchamel.* Béchamel is a thick white sauce and can be used, for example, in lieu of ricotta cheese when making lasagne. You also can spoon it over steamed endive in a buttered baking dish, sprinkle it with grated Parmesan cheese, and place under the broiler until lightly browned. When you add grated cheese to a hot *sauce béchamel,* you get the basic French cheese sauce, *sauce mornay.*

Sauce blanche can also be made with chicken or vegetable broth rather than milk. This white sauce is called *sauce velouté* and can be used in making crêpe fillings with poultry or even as a sauce for dishes such as chicken pot pie.

Basic White Sauce (Sauce Blanche or Béchamel)

A good, basic white sauce should be part of everyone's cooking repertoire.

Preparation time: 5 minutes

Cooking time: 10 minutes

Yield: 2 cups

2 tablespoons unsalted butter

2 tablespoons all-purpose flour

2 cups whole milk or chicken or vegetable broth

Salt and pepper to taste

1 Melt the butter in a saucepan over low heat. Blend in the flour and cook slowly, stirring, until the butter and flour foam without changing color, about 2 minutes. Remove from the heat.

2 Bring the milk or broth to a boil over medium heat. Add ¼ teaspoon salt. Slowly pour the hot liquid over the hot flour mixture, beating with a wire whisk until smooth.

3 Return to the stove and cook over medium-high heat until the sauce boils. Cook a minute longer. Remove from the heat and season with salt and pepper.

Vary It! *To make a cheese sauce (in French, Sauce Mornay), stir ½ cup grated Gruyère, Parmesan, or sharp cheddar cheese into the hot sauce until smooth in Step 3. Make sure to use milk rather than vegetable broth for this variation.*

Brown sauces

Like white sauce, brown sauce, or *sauce brune,* is made by mixing hot, rich beef or veal stock with brown *roux,* flour cooked in a small amount of butter until foamy and a rich golden brown color. The resulting sauce is perfect for serving over slices of roasted beef or veal, or perhaps turned into an even more flavorful *sauce duxelles* with the addition of sautéed mushrooms — perfect to serve with grilled beef or even meat loaf.

Brown Sauce (Sauce Brune)

This sauce is like a rich brown gravy. You can also use defatted pan drippings from a roast in lieu of part of the water for an even more intense, meaty flavor.

Preparation time:: 10 minutes

Cooking time: 35 minutes

Yield: 2½ cups

2 cups homemade or low-sodium canned beef broth

3 tablespoons minced onion

3 tablespoons minced carrots

1 tablespoon minced celery

½ cup dry red wine

2 sprigs parsley

2 tablespoons unsalted butter

1½ tablespoons all-purpose flour

Salt and pepper to taste

Book III

French Cooking

1 Bring the broth to a boil. Add the onion, carrots, celery, wine, and parsley. Lower the heat to a simmer and cook, covered, for 20 minutes. Strain and set aside.

2 Melt the butter in a saucepan over low heat. Blend in the flour and cook slowly, stirring, until the butter and flour foam and turn golden brown, about 4 to 6 minutes. Remove from the heat.

3 Slowly pour the hot broth over the flour mixture, beating with a wire whisk until smooth.

4 Return to the stove and cook over medium-high heat until the sauce boils. Cook a minute longer, remove from the heat, and season with salt and pepper.

Having problems getting your white or brown sauce right? Read the following tips for assistance:

- ✔ If the sauce is lumpy, the liquid or *roux* (cooked flour mixture) wasn't hot enough. Pour the sauce into a blender jar and blend until smooth.

- ✔ If the sauce is too thick, whisk in a small amount of hot milk or broth until the sauce reaches the desired consistency.

Mushroom Sauce (Sauce Duxelles)

You can use ordinary Paris mushrooms or what are typically called button white mushrooms in this recipe. If you want to vary the flavor and texture of this sauce, however, substitute cremini, shiitake, or even wild mushrooms.

Preparation time: *15 minutes*

Cooking time: *20 minutes*

Yield: *2½ cups*

1 tablespoon unsalted butter	*½ cup dry white wine*
4 ounces fresh mushrooms, trimmed and chopped	*2 cups Brown Sauce (see the recipe earlier in this chapter)*
1 small shallot, chopped	*3 tablespoons minced flat-leaf parsley*

1 Melt the butter over medium heat in a saucepan. Add the mushrooms and shallot and cook until soft.

2 Add the wine and reduce by half.

3 Add to the Brown Sauce and simmer for 5 minutes.

4 Stir in the parsley before serving.

Egg and butter sauces

Perhaps the most famous and best-known sauces in the world, hollandaise and bérnaise are the queens of sauces. Made with plenty of butter and egg yolks, these two aren't for calorie and fat counters; they're best reserved for special occasions.

The trick to making perfect *sauce hollandaise* and *sauce béarnaise* is to take each and every step slowly. The eggs need to heat gradually. Heat them too quickly, and you'll wind up with scrambled eggs!

For the eggs to absorb all the melted butter, you have to add a little at a time. Add too much, too quickly, and the sauce will curdle. Always let the sauce absorb the butter before adding more.

Always reheat hollandaise or bérnaise sauce over very low heat so that it doesn't curdle.

Béarnaise Sauce (Sauce Béarnaise)

Sauce béarnaise distinguishes itself from its lemony cousin, *sauce hollandaise,* in that it's more assertive and flavored with a reduction of dry white wine, white wine vinegar, shallots, and fresh tarragon. This flavorful sauce pairs wonderfully with grilled steaks or chicken, boiled or grilled fish, and egg dishes.

Preparation time: *15 minutes*

Cooking time: *25 minutes*

Yield: *Approximately 1½ cups*

¼ cup white wine vinegar	Salt
¼ cup dry white wine	3 egg yolks
1 small shallot, minced	2 tablespoons cold unsalted butter
3 tablespoons minced fresh tarragon	8 tablespoons (1 stick) unsalted butter, melted
⅛ teaspoon pepper	

Book III

French Cooking

1 Combine the vinegar, wine, shallot, 2 tablespoons of the tarragon, pepper, and a pinch of salt in a small saucepan. Bring to a boil over medium-high heat and reduce the liquid to 2 tablespoons. Watch the pan carefully as the mixture evaporates. Strain and set aside to cool to room temperature.

2 Beat the egg yolks in a medium saucepan until thick. Beat in the vinegar mixture. Add 1 tablespoon of the cold butter and warm the mixture over low heat, stirring until it thickens. Immediately remove from the heat and beat in the remaining tablespoon of cold butter.

3 Slowly whisk in the melted butter, a teaspoonful at a time, until the sauce is thick like heavy cream. Discard any milky residue from the bottom of the pan. Season with salt and pepper to taste. Add the remaining 1 tablespoon of tarragon. Serve warm, not hot.

Please do not be tempted to quickly add the melted butter in any of the butter-enriched sauces such as béarnaise or hollandaise. The addition of small amounts and constant whisking ensure a smooth, thick sauce.

Hollandaise Sauce

Hollandaise sauce, flavored with lemon juice, is delicious served with fresh vegetables such as steamed asparagus or artichokes. And don't forget about using it on top of eggs Benedict, a perfect brunch dish that consists of poached eggs and Canadian bacon on a toasted and buttered English muffin.

Preparation time: *10 minutes*

Cooking time: *10 minutes*

Yield: *Approximately 1½ cups*

3 egg yolks

1 tablespoon cold water

1 tablespoon lemon juice

Salt and pepper

2 tablespoons cold unsalted butter

12 tablespoons (1½ sticks) unsalted butter, melted

1 Beat the egg yolks in a medium saucepan. Beat in the water, lemon juice, and a pinch of salt. Add 1 tablespoon of the cold butter and warm the mixture over low heat, stirring until it thickens. Immediately remove from the heat and beat in the remaining tablespoon of cold butter.

2 Slowly whisk in the melted butter, a teaspoonful at a time, until the sauce is thick like heavy cream. Discard any milky residue from the bottom of the pan. Season with salt and pepper to taste. Serve warm, not hot.

Vinaigrette

Sauce vinaigrette, the salad dressing of choice in France, is a blend of quality extra-virgin olive oil and wine vinegar, seasoned with salt, freshly ground black pepper, and perhaps some finely minced shallots and a dollop of real Dijon mustard. What could be easier?

The key to a well-balanced salad dressing is to use the right proportion of vinegar to olive oil. Depending on your personal preference, a good rule is 2 parts olive oil to 1 part vinegar or, if you prefer a milder dressing, 3 parts olive oil to 1 part vinegar.

Make salad dressing in a clean jar for easy mixing and storage.

Vinaigrette

Depending on whether you like your salad dressing with a pronounced vinegar bite, choose either Version I or II, with Version I being the stronger of the two. Either dressing is also nice to use when marinating thinly sliced boneless chicken breasts for grilling.

Preparation time: *5 minutes*

Yield: *1 cup*

Version I	**Version II**
12 tablespoons (¾ cup) extra-virgin olive oil	*15 tablespoons (⅔ cup) extra-virgin olive oil*
6 tablespoons (¼ cup) red or white wine vinegar	*5 tablespoons (⅓ cup) red or white wine vinegar*
2 tablespoons Dijon mustard	*2 tablespoons Dijon mustard*
½ teaspoon salt	*½ teaspoon salt*
1 tablespoon minced shallots	*1 tablespoon minced shallots*

Place all the ingredients in a clean glass jar. Screw the lid on the jar and shake until the ingredients are well combined. Taste and add salt if needed.

Book III

French Cooking

Flavored butters (beurres composés)

Perhaps the simplest of all French sauces is butter, especially when flavored with things such as fresh garlic, herbs, or mustard. Flavored butters are very easy to prepare and keep for a few days in the refrigerator. With almost unlimited uses, a pat of flavored butter can be placed on a hot, grilled steak, chop, or chicken breast, adding amazing depth and flavor. Flavored butter can be melted and used to baste roasting poultry or root vegetables. Pieces can be stirred into a sauce, added to potatoes before mashing, or used to dress steamed vegetables or seafood. Flavored butter is also wonderful to spread on slices of bread cut from a crispy baguette.

Keep the following advice in mind when making flavored butter:

- ✔ For best results, always use unsalted, USDA AA Graded butter.
- ✔ The butter should be at room temperature for easy whipping and blending with other ingredients.

- The easiest way to cream butter is in a mixing bowl with an electric mixer.

- Use the freshest and best-quality ingredients.

- Use a spoon to fold the flavoring ingredients into the creamed butter.

- For easy-to-cut pats of butter, shape and refrigerate the butter in a log. To do so, take a 6-inch long piece of plastic wrap. Mound the flavored butter, about 1½ inches high × 1½ inches wide, on the longest edge of the plastic wrap, closest to you. Roll into a tight log and twist the edges. Refrigerate until chilled solid.

- Store well-wrapped flavored butters in the refrigerator. Use within 3 to 5 days, or slice into tablespoon-sized pieces, freeze on a baking sheet until hard, and then store in small freezer bags.

Parsley Butter
(Beurre Maître d'Hôtel)

The classic French blended butter, *beurre maître d'hôtel* is always wonderful to have on hand to enrich the flavor of a sauce or to place on top of a perfectly grilled piece of meat or fish.

Preparation time: *10 minutes*

Yield: *Approximately 10 tablespoons*

8 tablespoons (1 stick) unsalted butter	*3 tablespoons minced flat-leaf parsley*
1 tablespoon freshly squeezed lemon juice	*Salt and pepper to taste*

1 Cream the butter in a mixing bowl. Add the lemon juice to the creamed butter a drop at a time; if you add it any faster, it won't blend in well. Beat in the parsley and season with salt and pepper.

2 Roll into a log or place in a covered container, and refrigerate until ready to use.

Vary It! *To make herb butter (beurre de fines herbes), substitute a combination of your favorite fresh minced herbs for the parsley.*

Garlic Butter (Beurre d'Ail)

I like to use melted *beurre d'ail* to baste roasting chicken for a wonderfully rich garlic flavor and finish.

***Preparation time:*:** *10 minutes*

Yield: *Approximately 10 tablespoons*

8 tablespoons (1 stick) unsalted butter

4 small or 2 large cloves garlic, peeled and minced

Salt and pepper to taste

1 Cream the butter in a mixing bowl. Beat in the garlic and season with salt and pepper.

2 Roll into a log or place in a covered container, and refrigerate until ready to use.

Mustard Butter (Beurre de Moutarde)

For a perfect finish, try a pat of *beurre de moutarde* on a grilled pork chop or salmon steak.

***Preparation time:*:** *10 minutes*

Yield: *Approximately 10 tablespoons*

8 tablespoons (1 stick) unsalted butter

2 tablespoons Dijon mustard

Salt and pepper to taste

1 Cream the butter in a mixing bowl. Add the mustard to the creamed butter a teaspoon at a time. Season with salt and pepper.

2 Roll into a log or place in a covered container, and refrigerate until ready to use.

Book III

French Cooking

Stirring Up Soufflés as Light as Air

Puffed up and golden, a well-made soufflé is not as difficult to make as you may think. Made from a base or sauce comprised of milk, flour, and egg yolks, soufflés can be seasoned with cheese and served as entrees or made with sugar and other flavorings for dessert.

Soufflés get their height and light texture from the final addition of beaten egg whites that are gently folded in. In fact, properly beaten egg whites are the key to making a successful soufflé.

Soufflés are baked in tall, straight-sided soufflé molds made of porcelain, ceramic, or glass (see Figure 3-1). They puff up and turn golden during baking but begin to deflate as they cool, so plan accordingly and serve yours straight from the oven, using a large serving spoon.

Figure 3-1:
A porcelain
6-cup
soufflé
mold.

PORCELAIN
6 CUP SOUFFLÉ
MOLD

Knowing how to properly beat egg whites until stiff is the key to success for many recipes, especially soufflés. The following steps are a surefire bet for good results every time you beat egg whites, which must be beaten until they reach seven or eight times their normal volume:

- ✔ Check the expiration date on the egg carton and use only the freshest eggs possible.

- ✔ Egg whites must be at room temperature and free of all yolk. Separate eggs, one at a time, over a small bowl. Transfer the separated egg white to a large mixing bowl and let sit for 15 to 20 minutes to bring to room temperature. Egg whites that are too cold or that contain one tiny speck of yolk increase less in volume.

- ✔ Make sure that your mixing bowl is deep and wide enough to accommodate a sevenfold increase in the volume of the egg whites.

- ✔ All beaters and bowls must be washed well and contain no trace of fat or oil. Dry well with a clean kitchen towel.

✔ The easiest way to beat egg whites is with an electric mixer. Always start off on low speed so that you gently break up the egg whites. After 1 minute, or when the egg whites appear foamy, add a pinch of salt and begin beating on medium-high while tilting and rotating the bowl. Beat the egg whites around the sides of the bowl and up through the middle to incorporate as much air as possible.

✔ The egg whites are ready to use when they're shiny and stiff peaks form when the beaters are raised up (see Figure 3-2).

✔ So as not to deflate the beaten egg whites, fold into the remaining ingredients using a wide rubber spatula. Gently cut down through the center of the mixture to the bottom of the bowl and up and over toward the side (see Figure 3-3). Continue this process until the ingredients are combined. Don't worry if a few unmixed spots remain. The ingredients will all come together in the oven as the soufflé bakes.

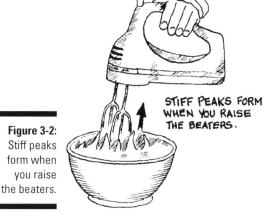

STIFF PEAKS FORM WHEN YOU RAISE THE BEATERS.

Figure 3-2:
Stiff peaks form when you raise the beaters.

FOLDING INGREDIENTS INTO EGG WHITES

SO AS NOT TO DEFLATE THE BEATEN EGG WHITES, FOLD INTO THE REMAINING INGREDIENTS USING A WIDE RUBBER SPATULA.

Figure 3-3:
Fold soufflé ingredients into beaten egg whites.

GENTLY CUT DOWN THE CENTER OF THE MIXTURE TO THE BOTTOM OF THE BOWL...

... AND UP AND OVER TOWARD THE SIDE. CONTINUE UNTIL THE INGREDIENTS ARE COMBINED.

Cheese Soufflé (Soufflé au Fromage)

The granddaddy of soufflés, a basic cheese soufflé makes a delicious lunch or light dinner entree. You can make it even more special by adding ingredients such as spinach, ham, and mushrooms.

Preparation time: *20 minutes*

Cooking time: *35 minutes*

Yield: *4 to 6 servings*

4 tablespoons plus 1 teaspoon unsalted butter

1 tablespoon grated Parmesan cheese

3 tablespoons all-purpose flour

1 cup whole milk, boiling

½ teaspoon salt

4 eggs, separated, plus 1 additional egg white, at room temperature

¾ cup (3 ounces) coarsely grated Gruyère, Swiss, or Parmesan cheese

1 Preheat the oven to 400 degrees. Using 1 teaspoon of butter, grease a 6-cup soufflé mold and sprinkle with the tablespoon of grated Parmesan cheese.

2 Melt the remaining 4 tablespoons butter in a saucepan over low heat. Stir in the flour and cook for 2 minutes. Do not let it brown. Remove from the heat. When the mixture stops foaming, slowly whisk in the hot milk and salt.

3 Whisk over medium heat until the milk thickens. Let boil for 1 minute and remove from the heat.

4 Beat in the egg yolks, one at a time, until smooth. Season with salt to taste. Cover and set aside.

5 Beat the egg whites and a pinch of salt in a large mixing bowl with an electric mixer until stiff peaks form.

6 Stir one-fourth of the stiffly beaten egg whites into the egg yolk mixture. Fold in the cheese. Gently fold in the remaining egg whites and scrape into the prepared mold. Gently tap the bottom of the mold on the table and smooth the top of the soufflé with a spatula.

7 Place the soufflé in the oven on the center rack. Lower the temperature to 375 degrees and cook for 30 to 35 minutes or until the soufflé puffs up about 2 inches above the rim of the mold, is golden brown, and tests done when a knife inserted in the center comes out clean. Serve at once.

Vary It! *Spinach Soufflé: Sauté ¼ cup of cooked, chopped frozen spinach, squeezed dry of all water, in 1 tablespoon of butter along with 1 tablespoon of minced onion. Add the sautéed spinach to the egg yolk mixture in Step 4. Continue with Steps 5 through 7. Ham and Mushroom Soufflé: Add 1 tablespoon snipped chives, ⅓ cup finely chopped boiled ham, and ¼ cup minced mushrooms sautéed in butter to the egg yolk mixture in Step 4. Continue with Steps 5 through 7.*

Cranking Out Crêpes with a Flip of the Wrist

If France had a national fast food, it would have to be crêpes. Don't think of the crêpe as a pancake; rather, think of it as a round, soft piece of flatbread to be filled with an endless variety of fillings or stacked and cut into wedges like a torte. Classic crêpe desserts like *crêpes suzette* are crêpes made with sugar that are then folded in quarters and dipped in a buttery orange sauce before being flambéed (see the Orange Dessert Crêpes recipe in Chapter 6 of Book III).

Crêpes are convenience food with a capital C. You can prepare the batter and store it in the refrigerator for up to 3 days before using. You can also prepare them earlier in the day, wrap them in a clean kitchen cloth, and then reheat them in the microwave before eating.

Though simple to make, crêpes require some preparation beforehand and a tiny bit of skill and practice.

- ✔ So that crêpes are tender and not chewy, the batter must rest for at least 2 to 3 hours, or better yet overnight, so plan accordingly.

- ✔ The crêpe pan must be hot so that the batter sets quickly and cooks evenly.

- ✔ So that crêpes come out thin, the batter should be not be thicker than heavy cream. If it's too thick, thin it with cold water until it reaches the proper consistency.

- ✔ After pouring batter into the hot pan, swirl it quickly so that the crêpes are evenly thin.

- ✔ There are two ways to flip a crêpe. Either use two small spatulas or do as I find easiest and quickly pull up and turn over using your fingers. Although you might feel like you're burning your fingers, it really is easier to flip the crêpes with your fingers. Just do it quickly.

- ✔ Stack cooked crêpes on a plate and cover with a clean kitchen cloth to keep them warm.

Book III

French Cooking

Basic French Pancake Batter
(Pâté à Crêpes)

Crêpe batter needs to rest for at least 2 to 3 hours before being used, so plan accordingly. For best results, read the preceding list of tips.

Preparation time: *5 minutes, plus at least 2 to 3 hours resting time*

Cooking time: *20 minutes*

Yield: *Approximately 12 crêpes (4 to 6 servings)*

1 cup cold milk	2 cups all-purpose flour
1 cup cold water	4 tablespoons (½ stick) unsalted butter, melted
4 eggs	
½ teaspoon salt	

1 Combine the milk, water, eggs, and salt in a blender jar and blend until smooth. Add the flour and butter and blend for 1 minute or until smooth. Pour into a large bowl, cover, and refrigerate overnight.

2 Remove the batter from the refrigerator and check the consistency; it should be thick, like heavy cream.

3 Heat a nonstick 8-inch crêpe pan or skillet over medium-high heat.

4 Hold the pan with one hand and lift it off the burner. With the other hand, pour ¼ cup of batter in the center of the hot pan and quickly begin to tilt the pan and swirl the batter so that it covers the bottom evenly in a thin layer. Place on the burner and cook for about 1 minute or until the edges begin to brown and the batter seems set on top.

5 Flip the crêpe. Cook for no longer than 30 seconds and remove to a plate. The top or good side of the crêpe should be evenly golden; the other side will be lighter in color and look different.

6 Repeat with the remaining batter.

7 Fill and roll each crêpe, or spread with a favorite filling, stack, and cut into wedges to serve.

Tip: Even though you use a nonstick pan to make the crêpes, you may need to occasionally brush the bottom and sides of the pan with a little butter so that the crêpes don't stick.

Vary It! Crêpes are also served in France for dessert. (See the recipe for Crêpes Suzette in Chapter 6 of Book III.) To make sweet French pancake batter (crêpes fines sucrées), add 5 teaspoons sugar and 3 tablespoons orange liqueur or brandy along with the eggs. Increase the melted butter to 6 tablespoons.

Savory Stuffed and Rolled Crêpes (Crêpes Farcies et Roulées)

Most savory crêpes are filled with a white or cheese sauce mixed with cooked vegetables or poultry, and then rolled.

Preparation time: *10 minutes*

Cooking time: *5 minutes*

Yield: *4 to 6 servings*

Cheese Sauce (see the recipe variation at the end of the Basic White Sauce recipe, earlier in this chapter)

Basic French Pancake Batter (see the recipe earlier in this chapter)

Filling options: 4 ounces mushrooms, sautéed in butter; 1 cup cooked and diced chicken or turkey; or 1 cup cooked, chopped spinach, well drained

2 tablespoons grated Parmesan cheese

1 Reserve ½ cup of the cheese sauce. Combine the remaining sauce with whatever you choose for your filling: the mushrooms, poultry, or spinach.

2 Place a big spoonful of the filling on the lower third of each crêpe and roll the crêpes up.

3 Place the crêpes in a shallow baking dish and spread the tops with the reserved sauce. Sprinkle with the Parmesan cheese and brown under the broiler for a minute or two.

Vary It! *Using this recipe, reserve ¾ cup of the cheese sauce. Spread the crêpes with the remaining sauce. Lay 3 cooked asparagus spears (2 on the bottom and 1 on top) at the bottom edge of each crêpe. Roll up tightly. Place in a shallow baking dish and spread the tops with the reserved sauce and 2 tablespoons Parmesan cheese. Brown under the broiler.*

Book III

French Cooking

Spinach, Mushroom, and Cheese Torte (Gâteau de Crêpes à la Florentine)

Gâteau de Crêpes à la Florentine is a quick and easy-to-make torte, made of stacked crêpes spread with a filling of cheese sauce prepared with spinach and mushrooms. Cut into thin wedges for appetizer servings or cut into quarters and serve as an entrée.

Preparation time: *15 minutes*

Cooking time: *25 minutes*

Yield: *8 appetizer portions or 4 entrée portions*

Cheese Sauce (see the recipe variation at the end of the Basic White Sauce recipe, earlier in this chapter)	1 cup cooked, chopped, frozen spinach, well drained
Basic French Pancake Batter (see the recipe earlier in this chapter)	½ teaspoon grated nutmeg
	Salt and pepper to taste
4 ounces mushrooms, sautéed in butter	3 tablespoons grated Parmesan cheese

1 Preheat the oven to 350 degrees.

2 Reserve 3 tablespoons of the cheese sauce. Combine the remaining sauce with the mushrooms and spinach. Season with the nutmeg and salt and pepper.

3 Place one crêpe in a shallow baking dish. Spread the crêpe with a layer of the filling. Cover with another crêpe and spread with more filling. Repeat this process, ending with a plain crêpe on top.

4 Spread the top crêpe with the reserved cheese sauce. Sprinkle with the Parmesan cheese. Bake for 25 minutes or until heated through and the top is golden brown.

5 Remove from the oven. To serve, cut into wedges.

Open-Faced Tarts: Savory and Sweet

As far as I'm concerned, one of the best contributions of French home cooking is its open-faced tarts, both savory and sweet. With only one crust to roll out, they are, for the most part, quick and easy to make. Savory tarts like quiche (and yes, real Frenchmen do eat quiche!) make for a great lunch or supper when paired with a green salad, a dry white wine, and fresh fruit. Sweet tarts are even better because you can bake the tart shell beforehand and then fill it with egg custard and fresh berries, or lemon or chocolate cream, before serving.

Unfortunately, some people are turned off by the idea of making pie crust and then having to handle it. Don't be! You'll be surprised at how easy these doughs are to work with. The key to getting a good crust is not to overwork the dough and to chill it before rolling it out and baking, so plan accordingly or, better yet, make the dough one day and the crust another.

For the most part, French-style tarts aren't as deep as the traditional American pie, so you may want to purchase a removable, false-bottom tart pan (see Figure 3-4) at your local housewares store.

Figure 3-4:
American-style pie tins versus removable, false-bottom tart and quiche pans.

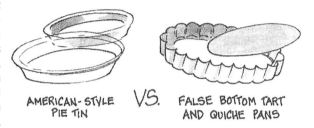

AMERICAN-STYLE PIE TIN VS. FALSE BOTTOM TART AND QUICHE PANS

Book III

French Cooking

You have a few options as far as the type of pan you can use when making pies, tarts, and quiches:

- Traditional American-style pie ties or pans are usually 8 to 9 inches in diameter, with sloping sides, and made from metal, glass, or ceramic. I prefer the old-fashioned yet readily available tinned steel or aluminum pans with perforated bottoms for even baking. Glazed ceramic pans are also a fine choice. These types of pans are best suited when making a deep-dish tart, such as a quiche. I also like to use my ceramic pan when making *clafoutis,* a custardlike fruit pie (see Chapter 6 of Book III).

- Removable-bottom tart pans are available in a wide variety of sizes, usually ranging in diameter from 9 to 11 inches, and made from tinned steel or steel or aluminum with a nonstick finish. The straight, 1-inch-high sides are fluted and folded under at the bottom, forming a lip that accommodates a removable false bottom. After baking, you can easily remove the cooled tart or quiche from the sides of the pan by supporting the bottom of the pan on the palm of your hand and gently pushing it up and away from the side ring. You can also purchase and use a removable bottom 8- to 9-inch, false-bottom quiche pan. With sloped, heavily fluted sides, these pans are approximately 2½ inches deep and make a deep-dish quiche. Removable, false-bottom tart and quiche pans make for a professional-looking presentation.

Savory Tart Dough (Pâté Brisée)

This is the dough you'll want to use when making a quiche or *pissaladière* (see Chapter 5 of Book III for the recipes).

Preparation time: *10 minutes, plus 3 hours chilling time*

Yield: *One 8- to 11-inch tart crust or shell*

2 cups all-purpose flour

½ teaspoon salt

¼ teaspoon sugar

8 tablespoons (1 stick) cold unsalted butter, cut into small pieces

3 tablespoons shortening, chilled

5 tablespoons ice water

1 Combine the flour, salt, sugar, butter, and shortening in a food processor bowl. Pulse a few times until the butter and shortening are cut into the flour.

2 With the processor running, pour the water through the feed tube. Process just until the dough begins to come together.

3 Turn the dough out onto the counter and gently knead 2 or 3 times until it forms a ball.

4 Flatten the dough into a ½-inch-thick disk. Wrap in plastic and refrigerate for at least 2 hours or overnight.

5 Remove the dough from the plastic wrap. Sprinkle both sides with flour and roll into a circle approximately ⅛ inch thick and 2 inches larger than the diameter of your pan.

6 Carefully lay the rolled-out dough over the rolling pin and position over an 8- to 11-inch tart pan, as shown in Figure 3-5. Center it and gently fit it into the pan by pressing the dough into the pan without stretching it. Fold the excess dough over inside edge of the pan so that the sides are slightly thicker. Press the dough up and over the sides so that the thickness is even throughout. Roll the rolling pin over the top of the pan to trim off any excess dough.

7 Place the pan with the dough in the refrigerator and chill for 1 hour before filling and baking, or baking blind, a technique I describe following this recipe.

Vary It! *To make sweet dough (pâté brisée sucrée) for fruit tarts and other desserts, increase the sugar to 4 tablespoons.*

Tip: Depending on the size pan you're using, you may have some leftover dough scraps. You can reroll them once and use them to make small, rustic fruit tarts. Flour and roll the dough out into a circle on a lightly greased baking pan. Place thinly sliced fruit in the center, 2 inches from the edge. Sprinkle the fruit lightly with flour and generously with sugar. Fold the 2-inch edge of dough over and toward the center, folding it in pleats as you do so. Bake in a preheated 400-degree oven until the crust is golden and the fruit is bubbling, approximately 30 to 40 minutes.

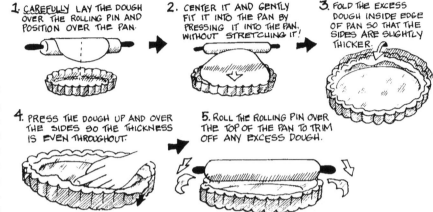

POSITIONING DOUGH IN A TART PAN

1. CAREFULLY LAY THE DOUGH OVER THE ROLLING PIN AND POSITION OVER THE PAN.

2. CENTER IT AND GENTLY FIT IT INTO THE PAN BY PRESSING IT INTO THE PAN, WITHOUT STRETCHING IT!

3. FOLD THE EXCESS DOUGH INSIDE EDGE OF PAN SO THAT THE SIDES ARE SLIGHTLY THICKER.

4. PRESS THE DOUGH UP AND OVER THE SIDES SO THE THICKNESS IS EVEN THROUGHOUT.

5. ROLL THE ROLLING PIN OVER THE TOP OF THE PAN TO TRIM OFF ANY EXCESS DOUGH.

Figure 3-5:
Follow these instructions when placing the dough in the pan.

You may want to fill a prebaked tart or pie shell with a prepared sweet or savory filling. If you bake the empty tart without anything in it, the pastry will shrink from the sides of the pan, and the bottom will bubble up. To keep this from happening, the crust must be *baked blind.* To do so, prepare the dough up through Step 7 in the Savory Tart Dough recipe, earlier in this chapter, and then continue as follows (see Figure 3-6):

1. **Prick the bottom of the chilled unbaked tart shell with a fork at ½-inch intervals.**

2. **Line the tart with a sheet of aluminum foil, pressing it against the sides of the pan.**

3. **Fill the tart shell with dried beans or rice, which will hold the dough to the sides of the pan.**

4. **Bake in a 400-degree oven for 8 minutes, or until the crust appears set. Carefully remove the foil and beans or rice from the pan. (Because you can't cook these beans or rice for eating, save them in a jar or plastic bag for other recipes that call for baking blind.)**

5. **Prick the bottom of the tart with a fork and continue baking for 3 to 5 minutes, or until the crust is lightly golden brown.**

6. **Remove from the oven and cool to room temperature before filling.**

Book III

French Cooking

BLIND BAKING PIE OR TART SHELLS

1. PRICK THE BOTTOM OF THE CHILLED UNBAKED TART SHELL WITH A FORK, ABOUT ½" APART.

2. LINE THE TART WITH A SHEET OF ALUMINUM FOIL, PRESSING IT AGAINST THE SIDES OF THE PAN.

3. FILL IT WITH DRIED BEANS OR RICE. THIS HOLDS THE DOUGH TO THE SIDES OF THE PAN.

4. BAKE IN A 400° OVEN FOR 8 MINUTES, OR UNTIL CRUST APPEARS SET. CAREFULLY REMOVE FOIL AND BEANS OR RICE FROM THE PAN.

5. PRICK THE BOTTOM OF THE TART WITH A FORK AND CONTINUE BAKING 3-5 MINUTES, OR UNTIL CRUST IS A LIGHT, GOLDEN BROWN.

6. REMOVE FROM THE OVEN. COOL TO ROOM TEMPERATURE BEFORE FILLING.

Figure 3-6:
Blind baking of tart or pie shells.

Chapter 4

First Impressions

A home-cooked meal in France usually con-sists of three to four courses, including sea-sonal fruit at the end of the meal. Although this may sound like a lot of work, it really isn't. The dif-ferent dishes are usually nothing too complicated, perhaps some soup, followed by grilled meat or fish served with a sauce or just a squeeze of fresh lemon, a green salad, crispy bread, and some fruit to finish things up.

As you see from the selection of recipes I've chosen for you in this chapter, the opening courses of a French meal are very straightforward and should complement the ensuing courses. The nice thing about these recipes is that some of them are hardy enough to stand on their own as an entrée for lunch or even a light supper. Sometimes nothing suits me better on a summer's evening than a *salade niçoise,* the perfect one-dish meal of steamed green beans and potatoes, quar-tered hard-boiled eggs, vine-ripened tomatoes, cucumbers, and olives, drizzled with vinaigrette. At other times, I want an al fresco dinner of thin slices of hearty *terrine paysanne,* served on sliced bread spread with Dijon mustard, and a tossed green salad with tomatoes from my garden. And I can't remember the number of times I've satisfied my hunger with a bowl or two of thick, vegetable *potage* on a cool fall evening.

Opening the Meal

A good meal should always start with just a little something to open up your appetite. Nothing too much, just enough to set the stage for the rest of the meal and to accompany *l'apéritif,* a glass of wine or beer, or perhaps home-made fruit-flavored fortified wine. At times, a small dish of briny olives will suffice or, better yet, some *tapénade,* a chopped olive spread from the south of France. Of the hundreds of possibilities, I've chosen three of my favorite recipes to share with you, including the light-as-air *gougères*.

Black Olive Spread (Tapénade)

Full of the sun-ripened Mediterranean flavors of Provence, *tapénade* comes from the Provençal word *tapéna* or capers, one of the briny-flavored ingredients used to make this spread. *Tapénade* is usually spread on toasted slices of country bread. I also like to place spoonfuls of the spread on small, unpeeled new potatoes boiled in salted water and then cut in half.

Preparation time: *10 minutes*

Yield: *Approximately 1¼ cups*

6 anchovies	*1 clove garlic, crushed*
2 cups pitted kalamata olives, drained	*6 tablespoons olive oil*
1 tablespoon capers, drained	*Salt and pepper to taste*
1 teaspoon Dijon mustard	

1 Place the anchovies, olives, capers, Dijon mustard, and garlic in a food processor. Process to a thick puree.

2 With the processor running, add the olive oil through the feed tube until just incorporated.

3 Season with salt and pepper.

Cheese Puffs (Gougères)

Highly addictive, *gougères* are light-as-air cheese puffs made with *pâté-à-chou,* the same type of dough used to make cream puffs. The size of Ping-Pong balls, *gougères* are quite easy to make and are wonderful served with predinner drinks or a glass of wine.

Preparation time: *10 minutes*

Cooking time: *20 minutes*

Yield: *Approximately 3 dozen*

1 cup water	*¼ teaspoon ground nutmeg*
5 tablespoons unsalted butter	*1 cup all-purpose flour*
1 teaspoon salt	*5 eggs, at room temperature*
¼ teaspoon pepper	*1 cup grated Gruyère or Swiss cheese*

1 Preheat the oven to 425 degrees.

2 Bring the water, butter, salt, pepper, and nutmeg to a boil in a medium-sized saucepan. Remove from the heat when the butter melts.

3 Add the flour and beat with a wooden spoon until the mixture comes away from the sides of the bowl, forming a thick, almost gluelike substance.

4 Stir in the cheese. Add 4 of the eggs, one at a time, beating until thoroughly incorporated into the dough. Beat the dough with a stiff spoon until shiny and firm. This takes some endurance on your part, but it's well worth the effort.

5 Drop well-rounded teaspoonfuls onto a greased baking sheet. Beat the remaining egg with ½ tablespoon water. Brush the tops of the cheese puffs with the egg wash.

6 Bake in the upper third of the oven for approximately 20 minutes or until the puffs are golden brown and doubled in size. Remove from the oven and serve immediately.

Tip: You can make gougères beforehand, freeze them, and then bake them at a later date. Simply prepare the recipe up to Step 5 and place the baking sheet in the freezer. When frozen, place the cheese puffs in a large plastic freezer bag. Bake the frozen cheese puffs according to Step 6. The baking time will be 5 to 7 minutes longer for frozen puffs.

Book III

French Cooking

Country Pâté (Terrine Paysanne)

Most French home cooks have their favorite tried-and-true recipe for *pâté,* a combination of ground or chopped meats, perhaps mixed with liver, herbs, and wine. After the ingredients are mixed together, they're packed into a loaf pan or porcelain *terrine* (a traditional oval, covered dish) and baked in hot water so that the outside doesn't form a browned exterior. Weighting and chilling the cooked *pâté* makes it firm and easier to slice.

Pâté is usually served as an appetizer or light meal. Thinly slice it and serve with tomato slices, *cornichons* (tiny French dill pickles), tiny pickled onions, slices of country bread (characterized by a good chewy crumb and a crisp crust), and Dijon mustard.

Preparation time: *Total of 24 hours (15 minutes actual preparation time, plus resting and overnight refrigeration)*

Cooking time: *1½ to 2 hours*

Yield: *8 to 10 servings*

1 pound ground pork	½ teaspoon mace, nutmeg, or allspice
1 pound ground veal	¼ teaspoon dried oregano
1 pound smoked pork shoulder butt, cut into ¼-inch dice	1 teaspoon salt
1 clove garlic, minced	½ teaspoon coarsely ground black pepper
6 juniper berries, chopped (optional)	½ cup dry white wine
1 teaspoon dried basil	2 tablespoons brandy or cognac
½ teaspoon dried thyme	6 to 8 strips lean bacon
½ teaspoon dried marjoram	2 large bay leaves

1 In a large mixing bowl, combine the ground pork, veal, pork butt, garlic, juniper berries (if desired), basil, thyme, marjoram, mace, oregano, salt, and pepper with both hands until the mixture is well combined and uniform. Add the wine and brandy. Mix well until the liquids are incorporated.

2 Line the bottom of a 6- to 7-cup loaf pan with 2 to 3 strips of the bacon. Spoon the *pâté* mixture into the pan. Pack down well so that there are no air pockets and the top is flat and smooth. Lay the bay leaves on top of the meat and pat down. Lay the remaining bacon strips on top of the pâté and refrigerate for 1 hour.

3 Preheat the oven to 350 degrees. Place the terrine in a larger baking pan. Place in the lower third of the oven. Fill the baking pan with boiling water so that it comes halfway up the sides of the terrine. Bake for 1½ to 2 hours. The *pâté* is done when it has shrunk from the sides of the pan and the surrounding liquid is clear yellow and not pink.

4 Remove the terrine from the water bath. Pour off any liquid from the terrine. Leave the *pâté* in the pan. Place a piece of folded foil on top. Place an unopened bottle of wine or a medium-sized can on its side on top of the *pâté* and press down. Cool to room temperature. Refrigerate overnight. Remove and discard the bacon and bay leaves before serving.

5 Cut into thin slices and serve on slices of country bread, toasted if desired, with Dijon mustard.

Ladling It Out: Classic French Soups

From golden-yellow chicken consommé to thick vegetable *potage,* the French hold soup in high regard. As is the case with most cuisines with close agricultural ties, the type of soup made depends on what fresh, locally grown vegetables are available at the market. Soup made with peas and lettuce is a classic spring soup, whereas leek and potato soup is a favorite in the fall, when these vegetables have made their way to market.

Enjoyed daily in many homes as an opening course, the four recipes that follow are true French classics.

Onion Soup (Soupe à l'Oignon)

Real, homemade *soupe à l'oignon* is probably the one soup most associated with French cooking. But genuine homemade onion soup has nothing in common with the packaged, dehydrated variety you're probably familiar with or, for that matter, the clumpy, cheesy impostor that most restaurants serve.

Preparation time: *15 minutes*

Cooking time: *90 minutes*

Yield: *6 servings*

Book III

French
Cooking

3 tablespoons unsalted butter	*⅔ cup dry sherry or white vermouth*
1 tablespoon olive oil	*4 cups beef stock or broth*
6 cups thinly sliced Spanish or Vidalia onions	*Salt and pepper to taste*
4 cloves garlic, thinly sliced	*12 slices hard-toasted French bread*
1 tablespoon dried thyme	*1 cup grated Gruyère or Swiss cheese*

1 Heat the butter and olive oil in a large saucepan over medium heat. Add the onions and garlic. Cover and cook over low heat for 15 minutes. Remove the lid and cook, stirring occasionally, for an additional 30 to 35 minutes, or until the onions are caramelized and a light golden brown,.

2 Add the thyme and sherry. Bring to a boil and cook for 2 minutes. Add the stock and bring to a boil. Lower the heat and simmer, covered, for 30 minutes. Season with salt and pepper.

3 Place 2 pieces of bread in each serving bowl. Ladle the soup over the bread. Serve with grated cheese.

Potato and Leek Soup (Potage Parmentier)

Potatoes and leeks were meant to be cooked together, as you can see in the recipe for this popular soup. Much simpler and humbler than its American counterpart, *vichyssoise,* this original version is simplicity at its best.

Preparation time: *10 minutes*

Cooking time: *45 minutes*

Yield: *6 to 8 servings*

1 pound all-purpose potatoes, peeled and diced

1 pound leeks, trimmed and washed well to remove dirt and grit; white and light green parts only (see Figure 4-1), thinly sliced

8 cups chicken broth

1 tablespoon salt

2 tablespoons minced parsley

2 tablespoons unsalted butter

4 tablespoons heavy cream

1 Combine the potatoes, leeks, broth, and salt in a large saucepan. Bring to a boil over high heat. Lower to a simmer and cook, partially covered, for 40 minutes.

2 Mash the potatoes and leeks against the side of the pot with a large spoon. Taste and add salt if necessary.

3 Before serving, stir in the parsley, butter, and cream.

Vary It! *This soup can be used as a master recipe for other vegetable soups. Try adding any of the following vegetables or a combination: 1 packed cup watercress leaves, ½ to 1 cup sliced or diced carrots, small cut string beans, cauliflower, or broccoli broken into small florets.*

Cleaning & Trimming Leeks

Figure 4-1: Preparing leeks for use.

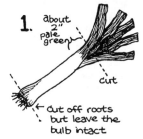
1. about 2" pale green
cut
cut off roots but leave the bulb intact

2. slit in half
still intact

3. rinse under running cold water
I'm gonna wash that grit right outta my leeks...

Split Pea Soup
(Potage Saint-Germain)

Split pea soup is comfort food. This humble soup is so satisfying and nourishing that I enjoy eating it best on a cold winter's night with a loaf of chewy country white or rye bread, a perfectly ripened pear, and a handful of walnuts. Split peas are readily available at the supermarket in the section where dried beans and legumes are sold.

Preparation time: *10 minutes*

Cooking time: *1 hour and 15 minutes to 2 hours and 15 minutes*

Yield: *6 to 8 servings*

2 tablespoons unsalted butter	1 small ham bone (optional)
1 medium onion, finely chopped	1 bay leaf
1 carrot, finely chopped	1 teaspoon dried marjoram
2 stalks celery, finely chopped	1 cup dry white wine
1 small turnip, peeled and finely chopped	5 cups water
1 clove garlic, finely chopped	Salt and pepper to taste
1 cup split peas	½ cup crème fraîche or sour cream

1 Melt the butter in a large saucepan over medium heat. Add the onion, carrot, celery, turnip, and garlic. Cook for about 10 to 15 minutes or until the vegetables are soft.

2 Add the split peas, ham bone (if desired), bay leaf, marjoram, wine, and water and bring to a boil. Cover and simmer until the peas are soft and falling apart. This can take anywhere from as little as 60 minutes up to 2 hours, depending on the split peas.

3 Remove and discard the ham bone and bay leaf. Season with the salt and pepper. Stir in the crème fraîche before serving.

Tip: *Crème fraîche is a fermented cream similar to sour cream — but at the same time very different. It is used in France to smooth out soups and sauces and is served drizzled over fresh fruit sprinkled with sugar. Homemade crème fraîche is easy to make. In a mixing bowl or 2-cup glass measuring cup, whisk together 2 cups heavy cream and 3 tablespoons cultured buttermilk. Cover with a clean dish towel and let sit at room temperature for 12 to 24 hours, or until the mixture thickens. Pour into a clean jar and refrigerate. Use within 10 days.*

Book III

French Cooking

Tomato Soup (Potage à la Tomate)

This soup is typical of most French seasonal soups. So rich in tomato flavor, it must have been created by a farmer's wife to take advantage of an overabundance of sun-ripened tomatoes at the end of the summer. Thickened with other vegetables, this soup is the essence of summer.

Preparation time: *15 minutes*

Cooking time: *30 minutes*

Yield: *6 to 8 servings*

4 large vine-ripened tomatoes, cored, seeded, and coarsely chopped

2 medium russet potatoes, peeled and diced

2 medium onions, chopped

2 cloves garlic, peeled and crushed

3 sprigs fresh flat-leaf parsley

2 sprigs fresh thyme or ½ teaspoon dried thyme

1 bay leaf

½ teaspoon salt

4 cups water

Pepper

2 tablespoons crème fraîche (see the information at the end of the Split Pea Soup recipe, earlier in this chapter) or sour cream

1 Combine the tomatoes, potatoes, onions, garlic, parsley, thyme, bay leaf, salt, and water in a saucepan and bring to a boil over medium-high heat. Reduce the heat and simmer for approximately 30 minutes, or until the vegetables are soft.

2 Either pass the soup through a food mill into another saucepan, or remove and discard the parsley, thyme, and bay leaf and puree in a blender.

3 Season with salt and pepper to taste. Stir in the crème fraîche or sour cream before serving.

Getting Your Greens and Veggies: Salads

In France, salads are served either before the entree or after it. Vegetables such as leeks, beets, and baby artichokes can be cooked, chilled, and served with a vinaigrette as a first course, sort of the vegetable served before the entree. On the other hand, just when you think you can't take another bite, a tossed green salad is usually served as a way of aiding digestion.

Many French salads are dressed with a simple vinaigrette, as found in Chapter 3 of Book III. This simple, uncomplicated mixture of extra-virgin olive oil and wine vinegar lets the produce flavors shine through.

Leeks in Vinaigrette
(Poireaux à la Vinaigrette)

Leeks are called the poor man's asparagus in Europe. A member of the allium or onion family, they look like thick scallions but have a sweeter, milder flavor. Because this salad is somewhat more substantial than tossed greens, I like serving it before a savory tart, such as a quiche, or a simple egg omelet.

Preparation time: *15 minutes*

Cooking time: *10 minutes*

Yield: *4 to 6 servings*

2 teaspoons salt

3 pounds whole leeks, trimmed and washed well to remove dirt and grit; white and light green parts only (refer to Figure 4-1)

½ cup vinaigrette (see Chapter 3 of Book III)

3 hard-boiled eggs

2 tablespoons minced flat-leaf parsley

Book III

French Cooking

1 Fill a 6-quart saucepan halfway with water. Bring to a boil and add the salt. Tie the leeks into bunches with kitchen string. Place in the pot of boiling water, reduce the heat, and simmer, covered, for 10 minutes.

2 Remove the cooked leeks with tongs and drain well in a colander.

3 Remove the string and place the leeks on a serving platter.

4 Remove the yolks from the hard-boiled eggs. Slightly mash the yolks with a fork and stir into the vinaigrette. Coarsely chop the egg whites and set aside.

5 Drizzle the vinaigrette over the leeks and then sprinkle the parsley over them. Top with the chopped egg whites.

Lentil Salad (Salade de Lentils)

Lentils are a favorite dried legume in France and contain more protein than meat does. They're used to make thick *potage* or an earthy salad such as this one. I particularly like to serve this salad with grilled garlic sausage as the people do in the Alsace region of France.

Preparation time: *15 minutes*

Cooking time: *20 to 30 minutes*

Yield: *4 to 6 servings*

1 pound du Puy or other small green lentils, picked over and rinsed

1 medium onion, peeled

6 sprigs parsley

1 bay leaf

½ cup vinaigrette (see Chapter 3 of Book III)

2 tablespoons Dijon mustard

Salt and pepper to taste

3 shallots, peeled and thickly sliced

1 Put the lentils in a saucepan with the onion, parsley, and bay leaf. Cover with enough cold water so that the water is 1 inch above the lentils. Bring to a boil. Reduce the heat to a simmer and cook, covered, until the lentils are tender. The exact cooking time will depend on the lentils, but you can figure about 20 to 30 minutes. Drain and discard the onion, parsley, and bay leaf. Return the lentils to the pot.

2 Combine the vinaigrette and Dijon mustard. Toss the lentils with the vinaigrette. Add the shallots and toss. Season with salt and pepper. Mound on a small platter or serving bowl and serve at room temperature.

Belgian Endive and Walnut Salad
(Salade de Chicorèe à l'Huile de Noix)

Growing endive is a two part process. First, the farmer plants and grows chicory, a bitter green that grows in bunches with very curly leaves. After the chicory is pulled from the soil, the root is cut off and planted in buckets or boxes of moist, very sandy soil and left to grow in a dark room. Eventually, the root produces a tightly closed bud, which is the endive.

Walnut oil is highly prized in France for its mild, nutty flavor that pairs so well with the fresh, bitter flavor and crispness of endive.

Preparation time: *15 minutes*

Cooking time: *10 minutes*

Yield: *4 to 6 servings*

3 heads Belgian endive	*Salt and pepper to taste*
2 tablespoons freshly squeezed lemon juice	*¼ cup toasted walnut pieces (see the tip at the end of the recipe)*
2 tablespoons walnut oil	

1 Remove and discard any discolored outer leaves from the endive. Halve the heads of endive lengthwise and cut out the bottom core. Cut vertically into ½-inch pieces.

2 Place the endive in a salad bowl. Toss with the lemon juice and walnut oil. Season with salt and pepper.

3 Sprinkle with the toasted walnuts and serve.

Tip: The easiest way to toast walnuts is in a skillet on top of the stove. Place a single layer of nuts in an appropriately sized pan. Heat over medium heat. Because you don't want the nuts to brown too much and become bitter, pay close attention and turn once when they begin to brown on one side. Remove from the heat when browned evenly on both sides. Let them cool to room temperature before using.

Book III

French Cooking

Curly Chicory and Poached Egg Salad with Bacon Vinaigrette (Salade Frisée aux Lardons)

This typical bistro salad is a popular working man's lunch. Because it contains ample protein from the egg and bacon and lots of vitamin-rich chicory, it can easily be served as an entrée for lunch or dinner, as well as a substantial salad preceding a light entrée such as grilled fish or chicken.

Preparation time: *15 minutes*

Cooking time: *10 minutes*

Yield: *4 servings*

1½ pounds curly chicory/endive or 2 small heads frisée lettuce

4 poached eggs (see Figure 4-2)

½ pound lean, thick-cut bacon, cut into ½-inch pieces

1 tablespoon extra-virgin olive oil

3 shallots, minced

5 tablespoons red wine vinegar

Salt and pepper to taste

1 Remove the light green or yellow-white leaves from the center of the chicory or *frisée.* Set aside and use the dark green leaves for another salad. Cut the center leaves into bite-sized pieces. Place an equal amount in 4 salad or soup bowls. Place a poached egg on top of each salad.

2 Place the bacon and oil in a large skillet. Cook over medium-high heat until the bacon is crisp. Add the shallots and cook for 30 seconds. Add the vinegar and cook a minute longer; then remove from the heat.

3 Divide the bacon evenly among the 4 salads. Spoon some of the vinaigrette from the skillet over each salad. Season with salt and pepper. Serve immediately.

Tip: *Poached eggs make for a quick and easy lunch or supper, especially if you happen to have some leftover cheese sauce, hollandaise sauce, or béarnaise sauce (all in Chapter 3 of Book III). Place the poached eggs on toast and spoon the warmed sauce on top. You also can serve the eggs over sautéed spinach.*

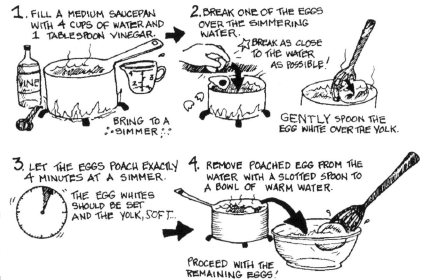

POACHING EGGS

1. FILL A MEDIUM SAUCEPAN WITH 4 CUPS OF WATER AND 1 TABLESPOON VINEGAR.

BRING TO A SIMMER

2. BREAK ONE OF THE EGGS OVER THE SIMMERING WATER.

BREAK AS CLOSE TO THE WATER AS POSSIBLE!

GENTLY SPOON THE EGG WHITE OVER THE YOLK.

3. LET THE EGGS POACH EXACTLY 4 MINUTES AT A SIMMER.

THE EGG WHITES SHOULD BE SET AND THE YOLK, SOFT...

4. REMOVE POACHED EGG FROM THE WATER WITH A SLOTTED SPOON TO A BOWL OF WARM WATER.

PROCEED WITH THE REMAINING EGGS!

Figure 4-2:
Poaching
eggs.

Book III

French Cooking

Potato Salad (Salade de Pommes de Terre)

This simple-to-make French potato salad is a delicious departure from the all-too-familiar mayonnaise variety. Cooking the potatoes in white wine and vinegar infuses them with even more flavor as they cook.

Preparation time: *15 minutes*

Cooking time: *20 minutes*

Yield: *4 to 6 servings*

2 pounds small red or new potatoes, pricked twice with a fork

1½ cups dry white wine

¼ cup white wine vinegar

1 teaspoon salt

1 small onion, finely chopped

4 tablespoons extra-virgin olive oil

2 tablespoons chopped flat-leaf Italian parsley

Salt and pepper to taste

1 Place the potatoes in a large pot with the white wine, vinegar, and salt. Bring to a boil and cook, covered, until tender, about 15 to 20 minutes.

2 Remove the potatoes with a slotted spoon to a serving bowl. Cut them into quarters. Sprinkle with the onion.

3 Bring the cooking liquid to a boil and reduce by half. Pour into a small bowl. Add the olive oil and parsley and whisk together. Season with salt and pepper. Pour over the potatoes and toss well. Serve warm.

Mediterranean Vegetable Salad (Salade Niçoise)

This dish, which originated in Nice, is one of my favorite entrée salads to make and eat on unbearably hot summer days. Because each vegetable is displayed on a bed of lettuce, you want to use the best-quality ingredients possible.

Preparation time: *20 minutes*

Cooking time: *20 minutes*

Yield: *4 to 6 servings*

1 pound green beans, trimmed and cut into 1½-inch pieces

1 pound small red or new potatoes, scrubbed well

4 eggs

1 large head Boston or green leaf lettuce, washed and dried

2 cans (7 ounces each) tuna packed in olive oil or vegetable oil

1 pint cherry tomatoes

1 cucumber, peeled and cut into ¼-inch slices

½ cup Niçoise or other brine-cured black olives

1 small red onion, cut into rings

¼ teaspoon dried thyme

½ cup vinaigrette

Salt and pepper to taste

1 Bring a large pot of water to a boil. Add the greens beans and cook until tender, about 4 to 5 minutes. Remove with a slotted spoon to a colander. Add the potatoes and eggs to the hot water and cook until the potatoes are tender, about 12 to 15 minutes. Remove with a slotted spoon to a colander and set the potatoes aside to cool. Peel and quarter the hard-boiled eggs and set aside.

2 Line a large serving platter or dish with the lettuce. Mound the cooled green beans on one half of the platter and the potatoes on the other. Mound the tuna in the center. Place the eggs, tomatoes, cucumbers, and black olives around the beans and potatoes. Place the onion slices on top of the salad.

3 Add the thyme to the vinaigrette and drizzle over the salad. Sprinkle with the salt and pepper. Serve immediately.

Book III

French Cooking

Chapter 5

The Main Event

In This Chapter

- Experimenting with egg dishes
- Turning out tempting tarts
- Concocting casseroles and gratins
- Seasoning meat, poultry, and seafood with a touch of France

The entrée, the center of the French meal, can vary dramatically from a piece of flaky-crusted quiche to a bowl of succulent lamb stew, depending on what you're in the mood for or what happens to catch your eye at the market that morning. The French know how to approach high-quality ingredients with the respect they deserve. From early on, home cooks are taught how to coax the flavor out of a cut of meat or piece of fish without overworking it. French food is definitely not a meat-and-potatoes cuisine, so things like egg dishes, savory tarts, and casseroles are also enjoyed as a main course, especially when matched with a complementing soup or salad.

Drawing from hundreds of possibilities, I have assembled a basic repertoire of tried-and-true recipes that a French home cook might draw from time and time again when cooking for friends and family.

Enjoying Eggs at Any Time of the Day

Although most Americans consider eggs as mainly breakfast food, the people of France enjoy eggs as a lunchtime entrée or as part of a light supper.

They're prepared simply, as an omelet with or without minced fresh herbs, or dressed up with the addition of cooked vegetables, meat, or even seafood. You also find eggs used in classic French dishes such as quiches and other savory tarts and soufflés.

When cooking with eggs, always use the freshest ones possible for best flavor and texture. If you have the good fortune to have access to free-range eggs from a local farm or farm stand, by all means go to the trouble and effort of purchasing them. Although they're a few cents more expensive, you'll be amazed how much more yellow the yolks are and how much clearer and less cloudy the whites seem.

Rolled Omelet with Herbs (Omelette aux Fines Herbes)

One of the first things a new cook learns how to make in a French kitchen is a basic rolled omelet. Plain or seasoned with herbs, the perfectly cooked omelet should be puffy and light.

Preparation time: *10 minutes*

Cooking time: *5 minutes*

Yield: *2 servings*

3 eggs	*Salt and pepper to taste*
1 tablespoon finely chopped fresh herbs, such as flat-leaf parsley and chives	*2 tablespoons unsalted butter*

1 Break the eggs into a shallow soup bowl. Beat with the herbs and salt and pepper. Add 1 tablespoon of the butter, cut into small pieces.

2 Melt the remaining tablespoon of butter in a small nonstick skillet over medium heat. Swirl the butter around the pan to evenly coat the bottom and sides.

3 When the butter melts, pour the beaten egg mixture into the hot pan. Quickly stir the eggs a couple of times so that they heat quickly. Let the mixture fill the bottom of the pan. Gentle lift the set eggs up from one side of the pan and begin rolling, or turning the omelet over itself, at least 3 times.

4 Tilt the pan away from you so that the omelet rests along one side of the pan. Once the omelet takes its shape and stays rolled, tilt the pan toward you to cook it on the other side. Remove and serve immediately.

Open-Faced Omelet with Peppers, Tomatoes, and Ham (Pipérade)

There's no denying that the origin of this hearty egg entrée is in the Basque region of France, which borders Spain. Basque cooking is known for its extensive use of peppers, onions, garlic, and tomatoes, as well as its excellent air-cured country ham, all of which join together in this delicious dish.

Preparation time: *10 minutes*

Cooking time: *30 minutes*

Yield: *4 servings*

4 slices prosciutto

2 tablespoons olive oil

2 red bell peppers, cored, seeded, and diced (see Figure 5-1)

1 green bell pepper, cored, seeded, and diced

1 large onion, sliced

1 clove garlic, thinly sliced

Salt and pepper to taste

14½-ounce can diced tomatoes

8 eggs

1 Heat a large nonstick skillet over medium heat. Warm each slice of prosciutto in the pan until it just begins to curl. Remove and place each slice on a dinner plate.

2 Heat the olive oil in the skillet over medium-high heat. Add the red and green peppers, onion, and garlic. Cook until soft, about 10 to 12 minutes. Season with salt and pepper. Add the tomatoes, cover, and cook over low heat for 10 minutes. Uncover and cook over high heat to evaporate any liquid. Taste and season with salt and pepper. Return heat to low.

3 Beat the eggs together in a mixing bowl. Season lightly with salt. Pour over the hot vegetables in the skillet. Stir to combine. Continue cooking until the eggs set, as if they were scrambled.

4 Spoon the eggs and vegetables over the ham and serve immediately.

Book III

French Cooking

How to Core and Seed a Pepper

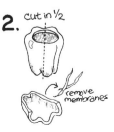

1. cut out stem

twist and pull out

2. cut in ½

remove membranes

3. Cut into lengthwise strips

4. For cubes, hold strips together and cut crosswise

Figure 5-1: Coring and seeding a bell pepper.

Having a Tart-to-Tart Talk

Tarts, both savory and sweet, are extremely popular in France. Regional differences also dictate the ingredients the home cook will use in tarts, which traditionally are made with a flaky crust and a smooth custard filling. For example, vine-ripened tomatoes and caramelized onions take the place of egg custard in the warm Mediterranean climate of Provence, while hearty, chewy bread dough is used in the Franco-Teutonic-influenced region of Alsace. Regardless of the method or ingredients, the results are delectable!

Cheese Tart (*Quiche au Fromage*)

Real men do indeed eat quiche in France. In fact, this savory, easy-to-make custard tart is a favorite entrée to prepare with whatever ingredients home cooks have on hand, including cheese, vegetables, and cured meat. Quiches are also a popular picnic food to make beforehand and eat at room temperature on a day out in the countryside or at an evening, open-air concert in the city.

Preparation time: *15 minutes, plus 3½ hours for pastry preparation, including 3 hours chilling time*

Cooking time: *30 minutes*

Yield: *6 to 8 servings*

Savory Tart Dough (see Chapter 3 of Book III)

2 eggs

3 tablespoons all-purpose flour

2 cups heavy cream

Salt and pepper to taste

2 cups (8 ounces) grated Gruyére or Swiss cheese

1 Prepare the Savory Tart Dough and bake blind.

2 As the pastry bakes, prepare the quiche filling. In a large mixing bowl, beat together the eggs. Add the flour and heavy cream and beat until smooth. Season with salt and pepper.

3 Sprinkle the cheese on the bottom of the prebaked pastry shell. Cover with the custard mixture and place on a rack in the upper third of the oven.

4 Bake at 400 degrees for 25 to 30 minutes or until the filling is set. Remove from the oven and let cool for at least 15 minutes before serving.

Vary It! *The great thing about quiche is that you can use an endless variety of different fillings. Some of my favorites are the following:*

Quiche Lorraine: Substitute the cheese with 8 slices of the thick-cut bacon diced and cooked until fat is rendered, but not crisp. Drain on a paper towel. Continue with Step 3.

Spinach Quiche (Quiche aux Éspinards): Substitute 1 cup of steamed, chopped spinach, drained well, for 1 cup of the cheese. Continue with Step 3.

Mushroom Quiche (Quiche aux Chapmpignons): Substitute 8 ounces sliced mushrooms, sautéed in butter, for 1 cup of the cheese. Continue with Step 3.

Tomato, Olive, and Anchovy Tart (Pissaladière)

True to their Mediterranean roots, the French of Provence shy away from using heat-sensitive fresh dairy products in their cooking, relying more on olive oil, vegetables, and cured fish, as in this fabulous *pissaladière*.

Preparation time: *15 minutes, plus 3½ hours for pastry preparation, including 3 hours chilling time*

Cooking time: *40 minutes*

Yield: *6 to 8 servings*

Savory Tart Dough (see Chapter 3 of Book III)	Salt and pepper to taste
4 tablespoons olive oil, plus additional for drizzling	3 medium tomatoes, thinly sliced
	8 anchovy fillets
2 pounds onions, thinly sliced	16 oil-cured black olives
2 cloves garlic, thinly sliced	
½ teaspoon dried thyme	

1 Prepare the Savory Tart Dough and bake blind.

2 As the pastry bakes, prepare the *pissaladière* filling. Heat the olive oil in a large skillet over medium heat. Add the onions and garlic and cook until soft and golden brown, about 20 minutes. Add the thyme and season with salt and pepper.

3 Spread the onion mixture on the bottom of the prebaked pastry shell. Layer the tomatoes on top of the onions. Season with salt and pepper. Place the anchovy fillets on top of the tomatoes as if you're dividing the tart into wedges. Scatter the olives on top and lightly drizzle all over with olive oil. Place on a rack in the upper third of the oven.

4 Bake at 400 degrees for 15 minutes, or until the filling is set. Remove from the oven and let cool for at least 15 minutes before serving.

Book III

French
Cooking

Onion and Bacon Pie (Flammkuche)

Chewy like pizza, *flammkuche* is distinctly an Alsatian specialty with both French and German influences. Spread thick with sautéed onions, crème fraîche, and chunks of smoked bacon, this pie is especially good on a cold night along with bowls of potato-leek soup and a good pilsner beer.

Preparation time: *2 hours, including rising time for the dough*

Cooking time: *30 minutes*

Yield: *6 to 8 servings*

2 cups all-purpose flour	6 slices thick-cut smoked bacon, diced
1½ teaspoons salt	4 tablespoons unsalted butter
2 tablespoons vegetable oil	3 pounds onions, thinly sliced
1½ teaspoons active dry yeast	Salt and pepper to taste
¾ cup warm water	1 cup crème fraîche or sour cream

1 Combine the flour, salt, and oil in the bowl of a food processor. Add the yeast. With the motor running, pour the water through the small hole in the feed tube. Process until the dough forms a ball. Process 60 seconds longer.

2 Place the dough in a large greased mixing bowl. Cover and let rise 1 to 1½ hours, or until doubled in size.

3 Prepare the filling while the dough rises. Cook the bacon in a large skillet over medium-high heat until the fat is rendered but not browned. Remove the bacon and drain on paper towels. Add the butter. When melted, add the onions and cook until soft and golden, about 20 minutes. Remove from the pan to a large bowl with a slotted spoon, draining away most of the fat. Season with salt and pepper. Let cool for 30 minutes. Stir in the crème fraîche. (For information on crème fraîche, see the Split Pea Soup recipe in Chapter 4 of Book III.)

4 Punch down the risen dough. Lightly flour and roll out into a 12-inch circle. Place on a 12-inch pizza pan. Spread the onion mixture over the dough. Scatter the bacon on top. Let rise 30 minutes.

5 Preheat the oven to 375 degrees. Place the *flammkuche* on a rack in the upper third of the oven. Bake for 30 minutes, or until the bottom of the crust is golden brown. Remove from the oven and let cool for at least 15 minutes before serving.

Calling on Your Creativity: Casseroles and Gratins

I especially admire French cooks for their ability to go to food shopping without a grocery list and plan a day's meals based on whatever is available at the market. By stopping at the different market stands, they see a wonderful meal unfolding right before their very eyes!

Casseroles and gratins, small baked dishes of almost anything imaginable cooked in a sauce, are the mainstay of French cooking and let cooks use the very best ingredients they can find. Some dishes are destined to be served as side dishes, while others are hearty enough to stand on their own. You can see for yourself what I mean by trying the four very distinct dishes I've selected.

Casserole of Scallops (Coquilles St. Jacques)

What could be more special than an easy-to-prepare casserole of sea scallops poached in a wonderful white wine and cream sauce, dotted with bright green specks of chives? Serve with lots of crusty bread to sop up the sauce.

Book III

French Cooking

Preparation time: *5 minutes*

Cooking time: *30 minutes*

Yield: *4 servings*

2 tablespoons unsalted butter	*½ cup heavy cream*
4 shallots, thinly sliced	*Salt and pepper to taste*
1 tablespoon plus 1 teaspoon flour	*1½ pounds sea scallops*
1 cup dry vermouth	*¼ cup snipped chives*
1 teaspoon Dijon mustard	

1 Preheat the oven to 500 degrees.

2 Melt the butter in a small saucepan over medium heat. Add the shallots and cook until soft. Stir in the flour. When the flour begins to foam, stir in the vermouth and mustard. Cook until the sauce thickens, about 4 to 6 minutes. Add the cream and season with salt and pepper. Cook until the sauce is heated through.

3 Place the scallops in a small Dutch oven or other covered baking dish. Spoon the sauce over the scallops. Cover and bake on the center oven rack for 10 minutes.

4 Remove from the oven. Stir in the chives and serve immediately.

Eggplant Casserole (Ratatouille)

Ratatouille, a hearty vegetable casserole from the Provence region of France, is made with the brightly colored and flavorful vegetables the area is known for. This dish is hearty enough to be served as a main course with salad, cheese, and thick slices of country bread or as a side dish with grilled meat, poultry, or fish.

Preparation time: *20 minutes*

Cooking time: *35 minutes*

Yield: *4 to 6 servings*

1 medium eggplant, peeled and diced (see Figure 5-2)

Salt and pepper to taste

5 tablespoons olive oil

1 medium zucchini, quartered lengthwise and diced

1 red bell pepper, cored, seeded, and diced

1 green bell pepper, cored, seeded, and diced

1 large onion, diced

2 cloves garlic, thinly sliced

14½-ounce can diced tomatoes

1 bay leaf

1 Place the eggplant in a colander. Sprinkle with salt and let sit for 30 minutes to drain off any acidity.

2 Heat 1 tablespoon of the olive oil in a large, covered skillet over medium-high heat. Add the zucchini and cook until soft, about 4 to 5 minutes. Season with salt and pepper. Place in a bowl and set aside.

3 Heat another 2 tablespoons of the olive oil in the skillet. Add the eggplant and cook until soft, 6 to 8 minutes. Place in the bowl with the zucchini.

4 Add the remaining 2 tablespoons of olive oil to the skillet. Add the red and green peppers, onion, and garlic and cook until soft. Add the diced tomatoes, season with salt and pepper, and cook for 5 minutes. Add the cooked zucchini, eggplant, and bay leaf. Cover and cook for 20 minutes over low heat. Remove the bay leaf. Taste and add salt and pepper if necessary.

Dicing an Eggplant

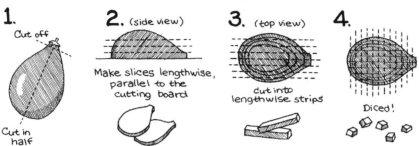

1. Cut off

Cut in half

2. (side view)

Make slices lengthwise, parallel to the cutting board

3. (top view)

cut into lengthwise strips

4.

Diced!

Figure 5-2:
Dicing an
eggplant.

Scalloped Potatoes (Gratin Dauphinois)

In almost any guise, potatoes are comfort food, especially when they're as creamy and cheesy as these French scalloped potatoes. Slice the potatoes as thin as possible before cooking in the milk, which will thicken almost immediately from the potato starch. These potatoes go especially well with roasted meats and poultry.

Preparation time: *15 minutes*

Cooking time: *60 minutes*

Yield: *4 to 6 servings*

2 pounds potatoes, peeled and thinly sliced	*1 teaspoon salt*
3½ cups milk	*¼ teaspoon pepper*
2 cloves garlic, peeled and minced	*½ cup coarsely grated Gruyère cheese*

1 Preheat the oven to 400 degrees. Butter a 2½-quart baking dish.

2 Combine the potatoes, milk, garlic, salt, and pepper in a large saucepan. Bring to a boil over medium-high heat.

3 Pour the potato mixture into the prepared baking dish and sprinkle with the grated cheese.

4 Place the dish on a baking sheet and bake on the center oven rack for 45 to 55 minutes, or until bubbly and golden brown.

5 Remove from the oven and let sit for 15 minutes before serving.

Book III

French
Cooking

Cauliflower Au Gratin (Chou-Fleur Gratiné)

A popular vegetable in France, cauliflower pairs extremely well when prepared *au gratin* in the oven with cheese sauce and crunchy, cheesy bread crumbs.

Preparation time: *15 minutes*

Cooking time: *45 minutes, including 15 to 20 minutes to cook the cauliflower, 10 minutes to cook the cheese sauce, and 25 minutes to bake*

Yield: *4 to 6 servings*

Cheese Sauce (see the Vary It! idea at the end of the Basic White Sauce recipe in Chapter 3 of Book III)	*2 tablespoons breadcrumbs mixed with 2 tablespoons grated Parmesan cheese*
1 medium cauliflower, trimmed, cut into florets, and cooked until tender	*2 tablespoons melted butter*

1 Preheat the oven to 375 degrees.

2 Spread one-third of the cheese sauce over the bottom of a 2-quart round or oval baking dish. Arrange the cauliflower in the dish and spoon the remaining sauce over it. Sprinkle with the breadcrumb mixture and drizzle with the melted butter.

3 Bake in the upper third of the oven for 20 to 25 minutes, or until bubbly and golden brown.

Grilling and Roasting Meat, Poultry, and Fish

Though perhaps not as carnivorous as their American counterparts, the French know how to perform wonders with even the lowliest cuts of meat. From simple pan frying or roasting to braising and stewing, French home cooks know the right methods to use to get the desired effect of fork-tender meat with as much flavor as possible. I include in this section some of the most popular classics from traditional French cooking, including hearty *boeuf bourguignonne* and *coq au vin,* as well as flaky whole fish cooked simply in a bed of salt.

Pan-Broiled Steak (Bifteck Sauté au Beurre)

These steaks are the perfect solution when short on time but big on hunger. Grilled in a quick minute or two on each side, these thin slices of tenderloin are then finished up with a simple *au jus* and butter sauce.

Preparation time: *10 minutes*

Cooking time: *15 minutes*

Yield: *4 to 6 servings*

4 thinly sliced beef tenderloin fillets, 6 ounces each

Salt and pepper

1½ cups Brown Sauce (see Chapter 3 of Book III)

Book III

French Cooking

1 Heat a heavy, large skillet, preferably cast iron, over high heat. Generously salt and pepper the steaks. Grill each steak a minute or two on each side, or until cooked as desired. Remove the steaks to a plate and cover to keep warm.

2 Add the Brown Sauce to the skillet. Bring to a quick boil, scraping the bottom of the skillet to remove any cooked-on particles.

3 Place each steak on a dinner plate. Spoon the sauce over each and serve immediately.

Roast Chicken (Poulet Rôti)

Every cuisine has its own version of roast chicken. Even browning and basting the bird ensures crispy skin and moist meat. In my opinion, roast chicken is the quintessential Sunday dinner entrée, which I like to serve with Scalloped Potatoes or Cauliflower Au Gratin (see the recipes earlier in this chapter) and a big green salad tossed in a vinaigrette.

Preparation time: *10 minutes*

Cooking time: *Approximately 1 hour and 30 minutes*

Yield: *4 to 6 servings*

3½- to 4-pound roasting chicken	1 small onion, chopped
Salt and pepper to taste	3 large shallots, thinly sliced
2 tablespoons unsalted butter	½ cup dry white wine
1 carrot, peeled and chopped	

1 Preheat the oven to 425 degrees.

2 Rinse the chicken under cold water and pat dry. Generously salt and pepper the cavity. Rub 1 tablespoon of butter on the breast skin. Generously salt and pepper the skin.

3 Place the chicken in a Dutch oven, breast side up. Scatter the carrots and onions around the chicken. Place on the center oven rack and roast for 15 minutes. Turn the chicken on the left breast and roast for 5 minutes, and then turn the chicken and roast on the right breast for 5 minutes. Place the chicken breast side up and baste with the pan juices. Lower the oven temperature to 350 degrees. Roast for 55 minutes longer, or when the juice runs clear when a thigh is pierced.

4 Place the chicken on a serving platter and cover with foil to keep warm. Remove and discard the carrots and onions. Pour the pan juices into a small bowl. Let the fat rise to the top and spoon off and discard all but 2 tablespoons of the fat, which you will place in the Dutch oven. Reserve the remaining cooking liquid.

5 Place the Dutch oven over medium heat. Add and cook the shallots in the 2 tablespoons of fat until soft. Add the wine to the pot. Bring to a quick boil, scraping the bottom of the pan to remove any cooked-on particles. Add the reserved pan juices. Boil until reduced by half.

6 Carve the chicken and serve with the sauce on the side.

Leg of Lamb (Gigot Rôti à la Moutarde)

Leave it to the French to know how to prepare such a humble cut of meat with so much flavor and aroma. The mustard seals in all the wonderful flavor of the lamb while at the same time keeping the meat tender and juicy. For maximum flavor, let the meat rest overnight with its mustard coating before roasting.

Preparation time: *10 minutes, plus at least 3 hours for the meat to rest before being roasted*

Cooking time: *Approximately 2 hours*

Yield: *4 to 6 servings*

Salt and pepper	1 teaspoon dried thyme
6-pound leg of lamb	2 carrots, chopped
½ cup Dijon mustard	1 large onion, chopped
2 cloves garlic, minced	1 cup beef or vegetable stock
1 tablespoon chopped rosemary needles, or 1 teaspoon dried rosemary	

1 Generously salt and pepper the lamb, rubbing the seasoning into the meat.

2 Combine the mustard, garlic, rosemary, and thyme in a small bowl. Brush over the leg of lamb. Place the meat in a roasting pan, cover with foil, and let the meat rest in the refrigerator at least 3 hours or overnight.

3 Preheat the oven to 450 degrees. Place the roasting pan in the center of the oven and roast for 20 minutes, turning and basting the meat every 5 minutes, or until it's browned all over.

4 Lower the heat to 350 degrees. Scatter the carrots and onions around the lamb and cook for 1¼ hours longer for medium rare or 1½ hours for well done.

5 Place the lamb on a serving platter and cover with foil to keep warm. Remove and discard the carrots and onions. Pour the pan juices into a small bowl. Let the fat rise to the top and spoon off. Reserve the remaining liquid.

6 Place a Dutch oven over medium heat. Add the stock to the pot. Bring to a quick boil, scraping the bottom of the pan to remove any cooked-on particles. Add the reserved pan liquid. Boil until reduced by half.

7 Carve the leg of lamb and serve with the sauce on the side.

Book III

French Cooking

Salt-Roasted Whole Fish (Le Poisson du Paludier)

Roasting fish in a shell of salt has been a popular cooking method for centuries. The salt absorbs the heat from the hot oven to cook the fish, which comes out moist and flaky with just the right about of saltiness. Don't skimp on the salt because the fish must be covered completely.

Preparation time: *30 minutes*

Cooking time: *20 minutes*

Yield: *4 servings*

4 whole fish, such as trout or sea bass, 1 pound each, cleaned with heads intact

Pepper

3 pounds kosher salt

16 bay leaves

Lemon wedges for serving

1 Preheat the oven to 400 degrees.

2 Rinse the fish under cold water and pat dry. Sprinkle the inside of the fish with pepper.

3 Cover the bottom of a 13-x-9-inch glass or ceramic baking dish with half the salt. Place 4 bay leaves in 2 rows where the fish will lie. Place the fish on top of the bay leaves. If necessary, trim the tails so that the fish fit in the pan.

4 Place the remaining bay leaves on top of the fish. Cover the fish with the remaining salt so that they're completely covered. Gently pat down.

5 Place the baking dish on the center rack of the oven and roast for 20 minutes.

6 Remove the fish from the oven. The salt will have formed a hard crust. Tap with a large metal cooking spoon to break and remove the top layer of salt. Check to see whether the fish are cooked. If not, return to the oven and cook for an additional 5 to 10 minutes.

7 Using two large spatulas, carefully lift the baked fish from the salt and place each on a serving plate. Carefully remove all the skin and any visible salt.

8 Lift the top fillet from each fish. Turn the fish over and remove the remaining fillet. Serve with the lemon wedges.

Savoring the Flavor of Stews

Popular since the days of hearth cooking, stews are still enjoyed today throughout all of France. Usually made with seasonal ingredients and inexpensive cuts
of meat or poultry that benefit from slow braising in a flavorful cooking liquid,
stews provide insight into the home cook's creativity and culinary skills.

Lamb Stew (Navarin d'Agneau)

Simplicity at its best, this stew benefits from very slow cooking, which makes the lamb
butter-tender and melting off the bone. Ask your butcher to cut the lamb into even-
sized pieces.

Preparation time: *15 minutes*

Cooking time: *2 hours*

Yield: *6 to 8 servings*

2 tablespoons olive oil

*3 to 3½ pounds lamb shoulder, cut into 2-inch
pieces*

Salt and pepper

1 medium onion, chopped

4 cloves garlic, minced

½ teaspoon dried thyme

1 bay leaf

1 cup water

4 carrots, peeled and chopped

2 cups frozen peas

1 Heat the olive oil in a Dutch oven over medium-high heat. Generously season the lamb
with salt and pepper. Add just enough lamb to cover the bottom of the pot and brown
on each side, about 10 minutes each. Remove the cooked meat to a large dish and
brown the remaining lamb in batches.

2 Return all the cooked meat and any accumulated juices to the pot. Add the onion, garlic,
and thyme and cook until the onion is soft. Add the bay leaf and water. Bring to a boil,
scraping the bottom of the pot to remove any cooked-on particles. Cover and simmer
for 1½ hours, or until the meat is tender.

3 Add the carrots and cook, covered, for 30 minutes. Add the peas and cook, covered,
20 minutes longer. Taste and, if necessary, season with salt and pepper before serving.

Book III

**French
Cooking**

Beef Stew (Boeuf Bourguignonne)

Perhaps the most famous of all stews, *boeuf bourguignonne* is chunks of beef that are browned and then slowly braised in red wine until the meat is fork-tender.

Preparation time: *20 minutes*

Cooking time: *Approximately 3 hours*

Yield: *4 to 6 servings*

2 tablespoons olive oil	*2 tablespoons all-purpose flour*
5 slices thick-cut bacon, cut into 1-inch pieces	*2 cups dry red wine*
2 pounds beef chuck, cut into 1-inch cubes	*1 cup beef broth*
1 carrot, peeled and sliced	*1 tablespoon tomato paste*
1 large onion, chopped	*16 ounces white mushrooms, sautéed in butter*
2 cloves garlic, minced	*2 tablespoons minced flat-leaf parsley*
1 teaspoon dried thyme	*8 ounces cooked broad noodles for serving*
Salt and pepper to taste	

1 Heat the oil in a Dutch oven over medium-high heat. Add the bacon and cook just until the fat melts but doesn't brown. Remove to a plate. Add just enough beef to cover the bottom of the pot and brown evenly on each side. Remove to a plate and continue with the remaining meat.

2 Add the carrot, onion, garlic, and thyme to the pot. Cook until the onion is soft. Return the meats to the pot. Heat, stirring constantly. Season with salt and pepper. Sprinkle with the flour and cook until the bacon and beef are well browned. Add the wine, broth, and tomato paste. Bring to a boil, scraping the bottom of the pot to remove any cooked-on particles. Cover and simmer 3 hours, or until the meat is tender, stirring occasionally.

3 Remove the meat with a slotted spoon and set aside. Spoon off any fat from the sauce. Bring the sauce to a boil and reduce to approximately 2 cups. Taste and add salt and pepper if necessary. Return the meat to the pot along with the mushrooms. Stir in the parsley. Serve over the noodles.

Stewed Chicken (Coq au Vin)

This dish was most likely created years ago by some farmer's wife as a way to tenderize an old laying hen or rooster. The chicken pieces are browned and slowly braised in red wine until the meat is falling off the bone. The cooking liquid is then reduced and thickened to make a flavorful sauce with pieces of bacon, pearl onions, and sliced mushrooms. Serve with lots of crusty bread.

Preparation time: *15 minutes*

Cooking time: *Approximately 1 hour*

Yield: *4 to 6 servings*

1 tablespoon olive oil	1 cup chicken broth
4 slices thick-cut bacon, diced	1½ teaspoons tomato paste
Salt and pepper	1 bay leaf
3-pound frying chicken, cut into serving pieces (see Figure 5-3)	1 tablespoon cold water
	1 tablespoon cornstarch
12 pearl onions, peeled	8 ounces mushrooms, sliced (see Figure 5-4) and sautéed in butter
2 garlic cloves, crushed	
½ teaspoon dried thyme	2 tablespoons minced flat-leaf parsley
3 cups dry red wine	

1 Heat the oil in a Dutch oven over medium-high heat. Add the bacon and cook just until the fat is rendered, but do not cook until crisp. Remove to a plate. Generously salt and pepper the chicken pieces. Brown in the hot fat in two batches.

2 Place all the cooked chicken and bacon in the pot. Add the onions, garlic, and thyme and cook for 2 minutes. Add the wine, broth, and tomato paste. Bring to a boil, scraping the bottom of the pot to remove any cooked-on particles. Add the bay leaf. Cover and simmer for 25 minutes, or until the chicken is tender.

3 Remove the chicken with a slotted spoon and set aside. Spoon off any fat from the sauce. Bring the sauce to a boil and reduce to approximately 2 cups. Taste and season with salt and pepper.

4 Combine the water and cornstarch in a small bowl. Stir into the sauce and cook until thickened. Return the chicken to the pot along with the mushrooms. Stir in the parsley.

Book III

French Cooking

Cutting Up a Raw Chicken

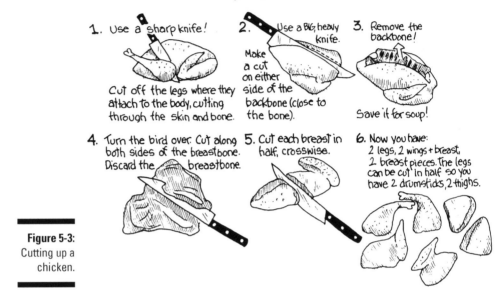

1. Use a sharp knife!

   Cut off the legs where they attach to the body, cutting through the skin and bone.

2. Use a BIG, heavy knife.

   Make a cut on either side of the backbone (close to the bone).

3. Remove the backbone!

   Save it for soup!

4. Turn the bird over. Cut along both sides of the breastbone. Discard the breastbone.

5. Cut each breast in half, crosswise.

6. Now you have: 2 legs, 2 wings + breast, 2 breast pieces. The legs can be cut in half so you have 2 drumsticks, 2 thighs.

Figure 5-3: Cutting up a chicken.

How to Trim and Slice Mushrooms

Figure 5-4: Slicing mushrooms.

1. wipe away dirt using a paper towel or a dish towel

2. Cut off stem

3. slice

Fisherman's Stew (Bouillabaisse)

This is the type of stew mostly likely made by a fisherman after cleaning his catch. The base of the stew is a tomatoey fish stock made with the most flavorful parts of the fish that are usually not eaten, such as the head, fins, and bones. After all the flavor is extracted and the stock strained, you quickly poach choice pieces of fish and seafood in the broth.

Preparation time: *20 minutes*

Cooking time: *50 minutes*

Yield: *4 servings*

2 tablespoons olive oil

1 large onion, chopped

3 cloves garlic, peeled and crushed

14½-ounce can diced tomatoes

2 pounds fish heads, bones, tails, and fins

4 parsley sprigs

1 basil sprig

¼ teaspoon fennel seeds

1 bay leaf

½ teaspoon dried thyme

1 strip of orange peel

1 tablespoon salt

¼ teaspoon pepper

10 cups water

3 pounds mixed fish, such as cod, scrod, flounder, halibut, or whiting, skinned, boned, and cut into bite-sized pieces

12 littleneck or cherrystone clams, scrubbed clean and soaked to remove sand

12 mussels, scrubbed clean and soaked to remove sand

12 sea scallops

Rounds of hard-toasted French bread

4 tablespoons minced flat-leaf parsley

1 Heat the olive oil in a 6-quart saucepan over medium heat. Add the onions and garlic and cook until soft. Add the diced tomatoes and cook until most of the liquid evaporates. Add the fish heads, bones, tails, and fins and the parsley, basil, fennel, bay leaf, thyme, orange peel, salt, pepper, and water. Bring to a boil over high heat and cook for 30 minutes.

2 Strain the soup into another saucepan, squeezing all the liquid out of the ingredients. Discard all solids. Season the soup with salt and pepper to taste.

3 Bring to a boil. Add the fish pieces and cook for 5 minutes. Add the clams, mussels, and scallops and cook for 5 minutes longer.

4 Place a couple of toasted bread rounds in 4 shallow soup bowls. Place some fish and shellfish in each plate. Ladle the soup on top of each and sprinkle with some of the minced parsley before serving.

Chapter 6

Sweet Endings

In This Chapter

- Upside down over apple tart
- Finishing your dinner in flames
- Making soufflés that rise to the occasion

*P*astry shops and cafés abound all over France. You would think that the French did nothing all day but eat sweets — everything from picture-perfect fruit tarts and jewel-like pastries, to exquisitely formed bonbons and truffles. Surprisingly, the favorite end to many a French meal is nothing more than a perfectly ripe piece of fruit and perhaps a piece of cheese, followed by a demitasse of black coffee as a digestive. Cakes and baked goods are usually eaten as a separate meal either late in the afternoon or on special occasions.

With such wonderful cakes and pastries available at local bakeries, home baking is kept simple, with rustic fruit tarts and cakes made with fruit from the home baker's own orchard or backyard garden. On very special occasions, the cook may go all out and surprise everyone with a light-as-air dessert soufflé or flambéed *crêpes*.

Because Americans expect a little something sweet at the end of a good meal, I include a few simple-to-make desserts that a French home cook might prepare to end a special meal or serve to a gathering of friends. I also suggest that you try your hand at the Crème Caramel recipe found in Chapter 6 of Book II. As with many recipes, the origin of this dessert is debatable; France, Italy, and Spain all claim this dessert as one of their own.

Apple Tart (Tarte Tatin)

Tradition has it that this tart was developed by two innkeeper sisters who were running low on fuel to keep their oven going. Needing to make some apple tarts, they decided to cook the apples in sugar on the stovetop, cover them with crust, and "bake" the tarts covered with a pot lid. Regardless of the why or where, the resulting tart is delectable. In this recipe, the apples are still caramelized on top of the stove, but after the pastry is laid on top, the tart is baked in the oven until golden.

Preparation time: *15 minutes*

Cooking time: *40 minutes*

Yield: *6 to 8 servings*

1 sheet frozen puff pastry, thawed

6 tablespoons butter, cut into slices

⅔ cup sugar

Approximately 6 to 7 large Golden Delicious apples, peeled, cored, and quartered (see Figure 6-1)

1 Roll the puff pastry until ⅛ inch thick. Cut into an 11-inch circle. Place on a baking sheet lined with wax paper. Prick the pastry with a fork and refrigerate until ready to use.

2 Melt the butter in a large cast-iron skillet over medium heat. Add the sugar and cook until the sugar melts and caramelizes. When the sugar looks like liquid caramel, remove it from the heat.

3 Preheat the oven to 375 degrees. Carefully arrange the apple quarters on top of the caramel, packing them in as tightly as possible. Cook over medium heat until the apples are tender. Do not stir or move the apples!

4 Place the puff pastry circle on top of the apples. Use the end of a wooden spoon to tuck the edges into the pan.

5 Place on the center rack in the oven and bake for 15 to 20 minutes, or until the pastry is golden.

6 Remove the pan from the oven. Let sit for 5 minutes. Place a large serving plate on top of the pan. Over the kitchen sink and in one swift motion, flip the pan over so that the tart is apple side up on the plate. Replace any apples that have stuck to the pan. Drizzle any remaining syrup over the apples. Serve warm.

Vary It! *In addition to the traditional apple tarte tatin, I like to make banana and mango versions. To make a banana tarte tatin, slice 4 underripe bananas into ¾-inch-thick slices. Follow recipe Steps 1 and 2. In Step 3, eliminate the apples and cover the bottom of the pan with banana slices. Cook over low heat until the caramel covers the bottom of the pan. Proceed with Steps 4 through 6. For a mango version, replace the bananas with 2 diced, almost ripe mangoes. Cook over low heat until the mangoes release their juices and combine with the hot caramel. Spread evenly over the bottom of the pan. Proceed with Steps 4 through 6.*

Tip: *Homemade puff pastry is laborious to make. Pepperidge Farm makes a very acceptable version available in the freezer section of your local supermarket. It comes 2 sheets to a box. If you want, you can also use the sweet tart pastry dough in Chapter 3 of Book III (see the Vary It! idea at the end of the Savory Tart Dough recipe) rather than the puff pastry.*

Peeling and Coring an Apple

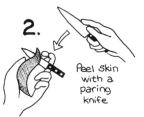
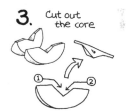

Figure 6-1:
Peeling and
coring an
apple.

Book III

**French
Cooking**

Apple Custard Cake
(Clafoutis aux Pommes)

This is, hands down, my all-time favorite apple dessert. *Clafoutis* is like a not-too-sweet custardy cake made with lots of fresh fruit. Although *clafoutis* is traditionally made with sweet cherries, I find that recipe a nuisance because you have to spit out the pits. Instead, I prefer *clafoutis aux pommes,* which is made with crisp, sautéed autumn apples. Better served warm, leftover *clafoutis* heats up easily in the microwave.

Preparation time: *15 minutes*

Cooking time: *40 minutes*

Yield: *6 to 8 servings*

2 tablespoons butter

6 cups peeled apple slices (use a crisp, not-too-sour variety of apple, such as Jonagold or Golden Delicious)

½ cup milk

3 eggs

⅓ cup all-purpose flour

¼ cup sugar

2 tablespoons brandy

¼ teaspoon baking powder

Pinch of cinnamon (optional)

1 Preheat the oven to 350 degrees.

2 Melt the butter in a large skillet over medium heat. Add the apples and cook until tender, 6 to 8 minutes. Arrange the apple slices in a 2-quart glass or ceramic baking dish.

3 Combine the milk, eggs, flour, sugar, brandy, and baking powder in a blender jar or combine in a bowl, using an electric hand mixer. Blend until smooth.

4 Pour the batter over the apples. Sprinkle with cinnamon, if desired.

5 Bake for 40 to 45 minutes or until a knife inserted comes out clean. Serve warm.

Vary It! *Peach clafoutis and pear clafoutis are equally delicious. Simply substitute firm peach or pear slices for the apples in Step 1.*

Lemon Tart *(Tarte au Citron)*

There's always room for a thin slice of bittersweet lemon tart at the end of a meal. Simple to make, this sunshine-yellow tart is so impressive looking that people will think it came from a Parisian bakery and not your oven.

Preparation time: *15 minutes*

Cooking time: *25 minutes*

Yield: *6 to 8 servings*

Sweet Tart Dough (see the Vary It! idea at the end of the Savory Tart Dough recipe in Chapter 3 of Book III)

4 eggs

2 egg yolks

¼ cup sugar

½ cup freshly squeezed lemon juice (about 3 lemons)

¼ cup crème fraîche (see the information at the end of the Split Pea Soup recipe in Chapter 4 of Book III) or heavy cream

1 tablespoon melted butter

1 Prepare the Sweet Tart Dough shell up through Step 7 and bake blind.

2 As the pastry bakes, prepare the lemon filling. In a large mixing bowl, beat together the eggs, egg yolks, sugar, lemon juice, and crème fraîche until smooth. Stir in the melted butter.

3 Place the prebaked pastry shell on the oven's center rack. Fill with the lemon filling mixture. Bake for 20 to 25 minutes, or until the filling is set. Remove from the oven and let cool to room temperature before chilling for at least 2 hours before serving.

Orange Dessert Crêpes (Crêpes Suzette)

The rage of American dinner parties in the 1950s and early 1960s, *crêpes suzette* are almost as easy to make as a box cake mix, especially if you make the crêpes early in the day and assemble the dessert right before serving. Be forewarned: These orange-flavored, buttery crêpes are addicting!

Preparation time: *15 minutes*

Cooking time: *30 minutes*

Yield: *4 to 6 servings*

Sweet French Pancake Batter (see the Vary It! idea at the end of the Basic French Pancake Batter recipe in Chapter 3 of Book III)

8 tablespoons (1 stick) unsalted butter

½ cup sugar

2 tablespoons grated orange zest

1 cup freshly squeezed orange juice

4 tablespoons Grand Marnier

1 Prepare the sweet French pancake batter as indicated in Chapter 3 of Book III, folding the crêpes in quarters as you remove them from the pan. Keep them covered on a large plate with a clean kitchen towel.

2 Fold the crêpes in quarters. Melt 4 tablespoons of the butter in a large skillet over medium heat. Add ¼ cup of the sugar and stir until melted. Add 1 tablespoon of the orange zest and ½ cup of the orange juice. Stir well and bring to a simmer. Add half the folded crêpes, turning gently to coat with the sauce.

3 Finish the sauce by adding 2 tablespoons of the Grand Marnier, allowing it to warm for a few seconds. Remove from the heat. Light a match and, holding the match in one hand, grab the pan with your other hand and slightly tilt pan away from you so that the sauce accumulates in that part. Ignite the sauce with a match. Be careful because the flames will rise high as the alcohol burns off! Place the pan on a flat, heatproof surface. When the flames die down, serve the crêpes, spooning the sauce over them.

4 Repeat Steps 2 and 3.

Chocolate Soufflé
(Soufflé au Chocolat)

Nothing is more special (or romantic, depending on whom you're dining with) than a chocolate soufflé straight from the oven. For best results, see the tips in Chapter 3 of Book III on how to properly beat egg whites, the key to a perfect soufflé!

Preparation time: *15 minutes*

Cooking time: *20 to 25 minutes*

Yield: *4 servings*

⅓ cup sugar, plus additional for sprinkling	6 egg whites
5 ounces bittersweet chocolate, chopped	Pinch of salt
3 egg yolks at room temperature	

1 Preheat the oven to 375 degrees. Butter a 6-cup soufflé mold and sprinkle with sugar. Shake out any excess.

2 Melt the chocolate in a metal bowl over a saucepan of simmering water. Remove the bowl from the heat and stir in the egg yolks, one at a time.

3 Using an electric mixer, beat the egg whites with a pinch of salt on medium speed until soft peaks form. Gradually add the ⅓ cup of sugar, beating at medium speed, and then begin to beat on high until stiff peaks form.

4 Stir about 1 cup of the beaten egg whites into the chocolate mixture to lighten it. Gently fold the mixture into the remaining whites, using a rubber spatula.

5 Spoon the mixture into the prepared soufflé mold. Bake on the center oven rack until puffed and crusted on top but still jiggly in the center, 20 to 25 minutes. Serve immediately.

Book IV

Greek and Middle Eastern Cooking

The 5th Wave   By Rich Tennant

"It says here that because Persephone ate a pomegranate seed she had to spend all year in the Underworld except for 4 months each year that she spent with her mother. Some scholars say it was 6 months. It probably just _felt_ like 6 months."

In this book . . .

*I*f you love Greek and Middle Eastern food but feel that cooking it's all Greek to you, this section will help you get a handle on this simple yet hearty cuisine. It's mostly a matter of familiarizing yourself with some unfamiliar spices and picking up some new ingredients and techniques. You'll be surprised at how easy it is to whip up a dish of hummus or make a delicious entree of stuffed grape leaves. The only hard part is pronouncing the names of all the new spices and ingredients you'll be using! And don't forget to try the baklava!

Contents at a glance

Chapter 1

Inside a Greek and Middle Eastern Kitchen

In This Chapter

▶ Looking at a cuisine defined and shaped by history

▶ Defining Greek and Middle Eastern cooking

▶ Cooking like the locals

Due to the geographical location of the region and its rich history of conquer and rule, there seems to have always been a constant exchange of ideas and culture between the countries that today make up the Middle East and southeastern Europe. These countries include Iran, Iraq, Jordan, Lebanon, and Syria in western Asia; Egypt, Tunisia, and Morocco in northern Africa; and Greece and Turkey. The borders that separate these nations today are more political than culinary.

Called the "fertile crescent" for good reason, the geographic area comprised today of the countries of Iraq, Syria, Jordan, and Lebanon was well known in ancient times for its irrigated fields of grains and cereals, fruits and vegetables, and livestock. As should be expected, a rich agricultural area such as this led the way to refined culinary skills and the great cuisine of the Middle East and ultimately Greece and Turkey, too.

At the crossroads to the Mediterranean and the rest of Europe, Greece, its culture, and its cuisine reflect a melting pot of European customs to the west, combined with the influence of its Arabic neighbors to the east. Life in this beautiful and magical part of the world has never been easy. Although Greece is a country proud of its ancient past, it has been invaded and conquered over the centuries, and the Greek people have endured political and economic hardships since the beginning of time. This strife is evident in the stoic character of the Greek personality, as well as in Greek cooking, where the need to use what is available, combined with influences of the East, has left its mark on the Greek kitchen.

Cooking by the Season and the Region

A peninsula surrounded by crystal-clear blue water and 1,400 islands outside of its modern, urban centers, Greece still remains a country of charming Mediterranean whitewashed villages and monasteries. The towns seem to cling to the crags and bluffs of an enchanting and sun-drenched landscape that can also be inhospitable and parched at times.

Because agricultural and seafaring traditions are as important today as they were centuries ago, Greek and Middle Eastern cooking continues to revolve around the bounty that Mother Nature provides. Simple yet hearty cooking continues to be the norm. Geography, as well as religious dietary traditions, dictates what is eaten and when.

The new growing season arrives early in Greece and the Middle East. Spring heralds the awakening of the land from the hot, dry days of summer long gone by and the cool, usually wet few weeks of autumn and winter that follow. As the days get warmer, the ochre countryside turns green, and the barren almond, peach, plum, quince, and cherry trees soon bear white or pink blossoms. The branches of the ever-hearty fig tree turn green with leaves and plump little figlets. Slowly but surely, fresh produce items — including citrus fruits, candy-sweet dates and persimmons, jewel-like pomegranates, fragrant quince, meaty nuts, wild herbs, greens, and honey — make their way to market from the countryside from mid-spring through mid-autumn.

Almost every fresh food has its own season and place in time, as well as in the Greek and Middle Eastern kitchen. Even now — with improved transportation and new technology in growing techniques — this region of the world remains faithful to the time-worn, culinary traditions of years gone by.

Religion also mandates what is eaten and when. In fact, it's said that in Greece, you're either fasting or celebrating. For example, during the 40 days of Lent, Greeks fast on certain holy days and abstain from all meat and dairy products, only to be followed by the great feast and celebration that is Easter, when roasted baby lamb, sweet and savory cheese pies, and desserts are once again enjoyed. In the Middle East, religious observances, such as Ramadam, also require strict fasting, followed by elaborate meals of family favorites, including the requisite roasted baby lamb or goat.

Getting Fresh: Buying the Best Ingredients

Most home cooks, even those living in urban centers, shop daily so that they have only the freshest ingredients when preparing the day's meals. Most neighborhoods and villages have a variety of food stores and shops that specialize in one thing, such as the local bread bakery, the greengrocer, the butcher, the fishmonger, and so on.

Buying locally from a small shopkeeper usually assures cooks of getting the best quality for their money. In this day and age of supermarket giants, the shopkeepers know that the best way to compete for customers is to keep them satisfied with fresh, high-quality food products.

Although grocery shopping every day may not be practical from a time stand-point, focusing on seasonal produce and shopping at specialty retailers make sense when you want to get the best taste from the foods you cook.

The following are some general pointers to getting the very best when you want to cook like a genuine Greek or Middle Eastern cook:

- First and foremost, don't purchase any produce or seafood that comes packaged on a plastic tray and wrapped in clear wrap. When food comes prepackaged, you can't use any of your senses, except sight, to see whether it's any good.

- Always feel whatever you buy. Fruit and vegetables should feel heavy for their size. If not, they are probably dry inside and will be tasteless. In general, avoid very hard or very soft produce, which usually means that it's overripe and perhaps even borderline spoiled.

- Look to see and feel whether the fruits and vegetables have any soft spots. Such spots are a sign of bruising or possible spoilage. This advice also holds true with large produce items, such as watermelons.

- Smell it before you buy it. Summer fruits, such as peaches, nectarines, some plums, and melons, should have a pleasant, sweet smell. If scent-less, they may not be ripe, while a strong smell could mean that they're overripe.

- Seafood should not smell fishy! In fact, if anything, it should have no smell at all.

- Fish should have their heads on them. Their eyes should be clear, bright, and shiny. If you see any mushy spots, put it down and walk away!

- Buy cheese and other dairy products from a reputable store that has a high turnover. Also, never be afraid to ask for a taste. Avoid moldy and smelly cheese unless it's supposed to be that way!

- If possible, avoid purchasing olives in jars and cans. The quality of olives varies, depending on how they were processed and prepared. If at all possible, buy olives from a retailer that sells them loose, by the pound. Always sample the olives to make sure that they're firm, not mushy, and that you like the flavor.

- The brand of olive oil you purchase and use is also a matter of personal preference, especially when dressing salads and vegetables. When trying a new brand, purchase the smallest bottle possible to see whether you like it.

- Loaves of bread should have a hard, crisp crust and not be rubbery or soft. Tap on the crust. You should hear a hollow sound; if not, the bread may not be fresh. Flatbread should be soft and flexible.

Greece's early culinary traditions

When you think of Greece, the first thing that comes to mind is probably the majestic ruins of its ancient empire. For 200 years, from 500 B.C. to 300 B.C., while the rest of the world lived under a cloud of cultural and political darkness, the ancient Greeks of Athens and Sparta became the citizens of the center of the Western world with its prolific creation of literature, philosophy, mathematics, architecture, the arts, and politics. And while the rest of Europe was gnawing on bones, the citizens of ancient Greece were enjoying culinary splendors unlike that ever seen before in recorded history. Agriculture flourished under the Greeks, who planted olive trees and grape vines throughout the Greek peninsula and the conquered territories of the Mediterranean basin.

Meats were marinated in olive oil, lemon juice, and wild honey and then grilled with wild herbs and served with fragrant sauces. Elaborate seafood dishes were created, using the bounty from the sea. Wonderful sweets were made with honey and nuts and flavored with spices from the Orient.

Chapter 2

Ingredients for Greek and Middle Eastern Cooking

In This Chapter

▶ Sampling Greek and Middle Eastern spices

▶ Adding salt and pepper

▶ Finding out about olive oil

▶ Shopping for butter and cheeses

*T*he culinary exchange that has taken place over thousands of years between the East and the West has provided the world with the rich culinary traditions of Greece, Turkey, and the Middle East. Some similarities exist between the different cuisines, including the use of fragrant herbs and spices to flavor both savory and sweet dishes, as well as the extensive use of fresh fruits and vegetables and fermented dairy products.

Fortunately for home cooks in the United States, many of these ingredients are readily available today at your local supermarket or at specialty food stores.

Herbs and Spices

Since ancient times, the regions known today as the eastern Mediterranean and the Middle East have been famous for their herbs and spices. In fact, wasn't Columbus looking for a shortcut to reduce the amount of time it took to go to and from Europe to Asia and then back again? Traders had to travel for months at a time in caravans to bring back the fragrant herbs and spices that were in such high demand. These herbs and spices, grown throughout these two regions, have played a fundamental role in shaping their distinct cuisine. Even humble lentil or dried fava bean dishes from Palestine and Egypt are transformed into steaming, aromatic delights when seasoned with fragrant cumin. Savory casserole dishes from Greece and Turkey are subtly seasoned with the flavor of cinnamon. Strong, thick Arabic coffee, served black without sugar, becomes fragrant with the sweet aroma and flavor of cardamom pods.

Fortunately for today's home cook, most of these highly prized herbs and spices are readily available at your local supermarket or by mail order or e-mail from reputable spice companies. In addition to using herbs and spices, Greek and Middle Eastern home cooks also purchase and use spice mixes or blends. Although these may be more difficult for you to obtain locally, you can easily make them at home when you have the right spices in your pantry.

Aleppo pepper

These dried, crushed Middle Eastern chile-type peppers impart a gentle heat when added to food. If not readily available, combine an equal amount of crushed, hot red pepper with paprika, preferably Spanish.

Harissa

The condiment of choice in North Africa, *harissa* is traditionally stirred into olives, stews, soups, and salads. It's also an ingredient in *tagine,* the traditional North African dish of braised meat or poultry and vegetables, served with *couscous,* steamed semolina pasta. See Chapter 5 of Book IV for the recipe for Tagine of Chicken with Lemons and Olives.

Preparation time: *10 minutes*

Cooking time: *1 to 2 minutes*

Yield: *Approximately* *⅓ cup*

1 teaspoon ground coriander

½ teaspoon ground cumin

3 tablespoons paprika

1 tablespoon crushed hot red pepper flakes

2 cloves garlic, minced

½ teaspoon salt

1 tablespoon olive oil

1 Combine the coriander, cumin, and paprika in a small nonstick skillet. Over low heat, warm until just fragrant. Remove from the heat and let cool to room temperature.

2 In a small bowl, combine the spice mixture, red pepper flakes, garlic, salt, and olive oil. The mixture will be very thick. Taste and add salt if necessary.

3 Store in a small glass jar in the refrigerator, for up to 1 month.

Spicy Harissa-Marinated Olives

Add a kick to some brine-cured black olives (not California, water-packed type) by adding some harissa. Serve along with cocktails or beer, or as one plate of *meze* (Greek or Middle Eastern appetizers).

Preparation time: *5 minutes, plus 24 hours for olives to marinate*

Yield: *2 cups*

2 cups brine-cured, unpitted black olives	½ teaspoon fennel seeds
2 tablespoons harissa (see the preceding recipe	

1 Combine the olives, harissa, and fennel seeds in a glass jar.

2 Cover tightly and store in the refrigerator at least 1 day before serving, up to a month.

Bay leaf

A member of the evergreen family, this aromatic herb imparts a wonderful flavor when used in cooking. Bay leaves are oval leaves approximately 2 to 3 inches long. Although fresh bay leaves aren't always readily available, you can find dry leaves sold in jars with other dry herbs and spices. A leaf or two is usually all you need when cooking. Bay leaf combines well with other traditional Mediterranean herbs, such as oregano, parsley, rosemary, and thyme.

Book IV

Greek and Middle Eastern Cooking

Cardamom

Ranked as one of the most expensive spices in the world, the popular Middle Eastern spice cardamom is used in baked goods and to make Arabic coffee. It's available in pods, seeds, or ground form.

Cinnamon

A popular spice worldwide in both savory and sweet dishes, cinnamon is used either ground or as pieces of rolled bark or sticks. When buying stick cinnamon, try to find the more brittle, aromatic version rather than the harder, tightly rolled sticks.

Coriander

Coriander is a member of the parsley family. The green leaves (cilantro) and seeds are widely used in Cypriot and Middle Eastern cooking.

Cumin

Whole and ground cumin seeds have been used from ancient times in Middle Eastern cooking. This popular spice, originally from Egypt, is used in preparing stews and when marinating meats for grilling and roasting.

Dill

Snipped fresh dill is a popular herb in Greek cooking. Native to the Mediterranean region, dill appears in soups, salads, and roasted dishes.

Fennel

Not to be confused with the fresh, light green bulb, dried fennel seeds taste of anise and licorice and have been used in Greece since ancient times for cooking and medicinal purposes. Use judiciously, because a little goes a long way.

Figs

Growing wild throughout most of Greece and parts of the Middle East, figs, both green and purple, are enjoyed either fresh or dried. Drying figs in the sun enhances their natural sweetness. You can eat them as is, or you can cut a small slit in them and stuff them with something as simple as a toasted whole almond or an exotic mixture of nuts and spices.

Stuffed Dried Figs

Figs have played an important part in the history of this region since Biblical times, when Adam and Eve were clothed only in fig leaves. Figs are available in both black and white varieties and can be enjoyed both fresh and dried. Fig trees usually bear fruit twice a year. Calimyrna figs are wonderfully sweet and chewy when dried, and pair very nicely with nuts and spices in this recipe.

Preparation time: *15 minutes*

Cooking time: *20 minutes*

Yield: *1 pound*

1 pound dried Calimyrna figs

2 tablespoons fennel seeds

1⅓ cups chopped walnuts

Grated zest of 1 lemon

1 tablespoon ground cinnamon

1 Preheat the oven to 325 degrees.

2 Place the fennel seeds in a small plastic bag. Gently crush the seeds by rolling a rolling pin over then. Combine the crushed seeds with the walnuts, lemon zest, and ground cinnamon in a small bowl.

3 Slit the bottom of each fig. Place a small amount of the nut and spice mixture in each one and pinch closed.

4 Place the stuffed figs on a baking sheet. Bake for 15 minutes.

5 Cool to room temperature. Store in a glass jar for up to 6 months.

Mastic

This resinous gum produced by a small evergreen looks like small yellow pebbles or stones. Crushed into a powder with a pestle and mortar, it's used to flavor sweet and stews. In Greece, it's also used to flavor a liqueur called *mastíha*.

Mint

Mint is used throughout the eastern Mediterranean and Middle East in both its fresh and dry states. It's used in meat and vegetable dishes and salads and is steeped in boiling water for tea.

Orange and rose waters

Distilled from orange or rose blossoms since ancient times, these "waters" have been traditionally used in both savory and sweet dishes, imparting a fragrant, exotic flavor and aroma.

Oregano

Wild-grown Greek oregano is known for its fragrant smell and tangy, pronounced flavor. Appreciated since ancient times, dried Greek oregano is widely available today at many supermarkets and specialty food stores.

Parsley

Always use fresh parsley and never the dried version, which is tasteless and a terrible color of gray. Available in two varieties, curly-leafed and flat-leafed, the latter is the preferred one to use when cooking because it has more flavor and is easier to chop or mince. Remove the leaves from the stems and chop or mince them only. Rather than discard the stems, tie them together with other herbs to use as part of a *bouquet garni*. Parsley is usually used as a flavoring ingredient in recipes such as a marinade for lamb, or it's added at the end of preparing a dish such as a sauce or soup in order to enjoy its maximum flavor and bright green color.

Rosemary

A member of the evergreen family, this aromatic herb imparts wonderful flavor to almost everything, especially roast meats and fish. Great with lamb and oily fish, such as sardines and mackerels, rosemary is usually paired with garlic, olive oil, and other Mediterranean herbs to make a fragrant marinade.

Sesame seeds

Another prized flavoring used in the Middle East since ancient times, sesame seeds are used in breads and cookies and for making *tahini,* a paste made from ground roasted sesame seeds. Tahini is used in sweets as well as in savory dishes such as hummus (see Chapter 3 of Book IV) and the following Tahini with Yogurt Dip.

Tahini with Yogurt Dip

This dip couldn't be easier to make. Try serving it with warm pita bread triangles or fresh vegetable crudités.

Preparation time: *5 minutes*

Yield: *2¼ cups*

1 cup tahini	*Salt*
1¼ cups drained or Greek-Style Yogurt (see Chapter 3 of Book IV)	

Combine the tahini and yogurt in a mixing bowl. Taste and add salt if necessary.

Book IV

Greek and Middle Eastern Cooking

Sumac

The dried crushed berries from a type of nonpoisonous sumac tree, sumac has a pleasant sour-lemony taste. It's usually combined with other spices and used as an seasoning.

Many varieties of poisonous sumac grow wild throughout North America. To avoid a health risk, use only sumac purchased from a spice purveyor or Middle Eastern specialty food retailer.

Za'atar

This is a popular blend of herbs and spices that is sprinkled on bread or used as a seasoning in cooked meat dishes.

Za'atar Seasoning Mix

Za'atar is readily available at market stalls and spice shops throughout the Middle East. Although available at some specialty food stores in the United States, the odds of finding it at your local supermarket are remote. Nevertheless, you can easily prepare a za'atar seasoning mix at home.

Preparation time: *10 minutes*

Cooking time: *1 to 2 minutes*

Yield: *Approximately ⅓ cup*

2 tablespoons sesame seeds

4 teaspoons dried thyme

½ teaspoon dried oregano

2 teaspoons dried sumac

1 teaspoon kosher salt

1 Toast the sesame seeds in a small nonstick skillet over medium-high heat, shaking to toast evenly. Remove from the heat when the sesame seeds turn golden brown. Remove to a bowl and cool to room temperature.

2 Add the thyme, oregano, sumac, and salt. Store in a tightly covered jar.

Khoubiz Seasoned with Za'atar

Za'atar seasoning is commonly sprinkled on oiled *khoubiz,* the Arabic name for flatbread, before baking. To simplify things, I've come up with an easier-to-make version that uses store-bought pita bread that is heated in the broiler on both sides and then spread with an olive oil-za'atar mixture. This bread is delicious eaten alone, with grilled meat, or with the Tahini and Yogurt Dip (see the recipe earlier in this chapter), Hummus (see Chapter 3 of Book IV), or Baba Ghanoush (see Chapter 4 of Book IV).

Preparation time: *10 minutes*

Cooking time: *15 minutes*

Yield: *6 seasoned khoubiz*

3 tablespoons za'atar seasoning mix

¼ cup extra-virgin olive oil

6 soft large pita breads

1 Preheat the broiler.

2 Combine the za'atar seasoning mix and olive oil in a small bowl.

3 Place the pita bread on a baking pan and broil for approximately 1 to 2 minutes on both sides, or until golden around the edges.

4 Spoon the za'atar and olive oil mixture on top of the pita bread and spread evenly.

5 Serve immediately.

Salt and Pepper

I usually like to generously salt and pepper food as I cook. For best results, I pat dry meat and poultry before seasoning. Nothing is worse than underseasoned foods, especially those that lack salt. Sure, you can always add more salt to taste as you sit down to eat, but quite honestly, the food doesn't taste the same. As with everything in life, you do have some options when it comes to salt and pepper.

Salt

Most Greek and Middle Eastern cooks use sea salt collected from salt farms of shallow ponds of seawater along the Mediterranean. Imported sea salt is readily available at most gourmet food stores, but averaging around $7 to $8 a pound, it's very costly when compared to, say, kosher salt at $1.99 for a 3-pound box. I prefer to use kosher salt over ordinary table salt because it doesn't contain any of the additives used in table salt, so it flows better. Kosher salt also has a "cleaner" salt flavor and doesn't dissolve as quickly as regular salt, the cause of wilted salad greens.

In addition to seasoning food, salt has been used to preserve food. A few types of commonly salted foods are capers (the buds of the wild caper bush that are either pickled or packed in salt), salted cod, and North African salt-preserved lemons, which are used as a condiment and an ingredient in cooking.

Book IV

Greek and Middle Eastern Cooking

Salt-Preserved Lemons

Home cooks in Morocco and other North African countries, which have an abundance of citrus fruits and salt, have been preserving lemons for generations by packing them in salt. The salt slowly draws out the juice as the lemon is preserved in its own salty juice. Cooks use the preserved lemons chopped up as a savory condiment. The bright yellow lemons, packed in a jar, are also a wonderful reminder of the warm days of summer.

Preparation time: *20 minutes*

Yield: *6 preserved lemons*

7 lemons	*Kosher salt*

1 Find a glass jar large enough to hold 6 of the lemons. Fill with boiling water to sterilize. Pour out the water and dry with a clean kitchen towel.

2 Juice 1 lemon. Set aside.

3 Scrub the remaining 6 lemons under cold water with a kitchen brush.

4 Cut each lemon, 4 times vertically, starting from the bottom to the stem, without cutting all the way up; the pieces should remain attached at the stem.

5 Pack the lemons in the glass jar, layering them with kosher salt so that they're completely covered. Drizzle the reserved lemon juice over the top of the lemons and salt.

6 Cover tightly and store in a cool, dark place for 2 weeks before using.

7 To use the lemons, remove from the salt and run under cool running water. Pat dry. Use as called for in the recipe. Preserved lemons will keep for up to 3 months when packed in salt.

Moroccan-Cured Olives

The salty-acid flavor of the salt-preserved lemons adds a pleasant contrast and freshness to the olives. Allow time to let the olives marinate at least overnight.

Preparation time: *5 minutes, plus 24 hours for olives to marinate*

Yield: *Approximately 1¼ cups*

½ Salt-Preserved Lemon (see the preceding recipe)	*1 tablespoon olive oil*
	1 bay leaf
1 cup Spanish green manzanilla or anchovy-stuffed olives	

1 Mince the preserved lemon half.

2 Drain the olives. Mix with the minced preserved lemon and olive oil.

3 Place the bay leaf in a small glass jar. Spoon in the olive mixture.

4 Cover tightly and store in the refrigerator at least 1 day before serving, up to a month.

Pepper

One of the most important and sought-after spices brought back to Europe by traders hundreds of years ago, black pepper continues to be imported from the subcontinent of Asia. For maximum flavor, I always use black pepper in the form of whole peppercorns ground in a pepper mill that allows me to adjust the grind to my liking. For example, when finishing up a dish, I might prefer to use coarsely ground pepper rather than finely ground.

Olive Oil

Excellent-quality olive oil is milled throughout Greece and many Arabic countries in North Africa and parts of the Middle East. In fact, it is believed that olives were first cultivated in the Greek Isles thousands of years ago and brought by the ancient Greeks to other parts of the Mediterranean, where the olive and olive oil industry flourished and continues to do so.

Greek and Tunisian olive oils are dark green and extremely fruity in flavor. It is the fat of choice in the region and is used in savory dishes as well as in some sweets.

Book IV

Greek and Middle Eastern Cooking

Greek olives

In addition to having ripe olives suitable for pressing into oil, Greece is also known to have some of the best eating olives in the world. Many of them are available at your local supermarket or at Greek or Middle Eastern specialty food stores.

The best-known and most readily available olive is the *kalamata,* a tear-shaped olive that is usually packed in brine or oil. Depending on when the olives were picked and their stage of ripeness, they may be green, purple, or black. Other Greek olives you may be able to find are *nafplion* and *pelion.* These two varieties are green and cured and packed in a salty brine.

Olive oil is made in fall and early winter by cold pressing the oil from tree-ripened olives using only mechanical force or pressure. The crème de la crème of olive oil is called extra-virgin. To be labeled "extra-virgin," the oil must be from the first cold pressing and have an acidity content of less than 1 percent. If greater, the oil is filtered and blended with other olive oil to mellow the flavor. Extra-virgin olive oil is naturally more expensive and is a better quality oil.

Greek or Tunisian olive oil, unlike Italian and Spanish olive oils, is not readily available and may require a trip to a Greek or Middle Eastern specialty food store. A good Spanish extra-virgin oil is a good substitute.

Butter

Although most Greek and Middle Eastern recipes call for olive oil, butter is also used in baked goods, especially those made with phyllo dough. I recommend that you use Grade AA unsalted butter for the best results and flavor.

When butter is melted and cools, the milk solids separate from the butterfat and sink to the bottom of the pot or container. Some Arabic recipes call for *ghee,* the butterfat only, with the milk solids being discarded.

Cheese

Excellent cheeses, made primarily from goat's milk and sheep's milk, or a combination of the two, are made throughout Greece and some Middle Eastern countries. The goats and sheep are allowed to graze in fields and mountains eating wild grasses and flowers in these countries, which have a long tradition of animal husbandry and herding. Made primarily from unpasteurized milk, these artisan-made cheeses all have distinct qualities and characteristics based on where the animals grazed. These cheeses can be fresh and soft, such as *labaneh,* or yogurt cheese balls (see Chapter 4 of Book IV), or hard and cured, such as *kasséri.* Here are some cheeses from Greek and Middle Eastern countries:

- **Feta:** Perhaps the best known of all Greek cheeses, authentic feta is made primarily from fresh sheep's milk mixed with a small amount of goat's milk. A fresh white curd cheese, feta may be soft, medium, or hard when sold. To stay fresh, feta should be stored in its salty brine. Although feta is usually eaten with bread and olives as part of a meze (which I discuss in Chapter 4 of Book IV), it is also used as a key ingredient in savory tarts, salads, and dishes such as garides saganaki, a delicious shrimp baked in tomato sauce with feta (see the recipe in Chapter 5 of Book IV).

If a recipe calls for hard or grated feta, let the cheese sit on an uncovered plate in the refrigerator overnight.

- **Haloumi:** This semihard sheep's milk cheese is somewhat elastic, such as mozzarella, and is a favorite in Greek and Cypriot cooking for grilling and frying.

- **Kasséri:** Made from goat's milk, kasséri is a semihard cheese similar in texture and taste to a good cheddar. You can eat it as a table cheese or dust it in flour and pan-fry it in olive oil.

- **Kefalotyri:** This hard cheese is usually made from a combination of sheep's milk and cow's milk. It's usually grated and served over pasta or in casserole dishes. Imported Italian pecorino Romano cheese is a good substitute.

The following are some suggestions when purchasing cheese:

- **Search for only fresh cheeses.** Shop from a store that handles the cheese properly and does a brisk business so that nothing sits around for very long. A wedge cut to order is fresher than a precut and wrapped wedge.

- **Taste everything before you buy.** Good cheese shops unwrap cheeses and cut off small slices for you to sample.

- **Buy Greek.** Buy imported Greek cheese whenever possible, although very respectable sheep's milk and goat's milk soft cheeses are being made in North America by small, independently owned and operated dairies, and are worth sampling, too.

Book IV

Greek and
Middle
Eastern
Cooking

Chapter 3

Mastering a Few Simple Techniques

In This Chapter

▶ Working with phyllo dough

▶ Acquainting yourself with quince

▶ Making thick and tangy Greek-style yogurt

▶ Putting dried legumes and beans to use

Greek and Middle Eastern cooks cook from the heart, using generation-old recipes that have been passed down from mother to daughter over the years. Many recipes are never even written down, having been learned from standing in the kitchen at a mother's side.

Using the very best ingredients available, many times grown or raised by the cook or her family, the dishes from this part of the world are usually uncomplicated and straightforward. A simple dish of wild greens — picked the same day, served with braised beans, and drizzled with the family's own cold-pressed extra-virgin olive oil — can smell and taste as good as, if not better than, any dish prepared and served in a five-star restaurant.

Although you don't need to raise your own food to prepare authentic Greek and Middle Eastern dishes, you can use some special techniques to help ensure that your meals come out as authentic as possible. I explain some of those techniques in this chapter.

Getting the Feel of Phyllo Dough

Almost anyone who has eaten Greek food is familiar with that wonderful Greek specialty *spanakopita*, or spinach pie (see the recipe in Chapter 5 of Book IV), or the most renowned of Greek sweets, *baklava* (see the recipe later in this chapter). While one is savory and the other sweet, both are recognizable from their baked-up, golden, crispy appearance, a tell-tale sign that they're made from phyllo or, as it is sometimes spelled, filo, dough.

Phyllo (which means *leaf* in Greek) dough is finely rolled and stretched sheets of wheat dough. Paper-thin and almost translucent, the sheets are approximately 12 × 20 inches and are stacked, rolled, wrapped, and then frozen. Phyllo dough is readily available for purchase at most supermarkets and at Greek and Middle Eastern specialty food stores.

Because the dough is already rolled and cut, phyllo is easy to work with when handled properly. Be aware, however, that the sheets of dough are so thin that they dry out quickly and can tear, leading to less than satisfactory results. Based on my own experience and that of Greek-American home cooks to whom I've spoken, I put together for you this list of tips for working with phyllo:

- ✔ Plan accordingly. Frozen phyllo dough has to defrost several hours or overnight in a tightly sealed package before you use it.

- ✔ Always defrost the dough in the refrigerator. If not, the outer sheets may become sticky from condensation in the package as it defrosts. Sticky sheets usually tear as you try to separate them.

✔ Because the dough tends to dry out so quickly, prepare the filling mix-ture and other ingredients while the dough defrosts. Cool filling mixtures to room temperature before using.

✔ Bring the dough to room temperature before using.

✔ To remove the phyllo dough from the package, carefully slit one end of the inner plastic bag. Save it to repack any leftover dough. Remove the defrosted dough from the package and carefully unroll it slowly so you don't tear it. Set the entire stack of phyllo on a large tray or clean kitchen towel.

✔ The sheets of dough are so thin that they'll begin to dry out almost immediately. The dry phyllo will then crack and be almost impossible to work with. Therefore, always cover the dough immediately with a sheet or two of wax paper or a clean, dampened kitchen cloth, wrung out well, making sure that the edges of the dough are well protected.

✔ Phyllo dough is usually a fat-free product. When baking with it, you usu-ally need to brush the individual sheets with melted, clarified butter.

✔ Don't fret if the dough gets small tears or cracks in it. The dough is so thin that such cracks are inevitable. Simply brush the area with melted butter, patch up the problem area with a small piece of dough, and brush over it again with some more butter.

✔ Never wet or brush the phyllo sheets (or "leaves," as the Greeks refer to them) with water. Doing so can cause the phyllo to fall apart.

✔ Because pastries using phyllo are made with melted butter, always bake them on a pan with a lip to catch any runoff.

✔ Unused, leftover phyllo sheets can be rerolled and placed in the original plastic bag. Tape to seal the end and place back in the box. Store in the refrigerator for up to a week or refreeze for up to 3 months.

Book IV

Greek and Middle Eastern Cooking

Baklava

The most famous of Greek pastries, baklava is a diamond-shaped pastry made of layers of buttery, crisp phyllo filled with sweetened nuts and bathed in a honey-enriched syrup. The contrast of textures and flavors makes this dessert unique and a special treat.

The recipe is somewhat labor intensive, so plan accordingly to allow the phyllo dough to defrost and to let the baked baklava absorb the honey syrup overnight before serving.

Preparation time: *1 hour, plus overnight for baklava to absorb honey syrup*

Cooking time: *1 hour and 30 minutes*

Yield: *Approximately 30 pieces*

1¾ cups granulated sugar	1½ cups finely chopped almonds
1½ cups water	2 teaspoons ground cinnamon
¼ cup honey	⅛ teaspoon ground cloves
1 small strip lemon peel	1-pound package (about 20 sheets) frozen phyllo dough, defrosted overnight
1 small cinnamon stick	
3 whole cloves	¾ cup (12 tablespoons) melted, unsalted butter
2 teaspoons freshly squeezed lemon juice	
1½ cups finely chopped walnuts	

1 Prepare the syrup by combining 1½ cups sugar, water, and honey in a small saucepan. Bring to a boil over medium-high heat. Add the lemon peel, cinnamon stick, and whole cloves. Lower the heat to a simmer and cook, covered, 20 minutes. Remove from the heat and let cool to room temperature. Add the lemon juice. Pour through a fine mesh strainer before using.

2 Preheat the oven to 350 degrees.

3 Combine the walnuts, almonds, the remaining ¼ cup sugar, ground cinnamon, and ground cloves in a small bowl and set aside.

4 Unroll the defrosted phyllo dough. Place on a clean kitchen cloth. If necessary, cut sheets to fit a 13-x-9-x-2-inch pan. Cover with wax paper or a dampened kitchen cloth, wrung out well, so that the phyllo dough doesn't dry out.

5 Brush the bottoms and sides of a 13-x-9-x-2-inch baking pan with some of the melted butter.

6 Place one sheet of phyllo dough on the prepared pan. Brush with melted butter and top with another sheet of dough. Repeat the process 6 more times so that you have a stack of 8 buttered sheets.

7 Sprinkle 1 cup of the nut mixture over the buttered stack of phyllo.

8 Cover with a sheet of phyllo dough. Brush with melted butter. Top with 2 more sheets of phyllo, brushing each with butter.

9 Sprinkle another cup of the nut mixture over the buttered stack of phyllo.

10 Cover with a sheet of phyllo dough. Brush with melted butter.

11 Sprinkle the remaining nuts over the buttered stack. Top with the remaining sheets of buttered phyllo (approximately 9 more sheets, depending on brand and package size). Make sure that the top sheet is clean, without any tears. Brush with melted butter.

12 Holding a sharp knife vertically, cut the unbaked baklava into diamonds (see Figure 3-1).

13 Bake on the center oven rack for approximately 75 minutes, or until the top is golden brown and the layers are puffed up.

14 Remove from the oven. Carefully spoon half of the prepared syrup over the baked baklava. Let sit for 5 minutes. Spoon the remaining syrup over the baklava. As soon as the baklava is cooled to room temperature, cover with foil and let sit overnight before serving.

Tip: *Most 1-pound packages of phyllo dough come packaged approximately 20 to 25 sheets to a box. If the sheets are larger than the size of your pan, cut through the stack of unrolled sheets so that they fit properly. Overlap them slightly as you place them in the pan.*

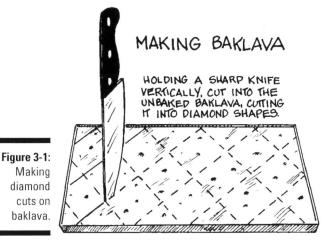

Figure 3-1:
Making diamond cuts on baklava.

MAKING BAKLAVA

HOLDING A SHARP KNIFE VERTICALLY, CUT INTO THE UNBAKED BAKLAVA, CUTTING IT INTO DIAMOND SHAPES.

Book IV

Greek and Middle Eastern Cooking

Taming the Quince

Enjoyed throughout the Mediterranean and Middle Eastern regions for well over 4,000 years, the quince (see Figure 3-2) is a hard, yellow fruit that looks like a cross between an apple and a pear. Quinces are never eaten raw. Extremely fragrant when ripe, they are also a very dry and astringent fruit and need to be cooked in liquid with a lot of sugar.

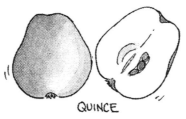

Figure 3-2:
The quince isn't meant for eating raw.

QUINCE

Greek home cooks like to poach slices of quince in sugar syrup flavored with strips of lemon peel and cinnamon sticks. The resulting compote is often spooned over plain, thick Greek yogurt.

Quinces are high in pectin, a natural thickening agent, so cooks throughout the Mediterranean region use quince to make a solid jamlike sweet that is sliced and eaten as dessert, either alone or with a piece of semifirm cheese. Because quinces are so high in pectin, the leftover cooking water can also be boiled down with sugar to make a delicious quince jelly.

Available in the fall at most greengrocers, quinces aren't as readily available in the United States and cost about $2 each.

Quince Paste (Kythonopasto)

This is, hands down, my favorite quince recipe and dessert. I first discovered it while living in Spain. It's also made and enjoyed in Portugal, France, Italy, and, naturally, Greece. Although every home cook has her own favorite version, the one that follows provides the best results, in my opinion. Don't be turned off by the long cooking time. It won't seem so long if you cook the quince while you do some other kitchen task. The bay leaves that cover the quince at the end of the recipe add an intriguing flavor.

Special tool: *Food mill*

Preparation time: *20 minutes*

Cooking time: *1 hour*

Yield: *Approximately 40 pieces*

2½ pounds quince

½ cup freshly squeezed lemon juice

2¼ cups granulated sugar

3 dried bay leaves

1 Core the quinces but do not peel. Cut into chunks and place in a 3-quart saucepan. Add the lemon juice and just enough water to cover the quinces.

2 Bring to a boil over high heat. Lower the heat and simmer, covered, 30 to 40 minutes, or until very soft.

3 Using a slotted spoon, remove the cooked quinces to a food mill (see Figure 3-3). Discard the cooking liquid or use to make quince jelly (see the tip at the end of the recipe). Process the fruit pulp into the saucepan. Discard the peel.

4 Add the sugar and stir well. Bring to a boil over medium heat, stirring constantly.

5 Lower the heat to a simmer and continue cooking, stirring constantly until the mixture thickens to an oatmeal-like consistency and begins to come away from the sides of the pot. (This step can take approximately 20 to 25 minutes.) The mixture is done when a spoonful turned upside down does not fall off the spoon.

6 Line a 4-cup loaf pan with a sheet of wax paper. Pour the quince into the pan and spread evenly with a spatula. Let sit, uncovered, for 3 hours or overnight.

7 When solidified, turn the pan over and remove the quince. Store in a tightly sealed container with 3 dried bay leaves.

8 To serve the quince, slice in pieces approximately ½-inch thick. Cut into squares and roll in granulated sugar.

Tip: Use the leftover water from cooking the quince to make quince jelly. To do so, pour the liquid through a fine mesh strainer into a small saucepan. Bring to a boil over high heat and reduce by half. Measure to see how much liquid you have. Return the liquid to the pot with an equal amount of sugar. Bring to a boil over high heat. Lower to a simmer and cook until syrupy. Test to see whether it's done by dribbling a small amount on a saucer. If the liquid sets quickly, like jelly, remove from the heat; if it doesn't set quickly, cook longer. When done, pour into an appropriate-sized glass jar and let cool to room temperature.

Book IV

Greek and
Middle
Eastern
Cooking

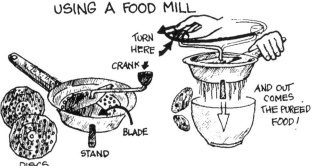

USING A FOOD MILL

Figure 3-3:
A food mill can come in handy when making quince paste.

TURN HERE

CRANK

DISCS

STAND

BLADE

AND OUT COMES THE PUREED FOOD!

Producing Greek-Style Yogurt

Thick, tangy, plain yogurt is a staple in Greek and Middle Eastern diets and kitchens. In some Arabic-speaking countries, it's mixed with cold water to make a refreshing beverage called *aryaan*. Greek cooks use it in cooking, not unlike using sour or heavy cream.

Making yogurt, which is nothing more than fermented milk, was a necessary method for preserving milk in this temperate part of the world. Home cooks in Greece and the Middle East can purchase excellent-quality, commercially produced yogurt made from a combination of sheep's and cow's milk. Nevertheless, this yogurt is very different from what people in the United States may be accustomed to. It's almost as thick as sour cream and never watery. To achieve this consistency, the yogurt is strained to remove some of the whey. The yogurt doesn't contain thickening agents like gelatin or cornstarch, so the clean, fresh flavor of the milk shines through.

Greek-Style Yogurt (Yaoúrti)

Imported yogurt from Greece and locally made Greek-style yogurt have been appearing more and more on the shelves of high-end supermarkets and specialty food stores. Once you try it, there's no going back to the pasty, thin versions of yogurt you've probably become so accustomed to over the years.

Don't despair if you can't find the Greek variety where you live. You can make a pretty respectable substitute at home by straining plain yogurt, even though it may not be identical to Greek yogurt. (See Figure 3-4 for an illustration of making Greek-style yogurt.) To do so, carefully read the label and look for a reliable brand of whole-milk plain yogurt that lists milk and active cultures as the only ingredients. After you have that product, you're ready to get started.

Special tool: *Cheesecloth or paper coffee filter*

Preparation time: *12 hours*

Yield: *Approximately 1¼ cups*

*2 cups plain active-culture whole-milk yogurt
with no additives or flavorings*

1 Line a large mesh strainer with several layers of cheesecloth or a paper coffee filter.

2 Place the strainer over a large bowl. Spoon the yogurt into the prepared strainer.

3 Cover with plastic wrap and let drain in the refrigerator overnight.

4 Discard the liquid in the bowl and spoon thickened yogurt into a clean, dry glass jar.

Figure 3-4:
Making
Greek-style
yogurt.

Cooking Dried Beans and Legumes

For centuries, dried beans and legumes have been a main source of protein in Greece and many Middle Eastern countries. Beans, lentils, and dried peas are used in soups and stews and are also used to make spreads and dips.

All beans grow enclosed in a pod. Some are picked when they're still "green" or fresh, but others are picked only after they've dried on the plant. Dried beans have all of the water removed from them so that they will not rot and spoil. This doesn't mean that they'll last forever. Dried beans that are less than a year old cook better than older ones. They'll hydrate quicker and be more tender; old beans just never seem to get tender enough. Because beans unfortunately don't come with an expiration date, purchase them only from stores that you know have a high turnover rate.

Cooks have many theories as to whether dried beans should be soaked before cooking and for how long. Because you can never be certain how old the beans are, it's always better to soak them before cooking to assure the best results (lentils are the only dried beans that can be cooked without any soaking). I share with you the two most commonly used soaking methods. Regardless of the method used, always pick through the beans to remove foreign particles such as pebbles, dirt, or twigs; then rinse in a colander with cold water.

Book IV

Greek and Middle Eastern Cooking

Soaking beans overnight

Use this method if you want to cook beans the next day. Place beans in a large bowl. Pour in enough room-temperature water so that the beans are covered by about 2 inches. Let sit overnight. Drain the beans and cook.

Soaking beans in a hurry

Use the quick soak method if you need beans the same day. Place the beans in a large pot. Add enough water to cover the beans by 2 inches. Bring the water to a boil over high heat. Boil for 2 minutes. Remove from the heat and let sit for 1 hour to hydrate. Drain the beans and cook.

Cooking the soaked beans

Here are the steps for cooking 1 pound of soaked beans:

1. **Place the beans in a large pot and add just enough water to cover the beans by 2 inches.**

2. **Add 2 bay leaves and a small peeled onion.**

3. **Bring the water to a boil over high heat.**

4. **Lower to a simmer and cook, covered, for approximately 1 hour.**

5. **Test the beans to see whether they're tender.**

   If not, re-cover and cook longer, testing every 15 minutes or so until tender, adding more hot water if necessary.

Never add salt to the soaking or cooking water when initially preparing beans. Salt prevents the skin from softening, making for a tough, not-too-tender bean. Always season the beans after they're done cooking. Like little sponges, they'll absorb the salt quite quickly and be flavorful.

Hummus

People throughout all of Greece and the Middle East seem to enjoy hummus, a smooth chickpea spread. Chickpeas, also known as garbanzo beans, are one of the oldest known dried legumes, and they appear in numerous culinary guises. Making hummus in a food processor is a breeze. Serve with warm pita bread triangles.

A key ingredient to this recipe, tahini, can be found in some supermarkets, usually in the same section where peanut butter is sold. Also check your local health food or specially gourmet food stores.

Preparation time: *15 minutes*

Yield: *Approximately 1¼ cups*

2 cups cooked chickpeas, drained

⅓ cup tahini (sesame seed paste), or ¼ cup olive oil

¼ cup freshly squeezed lemon juice

1 teaspoon salt

2 cloves garlic, peeled

1 tablespoon olive oil

1 pinch of paprika

1 Combine the chickpeas, tahini, lemon juice, salt, and garlic in a food processor bowl.

2 Cover and process until smooth, stopping to scrape the sides of the bowl as needed.

3 Transfer the mixture to a serving bowl. Drizzle the 1 tablespoon of olive oil over the hummus and sprinkle with paprika.

Chapter 4

First Impressions

In This Chapter

▶ Sampling the small dishes of Greek and Middle Eastern cooking

▶ Making garden-fresh salads and soups from the region

*F*amily and food are the cornerstones of Greek and Middle Eastern life. Whereas some cultures eat to live, Greeks and Middle Easterners live to eat. In fact, as in most Mediterranean cultures, food and meals are associated with special occasions, milestones, and the love and care that a family shares with its members.

Even the simplest and humblest of meals starts off with a little something to whet the appetite and to set the stage for the meal to come — a piece of dried sausage, some olives, some cured fish, or cheese. Nothing too elaborate, just something to tantalize the taste buds a bit. But as simple as it may be, it also shows the care and love that go into preparing a meal.

Cooks of the region also like to showcase the wide range and variety of fresh, seasonal greens and vegetables by turning them into flavorful salads and soups that accompany a meal. In Greece, it's even customary to forage in the countryside for wild herbs and greens.

Meeting over Mezedes: Petite Portions

Although most Greek families get together at home for holiday and other important celebrations, the café is where they meet their friends and neighbors to catch up and socialize. Social life in Greece revolves around the café, be it in a small town or village or an urban neighborhood. Most importantly though, the café is where — over a glass or *ouzo* (anise-flavored Greek liqueur), wine, or beer — people share a plate or two of *mezedes* (the plural of *meze),* small plates of savory foods that Greeks, as well as the Turks and some Middle Easterners, eat as snacks or as appetizers before the start of a big meal.

Although *mezedes* can be as simple and humble as a few brine-cured olives or a slice of feta cheese and a chunk of bread, they can also be as elaborate as stuffed grapes leaves, roasted eggplant, or refreshing *tzatziki.* In many cases, bars and cafés become known for their *mezedes* more than their ambiance. People agree to meet at "the bar around the corner near the church that has those great grilled lamb sausages" or "that place down by the pier that has the freshest grilled squid in town."

Some of my most memorable meals have been made up of small plates consisting of a variety of hot and cold dishes. In fact, the first time I had *mezedes* was, of all places, in London. It was a late summer's evening, and I was walking past an outdoor café. The tables were covered with small dishes of food. The variety and aromas were amazing. There wasn't a single table to be had, but I returned the next night and had the best meal of my trip. In assembling the *mezedes* for this chapter, I've thought back to that night and tried to re-create that moment for you with these recipes.

Potato and Garlic Spread (Skordalia)

This thick, creamy garlicky spread is served all over Greece as a popular *meze* with pita bread, although I also enjoy serving it in the summer with a bowl of raw baby carrots. This unique combination of stale bread, almonds, and potato provides insight into the "waste not, want not" mentality of the frugal Greek home cook.

Preparation time: *30 minutes*

Yield: *About 2 cups*

2 cups cubed day-old Italian bread	*1 medium potato, boiled, peeled, diced, and mashed*
⅓ cup ground blanched almonds	
4 cloves garlic	*Salt and pepper to taste*
3 tablespoons freshly squeezed lemon juice	*Pita bread*
½ cup extra-virgin olive oil	

1 Moisten the bread with a small amount of water until it's moist but not sopping wet. Gently press on the bread to squeeze out excess water.

2 Place the moistened bread, almonds, garlic, and lemon juice in the bowl of a food processor. Process until smooth.

3 With the food processor running, add the oil through the feed tube. Process until thick and smooth.

4 Scrape the mixture into a mixing bowl. Fold in the mashed potato. Season with salt and pepper and serve with warm pita bread.

Roasted Eggplant Dip (Baba Ghanoush)

Baba ghanoush is a delicious, popular Middle Eastern dish of roasted, charred eggplant pureed and mixed with tahini (see Chapter 2 of Book IV), garlic, and lemon juice. You find it quite frequently as part of a selection of *mezedes* in Greek and Arabic restaurants.

Preparation time: *15 minutes*

Cooking time: *15 minutes*

Yield: *About 2 cups*

1 large eggplant, about 1½ pounds	*1 tablespoon olive oil*
¼ cup tahini	*Salt and pepper to taste*
1 clove garlic, peeled and minced	*2 tablespoons minced flat-leaf parsley*
3 tablespoons freshly squeezed lemon juice	*Pita bread*

1 Preheat the oven broiler.

2 Prick the eggplant a few times with a fork. Place on a foil-lined baking pan. Place on the top oven rack. Broil on all sides until the skin is charred and the eggplant collapses.

3 Carefully cut the hot eggplant in half. Scoop out the flesh and place in a large colander placed over a bowl to drain any of the bitter liquid.

4 Mash the eggplant in a large mixing bowl with a hand-held potato masher or kitchen fork.

5 Combine the tahini, garlic, lemon juice, and olive oil in a small bowl. Add to the pureed eggplant, season with salt and pepper, and stir to combine well.

6 Spoon into a shallow serving dish. Sprinkle with the minced parsley and serve with warm pita bread.

Book IV

Greek and Middle Eastern Cooking

Cucumber and Yogurt Salad (Tzatziki)

This classic Greek salad of cool cucumbers and thick yogurt makes a refreshing addition to any lineup of *mezedes*. I also like to serve it as an accompaniment to grilled meats like lamb kebabs and burgers.

Preparation time: *15 minutes*

Yield: *About 2 cups*

1¼ cups Greek-Style Yogurt (see Chapter 3 of Book IV)

1 large cucumber, peeled, seeded, and chopped

2 cloves garlic, minced

2 teaspoons chopped fresh mint leaves

2 teaspoons snipped fresh dill

1 tablespoon white wine vinegar

1 tablespoon extra-virgin olive oil

Salt and pepper to taste

Crudités or pita bread

Combine the yogurt, cucumber, garlic, mint, dill, vinegar, and olive oil in a mixing bowl. Season with salt and pepper. Serve with crudités or warm pita bread.

Yogurt Cheese Balls (Labneh Makbus)

Before the days of refrigeration, fresh cheese made from thickened yogurt was made throughout the Middle East. Fermented milk was drained until it was the consistency of cream cheese, and then it was rolled into small balls and packed in jars filled with olive oil so it didn't spoil.

Still popular throughout parts of the region, *labneh makbus* are delicious, especially as they pick up additional flavor from the olive oil and bay leaf. Spread these balls on warm bread. Don't be put off by the long prep time; 90 percent of it is spent letting the yogurt drain in the refrigerator.

Special tool: *Cheesecloth or paper coffee filter*

Preparation time: *72 hours*

Yield: *Approximately 10 to 12 cheese balls*

2 cups plain active-culture, whole-milk yogurt with no additives or flavorings	1 bay leaf
	Olive oil
Salt to taste	Pita or flatbread

1 Line a large mesh strainer with several layers of cheesecloth or a paper coffee filter.

2 Place the strainer over a large bowl. Spoon the yogurt into the prepared strainer.

3 Cover with plastic wrap and let drain in the refrigerator for 48 hours.

4 Season the yogurt with salt.

5 Roll the yogurt cheese into 1-inch balls. Place on a plate and refrigerate overnight uncovered, until firm.

6 Find a glass jar large enough to hold the balls of yogurt cheese (about a 2-cup capacity jar should do). Fill with boiling water to sterilize. Pour out the water and dry with a clean kitchen towel.

7 Pack the cheese in the jar. Add the bay leaf. Pour in the olive oil until the cheese is covered.

8 Place the cover on the jar. Store in the refrigerator.

9 Before serving, bring to room temperature. Place some of the cheese balls on a plate with some of the oil.

10 Mash the cheese with some of the oil to soften it. Spread the mixture on pieces of warm pita or flatbread.

Vary It! *A quick and easier version of labneh makbus is the simple-to-make yogurt cheese spread, labneh. Follow the above recipe up to Step 4. Place the thickened yogurt cheese in a small, shallow bowl. Spread on warm flatbread. Drizzle with olive oil.*

Feta Cheese and Roasted Pepper Spread

This beautifully reddish orange cheese spread is addictive. It combines two of my favorite ingredients used in Greek and Arabic cooking: feta cheese and roasted red peppers. The addition of pickled peppers adds a jolt of warmth to this delicious spread. Serve with warm pita bread or thin slices of country whole-wheat bread.

Preparation time: *10 minutes*

Yield: *About 2 cups*

1 pound feta cheese	*2 tablespoons freshly squeezed lemon juice*
5 tablespoons extra-virgin olive oil	*Black pepper to taste*
1 roasted red pepper (from a jar)	*Pita bread*
2 tablespoons pickled jalapeño slices, drained	

1 Crumble the feta cheese into a blender jar or food processor bowl. Add 2 tablespoons of the olive oil. Pulse until creamy.

2 Add the pepper and jalapeños and pulse until well combined.

3 Add the remaining 3 tablespoons of olive oil and the lemon juice. Pulse until smooth. Season with the black pepper. Serve with warm pita bread.

Stuffed Grape Leaves (Dolmades Nistisimi, Dereve Pattoug)

Stuffed grape leaves, a recipe that's a perfect example of using easily available ingredients, have been served throughout Greece and the surrounding area for centuries. This recipe uses grape leaves prepared in brine as an edible wrapper for a sweet and savory mixture of rice, herbs, dried currants, and pine nuts. Although other versions are made with ground lamb, I prefer this vegetarian version.

Stuffed grape leaves can be served as one of many *mezedes* or as part of a Greek salad (see the recipe later in this chapter). I also like to serve them as a light meal with some feta cheese and sliced tomatoes, with the whole thing sprinkled with a bit of salt and oregano and drizzled with extra-virgin olive oil. Accompany with warm pita bread or other flatbread. Stuffed grape leaves are called *dolmades nistisimi* in Greece and *dereve pattoug* in Armenia.

Preparation time: *60 minutes*

Cooking time: *30 minutes*

Yield: *Approximately 40 pieces*

1 cup olive oil	*¼ teaspoon black pepper*
1 large onion, chopped	*2 jars (8 ounces each) brine-packed grape leaves, drained*
½ cup chopped mixed fresh herbs such as flat-leaf parsley, mint, and dill	*1½ cups water*
⅔ cup short-grain rice	*⅓ cup freshly squeezed lemon juice*
¼ cup dried currants	*Lemon wedges (optional)*
¼ cup pine nuts	*Greek-Style Yogurt (optional)*
1 tablespoon salt	

1 Heat ½ cup of the olive oil in a large skillet over medium-high heat. Add the onion and cook until soft. Add the herbs, rice, currants, pine nuts, salt, and pepper. Cook for 5 minutes longer. Remove from the heat.

2 Blanch the grape leaves in batches in a 6-quart pot of boiling water for approximately 1 minute. Rinse under cold water and drain. Place the leaves on a clean work surface, shiny side down. Remove any stems with scissors. Cover the bottom of the pot with a single layer of grape leaves, being sure to use any torn leaves first.

3 Place a tablespoon of filling near the stem of each remaining grape leaf. Roll once. Fold in the two sides of the leaf and continue rolling, as shown in Figure 4-1. Place the stuffed grape leaves, seam side down, in the pot lined with grape leaves, in tightly packed rows. When the bottom is covered, begin making a second layer.

4 Cover the grape leaves with the remaining ½ cup olive oil, the water, and lemon juice. If the leaves aren't completely covered in liquid, add additional water.

5 Invert a heavy plate on top to keep the grape leaves from unrolling. Cover the pot and bring the liquid to a boil. Lower the heat and simmer for 30 minutes.

6 Remove from the heat and let cool to room temperature. Serve on a plate with lemon wedges and thick Greek-Style Yogurt (see the recipe in Chapter 3 of Book IV), if desired.

Book IV

Greek and Middle Eastern Cooking

Wrapping Stuffed Grape Leaves

Place the leaves on a board.

Wrap the leaves around the mixture,

DON'T WRAP TOO TIGHTLY!

I'm stuffed

Figure 4-1: Stuffing grape leaves.

and drop about 2 teaspoons of the rice on each leaf.

rolling and folding the ends.

Swooning Iman (Iman Bayildi)

The history behind this recipe is unique. Rumor has it that this dish was prepared by a Greek cook for an Ottoman iman. The ruler was so taken by the aroma and taste of the dish that he became lightheaded and began to swoon, thus giving the recipe its name! I hope that this meltingly delicious combination of Mediterranean ingredients has the same effect on you, too!

Preparation time: *45 minutes*

Cooking time: *60 minutes*

Yield: *8 appetizer servings*

8 long, small Italian eggplants	*¼ cup chopped flat-leaf parsley*
½ cup extra-virgin olive oil	*Salt and pepper to taste*
3 medium onions, thinly sliced	*2 tablespoons freshly squeezed lemon juice*
4 cloves garlic, minced	*½ cup water*
14.5-ounce can diced tomatoes	

1 Cut the stems off the eggplants. Cut alternating thin strips of skin from the eggplants so that they look like they have stripes. Cut a deep slit lengthwise into the eggplants, stopping short of the two ends and the bottom.

2 Place in a bowl of well-salted cold water and let sit for 30 minutes.

3 Heat 2 tablespoons of the olive oil in a large covered deep pan over medium-high heat. Add the onions and cook until soft. Add the garlic and cook a minute longer. Remove to a bowl. Add the tomatoes and parsley. Season with salt and pepper.

4 Drain the eggplant. Squeeze out the moisture and pat dry. Heat the remaining oil in the pan over medium-high heat. Add the eggplant and brown on all sides. Remove the pan from the heat. Turn the eggplant so that the slit side is up. Spoon the onion and tomato mixture over the eggplant, being sure to get some into the slits. Combine the lemon juice and water and pour over the eggplant.

5 Cover and cook at a simmer for 45 minutes.

6 Cool to room temperature before serving.

Falafel

Street food in many Arabic countries, *falafel* is a delicious Arabic fast food of fried balls (or patties) of ground and seasoned chickpeas stuffed into a pita bread with lettuce, tomatoes, and a tahini sauce. It's amazingly easy to make. The chickpeas are soaked overnight and not cooked before being ground up in the food processor with the other ingredients.

Preparation time: *30 minutes, plus overnight for soaking the chickpeas*

Cooking time: *15 minutes*

Yield: *4 servings*

1¼ cups dried chickpeas, soaked overnight in room-temperature water	¼ teaspoon ground cayenne pepper
	2 tablespoons all-purpose flour
1 medium onion, chopped	Vegetable oil for frying
2 cloves garlic, minced	**For serving:**
¼ cup packed flat-leaf parsley leaves	4 pita breads, warmed
2 teaspoons ground cumin	2 cups iceberg lettuce, shredded
½ teaspoon ground coriander	1 tomato, cored and diced
1½ teaspoons salt	½ cup Tahini with Yogurt Dip (see Chapter 2 of Book IV)
½ teaspoon baking soda	

1 Drain the chickpeas. Place in a food processor bowl and coarsely chop.

2 Add the onion, garlic, parsley, cumin, coriander, salt, baking soda, and cayenne pepper. Process until finely chopped.

3 Place the mixture in a bowl and add the flour.

4 With wet hands, form 4 patties, about 3 inches in diameter.

5 Fill a large nonstick skillet with ½ inch of the vegetable oil. Heat over medium-high heat. Fry the falafels on each side until golden brown. Drain on paper towels.

6 Open one edge of the pita breads. Place a quarter of the lettuce and tomatoes in each. Place a falafel in each pita bread. Drizzle the falafel with some of the Tahini with Yogurt Dip.

Vary It! Sometimes I like to serve falafel as an appetizer. To do so, roll the mixture into small bite-sized balls and fry them until golden brown. Serve on a bed of lettuce and diced tomato. Drizzle generously with some of the sauce.

Book IV

Greek and Middle Eastern Cooking

Using Nature's Bounty for Salads and Soups

Greece and many Arabic countries share a similar culinary heritage based on a long growing season, which translates into a rich abundance of vibrant vegetables waiting to be turned into delectable salads and satisfying soups. Starting off with what seemed like an endless list to choose from, I've narrowed it down and chosen the most classic and familiar recipes for you to prepare and share with your family and friends. I can't stress enough the importance of choosing the freshest of ingredients for the best results when preparing these recipes.

Greek Salad (Salatà Eliniki)

People who haven't ever sampled a Greek salad don't know what they're missing. When properly made, a Greek salad should be a combination of lettuce, tomatoes, onions, and cucumbers, livened up with the tangy addition of Greek olives, feta cheese, and a fresh vinaigrette made with a wine vinegar and lemon juice.

Preparation time: *15 minutes*

Yield: *4 servings*

1 large head romaine lettuce	*½ cup crumbled feta cheese*
½ cup snipped fresh dill	*¼ cup extra-virgin olive oil*
1 small red onion, cut into thin rings	*1 tablespoon red wine vinegar*
1 cucumber, peeled, seeded, and thinly sliced	*1 tablespoon freshly squeezed lemon juice*
1 large tomato, cored and diced	*1 teaspoon dried oregano*
½ cup kalamata olives	*Salt and pepper to taste*

1 Lay the romaine lettuce on a cutting board. With leaves still intact, cut into a ½-inch shred. Place in a colander or salad spinner. Wash and dry well.

2 Scatter the lettuce on a platter. Sprinkle with the dill. Cover with the onion rings, cucumber, tomatoes, olives, and feta cheese.

3 In a small bowl, whisk together the olive oil, vinegar, lemon juice, oregano, and salt and pepper. Pour the dressing over the salad and serve.

Arabic Sweet Pepper Salad

People throughout Greece and the Arabic world enjoy large, bright red, sun-ripened bell peppers roasted over a wood fire until their skins are blackened. When allowed to sit, the charred skins come off easily to reveal the sweet, cooked, red flesh of the peppers, which are added to many dishes. The peppers are also combined with olive oil and vinegar to make a wonderfully delicious Arabic salad.

Preparation time: *20 minutes*

Cooking time: *20 minutes*

Yield: *6 servings*

5 red bell peppers	¼ cup white wine vinegar
1 green bell pepper	2 teaspoons salt
½ cup extra-virgin olive oil	2 cloves garlic, thinly sliced

1 Preheat the oven broiler. Place the red and green peppers on a foil-lined baking pan. Place directly under the broiler heat. Broil on each side until charred and blistered. Remove the peppers. Place in a large bowl. Cover and let sit for 10 minutes.

2 Remove the stems, charred skin, and seeds. Tear the peppers into strips and place in a large bowl with any accumulated liquid.

3 In a small bowl, whisk together the olive oil, vinegar, and salt. Pour over the peppers. Add the garlic. Toss well. Cover and let sit at least 2 hours before serving. Taste and add salt if necessary.

Carrot Salad

This brilliantly orange-colored salad from Morocco and Tunisia combines the culinary elements of the Mediterranean region with the exotic spices of the East, which were brought to the region hundreds of years ago by traders. Serve as a side dish or as part of a collection of *mezedes*.

Preparation time: *15 minutes*

Cooking time: *10 minutes*

Yield: *4 servings*

2 cups water

1 pound carrots, peeled and sliced diagonally into ¼-inch pieces

¼ cup extra-virgin olive oil

2 tablespoons freshly squeezed lemon juice

1 clove garlic, minced

1½ teaspoons sugar

1 teaspoon paprika

½ teaspoon salt

½ teaspoon ground cumin

⅛ teaspoon ground cinnamon

1 pinch of cayenne pepper

1 tablespoon minced flat-leaf parsley

1 Bring the water to a boil in a 2-quart saucepan. Salt the water. Add the carrots and cook until crisp-tender, about 5 to 8 minutes.

2 Drain the carrots and place in a serving dish.

3 In a small bowl, whisk together the olive oil, lemon juice, garlic, sugar, paprika, salt, cumin, cinnamon, and cayenne pepper. Drizzle over the carrots and toss well.

4 Sprinkle the carrot salad with the minced parsley before serving.

Bulghur Wheat and Parsley Salad (Tabbouleh)

Tabbouleh, a refreshing bulghur wheat and parsley salad, is a popular Arabic salad. The main ingredient is bulghur wheat, which is wheat kernels that have been steamed, dried, and crushed. When soaked, they plump up and have a chewy texture and nutty taste. Bulghur is also extremely tasty when soaked in lemon juice and then mixed with lots of coarsely chopped parsley leaves, green onions, and tomatoes, as in this tabbouleh salad.

Preparation time: *20 minutes, plus 2 hours to let the bulghur soften*

Yield: *Approximately 30 pieces*

1 cup fine bulghur

2 cups water

1⅓ cups freshly squeezed lemon juice

3 bunches scallions, trimmed and thinly sliced

3 cups flat-leaf parsley leaves, coarsely chopped

3 vine-ripened tomatoes, cored and chopped

½ cup extra-virgin olive oil

Salt to taste

1 Combine the bulghur, water, and 1 cup of the lemon juice in a large glass bowl. Cover and let sit about 2 hours, or until the bulghur has absorbed most of the liquid and is soft.

2 Drain the bulghur in a sieve. Gently press to remove any excess liquid.

3 Combine the soaked bulghur in a large glass bowl with the scallions, parsley, tomatoes, olive oil, and the remaining ⅓ cup lemon juice. Season with salt and toss well.

Egg and Lemon Soup
(Avgolemono Soupa)

The combination of chicken-and-rice soup, eggs, and lemon juice is popular in parts of the Mediterranean. This Aegean classic goes back to the days of the ancient Greeks. The eggs are beaten separately until the whites are stiff. The egg-lemon mixture is then stirred into the hot soup, adding both body and rich flavor.

Preparation time: *10 minutes*

Cooking time: *25 minutes*

Yield: *6 servings*

6 cups homemade or store-bought low-sodium chicken broth

⅓ cup short-grain rice

3 eggs, separated

Pinch of salt

Juice of 1 lemon

1 Bring the broth to a boil in a saucepan. Add the rice. Lower the heat to a simmer and cook, covered, until the rice is tender, about 15 to 20 minutes.

2 While the rice cooks, beat the egg whites in a large bowl with the pinch of salt until stiff. Beat the egg yolks and lemon juice separately. Fold into the stiffened egg whites.

3 Slowly pour 2 cups of the simmering broth into the egg mixture, stirring constantly.

4 Pour the egg mixture into the remaining broth in the pot, stirring constantly. Serve immediately.

White Bean Soup (Fasolátha, Fasulye Plaskisi)

Although Greece and Turkey were political and military rivals for centuries, these two countries share many culinary influences. The following hearty bean and vegetable soup recipe is nearly identical in both countries, with the exception that a Turkish home cook finishes it up with the optional cayenne pepper and lemon juice. This soup is called *fasolátha* in Greece and *fasulye plaskisi* in Turkey.

Preparation time: *15 minutes*

Cooking time: *45 minutes*

Yield: *4 to 6 servings*

4 tablespoons olive oil	1 bay leaf
1 large onion, chopped	5 cups water
2 cloves garlic, minced	Salt and pepper to taste
3 carrots, peeled and diced	3 tablespoons minced flat-leaf parsley
3 stalks celery, trimmed and diced	Pinch of cayenne pepper (optional)
1 cup diced canned tomatoes	2 tablespoons freshly squeezed lemon juice (optional)
2 cans (15 ounces each) white kidney beans, drained and rinsed under cold water	

1 Heat the olive oil in a large saucepan over medium-high heat. Add the onion and garlic. Cook until the onion is soft. Add the carrots and celery. Cook for 2 minutes, stirring constantly. Add the tomatoes and cook for 2 minutes.

2 Add the beans, bay leaf, water, and salt and pepper. Bring to a boil, lower the heat to a simmer, and cook, covered, for 20 minutes, or until the carrots and celery are tender.

3 When ready to serve, taste and add salt and pepper if necessary. To thicken the soup, mash some of the beans and vegetables against the side of the pot with the back of a large spoon. (The Turkish version has more mashed beans and vegetables, making for a thicker consistency.)

4 Stir in the parsley and, if desired, the cayenne pepper and lemon juice.

Book IV

Greek and Middle Eastern Cooking

Pilaf

A mixture of pan-browned fine egg noodles and rice, pilaf is enjoyed throughout the Arabic countries that border the Mediterranean, as well as Turkey and Armenia. Fluffier than regular cooked rice, pilaf is usually served as an accompaniment to grilled meats like kebabs (see Chapter 5 of Book IV).

Preparation time: *15 minutes*

Cooking time: *60 minutes*

Yield: *6 to 8 servings*

3 cups low-sodium chicken broth	*8 ounces fine egg noodles*
3 cups water	*2 cups short-grain rice*
7 tablespoons unsalted butter	*Salt and pepper to taste*

1 Bring the broth and water to a boil over medium-high heat in a 3-quart covered saucepan.

2 Melt the butter in a 3-quart pot over medium heat. Add the noodles and cook, stirring constantly, until golden brown. Remove from the heat and stir in the rice. Season with salt and pepper.

3 Return to medium heat. Add the hot broth. Cover and cook, undisturbed, 30 minutes.

4 Remove from the heat and let sit 10 minutes undisturbed. Fluff the rice and noodles with a large spoon and serve immediately.

Chapter 5

The Main Event

In This Chapter

- Baking savory one-dish meals
- Preparing meat, poultry, and seafood entrées

As in most cuisines, the main course in Greek and Middle Eastern cooking is the highlight of any meal. Fresh produce, milk-fed lamb, and time-treasured methods of preparation combine to turn even the simplest of dishes into something extremely special.

Running the gamut from flaky phyllo dough pies stuffed with savory fillings to casseroles and grilled meats, these recipes represent the history of the region on a plate, combining the many cultural and political influences of the past 4,000 years that have shaped the identity and cooking of this part of the world.

Savory Pies and Baked Dishes

Pites, or the wonderful stuffed pies the Greeks are rightly known for, have evolved from ancient times from simple, grilled flatbreads topped with vegetables and wild herbs and drizzled with olive oil, to the elaborate yet easy-to-prepare creations enjoyed today throughout Greece and other countries in the region.

These pies and casseroles are the mainstay of Greek cooking and are among some of the most popular imports of Greek cooking today.

Spinach and Cheese (Spanakopita)

Spanakopita is the best known of all the Greek savory pies, and rightfully so. Sandwiched between thin layers of crisp, buttery phyllo dough is a delicious blend of green spinach leaves, herbs, and cheese. A classic Greek creation, *spanakopita* is convenience food at its best. Cut into small squares, it makes a wonderful *meze* (an appetizer-like food), or cut into large pieces, it's a delicious and satisfying main course, especially when served with a classic Greek Salad or a Sweet Pepper Salad (see the recipes in Chapter 4 of Book IV).

Preparation time: *30 minutes*

Cooking time: *60 minutes*

Yield: *8 servings*

2 pounds fresh spinach, trimmed of stems, coarsely chopped, and washed well but not dried

4 tablespoons olive oil

1 medium onion, chopped

4 scallions, trimmed and thinly sliced

4 tablespoons chopped flat-leaf parsley

4 eggs, lightly beaten

½ cup grated Parmesan cheese

1 cup crumbled feta cheese

¼ teaspoon grated nutmeg

Salt and pepper to taste

10 sheets frozen phyllo dough (about half a 16-ounce package), defrosted overnight

6 tablespoons unsalted butter, melted

1 Preheat the oven to 350 degrees.

2 Place the wet spinach in a large covered pot. Let it cook in its own liquid over medium heat for 5 to 6 minutes, or until wilted. Drain well in a colander, pressing on the spinach with the back of a large kitchen spoon to squeeze out as much liquid as possible.

3 Heat the olive oil in a large skillet over medium-high heat. Add the onion and cook until soft. Add the scallions and cook for 2 minutes longer.

4 Place the drained spinach in a large bowl with the cooked onions. Add the parsley, eggs, Parmesan cheese, feta cheese, and nutmeg. Generously season with salt and pepper. Combine well.

5 Unroll the defrosted phyllo dough. Place on a clean kitchen cloth. If necessary, cut sheets to fit a 13-×-9-inch pan. Cover with wax paper or a dampened kitchen cloth, wrung out well, so that the phyllo dough doesn't dry out as you're working.

6 Brush the bottom and sides of a 13-×-9-×-2-inch baking pan with some of the melted butter.

7 Place 1 sheet of phyllo dough on the prepared pan. Brush with melted butter and then top with another sheet of dough. Repeat the process 4 more times so that you have a stack of 5 buttered sheets.

8 Spread the spinach filling over the top of the phyllo.

9 Cover with a sheet of phyllo dough. Brush with melted butter. Top with the remaining 4 sheets of phyllo, brushing each sheet with butter. Tuck the edges down into the pan. Sprinkle the top sheet with some water so that it doesn't curl up.

10 Cut the pie with a sharp knife into 8 pieces. Bake on the center oven rack for 45 to 50 minutes, or until puffed and golden brown.

11 Remove from the oven and let cool for 10 minutes before cutting into pieces.

Baked Macaroni Casserole (Pasticcio)

Every Greek cook has his own favorite version of the country's beloved *pasticcio,* a delicious layered casserole dish of meat sauce flavored with sweet wine, cinnamon, cooked pasta, and a cheesy, white sauce that eventually forms a custardlike cover on top when baked. Although the name of the dish is Italian for *a mess,* I prefer to layer the ingredients rather than mix them together, making for an attractive presentation when served.

Preparation time: *30 minutes*

Cooking time: *1 hour and 20 minutes*

Yield: *8 to 10 servings*

4 tablespoons olive oil	28-ounce can tomato sauce
1 large onion, chopped	4 tablespoons unsalted butter
1½ pounds lean ground beef or lamb	4 tablespoons all-purpose flour
1 teaspoon ground cinnamon	4 cups whole milk
1 tablespoon salt	2 eggs, lightly beaten
½ teaspoon pepper	1 cup grated Parmesan cheese
1 cup sweet Marsala wine	1 pound ziti, cooked al dente

1 Heat the olive oil in a large saucepan over medium-high heat. Add the onion and cook until soft. Add the ground beef and cook until no longer pink, breaking up any large pieces with a spoon. Add the cinnamon, salt, pepper, and wine. Bring to a boil and let cook for 1 minute. Stir in the tomato sauce. Bring to a boil. Lower the heat to a simmer and cook, covered, for 20 minutes.

2 While the tomato sauce mixture cooks, prepare the white sauce: Melt the butter in a large saucepan over low heat. Blend in the flour and cook slowly, stirring until the butter and flour foam without changing color, about 2 minutes. Remove from the heat. Bring the milk to a boil over medium heat. Slowly pour the hot liquid over the hot flour mixture, beating with a wire whisk until smooth. Add the eggs and grated Parmesan cheese. Return to the stove and cook over medium-high heat until the sauce boils. Cook a minute longer. Remove from the heat and season with salt and pepper to taste.

3 Add ½ cup of the white sauce to the cooked tomato sauce. Stir well.

4 Preheat the oven to 400 degrees.

5 Grease a 13-×-9-inch baking pan. Spread half the cooked pasta in the pan. Cover with the tomato sauce. Cover with the remaining pasta. Spoon the white sauce over the pasta. Smooth with a spatula to cover completely.

6 Place in the oven and bake for 50 minutes, or until golden brown on top.

7 Let stand for 10 minutes before cutting into pieces.

Eggplant Casserole (Moussaka)

Imagine a lasagna made with fried eggplant slices rather than pasta, and you'll have a *moussaka*, a popular Greek casserole dish. A *moussaka* shows how a small amount of meat and lots of vegetables can make for a very satisfying and delicious entree.

Preparation time: *30 minutes*

Cooking time: *1 hour and 5 minutes*

Yield: *8 to 10 servings*

4 eggplants, about 1 pound each, peeled and cut lengthwise into ¼-inch-thick slices

4 tablespoons olive oil

3 large onions, thinly sliced

2 cloves garlic, minced

1 green bell pepper, cored, seeded, and diced

1 pound lean ground beef

½ teaspoon ground cinnamon

1 tablespoon salt

½ teaspoon pepper

1 cup Marsala wine

28-ounce can tomato sauce

Vegetable oil for frying eggplant

1⅓ cups plain yogurt

4 eggs

1 cup whole milk

⅓ cup grated Parmesan cheese

1 Sprinkle the eggplant slices with salt and let them sit in a colander for 1 hour to extract any bitter juices.

2 Heat the olive oil in a large saucepan over medium-high heat. Add the onions, garlic, and green pepper. Cook until the onions and peppers are soft. Add the ground beef and cook until no longer pink, breaking up any large pieces with a spoon. Add the cinnamon, salt, pepper, and wine. Bring to a boil and let cook for 1 minute. Stir in the tomato sauce. Bring to a boil. Lower the heat to a simmer and cook, covered, for 20 minutes.

3 Dry the eggplants thoroughly. Heat ¼ inch of vegetable oil in a large skillet over medium-high heat. Cook the eggplant slices until golden brown on both sides. Drain on absorbent paper. Add more oil to the pan as needed.

4 Preheat the oven to 400 degrees.

5 Place a layer of eggplant on the bottom of a 13-x-9-inch baking dish. Cover with some meat sauce. Continue layering the eggplant and the meat sauce, ending with a final layer of eggplant.

6 Mix the yogurt together with the eggs, milk, and Parmesan cheese. Pour over the eggplant.

7 Place in the oven and bake for 40 to 50 minutes, or until golden brown on top.

8 Let stand for 10 minutes before cutting into pieces.

Book IV

Greek and Middle Eastern Cooking

Braised and Grilled Meat, Poultry, and Fish

Religious influence has played a major role in the lives of Greeks and Middle Easterners in determining when and what meats they eat. Faced with what at times seems like endless days of fasting and abstinence, the Greeks have found a bountiful alternative to meat in the form of seafood fished from its seemly endless miles of coastline. Fish and seafood also have sustained the Greeks through centuries when times were difficult and other food offerings were meager.

Although pork is served in Greek homes, it's forbidden in the Muslim kitchens in the Middle East for religious and dietary reasons. Beef is not as common in this dry part of the world as in the United States. Although cattle need fields and fields of green pasture land to graze on, sheep and goats are not as finicky and thrive well on wild herbs and the little green found in the countryside where they graze.

The Greeks and Middle Easterners are experts in the preparation of lamb and goat. The meat is usually prepared as it has been since the days of ancient Athens and Sparta and Alexander the Great. Traditionally mixed with wild herbs, lemons, and vibrant-tasting, locally pressed olive oil, the meat is then grilled over wood fires or stewed with sun-ripened tomatoes and herbs.

Lamb Kebabs
(Souvlakia, Sis Kebab)

Grilling cubes of lamb is perhaps one of the oldest ways to prepare meat in this area of the world. Marinating the meat not only gives it flavor but also tenderizes it. Sometimes I like to alternate pieces of onion and green pepper with the marinated meat chunks. These lamb kebabs are known as *souvlakia* in Greece and *sis kebab* in Turkey.

Special tools: *Skewers*

Preparation time: *20 minutes, plus overnight for marinating the lamb*

Cooking time: *10 minutes*

Yield: *8 servings*

1 large onion, minced	*Grated zest and juice of 1 lemon*
3 bay leaves	*1/3 cup olive oil*
2 sprigs fresh thyme, leaves removed and coarsely chopped	*2 pounds lean boneless lamb, cut into 3/4-inch cubes*
3 sprigs fresh rosemary, needles removed and coarsely chopped	*Salt and pepper to taste*
	Lemon wedges, for serving

1 Mix together the onion, bay leaves, thyme, rosemary, lemon zest and juice, and olive oil in a large mixing bowl. Add the lamb cubes. Season with salt and pepper and toss well.

2 Cover and marinate in the refrigerator overnight.

3 Prepare a grill or preheat the oven broiler.

4 Drain the meat, pat dry, and thread onto skewers. Arrange on a grill rack or broiler and cook for about 10 minutes, until browned, turning occasionally.

5 Serve over Pilaf (see Chapter 4 of Book IV) with lemon wedges and Yogurt Sauce (see the recipe later in this chapter).

Vary It! *If you happen to have a large rosemary bush in your herb garden, prune it and use the thicker branches as skewers for the lamb by cutting them into 8-inch lengths and removing the needles.*

Book IV

Greek and Middle Eastern Cooking

Lamb Burgers (Yaourtlou Kebap) with Yogurt Sauce

Because meat is a precious commodity in Greece, small scraps unsuitable for grilling or roasting are usually chopped fine and turned into savory patties. Not unlike a perfect burger, the patties are then grilled and served nestled in a warm pita bread. Serve with a delicious yogurt sauce flavored with mint and garlic that complement the flavor of the meat.

Preparation time: *20 minutes*

Cooking time: *12 minutes*

Yield: *4 servings*

1 pound ground lean lamb or beef

1 egg

2 slices day-old white bread, torn into very small pieces

1 small onion, minced

2 tablespoons freshly squeezed lemon juice

1 tablespoon minced flat-leaf parsley, or 1 tablespoon mint

1 teaspoon salt

⅛ teaspoon pepper

4 small pita breads

2 small vine-ripened tomatoes, sliced

2 small green bell peppers, cut in rings

1 red onion, thinly sliced

Yogurt Sauce

1 Preheat a grill or preheat the oven broiler.

2 Combine the lamb, egg, bread, onion, lemon juice, parsley, salt, and pepper in a mixing bowl. Form into 4 patties about ¾-inch thick.

3 Grill for about 6 minutes on each side, or until done.

4 Split the pitas to form a pocket. Transfer the burgers to pita pockets and top with tomatoes, bell peppers, and onion. Serve the burgers with Yogurt Sauce (see the following recipe.)

Yogurt Sauce

This classic yogurt sauce adds a refreshing touch to grilled lamb and other meats. I even use it to marinate boneless legs of lamb overnight. I then roast the lamb in a 350-degree oven until it's rosy pink in the center.

Preparation time: *10 minutes*

Yield: *1½ cups*

1½ cups Greek-Style Yogurt (see Chapter 3 of Book IV)

1 clove garlic, minced

¼ teaspoon salt

3 tablespoons shredded fresh mint leaves

Mix together the yogurt, garlic, salt, and mint in a small bowl. Let sit at room temperature 30 minutes before using to allow the flavors to mix.

Braised Lamb Sauce over Pasta

Contrary to popular belief, pasta is eaten and enjoyed regularly not only in Italy but also in Greece and other parts of the Middle East. Pasta-making is a tradition borrowed from the Arabs, who taught the people of the Mediterranean basin how to grow wheat in irrigated fields. Home cooks in many small villages still make their own pasta.

As you might expect, this Greek recipe is made with chunks of lamb and is almost stew-like in consistency.

Preparation time: *30 minutes*

Cooking time: *40 minutes*

Yield: *6 to 8 servings*

4 tablespoons olive oil

1 medium onion, thinly sliced

1 clove garlic, thinly sliced

1 pound lean boneless lamb, cut into ¾-inch cubes

Salt to taste

1 red bell pepper, cored, seeded, and thinly sliced

1 yellow bell pepper, cored, seeded, and thinly sliced

¾ cup dry white wine

28-ounce can tomato puree

1 teaspoon coarsely ground black pepper, plus more to taste

1 cup Greek-Style Yogurt (see Chapter 3 of Book IV)

1 pound penne, cooked al dente

1 Heat the olive oil in a large skillet over medium-high heat. Add the onion, garlic, and lamb. Cook until the lamb is browned. Season with salt.

2 Add the red and yellow peppers and cook until they begin to soften. Raise the heat to high and add the wine. Cook for 1 minute. Reduce the heat to a simmer.

3 Add the tomato puree and the black pepper. Season with salt. Cover and simmer for 30 minutes, or until the lamb is fork-tender. Taste and add more salt and pepper if necessary.

4 Stir in the yogurt and remove from the heat.

5 Serve the sauce over the cooked pasta.

Book IV

Greek and Middle Eastern Cooking

Tagine of Chicken with Lemons and Olives

Although the Arabic countries of North Africa aren't actually part of the Middle East, they share many culinary traditions with their southern European neighbors and fellow Arabs to the east. *Tagines,* or dishes of stewed or braised meats, poultry, and vegetables, are popular entrées in Morocco, Algeria, and Tunisia, and they're simple to prepare.

Preparation time: *20 minutes*

Cooking time: *2 hours*

Yield: *4 to 6 servings*

4 tablespoons olive oil	*½ teaspoon pepper*
1 large onion, thinly sliced	*3½-pound chicken, skin removed, cut into serving pieces*
1 clove garlic, thinly sliced	
1½ tablespoons minced flat-leaf parsley	*1 Salt-Preserved Lemon (see Chapter 2 of Book IV), quartered*
1 tablespoon minced cilantro	*⅓ cup Moroccan-Cured Olives (see Chapter 2 of Book IV)*
1 teaspoon salt	

1 Heat the olive oil in a Dutch oven or a heavy-bottomed pot with a tight-fitting cover over medium-high heat.

2 Add the onion, garlic, parsley, cilantro, salt, and pepper. Stir to mix.

3 Add the chicken pieces and turn to coat.

4 Place the lemon pieces on top of the chicken and cover.

5 Lower the heat and simmer about 2 hours, or until the chicken tests done, turning periodically.

6 Place the chicken pieces on a serving dish.

7 Bring the cooking liquid to a boil and reduce by half.

8 Add the olives and heat through.

9 Pour the sauce and olives over the chicken and serve with couscous, which absorbs the sauce (see the following tip).

Tip: A staple of North Africa, couscous is a type of pasta made from semolina flour. When making couscous in the traditional manner, Arabic women mix the semolina with a small amount of water to make a paste. They then rub the paste through a fine mesh screen. The resulting dried pellets are sun-dried and stored for later use. Fortunately, today you can purchase commercially made couscous at most supermarkets, usually in the aisle with the rice and noodle mixes.

Baked Shrimp with Tomatoes and Feta (Garides Saganaki)

The following recipe, popular in many Greek restaurants both in Greece and the United States, is surprisingly simple to make. Consisting of shrimp baked with tomatoes and feta, it was reportedly created by one of the many restaurants on the island of Santorini and shows off the best of Santorini's ingredients. Santorini is one of the most famous and beautiful of the many Greek islands. Enjoyed by visitors for centuries, Santorini is renowned for its villages of whitewashed houses and cobblestone streets, as well as the turquoise blue water of its beaches.

Preparation time: *15 minutes*

Cooking time: *20 minutes*

Yield: *6 servings*

4 tablespoons olive oil	*½ cup finely diced tomato, drained well*
1 medium onion, chopped	*Salt to taste*
½ teaspoon crushed hot red pepper	*⅔ cup crumbled feta cheese*
3 cloves garlic, minced	*¼ cup chopped flat-leaf parsley*
1½ pounds large shrimp, peeled, with tails on and deveined	

1 Preheat the oven to 400 degrees.

2 Heat the olive oil in a large skillet over medium-high heat. Add the onion and cook until soft. Add the hot pepper and garlic. Add the shrimp and cook for 2 minutes. Add the tomato and cook for 2 minutes longer. Season with salt.

3 Spoon the shrimp and sauce into a 13-x-9-inch baking dish, large enough to accommodate a single layer. Bake for 10 minutes. Sprinkle with the feta cheese and bake for 2 minutes longer. Sprinkle with the parsley before serving.

Book IV

Greek and Middle Eastern Cooking

Baked Fish Served with Rosemary Potatoes

Fish is often cooked with few accompaniments to let the flavor of the fish and the sea shine through. Greek cooks often grill fish over a wood fire or fry it in olive oil, but in this recipe, the fish is baked in a briny sauce of tomatoes, olives, and capers as a way to capitalize on the natural salty flavor of the sea's bounty.

Preparation time: *20 minutes*

Cooking time: *45 minutes*

Yield: *6 servings*

Approximately 4 pounds of fresh fish steaks, such as cod or tuna, or small whole red snapper, gutted and scaled

4 tablespoons olive oil

2 large onions, thinly sliced

4 cloves garlic, thinly sliced

14.5-ounce can diced tomatoes

1 bay leaf, crushed

¼ teaspoon dried thyme

Salt and pepper to taste

⅓ cup chopped kalamata olives

2 tablespoons capers

1 small fresh fennel, tops only, coarsely chopped (about ¾ cup)

1 Preheat the oven to 350 degrees.

2 Place the fish in an oiled 13-×-9-inch baking dish.

3 Heat the olive oil in a large skillet over medium-high heat. Add the onions and garlic. Cook until the onion is soft.

4 Add the tomatoes, bay leaf, thyme, and salt and pepper. Cover and simmer until the sauce is thick, about 10 minutes. Add the olives, capers, and fennel.

5 Pour the sauce over the fish and bake for approximately 30 minutes, or until done. Serve immediately with the Rosemary Potatoes (see the following recipe).

Rosemary Potatoes

This recipe is the perfect accompaniment to almost any grilled or roasted dishes, be it meat or seafood. Wild herbs, such as the rosemary in this recipe, grow in abundance throughout Greece and are used in many dishes of that country.

Preparation time: *10 minutes*

Cooking time: *5 to 8 minutes*

Yield: *6 servings*

1½ pounds baby potatoes

1 cup olive oil

1 tablespoon rosemary needles only, coarsely chopped

Salt to taste

1 Peel and wash the potatoes well.

2 Heat the olive oil in a large skillet over medium-high heat. Add the potatoes. Stir immediately and cover the pan with a lid.

3 Cook for 15 to 20 minutes or until the potatoes are browned and fork-tender. Sprinkle the potatoes with the rosemary. Using a slotted spoon, remove the potatoes to a serving dish. Sprinkle with salt and serve immediately.

Chapter 6

Sweet Endings

In This Chapter

▷ Flavoring desserts with products from nature
▷ Baking cookies that melt in your mouth

Recipes in This Chapter

▷ Mock Kataifi Nut Pastries
▷ Rice Pudding (Rizógalo, Gatnabour)
▷ Butter Cookies (Kourabiedes, Kurabia, Ghiraybah)
▷ Yogurt Cake (Yaourtopita, Yogurt Tatlisi)

🍴 🥄 🍳 🍶 🍐 🐦

Although most Greek and Arabic meals traditionally end with sun-ripened fresh or dried fruit, Greeks and Middle Easterners do have a sweet tooth. Buttery-rich pastries filled with nuts, melt-in-your-mouth cookies, and moist cakes abound throughout the region. Homemakers have their own cherished recipes that have been handed down from mother to daughter. Holidays are occasions for preparing special cakes, breads, or cookies served only at certain times of the year. Although people in the United States are used to a daily indulgence of sweets, Greek and Middle Eastern cooks usually prepare and serve sweet homemade desserts only on special occasions or when company calls. In fact, sweets are an important symbol of hospitality in Greek and Arabic homes and are usually served with strong, thick coffee or an herbal tea.

The recipes that follow cross over many ethnic and geographic boundaries and are enjoyed, for the most part, throughout the region. Flavorings from nature, such as honey, lemon, and cinnamon, are quite prevalent and appear in many different recipes.

Mock Kataifi Nut Pastries

Finely shredded pieces of phyllo dough, or *kataifi,* are a favorite Greek and Middle Eastern ingredient to use in making baklava-like pastries. When baked, it crisps up and closely resembles shredded wheat, which makes for an ideal and readily available substitute for phyllo and which is what you use in this recipe.

Preparation time: *20 minutes*

Cooking time: *30 minutes*

Yield: *24 pieces*

1½ cups plus 1 tablespoon granulated sugar	2 teaspoons freshly squeezed lemon juice
1½ cups water	15-ounce box large shredded wheat
¼ cup honey	1½ cups lukewarm whole milk
1 small strip lemon peel	1 cup (2 sticks) unsalted butter, melted
1 small cinnamon stick	2 cups chopped walnuts
3 whole cloves	¼ teaspoon cinnamon

1 Prepare the syrup by combining the 1½ cups sugar, water, and honey in a small saucepan. Bring to a boil over medium-high heat. Add the lemon peel, cinnamon stick, and cloves. Lower the heat to a simmer and cook, covered, for 20 minutes. Remove from the heat and let cool to room temperature. Add the lemon juice. Pour through a fine mesh strainer before using.

2 Preheat the oven to 375 degrees. Generously butter a 9-x-13-inch baking dish with some of the melted butter.

3 Quickly dip half of the shredded wheat, one at a time, into the lukewarm milk. Let the excess milk drip back into the bowl. Break the softened shredded wheat in half horizontally and cover the bottom of the prepared pan.

4 Combine the walnuts, 1 tablespoon sugar, and cinnamon in a bowl and sprinkle on top of the shredded wheat.

5 Place the remaining shredded wheat, dipped in the milk and split in half, over the nut mixture.

6 Spoon the melted butter evenly over the top.

7 Bake on the middle oven rack for 7 minutes. Remove from the heat and cover with foil. Let cool until lukewarm.

8 When the shredded wheat is lukewarm, spoon the syrup over the pastry. Re-cover with foil and cool to room temperature.

9 Cut with a sharp knife into 24 pieces.

Rice Pudding (Rizógalo, Gatnabour)

Traders spread rice throughout the Mediterranean region and Middle East hundreds of years ago. Today, rice appears not only in savory dishes such as Stuffed Grape Leaves and Pilaf (both recipes are in Chapter 4 of Book IV) but also in sweets such as rice cakes and cookies, as well as in puddings, like this one, scented with lemon peel and cinnamon. Rice pudding is called *rizógalo* in Greece and *gatnabour* in Armenia.

Preparation time: *5 minutes*

Cooking time: *1 hour and 10 minutes*

Yield: *8 servings*

1 cup water	*2 small strips lemon peel*
¾ cup short-grain rice	*1 small cinnamon stick*
4 cups whole milk	*½ cup granulated sugar*

1 Bring the water to a boil in a small saucepan. Add the rice and cook over low heat until the water is absorbed.

2 Bring the milk to a boil in a medium-sized saucepan with the lemon peel and cinnamon stick. Add the cooked rice to the hot milk and simmer, covered, for 40 minutes, stirring frequently.

3 Remove and discard the lemon peel and cinnamon stick. Add the sugar. Stir well and cook for 15 minutes longer.

Butter Cookies (Kourabiedes, Kurabia, Ghiraybah)

These are the ultimate butter cookies. Buttery and light, they literally melt in your mouth. In many countries, they're prepared and served on special occasions, such as Christmas and weddings, but in Arabic countries, they're served to celebrate the end of a fast. These cookies are called *kourabiedes* in Greece, *kurabia* in Armenia, and *ghiraybah* in the Middle East.

Preparation time: *15 minutes, plus 1 hour for chilling the dough*

Cooking time: *12 to 15 minutes a batch*

Yield: *Approximately 48 cookies*

1 cup (2 sticks) unsalted butter, at room temperature

½ cup confectioners' sugar, plus additional for sprinkling on baked cookies

½ teaspoon vanilla extract

2 cups all-purpose flour

½ teaspoon baking powder

Pinch of salt

½ cup very finely chopped walnuts

1 Beat the butter in a large bowl with an electric mixer until light in color and creamy. Add the confectioners' sugar and vanilla and beat until fluffy and well blended.

2 Sift together the flour, baking powder, and salt. Gradually add to the butter mixture along with the walnuts. Stir until well combined.

3 Cover and refrigerate until the dough is firm enough to shape into balls, about 1 hour.

4 Preheat the oven to 350 degrees.

5 Pull off pieces of dough and roll into 1-inch balls. Place on a lightly buttered baking sheet, about 1 inch apart.

6 Bake on the center oven rack for 12 to 15 minutes, or until lightly golden.

7 Remove from the oven and cool on a rack until the cookies are slightly firm.

8 Place the cookies on a cooling rack and generously sprinkle with confectioners' sugar.

Yogurt Cake (Yaourtopita, Yogurt Tatlisi)

This wonderfully moist cake (called _yaourtopita_ in Greece and _yogurt tatlisi_ in Turkey) tastes even better when served the day after it's made. It was probably first created by some farm wife to take advantage of an abundance of ingredients such as fresh eggs from her hens, homemade yogurt from the family's sheep or goats, honey from hives strategically positioned near nut and citrus trees, and the yellow lemons that grow under the hot — and at times, brutal — Mediterranean sun.

Preparation time: _20 minutes_

Cooking time: _50 to 55 minutes_

Yield: _8 to 10 servings_

¾ cup (1½ sticks) unsalted butter, at room temperature

1 cup granulated sugar

Grated zest of 1 lemon

5 eggs, separated

1 cup plain yogurt

2¼ cups all-purpose flour

2 teaspoons baking powder

½ teaspoon baking soda

Pinch of salt

Syrup:

1 cup granulated sugar

1½ cups water

3 tablespoons honey

4 small strips lemon peel

1 tablespoon freshly squeezed lemon juice

_1_ Preheat the oven to 350 degrees. Butter and flour an 8- to 9-inch tube pan.

_2_ Beat the butter, sugar, and lemon zest in a large bowl with an electric mixer until light in color and fluffy. Add the egg yolks, one at a time, beating well after each addition. Add the yogurt and mix until well combined.

_3_ Sift together the flour, baking powder, and baking soda. Fold into the butter mixture. Stir until well combined.

_4_ Beat the egg whites with a pinch of salt until stiff. Fold into the batter.

_5_ Spoon the cake batter into the prepared cake pan. Bake on the center rack for 50 to 55 minutes, or until the cake is golden and tests done when a toothpick is inserted.

_6_ While the cake bakes, prepare the syrup by combining the sugar, water, and honey in a small saucepan. Bring to a boil over medium-high heat. Add the lemon peel. Lower the heat to a simmer and cook, uncovered, for 10 minutes. Remove from the heat and let cool to room temperature. Add the lemon juice.

_7_ Remove the baked cake from the oven. Cool in the pan on a wire rack for 5 minutes. Invert the cake on a serving plate.

_8_ Slowly spoon the syrup evenly over the entire cake. Let the cake cool to room temperature before serving.

Book IV

Greek and Middle Eastern Cooking

Book V
Indian Cooking

The 5th Wave   By Rich Tennant

©RICHTENNANT

"I just don't think asking for chutney ketchup on your hamburger reflects a full appreciation of Indian cuisine."

In this book . . .

*I*ndian food is one of the more exotic cuisines we cover in this book, and most Americans are used to sampling it only in restaurants. But you can make the transition to cooking Indian food in your home. You'll be surprised at how easy it is, once you stock up on a few intriguing spices. Whether you want to stick to some basic curries, try your hand at samosas, or create some delicious rice pudding, this book gets you going in the right direction. Remember that Indian culture has a strong tradition of vegetarianism, so it's a good place to start if you want to expand your vegetarian repertoire.

Contents at a glance

Chapter 1

Basics of Indian Cooking

Most people's experience with Indian food can be summed up in three words: curry, curry, curry. But Indian cuisine is as varied as India's geography, climate, religion, and culture. From the meaty, warm tandoori dishes of Northern India to the mostly vegetarian, saucy Southern *dals* (legume-based dishes), no two of India's regions are alike.

What they do all share is a reliance on locally available foods. For example, in the south, rice grows in abundance. The southern population tends to prepare more liquid curries and sauces because rice is a highly absorbent, always present element at virtually every meal. In the north, where wheat is grown, the sauces are thicker and served with unleavened flat bread, or *parantha*. Additionally, southern farmers enjoy heavy rainfall and a seemingly endless array of vegetables, making a vegetarian diet very common. While their northern neighbors at the foothills of the Himalayas add lamb to their diet, their coastal cousins enjoy fish and other seafood regularly.

The influence of religion on eating habits can't be ignored. Hindus and Sikhs do not eat beef, as they regard the cow as a sacred animal. Specific sects of Hinduism are strict vegetarians and won't eat food that even resembles meat (such as tomatoes, beets, and watermelon) or foods that are often associated with meat (such as onions and garlic). Other religions within India (primarily Muslims and Jews) are prohibited from eating pork.

The Principles of Indian Cooking

Indian cooking is characterized by flavors and aromas unlike any other cuisine. Those flavors and aromas come from the varied spices, combinations and preparations, and a reliance on simple ingredients. Indian cooks let the spices do the work and flavor their foods. And no two Indian cooks cook exactly alike, so there's really no wrong way to do it! How's that for empowerment! Keep in mind a few basic principles, and you will be cooking like an Indian pro in no time.

Spices rule, guests drool

Despite the variety in climate, geography, and culinary traditions, one unifying element of Indian cooking is its reliance on herbs, spices, and spice blends. Their fragrance and aromatic properties are essential to Indian cuisine. A single spice can be treated a number of different ways (whole, ground, fried, roasted, or roasted and then ground) before being added to a dish, giving the finished product significantly different flavors and aromas. Additionally, different parts of an herb (the root, seeds, or leaves) can be used to add distinctively different flavors and aromas to the finished dish.

Buy fresh, seasonal, local ingredients

One reason for the differences among the styles of Indian cooking is the availability of ingredients. Use that same principle to your advantage. Shop farmer's markets when weather permits to find the best zucchini for your chutney or the best cauliflower for your pakoras. Try whole foods markets to find a wide variety of rice and legumes available to purchase in bulk. If you put good stuff in, you get good stuff out!

Experiment!

Although many dishes are staples of a particular region, no two preparations are identical. Different families within a particular village make a dish their own by creating their own custom spice blends. These blends are closely guarded family secrets. Don't be afraid to try creating some blends yourself.

Keep it simple

Although Indian food isn't difficult to prepare, it can be time-consuming. You don't have to create everything from scratch to have an authentic Indian meal. Don't be afraid to try some store-bought spice blends, marinades, chutneys, and cheese to use with the recipes in this book. Even if you can't find an

Indian grocer close to home, many gourmet shops and even mainstream supermarkets have expanded their Asian offerings to include more than soy sauce and chow mein noodles.

Maintain balance during menu planning

Indian meals maintain a balance between wet and dry dishes, like the balance between wet, saucy curries and dry rice. They also soothe warm, spicy dishes with cooling *raitas* (flavored, savory yogurts) and chutneys.

Four distinct Indian culinary regions

As with any country, India's culinary regions are known for their own delicacies. However, you may have a tough time finding a restaurant that serves these delicacies in the home region. Culturally, Indians usually leave the regional cooking at home and venture out for what they don't make at home. So a family in the southern state of Goa would not go to a restaurant down the street to try a Goan vindaloo curry. They would prefer their own family recipe, but would dine in a restaurant to sample the northern tandoori delicacies. Here's a brief overview of the various culinary regions in India.

Northern India (roughly made up of the six states of Madhya Pradesh, Uttar Pradesh, Haryana, Punjab, Himachal Pradesh, and Jammu and Kashmir) boasts the most familiar mix of regional dishes, including the ever-popular tandoori-style cooking. The typical Indian restaurant in the West owes most of its menu selections to this region, including *koftas* (spicy meatballs), *kormas* (meats braised in creamy sauces of yogurts and fruits), and the luxuriously chewy, leavened bread, *naan*. Garam masala is a typical spice blend used here, more warming than fiery. Basmati rice is the favorite choice in the north, but breads are the primary starch in this wheat-growing region.

Southern India's cuisine is characterized by fiery spice blends, such as vindaloo, and a reliance on legumes, including lentils and chickpeas. This region is comprised of the states of Andhra Pradesh, Karnataka, Goa, Tamil Nadu, and Kerala. Although the southern diet is primarily vegetarian, the people here may add meat for celebrations and special occasions. Rice grows well here, and the fragrant jasmine variety is present in almost every dish during a meal, even dessert!

The states of Orissa, Bihar, West Bengal, Assam, Meghalaya, Tripura, Mizoram, Manipur Nagaland, and Arunachal Pradesh make up **Eastern India**. Famous for Darjeeling tea and Mother Teresa, this hot, humid region along the Bay of Bengal has cultivated as many as 50 different varieties of rice. Coconuts and bananas are popular ingredients; coconut milk often substitutes for cow's or goat's milk.

Rajasthan, Gujarat, and Maharashtra compose **Western India**. Dairy products, including yogurt, buttermilk, cow's milk, and goat's milk, are staples in the western diet. Along the coastline of the Arabian Sea, you can sample the popular "Bombay Duck," which is actually a small, transparent fish. You'll also find a dizzying array of pickles, served with every meal.

Traditionally, Indian meals are served family style. All items, including desserts, are present at the table simultaneously, served on large platters called *thalis,* or sometimes on banana leaves (very handy, and much more environmentally friendly than paper plates). And although a few serving utensils are present, guests eat almost everything with their hands (well, actually, just the right hand; the left is reserved for other, shall we say, necessary functions).

Tools of the Trade

To make the most of the recipes in this book, you don't need any specialty equipment. But I describe some items that a typical Indian kitchen would have and then give you ways to get around using them.

Kadhai (Indian wok)

The Indian wok, or *kadhai,* looks like a cross between a Chinese wok and a round-bottom casserole (see Figure 1-1). It's typically made out of cast iron or stainless steel, but occasionally it has a copper bottom. It's very useful for deep-frying, stir-frying vegetables, and cooking curries.

Figure 1-1:
An Indian-
style wok.

KADHAI

If you choose to purchase a kadhai, you must season it before its first use, just as you season a Chinese wok. For details, check out Chapter 1 of Book VI. After each use, heat the kadhai briefly over low heat to thoroughly dry it. You could also just use a casserole pan or wok instead.

Enamel-coated cast-iron cookware

This type of cookware is great for all types of cooking, not just Indian. You can deep-fry and then go from the stovetop to oven without changing pans if necessary. If you don't already own any of this cookware, it's definitely worth the investment. You can find these pieces at a wide variety of stores (including discount, department, gourmet, and online) at a wide variety of prices. My grandmother swears by her set that now sells for around $200 per pan, and she has been cooking with it for more than 40 years. However, I've found that the "popularly priced" versions provide a great value and get the job done. If you have to pick one size, I'd recommend a large one, in the 5- to 7-quart range. You can use this for creating curries and dals, braising meats, and deep-frying.

Spice grinder

Spices are the single most important element in preparing Indian cuisine; so naturally, processing them properly is critical to your success. A coffee grinder is a perfect choice for grinding spices.

However, (and I can't stress this point enough) *do not* use the same grinder that you grind coffee with. That is, unless, you happen to like essence of peppercorns, coriander, and cumin mixed with your Columbian Supremo. I'm not a huge fan, but hey, if you're into that sort of thing, go for it.

Mortar and pestle

When you need to roughly grind spices, meaning create chunky, non-powdery spice blends, a mortar and pestle can come in very handy. This tool is also good for mashing fresh herbs, such as cilantro and mint. Many gourmet shops carry mortars and pestles, and I recommend finding a set that is dishwasher safe and fairly heavy. Because you're actually grinding the spices by hand, the extra weight of the pestle can really improve the process and final product.

Food processor

You may be surprised to discover that Indian food is not traditionally prepared by using a food processor. (Sorry to spoil the illusion, but this handy little device is fairly new on the scene.) However, it is invaluable in creating spice blends, slicing onions, processing dals into paste, kneading dough, creating marinades, you name it. If it could only read and follow the recipes in this book, you could kick your feet up, take a snooze, and wake up to your own Indian feast. But, alas, all fantasies can't come true, and you have to do some of the work here.

Blender

A blender can be very helpful for mixing raitas, grinding nuts, and pureeing fillings. If you have to choose between this and a food processor, though, stick with the food processor. It's more versatile. Personally, I find that it's nice to have two separate appliances to dirty up simultaneously, so I keep them both handy, busy, and, well, frankly, dirty.

Nonstick skillets and saucepans

These items are great general all-purpose pans for frying spices, boiling vegetables, making cheese, melting butter, making sauces, and almost anything else you need to do.

Tandoori oven

For newcomers to Indian cuisine, the tandoori oven is probably *the* quintessential Indian cooking tool. However, many Indian homes don't even have one. Basically, the tandoori oven is the Indian version of a barbecue grill, without the grate. It's made of steel, lined with clay, and then buried in the ground. Hot coals are placed in the bottom of the tandoori, and then skewers of marinated meats or vegetables are placed inside. Breads, such as the sumptuous naan, are slapped to the inside of the clay-sided oven to cook. This unique cooking environment creates delicious results. For the recipes in this book that are traditionally cooked in a tandoori oven, I substitute a grill or oven as appropriate. Figure 1-2 shows a traditional and a modern tandoori oven.

Figure 1-2:
Traditional and modern tandoori ovens.

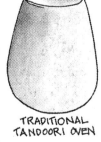

TRADITIONAL TANDOORI OVEN

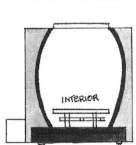

MODERN TANDOORI OVEN

INTERIOR

Pressure cooker

A pressure cooker isn't a requirement when preparing Indian food, but it can definitely speed up your prep time when you're in a hurry. When you're working with dried legumes, lentils, chickpeas, and the like, consider using a pressure cooker to get your dals tender and your pilafs fluffy. For information on purchasing and using a pressure cooker, check out *Pressure Cookers For Dummies* by Tom Lacalamita (published by Wiley).

Chapter 2

Masala and Other Must-Have Ingredients

A cook is only as good as his/her last dish. And a curry is only as good as its masala, or spice blend. But before you can venture out on your own, you need to grasp the basics. Herbs and spices are the building blocks of every Indian dish. Whether they're grown at home or purchased on the street at the spice grinder, their preparation and combination is key to the finished dish.

Chutneys, pickles (similar to Western relishes), and *raitas* (cooling, yet flavorful yogurt based sauces) are used in combinations as unique as the individual diner to create a different culinary experience at the same table. Using condiments is a great way for guests to get in on the experimentation fun.

And where would an Indian meal be without the omnipresent basmati rice? (Likely, a saucy, soupy mess, is my guess.) Various regions use rice more or less often depending on its availability. The northern wheat growing region relies on bread more regularly than the southern cousins. But even in the north, rice is usually present with at least one meal.

Herbs and Spices Are Twice as Nice (And Necessary)

In India, the importance of any particular herb or spice varies by region, so I list them in this section alphabetically by their English names. Because 15 official languages and more than 1,000 dialects are spoken on the Indian subcontinent, I include the most common Indian name(s) in parentheses. Also, in the whole of Indian cooking, many, many, many more ingredients are used regularly, but I don't have room to cover them all. I include some that aren't used regularly in the West, and some that are used in the West, but used differently in India.

The difference between an herb and a spice is subtle. Throughout history, the term "spice" described aromatic plants found in tropical regions (such as cloves, pepper, and cinnamon), while the term "herbs" was reserved for leaves and seeds of temperate-zone plants (such as oregano, basil, and mint). However, in common usage, the term "spice" can encompass all of these seasonings, including dehydrated vegetables and spice blends. As a rule, Indian cooks use spices dry, but herbs and vegetables fresh.

Ajwain seeds (carom seeds, ajowan, bishop's weed)

Ajwain seeds are tiny purple brown or red brown seeds with a lighter brown stripe. You can find them whole or ground. When crushed or ground, ajwain has a pungent smell very similar to thyme, with a flavor closer to cumin. Primarily used in savory dishes with lentils, chickpeas, breads, pickles, and samosas, ajwain is thought to aid in digestion and relieve stomachaches.

Asafetida (asafoetida, heeng, hing)

Asafetida is a combination of various dried gum resins, or saps, from the roots of a fennel-like plant. You'll find it in Indian markets in either lump form or powder. While in its lump form, it's fairly odorless, but the grinding process helps it make a pungent statement. The lump asafetida will last for years, but store it separately in an airtight container or it will quickly overpower its roommates. The powder loses its potency quickly, so grind only what you need. When fried in hot oil or *ghee* (clarified butter), asafetida mellows, giving the fat a rich, oniony flavor. Hence, it's never used in conjunction with onions.

Basil (tulsi)

In Indian cooking, basil is used only fresh because the dried herb loses too much aroma and flavor. The variety typically used in India, holy basil, is a bit sharper than the sweet basil familiar in the West. Hindus consider basil holy because of its association with their god, Vishnu. Holy basil is often grown in Indian homes.

Cardamom (elaichi, choti elaichi, kali, or badi elaichi)

A quintessential Indian ingredient, cardamom comes in a couple different forms and has virtually limitless uses. The distinctive green cardamom is the smaller of the two varieties, with pods from ¼ to ½ inch long. Each pod contains approximately 15 to 20 tiny black seeds that have a distinctive aroma similar to menthol or eucalyptus. You can find them as whole pods, seeds, or dried and prepowdered for your convenience. However, if you buy it powdered, you miss out on a host of ingenious uses for the discarded pods (used to infuse oil or steeped in water to soothe colicky babies) and whole seeds (after-dinner mint or gum).

Black cardamom is larger than its green cousin, ¾ to 1 inch long, with husky dark brown skin. It has a mellower, nuttier flavor than the green. Black cardamom is a key ingredient in garam masala. You can usually find these flavorful Indian must-haves only as whole seed pods. Figure 2-1 shows some pods.

Figure 2-1:
Cardamom pods are usually crushed or ground before being used.

CARDAMOM PODS

Coriander (dhania, sookha)

Coriander is another name for cilantro or Chinese parsley. Indian cooks typically use the dried seeds of the coriander plant, ground or whole, in a variety of spice blends, or masalas. Characterized by the sweet, piquant taste of cilantro, the coriander seed has a slightly citrus, nutty aroma. In addition to its wonderful flavor and fragrance, the ground powder is an excellent thickening agent for sauces.

Fresh coriander leaves or greens are used as a garnish or as a late-addition ingredient to give an extra punch of flavor. Don't waste your time with the dried variety; the resulting dishes completely lack any of the hallmark flavor or aroma of the fresh. It does, however, freeze reasonably well. Use your food processor to create a quick puree with fresh leaves and tender stems, mixed with a little bit of water. Then freeze the resulting aromatic liquid in ice cube trays so that you can use as little or as much as you need later.

Cumin (jeera, zeera)

White cumin is the cumin most often found in Indian homes. It is often dry-roasted as a seed or used in its powdered form and sprinkled over finished dishes. Despite its name, white cumin is yellowish-brown in color, with a distinctive nutty aroma.

Black cumin (or royal cumin) is tougher to find and more expensive. It has a mellower flavor that's more peppery than nutty and doesn't usually require roasting.

Traditionally, white and black cumin are not used interchangeably because they have two distinct flavors. I'm not saying that if you do substitute one for the other, you'll start an international culinary incident — just don't invite me over for dinner.

Fenugreek (methi, kasoori methi, patta)

The fenugreek "seed" is actually a legume, but because of its extreme aroma, reminiscent of the sweetness of maple syrup, and surprising bitter taste, it's categorized as a spice. The seeds are rectangular and brownish-yellow in color, about the size of mung beans.

Fenugreek is grown in many Indian homes, where the women of the household preserve the dried leaves for later use. Unlike many herbs, these watercress look-alikes hold their aroma fairly well, and the dried leaves, usually with the tougher stems removed, are often cooked with veggies throughout the cooler months. When they are in season, the leafy fresh greens are cooked like you would cook other greens, such as mustard greens or kale.

In Indian cooking, as with many ethnic cuisines, spices are selected not only for obvious reasons, such as their flavor and irreplaceable aromatic properties. They're also selected for their healing, soothing properties. Indians use fenugreek as a digestive aid. Additionally, it's believed to help nursing moms meet the needs of even the most demanding newborns.

Mango (amchur)

Dried green mangoes are used either in pulp pieces or ground. Amchur acts as a flavor catalyst for other spices. It's often used as a souring agent, giving chutneys and other dishes a distinctive tang. It's also an excellent tenderizer for meats.

Mint (podina)

Mint is not the tea and dessert spice in Indian cooking as it traditionally is in the West. It's often used in India in savory chutneys, chilled appetizers, and fragrant pilafs. Mint also graces the occasional meat dish, primarily lamb or goat items. With a pleasing but mild taste and delicate aroma, mint is not often used dried.

Ginger (sonth, adrak)

In Indian cooking, fresh gingerroot is often used. It's the same tuberous rhizome (or knobby, lumpy-looking plant root) that you might recognize from Chinese and Japanese cooking. Peel the brown skin from the root with a vegetable peeler, much like you would a carrot, and then shred the "meat" or grind it into a thick paste. Alternatively, you can very finely chop it or process it with your food processor.

Indian cooks often dry the peeled gingerroot in the sun and then grate or grind the dried root into a powder. Despite ginger's sweet, citrus smell, it packs a pungent, piquant taste. In addition to its flavor and aromatic properties, the powdered form is a thickening agent common in vegetarian dishes.

The following recipe features ginger. Used universally in India and ground fresh every time the need arises (which is 2 to 3 times on an average day), this paste is almost the first task of the morning cooking ritual. Once made, it gets added to breakfast breads and to whatever else is the savory call of the morning. Making it in bulk at one time and having it available, in my opinion, makes cooking easier.

Basic Ginger-Garlic Paste (Pissa Adrak-Lussan)

When making this paste, which appears in a few other recipes in this book, there's one thing I do that is out of the norm — I mix in some oil. The purists may not agree, but I find that it increases the refrigerator life of the paste and, more importantly, the paste does not darken but retains its original color.

Preparation Time: *5 minutes*

Yield: *Makes about 1½ cup*

1 cup quarter-size slices peeled fresh ginger	*1 to 3 tablespoons water*
1 cup fresh garlic cloves, peeled	

In a food processor or a blender, process together the ginger and garlic to make a smooth paste, adding the water as needed for blending. Transfer to an airtight container, mix in some oil (vegetable, peanut, or olive) until it forms a ⅛-inch layer on top of the paste, and refrigerate up to 15 days or freeze up to 6 months.

Tip: *Cut the ginger crosswise, across the grain, into thin slices, or you'll get long fibers in the paste. Also, make sure the storage containers you use are really airtight, so your whole refrigerator doesn't smell of garlic.*

Mustard (rai, sarsoon)

Indian mustard seeds look like huge poppy seeds, with colors ranging from ochre yellow to dark brown or nearly black. It has a pungent aroma when ground and cooked, with a lightly sour, bitter taste. The seeds are available whole or powdered. Mustard seed is an essential component of vindaloo, the famous Goan spice blend. The flavor of the seeds changes substantially when they're fried in oil. They take on sweet and nutty characteristics rather than their original bitter properties. For more information on frying spices, see Chapter 3 of Book V.

Mustard oil is prized for the delicate flavor it imparts to pickles. And the greens often star in their own veggie-only dish. Many believe that mustard oil helps in curing the common cold. You can find mustard oil in many Indian and Asian markets and health food stores.

Peppers (mirchi, tazi hari)

Both fresh and dried peppers are used extensively in preparing most Indian dishes. Serranos and jalepeños are both good substitutes for Indian green hot peppers. If you want something even a bit milder, try a large Anaheim pepper or green chile. Both of these peppers offer pepper flavor without a serious bite. You can find them in most grocery stores, Asian markets, and Indian and Mexican groceries.

The smaller red dried peppers can be used whole or ground. The ground variety is typically labeled as cayenne pepper and is a major component of chutneys and pickles.

As a rule, the smaller the pepper, the hotter the flavor. Choose your pepper according to your own tolerance. If you like your guests, you might take their preferences into account as well. You can further control the heat by keeping or removing the seeds. The seeds boast the majority of the heat. Also, *always* wear gloves when working with fresh peppers. Remove your gloves and wash your hands thoroughly before touching your eyes, face, or other sensitive parts of your (or anybody else's) body.

Tamarind (imli)

Tamarind is most often used as an extract. The pulpy pods are dark brown, with a sour, pruney flavor. The pulp from the pod is used to create the tamarind "cakes" often seen in Indian groceries. You rehydrate the cakes by soaking them in boiling water. Let the cakes steep in the water until cooled and then strain the mixture, reserving the liquid. Discard the leftover pulp cake.

Indian cooks use this liquid as an acidic agent, much like Western cooks use lemon juice. It's a common ingredient in beverages, chutneys, dals, and many veggie dishes.

Watch out for the prepackaged tamarind products, such as paste, concentrate, and puree. Most recipes that call for tamarind need the souring properties of tamarind to work their magic on a dish. The prepackaged stuff is usually loaded with sweeteners, making it unsuitable for many recipes.

Turmeric (haldi)

Turmeric is the primary ingredient in store-bought curry. It imparts a distinctive yellow color and a woody aroma to a dish. This dried root of the ginger family has thicker, rougher skin than ginger, and its rich internal color is similar to a yam or a sweet potato.

Masala: The Ingredients Behind the Ingredient

Masala is a key ingredient in many, many Indian dishes. It literally means, "spice blend." It can refer to the wet blend of spices or to the spice paste made by combining and grinding herbs, seasonings, and spices. Or masala may describe a powdered combination of ground seasonings. The type of masala used differentiates the finished product and defines the dish. Here are some of the most basic, well-known blends.

Garam masala and chaat masala

Most important of all spice blends is garam masala. No longer a staple only in Indian markets, garam masala is now commercially packaged by mainstream spice companies and available in just about any large grocery store. Garam means "warm" and accurately describes this blend. It's characterized by warming rather than biting, piquant flavors. This blend carries some familiar ingredients you probably have in your cupboard, including cinnamon, black pepper, and cloves, as well as the Indian essentials, black and green cardamom. Garam masala is usually added at the end of cooking, and Indian cooks generously sprinkle this masala over a finished dish. Most regions (and most families!) in India have their own version of this popular masala. Try this recipe and experiment with your own.

Chaat is the term to describe salads or snack dishes infused with a complex mix of sweet, salty, tangy, and spicy flavors, and always seasoned with some form of the spice blend called *chaat masala.* Of course, there are countless variations throughout India. Home cooks and professional chefs also use it to jazz up salads, fresh fruits, and fruit juices, and it can be added to dishes to "save" them when their flavors don't seem to be quite right. In this one rare instance, if not using homemade, I recommend trying commercially packaged chaat masala sold at Indian supermarkets.

Curry: Spice or sauce?

In Indian cooking, the word *curry* comes from the Tamil word *kahri,* which refers to any dish with a sauce or gravy. So a curry isn't a curry because it contains the particular blend of spices known as curry powder. It's the finished soupy concoction with its delicate combination of dry spices, wet herbs, meat, veggies, legumes, and so on that *is* curry. The commercially available spice blend known as curry powder originated with British soldiers attempting to re-create flavors and dishes they enjoyed while stationed in India.

Garam Masala

Garam masala, meaning hot spices in Hindi, is a dark brown, spicy-hot blend that is believed to induce internal heat in the body. Made with four basic spices — cloves, cinnamon, black and/or green cardamom, and black peppercorns — garam masala is available in many different forms. Every region — in fact, every family — has its own unique variation. Just a pinch of this masala, sprinkled over dishes as a garnish before serving, adds tremendous fragrance and flavor. It also adds complex nuances to dry-rubs and marinades. Garam masala is now found even in supermarkets, but homemade is always preferred.

Preparation Time: *1 minute*

Cooking Time: *2 minutes*

Yield: *Makes about 1½ cup*

⅓ cup ground cinnamon

⅓ cup ground freshly black pepper

¼ cup ground black cardamom seeds

¼ cup ground cloves

3 tablespoons ground green cardamom seeds

In a medium cast-iron or nonstick skillet, roast together all the spices, stirring and shaking the pan over medium heat until heated through, about 2 minutes. Let cool, then store in an airtight container in a cool, dark place, about 1 month at room temperature or about 1 year in the refrigerator.

Chaat Masala

This classic spice blend is made with an unrivaled combination of some of India's most intriguing herbs and spices, featuring mango powder, dry-roasted cumin seeds, and black salt at its base.

Preparation Time: *5 minutes*

Cooking Time: *2 minutes*

Yield: *Makes about 1½ cup*

⅓ tablespoons cumin seeds, dry-roasted and ground

¼ cup mango powder

3 tablespoons dried mint leaves, ground

2 tablespoons tamarind powder

2 tablespoons ground ginger

2 tablespoons ground ajwain seeds

1 to 2 tablespoons salt, or to taste

1 tablespoon ground black salt

1 tablespoon citric acid

1 to 3 teaspoons cayenne pepper, or to taste

1 teaspoon ground asafoetida

Prepare the cumin seeds. Then, in a medium cast-iron or nonstick skillet, roast together all the spices, stirring and shaking the pan over medium heat until heated through, about 2 minutes. Let cool, then store in an airtight container in a cool, dark place, about 1 month at room temperature or about 1 year in the refrigerator.

Curry powder

Curry powder is widely available in supermarkets and is one of the best known masalas in the West. However, making your own is very simple, and the resulting product is much better than the commercial varieties. You can use this ingredient in the recipes in this book or add an authentic Indian flair to other dishes calling for curry powder.

Basic Curry Powder (Kari ka Masala)

You can buy your curry powder at the market or make this simple mixture of spices that I use in my kitchen.

Preparation Time: *5 minutes*

Yield: *Makes about 1½ cups*

1 cup ground coriander seeds

⅓ cup ground cumin seeds

2 tablespoons ground turmeric

1 tablespoon ground paprika

1 tablespoon ground cayenne pepper (optional)

1 tablespoon ground dried fenugreek leaves

Put all the spices in a bowl and mix them together with a spoon. Store in an airtight container in a cool, dark place, about 1 month at room temperature or about 1 year in the refrigerator.

Chutney

Chutney is an Indian condiment much like a relish. You can make fresh sweet or savory vegetable chutneys, reminiscent of Mexican salsa, as well as fiery, aromatic chutneys. The nearest Indian equivalent to Western chutneys is the Indian sweet/hot chutney. Typically, chutneys are prepared fresh and have a shelf (or refrigerator) life of a couple weeks. The preserved variety (usually sweet/hot and made with sugar and vinegar) can last up to a year if properly stored. Most Indian chutneys are some combination of raw herbs and spices, diced or shredded fruits and/or vegetables, and chiles or red pepper. Here are a couple basic recipes to get you started. Feel free to experiment with flavors and spices as you build your confidence.

Basic Green Chutney
(Hari Chutni)

This pureed blend of herbs, spiked with fresh green chile peppers and lime juice, is universal all over India, with each family adding its own special touch and ingredients. Though you can use any onions, I prefer using just the scallion greens for their mild flavor and their deep green color. Another popular addition to this chutney is garlic, but to me it overpowers the flavors, so I generally don't use it. Add 1 to 3 fresh cloves, if you wish.

Preparation Time: *5 minutes*

Yield: *Makes about 1½ cups*

2 to 5 fresh green chile peppers, such as serrano, stemmed

6 to 8 scallions, just the green parts, coarsely chopped

1 cup fresh mint leaves, trimmed

2 to 3 cups coarsely chopped fresh cilantro, including soft stems

3 to 4 tablespoons fresh lime or lemon juice

1 teaspoon sugar

1 teaspoon salt, or to taste

½ teaspoon freshly ground black pepper, or to taste

1 In a food processor or blender, process together the green chile peppers and scallion greens until minced. Add the mint and cilantro to the work bowl and process, stopping a few times to scrape the sides with a spatula, until pureed. As you process, drizzle the lime juice through the feeder tube into the work bowl and process until the chutney is smooth.

2 Add the sugar, salt, and pepper and process once again. Adjust the seasonings. Transfer to a bowl and serve immediately, refrigerate about 10 days, or freeze up to 6 months.

Cilantro-Lime Chutney (Dhania Chutni)

Join the countless millions of Indians (including me) for whom this mild chutney, powered with the fragrance and taste of fresh cilantro, is the ultimate. You'll find a version of it in every home, no matter where you are in India.

It's so good, it shouldn't be limited to Indian food, either. Try it in sandwiches, tacos, and burritos, with fresh vegetables, fried or baked appetizers, in salads, steamed vegetables, or rice *pullaos* (pilafs), or simply serve it on the side with grilled foods.

Preparation Time: *15 minutes*

Yield: *Makes about 2 cups*

½ teaspoon cumin seeds, dry-roasted and coarsely ground

1 teaspoon Chaat Masala (see the recipe in this chapter or use store-bought)

3 to 5 fresh green chile peppers, such as serrano, stemmed

4 quarter-size slices peeled fresh ginger

1 small green bell pepper, coarsely chopped

5 to 6 scallions, green parts only, coarsely chopped

3 cups firmly packed, coarsely chopped fresh cilantro, including soft stems

½ cup fresh mint leaves

2 to 3 tablespoons fresh lime or lemon juice

1 teaspoon sugar

1 teaspoon salt, or to taste

1 Prepare the cumin seeds and the Chaat Masala. Then, in a food processor or a blender, blend together the green chile peppers, ginger, bell pepper, and scallion greens until minced. Add the cilantro and mint to the work bowl and process, scraping the sides with a spatula a few times, until pureed. As you process, drizzle the lime juice through the feeder tube into the work bowl and process to make a smooth chutney.

2 Add the Chaat Masala, sugar, and salt and process again. Adjust the seasonings. Transfer to a bowl and lightly mix in the cumin with some of it visible as a garnish. Serve immediately, refrigerate about 10 days, or freeze up to 6 months.

Pickles

Indian pickles are mainstays at Indian meals. They're quite a bit different from the pickled cucumbers of the West. Indian cooks create pickles from many different fruits and vegetables, including green mangoes, tomatoes, lemons, and limes. Their strong flavors demand that they be eaten in small quantities as an accompaniment to a meal.

Quick Mango Pickle
(Aam ka Achaar)

As children growing up in New Delhi, we loved this pickle. Our neighborhood *halvai* (a professional snack and sweet maker) always served it with his breakfast plate of *poori-aalu* (deep-fried breads and potatoes). The *poori-aalu* was delicious, but his pickle, with its fragrant and sour undertones, was always the greater attraction.

Most authentic mango pickles are made with the mango peel left on, but because here you peel the mangoes, this takes much less time to cure.

Preparation Time: *10 minutes*

Cooking Time: *40 minutes*

Yield: *Makes about 2 cups*

2½ teaspoons cumin seeds	*1 cup mustard or olive oil*
1¼ teaspoons fennel seeds	*3 large cloves fresh garlic, coarsely chopped*
1 teaspoon black mustard seed	*1 teaspoon black peppercorns, coarsely ground*
¾ teaspoon kalonji seeds	
½ teaspoon fenugreek seeds	*1 teaspoon ground turmeric*
2 large unripe green mangoes (about ¾ pound each), washed and wiped dry	*⅛ teaspoon ground asafoetida*
	1 tablespoon salt, or to taste

1 In a medium cast-iron or non-stick skillet, roast the cumin, fennel, mustard, kalonji, and fenugreek seeds, shaking and stirring the pan over medium-high heat for about 2 minutes. Let cool.

2 With a vegetable peeler, peel the mango, then cut the fruit around the center seed into thin ½-inch-by-2-inch pieces. Heat the oil in a large non-stick wok or saucepan over medium-high heat and add the garlic, the roasted seeds, peppercorns, turmeric, and asafoetida. They should sizzle upon contact with the hot oil.

3 Quickly add the mangoes and the salt, reduce heat to medium and cook, stirring, until the mangoes absorb all the flavors, 15 to 20 minutes. Let cool and allow to marinate at room temperature at least 2 days before serving. Store in the refrigerator about 1 month. Serve chilled or at room temperature.

Sun-Cured Pickled Lime (or Lemon) Wedges (Nimboo ka Achaar)

It's hard to find an Indian home without an array of fresh lime or lemon pickles. Indian limes are yellow and thin-skinned — just a little larger than Key limes. They are easy to juice and cure faster than their American counterparts. Here I use the varieties of limes and lemons available in the United States; they are still delicious.

Pickles are traditionally cured outside in the sun for several weeks, but you can set the jar in a sunny part of your kitchen. The pickle will take an extra 7 to 10 days, unless you move it as the sun rays move.

With indefinite staying power, this pickle actually improves with age as the juices turn darker, thicken, and actually transform into jelly and eventually into fine crystals. At this point, this pickle becomes an age-old Indian home remedy for indigestion, stomach upsets, and nausea.

Preparation Time: *5 minutes*

Cooking Time: *15 to 20 days*

Yield: *Makes about 4 cups*

20 to 24 fresh limes (about 2 pounds)

½ cup peeled and minced fresh ginger

¼ cup salt

2 tablespoons coarsely crushed ajwain seeds

4 cups fresh lime or lemon juice (from 20 additional limes)

1 small piece muslin or 4 layers cheesecloth (enough to cover the mouth of the jar)

1 Wash and wipe dry the limes. Cut each one into 8 wedges and place in a large sterile glass jar. Mix in the ginger, salt, and ajwain seeds; cover the jar with your palm or the lid; and shake vigorously to mix.

2 Uncover, add the lime juice, and shake the jar again. (The juice should cover the limes by about ½ inch; if not, add some more lime juice.) Cover the jar with the muslin, securing it with a rubber band, and place in a warm, sunny spot in the kitchen or outside in the sun. (If the pickle jar is outside in the sun, bring it inside in the evening.)

3 Shake the jar once or twice each day, until the lime wedges are soft and light buff in color, and the juices are thick, 15 to 20 days. This pickle stays fresh at room temperature almost indefinitely.

Vary It! *Along with ajwain seeds, add 1 tablespoon each ground cumin and coriander, and 1 teaspoon coarsely ground black pepper.*

Raita

Fiery curries, spicy dals, and piquant biryanis (layered rice casseroles) all can be soothed with a dash of cooling raita. Raitas are fragrant and aromatic (like 99 percent of Indian dishes), but without the heat that characterizes the rest of the cuisine. These creamy yogurt blends still pack a ton of flavor and are a favorite dish served at most meals as a condiment or eaten by itself.

Cucumber and Radish Raita (Kheera aur Mooli ka Raita)

Almost like a salad, this has lots of colorful vegetables, adding a light crunch to the otherwise smooth yogurt. After grating and chopping, you should have about 3 cups of the vegetables, but the proportions don't have to be precise.

Preparation Time: *15 minutes*

Yield: *Makes 4 to 6 servings*

1 teaspoon Chaat Masala (see the recipe in this chapter or use store-bought)

2 cups nonfat plain yogurt, whisked until smooth

2 to 4 seedless cucumbers, grated (peeled or unpeeled)

12 to 15 red radishes, grated and squeezed

1 large firm tomato, finely chopped

1 fresh green chile pepper, such as serrano, minced with seeds

½ teaspoon salt, or to taste

½ teaspoon freshly ground black pepper, or to taste

½ teaspoon ground paprika

Cilantro or mint leaves

Prepare the Chaat Masala. Place the yogurt in a serving bowl. Add the cucumbers, radishes, tomato, green chile pepper, Chaat Masala, salt, and pepper and stir to mix well. Garnish with the paprika and cilantro or mint leaves, and serve.

Legumes and Rice

Legumes is a big fancy word for beans and peas. This group of protein-rich foods includes lentils, chickpeas, mung beans, soybeans, black-eyed peas, split peas, kidney beans, pinto beans, and any other bean or pea you can think of. Legumes are the cornerstones of the Indian vegetarian diet, and even among those families that eat meat, legumes are ever-present elements of virtually every meal.

Part of the reason that they're consumed in such great volume is their versatility. Dried legumes, particularly chickpeas, are ground and used as flour to create pakoras, or batter-fried fritters, and wafers. Legumes are boiled, then pureed, flavored with spices, and served as dips and condiments. Indian cooks soak them and then cook them in hearty stews and curries with or without meat.

While the term *dal* can be used to describe the actual legume itself, typically just smaller or split hulled varieties, *dal* also refers to any dish whose primary ingredient is legumes.

Lentils (masoor, toovar dal, masar dal, toor dal)

Lentils are the most commonly consumed legumes in India. They come in several colors and varieties and are distinguished by their stages of processing (such as whole, with skin, and without skin). Typically, they're seeds shaped like half moons. After their skin is removed, the seeds can reveal their vibrant colors, including golden yellow and pink varieties. The skinless variety cooks much faster than the lentils with skin. But be sure not to overcook the skinless variety because they get very mushy.

Chickpeas (kabuli channa, safaid channa, channae)

Chickpeas, also known as garbanzo beans, are available in the familiar tan variety and the less common black variety. Both are heart-shaped, full (rather than split) beans with a nutty flavor and firm texture. Black chickpeas are slightly more nutritious than their tan cousins.

Besan flour, or chickpea flour, is a primary component of pakora dough, as well as a terrific thickening agent. If you can't find besan flour at your local market, you can easily make your own. Use your handy spice/coffee grinder to grind dried chickpeas. Sift the ground flour with a fine mesh sieve and regrind the big chunks until you get the consistency you need.

Mung beans (moong dal, sabat moong)

The small, green, kidney-shaped mung bean is the most highly digestible of the legumes popularly used in Indian cooking. Most recipes recommend using the skinned and split version of the bean, but the whole bean (sabat moong) is served in the north and west of India.

Rice

Rice is a staple for two-thirds of the world's population. Given India's varied geography and climate, it's no surprise that many varieties of rice are successfully cultivated. Rice is not as nutrient-rich or complex as some other carbohydrates, but when eaten in conjunction with the rest of the Indian diet, rice helps maintain a healthful balance.

The most highly prized of the Indian rice varieties is the delicately thin, long-grain basmati, or "Queen of Fragrance" in Hindi. Basmati rice exhibits a nutty flavor and a serious aroma. Although basmati rice is delicious, it's a bit more complicated to make than its highly polished and processed Western counterpart. For the full scoop, check out Chapter 3 of Book V.

After the basic rice is prepared, Indian cooks create wonderful, fragrant pullaos, or pilafs, and rich, delicious casserole-like biryanis.

Chapter 3

Mastering a Few Simple Techniques

So you bought all your spices, got your pots and pans together, and are ready to tackle your first recipe. How do you get authentic Indian aromas to emanate from your kitchen? Much of the famed fragrance comes from preparing the ingredients you add to the dishes.

Indian cooks prepare all ingredients before beginning a recipe. It's just like the French technique of *mis en place (MEEZ on plass)*, which means "everything in its place." Cucumbers are diced, spice blends are roasted, and onions are sliced — all before the cooking begins. Because the heart of Indian cooking depends on the spice flavors, you want your cumin seeds ground or your mustard seeds fried before you need them. If you're in the middle of a recipe and leave your skillet too long while searching for the next ingredient, you can ruin the flavor of the whole thing.

Preparing Spices

Spices are the very essence of Indian cooking. Indian cooks rarely use a spice "as-is." Their careful and varied preparation elicits the intoxicating fragrances and complex flavors that are the hallmark of Indian cooking. Whether you're creating your own spice blend or following a recipe, these techniques can help you get the most out of your spices.

Roasting spices, flour, and nuts

Roasting spices significantly changes the complexity of their flavors and aromas. Roast whole seeds and then grind to make a powdered spice for more variety. Some spice blends call for roasting spices first and then grinding; others require you to combine first and ask questions later, er, I mean, and roast later. But they all follow a very similar process. One of the key factors in this preparation is the absence of fat. For this reason, the process is sometimes called dry roasting.

Roasting whole spices and nuts

When roasting whole spices, roast each type of spice separately. Because whole coriander seed is larger than cumin seed, coriander must be roasted a bit longer for the best flavor. Use the same rule for roasting nuts. If you must roast different types of nuts together, coarsely chop them so that they're similarly sized. Just follow these steps:

1. **Preheat a heavy skillet over medium-high heat for at least 2 minutes.**

2. **Add the spices, stirring constantly, until they turn a shade or two darker and release their aroma, typically, 1 to 2 minutes.**

If you're grinding your spices after roasting, cool the spices a few minutes before grinding.

Roasting ground spices and flour

When roasting ground or powdered spices, the spice bits are about the same size, so you can usually throw it all in the same pan. However, if the recipe calls for the spices to be roasted separately, there's probably a good reason for it. Try this method as is before going off on your own.

1. **Preheat a heavy skillet over medium-high heat for at least 2 minutes.**

2. **Add the spices, stirring constantly, until they start to brown.**

3. **Reduce the heat to low and continue to roast another minute.**

4. **Remove from the heat and transfer to another container to cool.**

Frying spices

Typically, spices are fried as the first step of a recipe. The major difference between roasting and frying spices is the addition of oil. Some spices, such as mustard seed, pop much like popcorn when fried, releasing a truly wonderful aroma and surprising (often mellow) flavor. Cardamom pods brown quickly and puff up. The oil used for frying is delicately infused with the flavor of the spices. The resulting dish relies on this vital step. One simple vegetable dish that utilizes this fragrant oil is known as *bhujia*. Vegetables are simply fried in the aromatic, spiced oil, with no additional sauce. Delicious!

Here's how to fry spices (see Figure 3-1):

1. **Place a few tablespoons of oil in a preheated, heavy skillet over medium-high heat.**

2. **Heat the oil until it's almost smoking.**

3. **Fry each type of spice separately in batches, until browned, typically not more than 2–3 minutes.**

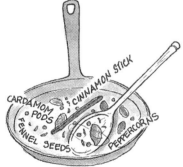

Figure 3-1:
Frying
spices in a
cast-iron
skillet.

Keep your skillet's lid handy when frying spices that pop, such as mustard seeds. It can help catch any seeds that are trying to escape and, more importantly, protect you from the extremely hot oil. If you've ever fried bacon, you know what I'm talking about. Ouch!

Crushing spices

A mortar and pestle (which I discuss in Chapter 1 of Book V) are your best tools when crushing spices. Spices and herbs can be smashed and crushed together to create chunky fragrant pastes and wet spice blends. Alternatively, if you don't have a mortar and pestle, seal your spices in a resealable plastic bag and pound with a kitchen mallet or rolling pin.

Grinding spices

For centuries, Indian cooks ground spices by hand. Many still perform this time-honored ritual daily. But today, technology is our friend, and Indian cooking is no exception. A coffee grinder is your best Western substitute for the elbow grease used in a traditional Indian kitchen. Use a coffee grinder (but not the same one you use to grind your favorite coffee beans) to grind the spices. Sift the ground spice with a fine mesh sieve and regrind the big chunks until you get the consistency you need.

Cooking with Basmati, Paneer, and Ghee — Oh Gee!

No Indian culinary day is complete without basmati rice, paneer (firm cheese), and ghee (clarified butter). While some busy families no longer make their own paneer and ghee, they are staples in the Indian home. In the West, paneer and ghee are available in most Indian groceries and some specialty markets. But they are both very simple to make, so give it a try!

Basmati rice

The most highly prized of the Indian rice varieties is the delicately thin, long grain basmati, or "Queen of Fragrance" in Hindi. Basmati rice exhibits a nutty flavor and serious aroma. It's a bit more complicated to prepare, but the end result is definitely worth the effort.

Before cooking basmati, you must thoroughly rinse it. Rinsing removes the excess starch and remaining husks. Here's how:

1. **Place the basmati in a bowl and fill the bowl with cold water.**

2. **Gently agitate the water with your hands and then drain the rice.**

3. **Repeat this process 3 to 4 times until your water is clear.**

   Remove the floating husks and hulls so that they don't make it into the cooking pot.

Steamed Basmati Rice (Ooblae Chaval)

With no additional flavors and seasonings, the celebrated flavors of basmati rice truly shine through. It is important to soak the rice before cooking with this method to ensure fluffy, individuated grains.

Preparation Time: *30 minutes*

Cooking Time: *30 minutes*

Yield: *Makes 4 to 6 servings, or about 4 cups*

1¼ cups basmati rice, sorted and washed in 3 to 4 changes of water

2⅓ cups water

Cilantro sprig, for garnish (optional)

1 In a medium bowl, soak the rice in the water, about 30 minutes.

2 Put the rice and the water in a medium saucepan and bring to a boil over high heat. Reduce the heat to the lowest setting, cover the pan (partially at first, until the foam subsides, then snugly), and cook until the rice is done, 10 to 15 minutes. Do not stir the rice at all. Remove the pan from the heat and let the rice rest undisturbed about 5 minutes. Transfer to a serving platter, fluff lightly with a fork, and serve with a sprig of cilantro, if you like.

I always make more basmati than I think I'll need so that I'll have extra to make biryani, a casserole-like layered rice dish. For a taste of this delicious dish, try Hyderabadi Layered Rice with Mixed Vegetables in Chapter 6 of Book V.

Paneer cheese

Paneer cheese is a staple of the Indian diet. Paneer resembles firm tofu, with a light flavor reminiscent of fresh mozzarella. The delicate cheese curds are formed as the milk fat separates from the whey. Because the milk fat is essential to the process, I recommend that you use only whole milk (skim or even 2 percent milk won't do the trick). The curds are strained and pressed into cakes that are cubed and then sometimes fried. The light, delicate flavor of paneer blends well with a variety of savory dishes and curries.

Paneer Cheese

Paneer cheese doesn't melt when heated, although too much stirring will cause it to break. Freshly made paneer cheese, warm and right out of the cheesecloth, is much prized for its own taste. Indians love it just by itself, or dressed with a little chaat masala, a savory and spicy seasoning blend that instantly perks up flavors, and fresh herbs. When making paneer cheese, use only heavy-bottomed aluminum or anodized metal pans, and to avoid accidental spills, add the curdling agent almost as soon as you see bubbles rising in the milk. As an alternative, you can buy paneer cheese in the refrigerator section of Indian markets.

Preparation Time: *45 minutes*

Yield: *Makes 8 ounces or about 30 1¼-inch pieces*

½ gallon lowfat or whole milk

2 cups plain yogurt, nonfat or any kind, whisked until smooth, or 1/4 cup fresh lemon juice, or a mixture of both

1 (2-foot-square) piece of fine muslin or 4 layers of cheesecloth

1 Place the milk in a large, heavy saucepan and bring to a boil, stirring gently, over high heat. Before the milk boils and the bubbles spill over, mix in the yogurt or the lemon juice, and continue to stir until the milk curdles and separates into curds and whey, 1 to 2 minutes. Remove from the heat.

2 Drape the muslin or cheesecloth over a large pan and pour the curdled milk over it. As you do this, the whey drains through the cloth into the pan, and the curdled paneer cheese remains in the cloth.

3 With the paneer cheese still inside it, pick up the cloth from the pan and tie the ends of the cloth around the kitchen faucet to drain, making sure that the cheese is a few inches above the bottom of the sink. Allow to drain 3 to 5 minutes.

4 Remove from the faucet and gently twist the cloth snugly around the cheese, and then place the cheese between two salad-size plates (or any other flat surfaces), with the twisted cloth edges placed to one side, out of the way. Place a large pan of water on the top plate and let the cheese drain further, 10 to 12 minutes. (Do this close to the sink or within a baking pan, or you'll have a mess to clean up.)

5 Remove the pan of water from the paneer cheese (which, by now, should have compressed into a chunk), cut into desired shapes and sizes and use as needed. Store in an airtight container in the refrigerator 4 to 5 days or freeze up to 4 months.

Vary It! *Paneer cheese can also be made with about ½ cup fresh or bottled lemon or lime juice, 3 to 4 tablespoons white or any other vinegar, or 1 quart buttermilk. Lemon juice and vinegar will yield about 61/2 ounces of paneer cheese, and the buttermilk will yield about 8 ounces. Paneer cheese can also be made with non-dairy soy milk (made from bean curd or tofu) or with a mixture of soy milk and milk. Make both these variations as you would with milk, and follow the directions above.*

Ghee

Traditionally made with butter from water buffalo milk, *ghee* is a clarified butter that's a staple in most Indian homes. You can make it too, even if you don't have a water buffalo. Ghee is simple to make from cow's milk and invaluable for adding flavor to vegetable dishes and marinades. Use it in conjunction with other fats such as olive oil to get the flavor but save some cholesterol. After you master the technique, try adding fresh herbs (such as coriander or basil) at the end of the cooking process.

Indian Clarified Butter (Ghee)

Ghee, interchangeably called desi, usli, or khara ghee in India, is very easy to make at home and can also be purchased at Indian markets.

Preparation Time: *1 minute*

Cooking Time: *20 minutes*

Yield: *Makes about 2 cups*

1 pound unsalted butter	*One 1-foot-square piece of fine muslin or 4 layers of cheesecloth*

1 Place the butter in a heavy, medium saucepan and simmer, stirring occasionally, over medium-low heat until the milk solids turn golden and settle to the bottom of the pan, 15 to 20 minutes. (At first the butter will start to foam, but as it simmers, the foaming will eventually subside.) Once this happens, pass everything through the cheesecloth or a fine-mesh strainer into a sterilized jar.

2 Do not discard the leftover milk solids. Store them at room temperature about 2 days or in the refrigerator about 6 months. Or combine with whole-wheat flour to make *paranthas* (griddle-fried breads) or add by the teaspoon to flavor soups, rice, or steamed vegetables.

Vary It! *To make flavored-infused ghee, add any of the following herbs, spices, or combinations to the pan along with the butter. After straining the ghee and removing any large spices, such as cardamom pods and cinnamon, use the milk solids in other dishes.*

¼ cup minced fresh mint leaves	*2 teaspoons cumin seeds, 2 black cardamom pods, crushed lightly to break the skin, and 2 (1-inch) sticks cinnamon*
½ cup minced fresh curry leaves plus ¼ teaspoon ground asafoetida	
1 teaspoon dried fenugreek leaves	*1 teaspoon black peppercorns and 1 teaspoon ajwain seeds*
2 tablespoons peeled and minced fresh ginger	
1 tablespoon coarsely chopped garlic	

Mastering Indian Cooking Techniques

Once you master spice preparation, these techniques help you put it all together. You can refer to the different techniques as the recipes call for them, but you might want to quickly read over this section to familiarize yourself with them. I've made a few changes from purely authentic preparations to take advantage of Western conveniences, such as using aluminum foil rather than dough in the dum preparation. But you shouldn't have trouble getting authentic results.

Deep-frying

Just as the name suggests, deep-frying involves cooking foods in generous amounts of hot fat, typically vegetable or peanut oil. You need a heavy, deep pan, such as the Indian kadhai (which I discuss in more detail in Chapter 1 of Book V). If you don't have a kadhai, a heavy, enamel-coated, deep, cast-iron pot will do the trick. Select a pot with a capacity of 6 to 8 quarts. You need at least 3 inches of oil, so depending on the diameter of your pot, you may need as many as 4 to 6 cups.

Optimal frying temperature for cooking most Indian delicacies is about 325 or 350 degrees; some recipes use a bit higher temperature, and I note it when necessary. Use a candy thermometer to watch the precise temperature, or fry a test piece of food. If your oil's too hot, the outside will cook, but the inside will not. If your oil's not hot enough, the food will absorb too much oil, making for soggy fritters and the like. Try to fry ingredients at or close to room temperature when possible, as cold ingredients bring down the temperature of the oil. If you'd like to try your hand at deep-frying, check out the recipe for Traditional Stuffed Triangular Pastries in Chapter 4 of Book V.

Braising (korma)

Indian braising, or *korma,* is similar to Western braising. However, although Westerners use a stock and fats, Indian cooks create rich thick, stewlike braising liquids. Made from yogurts, creams, and purees, these special-occasion dishes are more subtly spiced than a curry. The meat or other main ingredient marinates for hours in the refrigerator submerged in the braising liquid and then slow cooks, usually covered on the stovetop, to perfection.

Pot roasting (dum)

Dum, Indian pot roasting, is characterized by frying fragrant spices in a good amount of fat. Indian cooks lightly brown the meat or other main ingredient in the fat. Briefly increase the heat to create steam, and then cover and tightly seal the pot with aluminum foil. Reduce the heat to low, allowing the meat to essentially steam in the fragrant vapors of the herb-infused fat or butter.

Dum is also used as a finishing technique for some kormas (see the preceding section) and pilafs. It allows meats or rice to rest before serving, creating moist and plump finished dishes. To finish your korma with dum, seal your pot with aluminum foil and place the entire pot in a preheated 300-degree oven for 20 to 30 minutes. For a firsthand look at dum, try it with Basic Pan-Roasted Lamb Curry in Chapter 5 of Book V. The technique will make the lamb even more tender and juicy.

Tandoori cooking

The tandoori oven and blend of tandoori spices and marinades characterize tandoori cooking. Basically, the tandoori oven is the Indian version of a barbecue grill. For more about this device, see Chapter 1 of Book V. Because home versions of this amazing piece of equipment aren't practical for everyone to own, a grill (preferably charcoal rather than gas) or an oven is the best choice.

Tandoori food is known for its bright red color and earthy, robust flavors. Although you can't get quite the same flavor without the tandoori oven, you can re-create the color. The tandoori marinade (like all spice blends) varies to some extent, but most marinades include yogurt and paprika or cayenne pepper. To try my version, check out Grilled Tandoori Chicken in Chapter 5 of Book V.

Chapter 4

Starters, Snacks, and Sides

In This Chapter

▶ Making your own Indian breads

▶ Frying up tasty fritters

▶ Treating your vegetables right

*O*ne of my favorite things about Indian cooking is the variety — the variety of spices, flavors, aromas, techniques, and, most importantly, the variety of occasions for eating. The people of India have the usual special events, such as weddings, birthdays, and the like. But they also build snack time into their daily lives. Teatime is a perfect time for pakoras and samosas. Or they take a break from the day and have some parantha and chutney. And don't forget to somehow work a raita into a hot day.

Indian meals are served family style, and all dishes are placed on the table simultaneously, including the ones in this chapter. So although the terms "starters" and "sides" aren't completely applicable to Indian culture and cooking, it's helpful to separate the supporting cast of characters from the star of the show, so to speak.

Breads and Wafers

Northern India is known as the breadbasket of India. The people of this region have bread with almost every meal, so the bread-making process is a daily ritual for many families, typically the wives and daughters. In other regions, rice is the omnipresent accompaniment, and bread is the accent for special occasions. Regardless of how often you choose to prepare it, these Indian breads are always a special treat.

Indians traditionally eat with their hands. These breads are the disposable (or digestible) flatware of choice. Load them with tender dals or savory curries, roll them up, and enjoy.

Lentil wafers (paapad, paapadum)

You'll find these delectable snacks in Indian markets. These tortilla-shaped delights come prepackaged, just like the tostada (flat taco) shells you can find in a Mexican grocery. They're lighter and crispier than a tostada shell, with much more nutritional value because they're made from one of the world's most perfect foods: the protein-rich lentil. Because the commercial variety of this everyday snack is widely available (and delicious!), I include a few recommendations for heating, toasting, and roasting them rather than directions for creating them from scratch. Serve them at your next party with spicy chutney as the Indian equivalent of chips and salsa!

Here are tips on roasting the wafers:

- **Flame roasting:** Using tongs, hold each paapad over the flame and roast it, beginning with the edges and moving toward the center.

- **Oven or toaster oven:** Place under the preheated broiler until crisp — no more than 35 seconds — making sure that the edges don't burn.

- **Toaster:** Toast as you would a slice of bread, turning the paapad to make sure that the edges get browned.

- **Microwave oven:** Cook on high power about 1 minute, watching to make sure the paapad doesn't burn or begin to smoke. (This method is so quick and easy that you may find yourself making them this way all the time at home and even start a new trend at the office — if you have a microwave.)

- **Deep-frying:** Follow the directions for deep-frying (see Chapter 3 of Book V), making sure to drain each paapad well. Typically, the oil used for paapad frying is not reusable because it gets gelatinized in the process.

Griddle-fried breads (parantha)

These buttery layered breads are an accompaniment to special meals. They're traditionally fried on a *tava,* or Indian griddle, but I find that a stove-top or electric griddle is a good substitute. My electric griddle works well, and because it has a large cooking surface, I can fry 4 to 6 paranthas at a time. It saves load of time, and I can be in control of the temperature. I set it between 350 and 400 degrees.

Basic Griddle-Fried Breads
(Saada Parantha)

Made with a whole-wheat flour and water dough, this recipe is the perfect example of a parantha at its most basic. When frying, keep the rhythm going — while one parantha is on the griddle being cooked, prepare the next one. Doing so will save you a lot of time, but be sure to watch both.

Although freshly made paranthas are best, they can be cooked a few hours before serving. Allow 2 to 3 per person.

Preparation time: *4½ hours*

Cooking time: *5 minutes*

Yield: *Makes 10 to 12 breads*

2 cups stone-ground durum whole-wheat flour plus 1 cup for coating and dusting

About 1 cup water or nonfat plain yogurt, whisked until smooth

3 to 4 tablespoons oil or melted ghee or butter, for basting

1 Place the 2 cups flour in a mixing bowl, add 1cup water or yogurt, and mix with your clean fingers in round circular motions, until it starts to gather. (Add 1 or 2 tablespoons more flour if the dough seems sticky, or some water if it seems too firm.)

2 Knead for about a minute, pressing your knuckles lightly into the dough, spreading the dough outward, and then gathering the ends together toward the center with your fingers. Push down the center and then repeat pressing and gathering a few times until you have a soft and pliable dough that doesn't stick to your fingers. Cover and let it rest at least 1 hour and up to 4 hours at room temperature. (Doing so allows the wheat gluten to develop.) If keeping for a longer period, refrigerate the dough.

3 Preheat the tava or griddle over medium-high heat (350 and 400 degrees) until a sprinkling of the flour immediately turns dark brown. Wipe off the flour and proceed. While the tava is heating, with lightly oiled hands divide the dough into 10 to 12 round balls (depending on the size of the parantha you like). Cover with foil to prevent drying.

4 Working with each ball of dough separately, place in the bowl with the dry flour, flatten it with your fingertips, and coat well with the dry flour. Transfer to a cutting board or any other clean flat surface and, with a rolling pin, roll into a 6- to 7-inch circle of uniform thickness. (If the dough sticks to the rolling surface, dust with more flour.) Baste the top of the dough with ghee and fold into a circle.

5 Place the rolled parantha on the hot tava or griddle. Turn over when it is slightly cooked and dotted with tiny golden spots on the bottom, about 1 minute. When the other side is covered with larger brown dots, turn it over, and brush lightly with oil. Flip it over again and fry the oiled side about 30 seconds. Similarly, baste and fry the other side another 30 seconds. There should be a total of 4 turns.

6 Remove from the griddle and serve.

Oven-grilled leavened bread (naan)

Naan may be the most memorable Indian bread available in restaurants in the West. Its teardrop shape is unusual, and its texture is somewhere between that of a flour tortilla and hand-tossed pizza dough. Naan is finished by brushing it with ghee, or clarified butter, so, enough said, it's gotta be good.

The tandoori oven helps give naan its distinctive earthy flavor and aroma. You can get similar results without the tandoori oven by using a broiler. Use this recipe with a pizza stone (rather than a broiler pan), if you have one, to create an even more authentic crust. Although this bread is delicious, it's pretty tough to beat the authentic tandoori variety. Check with the chef at your local Indian restaurant to see whether he or she may be willing to sell you naan made in the tandoori to take home for your next party. At the very least, the chef will probably let you sneak a peek at the oven and watch how it's made.

Basic Oven-Grilled Leavened Breads (Tandoori Naan)

This basic recipe is made with refined all-purpose flour and is cooked under the broiler. These naans have yogurt in the dough. For a vegan alternative, use water in its place.

Preparation time: *4 hours*

Cooking time: *5 minutes*

Yield: *10 to 12 breads*

2 teaspoons active dry yeast	*2 cups all-purpose flour, or bread flour*
1 teaspoon sugar	*¼ teaspoon salt, or to taste*
¼ cup warm water (about 110 degrees)	*1 cup all-purpose flour in a medium bowl or a pie dish, for coating and dusting*
½ cup nonfat plain yogurt, whisked until smooth	*¼ cup melted butter or ghee, for basting (optional)*
2 tablespoons vegetable oil	

1 For the dough, dissolve the yeast and sugar in the warm water and set aside until frothy, about 5 minutes. Mix in the yogurt and oil.

2 Place the flour and salt in the food processor and process until mixed. With the motor running, pour the yeast mixture into the work bowl in a thin stream and process until the flour gathers into a ball and the sides of the processor are clean. (If the dough seems too sticky, add some more flour through the feeder tube, or add some more yogurt if the dough is dry and hard.) Transfer to a large bowl, cover with plastic wrap or the lid of the bowl, and place in a warm draft-free spot until it doubles in volume, 3 to 4 hours. (This allows the yeast to ferment and multiply, causing the dough to rise.) If keeping for a longer period, refrigerate the dough.

3 To roll and grill the naan breads, with clean, lightly oiled hands, divide the dough equally into 10 to 12 balls and cover with foil to prevent drying. Working with each ball of dough separately, place in the bowl with the dry flour, flatten it with your fingertips, and coat well with the dry flour. Then transfer to a cutting board or any other clean flat surface and, with a rolling pin, roll into a 7- to 8-inch triangle. (If the dough sticks to the rolling surface, dust with more flour.)

4 Place on large baking trays or, if you have a separate broiler, place on the broiler trays — 3 to 4 per tray. With a basting brush or your fingers, lightly baste the top of each naan with water. (Doing so prevents them from drying out.)

5 Preheat the oven to broil or preheat the broiler, and place the trays, one at a time, 4 to 5 inches below the heating element and broil until small brown spots appear on the top surface, about 1 minute. With a spatula, carefully, turn each naan over and cook until the other side is golden, about 30 seconds. Transfer the naan breads to a platter, baste lightly with butter, if desired, and serve hot.

Samosas

Samosas are the triangular, stuffed, deep-fried savory pastries available just about anywhere in India. From street vendors to Grandma's house, these tasty packets are a favorite. They're more similar to a stuffed wonton than to an egg roll. In fact, to save time, you can skip the dough recipe and use wonton or egg roll wrappers instead. Of course, the flavor will be different, but the concept is the same.

For a word about deep-frying, check out Chapter 3 of Book V.

I include some traditional (and hopefully familiar) fillings. But don't be afraid to experiment with your own fillings. If your family finds a favorite dal, or chunky legume-based dish, use it here. Just make sure that you do the following:

- ✔ Mince the ingredients finely. Consider using your food processor.

- ✔ Use fairly dry rather than soupy fillings. Soupy fillings make soggy samosas. And nobody likes a soggy samosa.

- ✔ Precook the ingredients before stuffing the samosas. The frying process fries the dough but only heats the filling. Don't rely on it to cook your filling.

Traditional Stuffed Triangular Pastries (Samosae)

There are three basic steps to making samosas: making the pastry dough, filling the samosas, and deep-frying them. As for the filling, you can use just about any dry-cooked vegetable or meat, as long as it's finely chopped or minced and cooked.

Preparation time: *Up to 5 hours*

Cooking time: *10 minutes*

Yield: *24 pieces*

1 recipe any Samosa Filling (see the recipes later in this chapter)	*½ teaspoon salt, or to taste*
	About ⅓ cup water
1½ cups self-rising flour	*1 cup all-purpose flour in a medium bowl or a*
3 tablespoons vegetable oil	*pie dish, for coating and dusting*
½ teaspoon coarsely ground ajwain seeds	*1½ to 2 cups peanut oil for deep-frying*

1 Prepare the filling. Then prepare the dough: Place the self-rising flour, oil, ajwain seeds, and salt in a food processor and pulse a few times to mix. With the motor running, pour the water in a slow stream and process until the flour gathers into a semifirm ball that doesn't stick to the sides of the work bowl. Remove to a bowl, cover with plastic wrap or a lid, and let rest at least 1 hour and up to 4 hours. (This allows the gluten to develop.) If keeping for a longer period, refrigerate the dough.

2 To roll and assemble: Lightly oil your clean hands (to prevent the dough from sticking to them), then divide into twelve 1½-inch balls. Cover with aluminum foil and set aside. Working with each ball separately, flatten it into a disk with your fingertips, coat well with dry flour, and then roll with a rolling pin into a 6- to 7-inch circle of uniform ⅛-inch thickness. If the dough sticks to the rolling surface, coat once again with flour.

3 Cut the circle in half and brush with water about ½-inch in, along the straight edge. Pick up the two corners and place one over and around the other along the straight edge and then press along the straight edge to seal, making a cone. Also pinch the point of the cone to seal. Alternatively, fold in half, sealing the straight edge to make a simpler cone.

4 Hold the cone between your thumb and forefinger, with the pointed side down toward the work surface. Fill the mouth of the cone with 2 to 3 tablespoons of filling. Brush the edges of the mouth of the cone with water and press them together to seal. You should end up with a stuffed triangular pastry. Cover with foil and set aside until ready to fry. Repeat with all the other balls of dough.

5 To fry: Heat the oil in a wok or skillet over medium-high heat until it reaches 325 to 350 degrees on a frying thermometer, or when a small piece of the dough dropped into the hot oil rises to the top after 15 to 20 seconds. Place the samosas in the wok, as many as it can hold at one time without crowding, and fry, turning them a few times with a slotted spatula, until crispy and golden on all sides, 4 to 5 minutes. (If the samosas brown too quickly, it means the heat is too high; lower it.) Transfer to paper towels to drain and then serve.

Vary It! *For bite-size servings, in Step 2 divide the filling and dough into 48 balls. Roll each ball of dough into a 2-inch circle, stuff with a teaspoon of filling, wrap, and then fry according to directions, about 2 minutes or until golden.*

Potato Filling (Samosae mein bharnae kae Aalu)

Although any type of dry-cooked vegetable or meat makes for delicious samosa fillings, there are some traditional ones. Potatoes are tops on the list.

You can also use this samosa filling to stuff vegetables such as tomatoes, eggplants, bell peppers, and others, and even serve as a side dish. You can use any of the dry-cooked potato dishes in the book to fill your samosas.

Preparation time: *5 minutes*

Cooking time: *45 minutes*

Yield: *About 4 cups*

4 to 5 medium russet (or any) potatoes (about 1½ pounds)

2 tablespoons peanut oil

2 teaspoons cumin seeds

½ teaspoon coarsely ground fenugreek seeds

2 tablespoons peeled and minced fresh ginger

1 to 3 fresh green chile peppers, such as serrano, minced with seeds

1½ tablespoons ground coriander

½ teaspoon salt, or to taste

½ teaspoon garam masala

¼ cup finely chopped fresh cilantro, including soft stems

1 teaspoon mango powder

1 Cook the potatoes in lightly salted boiling water to cover until tender, about 20 minutes. Drain, let cool, and then peel and finely chop. Heat the oil in a large nonstick wok or saucepan over medium-high heat and add the cumin seeds; they should sizzle upon contact with the hot oil. Quickly add the fenugreek seeds and mix in the potatoes.

2 Stir about 2 minutes, add the ginger, green chile peppers, coriander, salt, and garam masala, and stir occasionally until the potatoes are golden, about 10 minutes.

3 Add the cilantro and mango powder and cook for another 5 minutes. Remove from the heat and let cool before using.

Vary It! *Mix in ½ cup thawed frozen peas, 1 cup finely chopped fresh spinach, or ½ cup soaked red lentils (dhulli masoor dal) along with the potatoes. Adjust the seasonings.*

Spicy Mixed Vegetable Samosa Filling (Samosae mein bharnae ki Sabziyan)

Mix at least three vegetables — carrots, beans, mushrooms, potatoes, peas, cauliflower, or any others you fancy. The underlying flavor of this filling comes from the special kadhai masala blend, which has fenugreek, fennel, and pomegranate seeds. It's named for a blend of spices often used in foods fried in the *kadhai* (Indian wok).

Preparation time: *10 minutes*

Cooking time: *15 minutes*

Yield: *About 4 cups*

1½ to 2 tablespoons Spicy Masala for Wok-Cooked Foods (see the following recipe)

2 tablespoons vegetable oil

1 medium onion, finely chopped

1 to 3 fresh green chile peppers, such as serrano, minced with seeds

1 tablespoon peeled and finely chopped fresh ginger

4 cups finely chopped mixed fresh or frozen vegetables

½ teaspoon salt, or to taste

Freshly ground black pepper to taste

1 Prepare the Spicy Masala. Heat the oil in a large nonstick wok or saucepan over medium-high heat and add the Spicy Masala; it should sizzle upon contact with the hot oil. Quickly add the onion and stir about 2 minutes.

2 Add the green chile peppers, ginger, vegetables, salt, and black pepper; cook over medium heat the first 2 to 3 minutes and then over medium-low heat until the vegetables are soft, 5 to 7 minutes more. Remove from the heat and let cool before using.

Spicy Masala for Wok-Cooked Foods (Kadhai Masala)

Associated with meat, vegetable, and paneer cheese dishes made in a heavy, round-bottomed wok known as the kadhai, this blend, though very much like a curry powder, is known and marketed specifically for its outstanding fragrance. To use, pan-cook sliced onion, ginger, garlic, and bell peppers, add 1 to 2 tablespoons of the spice mixture, and cook, stirring, until fragrant. Add your choice of meat, vegetable, or paneer cheese and finish cooking.

Preparation time: *5 minutes*

Yield: *About 1¼ cups*

½ cup coarsely ground coriander seeds

2 tablespoons ground dried fenugreek leaves

2 tablespoons ground dried mint leaves

2 tablespoons ground cumin seeds

1 tablespoon ground fennel seeds

1 tablespoon ground ginger

1 tablespoon mango powder

1 tablespoon ground dried pomegranate seeds

1 tablespoon cayenne pepper

1 teaspoon ground paprika

1 teaspoon ground black cardamom seeds

1 teaspoon ground nutmeg

1 teaspoon ground black salt

Put all the spices in a small bowl and mix them together with a spoon. Store in an airtight container in a cool, dark place, about 1 month at room temperature or about 1 year in the refrigerator.

Pakoras

Think of pakoras as India's answer to onion rings or fried mushrooms. (Not that onion rings really need an answer; they pretty much speak for themselves.) Pakoras and Western fried veggies share many characteristics: chopped or sliced vegetables, a coating of batter, and deep-frying to perfection. The batter, made with chickpea flour (also called besan flour), is the crucial difference. For more about besan flour, see Chapter 2 of Book V. Besan flour is heavy and tends to clump as it sits. Sifting the besan flour is key to creating a nice smooth batter, the hallmark of any good pakora.

Fry pakoras at a slightly higher temperature than the temperature described in Chapter 2 of Book V, around 375 degrees. If possible, try to use small, maybe 2-inch, pieces when starting out. You can use larger pieces, but you must double-fry them and let them rest a few minutes between fryings. Without the resting period, the outside will burn and the inside will be underdone.

Basic Batter for Pakora Fritters
(Pakorae ka Besan)

This is the most basic batter for pakora fritters, to which you can add as many or as few herbs and spices as you wish. With no other additions, this basic recipe forms a light, crisp coating around a large array of foods. More than anything else, it is the consistency of the batter that is really important. Thick, it will be doughy; thin it will not coat properly.

Preparation time: *5 minutes*

Yield: *40 to 50 fritters*

½ cup chickpea flour (besan)

⅓ teaspoon salt, or to taste

⅛ teaspoon baking soda

⅓ to ½ cup water

1 Sift the chickpea flour into a medium bowl, add the salt and baking soda, and mix well.

2 Add water to make a smooth batter of medium consistency. If the batter is thin, add some more chickpea flour; if it seems too thick, mix in some more water. The batter is now ready.

Cauliflower Pakora Fritters with Cilantro (Gobhi kae Pakorae)

This is one of thousands of variations on the vegetable pakora. Cauliflower is a nice firm vegetable that holds its shape well and lets the batter cling to it, so it's a good one to start with. You can use any vegetables from your own summer harvest, such as bell peppers, squash, or eggplant. Tender greens (such as mustard or spinach) also work well, but frying the leaves is a delicate job, so take a little extra time and practice.

Cauliflower can be cut into all types of pieces — large or small florets or thick or thin stem slices. Just remember that while the thin, small pieces are fine at the first go, the larger, thicker ones will need to be double-fried.

Preparation time: *15 minutes*

Cooking time: *20 minutes*

Yield: *20 to 25 pieces*

1 teaspoon Chaat Masala (see Chapter 2 of Book V)

1 large head cauliflower (about 1½ pounds), cut into 2-inch florets

½ teaspoon salt, or to taste

½ teaspoon hot red pepper flakes, or to taste

1½ recipes Basic Batter for Pakora Fritters (see the preceding recipe)

1 to 2 tablespoons chickpea flour

¼ cup minced fresh cilantro, including soft stems

1 to 3 fresh green chile peppers, such as serrano, minced with seeds

¼ teaspoon garam masala

½ teaspoon coarsely ground ajwain seeds

1½ to 2 cups peanut oil for deep-frying

¼ cup mustard oil for deep-frying

1 Prepare the Chaat Masala. Place the cauliflower florets in a bowl and toss with salt and red pepper flakes. Set aside to let the flavors blend. Prepare the basic batter. Mix in the chickpea flour, cilantro, green chile peppers, garam masala, and ajwain seeds.

2 In a wok or skillet, heat the oil to 350 to 375 degrees.

3 Add the florets to the batter and mix lightly with your fingers. Working with each piece separately, shake off the excess batter by tapping it gently against the side of the bowl. Then carefully place the battered floret into the hot oil with your fingers (or tongs). Be as gentle as possible to avoid oil splatter. Add as many pieces as the wok can hold without crowding, and fry each batch, turning a few times with a slotted spoon, until crispy and golden on all sides, about 2 minutes. Transfer to paper towels to drain. Repeat the process with the remaining pieces.

4 Let cool and then press each fritter between the palms of your hands to flatten. As you do this, the batter coating will break and reveal parts of the florets. Refry the dense florets in hot oil until the pakoras are lightly browned and crisp, 1 to 2 minutes. Drain on paper towels. Transfer all the fried pakoras to a serving platter, sprinkle the Chaat Masala on top, and serve.

Traditional Chicken Pakora Fritters
(Murgh kae Pakorae)

This recipe for Chicken Pakoras works well with other meats as well. Try it with tender cuts of beef or marinate tougher cuts in the refrigerator overnight before cooking.

If you're convinced that you know what fried chicken tastes like, just wait till you try this finger-licking-delicious recipe!

Preparation time: *15 minutes*

Cooking time: *20 minutes*

Yield: *10 to 15 pieces*

2 tablespoons Basic Ginger-Garlic Paste (see the recipe in Chapter 2 of Book V or use store-bought)

2½- to 3-pound chicken, skinned and cut into serving pieces (discard the back and wings)

2 cups water

1 teaspoon garam masala

½ teaspoon salt, or to taste

½ teaspoon Chaat Masala (see the recipe in Chapter 2 of Book V or use store-bought)

1 teaspoon dry-roasted and coarsely ground cumin seeds

1 recipe Basic Batter for Pakora Fritters (see the recipe earlier in this chapter)

2 tablespoons minced fresh cilantro, including soft stems

1 tablespoon ground coriander

1 teaspoon ground cumin seeds

½ teaspoon hot red pepper flakes, or to taste

½ teaspoon coarsely ground ajwain seeds

1½ to 2 cups peanut oil for deep-frying

1 Prepare the ginger-garlic paste. Then place the chicken, water, ginger-garlic paste, garam masala, and salt in a small saucepan and bring to a boil over high heat. Reduce the heat to medium-low, cover the pan, and simmer until the chicken is tender and all the water has been absorbed, 15 to 20 minutes. If the chicken cooks before the water dries up, uncover the pan and cook until the chicken is completely dry. Let cool, remove the bones, and cut into smaller pieces, if you wish.

2 Meanwhile, prepare the Chaat Masala and the dry-roasted cumin seeds. Then, prepare the basic batter, and mix in the cilantro, coriander, cumin, red pepper flakes, and ajwain seeds.

3 Add the chicken to the batter, making sure each piece is thoroughly coated. Heat the oil in a wok or skillet to 350 to 375 degrees.

4 Using tongs or your fingers, tap the excess batter off each chicken piece and gently place it in the oil one piece at a time. Add as many pieces as the wok can hold without crowding, and fry each batch, turning a few times with a slotted spoon, until crispy and golden on all sides, about 2 to 3 minutes. Transfer to paper towels to drain. Repeat the process with the remaining pieces.

5 Transfer to a platter and sprinkle with the roasted cumin and Chaat Masala.

Veggies on the Side

The vegetarian diet is a favorite among Indian people. It's entrenched in their culture through religious beliefs and economic necessity. In a country where meat can cost five times more than vegetables, you learn to get by with the vegetables.

As unusual as it may seem to Westerners, Indian cooks have thousands of ways to prepare vegetables, ensuring that variety is present at every meal. Varying the preparation method, the spice blends, and the condiments served makes each meal a unique experience. Here are just a few of the Indian staples.

Spicy Potatoes with Onions and Tomatoes (Aalu, Pyaz aur Tamatar)

A workhorse dish, this recipe is the daily side dish that is as good as gourmet food when you're hungry.

Preparation time: *5 minutes*

Cooking time: *45 minutes*

Yield: *4 to 6 servings*

4 medium russet potatoes (about 1¼ pounds)	*½ teaspoon ground cumin*
2 tablespoons vegetable oil	*¼ teaspoon ground turmeric*
2 teaspoons melted ghee (optional)	*¼ teaspoon ground paprika*
1 large onion, finely chopped	*¾ teaspoon salt, or to taste*
1 to 3 fresh green chile peppers, such as serrano, minced with seeds	*½ cup finely chopped fresh cilantro, including soft stems*
1 large tomato, finely chopped	*¼ teaspoon garam masala*
1 tablespoon ground coriander	

1 Boil the potatoes in water to cover until tender, about 20 minutes. Drain, let cool, peel, and cut into ½-inch pieces.

2 Heat the oil (and ghee, if using) in a large nonstick wok over medium-high heat and cook the onion, stirring frequently, until golden, 5 to 7 minutes. Add the green chile peppers and tomato and cook until most of the juices evaporate, 3 to 4 minutes.

3 Add all the spices and salt. Cook, stirring, about 1 minute, and then add the potatoes and cilantro and cook over high heat until heated through. Reduce the heat to medium-low and cook until the potatoes are well mixed with the onions and tomatoes, and the oil separates to the sides, about 10 minutes. Transfer to a serving dish, sprinkle the garam masala on top, and serve.

Mashed Fire-Roasted Eggplant
(Baingan ka Bhartha)

Seasoned just with salt, this authentic home-style specialty is a textured eggplant mash with lots of natural flavor. It has no resemblance to the heavily creamed and spiced *bhartha* (mashed eggplant) dishes that you find in Indian restaurants. Present it as a dip for fresh vegetables and in sandwiches in place of grilled eggplants.

Preparation time: *20 minutes*

Cooking time: *30 minutes*

Yield: *4 to 6 servings*

2 medium oval-shaped eggplants (about ¾ pound each)

3 tablespoons vegetable oil

5 to 7 fresh green chile peppers, such as serrano, whole (puncture skin to prevent bursting), or mince 1 pepper

1 large onion, finely chopped

2 large tomatoes, finely chopped

1½ cups finely chopped fresh cilantro, including soft stems

1 teaspoon salt, or to taste

1 Wash, dry, and lightly oil your hands. Rub them all over the surface of each eggplant. With the tip of a sharp knife, puncture the skin in a few places. Place the eggplants over the hot coals of a grill or over the direct flame of a kitchen stove burner (cover the bottom plate with aluminum foil), and roast, turning with tongs as the sides blacken, until the eggplants are soft and the skin is completely charred 5 to 7 minutes. Transfer to a bowl and let cool.

2 When cool enough to handle, peel off the charred skin of the eggplants and discard. Work close to the kitchen sink because you may need to rinse your fingers as you go along. Do not wash the eggplant. Mash the pulp with your hands or a fork until somewhat smooth but still lumpy. Strain any juice that may have collected in the bowl. You may save the juice for other recipes if you like, but you don't need it for this recipe.

3 Heat the oil in a large wok or saucepan over medium-high heat, add the green chile peppers and onion, and cook, stirring, until golden, about 7 minutes. Add the tomatoes and 1 cup cilantro and cook, stirring occasionally, until the tomato juices evaporate, about 5 minutes.

4 Mix in the eggplant pulp and salt. Reduce the heat to medium-low and cook, stirring occasionally, about 15 minutes. Mix in the remaining ½ cup chopped cilantro during the last 5 minutes. Transfer to a serving dish, dig out the chile peppers, and place them on top as a garnish (and a warning), and serve.

North Indian–Style Mixed Vegetable Stir-Fry (Uttar ki Jhalfrezi)

This dish features lots of mildly spiced vegetables supported with fresh tomatoes that just melt in your mouth, along with tandoori chicken and naan breads.

Like kadhai dishes, jhalfrezi dishes are about flavors. Whether you make them with vegetables, chicken, meat, seafood, or paneer cheese, they all have lots of vegetables, tomatoes, and vinegar (or lemon juice), and are mostly served in Indian restaurants but are easy enough to be made at home. Variations of this dish are made all over India, with coriander and turmeric in the north, curry leaves and coconut in the south.

Preparation time: *10 minutes*

Cooking time: *15 minutes*

Yield: *4 to 6 servings*

2 tablespoons Basic Ginger-Garlic Paste (see the recipe in Chapter 2 of Book V or use store-bought)

3 tablespoons peanut oil

1 teaspoon cumin seeds

¼ teaspoon coarsely ground ajwain seeds

2 small onions, cut into ¾-inch pieces

1-inch piece fresh ginger, peeled and cut into thin matchsticks

1 to 3 fresh green chile peppers, such as serrano, minced with seeds

1 tablespoon ground coriander

½ teaspoon cayenne pepper, or to taste

¼ teaspoon ground turmeric

3 to 4 cups mixed vegetables, such as cauliflower, potatoes, carrots, green beans, green bell peppers, and peas, cut into ¾- to 1-inch pieces

1 teaspoon salt, or to taste

4 small tomatoes, cut into 6 wedges each

1 to 2 tablespoons distilled white vinegar

½ cup finely chopped fresh cilantro, including soft stems

½ teaspoon garam masala

1 Prepare the Ginger-Garlic Paste. Heat the oil in a large nonstick wok or saucepan over medium-high heat and add the cumin and ajwain seeds; they should sizzle upon contact with the hot oil. Quickly add the onions and ginger, and cook about 1 minute. Add the Ginger-Garlic Paste and cook another minute.

2 Mix in the coriander, cayenne pepper, and turmeric, add the vegetables and salt, and cook, stirring, until golden, about 5 minutes.

3 Add the tomato wedges, stir 1 minute, cover the pan, reduce the heat to medium, and cook until the vegetables are crisp-tender, about 5 minutes. Add the vinegar and cilantro, stir 1 minute, transfer to a serving dish, mix in the garam masala, and serve.

Chapter 5

The Main Event

In This Chapter

- Discovering the secrets of classic Indian dishes
- Creating killer curries
- Taking vegetarian dishes to new heights
- Getting the most out of dals

Indian meals are often shared with friends and families. Indian cooks develop strategies for stretching dishes further when unexpected company arrives. They rely on condiments (like chutneys and pickles), a wide variety of vegetable dishes, and a few mainstay meats to create elaborate banquets. Their love of fresh ingredients and traditional techniques is passed from generation to generation.

Despite the variety offered at the Indian table, invariably some dishes take center stage. Whether you're new to Indian cuisine and cooking, or next in line for job of the executive chef to the maharaja, the dishes in this chapter are must-haves in your Indian cooking lineup.

Classic Standards

Indian restaurants in the West celebrate the northern Indian cooking style. Characterized by the tandoori oven, sumptuous breads, and special spice blends, northern Indian cooking gives us these familiar favorites.

I substitute an oven or grill for the authentic tandoori oven, but I hope that you'll still find these versions tasty and satisfying.

Grilled Tandoori Chicken (Tandoori Murgh)

Whenever the words "tandoori chicken" are mentioned, a dramatically red chicken may flash before your eyes. This arresting red color, however, is purely for visual appeal. The chicken's real flavor comes from the marinade, and its smoky richness from the juices and marinades as they drip onto hot coals. (For best flavor, marinate the chicken the day before cooking or leave enough time for the two marinating steps.)

Authentically, this chicken should be roasted whole in a tandoor, but the best alternatives are an outdoor grill, a smoker, a rotisserie, and, failing all those, the oven or broiler. This recipe offers directions for grilling, broiling, and roasting. For the outdoor grill and the oven, you can either roast a whole chicken or, for ease and convenience, use serving-size pieces.

Preparation time: *15 minutes, plus at least 8 hours for marinade*

Cooking time: *25–35 minutes*

Yield: *4 to 6 servings*

2½- to 3-pound whole chicken, skinned	1 teaspoon garam masala
2 tablespoons fresh lime or lemon juice	1 teaspoon ground dried fenugreek leaves
½ teaspoon salt, or to taste	½ teaspoon ground cumin
2 tablespoons Basic Ginger-Garlic Paste (see Chapter 2 of Book V or use store-bought)	1 teaspoon ground paprika
⅓ cup nonfat plain yogurt, whisked until smooth	¼ teaspoon cayenne pepper, or to taste
	⅛ teaspoon ground turmeric
2 tablespoons heavy cream	1 tablespoon melted butter for basting
1 tablespoon peanut oil	Scallion whites
	Lemon wedges

1 Leaving the chicken whole, with a sharp knife make deep, 1½-inch cuts all over the chicken — 3 on each breast, 3 on each thigh, and 2 on each drumstick — and then place in a nonreactive dish. In a small bowl, mix together the lime juice and salt and rub it over the chicken, making sure to reach inside the cuts. Cover with plastic wrap and marinate in the refrigerator about 2 hours. Meanwhile, prepare the ginger-garlic paste.

2 After the chicken has marinated, in another small bowl, mix together the yogurt, cream, oil, ginger-garlic paste, garam masala, fenugreek leaves, and cumin.

3 Heat the oil in a small nonstick saucepan over medium-high heat until hot but not smoking. Remove from the heat and add the paprika, cayenne pepper, and turmeric. Mix the spiced oil into the yogurt mixture. Rub the yogurt well over and inside the chicken. Cover with plastic wrap and marinate in the refrigerator, at least 8 and up to 24 hours.

4 **To grill:** Preheat the grill to medium-high (about 375 to 400 degrees). Grill, turning the chicken as needed, until the meat is soft and charred in a few places and opaque inside, 20 to 25 minutes. Baste with the melted butter and grill, turning, another 3 to 5 minutes.

To broil: Preheat the broiler. Place the marinated chicken (whole or cut up into serving pieces) on a roasting or broiler pan with a tray underneath to catch the dripping juices, and broil in the lower center section of the oven or broiler (about 10 inches from the heat source) until the chicken is opaque inside when tested with a knife, 25 to 30 minutes. Turn a few times and watch the heat. If the chicken browns too quickly, cover with foil.

To bake (with a gas oven): Preheat the oven to 375 degrees. Cut the chicken into serving pieces and place on a roasting rack with a tray underneath to catch the juices. Bake, covered with aluminum foil, in the center section of the oven until the chicken is lightly browned and the meat is soft and opaque inside when tested with a knife, 30 to 35 minutes. Turn and baste the pieces with the butter a few times while they're cooking.

5 Transfer to a serving platter, garnish with the scallions and lemon wedges, and serve whole or quartered.

Fried Onion Paste
(Talae Pyaz ka Masala)

This paste, used mostly for the richer northern, Mughlai-type dishes, gives everyday curries a distinctive rich quality that sets them apart from the usual fare. Even though the onion, ginger, and garlic are deep-fried, this paste is not as rich as the word "fried" implies. The fried ingredients are drained on paper towels and then ground to make a paste.

To use, add spices to the paste and then simmer with water, buttermilk, whisked yogurt, or light cream, for all types of meats, especially *kofta* (fried minced meat balls).

Preparation time: *15 minutes*

Cooking time: *10 minutes*

Yield: *About 1 cup*

1 cup melted ghee or vegetable oil for deep-frying

6 to 8 quarter-size slices of peeled fresh ginger

4 large cloves fresh garlic, peeled

1 large onion, cut in half lengthwise and thinly sliced

½ cup nonfat plain yogurt

1 Heat the oil in a large nonstick saucepan over medium-high heat and fry the ginger and garlic until golden, about 2 minutes. Add the onion and fry until everything is well browned, about 5 minutes. (Reduce the heat if the browning occurs too quickly.) Remove to paper towels to drain and reserve the ghee or oil for another purpose.

2 Transfer to a blender or a food processor, add the yogurt, and process to make a thick, smooth paste. Transfer to an airtight container and refrigerate up to 5 days or freeze up to 3 months.

Basic Chicken Tikka Kabaabs (Murgh Tikka)

Skinless, boneless pieces of tandoor-grilled chicken, flavored with one of the countless Indian marinades, are popular items on restaurant menus and are quite easy to enjoy at home, as well. Granted, you may not have a tandoor, but you do have grilling options, an oven, and, if all else fails, a saucepan.

Special tool: *8 to 10 metal skewers or bamboo skewers, soaked in water at least 30 minutes*

Preparation time: *1½ hours plus 6–24 hours for marinade*

Cooking time: *30 minutes*

Yield: *4 to 6 servings*

1 recipe Creamy Chicken Tikka Marinade (see the following recipe)

2 pounds skinless, boneless chicken breasts, cut into 1½-inch pieces

1 recipe Kabaab and Tikka Finishing Glaze (see the recipe later in this chapter)

2 cups shredded greens, such as romaine or green leaf lettuce

Lemon wedges

Tomato wedges

Scallions, thinly sliced

1 to 2 fresh green chile peppers, such as serrano, stemmed, seeded, and thinly sliced

1 Prepare the marinade. Then place the chicken in a large nonreactive bowl, add the marinade (saving about ¼ cup to use for basting as you grill), and mix well, making sure that all the pieces are well coated. Cover the bowl and marinate the chicken in the refrigerator, at least 6 and up to 24 hours. (To prevent potential salmonella contamination, never marinate poultry, meat, or seafood at room temperature.)

2 When ready to cook, prepare the finishing glaze and set aside. Then thread the marinated pieces of chicken on skewers (4 to 5 pieces per skewer) and discard the used marinade. (If you prefer, immediately boil the marinade for about 5 minutes and use it as a sauce. Boiling kills any bacteria.)

3 Preheat a grill over medium-high heat to 375 to 400 degrees and grill, turning and rotating the chicken until lightly charred on all sides and tender, about 20 minutes. Baste occasionally with the reserved marinade. During the last minute or so, baste with the finishing glaze. Transfer to a platter lined with shredded greens. Garnish with lemon and tomato wedges, sliced scallions, and green chile peppers, and serve.

Vary It! *Place the skewered pieces in a broiler tray and grill about 8 inches from the heating element, until charred all over. Then heat the oven to 450 degrees, cover the skewers with foil, and bake until the chicken is soft and tender, about 25 minutes.*

Creamy Chicken Tikka Marinade (Murgh Tikka — Malai)

Malai is clotted cream. Because it's not readily available, I use heavy cream instead. No matter what you use, the end result is a marinade that yields pale-white, smooth, and delicate tikka kabaabs.

Preparation time: *50 minutes*

Yield: *4 to 6 servings*

2 tablespoons Hyderabadi Ginger-Garlic Paste (see the recipe later in this chapter)	*1 large egg (or 2 egg whites), lightly beaten*
1 teaspoon freshly ground white pepper	*2 fresh green chile peppers, such as serrano, coarsely chopped*
1 teaspoon salt, or to taste	*1 tablespoon cornstarch*
¼ cup heavy cream	*⅛ teaspoon ground mace*
¼ cup grated Pepper-Jack cheese	*⅛ teaspoon ground nutmeg*

1 Prepare the ginger-garlic paste. In a large nonreactive bowl, combine the paste, white pepper, and salt, rub the chicken pieces with this mixture, and set aside for 30 to 40 minutes.

2 In a blender, blend together the cream, cheese, egg, chile peppers, cornstarch, mace, and nutmeg, and blend until smooth. Add to the chicken and mix well.

Kabaab and Tikka Finishing Glaze

Before they're finished, all tandoor-cooked kabaabs and tikkas are basted with a special finishing glaze that is made with seasoned ghee, butter, or oil and, occasionally, lemon juice. Brushed on the foods during the last few minutes, while the meat is still in the tandoor (or on your grill), this glaze really jazzes up the flavors and gives the food a brilliant shine.

Preparation time: *5 minutes*

1 to 2 tablespoons melted butter or any vegetable oil, mixed with ½ teaspoon Asian sesame oil or ghee	*¼ teaspoon ground black salt, or to taste*
	One of the following:
2 tablespoons fresh lemon or lime juice, or vinegar	*½ to 1 teaspoon dry-roasted and coarsely ground cumin or black peppercorns*
½ teaspoon dried fenugreek leaves	*1 teaspoon Chaat Masala (see the recipe in Chapter 2 of Book V or use store-bought)*

To the butter, add the lemon juice, fenugreek leaves, and salt. Mix in the cumin or Chaat Masala.

Grilled Chicken in Spicy Sauce (Murgh Tikka Masala)

This dish, called *murgh tikka masala,* has multiple levels of delectable flavor. It's made with grilled boneless cubes of chicken *(tikkas)* simmered in a full-bodied and spicy curry sauce. Make the *tikkas* a day ahead — serve some with chilled beer or wine and then make this curry the next day. You can also make this recipe with any leftover grilled chicken, meat, or fish. If you're using fish, add it just minutes before serving or it will disintegrate in the sauce.

Preparation time: *2 hours*

Cooking time: *30 minutes*

Yield: *4 to 6 servings*

½ recipe Basic Chicken Tikka Kabaabs (see the recipe earlier in this chapter), made with Creamy Chicken Tikka Marinade (see the recipe earlier in this chapter)

2 large tomatoes, coarsely chopped

½ cup coarsely chopped fresh cilantro, including soft stems, plus more for garnish

½ cup (½ recipe) Fried Onion Paste (see the recipe earlier in this chapter)

1 tablespoon coriander

1 teaspoon ground cumin

2 teaspoons dried fenugreek leaves

1 teaspoon ground paprika

1 teaspoon garam masala

1 teaspoon salt, or to taste

1 cup water

½ cup heavy cream

1 Make the tikka kabaabs and cut them into smaller pieces if you wish. Then make the Fried Onion Paste (reserving the ghee).

2 In a food processor, process together the tomatoes and cilantro until pureed.

3 Place the onion paste, along with 1 tablespoon of the ghee in which the onion paste was fried. Add the pureed tomatoes and cook, stirring, over medium-high heat until all the juices evaporate, about 7 minutes.

4 Add the coriander, cumin, fenugreek leaves, paprika, garam masala, and salt and stir about 1 minute. Then add the water and the grilled chicken kabaab pieces and simmer about 5 minutes. Add the cream and simmer another 5 minutes to blend the flavors. Transfer to a serving dish, garnish with some chopped cilantro, and serve.

Marinated Lamb Kabaabs (Boti Kabaabs)

Lamb is virtually the *only* red meat in India. The sacred cow is rarely used for food. In the West, the term *mutton* refers to mature sheep meat, but in India, it can refer to sheep or goat meat, neither of which is very tender. Both are standard fare for those families that eat meat.

Boti is a piece of bone-in meat. The authentic version of these kabaabs calls for bone-in pieces, although over the years this has changed and boti kabaabs all over India are now made with boneless meat. My recipe here uses boneless leg of lamb.

For a true and authentic version, ask your butcher to trim and cut lamb shanks into 1½-inch pieces.

Special tool: *6 metal skewers or bamboo skewers, soaked in water at least 30 minutes*

Preparation time: *15 minutes*

Cooking time: *20 minutes*

Yield: *4 to 6 servings*

1½ to 2 pounds boneless leg of lamb, all visible fat trimmed, cut into 1½-inch pieces

½ cup nonfat plain yogurt, whisked until smooth

¼ cup Basic Ginger-Garlic Paste (see Chapter 2 of Book V or use store-bought)

¼ cup fresh lemon or lime juice

1 tablespoon vegetable oil

1 tablespoon ground coriander

1 tablespoon ground cumin

2 teaspoons garam masala (see Chapter 2 Book V)

1 teaspoon cayenne pepper, or to taste

1½ teaspoons salt, or to taste

1 tablespoon melted unsalted butter

2 tablespoons finely chopped fresh cilantro, including soft stems

1 With a fork, prick each piece of lamb all over and place in a large nonreactive bowl. In another bowl, mix together the yogurt, ginger-garlic paste, lemon juice, oil, coriander, cumin, garam masala, cayenne pepper, and salt. Add the yogurt mixture to the lamb pieces. Mix well, making sure that all the pieces are coated with the marinade. Cover and marinate in the refrigerator about 24 hours.

2 Thread the marinated pieces of lamb on metal or bamboo skewers (4 to 5 pieces per skewer) and discard the marinade. (If you absolutely must, immediately boil the marinade for about 5 minutes and use it in sauces. Boiling kills any bacteria.)

3 Preheat a grill on medium-high heat (375 to 400 degrees) and grill, turning the skewered pieces over until they're lightly charred and very tender, about 20 minutes. During the last minute or so, baste with the melted butter. Remove to a serving platter, garnish with the cilantro, and serve.

Curries

Curry is almost always cooking in the typical Indian home.

Thanks to the distinct fragrance and aroma of Indian food, curry powder is synonymous with Indian food in the mind of many Westerners. However, most dishes contain many other spice blends. Any dish with a gravy or sauce is commonly referred to as a *curry* in Indian cooking, whether or not it has the famed spice blend familiar to Westerners. For more about the curry versus curry powder distinction, see Chapter 2 of Book V.

Curries are great for entertaining because you can prepare them in advance and, like soups and stews, they only get better with age. Served with fragrant basmati rice (see Chapter 3 of Book V), curries are sure to please your guests.

Basic Pan-Roasted Lamb Curry (Bhunnae Gosht ki Kari)

In this basic curry, the meat is stirred and roasted until well browned. In India, this dish is customarily made with bone-in pieces, but because I noticed people fishing for the boneless ones in the thick curry pool, I make this recipe with boneless pieces. Of course, the addition of a few bone-in pieces (such as lamb shanks or chops) will add more flavor to this curry.

Preparation time: *10 minutes*

Cooking time: *2 hours*

Yield: *4 to 6 servings*

3 tablespoons vegetable oil

1 large onion, finely chopped

1 tablespoon peeled and minced fresh ginger

2 large cloves fresh garlic, minced

2 large tomatoes, finely chopped

2 tablespoons ground coriander

2 teaspoons garam masala

1 teaspoon ground cumin

¼ teaspoon ground turmeric

½ teaspoon dried cayenne pepper, or to taste

2 pounds boneless leg of lamb or beef (rump, brisket, or sirloin), all visible fat trimmed and the meat cut into 1½-inch pieces

1 teaspoon salt, or to taste

1½ cups nonfat plain yogurt, whisked until smooth

3 to 4 cups water

1 teaspoon dried fenugreek leaves

3 to 4 cups water

¼ cup chopped cilantro

1 Heat the oil in a large nonstick wok or saucepan and cook the onions, stirring as needed, initially over high heat for the first 3 to 5 minutes and then over medium-low heat until well-browned, about 12 minutes.

2 Add the ginger and garlic and stir about 1 minute. Add the tomatoes and cook until most of the juices evaporate, about 5 minutes.

3 Add the coriander, garam masala (save ¼ teaspoon for garnish), cumin, turmeric, chile powder, and cayenne pepper and stir about 30 seconds. Mix in the lamb and salt, and stir, initially over high heat the first 3 to 5 minutes, and then over medium-low heat until the lamb is well browned and fragrant, 15 to 20 minutes.

4 Add the yogurt, a little at a time, while stirring constantly to prevent it from curdling, and cook until it's completely absorbed, about 5 minutes. Add the water, cover the pan, and cook until the lamb is fork-tender (adding more water, if necessary) and the sauce is as thick or as soupy as desired, 50 to 60 minutes. Add the fenugreek leaves during the last 5 minutes of cooking.

5 Transfer to a serving dish, lightly mix in the cilantro, sprinkle the reserved ¼ teaspoon garam masala on top, and serve hot.

Vary It! *If you're in a hurry, after Step 3, transfer everything (just before you add the yogurt) to a pressure cooker, cook over high heat until the regulator indicates high pressure, and then cook about 2 minutes more. Allow the pot to depressurize, 12 to 15 minutes. Carefully open the lid, add the yogurt, and stir until it is absorbed. Add the fenugreek leaves and continue with Step 5.*

Paneer Cheese Curry with Coconut Milk (Paneer Korma)

Paneer is the delicious homemade cheese used in many Indian dishes. This curry is much closer to a korma than to a traditional curry, meaning that the sauce is thicker and not as soupy. For more information about kormas, see Chapter 3 of Book V. Braising the paneer in coconut milk gives the finished dish a much different consistency than the yogurt and spice curries in this chapter.

Here, paneer is braised in coconut milk with many whole spices. Because this is a rich entrée, you may want to reserve it for special occasions. But then again, it's so satisfying and delicious, you may not.

Preparation time: *20 minutes*

Cooking time: *30 minutes*

Yield: *4 to 6 servings*

1 cup canned coconut milk

8 ounces (1 recipe) Paneer Cheese (see the recipe in Chapter 3 of Book V or use store-bought)

¼ cup Dessert Masala (see the recipe in Chapter 6 of Book V)

1 small onion, coarsely chopped

2 to 3 large cloves fresh garlic, peeled

5 to 6 quarter-size slices peeled fresh ginger

1 to 3 fresh green chile peppers, such as serrano, stemmed

10 raw cashews, coarsely chopped

1 large tomato, coarsely chopped

2 tablespoons vegetable oil

2 bay leaves

1 teaspoon cumin seeds

1 stick cinnamon, 1 inch long

4 green cardamom pods, pounded lightly to break the skin

4 cloves

⅛ teaspoon ground nutmeg

⅛ teaspoon ground mace

1 teaspoon ground coriander

1 teaspoon garam masala

1 cup frozen peas, thawed

1 teaspoon salt, or to taste

Freshly ground black pepper, for garnish

1 Prepare the Paneer Cheese and then cut into 1½-by-½-inch-thick rectangles. Prepare the Dessert Masala.

2 In a food processor or a blender, process together the onion, garlic, ginger, green chile peppers, and cashews about 1 minute to make a smooth paste. Transfer to a bowl, add the tomato to the food processor, and process until puréed.

3 Heat the oil in a large nonstick wok or saucepan over medium-high heat and cook the bay leaves, cumin, cinnamon, cardamom pods, and cloves, stirring, until fragrant, about 1 minute. Reduce the heat to medium and add the nutmeg and mace and then the coriander and garam masala. Stir about 30 seconds, add the onion paste, and cook, stirring, until well browned, about 10 minutes.

4 Add the pureed tomato and cook, stirring constantly, until the juices evaporate, about 3 minutes. Add the paneer cheese, peas, salt, and coconut milk. Cover the pan, lower the heat, and simmer until the paneer pieces are soft and the sauce is thick, 10 to 15 minutes. Transfer to a serving dish, garnish with black pepper, and serve.

Tip: *Because making paneer cheese is a process unto itself, I highly recommend doing this at least a day ahead of time, or choosing the commercially available prepackaged varieties available in Indian markets and some specialty markets.*

Goan-Style Spicy Chicken Curry
(Murgh Vindaloo)

Vindaloo is the Goan (from Goa, a southern Indian state) word for "with vinegar." Vindaloo curries are famous for their fiery spice blends and unique flavors influenced by the Portuguese settlers of the region. You can turn down the heat a bit by leaving the peppers whole and removing them before serving, or by leaving them out of the dish completely. You can also substitute a little cayenne pepper for the whole peppers to find a balance between hot and I-want-to-rip-my-tongue-out-of-my-head-please-just-let-me-die.

Preparation time: *15 minutes plus 4–24 hours for marinade*

Cooking time: *30 minutes*

Yield: *4 to 6 servings*

1 tablespoon Goan Vindaloo Powder (see the following recipe)	1 teaspoon salt, or to taste
3 dried red chile peppers, broken (optional)	¼ teaspoon ground turmeric
4 large cloves fresh garlic, peeled	2 large tomatoes, coarsely chopped
6 quarter-size slices peeled fresh ginger	15 to 20 fresh curry leaves
1 large onion, coarsely chopped	2½- to 3-pound chicken, skinned and cut into serving pieces (discard the back and wings)
¼ cup distilled white vinegar	2 tablespoons peanut oil
1 teaspoon garam masala plus ¼ teaspoon for garnish	¼ cup finely chopped cilantro

1 Prepare the vindaloo powder. Then, in a food processor or a blender, process together the red chile peppers (if desired), garlic, ginger, onion, and vinegar until smooth. Add the vindaloo, garam masala, salt, and turmeric and process to make a smooth paste. Remove to a bowl and then process the tomatoes and curry leaves until pureed.

2 Place the chicken in a large nonreactive bowl. Add the chile pepper-onion-vinegar paste and mix well, making sure that all the chicken pieces are well coated. Cover and marinate in the refrigerator at least 4 and up to 24 hours.

3 Heat the oil in a large nonstick saucepan over medium-high heat and add the marinated chicken, plus all the marinade. Cook, stirring, until golden, about 10 minutes.

4 Add the pureed tomatoes and cook, stirring as needed, until the chicken is tender and the sauce thick, about 10 minutes. (Add up to ½ cup water for a thinner sauce.) Transfer to a serving dish, garnish with the chopped cilantro and the ¼ teaspoon garam masala, and serve.

Vary It! To make a dry vindaloo, when you reach Step 3, cook the chicken until tender and completely dry, about 30 minutes. Do not add tomatoes.

Goan Vindaloo Powder (Vindaloo ka Masala)

This masala reflects the Portuguese influence in the western state of Goa, which was under Portuguese rule from 1510 to 1961. It's primarily used in a unique Goan curry called *vindaloo,* meaning "with vinegar." The vinegar isn't part of this dry mixture of spices, but it is an essential, separate ingredient that gives vindaloo curries a unique taste, distinguishing them from other curries.

Cooking time: *2 minutes*

Yield: *About 1½ cups*

4 to 6 dried red chile peppers, such as chile de arbol, broken

¾ cup coriander seeds

¼ cup cumin seeds

2 tablespoons black cumin seeds

2 tablespoons black peppercorns

1 tablespoon fenugreek seeds

2 teaspoons mustard seeds

1 teaspoon ground turmeric

1 teaspoon ground black cardamom seeds

1 teaspoon ground cloves

1 teaspoon ground cinnamon

1 In a medium cast-iron or nonstick skillet, roast together the red chile peppers, coriander, cumin, black cumin, peppercorns, fenugreek, and mustard seeds, stirring and shaking the pan over medium heat until a few shades darker, about 2 minutes.

2 Let cool and then grind in a spice or coffee grinder to make a fine powder. Transfer to a bowl and mix in the turmeric, cardamom, cloves, and cinnamon. Store in an airtight container in a cool, dark place, about 1 month at room temperature or about 1 year in the refrigerator.

Basic Chicken Curry
(Har-Roz ki Murgh Kari)

Perfect when served with rice or bread and easy enough to cook every day, this traditional chicken curry is usually the first one taught to all novice Indian cooks. Once you understand the basic procedure, you can vary it as you like.

Preparation time: *15 minutes*

Cooking time: *1 hour*

Yield: *4 to 6 servings*

3 large cloves fresh garlic, peeled

6 quarter-size slices peeled fresh ginger

1 large onion, coarsely chopped

2 large tomatoes, coarsely chopped

½ cup coarsely chopped fresh cilantro, including soft stems

1 to 3 fresh green chile peppers, stemmed

3 tablespoons vegetable oil

2 bay leaves

5 green cardamom pods, crushed lightly to break the skin

2 sticks cinnamon, 1 inch long

1½ tablespoons ground coriander

1 teaspoon ground cumin

1 teaspoon garam masala plus ¼ teaspoon for garnish

½ teaspoon ground turmeric

1 teaspoon salt, or to taste

¼ teaspoon freshly ground black pepper, or to taste

½ cup nonfat plain yogurt, whisked until smooth

2½- to 3-pound chicken, skinned and cut into serving pieces (discard the back and wings)

1 cup water, or more as required

Cilantro sprigs

1 In a food processor, process together the garlic, ginger, and onion until minced. Remove to a bowl. Then process together the tomatoes, cilantro, and green chile peppers until smooth. Remove to another bowl and set aside.

2 Heat the oil in a large pan over medium-high heat and cook the bay leaves, cardamom pods, and cinnamon, stirring, about 30 seconds. Add the onion-garlic mixture and cook until browned, about 7 minutes. Add the tomato-cilantro mixture and continue to cook, stirring, until all the juices evaporate and the oil separates to the sides, about 7 minutes.

3 Add the coriander, cumin, 1 teaspoon garam masala, turmeric, salt, and black pepper. Mix in the yogurt, stirring constantly to prevent it from curdling, and cook, stirring, until it's incorporated into the sauce.

4 Add the chicken pieces and stir about 5 minutes to brown them. Then add 1 cup water, cover the pan, and cook over high heat, about 5 minutes. Reduce the heat to moderate and cook until the chicken is tender and the sauce thick, about 30 minutes, turning the pieces over a few times and adding more water if you prefer a thinner sauce. Transfer to a serving dish, garnish with garam masala and cilantro, and serve.

Vegetarian Dishes

Historically speaking, much of the Indian diet has been vegetarian based. Religious, cultural, and economic realities continue to reinforce this lifestyle. And today, *hundreds of millions* of Indians are strict vegetarians. In fact, there are more Indian vegetarians than there are Americans — not American vegetarians, I mean the entire population of the United States, carnivores and vegetarians combined. So it's no wonder that the care and attention Indians give to their vegetable dishes result in a level of sophistication unparalleled in the West. Here are some common dishes you've probably tried at your favorite Indian hangout.

Hyderabadi Layered Rice with Mixed Vegetables (Sabz Biryani)

Here's a classic example of the Indian special-occasion dish, *biryani*. Biryani is sort of like a casserole, but it enjoys a level of prestige in India well above the tuna-noodle concoction your mother made. Often part of celebrations, including weddings, biryanis are also great dishes for entertaining because you can make them ahead and avoid the last-minute rush often associated with cooking rice.

Preparation time: *45 minutes*

Cooking time: *1 hour*

Yield: *4 to 6 servings*

1 tablespoon Hyderabadi Ginger-Garlic Paste (see the recipe later in this chapter)

4 cups (1 recipe) Steamed Basmati Rice (see Chapter 3 of Book V)

¼ teaspoon saffron threads

¼ cup milk (any kind)

½ cup coarsely chopped mixed raw nuts, such as almonds, pistachios, cashews, and walnuts

2 tablespoons melted ghee, or 1 tablespoon each ghee and peanut oil

2 sticks cinnamon, 1 inch each

6 whole cloves

5 green cardamom pods, crushed lightly to break the skin

2 bay leaves

1 medium onion, cut in half lengthwise and thinly sliced

1 to 3 fresh green chile peppers, such as serrano, minced with seeds

3 to 4 cups washed and chopped mixed fresh vegetables, such as green beans, carrots, potatoes, eggplant, and peas

1 cup nonfat plain yogurt, whisked until smooth

1 to 2 tablespoons fresh lime juice

½ cup finely chopped fresh cilantro, including soft stems

2 tablespoons finely chopped fresh mint leaves

½ teaspoon ground green cardamom seeds

1 Prepare the ginger-garlic paste and the rice. Meanwhile, soak the saffron in the milk for 30 minutes or longer. Place the nuts in a small skillet and dry-roast them over medium heat, stirring and shaking the pan, until golden, about 3 minutes. Reserve.

2 Heat the ghee (or ghee and oil) in a large nonstick wok or saucepan over medium-high heat and add the cinnamon, cloves, cardamom pods, and bay leaves and cook, stirring, until fragrant, about 1 minute. Add the onion and cook, stirring, until browned, about 7 minutes. Mix in the ginger-garlic paste and green chile peppers and cook, stirring, 1 minute.

3 Add the vegetables and cook, stirring, 5 to 7 minutes. Then add the yogurt, a little at a time, stirring constantly to prevent it from curdling, and cook until most of it is absorbed, about 5 minutes. Remove from heat.

4 Preheat the oven to 350 degrees. To assemble the biryani, baste the bottom of a clear oven-safe dish with some of the juices from the vegetables and spread half the rice in the pan. Layer all the vegetables over the rice and top with the lime juice, cilantro, and mint. Then spread the remaining half of the rice over the vegetables.

5 Drizzle the saffron milk over the rice and cover well with aluminum foil. Bake the rice until the grains are soft and the flavors are well blended, about 30 minutes. Remove from the oven, fluff the rice lightly with a fork, garnish with the roasted nuts and cardamom seeds, and serve.

Hyderabadi Ginger-Garlic Paste (Hyderabad ka Pissa Adrak-Lussan)

This fragrant variation of the basic ginger-garlic paste contains three times more ginger than garlic. This is a well-guarded secret that gives the southeastern Muslim-style Hyderabadi cuisine its characteristic flavors and silky smooth sauces.

Preparation time: *5 minutes*

Yield: *About 1½ cups*

¾ pound fresh ginger, peeled and cut crosswise into thin round slices

¼ pound fresh garlic cloves, peeled

1 to 3 tablespoons water

In a blender (not a food processor), blend together the ginger and garlic until smooth, adding the water as needed for blending. Transfer to an airtight container and refrigerate up to 10 days or freeze up to 6 months.

Spinach with Paneer Cheese
(Saag Paneer)

After you've tried this recipe, ordinary creamed spinach will never be the same. This dish is available almost daily at my favorite Indian restaurant. The authentic recipe calls for the paneer pieces to be deep-fried, another step I avoid. If you wish, lightly fry the paneer pieces until they're just golden. This firms up the pieces, so you don't have to be as careful when stirring.

Preparation time: *15 minutes*

Cooking time: *45 minutes*

Yield: *4 to 6 servings*

8 ounces (1 recipe) Paneer Cheese (see Chapter 3 of Book V), or use store-bought

2 small bunches (about 1 pound) fresh spinach, trimmed of roots only, washed well and coarsely chopped

1 large onion, coarsely chopped

4 quarter-size slices peeled fresh ginger plus one 1-inch piece peeled and cut into thin matchsticks

3 large cloves fresh garlic, peeled, plus 1 clove garlic, minced

¼ cup water

2 tablespoons vegetable oil

1 tablespoon melted ghee

2 sticks cinnamon, 1 inch long

5 green cardamom pods, crushed lightly to break the skin

1 tablespoon ground coriander

1 teaspoon garam masala

1 teaspoon dried fenugreek leaves

½ teaspoon salt, or to taste

¼ cup plain yogurt (any kind), whisked until smooth

1 to 2 tablespoons unsalted butter, at room temperature

4 whole dried red chile peppers, such as chile de arbol

½ teaspoon ground paprika

1 Prepare the paneer cheese and cut it into 1-by-½-inch squares.

2 Place the spinach, onion, ginger slices, whole garlic, and water in a large nonstick saucepan. Cover and bring to a boil over high heat. Reduce the heat to medium-low, cover the pan, and simmer until the spinach is wilted and the onion tender, about 10 minutes. Let cool and then pulse lightly in a food processor until just minced (do not make a smooth puree). Return to the pan.

3 Heat the oil and ghee in a small saucepan over medium-high heat and cook the cinnamon, cardamom pods, and ginger matchsticks, stirring, until the ginger is golden, 1 to 2 minutes. Add the minced garlic, coriander, garam masala, fenugreek leaves, and salt and stir a few seconds. Then add the yogurt, a little at a time, stirring constantly to prevent curdling. Immediately transfer to the spinach, cover, and simmer over medium heat, 10 to 15 minutes.

4 Add the paneer cheese to the pan and stir gently to mix, trying not to break the pieces. Cover and simmer, stirring occasionally, about 10 minutes to blend the flavors. Transfer to a serving dish.

5 Heat the butter in a small saucepan, add the dried chile peppers, and cook, stirring, until golden, about 30 seconds. Remove the pan from the heat, add the paprika, immediately add to the spinach dish, and swirl lightly to mix, with parts of the chile peppers visible as a garnish. Serve hot.

All Dal'd Up with No Place to Go

Dal is the Indian word for legumes, which is a fancy English word for lentils, beans, and peas. Dal can refer to either the legume itself, or a dish made with legumes. Due to the high rate of vegetarianism in India, dals account for an astonishing proportion of the Indian diet. And Indians account for an astonishing proportion of worldwide dal eaters, more than 50 percent. For information about the specific legumes used in these recipes, see Chapter 2 of Book V.

Most dal recipes refer to dried dal and require you to wash and sort the dal before beginning. These little protein-packed tidbits take a while to cook, but you can speed up the process by soaking them for a few hours or overnight, or by using a pressure cooker. For more information on using pressure cookers, see *Pressure Cookers For Dummies* by Tom Lacalamita (published by Wiley Publishing).

Chickpeas with Ginger, Garlic, and Chaat Masala (Channa-Chaat Masala)

Chickpeas are garbanzo beans. They often take longer to cook than other dals, so this recipe calls for canned garbanzo beans. Rinse them before adding them to the dish. Many supermarkets now carry a line of fresh legumes, including chickpeas, in the fresh produce section. They have a better flavor than their canned counterparts, but still save time over the dried varieties.

Preparation time: *10 minutes*

Cooking time: *15 minutes*

Yield: *4 to 6 servings*

1 teaspoon Chaat Masala (see the recipe in Chapter 2 of Book V or use store-bought) (can use more to taste)	½ teaspoon dried fenugreek leaves
2 tablespoons peanut oil	4 cans (15½ ounces each) chickpeas, drained and rinsed well
5 to 7 fresh green chile peppers, such as serrano, skin punctured to prevent bursting	⅓ cup water
2 teaspoons cumin seeds	1 to 2 tablespoons fresh lime or lemon juice
2 tablespoons peeled minced fresh ginger	½ cup finely chopped fresh cilantro, including soft stems
1 large clove fresh garlic, minced	Tomato wedges for garnish
1½ tablespoons ground coriander	Sliced scallions for garnish
½ teaspoon ground cumin	Chopped cilantro for garnish

1 Prepare the Chaat Masala. Then heat the oil in a large nonstick wok or skillet over medium-high heat and cook the green chile peppers, stirring gently, about 30 seconds (stand back in case they burst). Add the cumin seeds; they should sizzle upon contact with the hot oil. Quickly add the ginger and garlic and stir about 30 seconds.

2 Add the coriander, cumin, and fenugreek leaves and stir momentarily. Mix in the chickpeas and water. Cover and cook over medium heat until the chickpeas are soft, about 4 minutes. Add the lime juice, chaat masala, and cilantro and cook, stirring, another 5 minutes. Transfer to a serving dish, mix in the tomato wedges, scallions, and cilantro, and serve.

Dry-Cooked Red Lentils with Cumin Seeds (Sookhi Dhulli Masoor Dal)

Red lentils are the hulled version of the more familiar brown lentil. This hulled variety cooks incredibly fast. The red lentils and beets combine to make a spectacular visual display in this dish. This lentil dish, more like a rice pilaf than a soup, is made with pre-soaked whole red lentils (split red ones are fine, too). For a vivid color presentation, throw in some beets, but avoid turmeric (which is usually a must in dal dishes) because it colors everything yellow.

Serve with a soft-cooked vegetable side dish, such as a bhartha (see the Mashed Fire-Roasted Eggplant recipe in Chapter 4 of Book V), or present it atop lettuce leaves as a salad.

Preparation time: *2 hours*

Cooking time: *15 minutes*

Yield: *4 to 6 servings*

1 cup red lentils (dhulli masoor dal), sorted and washed in 3 to 4 changes of water

2 cups water

¼ cup cooked and minced fresh or drained canned beets

2 tablespoons vegetable oil

3 to 5 dried red chile peppers, such as chile de arbol

1½ teaspoons cumin seeds

1 tablespoon peeled minced fresh ginger

2 teaspoons ground coriander

½ teaspoon ground cumin

½ teaspoon garam masala

½ teaspoon salt, or to taste

¼ cup finely chopped cilantro, including soft stems

1 tablespoon fresh lime or lemon juice

4 scallions, finely sliced

1 Place the dal, water, and beets in a bowl and allow to soak about 2 hours or longer.

2 Heat the oil in a medium nonstick saucepan over medium-high heat and cook the red chile peppers until golden, about 1 minute. (Stand away from the pan, in case they burst.) Add the cumin seeds; they should sizzle upon contact with the hot oil. Quickly add the ginger and stir, about 1 minute.

3 Add the coriander, cumin, and garam masala. Mix in the dal plus all the water and the salt, and cook over high heat until the water evaporates and the dal is tender, about 5 minutes. Stir a few times with a fork just to fluff it, taking care not to break the dal.

4 With a fork, gently mix in the cilantro and lime juice, cover the pan, and set over low heat about 2 minutes to blend the flavors. Transfer to a serving dish, lightly mix in the scallions, and serve.

Yellow Mung Beans with Sautéed Onion and Ginger (Dhulli Mungi ki Dal)

Mung beans are highly digestible, and this dish is no exception. These tiny legumes are skinless and cook very quickly, making this an easy weekday dish, no matter how busy your schedule. If you'd like to lose some of the heat of this dish, chop the green chile peppers and remove the seeds and ribs. Most of the heat lives there.

Yellow mung dal is a hands-down favorite in northern India. Considered light and easy to digest, this quick-cooking dal is comfort food par excellence. It marries well with whole-wheat *chapatis* (whole-wheat griddle breads) and with rice — the two food staples of India.

Preparation time: *5 minutes*

Cooking time: *35 minutes*

Yield: *4 to 6 servings*

1 cup yellow mung beans (dhulli mung dal), sorted and washed in 3 to 4 changes of water

3½ to 4 cups water

3 to 5 whole fresh green chile peppers, such as serrano

¼ teaspoon ground turmeric

¾ teaspoon salt, or to taste

¼ cup finely chopped fresh cilantro, including soft stems

2 tablespoons peanut or canola oil

1 teaspoon melted ghee (optional)

1 teaspoon cumin seeds

½ small onion, finely chopped

1 tablespoon peeled minced fresh ginger

1 tablespoon ground coriander

½ teaspoon ground cumin

¼ teaspoon ground paprika

Freshly ground black pepper

1 Place the dal, 3½ cups water, green chile peppers, turmeric, and salt in a medium saucepan and bring to a boil over high heat. Reduce the heat to medium and cook the dal, uncovered, stirring occasionally and watching carefully that it doesn't boil over, about 10 minutes. Reduce the heat to low, add the remaining water, if needed, and simmer until the dal is soft and creamy, about 15 minutes. Mix in the cilantro during the last 5 minutes of cooking. Transfer to a serving bowl, cover, and keep warm.

2 Heat the oil (and the ghee, if desired) in a small saucepan over medium-high heat and add the cumin seeds; they should sizzle upon contact with the hot oil. Quickly add the onion and cook, stirring, until golden, about 1 minute. Add the ginger and cook another minute. Then add the coriander and cumin and stir about 30 seconds. Remove the pan from the heat and add the paprika. Immediately pour the *tarka* (sizzling flavor topping) over the warm dal and swirl lightly to mix, with parts of it visible as a garnish. Top with black pepper and serve.

Chapter 6

Sweet Endings

*W*esterners may find Indian sweets a bit tough to love because they're typically, well, not sweet — not in the Western sense of the word, anyway. Indian desserts are characterized by many of the same spices that flavor their other foods. Cardamom, rose water, and even saffron all have a place in traditional Indian sweets.

You won't find their milk fudge *(burfee)* loaded down with sugar, or their fried milk rolls *(gulaab jamun)* rolled in cinnamon and sugar after frying. Indian cooks use the whole range of spices, herbs, and nuts available to them to create their desserts.

Most homemade desserts are milk based, using some version of condensed milk, called either *rabdi* or *khoa,* depending on how condensed it is. More elaborate desserts, such as *jalebis,* India funnel cakes, are left to the *halvais,* or professional sweet makers.

Punjabi Rice Pudding (Kheer)

If you think that adding cinnamon to your rice pudding is on the culinary cutting edge, wait until you try this *kheer,* or rice pudding. The northern state of Punjab lends its name to this classic Indian dessert. Green cardamom lends its menthol aroma. The subtle blends of saffron and rose water, along with the garnish of silver leaf, or *verk,* make for a quintessential Indian dessert experience (or experiment, depending on your point of view).

Preparation Time: *40 minutes, and chill for 4 hours*

Cooking Time: *45 minutes*

Yield: *Makes 4 to 6 servings*

½ cup Dessert Masala (later in this chapter)	½ cup sweetened condensed milk
½ cup blanched and slivered raw almonds	½ teaspoon ground green cardamom seeds
¼ teaspoon saffron threads	2 drops rose essence
½ gallon whole milk	6 (4-inch) silver leaves (optional)
½ cup basmati rice, sorted and washed in 3 to 4 changes of water	

1 Prepare the Dessert Masala and the almonds. In a small bowl, soak the saffron threads in ¼ cup milk for about 30 minutes.

2 Place the milk and the rice in a large, heavy wok or saucepan and bring to a boil over high heat. Reduce the heat to medium-low and simmer, stirring and scraping the bottom and the sides of the wok often, until the rice is very soft and the milk is reduced by at least half, about 35 minutes. Stirring and scraping is crucial to prevent the milk from scalding and adding a burned flavor to the pudding.

3 Mix in the almonds, condensed milk, cardamom seeds, and half the Dessert Masala. Continue to cook, stirring, 5 to 7 minutes. Add the rose essence, saffron and saffron-infused milk, and transfer to a serving dish. Let cool and garnish with the silver leaves and the remaining Dessert Masala. Refrigerate at least 4 hours and serve chilled.

Dessert Masala (Mithai ka Masala)

Along with raisins and nuts, certain fragrant seasonings are crucial to Indian desserts —
cardamom, saffron, rosewater, and, occasionally, a touch of black pepper. Although
each dessert can be customized, the following standard mixture can be added to almost
all desserts. This pale green mixture is also a spectacular garnish over entrees such as
rice, casseroles, and white curry dishes. A tablespoon of this stirred into hot milk is
also really delicious. I often sprinkle it over vanilla, strawberry, or other fruit-flavored
ice creams, and even over Indian banana fudge (burfee) and crème brûlées.

Preparation Time: *5 minutes*

Yield: *Makes about 1½ cups*

*1 teaspoon saffron threads, dry-roasted and
coarsely crushed*

1 cup shelled raw pistachios

½ cup shelled raw almonds, coarsely broken

¼ cup cashews, coarsely broken

*1 tablespoon coarsely ground green
cardamom seeds*

*1 teaspoon coarsely ground black
cardamom seeds*

1 Prepare the saffron. Then, in a spice grinder or in a small food processor, pulse together
the pistachios, almonds, and cashews in one or two batches, to make a coarse powder.

2 Mix in the green and black cardamom seeds and the saffron. Store in an airtight container, about 3 months in the refrigerator or 1 year in the freezer.

Mango Ice Cream Dessert

This is likely the easiest and most familiar dessert I include in the book. Mangoes are available in the summer in India but used in a variety of ways throughout the year. The tart, unripe green mango is dried and lends its sour properties to many dishes, like a spice. The fresh green mango can be pickled, which preserves it to be enjoyed year-round. But the ripe, sinfully sweet mango is the one people wait for all year long.

Preparation Time: *1 hour*

Yield: *Makes 4 to 6 servings*

1 large ripe mango	*1 to 2 drops mango essence*
1 cup canned mango pulp	*1 pint vanilla ice cream*

1 With a vegetable peeler, peel the mango, then cut the fruit around the center seed into ½-inch pieces. Then, in a medium bowl, mix together the mango pieces, the canned mango pulp, and the mango essence, and chill at least 1 hour.

2 To serve, place rounded scoops of ice cream in a serving platter and top with the prepared mango mixture.

Vary It! *Mix 1 cup canned mango pulp into 1 pint softened vanilla ice cream and freeze. Peel and cut 2 large mangoes into 1-inch pieces and serve alongside the ice cream.*

Traditional Dark Brown Milk Rolls in Saffron Syrup (Gulaab Jamun)

Gulaab jamuns look like overgrown doughnut holes soaked in sugary syrup. One taste (or smell) and you'll agree that they're more than that. Although the texture is similar to doughnuts, the juxtaposition of the bitter saffron with the sugar and the aroma of the cardamom are intoxicating. I enjoy a Krispy Kreme doughnut as much as the next person, but traditional gulaab jamuns are the full sensory experience that no doughnut can compete with. Other traditional presentations include using rose water in place of the saffron.

For ideal flavor and texture, do not replace the shortening with oil. You could, however, use ghee if you wish. Also, monitor the temperature carefully, making sure that it remains between 300 to 325 degrees. It is crucial to fry the gulaab jamuns at a low temperature for a longer time to ensure that the centers get cooked and the gulaab jamuns don't collapse when added to the syrup.

Preparation Time: *15 minutes*

Cooking Time: *30 minutes*

Yield: *Makes 15 pieces*

1 cup instant nonfat dry milk

½ cup all-purpose flour

¾ teaspoon baking powder

*1 teaspoon coarsely ground green
cardamom seeds*

1½ cups sugar

*¼ cup (½ stick) unsalted butter, at room
temperature*

*⅓ cup plain yogurt (any kind), whisked until
smooth*

*2 to 3 cups melted vegetable shortening,
for deep-frying*

2 cups water

½ teaspoon saffron threads

*1 to 2 tablespoons coarsely chopped raw
pistachios*

1 In a food processor, add the dry milk, flour, baking powder, ½ teaspoon cardamom seeds, and 1 tablespoon sugar and pulse a few times to mix. Add the butter and process until the mixture resembles bread crumbs, about 30 seconds.

2 With the food processor running, add the yogurt in a thin stream through the feed tube and process until everything gathers into a ball. The dough should be soft and somewhat sticky; if it seems too sticky, add some more dry milk.

3 With lightly buttered clean hands, divide the dough into 15 equal portions. Shape each portion either into a log about 1½ inches long and ½ inch wide, or into a ball. Make sure the pieces are smooth and free of cracks. Cover with a piece of aluminum foil and set aside.

4 Heat the shortening in a large, heavy wok over medium-high heat until it reaches 325 degrees on a frying thermometer or until a piece of dough dropped into the hot oil rises to the top after 30 to 40 seconds. Do not make the oil any hotter; the gulaab jamuns need to be fried long and slow. (If you can, leave the thermometer in the wok and carefully monitor the temperature as you cook; it should remain between 275 to 325 degrees. Turn off the heat if it goes any higher.) Add half the gulaab jamuns and fry, stirring and turning gently with a slotted spatula, until they are dark brown, about 5 minutes. Remove to paper towels to drain.

5 Place the water, saffron, and the remaining sugar and cardamom seeds in a skillet or wok and bring to a boil over high heat. Reduce to medium-low and simmer, about 5 minutes. Add the fried rolls to the syrup and continue to simmer until they soak up the syrup, swell and become soft, and the sugar syrup becomes very thick, 15 to 20 minutes. Transfer to a serving dish, sprinkle the pistachios on top, and serve hot or at room temperature.

Sweet Mango-Yogurt Cooler
(Lussi, Lassi)

Yogurt is used in many ways in Indian cooking. From cooling raitas and savory marinades to velvety curries, there's seemingly no end to its usefulness. It's no surprise that yogurt has a special place in the world of Indian desserts.

Lussi, a cold beverage that always contains both yogurt and water, can be flavored with just about any sweet, savory, bitter, or even spicy ingredient. Yogurt's the perfect cooling palette to test the boundaries of your spice artistry. I include the sweet variety made with India's favorite fruit, the mango.

Mango essence may sometimes be sold in Indian markets as mango-milk essence. It is very strong, so add carefully when using it. You can also make this recipe with nectarines, peaches, bananas, strawberries, and any other berries.

Preparation Time: *5 minutes*

Yield: *Makes 2 servings*

2 cups plain yogurt, any kind

1 cup chopped fresh ripe mango or canned mango pulp

½ cup crushed ice or ice cubes, plus more for serving

1 tablespoon sugar

1 drop mango essence (optional)

1 Place the yogurt, mango, ½ cup ice, sugar, and mango essence in a blender and blend until frothy.

2 Divide into 2 glasses and serve cold over crushed ice.

Book VI
Chinese Cooking

The 5th Wave   By Rich Tennant

"It's General Gau's Stranger Flavored Chicken prepared by Mrs. Howel's odd looking husband."

In this book . . .

You may think everything you need to know about Chinese cuisine can be summed up in three phrases — egg rolls, wonton soup, and fried rice — but I intend to expand your horizons and allow you to experience the wide range of traditional Chinese cuisine. I show you how to select the perfect wok for your needs and give you pointers on the basic techniques of Chinese cooking. And then I open up an exciting new world of exotic, tasty, and wholesome dishes. From Fried Rice to Mu Shu Pork, Chinese cooking is great fun and great food!

Contents at a glance

Chapter 1

How to Think Like a Chinese Chef

*I*f your idea of Chinese cooking is egg rolls, wonton soup, and fortune cookies, you're about to get quite a wake-up call. One of the most diverse and unique of the world's cuisines, Chinese cooking offers an endless variety of flavors, textures, shapes, and cooking techniques. But don't let that variety overwhelm you; at the heart of even the most elaborate imperial dish lie a no-nonsense simplicity and some common ingredients.

Just follow some basic guidelines, and you can sharpen your Chinese culinary instinct and turn the contents of your pantry into authentic Chinese treats at the same time. It's this openness to invention that makes Chinese cuisine truly egalitarian. Power to the people!

The Three Tenets of Chinese Cooking

You don't have to be well versed in Confucianism or Taoist principles to think like a Chinese chef, and you don't have to master fancy cooking techniques or buy a ton of kitchen equipment either. You really need only a few simple tools and the willingness to follow a few basic guidelines — not rules — that all Chinese cooks first followed as children in their own parents' kitchens.

Keep it in balance

The Chinese pay a great deal of attention to contrast and harmony in their everyday existence. Balancing *yin* (feminine, soft, cold, and wet forces) and *yang* (masculine, bright, hot, dry, and vigorous forces) is a way to achieve harmony in your life, as well as your culinary creations. These two elements complement each other, and a thorough understanding of them goes a long way toward understanding the Chinese philosophy in the kitchen.

So how does this harmony translate to food? Chinese classify bland, low-calorie foods as yin, whereas richer and fattier items fall within the yang category. By harmonizing the yin and yang ingredients in a dish, the cook creates a good meal that maintains a healthy balance. If this concept sounds a bit too abstract, consider the popular dish sweet-and-sour pork — a clear example of the yin/yang balance of taste (sweet is yin, and sour is yang).

Balancing isn't restricted to taste alone. You can create texture contrast by combining soft, steamed items with crispy, fried ones. Or how about contrasting the color scheme with the spiciness in a single dish? Cooking techniques as opposite as deep-frying and steaming can join forces to create meals that are not only tasty but also philosophically stimulating.

Cook seasonally, buy locally

For much of China's history, its people have had to adapt their daily menus to the ingredients available in their own gardens and at local markets on that particular day. Chinese home cooks somehow managed to turn this liability into an asset, taking limited, simple ingredients and turning them into masterpieces. The popularity of wheat-flour dumplings and noodles and of root-based dishes in northern China, the deft preparation of fresh seafood in the regions running along the country's coast, and the prevalence of fresh produce and rice dishes in the semitropical south are all examples of the use of local, seasonally accessible foods.

Perhaps the best place to start is at your local farmers market. Always ask what's in season. Fruits and vegetables that are in season are abundant and at their peak of flavor, color, and texture; while those out of season are few, and their quality can be questionable. Go with the numbers, and you have a better chance at getting high-quality ingredients.

Many substitutes are available for the traditional ingredients and cooking tools used in Chinese cuisine. But there's no substitute for freshness. None.

If all else fails, improvise!

Chinese chefs are experts in developing endless alternatives in ingredients and cooking methods in the face of scarcity and hardship. If you want to cook like the Chinese, adopt a flexible approach when it comes to the availability of ingredients.

The next time you can't find a particular ingredient, don't give up on the whole recipe. Use your imagination to scope out attainable items that can take the place of ones not quite at peak freshness or still on the dock in Shanghai. No one but you will know the difference.

In all Chinese markets, you find an array of dried, pickled, salted, bottled, canned, or otherwise-preserved counterparts for seasonal or less readily available ingredients. Take advantage of the assortment and stock up on dried noodles, grains, and dried black mushrooms, for starters.

Tools of the Trade

Stepping into a typical kitchen in China may feel like a journey back in time. You probably won't find too many modern conveniences such as microwave ovens, food processors, or pots and pans in all different sizes to fit every dish. You may not even find an oven! The typical Chinese kitchen (see Figure 1-1) hasn't changed much over the centuries simply because it doesn't need to. Why change when the traditional method still works? Chinese cuisine is a simple cuisine, and so, naturally, are its essential kitchen accoutrements.

Many skilled Chinese cooks get by with nothing more than a wok, a matching lid, a spatula, a chef's knife, and a heavy-duty cutting board. A really well-stocked Chinese kitchen may come with a ladle, a bamboo steamer, a claypot, a few pots, and, of course, lots and lots of chopsticks.

Book VI

Chinese Cooking

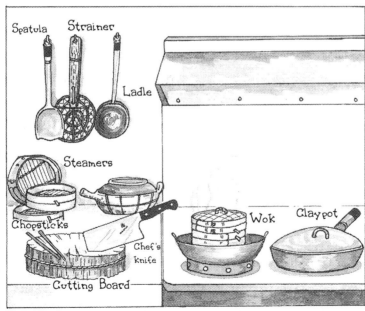

Figure 1-1:
The kind of traditional well-stocked kitchen that you can find all over China.

TRADITIONAL CHINESE KITCHEN SCENE

Before you run to your housewares store and snap up every gadget necessary to create a top-notch Chinese kitchen, consider that you may already have several of these items. Furthermore, you may be surprised at how easily you can adapt everyday Western cooking tools to make authentic-tasting Chinese dishes. If you decide to purchase a few items, choose high-quality pieces that will last as long as Chinese cooking has. Here's what you may want to buy new and what you can improvise from your current kitchen stock.

The wok

The wok (refer to Figure 1-1) is the single most essential and functional piece of equipment in the Chinese kitchen. The traditional concave, bowl-shaped pan can do the job of a number of pots and pans. It stir-fries, steams, deep-fries, boils, simmers, braises, smokes, and can also pop your corn. In a pinch, it can even be a portable kitchen sink!

Woks come in all sizes, ranging in diameter from 9 inches for small home woks, to 24 inches for restaurant woks, to the massive 4-foot woks that you can find in Buddhist temples. For family use, I suggest a deep 12- or 14-inch wok, which should give you enough room to prepare a hearty stir-fry for four to six people.

Rinse your wok after each use with water only; use no soap or, at the very most, a little soapy water. You don't have to scrub it very vigorously after each use. If the wok rusts, scour it with an abrasive cream or fine salt to remove the surface rust. Before storing your wok, make sure to thoroughly dry it by setting it over low heat on the cooktop for a couple minutes. Then rub a little oil into the surface if you don't plan to use it for a few weeks.

The Chinese chef's knife

The Chinese have used a type of single-blade food processor in the kitchen since centuries before the invention of electricity. What's more, this age-old food processor is a lot easier to clean and store than an electric model. It is the Chinese chef's knife (refer to Figure 1-1).

The modest chef's knife, with its large, wide blade and slightly curved edge, is the ideal slicer, dicer, shredder, and mincer. In addition to cutting and dicing, you can tenderize meats by pounding them with the dull side of its blade. You can use the flat of the blade as a scooper and smasher for herbs and spices such as garlic and ginger. Even the handle comes in handy: Use it to crush black peppercorns, Sichuan peppercorns, and other dried spices.

But before you rush out to buy your first Chinese chef's knife, take into account these purchasing and usage guidelines that will keep you chopping effectively for years to come:

- ✔ Select a Chinese chef's knife that is made from quality, high-carbon stainless steel and feels comfortable and well balanced in your hand. Don't pick a knife that feels awkward or heavier on one end than the other.

- ✔ The knife's center of gravity should be right where the wooden part of the handle meets the metal part of the blade.

Once you find the knife of your dreams, what's the secret to the lightning-fast chopping skill and accuracy of an accomplished Chinese master chef? Three words — practice, practice, practice.

Any professional chef will tell you that a sharp knife is a safe knife. Always make sure that your knife holds its sharp edge and that it sharpens easily when needed. Your chef's knife is not a heavy cleaver for hacking through dense bones; that will ruin its edge. You can use your knife for cutting poultry carcasses, but not bones and joints of beef, lamb, and pork. Protect your knife's blade during storage; knocking it against other knives and tools can dull it quickly. After using it, clean your knife with hot, soapy water, rinse it, and wipe it dry. To preserve its wooden handle, never soak your chef's knife in water and never put it in the dishwasher.

The cutting board

A good, solid hardwood cutting board preserves not only your knife's edge but also your countertops. My mom's cutting board was actually the cross section of a pine tree — how's that for cooking with nature? But you don't have to fell a tree for a cutting board. You can simply visit your favorite department, discount, or grocery store. There, you'll find a wide assortment of cutting boards in all sizes, materials, and weights to suit your kitchen. And if you make a trip to a well-appointed Chinese market, you can actually find one of those tree-trunk cutting boards, perfect for that rustic kitchen look.

No matter which type of board you select — hardwood or plastic — work with it only on a steady, level surface that doesn't tip or slip. Placing a damp cloth on the work surface underneath the board gives it traction. Be sure to follow my first rule on chopping board usage: "Those who won't lift a finger to assure stability of their board now won't have too many fingers to lift later."

Always clean your cutting board thoroughly with hot, soapy water between uses. This advice is especially important when you're switching from raw meat and poultry preparation to vegetable preparation. A thorough cleaning is the most effective way to prevent cross-contamination. Investing in two different boards is another possibility. To remove the odors of strong foods, thoroughly wash your cutting board and then rub the cutting surface with a freshly cut lemon half.

The spatula and the ladle

The wok's unique shape led to the Chinese development of the long-handled, shovel-shaped metal spatula (refer to Figure 1-1), whose perfectly curved scoop fits the wok's sloping sides. The spatula makes quick stirring and tossing of foods a snap, preventing burning. With its shovel-type base, it also doubles as a serving utensil. The ladle (refer to Figure 1-1) often works with the spatula to help toss and scoop meats and vegetables quickly while they're cooking.

The strainer or skimmer

When deep-frying or scooping out the food in your wok, use a wire strainer or skimmer (refer to Figure 1-1). The Chinese like to call them "spiders." A typical Chinese skimmer is a shallow, copper-wire mesh bowl attached to a long, flat bamboo handle. But if you can't find this traditional variety of skimmer, any strainer or basket with a handle long enough to keep you a safe distance from the hot oil will do. A 6- or 8-inch skimmer is most functional. To clean the bamboo-handled variety, just rinse it in hot, soapy water and dry.

The steamer

Steaming is a popular way to cook many healthy and tasty Chinese dishes. Traditional basket steamers, for use in a wok, are made of bamboo (refer to Figure 1-1) and come in different sizes perfect for using in different sizes of woks. Nowadays, you can find aluminum or stainless steel steamer sets that resemble double boilers, but with perforations in the top tier's base. Chinese chefs generally prefer the age-old bamboo variety, which have woven lids that allow excess steam to escape without condensing and dripping back onto the food. You can buy a few of these steamers and only one lid and then stack the baskets one atop the other to steam or to reheat several dishes at one time.

When shopping for a steamer basket, choose one slightly smaller than your wok's diameter; a 12-inch steamer works well in a 14-inch wok, for example. After each use, simply wash, rinse, and thoroughly dry it before storing in an open shelf or cupboard for maximum air circulation. (Keep it cooped up and it may develop mildew.)

The claypot casserole

The best way to serve a slowly cooked, stewed, or braised Chinese dish is in a rustic-looking earthenware pot commonly called a Chinese claypot (refer to Figure 1-1). These covered casseroles usually have a dark brown, lead-free glaze on the inside, and an unglazed exterior that is sometimes encased in wire mesh for protection and strength. They come in all sizes, from small ones that are perfect for dinner for two (or one very hungry person!) to larger ones that can feed a big party of diners. If you don't have a claypot, use a heatproof, covered casserole as a substitute.

When purchasing a claypot, ask the salesperson to let you dip it in water to check for cracks or leaks, indicated by small bubbles floating to the water's surface. Before using a claypot, soak it (and its lid, if it has one) in water for several hours, drain, and then let it dry overnight. You don't have to soak it again after this. Never set an empty pot over direct heat, and never place a hot claypot on a damp, cool surface or in cold water; the sudden change of temperature may cause it to crack. You can use claypots in the oven, but make sure to warm them up beforehand so the oven's heat won't shock the clay.

Book VI

Chinese
Cooking

Chopsticks

No Chinese kitchen is complete without plenty of chopsticks. Long or short, wooden, bamboo, lacquer, plastic, bone, or ivory, these deceptively simple devices make excellent cooking and eating tools. Master their use, and you'll never miss having knives or forks at your dining table again. In most Chinese families, kids learn how to use chopsticks as soon as they're ready for solid food.

Although the Chinese don't object to modern cutlery, they do prefer to cut up meat in the kitchen and not at the dining room table. Confucius forbade enlightened people from bringing their knives and other weapons to the table. Hence Chinese chefs cut their food into bite-sized pieces behind the scenes so that refined diners need only lightly and effortlessly grasp the little morsels with their slender, elegant chopsticks.

Chopsticks aren't used just for eating. I use them to beat eggs for omelets, mix sauces, and give a good swirl to soups and broths. I even use them to stir-fry food in a wok. Chinese markets and cookware shops sometimes carry long cooking chopsticks that range anywhere from 1 to 1½ feet. These long sticks are great for cooks who "can't take the heat"; their added length keeps flames and the hot oil literally at arm's length. And because they're wooden or bamboo, they don't conduct heat like a metal spoon.

Chapter 2

Ingredients for Chinese Cooking

A trip to Chinatown always leaves me breathless. I'm amazed by the breadth of products I can find in the markets: farm-fresh produce, live fish and shellfish, and barbecued pork and Cantonese roast duck at crowded deli counters, among other treats. And the shelves at the packed-to-the-gills Chinese grocery stores contain every dry Asian ingredient imaginable. Even a culinary glutton such as myself can get a case of sensory overload.

You don't really need an entire Chinatown to stock your pantry. The single most positive retail food trend of the past decade (in my opinion, at least) has been the expansion of the average supermarket's Chinese ingredients section from just one shelf to, in many cases, a whole aisle. Granted, rare ingredients are bound to call for a trip into Chinatown, but check your local supermarket first, just in case. You can put the time you save to better use in your kitchen.

Market Forces: Where to Find Essential Chinese Ingredients

The Chinese are pros at shopping. My mom used to visit the local market twice a day. Back in those days, shopping twice daily was customary. How else could she get the freshest fruits, roots, gourds, and greens, often with clumps of earth still attached? If I could, I'd do the same, but a busy schedule and the lure of the modern supermarket sometimes get the best of me. I do make sure to get the best ingredients by making the most of my shopping trips, wherever they lead me. Usually, they lead me to the following types of stores:

✔ **Supermarkets:** Most stores have a specific aisle or aisles dedicated to Chinese sauces, pastes, vinegars, oils, and seasonings, as well as to rice, noodles, and preserved foods. Look for convenient, time-saving packaged mixes for soups and rice or noodle dishes.

✔ **Natural food stores and co-ops:** Chinese cuisine advocates lots of fresh, locally grown produce, plenty of grains, and soybeans and sprouts in all their forms. For that reason, Chinese food is a logical match for the current natural-foods trend in North America. It is, therefore, not surprising that many natural food stores carry a wide array of Chinese ingredients, especially items that are harder to find at conventional stores — certain soy and tofu products, wheat gluten, exotic mushrooms and fungi, and bulk spices, for example. Look for fresh produce at natural food markets; they often carry greens, sprouts, and leafy items that may not be so popular at major chain markets.

✔ **Chinatown markets:** I can't emphasize enough the wealth of Chinese cuisine and culture that you'll experience at these shopping heavens. Produce stalls and butcher and seafood shops carry the freshest ingredients. For prepared foods such as Chinese roast pork, crispy-skinned duck, or Chinese sausages, visit your friendly Chinese deli. You can't miss them because they usually hang their deli meats right behind glass windows.

Tell the server at the counter what and how much of an item you want. And don't be shy — if you see a piece of meat that's leaner and juicier, point to it. The server is there to take care of your needs and cater to your preferences. If only all shopping were so satisfying!

Getting Sauced: Classic Chinese Sauces and Condiments

If you were to create a library of Chinese ingredients, you'd have to build an entire wing for the sauces and condiments alone. Chinese cooks have thousands of pastes, potions, sauces, and seasonings at their disposal; and thanks to your supermarket's Asian food aisle, you can get in on some of that action yourself. These condiments are already prepared and conveniently packaged, too, so they let you inject real Chinese flavor into a dish without any fuss. Start your browsing with some of the following suggestions. (In the following list, the first Chinese pronunciation is Cantonese; the second is Mandarin.)

Black bean sauce (See tzup jeng; shi zhi jiang)

This ready-to-use sauce made of salted black beans and rice wine is a popular addition to dishes all over China, where its savory, slightly salty flavor sometimes gets a little kick from garlic and hot chiles. Add it to stir-fries and sauces near the end of their cooking times because the prepared sauce only needs to be heated through. This feature makes it a super time-saver for appetizers and quick meals. Refrigerate the jar after opening, and the sauce should last for about a year.

Char siu sauce (Tza siu jeng; cha shao jiang)

Because I'm such a fan of char siu, Chinese roast pork, I just love this thick, sweet and savory, ready-made sauce. A combination of fermented soybeans, vinegar, tomato paste, chile, garlic, sugar, and Chinese spices, it has a vibrant reddish brown color and an unmistakable flavor synonymous with Chinese barbecued spareribs and roast pork.

Use char siu sauce as you would Western barbecue sauce — in marinades, basting sauces, and dips for meats and poultry. And, of course, use it in barbecue cooking, where its sweet and spicy flavor livens up anything from grilled meats to vegetables. Refrigerate it after opening, and it will keep for about a year.

Chile pastes and sauces (Laut tziu jeng; la jiao jiang)

These fiery pastes and sauces come in a range of flavors, degrees of heat, and consistencies, but most are made from a blend of fresh and dried chiles and vinegar. Chile sauces and pastes run from mild to wild, so start slowly when adding them to stir-fries or noodle soups. The sweeter versions of chile pastes and sauces make nice accompaniments to roast chicken.

Most Asian markets sell an assortment of popular brands of chile pastes and sauces, some even coming from different countries. You may want to initiate yourself and your palate with a small bottle or jar because a little goes a long way. Refrigerate it after you've opened it, and it should keep for about a year.

Chile oil (Laut you; la you)

Another spicy addition to your Chinese pantry, this reddish orange oil comes from infusing whole, dried red chiles or crushed red pepper flakes in oil. Used primarily as a flavoring agent during cooking or as a condiment at the table, it has surprised many unexpected diners who didn't realize how much punch a few drops can pack. Be careful! Start by adding just a drop or two, and then add more if you have an asbestos tongue.

Chile oil is a perfect flavoring agent for stir-fries and, when combined with soy sauce, vinegar, and a little sugar or garlic, makes an eye-opening dipping sauce for dim sum and Chinese appetizers. Chile oil comes in small bottles, often with convenient, no-drip spouts. Store the bottles in a cool, dry place for up to several months.

Hoisin sauce (Hoi seen jeng; hai xian jiang)

This dark, rich, pastelike sauce is one of the most popular Chinese condiments in the West. Its spicy-sweet flavor and reddish brown color are great matches for Western roasts as well as for Asian stir-fries and barbecues. It's normally made from fermented soybeans, vinegar, garlic, sugar, and Chinese spices, all of which add to its complex flavor.

If you've ever had Peking duck or mu shu dishes, you've probably spread a thin coating of hoisin on the accompanying Mandarin pancakes or steamed buns. Hoisin also makes a great dipping sauce or barbecue sauce base. Try adding a little hoisin to your own sauce recipes to give them an intriguing Asian sweetness and smokiness. I prefer the big jars because I can never have enough of this stuff. In addition, the larger jars' wide mouths make serving the thick sauce easier. Refrigerate opened bottles or jars for up to a year.

Oyster-flavored sauce (Hou yeo; hao you)

The name of this sauce is a little deceptive: It really doesn't have a flavor much like oysters. Instead, the thick, brown, all-purpose sauce made from oyster extracts, sugar, seasonings, and cornstarch has sweet and smoky notes that make it indispensable in a wide variety of Chinese meat and vegetable dishes. This sauce is one of the most common ingredients in Cantonese cuisine. Whether drizzled over simple steamed Chinese broccoli and savory egg custards, mixed into a sizzling stir-fry or a wok of fried rice, or simply used as a dip for roast pork or chicken, oyster-flavored sauce enhances the natural flavors of any dish.

You'll find plenty of brands, sizes, and types of oyster-flavored sauce. You can even choose mushroom-based "oyster-flavored" sauces with the same smoky character as the original that should please vegetarians. Whichever kind you buy, refrigerate it after opening, and it will keep for a year.

Plum sauce (Suin mui jeng; suan mei chiang)

Although this sauce may look like something you'd want to spread on a piece of toast, it's made from a combination of salted plums, apricots, yams, rice vinegar, chiles, sugar, and other spices. These flavors make the sauce better suited as a dipping sauce for roast duck, deep-fried appetizers, and barbecued meats.

Depending on the brand, plum sauce (also known as "duck sauce" thanks to its popularity as a condiment for Cantonese roast duck) runs the gamut from sweet-tart to salty and from smooth to chunky and jamlike. Try all the varieties to find the flavor, composition, and consistency that you like best. I've found that certain styles go better with some dishes than others. It's really a mix-and-match ingredient. You can buy plum sauce in jars, bottles, and cans. Refrigerate jars and bottles after opening. Transfer the contents of an opened can to a storage container with a tightly fitting lid and refrigerate. All should keep for a year.

Rice wine (Mike tziu; mi jiu)

Chinese cookbooks regularly call for this amber-colored liquid from the fermentation of glutinous rice and millet. After 10 to even 100 years of aging, these wines have developed a delightful aroma that stir-frying helps release. Just remember to add the wine toward the end of cooking, or the high heat will flash off those pungent volatile notes. In braised "drunken" dishes, marinated in plenty of wine, the mildly acidic rice wine adds flavor while helping tenderize tough meats.

You can find rice wines from many locales and at many different quality levels. Generally speaking, the more expensive the wine, the better the quality. If you have a hard time finding Chinese rice wine, you can substitute dry sherry or Japanese sake. Once opened, all will keep for several months in a cool, dry place.

Sesame oil (Ma you)

You don't use this dark amber, aromatic oil pressed from toasted sesame seeds for cooking, but rather for the subtle and unmistakably Chinese flavor it gives to a finished dish. As with rice wine, its flavor and aroma can vaporize if exposed to high heat for a long time, so be patient and add it at the end of cooking.

Use sesame oil anywhere you'd like to add a nutty aroma and richness — marinades, salad dressings, and soups come to mind. The best-quality oils are 100-percent pure, as opposed to blends of sesame oil with a greater proportion of soybean oil. Whichever kind you choose, you can refrigerate it for up to several months after opening.

Sesame paste (Tzee ma jeng; zhi ma jiang)

This thick, peanut buttery, golden brown to light gray-brown paste made from toasted white sesame seeds plays an important role in Sichuanese dishes. Try it in your Sichuanese creations and in any other dish that could use a nutty flavor and aroma. It's also perfect for salad dressings and marinades. If the paste is too thick to add to dressings, sauces, or marinades, soften it with a little fresh oil or water.

If you can't find Chinese sesame paste, go ahead and substitute Middle Eastern tahini, made from untoasted white sesame seeds, or even peanut butter mixed with some sesame oil. If you do land some of this rich, flavorful paste, stir the layer of oil at the top of the jar back into the paste itself. Or, if you prefer it thicker, pour off the oil before each use, and then top off the jar with a fresh layer of sesame oil or lightly flavored vegetable oil before storing the paste in the refrigerator. It should keep there for several months.

Soy sauce (Jeng yeo; jiang you)

Anyone who has ever eaten in a Chinese restaurant, opened a Chinese cookbook, or paid Chinese cooking any attention at all must be well acquainted with soy sauce. Perhaps the single most important ingredient in Chinese kitchens, soy sauce plays a role in virtually every Chinese dish. The best-quality soy sauces, made from traditionally fermented soybeans and wheat, have a dark color emblematic of Chinese foods and a slightly sweet, mildly salty flavor that isn't overpowering or parchingly salty.

Soy sauce gives an unequivocally Chinese note to marinades, stir-fry sauces, braising liquids, roasting glazes, soups, and salad dressings. Chinese restaurants often serve a mixture of soy sauce and vinegar as a table condiment for roast meats and Chinese appetizers. Always choose a "naturally brewed" or fermented soy sauce rather than artificially colored and chemically processed soy sauces. Store soy sauce in a cool, dry place, or in the refrigerator if you're a slow user. Because they're fermented and contain plenty of salt, soy sauces are naturally preserved and will keep for several months. However, be mindful that they will darken and become more concentrated over time.

Dark soy sauce (Lo ceo; lao chou)

The addition of molasses and a bit of cornstarch gives a sweeter, more full-bodied flavor and a syrupy consistency to dark soy sauce. This is the soy sauce of choice for Shanghai-style, red-cooked meats and stewed dishes, as well as for any application that requires a richer, slightly sweet flavor and deeper mahogany color.

Book VI

Chinese Cooking

Many dark soy sauce bottles have labels that are solely in Chinese, but don't let that discourage you. The clerk at a Chinese market can locate a bottle for you. Dark soy sauce is not interchangeable with regular, although the two often appear together in recipes. If you've given up on finding a bottle of dark soy sauce, use a mildly sweet regular soy sauce, such as Kikkoman brand, as a substitute. As with regular soy sauce, store dark soy sauce in a cool, dark place, or in the refrigerator if you're a slow user, for up to a year.

Rice vinegar (Bok tzo; mi cu)

Compared to distilled white vinegar, rice vinegar is milder, less pungent, and sweeter. Popular Chinese rice vinegars range in color from clear or slightly golden to rich amber brown. "Seasoned" rice vinegars are spiked with sugar, which adds an even stronger sweetness.

Rice vinegar contributes the sweetness and sourness essential to sweet and sour sauces and also helps season cooked and raw vegetable dishes, salad dressings, and marinades. In addition to its specifically Chinese applications, rice vinegar gives vibrancy to foods from other cuisines as well, Japanese cuisine in particular. Store bottles of rice vinegar in a cool, dry place. They'll keep for several months, albeit with some loss in intensity and flavor. (If your rice vinegar smells slightly sour, good. It's supposed to!)

Black vinegar (Hok tzo; hei cu)

As a direct contrast to rice vinegar's mild flavor and color, black vinegar has a bold, sweet-tart, smoky flavor and a deep, dark color. The fermentation of a mixture of rice, wheat, and millet or sorghum gives black vinegar its unique characteristics. As an alternative to black vinegar's robustness, you can turn to Chinese red vinegar for a mild, light, and smooth flavor. The latter works just as well in just as many applications. Both black and red vinegar come in variously sized bottles. If you can't find either, substitute balsamic vinegar, but decrease the amount of sugar listed in the recipe. Store Chinese black and red vinegars in a cool, dry place for several months, although, as with rice vinegar, they will lose some flavor and intensity.

Spicing Up Your Life with Chinese Herbs and Spices

The Chinese have a long tradition of using herbs and spices to boost not only a dish's flavor but also its nutritional benefits. Walk into any Chinese herb shop or pharmacy and you'll quickly discover that the line between food and medicine in China is pretty blurry. So considering that the meal itself is often the medicine, you won't need that spoonful of sugar to help it go down. Just try adding some of the flavorful ingredients listed in this section.

Chinese five-spice powder (Ng heung fun; wu xiang fen)

The Chinese have long believed that the number five has special curative and healing powers, which is why this light cocoa-colored powder originally contained five specific spices. But nowadays, it contains quite a few more, including cinnamon, star anise, fennel, clove, ginger, licorice, Sichuan peppercorn, and dried tangerine peel.

Most grocery stores carry Chinese five-spice powder, either in jars or small plastic packages. If you can't find it in the spice section, give the trusty Chinese food section a try. Store loose powder in a jar with a tight-fitting lid in a cool, dry place, and it will keep for a year.

Chinese hot mustard (Gai mut; jie mo)

Most people who have had egg rolls in American-Chinese restaurants have given Chinese hot mustard a try. It's the condiment with the pungent, horseradish-like fireiness that goes so well with Chinese appetizers and cold meat platters. Try adding Chinese hot mustard to chicken salad dressings and dipping sauces for fresh vegetables.

Chinese hot mustards are available already prepared or in powdered form. Store the loose powder in a jar with a tightly fitting lid in a cool, dry place.

Store opened containers of prepared mustard in the refrigerator. Both will keep for several months.

Ginger (Geung; jiang)

No matter where or when I smell it, fresh ginger signals the prelude of Chinese cooking to me. This pale golden, knobby, hand-shaped rhizome (it's not actually a root, but rather a special type of underground-growing stem) has the perfect combination of enchanting aroma, spicy bite, and natural sweetness. Slice, julienne, mince, or grate fresh ginger for use in dressings, sauces, and marinades. And remember to include it in poultry, meat, seafood, and vegetable dishes. Choose ginger that's hard, heavy, and free of wrinkles and mold. It's available year-round. You can also find young ginger, which is more delicate in flavor and texture, during summer and fall. Store mature ginger in a cool, dry place for up to a couple weeks. Alternatively, peel and place it in a jar with rice wine sherry and refrigerate for up to several months.

Sichuan peppercorns (Fa tziu; hua jiao)

Black peppercorns are no substitute for these dried, reddish brown berries with a unique woodsy fragrance and pleasantly numbing tang. In fact, the two aren't even related. To give red-cooked dishes and stir-fries a distinctive Chinese flavor, stick with Sichuan when it comes to peppercorns.

The cuisine of western China relies a great deal on Sichuan peppercorns as well as Chinese five-spice powder. Get the most out of your Sichuan peppercorns by toasting a handful of them in a dry frying pan over low heat until they become fragrant and then add them to your recipe. You can work with either whole peppercorns or ones that are crushed to a fine or coarse powder in a mortar and pestle or spice grinder.

Sichuan peppercorns are available in plastic bags. Some packages label them "wild" or "red" pepper. But don't let the latter name confuse you — these are not the same things as red chile peppers. Store the peppercorns in a jar with a tightly fitting lid in a cool, dry place. They'll keep for several months.

Star anise (Bark gog; ba jiao)

Another essential in Chinese five-spice powder, star anise is hard to miss. These approximately 1-inch, star-shaped pods have points, each containing a shiny, mahogany-colored seed. Like the anise seed of the West, star anise has a licorice flavor that complements meats and poultry in red-cooked and barbecued dishes.

Most cooks use star anise to make rich braising sauces and stews. You don't want to eat the whole spice; just let it infuse the sauce or braising liquid with its warm, mild spiciness. Ground star anise goes into flavoring powders, Chinese five-spice powder being a fine example, and dipping sauces.

You can find whole and ground star anise in plastic packages and small jars. I challenge you to find a bag with no broken stars — it's impossible, given their delicate points. Nevertheless, eight broken points still equal one whole pod. Store whole and powdered star anise in separate jars with tightly fitting lids in a cool, dry place. They'll keep there for several months.

Canned, Dried, and Otherwise Preserved: Long-Lasting Chinese Ingredients

The Chinese are masters at making foods last for the long haul. When you've had as much experience battling Mother Nature and pesky foreign invaders as China's cooks have, you're bound to learn some preservation tricks. Even though the Western world's food supply is predictable and stable enough to make stockpiling long-lasting ingredients unnecessary, these preserved ingredients have become such important players in Chinese cuisine that omitting them will leave you with a less-than-authentic dish.

Tofu (Dou fu; do fu)

Tofu (also known as bean curd) is the chameleon of Chinese ingredients. It comes in a variety of textures, from silky-soft, which is best for soups and puddinglike dishes, to a dense yet slightly spongy firmness that stands up to hearty stir-fries and also works well cold and crumbled into salads. Its neutral taste lets it absorb the flavors of other foods and sauces like a sponge. No wonder it's such a popular meat substitute.

You can find soft, regular, or firm tofu in plastic containers and cartons in the refrigerated sections and produce departments of most supermarkets these days. Check the package for its best storage method and its expiration date. If you frequent Asian markets or health food stores, you may find tubs of water holding cubes of loose tofu. Store these cubes in a container with a tightly fitting lid, fill it with water, and refrigerate. It will keep for several days if you change the water daily. If your tofu develops a strong odor, discard it.

Chinese sausage (Larp tzoen; la chang)

Whenever I need to add a savory, flavorful, specifically Chinese note to a rice dish or stir-fry, I reach for Chinese sausages. You may have seen these slender, deep brownish-red, wrinkled links hanging from racks in Chinese deli windows. No matter which kind you buy, cook them before serving to bring the pork to a safe temperature and remove excess fat. A quick turn in a steamer, a pot of boiling water, or the wok with the rest of the stir-fry should do the trick.

Chinese delis sell sausages in pairs held together with colored string, the color representing the type of sausage. (Approximately four pairs give you a pound of sausage.) You can also find them in vacuum-sealed packages. Store them in your refrigerator in their original packaging or in a zippered plastic bag for up to a month, or freeze them for up to several months.

Baby corn (Siu gum soeun; xiao jin sun)

These little mellow-yellow gems never fail to impress diners — my sons can appreciate eating a vegetable that's just the right size for them. Normally 2 to 3 inches long and found in cans, baby corn, or young corn as it's sometimes called, is completely edible, cob and all. Another point for convenience!

Enjoy baby corn's sweet taste and crunchy texture in stir-fries, soups, and salads. I sometimes serve it on its own as a snack or part of a vegetable platter. When using canned baby corn, drain and rinse it under water to remove the salty canning brine. If the corn has a metallic taste, blanch the ears in boiling water.

After you open a can, transfer the ears to a container with a tightly fitting lid, fill it with water, and refrigerate. The baby corn will keep for a week if you change the water daily.

Bamboo shoots (Tzook soeun; zhu sun)

Another classic Chinese food ingredient, bamboo shoots come in so many forms — whole tips, young tips, sliced shoots, and diced shoots — that you should have no problem finding the variety that suits your tastes and your recipe. All of them have a mildly sweet flavor, but their individual textures vary with how much fiber the shoots contain. Young winter shoots are the most tender, while older, sliced shoots are more fibrous.

Most bamboo shoots in Western markets come in cans. As with other canned ingredients, you'll want to rinse them under water to remove excess salt, or blanch them to rid them of tinny flavors. Transfer the contents of an opened can to a container with a tightly fitting lid, fill it with water, and refrigerate for up to a week, changing the water daily. If you can find fresh shoots in bins of water in your market's produce section, try them. Store fresh shoots in your refrigerator the same way you would canned shoots.

Water chestnuts (Ma tike; ma ti)

Fresh water chestnuts are proof that you can't judge a book by its cover. These squat, dingy brown, pointy-topped tubers that are rarely bigger than golf balls have a sweet, slightly starchy taste and pale beige flesh that belies their homely exteriors. Many grocery stores carry cans of whole and sliced water chestnuts. They may not be as sweet as the fresh kind, but they keep their crunchy texture long after cooking, just like the fresh ones, making them perfect for stews as well as stir-fries and salads.

If you can find fresh water chestnuts, choose ones with no wrinkles or mold and store them in a breathable paper bag in the refrigerator for up to a week. You can also peel fresh ones and freeze them for up to a month. Treat the canned ones as you would any other canned ingredient: Drain and rinse them with cold water, blanch them if necessary, and store them for up to a week in the refrigerator in a container with a tightly fitting lid and enough water to cover them, changing the water daily.

Straw mushrooms (Tzo gu; cao gu)

These cute little mushrooms may look like props from the set of *Alice in Wonderland,* but I promise they're quite edible (and deliciously so). You're probably most familiar with the peeled variety — the kind that look like little toadstools with their brown, dome-shaped caps and thick, straw-colored stems. But Chinese cooks actually prefer the unpeeled variety, which resembles little brown eggs with a slightly flat bottom. The delicate sweetness and firm, meaty texture of the peeled and unpeeled mushrooms make either perfect for meat or vegetarian stir-fries.

Drain and rinse canned straw mushrooms before using and blanch them in boiling water if they still have that tinny flavor. Although most supermarkets carry only peeled straw mushrooms, keep your eyes "peeled" for the unpeeled variety that comes in cans and jars as well. To store the unused portion of a can, transfer the contents to a container with a tightly fitting lid, fill it with water, and refrigerate. If you change the water daily, the mushrooms should keep for a week.

Dried black mushrooms (Gon doan gu; gan dong gu)

You can find just as many types of dried mushrooms in Chinese markets as you can find dishes in which to use them. The favorite of most Chinese cooks is the dried black mushroom, the same one that the Japanese refer to as the shiitake. I just can't resist the rich, meaty texture and wild-mushroom flavor of these preserved treats, and judging by their popularity, I'm not alone! You can spot them by their tan undersides and brownish black caps, which are sometimes cracked in a chrysanthemum-shaped pattern and are sometimes smooth.

Before cooking, soak them in warm water until they're soft (usually half an hour to an hour will do) and then cut off the hard, knobby stem. Remember to strain and save that soaking liquid — it adds so much flavor to sauces and soups. After your dried mushrooms are rehydrated, chop them and add them to stuffings for poultry or dumplings. Larger slices work best in stir-fries, where their substantial texture can stand up to and complement the textures of other ingredients.

Dried black mushrooms are available in plastic packages in Asian markets. Increasingly, small specialty companies and organic farms are marketing them to large Western supermarkets and health food stores, so look for them in those outlets if you don't have an Asian market nearby. Store mushrooms in a tightly sealed container in a cool, dry place. They'll keep for several months.

Dried black fungus (Hok mook yee; gan mu er)

Not to be confused with dried black mushrooms, dried black fungus is actually a catchall term for different fungus varieties, including cloud ear, wood ear, and tree ear. Cloud ear fungus gets its name from its resemblance to clouds — apparently dark, black storm clouds. Wood ear and tree ear fungi grow on old pieces of wood and tree stumps, hence their imaginative names. No matter which type of dried, leathery-looking chips you choose, the slightly crispy/slightly gummy bite and smooth surface of black fungus add a whole new textural dimension to your dishes. And to boot, their bland flavor goes with just about any dish, from mu shu to wonton soup.

Soak dried black fungus in warm water until soft before using, and remove the knobby stem end. Because these thirsty characters really expand — up to three times their dried size — prepare only a few pieces for use in a recipe. Slice them into strips or bite-sized chunks depending on the texture and appearance you want. You can find whole or shredded dried black fungus in plastic packages. Look for the bags with small, thin ears, which are better quality than the thick, large ones. Store them in a tightly sealed container in a cool, dry place for up to several months.

Chapter 3

Mastering a Few Simple Techniques

*I*f the word *technique* sounds too technical, relax. You don't need to struggle with complicated techniques to cook like a true Chinese chef. Basic Chinese cooking techniques are never more complicated than the ones you already know and practice daily in your own kitchen. With a little planning and some practice (and practice is the fun part!), anyone can master Chinese cooking.

Getting a Grip on Your Knife

Those who are familiar with my cooking show know that I am quite fond of my Chinese chef's knife. I use it to slice, dice, and chop, and I can work up quite an appetite with all that exercise. But speed isn't everything. In fact, when it comes to knife skills, I recommend starting slowly and carefully.

Your *guiding hand,* the one not holding the knife, performs some pretty important functions, from guiding the food you're cutting, to keeping the knife from slipping, to controlling the size of the cuts you make. No matter what you do with your free hand, make sure to keep it out of the knife's way. When holding food, use your guiding hand's fingertips to steady the item while you keep your thumb back away from the blade. Tuck your fingertips under a bit so that your knuckles abut the blade's flat side. This hand position lets you slice, chop, and move the knife freely without putting those fingertips in danger.

Slicing

Hold the food securely on the cutting board, making sure that the fingers on your guiding hand are curled under and are out of the way of the knife's edge. Press straight down with the knife, slicing into the food to get pieces of the desired thickness.

Matchstick or julienne cutting

The words *matchstick* and *julienne* mean essentially the same thing: thin strips of food that are cut to the size of matchsticks. To julienne or matchstick-cut an ingredient, cut it into thin, even slices, stack them, and slice vertically through the stack to create a bundle of thin strips resembling matchsticks. If you want to julienne or matchstick-cut meat or chicken, I suggest chilling it in the freezer for about 15 to 20 minutes. Doing so firms the flesh and makes slicing more manageable.

Technically, julienned foods are cut to dimensions of ⅛ inch × ⅛ inch × 1 to 2 inches. But in Chinese cooking, we generally julienne or matchstick-cut items thinner — almost to shreds. The thinner the vegetables or meats, the quicker they cook, and that's important when using a quick-cooking method such as stir-frying (described later in this chapter). In addition to julienne- or matchstick-cutting ingredients very thinly, make sure that all ingredients in a recipe are cut to roughly the same size, which ensures that they'll cook at the same pace.

Cubing, dicing, and mincing

The main difference between cubes, dices, and minces is size. Other than that, they're all basically cube-shaped pieces of food. Cubes are the largest of the three, while dice can measure ¾ inch to ¼ inch. Mincing produces the smallest pieces, usually 1/16 inch. To cube, dice, or mince a food, first cut it into long sticks by using the julienne/matchstick technique described in the preceding section. Vary the sticks' cross-sectional dimensions depending on whether you want to cube, dice, or mince. Then cut across the sticks to create whatever size cubes you want.

Roll cutting

Roll cutting is a great technique for cutting long, cylindrical vegetables such as carrots, zucchini, and eggplants. To begin, cut a diagonal slice off the tip of the vegetable. Then roll it a quarter turn, make another diagonal cut along the same angle as the first, roll a quarter turn again, and make another cut.

Continue rolling and cutting until you come to the end of the vegetable. This convenient technique creates attractively shaped ingredients and exposes more of the food's surface to heat to speed cooking.

Parallel cutting

When you need to cut wide, thin slices from meats or slice a block of tofu into two layers, parallel cutting (illustrated in Figure 3-1) is your technique of choice. Place the piece of food near the edge of your cutting board and lay your guiding hand flat on top of it. With your other hand, hold your Chinese chef's knife at a slight angle *downward* so that it's not quite parallel to the board. Use a slow and careful back-and-forth motion to slice the food.

Book VI

Chinese Cooking

Figure 3-1: Parallel cutting into very thin slices.

When parallel cutting food into very thin slices, your fingers come awfully close to the knife's blade. Be very careful to keep that knife angled slightly downward and away from your hand.

Crushing

To release the essential oils in pungent ingredients such as garlic, ginger, or salted black beans, crush them. Doing so bursts the cellular "sacks" containing those oils. Place the ingredient on a cutting board and hold a knife over it horizontally with the blade's edge facing away from you. Then slap the flat of the blade onto the board with your free hand, crushing the food underneath it. Use the flat of the knife's blade as a scoop to pick up the newly crushed ingredient.

How's this for easy garlic and ginger peeling? Crush an unpeeled garlic clove by using the technique described in this section, and the peel will slide right off. Peeling ginger calls for a different skill. Although the skin of young ginger is so thin that you don't really need to peel it, older hand-shaped chunks of ginger — actually called *hands* — have thick, rough skin that you'll probably want to remove. Beware, however; most of ginger's flavor is concentrated right below its skin, so peeling too deeply may remove the flavor along with the skin. The solution? Use a teaspoon to scrape off the skin (gingerly, of course).

Scoring

Ever ordered a fish fillet and noticed the diamond pattern sliced into its surface? If so, you already know what happens when you score food. Simply make a few slightly angled cuts, about ⅛ inch deep, at the food's surface, being careful not to cut all the way through. These marks help the food cook faster and more evenly. You can also slip slices of garlic, herbs, and other aromatic flavorings into the score marks to enhance the flavor.

Tenderizing

Don't waste your money on a tenderizer hammer. Put your handy Chinese chef's knife to work instead. Use the blunt edge to pound tough cuts of meat in a crisscross pattern. This action helps break down some of the stronger fibers that give meat a tough texture.

Stir-Frying

This is the most common Chinese cooking technique. Its simplicity makes it the perfect starting point for novice cooks, too. In no time, you'll be hooked by the crispy textures, bright colors, and delicious flavors of stir-fried dishes. To keep up with the fast pace of this cooking method and get the best results, pay attention to the three cardinal rules of stir-frying:

- ✔ **Have everything chopped, measured, mixed, and within easy reach.** Stir-frying is a quick cooking method, leaving little time to reach into cabinets or chop ingredients after you start cooking.

- ✔ **Keep the heat high.** High heat gets the best stir-fry results. Intense cooking temperatures and the small size of stir-fry ingredients help your stir-fry go from stove to serving dish in no time. Keeping things hot also seals flavor, juices, and nutrients into the ingredients while leaving them crisp.

- ✔ **Rapidly toss and stir the ingredients to expose all their surfaces to the heat.** Don't load the wok with vegetables and meat and just stand there and stare at it. Good stir-fry dishes require plenty of elbow grease. Remember that it's *stir*-fry, not *stare*-fry!

And although each stir-fry recipe is slightly different, they all tend to follow the same basic pattern of steps:

1. **Preheat the wok, add the oil, and let it heat up.**

2. **Add the aromatic flavoring ingredients such as garlic, ginger, chiles, and green onions.**

   Cook these ingredients for a few seconds until they become aromatic and release their flavors into the oil.

3. **Add the meat or seafood.**

   If your home stove doesn't reach very high temperatures (which is likely if you have an electric range), you may want to let the meat rest in the hot wok for up to 1 minute to begin cooking its surface before you start stir-frying in earnest. After you do, remember to toss, stir, and toss some more. You're sealing in the juices and keeping the food from sticking.

   When the meat or seafood is done, you may want to remove it from the wok to a platter, or it will overcook and toughen. Cooking the meat or seafood first flavors the oil and releases juices into the wok, adding flavors to the vegetables that come next.

4. **Add the vegetables.**

   Add the dense, tough ones first, followed by the smaller, more tender ones. Continue tossing and stirring.

5. **When the vegetables are done, return the meat and any accumulated juices to the wok, along with the sauce called for in the recipe. Stir well and allow everything to heat through.**

   Chinese stir-fry sauces often call for the addition of a solution of cornstarch and water near the end of cooking. The solution helps thicken the sauce and gives it a smooth, glossy appearance. (For more on sauce-making basics, see Chapter 4 of Book VI.)

6. **Taste the dish to decide whether the seasonings are balanced.**

   Don't be shy about taste-testing — a perk of doing the cooking.

7. **Add a garnish that echoes one of the other ingredients in the dish: a green onion blossom for lamb with green onions, or some toasted, sliced almonds to decorate a dish of almond chicken.**

8. **Remove the wok from the heat, place the stir-fry on a serving platter, and get ready to take your bow!**

Steaming

Steaming is another popular cooking technique in China. Steam cooks foods quickly and lets their natural flavors come through. Nutritionists and weight watchers love it, too, because it introduces little or no fat and leaves the ingredients' nutrients intact. As if these advantages weren't enough, it's also easy to do.

Many steamers are readily available at your culinary store (see Chapter 1); however, you can make do, as I prefer to, with a wok or a large pan. Bring water to a boil in a large wok or pan with a rack in it. Place your food in a heatproof dish or glass pie plate and put that on the rack over the boiling water. Cover with a tight-fitting lid and let the moist heat circulate around the food, cooking it to a tender finish. Add water to the wok or pan if the level gets too low.

To tell whether my steamer is out of steam, I place a marble at the bottom before I start cooking. It quietly rolls around in the water while the level is high, but once that level reaches zero, it clangs against the bottom of the steamer to tell me that I need to add more water. The hotter the water, the better — boiling is best — but be careful to gently pour the water around the food or underneath the steamer basket into the bottom of the steamer.

Be especially careful when removing the lid from your steamer. Always open it away from you, letting the steam — which is hotter than boiling water — escape out of your way before you remove your food.

Blanching

Chinese cooks use blanching to precook many ingredients before the final cooking process. It softens tough, hardy vegetables, such as broccoli, carrots, and potatoes, and makes peeling vegetables and fruits such as tomatoes and peaches easier. Blanching is also a quick and easy way to get rid of the tinny, metallic taste of canned vegetables such as bamboo shoots, straw mushrooms, and water chestnuts.

Bring a wok of water to a boil and plunge the vegetables into the water for a few minutes until they're crisp-tender and their color has brightened. *Remember:* Blanching is not cooking, so remove your ingredients quickly from the wok and rinse them under cold water. Or better yet, plunge them into a cold water bath to stop the cooking and set the color.

Braising

When you combine simmering with stir-frying, you get braising, a cooking method that's especially effective with larger, tougher cuts of meat.

Braising is a two-step process. Stir-frying comes first: Lightly brown chunks of meat in a wok or pot to caramelize them. Do not overcrowd the pot with too much meat, or you'll lower the temperature and prevent all the pieces from contacting the cooking surface evenly.

After you've browned the meat, add the seasonings and braising liquid — stock, water, soy sauce, or rice wine. Bring this liquid to a boil, lower the heat to a simmer, cover, and cook gently for a couple hours (or whatever the recipe requires) so that the braising liquid's flavors permeate and tenderize the meat.

Deep-Frying

Deep-fried Chinese foods, including wontons, egg rolls, and sweet-and-sour dishes, are crowd pleasers inside China as well as outside. Who can refuse rich flavors and a crispy exterior contrasted with a moist, delicate inside? For easy deep-frying at home, follow these simple guidelines:

Book VI

Chinese Cooking

1. **Pour oil into a wok or deep-frying pan to a depth of about 2 inches and turn on the heat.**

2. **Regulate the oil temperature according to the recipe.**

   If the temperature is too hot, you'll burn the food or cook the outside too quickly before the inside has a chance to cook. If the temperature is too low, your foods will take a long time to cook, absorbing so much oil in the process that they end up soggy and greasy. Properly heated oil seals the food's surface, creating a crispy outer layer while fully cooking what's inside.

   How can you tell whether your oil has reached the correct temperature? Most electric frying pans come with a temperature control, thereby eliminating guesswork. You can also use a deep-frying thermometer to get an even more accurate measure. If you don't have either of these tools, I have an age-old trick that Chinese chefs have used for centuries: Dip the tip of a dry, wooden chopstick into the hot oil. If the oil bubbles around the chopstick, it's hot enough for the food.

3. **After the oil is hot enough, very carefully slide the food into the oil a few pieces at a time, pointing them away from your body. Don't add too much at once or you'll lower the oil temperature and end up with greasy food.**

   You don't want oil that's been heated to 300 degrees or hotter splashing on you. If you deep-fry in a wok, use a flat-bottomed one or stabilize a round-bottomed one by setting it in a ring stand.

4. **Turn the food frequently as it cooks to ensure even browning.**

   After the food floats to the top of the wok and stays there (some foods float initially but then sink), it's ready.

5. **Remove the food with a wire strainer or slotted spoon and drain on paper towels.**

Smoking

Like barbecuing and roasting, variations on smoking are at home both in Western and Chinese kitchens. Smoking is a flavoring technique that involves slowly cooking meats in an enclosed container with a smoky fire. The Chinese often smoke in a wok, using black tea leaves, citrus peel, raw rice, brown sugar, and whole spices to add flavor.

For easy smoking in your own home, line a large wok with foil and sprinkle in the smoking seasonings listed in the recipe. Place the meat on a rack inside the wok. Tightly cover the wok, turning the excess foil up to cover the wok's lid, sealing in the heat and flavor. Increase the heat and let the scented smoke permeate the meat, giving it a very distinctive smoky flavor. Follow the smoking time recommended in your recipe.

Chapter 4

Sauces and Dips

*Y*ou know the old saying, "the suit makes the man"? I think the better analogy is "the sauce makes the meal," and it's as true in Chinese cuisine as it is in French. But traditional Chinese sauces aren't the complicated reductions or egg- and cream-thickened concoctions of classic French cooking. Instead, the inventory of Chinese sauces and dips is based on simple, yet flavorfully potent, combinations of basic seasonings and widely available bottled sauces.

In Chapter 2 of Book VI, I introduce you to many of those prepared sauces available in supermarkets and Chinese groceries. Most of them work wonders on their own. Yet, by mixing a sauce, hoisin for example, with fresh garlic, ginger, dried chili peppers, and any of a number of other flavorings, Chinese cooks build an elegant sauce with complex character. Now it's your turn to do the same and experiment a little. You'll be amazed at all the creative sauces and dips you can make with just a few basic building blocks.

The beauty of most Chinese sauces and dips is that you can make them in quantity ahead of time and store them in tightly sealed containers in the refrigerator, where they'll keep for weeks at a time. Whenever you want to add a little sweet-and-sour to your pork with peppers, you can have that sauce prepared and ready to go without a lot of last-minute kitchen confusion.

Sauce Smarts

The strategy behind Chinese sauce making involves building a more complex sauce out of simpler elements. But achieving complexity of flavor while keeping the overall sauce balanced is key here. Just as in any other aspect of Chinese cuisine, when one flavor dominates all others — even if you really like that one flavor — you've missed the mark.

The following recipes guarantee that your Chinese sauces will hit the mark every time.

All-Purpose Stir-Fry Sauce

The culinary equivalent of a simple white shirt, this sauce goes with just about anything.

Preparation time: *15 minutes*

Cooking time: *5 minutes*

Yield: *About 1¾ cups*

⅔ cup soy sauce	¼ teaspoon white pepper
½ cup chicken broth	2 tablespoons cooking oil
⅓ cup Chinese rice wine	1 tablespoon minced garlic
3½ tablespoons sugar	1 tablespoon minced ginger
1 tablespoon sesame oil	2 tablespoons cornstarch dissolved in ¼ cup water

1 In a bowl, combine the soy sauce, chicken broth, rice wine, sugar, sesame oil, and white pepper.

2 Place a pan over high heat until hot. Add the cooking oil, swirling to coat the sides. Add the garlic and the ginger; cook, stirring, until fragrant, about 15 seconds.

3 Add the mixture from Step 1; bring to a boil. Reduce the heat to medium and cook for 1 minute. Add the cornstarch solution and cook, stirring, until the sauce boils and thickens.

Hot and Spicy Stir-Fry Sauce

Sometimes an all-purpose sauce needs a little bit of kick, and this variation of the standard all-purpose stir-fry sauce packs just such a wallop by way of two different types of pepper and a liberal dose of chile garlic sauce. Be sure to taste your sauce as you make it. That way, you can put the brakes on the hot chile if it gets a little too racy for you.

Preparation time: *15 minutes*

Cooking time: *7 minutes*

Yield: *1½ cups*

Book VI

Chinese Cooking

⅔ cup Chinese rice wine

⅓ cup soy sauce

⅓ cup chicken broth

3 tablespoons sugar

½ teaspoon white pepper

2 tablespoons thinly sliced green onions

1½ tablespoons chile garlic sauce

2 tablespoons cooking oil

1½ tablespoons minced garlic

1½ tablespoons minced ginger

2 tablespoons cornstarch dissolved in ¼ cup water

1 In a bowl, combine the rice wine, soy sauce, chicken broth, sugar, white pepper, green onions, and chile garlic sauce.

2 Place a wok or medium pan over high heat until hot. Add the cooking oil, swirling to coat the sides. Add the garlic and ginger; cook, stirring, until fragrant, about 30 seconds. Add the wine mixture, bring to a boil, reduce the heat to medium, and cook for 2 minutes. Add the cornstarch solution and cook, stirring, until the sauce boils and thickens. Let cool.

Sweet and Sour Sauce

North America's favorite Chinese restaurant sauce balances the flavors of any stir-fry, but it's especially good at cutting the richness of batter-dipped meats and fish, as well as deep-fried appetizers, such as egg rolls.

Preparation time: *15 minutes*

Cooking time: *15 minutes*

Yield: *2 cups*

½ cup water

½ cup ketchup

⅓ cup packed brown sugar

⅓ cup orange juice

⅓ cup rice vinegar

1½ tablespoons soy sauce

1½ teaspoons crushed dried red chiles

2 tablespoons cooking oil

2 tablespoons minced ginger

1½ tablespoons cornstarch mixed with ¼ cup water

1 In a bowl, combine the water, ketchup, brown sugar, orange juice, rice vinegar, soy sauce, and dried chiles.

2 Place a medium pan over high heat until hot. Add the cooking oil, swirling to coat the sides. Add the minced ginger and cook, stirring, until fragrant, about 20 seconds. Add the mixture from Step 1; bring to a boil and cook until the sugar dissolves. Add the cornstarch solution and cook, stirring, until the sauce boils and thickens.

Remember: *Sweet and sour sauce wouldn't be sweet and sour without an ample helping of acidic ingredients such as rice vinegar and orange juice. But any starch-thickened sauce becomes thin and watery if you add too much acid. So if you're playing with proportions, don't get out of hand when upping the sour.*

Master Sauce/Red-Cooking Sauce

Like a well-seasoned wok, this richly flavored sauce that hails from eastern China gets better with each use, so don't pour it down the drain after using it in a stew or a claypot casserole. Rather, strain it and store it in a tightly sealed container in the refrigerator or freezer (the latter if you'd like to keep it longer) until you're ready to red-cook again — and again, and again. Every item that you cook in it deepens and enriches the sauce with its own flavors. That's my idea of sauce recycling!

Preparation time: 15 minutes

Cooking time: 23 minutes

Yield: About 3½ cups

Book VI

Chinese Cooking

3 cups chicken broth	2 pieces dried tangerine peel or 4 pieces fresh orange peel
½ cup soy sauce	
⅓ cup dark soy sauce	2 tablespoons cooking oil
⅓ cup Chinese rice wine	8 slices ginger
¼ cup packed brown sugar	6 cloves garlic, crushed
2 whole star anise	1 tablespoon sesame oil

1 In a bowl, combine the chicken broth, soy sauce, dark soy sauce, rice wine, brown sugar, anise, and tangerine peel.

2 Place a medium pan over high heat until hot. Add the cooking oil, swirling to coat the sides. Add the ginger and garlic; cook, stirring, until fragrant, about 20 seconds. Add the broth mixture; bring to a boil, reduce the heat, cover and simmer for 20 minutes, stirring occasionally.

3 Stir in the sesame oil and remove from heat.

Remember: Some of the aromatics and fresh ingredients in a red-cooking sauce need replenishing now and again. The volatile flavors of dried tangerine peel, ginger, and garlic can "flash off," or vaporize, during cooking. Taste your sauce each time; if it seems a bit weak, by all means add fresh ginger, onions, soy, or any other flavoring ingredient that could use some refreshing.

All-Purpose Black Bean Sauce

This is truly a sauce for all seasons — and a seasoning for just about every situation. Try it with pork ribs, meat dishes, vegetable stir-fries, and especially with seafood. When it comes to pairing black beans with the flavors of the sea, anyone who's done any eating in Guangzhou can vouch that no match is better seasoned.

Preparation time: *9 minutes*

Yield: *About ¾ cup*

2 tablespoons black bean garlic sauce

1 tablespoon chicken broth

1 tablespoon sesame oil

1 tablespoon sugar

2 tablespoons sliced green onion

1 tablespoon minced ginger

1 teaspoon minced garlic

In a bowl, combine all the ingredients; stir to mix well.

Taking a Dip

The distinctions among sauces, dips, oils, and dressings isn't always very clear in Chinese cuisine — or in any cuisine, for that matter. But the recipes that follow provide you with plenty of pleasing condiments that are great for appetizer-dunking or splashing onto stir-fries and salads.

All-Purpose Dipping Sauce

Is it a sauce, or is it a dip? Who cares? When you have hoisin and Worcestershire sauces, ketchup, and two flavored oils contributing to this complex mixture, what you call it really doesn't matter. Its thick consistency makes it heavenly for fried finger foods, giving it a number-one rank in my list of favorite dips.

Preparation time: *3 minutes*

Yield: *About 2 cups*

1 cup ketchup

⅓ cup soy sauce

¼ cup hoisin sauce

¼ cup chicken broth

2½ tablespoons sugar or honey

2 tablespoons Worcestershire sauce

2 tablespoons sesame oil

1 teaspoon Chile Oil (see the recipe below)

⅛ teaspoon white pepper

Combine all the ingredients in a medium bowl and mix well.

Chile Oil

Sure, you can buy chile oil at the grocery store or Asian market. But when you make it yourself, you control its heat and its freshness — a real plus, because chile sauces lose some of their flavor over time. Keeping a bottle of this homemade chile sauce on hand for stir-fries, sauces, salad dressings, and dips saves you plenty of time. It even makes a mouth-watering dip on its own.

Preparation time: *5 minutes*

Cooking time: *1 minute*

Yield: *About 1¼ cups*

1 cup cooking oil

2 tablespoons sesame oil

2 tablespoons crushed dried red chiles

2 teaspoons crushed garlic

Place a small pan over high heat until hot. Add the cooking oil for about 1 minute. Remove from the heat and add the sesame oil, dried chiles, and garlic. Let stand overnight, strain out the seasonings, and then transfer to an airtight jar.

Book VI

Chinese Cooking

Chinese Mustard Dip

As sure as the Yangtze River flows to the East China Sea, an order of egg rolls will come with a little bowl of pungent Chinese mustard. Like sweet and sour sauce — another common egg roll accompaniment — Chinese mustard dip has a mild tartness that, along with the bite of the mustard itself, provides the perfect foil for deep-fried appetizers.

Preparation time: *7 minutes*

Yield: *About ¾ cup*

⅓ cup rice vinegar	*¾ cup dry mustard powder*
¼ cup water	*2 tablespoons sesame oil*
1 tablespoon sugar	*¾ teaspoon cooking oil*

In a small bowl, whisk all the ingredients to a smooth paste. Set aside for at least 1 hour before serving.

Note: *Like a fine wine, Chinese mustard improves with age. When you first mix up a batch, it may seem particularly sharp, a little bitter, and even powdery. But let it spend the night in a covered container in the fridge, and it will wake up mellowed, smooth, and ready to enhance the flavor of your egg rolls or fried wontons.*

Chapter 5

Rice and Noodles

*I*n China, rice reigns in the hot, humid paddies down south while amber waves of grain sway over the colder, drier plains up north. My recommendation: Take advantage of the wealth of both. Rice and wheat (and rice and wheat products) make up the bulk of the Chinese diet, and all the creative rice and noodle dishes that showcase these humble starches make carbo-loading a delicious idea. But if steamed and fried is all you know of rice, or if your idea of a Chinese noodle is the one Confucius used to come up with all those great sayings, you have some pleasant surprises in store.

Rice to the Occasion

In China, rice is such an important part of meals that any accompanying meat, fish, and vegetables dishes (what may be considered the main courses in the West) are really just icing on the cake. Rice creates a "cushion" that tones down the richness of heavier dishes, while its starchiness bulks up lighter ones. And although white rice is the most popular, the Chinese claim to grow and eat more than 3,000 different rice varieties, including brown rice. That's probably an inflated number, but it is a testament to rice's role in the cuisine.

Although simple white rice seems about as basic as you can get, the wide variety of rice cultivated and consumed in China proves that there's a lot more to this humble grain than meets the eye. But before you panic and run out to buy dozens of rice bins for your kitchen, remember that the most common types of rice fall within three fundamental categories:

✔ **Long-grain rice (Jim mike; chan mi):** Most southern Chinese turn to long-grain rice for everyday — and every-meal — use. Of all the rice varieties, it is the least starchy, which means that it cooks up dry and fluffy, with grains that separate easily. This quality makes long-grain rice the top choice for classic fried rice.

✔ **Medium-grain rice (Fong loi mike; fung lai mi):** Shorter than long-grain, medium-grain rice has fans in eastern China and Taiwan, as well as in Korea and Japan, where its higher starch content makes it sticky enough for sushi. When cooked (as you would long-grain rice, but with slightly less water), medium-grain rice is nuttier tasting and shinier than long-grain, as well as stickier and softer. To make it less sticky, use even less water in preparation. Most supermarket rice and bean aisles carry medium-grain rice in various-sized plastic and paper bags, as well as in woven sacks with a variety of labels.

✔ **Glutinous rice (Nor mike; nuo mi):** A variety of short-grain rice, uncooked glutinous rice resembles tiny, opaque, oblong pearls. It becomes soft, moist, translucent, sticky, and slightly sweet when cooked. No wonder it also goes by the names "sticky rice" and "sweet rice." Glutinous rice's starchiness and natural tendency to stick together as a soft paste make it perfect for puddings and fillings. Before steaming or boiling glutinous rice, do as the pros do and plump the grains a bit by soaking them in water for several hours to overnight. You can find glutinous rice in the rice and bean section and the Asian food aisle of your supermarket.

After you open the bag or box, store uncooked rice in a tightly sealed container in a cool, dry place for up to several months. Place cooled, cooked rice in a container with a tight lid and store it in the refrigerator for up to several days. Just drizzle a little water into the container and reheat the rice in the microwave. Or use it in the fried rice recipe that appears in this chapter.

If you bought the rice in a big bag imported from Asia, you may want to pick through the sack or bag first to weed out any rice hulls or pebbles that sneaked in from the paddy. Some less expensive types of rice also benefit from rinsing and draining several times before cooking. This is actually an old tradition in China, where the rhythmic motions of soaking the rice and rubbing the grains until the water runs clear is a calming, meditative process.

Perfect Steamed Rice

You too can make the fluffy, long-grain rice that you thought came only from Chinese restaurants — and you can make it the old-fashioned way. Just follow these stove-top instructions. (They come straight from the best rice cook I know: Mom.)

Preparation time: *3 minutes*

Cooking time: *16 minutes, plus 10 minutes for the rice to rest*

Yield: *4 servings*

2 cups long-grain rice   3 cups cold water

Book VI

**Chinese
Cooking**

1 Rinse the rice; repeat 2 or 3 times until the water is clear; drain well.

2 Place the rice in a 3-quart saucepan with a tight-fitting lid; add the water. Bring to a boil, uncovered, and cook over high heat for 2 minutes. Reduce the heat to low; cover and simmer for 9 minutes. Remove from the heat and let it stand, covered, for 10 minutes. Remove the cover and fluff the rice with a fork.

Remember: *Good rice comes to those who wait. Treasure those last 10 or so minutes of "sitting" time, as you let the cooked rice rest off the heat with the cover on. This leaves you with firm, fluffy rice; serve it too soon, and it will be soggy and overly starchy.*

Perfect Steamed Glutinous Rice

Steaming glutinous rice to a perfectly moist and sticky finish can be a bit of a — ahem — sticky proposition, especially considering that many bags of imported glutinous rice either don't have cooking instructions or print the instructions in Chinese or Japanese. Just follow these instructions, and you'll be a glutinous glutton in no time.

Preparation time: *Up to 8 hours or overnight for soaking the rice*

Cooking time: *25 minutes*

Yield: *4 servings*

1½ cups Chinese glutinous rice	*2 tablespoons water, for sprinkling*

1 Soak the glutinous rice for at least 8 hours or overnight; then drain it.

2 Prepare a wok for steaming (see Chapter 3 of Book VI).

3 Place the glutinous rice in a heatproof glass dish. Steam over high heat for 25 minutes. Sprinkle with water at 10-minute intervals to retain the moisture.

Remember: *Give the glutinous rice ample time to soak and absorb plenty of water — overnight is best. Doing so gives the plump little grains a chance to become even plumper, making the final dish moist and soft.*

Fried Rice

Leftovers get a makeover in this answer to the age-old question "What do I do with last night's rice?" Actually, the fluffy, slightly dry texture of fried rice practically depends on your using day-old — or at least not-straight-from-the-stove or -steamer — rice. Freshly cooked rice still contains so much moisture that when you stir-fry it with all the other ingredients, you end up with a wet, clumpy dish. Break up the clumps that form in the leftover rice by gently rubbing the grains between your fingers or breaking them apart with a wooden spoon or rubber scraper before stir-frying. Separate grains stir-fry more quickly and evenly than huge clumps.

Preparation time: *15 minutes*

Cooking time: *8 minutes*

Yield: *4 servings*

3 tablespoons cooking oil

2 eggs, lightly beaten

¼ teaspoon salt

⅛ teaspoon white pepper

3 cups cold, cooked long-grain rice, fluffed

¾ cup diced char siu (see Chapter 2 of Book VI)

¾ cup frozen peas and carrots, thawed

1½ tablespoons soy sauce

4 green onions, thinly sliced

1 Place a wok over high heat until hot. Add 2 tablespoons of the oil, swirling to coat the sides. Add the eggs, salt, and white pepper; cook until lightly scrambled. Use a spatula to move the eggs to the side. Add the remaining 1 tablespoon oil. Add the rice; stir for 2 minutes.

2 Add the char siu and peas and carrots; stir to mix well. Add the soy sauce and green onions; stir-fry for 1 minute.

Vary It! *Fried rice is meant to be one of those do-it-yourself dishes, so whatever looks good in your pantry is a potential fried rice ingredient. I chose the particular ingredients for this dish with the goal of creating a fried rice like those you get at Chinese restaurants. As you become more familiar with Chinese cuisine, take some chances and create your own fried rice dishes. For instance, if you want fried rice with shrimp, it's a short order to fill: Before you add the eggs, quickly stir-fry some shrimp until they begin to curl and turn pink. Set them aside, proceed with the recipe, and return the shrimp to the wok for a quick heat-through before serving.*

Noodling Around

Rice may be nice, but in the north and west of China, noodles are nicer. In fact, in much of northern China, where it's too cold and dry to grow rice, noodles are so common that, to a southerner like myself, rice seems downright rare in comparison. Traditionally thought of as snacks and small meals in the south, noodles still make classic lunchtime dishes in southern homes and restaurants. But in northern China, they're fair game any time of day.

Easy-to-Make Chow Mein

Actually, the whole point of chow mein ("stir-fried noodles" in Cantonese) is that it should be easy to make — a quick stir and toss, and there you have it. Remember, once you get down the basics of stir-frying, you're free to invent whatever chow mein creations strike your fancy. As with fried rice, what you put in this noodle dish is really up to you. Use this recipe to get your imagination (and your appetite) going.

Preparation time: *20 minutes*

Cooking time: *12 minutes*

Yield: *4 servings*

8 ounces fresh or dried Chinese egg noodles

6 ounces lean pork, thinly sliced

1 tablespoon oyster-flavored sauce

½ cup chicken broth

2 tablespoons dark soy sauce

2 teaspoons sesame oil

½ teaspoon sugar

3 tablespoons cooking oil

2 teaspoons minced garlic

3 bok choy (or any leafy Chinese greens), cut into 1½-inch pieces

1½ cups bean sprouts

3 green onions, cut into 2-inch pieces

1 In a large pot of boiling water, cook the noodles according to the package directions until barely tender to the bite; drain, rinse with cold water, and drain again.

2 Combine the pork and oyster-flavored sauce in a bowl; stir to coat. Let stand for 10 minutes.

3 Make a sauce by combining the chicken broth, dark soy sauce, sesame oil, and sugar in a small bowl.

4 Place a wok over high heat until hot. Add the cooking oil, swirling to coat the sides. Add the garlic and cook, stirring, until fragrant, about 10 seconds. Add the pork and stir-fry for 2 minutes.

5 Add the noodles and sauce; gently toss until heated through. Add the bok choy, bean sprouts, and green onions; cook for 2 minutes, stirring to mix well.

Remember: *Just as fried rice is great for using leftover rice, chow mein is a perfect opportunity for doing something with leftover noodles. However, unlike fried rice — which requires rice that's not brand-spanking new — chow mein comes out just as well with freshly cooked noodles.*

Vary It! *To save time, keep plenty of All-Purpose Stir-Fry Sauce or Hot and Spicy Stir-Fry Sauce, both from Chapter 4 of Book VI, on hand. Instead of making the sauce in the recipe, just add ⅓ cup chicken broth to ½ cup of either sauce and toss it with the noodles.*

Hong Kong–Style Pan-Fried Noodles

It's no wonder that this classic noodle creation from Hong Kong has almost as many fans in the West as it does in its rightful birthplace. The "pancake" of fried noodles topped with saucy meat and vegetables (or whatever else you like) has a smoky, caramelized flavor and a rich, crisply textured surface that no one can resist. Also, the pancake's combination of crispy outside and soft inside is the perfect embodiment of culinary balance of yin and yang.

Preparation time: *25 minutes*

Cooking time: *45 minutes*

Yield: *4 servings*

Book VI

Chinese Cooking

6 ounces medium raw shrimp, shelled and deveined

6 ounces sea scallops, halved horizontally

⅛ teaspoon white pepper

1¼ cups chicken broth

2 tablespoons oyster-flavored sauce

1 teaspoon sesame oil

¼ teaspoon sugar

1 tablespoon cornstarch

8 ounces fresh thin egg noodles

¼ cup cooking oil

1 tablespoon minced garlic

1 teaspoon minced ginger

4 fresh shiitake mushrooms, sliced

3 baby bok choy, quartered lengthwise

1 Combine the shrimp, scallops, and white pepper in a bowl.

2 Make a sauce by combining the chicken broth, oyster-flavored sauce, sesame oil, sugar, and cornstarch in a small bowl.

3 In a large pot of boiling water, cook the noodles according to the package instructions; drain, rinse with cold water, and drain again.

4 Place a 10- to 12-inch nonstick frying pan over medium-high heat until hot. Add 1 table-spoon of the cooking oil, swirling to coat the sides. Spread the noodles in the pan and press lightly to make a firm cake. Cook until the bottom is golden brown, about 5 minutes. Turn the pancake over, add 1 more tablespoon of the cooking oil around the edges of the pan, and cook until the other side is golden brown, 3 to 4 minutes. Remove to a serving plate and keep warm.

5 Place a wok over high heat until hot. Add 1 tablespoon of the cooking oil, swirling to coat the sides. Add the garlic and ginger; cook, stirring, until fragrant, about 10 sec-onds. Add the shrimp and scallops; stir-fry until the shrimp turn pink and the scallops are slightly firm, about 2 minutes. Remove and set aside.

6 Add the remaining 1 tablespoon cooking oil to the wok over high heat, swirling to coat the sides. Add the mushrooms; cook for 1 minute. Add the sauce and bring it to a boil. Add the baby bok choy; cover and cook for 1 minute. Return the seafood to the wok and stir to heat through. Pour on top of the noodle pancake and serve.

Chapter 6

First Impressions

*T*he Chinese may be the world champions of finger foods, and the proof is not in the pudding, but rather in the dim sum. Dim sums — the words literally mean "touches the heart" — are small, sweet or savory morsels that traditionally accompany morning tea in China. Chinese dim sum chefs have developed approximately 2,000 distinctive dim sum items over the centuries, so the definition of dim sum seems rather bland and inadequate. Some of these creations are so imaginative and intricate that you'll wonder whether they're fine food or fine art. My opinion is "both!"

Chinese soups are usually clear broths with some greens, a handful of dumplings, or a few strips of barbecued pork or chicken added for flavoring. Instead of a formal first course, they can be served together with other dishes at meals or as palate cleansers between courses. Diners sip them as a hot beverage, picking up the chopsticks only when they need to grab that hunk of shredded duck or bean curd from the bottom of the bowl. In comparison to heartier Italian minestrones or thick American split-pea porridges, Chinese soups are light and simple fares. That doesn't mean that Chinese cooks don't make hearty soups that could be meals in their own right. But even so, the typical Chinese soup is still a far cry from a thick chowder or a cream bisque.

Scrumptious Starters

What better way to start a meal, and this chapter, than with a few recipes for Chinese appetizer classics, as well as some updates on those traditional starter themes? I even include some Asian takes on Western favorites, too. So let's get the party rolling!

Cantonese Pickled Vegetables

This common Chinese side dish is normally served as a pre-meal appetizer but often isn't actually listed on restaurant menus. It highlights the Chinese knack for preserving perishable foods by pickling and brining.

Preparation time: *25 minutes (and 3 hours standing time)*

Yield: *4 to 6 servings*

1 cup julienned daikon (white radish)	*1½ teaspoons salt*
1 cup julienned carrots	*¼ cup rice vinegar or distilled white vinegar*
1 cup julienned cucumber	*2½ tablespoons sugar*

1 In a bowl, combine the daikon, carrots, cucumber, and salt; mix well. Let stand for 3 to 4 hours.

2 To make the pickling dressing, bring the vinegar and sugar to a boil in a small saucepan. Let cool.

3 Rinse the vegetables; drain well and return to the bowl. Add the vinegar mixture. Let it stand for another 3 hours at room temperature, or overnight in the refrigerator.

Tip: *Save the pickling dressing in a tightly covered container in the refrigerator for the next time you make pickled vegetables. You can even save the pickled vegetables in the fridge because they taste better after a day or two of chilling. Like a fine wine — and like a certain fine Chinese chef I see every time I look into the mirror — the more they age, the better they get!*

Chinese Chicken Salad

Guess what: Chinese chicken salad, like a number of dishes common in American-Chinese restaurants, is actually a Western invention. Even so, it's a simple, classic, and refreshing dish that successfully combines Asian flavors such as rice vinegar and sesame oil with the Western penchant for salads. Now, that's my idea of fusion cuisine. To keep the salad crisp and crunchy, be sure to dress it right before serving.

Preparation time: *30 minutes*

Cooking time: *7 to 8 minutes*

Yield: *4 to 6 servings*

⅓ cup rice vinegar	1½ cups shredded iceberg lettuce
2 tablespoons honey	1 cup julienned carrots
2 teaspoons hot pepper sauce or chile garlic sauce	½ red onion, julienned
2 teaspoons sesame oil	1½ cups shredded cooked chicken
1 teaspoon dry mustard	1 tablespoon toasted sesame seeds

1 To make the dressing, mix the rice vinegar, honey, hot pepper sauce, sesame oil, and dry mustard in a bowl and set aside.

2 Arrange the lettuce on a serving plate. In a small bowl, toss the carrots, onion, and chicken with the dressing. Place on top of the lettuce. Sprinkle with the toasted sesame seeds.

Vary It! *If you like your dressing richer and creamier, add 2 teaspoons chunky peanut butter and 1 tablespoon cooking oil to the other dressing ingredients and mix thoroughly. Or, to add extra crunch to the salad, deep-fry ¼-inch strips of wonton skins in 350-degree oil for a couple minutes until crisp and golden brown, and sprinkle them liberally over the top of the salad. If you don't feel like firing up the wok for deep-frying, just buy some already prepared crispy Chinese noodles — available in the Chinese food sections of most grocery stores — and sprinkle those on instead. A sprightly garnish of cilantro leaves improves the overall picture.*

It's a Wrap!

Much of dim sum making is all about wrapping. And as a future dim sum chef, you owe a great debt to the companies that produce and conveniently package fresh wrappers — they've done the work of rolling and cutting the dough for you. You can now find a wrapper with the right size, thickness, and shape to accommodate any appetizer you want to make.

- ✔ **Egg roll wrappers:** These classic wrappers are made from wheat flour, eggs, and water. The dough gets rolled into thin, large, pliable squares with a golden yellow, wheaty color. As the name implies, they are designed to wrap the crunchy American-Chinese restaurant favorite called the egg roll. But you can also wrap egg roll wrappers around other fillings: savory leftover vegetables and even dried fruit and crunchy nuts. Deep-fry these packages until they're golden brown, crispy-crunchy, and bubbly on the outside, and you have a tasty treat that dares you to stop at one. Dip the savory rolls in sweet-and-sour sauce or soy sauce for a complete treat.

- ✔ **Spring roll wrappers:** Unlike egg roll wrappers, spring roll wrappers contain no eggs — just wheat flour and water. Cooks pour the thin batter onto the wok surface and steam it to form a paper-thin pancake that is thinner than egg roll wrappers and a lighter, grayer color (due to the lack of eggs in the batter). Spring rolls also fry up crispier and have a smoother, lighter-textured surface.

  You can fill spring roll wrappers the same way you would egg roll wrappers — with precooked meats and vegetables — and then deep-fry them to make all kinds of delicious hot snacks. Dip them in a variety of different sauces such as soy sauce and Chinese hot mustard, or even Western Worcestershire sauce. Let your imagination guide you when enjoying these delicate delights.

  Don't try to make egg rolls with spring roll wrappers. Although the two are used in similar ways — and although many restaurants mistakenly call egg rolls spring rolls and vice versa — the finished items are not the same, nor are their respective wrappers.

- ✔ **Wonton and potsticker wrappers:** Like egg roll wrappers, wonton and potsticker wrappers contain eggs as well as wheat flour and water. Thus, they have the same texture and tawny color as their egg roll cousins. However, these wrappers are much smaller in size — usually around 3½ inches in diameter. They also come in a greater variety of thicknesses and shapes, from round, thin wrappers used to make siu mai, to the thicker wrappers for potstickers, and even to the traditional square shape used for wontons. The thickness and type of wrapper you choose depend ultimately on what you want to do with them. Thicker wrappers stand up better to deep-frying and pan-frying (they won't break when flipped inside the wok). Thinner wrappers work best in steamed dishes or as wrappers for soup dumplings.

If you can't find the round wrappers, just use a round cookie cutter or pair of scissors to cut a circle from a square wrapper. Store the wrappers in a zippered plastic bag in the refrigerator for up to a week or freeze them for up to several months. Defrost frozen wrappers in the bag so that they retain their moisture. When working with the wrappers, remove only a few from the bag at a time and cover the rest with a damp cloth to prevent drying.

Spring Rolls

The secret to making the perfect spring roll is having the oil hot enough, but not too hot. Make sure that you heat it to 360 degrees rapidly. Then comes the most important step: adding the spring rolls. Without them, all you have to show is a pot of hot oil! Serve the spring rolls hot with a dipping sauce. I recommend the All-Purpose Stir-Fry Sauce, the Sweet and Sour Sauce, or the Chinese Mustard Dip, all from Chapter 4 of Book VI, but any bottled dipping sauce works, too.

Preparation time: *1 hour*

Cooking time: *18 minutes*

Yield: *12 spring rolls*

Book VI

Chinese Cooking

6 dried black mushrooms	*⅛ teaspoon white pepper*
2 tablespoons cooking oil	*¼ cup chicken broth*
½ pound boneless pork, finely julienned	*1 cup bean sprouts*
1 cup shredded cabbage	*1½ teaspoons cornstarch dissolved in 1 tablespoon water*
2 green onions, coarsely chopped	*12 spring roll wrappers*
2 tablespoons oyster-flavored sauce	*Cooking oil for deep-frying*

1 Soak the mushrooms in warm water to cover until softened, about 20 minutes; drain. Discard the stems and thinly slice the caps.

2 To make the filling, place a wok over high heat until hot. Add the cooking oil, swirling to coat the sides. Add the pork; stir-fry for 2 minutes. Add the mushrooms and cabbage; stir-fry for 2 minutes. Add the green onions, oyster-flavored sauce, and white pepper; cook for 1 minute. Add the chicken broth and the bean sprouts; stir to coat. Add the cornstarch solution and cook, stirring, until the sauce boils and thickens. Remove from the heat and cool.

3 To make each spring roll, mound 2 heaping tablespoons filling across a wrapper (see Figure 6-1). Fold the bottom corner over the filling to cover and then fold over the right and left corners. Roll over once to enclose the filling. Brush the sides and top of the triangle with water. Fold over to seal. While filling the remaining spring rolls, cover the filled spring rolls with a dry towel to prevent drying.

4 In a wok, heat the cooking oil for deep-frying to 360 degrees. Carefully lower the spring rolls, several at a time, into the hot oil with a slotted spoon. Deep-fry, turning occasionally, until golden brown, 2 to 3 minutes. Remove with a slotted spoon; drain on paper towels.

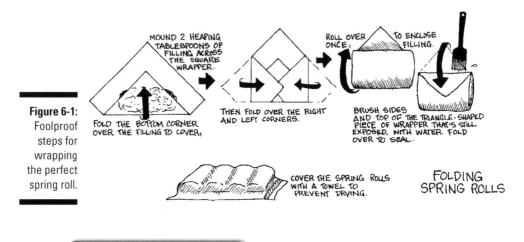

Figure 6-1: Foolproof steps for wrapping the perfect spring roll.

MOUND 2 HEAPING TABLESPOONS OF FILLING ACROSS THE SQUARE WRAPPER.

FOLD THE BOTTOM CORNER OVER THE FILLING TO COVER,

THEN FOLD OVER THE RIGHT AND LEFT CORNERS.

ROLL OVER ONCE, TO ENCLOSE FILLING.

BRUSH SIDES AND TOP OF THE TRIANGLE-SHAPED PIECE OF WRAPPER THAT'S STILL EXPOSED, WITH WATER. FOLD OVER TO SEAL.

COVER THE SPRING ROLLS WITH A TOWEL TO PREVENT DRYING.

FOLDING SPRING ROLLS

Crispy Wontons

One is never enough with these snacks. To save time, fold your crispy wontons in advance and then freeze them in a single layer on a baking sheet. If they touch while freezing, they tend to stick together; and when you try to separate them, they'll crumble. After the wontons have been individually frozen, you can store them in freezer bags. When you're ready, fry them straight from the freezer by using the instructions in this recipe, but just remember to let them fry a little longer because they'll need extra time to fully cook and brown. In fact, all these "wrappetizers" work well when made ahead, frozen individually, and fried later. Just goes to show how convenient Chinese cooking is.

Preparation time: *1 hour and 45 minutes*

Cooking time: *50 minutes*

Yield: *48 wontons*

¼ pound medium raw shrimp, shelled and deveined

¼ pound ground pork

6 whole water chestnuts, finely chopped

3 tablespoons minced green onions

2 tablespoons oyster-flavored sauce

2 teaspoons wine

1 teaspoon sesame oil

2 teaspoons cornstarch

48 wonton wrappers

1 egg, lightly beaten

Cooking oil for deep-frying

1 To make the wonton filling: With a cleaver, chop the shrimp into a fine paste (or use a food processor). Place the chopped shrimp in a bowl with the pork, water chestnuts, green onions, oyster-flavored sauce, wine, sesame oil, and cornstarch; mix well.

2 To make each wonton, place 1 heaping teaspoon filling in the center of a wonton wrapper, as shown in Figure 6-2; keep the remaining wrappers covered to prevent drying.

3 Brush the edges of the wrapper with the beaten egg; fold the wrapper in half to form a triangle and pinch the edges to seal.

4 Pull the two opposite corners together, moisten one corner with the egg, and overlap with another corner; press to seal. Cover the filled wontons with a dry towel to prevent drying.

5 In a wok, heat the cooking oil to 350 degrees. Deep-fry the wontons, a few at a time, turning occasionally, until golden brown, 3 to 3½ minutes. Remove with a slotted spoon and drain on paper towels. Keep them warm in a 200-degree oven while cooking the remaining wontons.

Book VI

Chinese Cooking

Vary It! *Making the filling for these wontons gives you a great opportunity to try dried black mushrooms. (See Chapter 2 of Book VI for an introduction to dried black mushrooms.) Most traditional wonton fillings include them, soaked and finely chopped to the same size as the rest of the filling's ingredients. If you're in a mushroom mood, go ahead and add some.*

Figure 6-2: Step-by-step instructions for wrapping crispy wontons.

PLACE 1 HEAPING TEASPOON OF FILLING IN THE CENTER OF THE WRAPPER.

BRUSH THE EDGES OF THE WRAPPER WITH THE BEATEN EGG.

FOLD THE WRAPPER IN HALF TO FORM A TRIANGLE. PINCH EDGES TO SEAL.

PULL 2 OPPOSITE CORNERS TOGETHER. MOISTEN ONE CORNER WITH EGG. OVERLAP WITH OTHER CORNER. PRESS TO SEAL.

FOLDING WONTONS

Potstickers

Not too long ago, potstickers, called "Beijing dumplings" in some places, were practically unheard of in the West. Not anymore, thankfully. These little dumplings have become almost as popular in American-Chinese restaurants as the tried-and-true egg rolls and wontons. The combination of steaming and pan-frying gives their wrapper's texture an irresistible balance between smooth and noodlelike on top, and crispy and caramelized on the bottom.

By the way, despite the name, I recommend that you brown the bottom of the dumplings without letting them stick to the wok or pan. Nonstick pans can help you prepare this recipe correctly. You want a potsticker, not a potstucker.

Preparation time: *1 hour*

Cooking time: *About 30 minutes*

Yield: *30 potstickers*

8 dried black mushrooms	*2 teaspoons Chinese rice wine*
4 cups shredded napa cabbage	*1 teaspoon sesame oil*
1 teaspoon salt	*1½ tablespoons cornstarch*
¾ pound ground pork, chicken, or beef	*¼ teaspoon white pepper*
4 green onions, chopped	*30 potsticker wrappers*
1½ tablespoons minced ginger	*3 tablespoons cooking oil*
2 tablespoons oyster-flavored sauce	*1 cup chicken broth*

1 Soak the mushrooms in warm water to cover until softened, about 20 minutes; drain. Discard the stems and mince the caps.

2 In a large bowl, toss the napa cabbage with the salt; squeeze to remove the excess liquid.

3 To make the filling, combine the mushrooms, napa cabbage, ground pork, green onions, ginger, oyster-flavored sauce, rice wine, sesame oil, cornstarch, and white pepper in a bowl; mix well.

4 To make each potsticker (see Figure 6-3), place a heaping teaspoon of the filling in the center of a potsticker wrapper; keep the remaining wrappers covered to prevent drying. Brush the edges of the wrapper with water; fold the wrapper in half, crimping one side, to form a semicircle. Pinch the edges together to seal. Set the potsticker, seam side up, in a baking pan. Cover the potstickers with a wet towel to prevent drying.

5 Place a wide frying pan over medium heat until hot. Add 1 tablespoon of the cooking oil. Add 10 potstickers, seam side up; cook until the bottoms are golden brown, about 3 minutes. Add ⅓ cup chicken broth; reduce the heat to low, cover, and cook until the liquid is absorbed, 4 to 5 minutes. Remove from the heat. Repeat with the remaining potstickers, cooking oil, and chicken broth.

Tip: Most potsticker wrappers come in 1-pound packages. The number of actual wrappers in a 1-pound package varies depending on the wrapper thickness. But because potsticker wrappers should be a little bit on the thick side to survive pan-frying without tearing, scope out those packages that appear to have fewer, thicker wrappers.

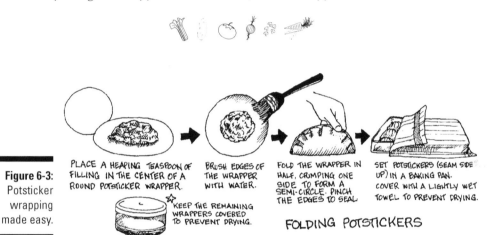

Figure 6-3: Potsticker wrapping made easy.

PLACE A HEAPING TEASPOON OF FILLING IN THE CENTER OF A ROUND POTSTICKER WRAPPER.

BRUSH EDGES OF THE WRAPPER WITH WATER.

FOLD THE WRAPPER IN HALF, CRIMPING ONE SIDE TO FORM A SEMI-CIRCLE. PINCH THE EDGES TO SEAL.

SET POTSTICKERS (SEAM SIDE UP) IN A BAKING PAN. COVER WITH A LIGHTLY WET TOWEL TO PREVENT DRYING.

☆ KEEP THE REMAINING WRAPPERS COVERED TO PREVENT DRYING.

FOLDING POTSTICKERS

Chinese Soup for the Soul and Body

Although soup is associated with home-cooked meals in every culture, the Chinese regard it as the premier comfort food. The recipe road to any good chicken stock has its secret twists and turns, and there are just as many paths as there are travelers. But a few key elements distinguish Chinese chicken broth from its Western counterpart. The key difference that sets the classic Chinese chicken broth apart from Western stocks is the lack of a *mire poix* — that classic French combination of onions, carrots, celery, and bay leaf that flavor Western broths. Instead, Chinese stocks get their flavors from ginger and green onion — maybe even a little rice wine if the cook's feeling frisky.

Chinese Chicken Broth

Don't even think of throwing away that chicken after you use it to make your broth! Although most of its flavor gets distilled into the stock, its shredded meat still makes a delicious treat when dipped in a little oyster-flavored sauce. Should you choose to make the stock with just the chicken, duck, or turkey bones, remember to use three to four carcasses — you need the extra bones to boost the stock's flavor.

Preparation time: *10 minutes*

Cooking time: *2 hours*

Yield: *About 9 cups*

1 whole chicken (about 3 pounds)	*⅛ teaspoon salt*
8 slices ginger, lightly crushed	*⅛ teaspoon white pepper*
6 green onions, halved	

1 Clean the chicken by removing the giblets and extra fat.

2 Place the chicken in a large pot and add enough cold water to cover. Add the ginger, green onions, salt, and white pepper; bring to a boil. Skim off any foam that forms. Reduce the heat and simmer, covered, for 2 hours. Strain.

Vary It! *Pork, fish, and ham bones, vegetable scraps, and any other flavorful ingredients lying around the kitchen are all fair game for making a rich, succulent Chinese soup stock, too.*

Tip: *Skimming the fat from the top of a warm or hot broth can be particularly tricky because, at high temperatures, the fat liquefies and blends right in with the broth. Refrigerating the pot of broth or placing it in an ice bath reduces the temperature to the point where the fat solidifies, allowing you to easily scoop it off the broth's surface.*

Egg Flower Soup

Sometimes called egg drop soup, this version of egg flower soup is surprisingly quick and easy to make. It's a great dish when your cupboards are almost bare and you just can't summon the energy to fix anything more complicated.

Preparation time: *12 minutes*

Cooking time: *About 15 minutes*

Yield: *4 to 6 servings*

Book VI

Chinese Cooking

6 cups chicken broth

1 tablespoon wine

¼ cup julienned carrots

1 cup snow peas, stem ends snapped off and fibrous strings removed

1 teaspoon cornstarch dissolved in 2 teaspoons of water

1 sheet 8-x-7-inch nori, cut into ⅛-inch strips

1 egg, lightly beaten

1 teaspoon sesame oil

⅛ teaspoon salt

⅛ teaspoon white pepper

1 In a medium soup pot, bring the chicken broth and wine to a boil. Reduce the heat and simmer for 5 minutes. Add the carrots and snow peas; cook for 30 to 40 seconds.

2 Add the cornstarch solution and cook, stirring, until the soup comes to a boil. Stir in the nori. Turn off the heat.

3 Slowly pour in the egg, stirring with a chopstick in a circular motion until long threads form. Stir in the sesame oil, salt, and white pepper.

Vary It! *To give this recipe a little bit more green, add baby bok choy, spinach, or any other leafy green that you like. And to create a more substantial soup for those meat lovers, a half cup of leftover barbecued pork, cooked shrimp, or ham lunch meat also makes a nice addition.*

Hot and Sour Soup

You can adjust the heat and bite of this Chinese restaurant classic by experimenting with the amounts of white pepper and vinegar you add. Keep in mind, however, that the Sichuan cooks who concocted it didn't name it hot and sour soup for nothing — like most of the foods from that region, it's supposed to be fiery. But finding the right balance between the hot and the sour tastes is still the secret to this creation.

Preparation time: *35 minutes*

Cooking time: *20 minutes*

Yield: *4 to 6 servings*

4 dried black mushrooms	⅔ cup white vinegar
2 cloud ears	1 tablespoon dark soy sauce
6 cups chicken broth	½ teaspoon salt
4 ounces pork, shredded	1 teaspoon white pepper
½ cup julienned bamboo shoots	4 tablespoons cornstarch dissolved in 5 tablespoons water
1 cup julienned firm tofu	

1 In separate bowls, soak the mushrooms and cloud ears in warm water to cover until softened, about 20 minutes; drain. Discard the stems of the mushrooms; cut the cloud ears and the mushroom caps into thin strips.

2 In a medium soup pot, bring the chicken broth to a boil. Add the pork, mushrooms, cloud ears, and bamboo shoots; cook for 3 to 4 minutes. Add the tofu, vinegar, soy sauce, salt, and white pepper; cook for 1 to 2 minutes. Add the cornstarch solution and cook, stirring, until the soup boils and thickens.

Tip: *To guarantee uniform cooking in this soup, cut all the ingredients into the same dimensions. In this case, that means cutting or shredding them into thin strips.*

Wonton Soup

Who doesn't crave a bowl of savory wonton soup? Maybe I should ask who does crave one right this moment. Lucky for you, you can make it yourself in a jiff with this simple recipe. Just use the wonton recipe in this chapter to prepare the wontons themselves — but don't fry them, of course — and you're well on your way to enjoying this ever-present Chinese restaurant favorite.

Preparation time: *10 minutes*

Cooking time: *12 minutes*

Yield: *4 servings*

Book VI

Chinese Cooking

20 premade wontons	*½ teaspoon sesame oil*
6 cups chicken broth	*1 teaspoon salt*
½ cup julienned carrots	*⅛ teaspoon white pepper*
4 to 6 whole baby bok choy, quartered lengthwise	

1 Bring a pot of water to a boil. Add the wontons and cook for about 4 minutes; drain.

2 In a medium soup pot, bring the chicken broth to a boil. Add the carrots and baby bok choy; cook until the vegetables are tender-crisp, 2 to 3 minutes. Add the sesame oil, salt, white pepper, and cooked wontons. Cook until they are heated through.

Tip: *Cook the wontons right before you add them to the soup — if you let them sit around too long, they'll stick together. If you wish, you can even cook them in the soup stock itself, but you may end up with a starchier, cloudier soup.*

Chapter 7

The Main Event

In This Chapter

- Cooking fish to perfection
- Making chicken, Chinese style
- Beefing up your menu
- Working wonders with tofu
- Cooking vegetables the right way

This chapter is the heart and soul of the book. I start by presenting the dishes that you know and love from menus at your favorite Chinese restaurants. In addition to those classics, this chapter includes a few dishes that may not be too familiar on this side of the Pacific, as well as updates and twists on the tried-and-true, just to keep you on your toes.

Swimming with the Best of Them: Seafood

Ah, fresh seafood! It's a topic near and dear to my heart, and even nearer to my stomach.

Cooking your fish with a Chinese accent is a lot easier than you may think. The Chinese love to steam fish because this simple cooking method accentuates the clean, natural flavor of the fish. Just add a little simple seasoning from a marinade of green onions, soy sauce, sugar, and pepper, and the result is pure magic.

Deep-frying is also a popular way to prepare fish in China. A particularly festive New Year's dish is a deep-fried whole fish garnished with green onions and topped with a sweet and sour sauce whose red color symbolizes life, energy, wealth, and prosperity. It makes me feel successful — and hungry — just thinking about it!

Braised Fish Hunan Style

Hunan province in central China is known for having spicy cuisine similar to that in neighboring Sichuan, and this recipe proves it. And even though both regions are miles from the nearest coast, their rivers and lakes provide plenty of freshwater fish perfect for pairing with the zesty sauce in this recipe.

Preparation time: *15 minutes*

Cooking time: *10 minutes*

Yield: *4 servings*

1 pound fish steaks or fillets, about 1 inch thick	1 teaspoon chile garlic sauce
1/4 teaspoon salt	1 teaspoon sesame oil
1/4 cup chicken broth	1/2 teaspoon soy sauce
2 tablespoons Chinese rice wine	2 tablespoons cooking oil
2 teaspoons black bean garlic sauce	1 green onion, thinly sliced
1 1/2 teaspoons sugar	1 teaspoon cornstarch dissolved in 2 teaspoons water

1 Cut the fish into 4 pieces. Pat the fish dry with a paper towel. Rub the salt all over; let stand for 10 minutes.

2 Make the sauce: Combine the chicken broth, rice wine, black bean garlic sauce, sugar, chile garlic sauce, sesame oil, and soy sauce in a bowl.

3 Place a wok over high heat until hot. Add the cooking oil, swirling to coat the sides. Reduce the heat to medium and add the fish; pan-fry until golden brown, about 2 minutes on each side.

4 Add the sauce and bring to a boil. Add the green onion, cover, and braise over low heat for 3 to 5 minutes. Add the cornstarch solution and cook, stirring, until the sauce boils and thickens.

Vary It! *Any type of firm, moist white fish works in this dish. Choose one with a slightly fatty texture to provide a counterpoint to the sauce's piquancy. My personal favorites are sea bass, cod, and halibut.*

Most of the seafood dishes on any Chinese restaurant menu feature some sort of shellfish: kung pao shrimp, wok seared scallops, crab with ginger and green onion, just to name a few. Chinese chefs crave shellfish of all sizes and shapes. Shrimp, scallops, crab, lobster, clams, oysters, and mussels all rank highly in their books. Whether steamed, fried, stir-fried, served with a savory sauce, or accompanied by a simple salt-and-pepper dip, shellfish sure get the royal treatment in China.

Sweet and Sour Shrimp

Book VI

Chinese
Cooking

Every American-Chinese restaurant has its own version of this North American favorite. Now you can make it at home by using the Sweet and Sour Sauce from Chapter 4 of Book VI. If you can't resist giving it a little more restaurant flair, add some colorful contrast with red and green bell peppers and juicy cubes of pineapple.

Preparation time: *12 minutes*

Cooking time: *10 minutes*

Yield: *4 servings*

1 pound medium raw shrimp, shelled and deveined (see the sidebar "In vein or not in vein" for instructions)	*2 stalks celery, cut at an angle, ¼-inch thick*
	⅔ cup Sweet and Sour Sauce (see Chapter 4 of Book VI)
1 teaspoon minced garlic	*¼ cup chicken broth*
1 teaspoon minced ginger	*½ cup canned pineapple chunks*
¼ teaspoon white pepper	*¼ cup crystallized ginger chips (optional)*
1½ tablespoons cooking oil	

1 Combine the shrimp, garlic, ginger, and white pepper in a bowl. Let stand for 10 minutes.

2 Place a wok over high heat until hot. Add the oil, swirling to coat the sides. Add the shrimp and cook until they turn pink, about 2 minutes. Remove and set aside.

3 Add the celery; stir-fry for 1 to 2 minutes. Add the Sweet and Sour Sauce and the chicken broth; cook until the sauce boils and reduces slightly. Add the pineapple and return the shrimp to the wok; stir to coat well.

4 To serve, place the shrimp on a serving plate and garnish with the ginger chips, if desired.

Coming out of their shells:
Easy instructions for shelling shrimp

I grew up eating shrimp cooked with the shell, tail, and even the head left on. Chinese cooks still normally prepare shrimp this way, for a number of reasons. For one, shrimp with the shells and head intact retain a more intense, fresh-shrimp flavor that you just can't get from shelled shrimp. Also, these little shields of armor protect the shrimp from being overcooked and help keep their shape.

But what if you find staring your shrimp in the face a little disarming and you would rather remove the shells in the kitchen than at the table? If so, you can easily take them off before cooking by following these steps and the instructions in the accompanying figure. By the way, the shells are excellent candidates for making a shrimp broth, so be sure to save them. (These instructions work equally well for raw and cooked shrimp.)

1. **Holding the shrimp by the tail with one hand, use the thumb and forefinger of the free hand to grasp the shrimp's legs and edge of the shell.**

2. **Simply pull the legs and shell off the shrimp. They should easily slip off in one piece.**

3. **Leave the shrimp's tail intact for a slightly fancier presentation or pull it off to save you work at the dinner table.**

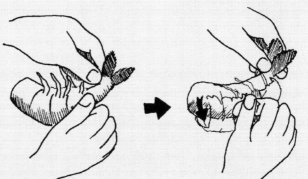

HOLD THE SHRIMP BY THE TAIL WITH ONE HAND. USE THE THUMB AND FOREFINGER OF THE FREE HAND TO GRASP THE SHRIMP'S LEGS AND EDGE OF SHELL.

PULL THE LEGS AND SHELL OFF THE SHRIMP. THEY SHOULD EASILY SLIP OFF IN ONE PIECE.

☆ LEAVE THE TAIL INTACT FOR A FANCIER PRESENTATION OR PULL OFF FOR A COMPLETELY NAKED SHRIMP.

PEELING SHRIMP

In vein or not in vein

Although the little black veins that run along the backs of shrimp aren't dangerous, poisonous, or otherwise hazardous to eat, they're definitely unappetizing. Most cooks remove these gritty, slightly muddy-tasting, and just plain ugly tubes before cooking the shrimp. If you're in a big pinch for time, you can safely leave them in the shrimp, but the resulting dish will suffer for it. And although most markets sell deveined shrimp — at a higher price, of course — extracting these mini-intestinal tracts yourself actually doesn't take much work.

You can buy little gadgets such as plastic deveiners at your local kitchen supply shop, but they're not much more helpful than a simple paring knife. Hold the shrimp under cold, running water and make a shallow slit with a knife down the shrimp's back along the line of the vein. Then wash the vein and grit away with the water, as depicted in the accompanying figure.

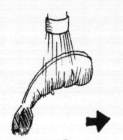

HOLD THE SHRIMP UNDER COLD, RUNNING WATER.

MAKE A SHALLOW SLIT WITH A KNIFE DOWN THE SHRIMP'S BACK ALONG THE LINE OF THE VEIN.

WASH THE VEIN AND GRIT AWAY WITH THE WATER.

DEVEINING SHRIMP

Book VI

Chinese Cooking

Crying Fowl: Poultry

In recent years, chicken has become the darling in Western kitchens. Consumers appreciate it as a healthy, versatile source of protein, inexpensive as well as nutritious, and low in fat when prepared the right way. Its mild character makes it the perfect partner to a variety of flavorings and cooking methods. Chinese cooks have recognized this versatility for ages. They fry, roast, steam, and boil the whole bird; stir-fry dices, shreds, or slices of it; mince it for dumpling stuffings; and turn its carcasses into luscious soups. It's the meat with a million uses!

Kung Pao Chicken

In recent years, kung pao chicken has gotten a bad rap in the Western press as a "typical fattening Chinese meal." The truth is, like any other dish, Chinese or otherwise, it's only as fattening as its ingredients and the techniques used to prepare them. Although some American-Chinese restaurants deep-fry the chicken pieces and add a generous portion of oil to the sauce, this is not how cooks in China normally prepare kung pao chicken. By stir-frying skinless lean chicken in minimal oil, you can create a lean, delicious dish that beats the stereotypes. Make sure to use skinned peanuts for this recipe.

Preparation time: *10 minutes*

Cooking time: *10 minutes*

Yield: *4 servings*

1 tablespoon oyster-flavored sauce	*1 teaspoon minced garlic*
1 tablespoon Chinese rice wine	*6 whole dried red chiles, halved*
½ teaspoon cornstarch	*1 red bell pepper, cut into ½-inch dice*
¾ pound boneless, skinless chicken, cut into ½-inch cubes	*1 green bell pepper, cut into ½-inch dice*
3 tablespoons chicken broth	*1 cup sliced bamboo shoots*
2 tablespoons white vinegar	*½ teaspoon cornstarch dissolved in 1 teaspoon water*
2 tablespoons dark soy sauce	*⅓ cup unsalted roasted peanuts, walnuts, or cashew nuts*
2 teaspoons sugar	
1½ tablespoons cooking oil	

1 Combine the oyster-flavored sauce, rice wine, and cornstarch in a bowl to make a marinade. Add the chicken and stir to coat. Let stand for 10 minutes.

2 Make a sauce by combining the chicken broth, vinegar, dark soy sauce, and sugar in a bowl.

3 Place a wok over high heat until hot. Add the oil, swirling to coat the sides. Add the garlic and chiles; cook, stirring until fragrant, about 10 seconds. Add the chicken and stir-fry for 3 minutes.

4 Add the red and green bell peppers and bamboo shoots; stir-fry for 1 minute. Add the sauce; bring it to a boil. Add the cornstarch solution and cook, stirring until the sauce boils and thickens. Add the peanuts and stir to coat.

Honey Garlic Chicken

Honey's smoothness mellows the intense flavor of 12 cloves of garlic in this simple stir-fry. Pairing the two may not seem like an obvious combination at first, but after trying this honey of a sauce, I bet you'll be sweet on it yourself.

Preparation time: *15 minutes*

Cooking time: *8 minutes*

Yield: *4 servings*

Book VI

Chinese Cooking

2 tablespoons oyster-flavored sauce	1 tablespoon dark soy sauce
1 tablespoon Chinese rice wine	2 tablespoons honey
1 teaspoon cornstarch	1½ tablespoons cooking oil
⅛ teaspoon Chinese five-spice powder	12 cloves garlic, crushed
1 pound boneless, skinless chicken, cut into 1-inch cubes	3 whole dried red chiles
⅓ cup chicken broth	1 cup cubed water chestnuts or jícama (½-inch pieces)

1 To make the marinade, combine the oyster-flavored sauce, rice wine, cornstarch, and five-spice powder in a bowl. Add the chicken and stir to coat. Let stand for 10 minutes.

2 To make the sauce, combine the chicken broth, soy sauce, and honey in a bowl.

3 Place a wok over high heat until hot. Add the oil, swirling to coat the sides. Add the garlic; cook, stirring, until golden brown, about 2 minutes. Add the chiles and cook until fragrant, about 10 seconds. Add the chicken and stir-fry until done, 4 to 5 minutes. Add the water chestnuts and the sauce; bring to a boil until the sauce reduces slightly and the chicken is fully glazed, about 2 minutes.

Remember: *If the thought of peeling 12 cloves of garlic drives you out of your own skin, remember that a good smash with the flat of your knife's blade makes quick work of slipping off those papery peels.*

Lemon Chicken

Another Cantonese classic, this citrusy treatment of chicken combines sweet and sour flavors with savory meats. No wonder you find versions of it on almost every Chinese restaurant menu in the West.

Preparation time: *15 minutes*

Cooking time: *15 minutes*

Yield: *4 servings*

⅓ cup chicken broth	¼ teaspoon white pepper
⅓ cup fresh lemon juice	¾ pound boneless, skinless chicken breasts, butterflied
½ teaspoon dark soy sauce	
¼ cup packed brown sugar	¼ cup cornstarch
2 teaspoons lemon zest	⅓ cup cooking oil
1 egg	1½ teaspoons cornstarch dissolved in 1 tablespoon water
½ teaspoon salt	
	1 teaspoon toasted sesame seeds

1 Make a sauce by combining the chicken broth, lemon juice, soy sauce, brown sugar, and lemon zest in a small saucepan; set aside.

2 In a bowl, beat the egg lightly with the salt and white pepper. Dredge the chicken with the cornstarch; dip into the egg batter and dredge in the cornstarch again. Let it stand for 5 minutes. Just before cooking, shake off the excess cornstarch.

3 In a wok, heat the oil until hot. Pan-fry the chicken, a couple pieces at a time, turning occasionally, until golden brown, about 3 minutes on each side. Remove with a slotted spoon and drain on paper towels.

4 Bring the sauce to a boil over medium heat; add the cornstarch solution and cook, stirring, until the sauce boils and thickens.

5 Cut the chicken across the grain into ½-inch slices. Place the chicken on a serving plate. Pour the sauce on top and sprinkle with the sesame seeds.

Tip: *The breast, with its tenderness and mild flavor, works best for lemon chicken, as does a simple garnish of lemon slices and cilantro. The lemon echoes the citrusy sauce, while the cilantro brings its own bright colors and flavor notes to the dish.*

Tip: *Toast the sesame seeds before adding them to this recipe. Toasting rids the seeds of any raw flavor and enhances their warm nuttiness. It gives them a prettier color, too.*

Moo-ve In and Pig Out: Beef and Pork

Throughout China's history, eating high on the hoof has been a real luxury. Meat is traditionally expensive and scarce; hence, the Chinese don't consume as much of it as Westerners do. But then, absence can make the meat grow fonder. Chinese cooks employ meats to complement and enhance, rather than overpower, the vegetables, starches, and other ingredients in dishes.

Even loyal porterhouse aficionados will be impressed by the Chinese style of meat eating. You'll be surprised by just how easy it is to stretch out a relatively small cut of meat when it's part of a meal's ensemble cast rather than its starring lead. So don't limit yourself to the same old T-bone and pork tenderloin. Give the Chinese way a try and see how quickly you trade in your carving knife for a pair of chopsticks.

When preparing meat for any of these recipes, remember to cut it across the grain. That means identifying the direction in which the meat's fibers run and making your slices perpendicular to that direction. Doing so makes for a more tender cut of meat and a much more forgiving chewing experience. The bundled fibers of a crosscut piece of meat essentially "unbundle" easily with chewing, whereas the long, stringy meat fibers of a chunk cut along the grain just never seem to break down no matter how long you gnaw on them. In fact, even the tenderest meat cut along the grain is a challenge to chew compared to a tougher cut of crosscut meat.

Although marinated and crosscut flank steak works well for stir-fry, I suggest more tender parts of the round and even the shoulder for other beef dishes. (Ask your supermarket's meat department manager to direct you to those more tender choices.) They contain plenty of collagen that, when braised or stewed for a long time, melts into the cooking liquid and sauce to give it a rich, mouth-pleasing, gelatinous texture that I absolutely adore. Even though the round may cost you a little more than some other cuts, the texture and flavor are more than worth the higher price.

Sweet and Sour Pork

This recipe pays its respects to one of the most popular dishes in American-Chinese restaurants, and it does a pretty good job of it to boot. Everything from the lightly crispy pork to the mildly tangy sauce with bell pepper, onion, and pineapple chunks will take you back to your favorite neighborhood spot for Chinese food. I take the liberty of making one change, however: Many restaurant versions dip the pork in a heavy batter before deep-frying. I've lightened the dish by coating the pork in a light dusting of cornstarch instead. This method is simpler and less greasy, but it still achieves that delightful crispiness that makes sweet and sour pork such a winner.

Preparation time: *12 minutes*

Cooking time: *15 minutes*

Yield: *4 servings*

1 cup Sweet and Sour Sauce (see Chapter 4 of Book VI)

¼ cup chicken broth

¾ pound boneless pork, cut into ¾-inch cubes

½ cup cornstarch

2 tablespoons cooking oil

½ cup diced onion (½-inch)

½ cup diced green bell pepper (½-inch)

¾ cup pineapple chunks

1 Combine the Sweet and Sour Sauce and chicken broth in a bowl.

2 Dust the pork with the cornstarch.

3 Place a wok over high heat until hot. Add 1 tablespoon of the oil, swirling to coat the sides. Add the pork and stir-fry until golden brown, about 3 minutes. Remove and drain on paper towels. Keep warm.

4 Return the wok to high heat; add the remaining oil, swirling to coat the sides. Add the onion; stir-fry for 2 minutes. Add the bell pepper; stir-fry for 1 minute.

5 Reduce the heat to medium-high. Add the sauce, stirring until the sauce boils and thickens. Return the pork to the wok and add the pineapple chunks; turn to heat through, about 1 minute.

Vary It! *Whether store-bought or homemade from the recipe in Chapter 4 of Book VI, any sweet and sour sauce that gets your mouth watering is good enough for this recipe.*

Mu Shu Pork

To make this simple pork, vegetable, and mushroom stir-fry officially mu shu, you should eat it the way people do in China and in Chinese restaurants. That means wrapping a few tablespoons of the meat and vegetable mixture in thin, crêpelike Mandarin pancakes that you've spread with some hoisin sauce. Chinese groceries carry the pancakes, and if you're lucky, your supermarket may have a selection as well. But if you can't find Mandarin pancakes, flour tortillas make a convenient substitute.

Preparation time: *25 minutes*

Cooking time: *15 minutes*

Yield: *4 servings*

Book VI

**Chinese
Cooking**

6 dried black mushrooms	*3 cups julienned cabbage*
4 cloud ears or wood ears (see Chapter 2 of Book VI)	*1 cup julienned carrots*
	2 green onions, julienned
¼ cup chicken broth	*1½ teaspoons cornstarch dissolved in 1 tablespoon water*
2 tablespoons soy sauce	
1 tablespoon cooking oil	*3 tablespoons hoisin sauce*
2 teaspoons minced garlic	*10 to 12 tortilla wraps*
½ pound boneless pork, julienned	

1 In separate bowls, soak the mushrooms and the cloud ears or wood ears in warm water to cover until softened, about 20 minutes; drain. Discard the mushroom stems and thinly slice the mushroom caps and the cloud ears.

2 Make the sauce by combining the chicken broth and soy sauce in a bowl.

3 Place a wok over high heat until hot. Add the oil, swirling to coat the sides. Add the garlic and cook, stirring, until fragrant, about 10 seconds. Add the pork and stir-fry until lightly browned, about 2 minutes. Add the mushrooms, cloud ears, cabbage, and carrots; stir-fry for 1 to 2 minutes. Add the green onions and sauce; bring it to a boil. Add the cornstarch solution and cook, stirring, until the sauce boils and thickens.

4 To eat: Spread ½ teaspoon hoisin sauce on a tortilla wrap and place about 1½ tablespoons mu shu mixture over the sauce and serve.

Vary 1t! *A quick glance at a Chinese restaurant menu shows that mu shu dishes are the picture of versatility: mu shu pork, mu shu chicken, mu shu vegetables, combination mu shu . . . you get the picture. So mu shu any way you want to, adding new ingredients and taking others out.*

Steamed Cabbage Rolls

Do you ever wonder why the cuisines of so many different cultures include at least some version of stuffed cabbage rolls? One bite of these tasty packets — plump with ground pork, shrimp, and crunchy water chestnuts and topped with a sauce made with the steaming juices — and you'll understand why they're such winners in China.

Preparation time: *1 hour*

Cooking time: *15 minutes*

Yield: *14 rolls*

7 large cabbage leaves	*2 tablespoons soy sauce*
½ pound ground pork	*¼ teaspoon white pepper*
¼ pound medium raw shrimp, shelled, deveined, and coarsely chopped	*1 teaspoon chile garlic sauce*
½ cup minced water chestnuts	*¾ cup chicken broth*
¼ cup minced green onions	*1 tablespoon oyster-flavored sauce*
2 tablespoons wine	*2 tablespoons cornstarch dissolved in 4 tablespoons water*

1 Bring a pot of water to a boil; blanch the cabbage leaves just until slightly limp, 5 to 7 minutes. Drain, rinse with cold water, and drain again. Cut the leaves in half and discard the thick center rib.

2 Make the filling by combining the ground pork, shrimp, water chestnuts, green onions, wine, soy sauce, and white pepper in a bowl.

3 Make the sauce by combining the chile garlic sauce, chicken broth, and oyster-flavored sauce in a small saucepan.

4 To make each roll: Place a cabbage leaf on a clean, flat work surface with the stem end facing you. Spread about 1 tablespoon of the filling in a band near the bottom of the leaf. Roll the leaf tightly to enclose the filling. Arrange the rolls on a heatproof dish in a single layer. (If you're a little rusty as to how to actually roll the cabbage rolls, the steps as illustrated in Figure 7-1 should help clear things up for you.)

5 Prepare a wok for steaming (see Chapter 3 of Book VI). Steam the rolls over high heat until the filling is no longer pink, 12 to 14 minutes. When the rolls are cooked, transfer them to a serving platter. Pour the steaming juices into the saucepan with the sauce. Bring to a boil. Add the cornstarch solution and cook, stirring, until the sauce boils and thickens.

6 To serve, pour the sauce over the rolls.

Tip: *Regular head cabbage, which is the best choice for this recipe, is very dense and compact, and the leaves are sometimes hard to remove without tearing. Try this trick to keep your cabbage leaves in one piece: Core the cabbage with a paring knife. Meanwhile, heat a pot of water to boiling. Slide the whole head of cabbage into the water and blanch for 1 minute; remove from the pot. Now that the cabbage has softened from blanching, easily lift off as many large leaves as you need. Remove the heart of the remaining cabbage, rinse with cold water until it's cooled, and save it for another recipe.*

Book VI

Chinese Cooking

Remember: *The recipe recommends that you blanch the individual cabbage leaves for 1 to 2 minutes before rolling. If you decide instead to blanch the whole head of cabbage as outlined in the preceding tip, reduce the blanch time for the individual leaves to just 1 minute.*

ROLLING STEAMED PORK AND CABBAGE ROLLS

Figure 7-1: Step-by-step instructions for neatly wrapping pork-stuffed cabbage rolls.

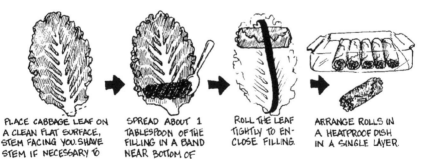

PLACE CABBAGE LEAF ON A CLEAN FLAT SURFACE, STEM FACING YOU. SHAVE STEM IF NECESSARY TO MAKE ROLLING EASIER.

SPREAD ABOUT 1 TABLESPOON OF THE FILLING IN A BAND NEAR BOTTOM OF THE LEAF.

ROLL THE LEAF TIGHTLY TO ENCLOSE FILLING.

ARRANGE ROLLS IN A HEATPROOF DISH IN A SINGLE LAYER.

Broccoli Beef

Even the most committed broccoliphobe will have a hard time resisting this popular restaurant dish. And because it's so easy to prepare, it makes a great quick and nutritious lunch when served over plain steamed rice. Try it — it'll make your mother proud.

Preparation time: *15 minutes*

Cooking time: *6 minutes*

Yield: *4 servings*

1 tablespoon soy sauce	1 tablespoon dark soy sauce
1 tablespoon Chinese rice wine	1 teaspoon sesame oil
2 teaspoons cornstarch	2 tablespoons cooking oil
¾ pound tri-tip or flank steak, thinly sliced across the grain	2 cloves garlic, thinly sliced
	8 ounces broccoli florets
2 tablespoons oyster-flavored sauce	¾ cup chicken broth

1 Make the marinade by combining the soy sauce, rice wine, and cornstarch in a bowl. Add the beef and stir to coat. Let stand for 10 minutes. Make the sauce by combining the oyster-flavored sauce, dark soy sauce, and sesame oil in a bowl.

2 Place a wok over high heat until hot. Add the cooking oil, swirling to coat the sides. Add the garlic and cook, stirring, until fragrant, about 10 seconds. Add the beef; stir-fry until barely pink, about 1 minute. Add the sauce and cook for 1 minute. Remove the beef and place in the center of a serving plate.

3 Add the broccoli and chicken broth to the wok. Cook until the broccoli is tender-crisp, about 3 minutes. Place around the beef and serve.

Beef Steak over Glass Noodles

The herbs and ingredients common to Southeast Asian cuisines such as Vietnamese easily spread across the borders and into the kitchens of southern China. As a result, mint — a favorite in Vietnamese kitchens — finds its way into many of the area's dishes. I incorporate some of this zesty herb into a recipe that pairs flank steak with glass noodles — also known as cellophane or bean thread noodles. No matter what you call them, these noodles add a pleasingly pliant, smooth texture to the dish, setting up a nice contrast with the crunchy nuts and bright flavor notes of the mint. Quickly simmering the glassy noodles with chicken broth and soy sauce infuses them with an extra facet of flavor as well.

Book VI

Chinese Cooking

Preparation time: *25 minutes*

Cooking time: *8 minutes*

Yield: *4 to 6 servings*

1 tablespoon Chinese rice wine	*4 ounces bean thread noodles*
2 teaspoons dark soy sauce	*1 cup chicken broth*
2 teaspoons soy sauce	*1 tablespoon soy sauce*
2 teaspoons cornstarch	*1½ tablespoons cooking oil*
1 teaspoon chopped mint leaves	*¼ cup chopped toasted nuts (peanuts or walnuts)*
¼ teaspoon ground black pepper	*1 teaspoon chopped mint leaves*
¼ teaspoon sugar	
¾ pound flank steak, sliced into 3-inch pieces, ¼ inch thick	

1 Make the marinade by combining the rice wine, dark soy sauce, 2 teaspoons soy sauce, cornstarch, mint leaves, pepper, and sugar in a bowl. Add the beef and stir to coat. Let stand for 10 minutes.

2 Soak the noodles in warm water to soften, about 5 minutes.

3 Place a wok over high heat until hot. Add the chicken broth, 1 tablespoon soy sauce, and noodles; cook until soft, about 3 minutes. Place the noodles on a serving platter.

4 Return the wok to high heat. Add the cooking oil, swirling to coat the sides. Add the beef and stir-fry until no longer pink, about 1 minute on each side.

5 To serve, place the beef on top of the noodles. Garnish with the toasted nuts and mint.

Healthy Tofu

Tofu (also known as bean curd) has gained popularity the world over despite its arguably bland flavor, texture, and shape. After trying a few inventive dishes made with this multifaceted product, skeptical Westerners are quickly convinced that you can't judge this book by its nondescript cover. Tofu agrees with almost any cooking method: The Chinese steam it, chill it, braise it, stir-fry, and deep-fry it. They scoop out its center to make a pocket for a variety of savory fillings. I especially love tofu's uncanny ability to adopt the flavor of whatever sauce or ingredient it's served with. This makes tofu the perfect "cheat meat" and a favorite of many vegetarians and meat eaters (including yours truly) alike. But meat mimicry is only the tip of the iceberg when it comes to cooking tofu. As unassuming as it may seem, tofu is a true culinary powerhouse.

Ma Po Tofu

The name of this classic Sichuanese dish actually means "pockmarked grandmother's bean curd," which doesn't quite do its deliciously bold flavors justice. But according to legend, hundreds of years ago, a pockmarked grandmother in Sichuan was known for her generosity to travelers and townsfolk despite being very poor herself. She also ran a tofu stall where she served the only dish she could afford to make — a combination of tofu cakes, a little ground meat, and the local spices and seasonings. Although her specialty had obviously humble origins, it was nothing to be ashamed of. Not only was her dish inexpensive and nutritious, but those who ate it thought it so unforgettable that Chinese cooks still make it centuries later, and it remains a regular item on Chinese restaurant menus today.

Preparation time: *15 minutes*

Cooking time: *5 minutes*

Yield: *4 servings*

6 ounces ground pork

1 tablespoon oyster-flavored sauce

½ cup chicken broth

1 tablespoon soy sauce

1 tablespoon white distilled vinegar

2 teaspoons sugar

1 teaspoon dried chile flakes

1 teaspoon sesame oil

2 tablespoons cooking oil

1 teaspoon minced garlic

1 teaspoon minced ginger

1 package (16 ounces) soft tofu, drained and cut into ½-inch cubes

1½ teaspoons cornstarch dissolved in 1 tablespoon water

1 Combine the ground pork and oyster-flavored sauce in a bowl. Let stand 10 minutes.

2 Make the sauce by combining the chicken broth, soy sauce, vinegar, sugar, chile flakes, and sesame oil in a bowl.

3 Place a wok over high heat until hot. Add the cooking oil, swirling to coat the sides. Add the garlic and ginger; cook, stirring until fragrant, about 10 seconds. Add the pork and stir-fry until lightly browned and crumbly, about 2 minutes. Add the sauce and bring it to a boil. Reduce the heat to medium and cook for 2 minutes.

4 Add the tofu and bring to a boil. Cook for 1 minute. Add the cornstarch solution and cook, stirring, until the sauce boils and thickens.

Remember: *Be gentle when draining soft tofu. You won't want to press it with a coffee can or cutting board.*

Book VI

Chinese Cooking

Tofu and Spinach

If you've never tried pressed tofu, this recipe, which pairs its firm texture with tender spinach, gives fabulous results. Because some types of pressed tofu are flavored with marinades or spices, you may want to use that kind in this recipe. But remember that you have to adjust the seasonings in the sauce according to the pressed tofu's seasonings. What's the best way to do this? Taste some of the pressed tofu and judge from there how to alter the oyster-flavored sauce, sugar, or chicken broth to suit your tastes. It's all a matter of training the tongue!

Preparation time: *12 minutes*

Cooking time: *5 minutes*

Yield: *4 servings*

2 tablespoons black vinegar or balsamic vinegar	1 pound spinach, washed and drained well
1 teaspoon sesame oil	½ cup thinly sliced carrots
½ teaspoon salt	4 ounces pressed tofu, cut into ¼-x-1-x-½-inch pieces
¼ teaspoon pepper	⅓ cup chicken broth
1 tablespoon cooking oil	¼ cup glazed walnuts
4 cloves garlic, sliced	

1 Make the sauce by combining the vinegar, sesame oil, salt, and pepper in a bowl.

2 Place a wok over medium-high heat until hot. Add the cooking oil, swirling to coat the sides. Add the garlic and cook, stirring, until fragrant, about 10 seconds. Add the spinach, carrots, and tofu; stir-fry for 1 minute. Add the chicken broth and stir to mix well. Add the sauce; cover and cook until the spinach is wilted, about 4 minutes. Discard the excess liquid and place on a serving platter. Garnish with the glazed walnuts.

Vary It! *Fresh, young pea shoots really work well in this dish, so if you can find some at a farmers market or Asian grocery store, give them a try. Also, to make it a meatier meal, add strips of ham with the vegetables and tofu.*

Vary It! *Pressed tofu is such a delicious treat, as well as an important part of this recipe. But many Western supermarkets don't carry this distinctly Asian ingredient. If that's the case in your neighborhood, make your own pressed and marinated tofu by pressing half a block of fresh tofu, leaving it to drain overnight. Then marinate it in ½ cup of dark soy sauce for 2 to 3 hours. Using about 1 tablespoon cooking oil, pan-fry the tofu until golden brown and pleasingly caramelized on the outside.*

The Green Revolution: Cooking Vegetables the Chinese Way

The Chinese have always been a step ahead of their time. Although Western nutritionists, doctors, and medical researchers now tell people to eat at least five servings of fruits and vegetables each day, the Chinese have been doing just that for thousands of years. And they never needed the coaxing of medical professionals to get them to do it either. Why? Because, when prepared the Chinese way — rapidly cooked and with an eye toward preserving their natural flavors — vegetables are just too delicious to resist. Whether stockpiling a winter's worth of rugged, Tianjin cabbage or quickly stir-frying fresh, delicate pea shoots from a backyard garden in Guangzhou, the Chinese have a million reasons (and recipes) to eat their veggies. Their mothers see to it. Mine certainly did.

A typical restaurant in the West may serve its guests a big, thick steak with just a spoonful of mashed potatoes and maybe a skimpy stalk of broccoli on the side. But if that kind of meal were served to a typical Chinese diner, it would go right back to the kitchen. A typical Chinese meal stars a variety of crisp, fresh vegetables — brightly colored greens and peppers, slender Asian eggplants, and exotic mushrooms and fungi that may look strange but still taste truly heavenly. Meats, if included in the cast at all, play more of a supporting role in this culinary production. They're there to accompany the lead vegetables on a stage whose set decoration is nothing more than a subtly designed sauce.

How to get the most out of your vegetables while cooking them the least

Years of practice at cooking vegetables have taught Chinese cooks that a light touch with flavor and texture works best when you're preparing fresh vegetables. So if you grew up with overboiled mushy green beans or anemic-looking canned corn, take heart that Chinese vegetable cooks have a lesson to teach you that will direct your diet toward much greener pastures. Just follow these suggestions:

1. **Give the leaves a good rinse in cool water and drain them thoroughly; a salad spinner helps with this step.**

2. **Chop the leaves into pieces a few inches long, making sure to keep the lengths fairly similar among all the pieces — doing so ensures even cooking.**

   If the stalks seem tender enough, go ahead and chop those, too, cutting the stalks at an angle to expose more surface area to heat during cooking.

3. **Prepare yourself for stir-frying, heating your wok beforehand and adding just enough oil to lightly coat the amount of greens you want to cook.**

   After the oil starts steaming a bit, gently tilt your wok to distribute it evenly across the surface. It doesn't hurt to drop in a clove of crushed garlic and a few slices of fresh ginger for flavor before adding the main ingredients.

   Keep in mind the three cardinal rules of stir-frying that I explain more fully in Chapter 3 of Book VI: Have all your ingredients prepared and organized beforehand, make sure that your wok is smoking hot when you add the food, and stir, stir, stir.

4. **Take the plunge: Add the vegetables to the ready-to-go wok and toss them immediately to fully coat with the oil.**

   Keep tossing and pay attention to how they begin softening and changing color — not wilting, but rather just gently relaxing — all the while releasing their own earthy aroma.

5. **Add your choice of seasoning: Pepper, salt, and sugar are foolproof options.**

   Then add a little bit of water or broth and put a lid on it — the wok, that is — to initiate the steaming that finishes the vegetable-cooking process.

6. **Within a couple minutes, lift that lid and feast your eyes on one of the simplest and most delightful culinary creations nature offers: fresh, green vegetables redolent with their own natural juices and aromas.**

   Taste and adjust the seasoning according to your liking, add a sauce during the final couple minutes if you wish, and get ready to eat!

Of course, other, more elaborate recipes are out there for you to try. But remember that the Chinese have cooked their greens for millennia by following these simple steps. If they can do it, so can you.

Stir-Fried Assorted Vegetables

Crisp and crunchy stir-fried vegetables are a delight to have at every dinner table. This recipe contains an assortment that you should find easily in any grocery store's produce department. I picked these particular ones not only for their great flavor (made even greater with a little All-Purpose Stir-Fry Sauce from Chapter 4 of Book VI) but also for their bright, rainbow colors.

Preparation time: *15 minutes*

Cooking time: *10 minutes*

Yield: *4 to 6 servings*

½ cup All-Purpose Stir-Fry Sauce (see the recipe in Chapter 4 of Book VI)

¼ cup chicken broth

2 tablespoons cooking oil

3 cloves garlic, lightly crushed

½ cup thinly sliced carrots

½ cup julienned red bell pepper

1 cup broccoli florets

1 large zucchini, roll cut

1 cup small white mushrooms, cleaned and halved

1 To make the sauce, combine the stir-fry sauce and the chicken broth in a bowl.

2 Place a wok over high heat until hot. Add the oil, swirling to coat the sides. Add the garlic and cook, stirring until fragrant, about 10 seconds. Add the carrots and red pepper; stir-fry for 2 minutes. Add the broccoli, zucchini, and white mushrooms; stir-fry for 2 minutes. Add the sauce and bring it to a boil, stirring until the vegetables are tender-crisp, about 3 minutes.

Vary It! *If you'd like, gently toss a few cubes of firm tofu with the vegetables in this dish. Tofu not only adds healthful protein but also gives the recipe a little more substance and bulk. And tofu's yielding texture provides the perfect counterpoint to the crunchy vegetables.*

Book VI

Chinese Cooking

Chinatown Chop Suey

"Miscellaneous odds and ends." That's the literal translation of the Cantonese words *chop suey,* and the combination of ingredients in this recipe for chop suey fits the bill perfectly. In fact, chop suey is a dish that really doesn't need a recipe at all. All you need is a refrigerator and pantry full of leftover vegetables, some seasonings and sauces, and even meat if you'd like.

Preparation time: *20 minutes*

Cooking time: *10 minutes*

Yield: *4 servings*

¾ cup chicken broth

2 tablespoons oyster-flavored sauce

1½ tablespoons Chinese rice wine

2 tablespoons cooking oil

1 tablespoon minced garlic

6 ounces boneless lean pork, thinly sliced

2 heaping cups diced green cabbage (1-inch pieces)

½ cup sliced water chestnuts

⅔ cup thinly sliced carrots

1 cup bean sprouts

2 green onions, cut at an angle into 1-inch lengths

1 tablespoon cornstarch dissolved in 2 tablespoons water

1 To make the sauce, combine the chicken broth, oyster-flavored sauce, and rice wine in a bowl.

2 Place a wok over high heat until hot. Add the cooking oil, swirling to coat the sides. Add the garlic and cook, stirring, until fragrant, about 10 seconds. Add the pork and stir-fry until lightly browned, about 2 minutes.

3 Add the cabbage, water chestnuts, and carrots. Stir-fry until tender-crisp, about 2 minutes. Add the bean sprouts and green onions and stir to mix well. Add the sauce and bring it to a boil. Add the cornstarch solution and cook, stirring, until the sauce boils and thickens.

Chapter 8

Sweet Endings

Chinese restaurant menus can run for pages, sometimes listing hundreds of dishes. Everything gets a fair shake — from soups and appetizers to meats and vegetables, from "sizzling platters" and claypot casseroles to countless interpretations on rice and noodles. But when it comes to desserts, you often find only the cursory plate of fortune cookies, maybe some caramelized bananas, or, as a sop to Westerners, ice cream.

Then again, after a deliciously satisfying Chinese meal, do you really need, or even want, a big slab of cheesecake? According to Chinese cuisine's balancing principles, an arsenal of light, mildly sweet, and usually fruit-based desserts is the more natural choice. Personally, I prefer to end a meal with a bowl of chilled fresh seasonal fruits. Dessert soups, served either chilled or warm, make refreshing finales, too; they often consist of tapioca pearls or sweetened nut pastes simmered in water, perhaps with a little coconut milk.

But just because you don't see as many desserts at a Chinese restaurant as you would at, say, a French one, don't assume that China doesn't have its own national sweet tooth. Visit any Chinatown bakery and you'll find enough tarts, cakes, candies, pastries, and sweet paste-filled buns to put your dentist's six kids through college. The difference is that the Chinese prefer leaving the tour de force desserts to the specialists — and to those times when they're really hungry for them, which isn't normally after a full meal.

You can also experience the pleasures of selected Chinese sweets at dim sum teahouses. Many of those bakery-based specialties, as well as sweet rice puddings and jiggly almond, coconut, or fruit jellies, play supporting roles to a pot of hot jasmine tea.

The recipes in this chapter contain a little bit of old and new and a little bit of East and West. By blending the best of China's lightly sweet philosophy with the richer Western dessert tradition, they do double duty as between-meal snacks and after-meal treats. Be sure to try your favorite Chinese restaurant standbys, but don't leave out the less familiar options.

Eastern Traditions

If your idea of the ultimate treat is a gooey chocolate cake or a triple-decker sundae with the works, traditional Chinese desserts may seem a bit on the light side. But give them a chance, and you will become a Chinese sweetie in no time.

A clean, fresh sweetness comes naturally to China's many fruit-based desserts; you don't need a ton of sugar or cream to get those flavors. The smooth texture of the steamed and tofu-based desserts will awaken your palate to a different post-dining experience. Give them a try, and you may find that you don't miss the apple pie à la mode.

Steamed Sponge Cake

Just as Chinese steamed buns raise a few Western eyebrows, steamed sponge cake may do the same. But this recipe for the Cantonese classic — straight from the kitchen of my good friend Trudy Cuan — makes a cake that's so light, fluffy, and pleasantly sweet that it'll have you raising your fork, instead of your eyebrows, for another bite.

Preparation time: *13 minutes*

Cooking time: *20 minutes*

Yield: *One 9-inch round cake*

4 large eggs	*1 cup all-purpose flour*
1 cup sugar	*2 tablespoons cooking oil*

1 Line the bottom of a 9-inch cake pan with plastic wrap and set aside.

2 Beat the eggs with an electric mixer until smooth, about 1 minute. Gradually add the sugar, beating well after each addition.

3 Slowly add ¼ cup flour at a time, mixing well after each addition. Continue to beat until fully incorporated. Add the cooking oil; beat to mix well.

4 Prepare a wok for steaming (see Chapter 3 of Book VI). Transfer the mixture into the cake pan. Set the pan into the wok; cover and steam for 20 minutes, or until a wooden toothpick inserted in the center comes out clean. Serve warm or cold.

Tip: *Resist the temptation to lift the wok's lid and peek at your steaming cake. The condensation on the lid will drip onto the cake, making it soggy. To avoid having to lift the lid to add steaming water, use a little bit more than usual before you start and keep a pitcher of hot water handy in case you need it. Carefully slide the lid to the side, leaving enough space to pour in the water. When the cake is done, quickly but gently lift and invert the lid to avoid splashing any condensation onto it.*

Sweet Tapioca Pearls

People usually have strong feelings about tapioca — and if you grew up on the gooey tapioca pudding served in school cafeterias, those feelings may be strongly negative. Get ready to redress your childhood tapioca issues with this delicious combination of starchy tapioca pearls and nutty-sweet taro root. Serve it warm or chilled.

Don't succumb to the temptation of using quick-cooking tapioca in this recipe because it simply won't give the same results as the pearls. Tapioca pearls are tapioca starch that has been processed into pellets ranging in size from ⅛ to ¼ inch. They're essential to both the creamy, pearly texture of the dessert and to its lustrous name.

Preparation time: 25 minutes

Cooking time: 30 minutes

Yield: 4 to 6 servings

6 cups water

2 cups (10 ounces) taro, cut into ¼-inch cubes

½ cup small tapioca pearls

1 cup sugar

1 cup coconut milk

⅛ teaspoon salt

1½ cups melon balls, about ¾ inch in diameter

1 In a large pot, bring 5 cups of the water to a boil. Add the taro and tapioca pearls; reduce the heat to medium. Cover and simmer for 25 minutes, adding additional water as needed.

2 When the tapioca pearls become translucent, add the sugar, coconut milk, and salt; cook for 3 minutes. Add the melon balls; cook to heat through, about 2 minutes.

Book VI

Chinese Cooking

Western Influences

In the hotels and upscale restaurants of Hong Kong, Beijing, and China's metropolitan capitals, chefs from around the world bring their own influences to local traditional dishes and ingredients. Not surprisingly, the collaboration has produced innovative, mouthwatering desserts.

This culinary approach to "foreign affairs" spread from the big cities to local bakeries in smaller towns, in part because the results were so irresistible. From there, they returned to the Western world, where they satisfy sweet-toothed Western tastes quite handily. As I always say, there's no better way to achieve cultural diplomacy than through cuisine.

Doing the mango tango

Peeling and deseeding a mango take a little practice, but with my tips, you'll never have to wait longer than you can bear to savor this fruit's sweetness:

1. **Stand the unpeeled mango on its pointy end with a narrow side facing you.**

2. **With a sharp knife placed slightly off the mango's center, steering clear of the large seed, slice vertically from top to bottom. Turn the mango around and make the same slice on the other side. Now you should have two cut slices of roughly equal size.**

3. **Lay the 2 slices cut side up on the counter and, using the tip of your knife, make diagonal cuts about ½ inch apart in a cross-hatch pattern on the mango slices. Take care not to cut through the peel.**

4. **Hold the mango slices so that your thumbs rest on the skin, and press the slices with your thumbs to invert the mango. Doing so creates a mango "flower" as the cross-hatched sections separate from one another.**

5. **Trim away the peel, and the flesh will fall away into perfectly formed chunks. Repeat these steps with the other slice.**

Mango Pudding

The sweet perfume and smooth texture of the mango turn a simple gelatin-based pudding into a sumptuous dessert. Served in individual ramekins, this pudding makes a particularly elegant presentation with an equally elegant flavor. Use the ripest mangoes you can find for maximum flavor.

Preparation time: *12 minutes*

Cooking time: *3 minutes*

Yield: *4 servings*

2 ripe mangoes, about 14 ounces each

1 cup water

1 cup whole milk

1 package unflavored gelatin

1 cup sugar

Lemon juice

Lemon wedges (optional)

1 Peel the mangoes and cut the flesh from the pits. Cut enough flesh into ½-inch cubes to make 2 cups. Place the chopped fruit into the blender with the water and puree until smooth.

2 Combine the milk, gelatin, and sugar in a medium saucepan and bring to a simmer over medium-low heat. Stir well with a whisk to dissolve the gelatin, about 3 minutes. Remove from the heat. Pour the pureed mangoes into the pan and mix well. Pour the mixture into a 1-quart mold or divide among 4 individual 1-cup ramekins or custard cups. Cover and refrigerate until firm, 3 to 4 hours, or overnight.

3 Squeeze a few drops of lemon juice on the pudding before serving. Garnish with lemon wedges, if desired.

Vary It! *If you're so inclined, make different flavors of fruit pudding with whatever sweet gems are ripe and ready. Just substitute a different fruit for the mango and proceed with the recipe.*

Caramelized Bananas

This common Chinese restaurant dessert is just the kind of sticky situation I crave, although "freezing" the fried bananas' syrupy coating with a dunk in ice water leaves you with less of a mess on your hands. You end up with a crackly, cooled candy glaze surrounding soft, piping-hot bananas at the center — the best of both worlds.

Preparation time: *10 minutes*

Cooking time: *20 minutes*

Yield: *4 servings*

1 tablespoon sesame seeds	Cooking oil for deep-frying
¼ cup all-purpose flour	7 tablespoons sugar
1 egg, lightly beaten	2½ tablespoons water
4 firm bananas	Ice cubes in cold water

1 Place the sesame seeds in a small frying pan over medium heat, shaking the pan frequently, until lightly browned, about 3 minutes. Immediately remove from the pan to cool.

2 Place the flour and egg in separate dishes.

3 Peel and cut the bananas into thirds. Just before deep-frying, coat the bananas in the flour, then in the egg, and back to the flour, shaking off the excess.

4 In a wok, heat the oil for deep-frying to 360 degrees. Using a pair of chopsticks or a slotted spoon, carefully lower the banana pieces into the hot oil. Deep-fry, a few pieces at a time, turning frequently, until golden brown, about 2 minutes. Remove with a slotted spoon and drain on paper towels.

5 To make the syrup, combine the sugar and water in a small saucepan. Cook over medium heat until the mixture caramelizes and turns to a pale straw color, about 8 minutes. (It is not necessary to stir, as the sugar should melt and incorporate into the water.) Immediately remove from the heat. (The syrup will continue to cook after you remove it from the heat, and the color will turn golden in a few seconds.)

6 Line a cookie sheet with wax paper or foil. Top with an oiled cooling rack. Lay the fried bananas on the rack, pour sugar syrup over the bananas, and then sprinkle with the sesame seeds. Using a pair of chopsticks, remove each piece of banana and immediately dip into the ice water so that the coating hardens. Gently place the bananas on a lightly greased serving plate and serve immediately.

Tip: *Even after you dunk the caramelized bananas into the ice water, they still may stick to the serving plate. Grease the dish with a little cooking oil or butter, and you won't leave any delicious bits stuck behind.*

Book VII
Japanese Cooking

The 5th Wave By Rich Tennant

"I think you meant to ask for more 'wasabi', not, 'Kemosabe'."

In this book . . .

*I*f you think Japanese cooking is all about sushi — or that sushi is all about raw fish — then prepare for an eye-opening experience. You'll find plenty to occupy your taste buds. And if you want to try your hand at making the various types of sushi at home, I walk you through the steps. And don't forget to save room for green tea ice cream!

Contents at a glance

Chapter 1

Choosing, Cooking, and Enjoying Japanese Food

In This Chapter

▶ Identifying what makes food quintessentially Japanese

▶ Looking at Japanese cooking philosophies

▶ Taking seasons into account

▶ Presenting Japanese foods in style

*W*hat makes Japanese food different from other cuisines? Many factors go into making a Japanese meal the special experience that it is. The quality of the ingredients, the care with which they are prepared, and the season in which they're served all help define Japanese food.

This chapter explores all these aspects and provides a brief introduction to techniques used in Japanese cooking as well as information on how to artfully present your Japanese food.

Exploring Typical Japanese Meals

Imagine a meal where every sense is considered. Your eyes are enticed by the colors and shapes of the food as well as by the interesting presentations of the food in bowls, on dishes, and on trays. Your sense of touch comes alive from touching a blood red lacquered tray, the raw edges of a blond wooden dish, and the smoothness of a multicolored ceramic cup. Various textures and temperatures caress your tongue and awaken your taste buds. You're fully aware of the silken texture and coldness of chilled tofu, the spicy hotness of *wasabi* — the popular Japanese horseradish condiment — and the warm crunchiness of freshly fried tempura. Add the loud (and very proper) slurp of soba noodles to the dinner table and make no mistake — you're eating a Japanese meal!

Three squares daily

For breakfast, many Japanese start their day with miso soup, a bowl of rice, maybe a rolled omelet, some salted fish, and pickled vegetables. That's not to say that the Western idea of a ham-filled croissant hasn't appeared in Japan, but soup and rice are still the classic way to start the day.

Lunch might include noodles of some sort — soba, udon, or ramen — as well as one-dish meals such as a rice bowl with meat and vegetables. A *bento box,* which is the Japanese equivalent of a lunch box, is a square or rectangular box with different compartments, each containing a different food. Typically, the box includes a rice dish, a high-protein dish (meat, chicken, or fish), some vegetables, and some sort of condiment.

I recently ate a bento box meal with four square compartments. The box was black lacquer; one square had a blue and white ceramic dish shaped like a lotus leaf set inside holding artfully arranged sashimi with shredded daikon radish. Another square contained vegetarian makizushi. The third square offered a small amount of pickles and a tiny covered ceramic dish, maybe 2 inches across, filled with daikon and salmon roe. When I removed the cover, it was like discovering a tiny box of glistening orange jewels. The final square had a rolled omelet as well as some additional sushi set on a bamboo mat, which fit perfectly inside the square. The meal was a delight for my eyes as well as my mouth!

Dinner at home is casual. Everyone gets his or her own bowl of miso soup and a bowl of rice, and various dishes are placed in the center of the table so that diners can serve themselves — a bit of meat, some vegetables, a pickled dish, that sort of thing. Fresh fruit and green tea round out the meal.

Japanese home cooking, like American home cooking, can be elaborate and quite special at times, but it's often just down-home cooking meant to nourish the family. The recipes in this book include common home-cooked foods, like soups and stews, as well as *nigirizushi* — those fingers of rice topped with fish — which, while often eaten in restaurants, is such an emblem of Japanese cuisine that I simply couldn't leave it out.

Japanese restaurant meals

Japanese restaurants that specialize in certain dishes include *teppanyakiya,* which are steakhouses; *okonomiyakiya,* which are pancake houses (where you won't find maple syrup because these pancakes are the savory variety); and, of course, sushi restaurants. Other types of restaurants and stands feature *yakitori* (grilled food), *sukiyaki* (hot-pot dishes), and *oden* (fish-cake stews). Japan has many distinctive cooking techniques and dishes, and the Japanese are justly proud of their cuisine.

Getting Started at Home

To help you start thinking like a Japanese home cook, here are some things to take into consideration. None of these ideas is difficult to master; it's just that the approach is slightly different from some other cuisines.

Think seasonally

Traditional Japanese cooking is dictated by the season, so in the spring you may find a dish with freshly harvested spinach (see Chapter 4), and in the summer a chilled soba dish may be offered (see Chapter 6). In the fall, deep-fried dishes appear (Chapter 7), and in the winter a one-dish simmered stew (Chapter 7) warms you right up.

The foods also are often arranged with the season in mind. So in the spring, you may find a carrot cut in the shape of a springtime blossom, while in the winter, you may eat a stew in a bowl that depicts a snow-capped peak.

Think fresh

Different areas of Japan feature different foods that take advantage of the fresh foods of the region. Coastal cities feature saltwater fish, for instance, while mountainous areas serve freshwater river fish. Many of the dishes have few ingredients, so each ingredient shines through and is at its best if it's as fresh as it can be.

Umami: The fifth taste experience

What is umami? Good question, and one that could be debated endlessly. Western science maintains that there are four basic taste sensations — sweet, sour, salty, and bitter — and that all of them have corresponding taste receptors in different locations on the tongue. The Japanese include *umami,* which they define as deliciousness or tastiness, as a fifth taste, with its own receptors on the tongue. It's hard to describe, although some people say that miso, with its rich, complex aromas and flavor, is high in the umami factor. Monosodium glutamate (MSG) is found naturally in some foods, such as konbu and green tea, to mention some Asian foods, and Parmesan cheese, to mention a more common foodstuff. These foods have the ability to enhance and heighten flavors and are often associated with the experience of umami. Another way to experience umami is to taste and smell a matsutake mushroom, which is said to have an incomparable and indescribably delicious taste. It's piney and woody, yet delicate and delicious, all at the same time — umami in one bite!

Think ingredient

Many a Japanese dish, sometimes an entire meal, is built around a specific ingredient, such as tofu. The tofu may be simmered in a broth, served raw with a seasoning, deep-fried and stuffed, and perhaps even grilled. In this way, the diner can experience all the different qualities of the main ingredient.

Whatever the main ingredient of the dish is, the other ingredients are there to support it. With *sashimi* (raw fish), for instance, it's all about the specific fish you're eating. The condiments, such as the *wasabi* (Japanese horseradish), grated daikon radish, and pickled ginger, are there to enhance the fish.

Think technique

Japanese cuisine is hugely varied, from rich stews to delicate sashimi. With the stews, cooking the different ingredients correctly is important so that they come together in the end in a pleasing way. When slicing sashimi, the difference between a thick slice and a translucent paper-thin slice affects how it feels on the tongue and in the mouth, not to mention how different the various thicknesses look. Neither is inherently wrong. It depends on the fish and the presentation; just be aware that every slice of the knife has an effect.

Making Presentation Count

The importance of presentation in the Japanese meal is paramount. Sashimi is never just heaped on a plate, and stews are not ladled into any old bowl.

The Japanese consider the shape and color of a dish to be important. For example, udon noodles, because of their curvy, swirling nature, should be placed in a bowl that enhances their movement. Deep burgundy-red tuna sashimi should be served on a plate that shows off the color and texture of the fish. Texture plays a role as well. I have some small teacups that are made from rough brown ceramic, but you place your lips on a triangular insert of smooth blue-and-white porcelain. This smooth texture greatly enhances the smooth, liquid nature of the tea as it slips into your mouth — a simple embellishment that makes a huge difference.

No, you don't have to go out and buy all new serving pieces. However, if you're going to make a Japanese soup for a special meal, for instance, consider buying some inexpensive covered bowls. The sensation of the glorious aroma and warm steam bursting forth as each guest lifts the lid will make your Japanese meal all the more enjoyable. Many Asian specialty stores have at least a small selection of bowls, plates, and spoons that are suitable for your Japanese meal.

Chapter 2

Inside the Japanese Kitchen

Daikon radishes over a foot long. Green and black seaweed. Soy products ranging from liquid to crunchy. Dark brown noodles. Hot horseradish and pickled vegetables. Fish both raw and cooked. Rice, rice, and more rice. Bamboo steamers, extra-long chopsticks (attached at the top!), razor-sharp cleavers, and rolling mats. These are just some of the intriguing ingredients and pieces of equipment found in the Japanese kitchen.

Introducing Japanese Ingredients

You may find that some ingredients in Japanese dishes, such as vegetable oil and certain varieties of fish, are familiar to you already. But other ingredients, such as *edamame* (soybeans) and *konbu* (kelp) may be new to you. Well, maybe you've encountered kelp while swimming in the ocean, but you may have never cooked with it before!

Commonly used vegetables

I start my description of Japanese ingredients with vegetables because they're so important to Japanese cuisine. This section is just a sampling of some of the more important ones featured in these recipes. Some are shown in Figure 2-1.

Bamboo shoots

Fresh *takenoko* (bamboo shoots) are used frequently in Japanese cooking. I often find them fresh in my local Asian market, but I prefer to use them already prepared. Fresh, they look like rugged reddish flower buds, tightly furled. They must be cooked very soon after harvesting, or they become tough, dry, and bitter. Because finding truly fresh bamboo shoots is so difficult, I suggest looking for parboiled ones in plastic bags in the refrigerator section of your Asian market or using the canned variety. Like many prepared veggies, prepared bamboo shoots don't have the brightness in flavor or texture of fresh, but they'll do just fine in the recipes in this book.

Daikon

This large white radish can be over 3 inches wide and over a foot long. It's often grated or cut into long strands and used as a delicious, crunchy condiment. If you've ever noticed a pearly white threadlike mound of something next to your sashimi, it's daikon. It has a fresh, peppery bite and is quite refreshing. Sometimes it's pickled, dyed bright yellow, and used in vegetable sushi rolls. Fresh daikon should be crisp and blemish free when you buy it; steer clear of any that are limp. Always peel it before using.

Ginkgo nuts

Called *ginnan* in Japan, ginkgo nuts are found fresh in Japanese markets in the fall. They come with a hard shell, and some preparation is involved — removing the shells, parboiling them, rubbing off the skins, and so on. I suggest buying vacuum-packed or ones in cans or jars, ready to use. Check Asian stores to find them. Ginkgo nuts add a delicious autumnal flavor to stews.

Hakusai

This Chinese cabbage is used in soups and stews. It's easy to find in many regular supermarkets as well as Asian markets, where it will most likely be labeled "Chinese cabbage."

Kabocha

This richly colored (dark orange), velvety textured winter squash adds an incredible richness to stews. It's fairly easy to find in regular supermarkets in the fall and winter. Look for a vegetable with a dark green skin that's shaped like a small pumpkin. I love this vitamin- and mineral-rich veggie in tempura. If you can't find it, you can substitute buttercup or butternut squash.

Lotus root

Called *renkon* in Japanese, this root vegetable, which has a lacy pattern when sliced, offers little taste, but it adds great visual interest to Japanese dishes. It is quite starchy and is often fried or used in simmered dishes. You can find the fresh variety in Asian markets, and you can also find it canned or frozen. When buying fresh, look for firm, unblemished vegetables. Peel, slice ¼-inch thick, and then drop in water that has a little rice vinegar added to prevent discoloration. Allow to soak for 5 minutes and then drop in boiling water and cook for about 2 minutes, until you can pierce it with a knife. Drain and it's ready to use.

Mushrooms

Fresh and dried mushrooms of many varieties are used in Japanese cooking. Shiitake, a large, meaty mushroom, is used both ways; while delicate mushrooms like enoki, which have very long, thin, edible stems and tiny caps the size of your pinkie nail, are better fresh. Many well-stocked supermarkets carry a variety of both fresh and dried, so you shouldn't have trouble finding what you need.

- ✔ **Fresh:** To use fresh mushrooms, just wipe them clean with a damp paper towel and remove any hard, woody stems. You can, however, reserve the stems for stock.

- ✔ **Dried:** To reconstitute dried mushrooms, place them in a bowl of warm water, place a lid or small plate on top of the mushrooms to keep them submerged, and allow to sit for 30 minutes. They're now ready to use in recipes; always follow instructions in individual recipes.

Dried mushrooms can be very expensive if purchased in small packages from supermarkets or specialty food stores. Conversely, Asian grocery stores often sell large bags very inexpensively, so put them on your list for the shopping trip to the Asian grocery store. They're even cheaper there than in the bulk section of natural foods markets.

Sweet potatoes

The Japanese have their own sweet potato. You may be able to find it fresh in an Asian grocery store, but you can easily substitute regular sweet potatoes. I always include them in my tempura. (For more information on tempura, see Chapter 7.)

Book VII

Japanese Cooking

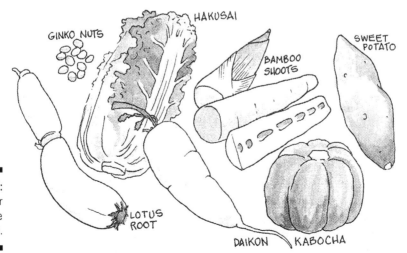

Figure 2-1:
Popular
Japanese
vegetables.

GINKO NUTS

HAKUSAI

BAMBOO SHOOTS

SWEET POTATO

LOTUS ROOT

DAIKON

KABOCHA

Seaweed and bonito flakes

Seaweeds, or sea vegetables, are very common to Japanese cuisine. The next few pages discuss the ones used in these recipes. Bonito flakes, a dried fish product, are often used in conjunction with sea veggies, so I describe them here too.

To store dried seaweed and bonito flakes, keep them dry in resealable plastic bags and store at room temperature.

Konbu

Sometimes spelled "kombu," this dark green giant kelp grows attached to the floor of the ocean. It is packaged in large strips, often folded over on themselves, and is the most frequently used sea vegetable in Japan due to the fact that it's always found in *dashi,* the ubiquitous Japanese stock. You can find the dried version in natural foods stores and Asian food stores. It is vitamin rich and very high in iodine and even offers some protein. Just wipe any dirt off with a damp cloth, and you're ready to go.

Konbu often has a powdery white coating, which is just natural salts and minerals. You don't have to wipe this off, and, in fact, you shouldn't because it provides flavor.

Konbu often comes in large strips that are over a foot long. Tearing it or cutting it is hard with a knife, but kitchen scissors make the job easy. Just cut off the pieces that you need.

Nori

Rectangular sheets of *nori,* sometimes called *laver,* of approximately 8 × 7 inches, come in packages that contain a stack of the dark green, almost black, sheets. This is the seaweed that you see wrapped around the outside of sushi rolls. All seaweeds have a lot of vitamins, but nori is the highest in vitamin A. Nori is traditionally eaten for breakfast with a little soup and rice; it's simply toasted and served — sort of a Japanese toast! You also find nori crumbled over soups.

Nori has two sides; one is shinier than the other side. When using nori to make *makizushi* (sushi rolls), roll them with the shiny side facing out; that is, place the shiny side down on your bamboo rolling mat.

Nori is best if served lightly toasted. Some packages claim that the nori is already toasted, but you should toast your own right before using. It is very easy to do: Turn on a burner and pass the sheet of nori several inches over the heat until it turns from dark green to an even darker green. You just hold a corner with your fingers and slowly pass it back and forth over the burner. Take care to toast it evenly and do not allow it to burn. It takes only seconds; make sure to toast both sides.

Wakame

Yet another sea vegetable, the *wakame* used in these recipes is fresh or fresh-frozen and used in salad, which is a quite common use of this seaweed. It's also used frequently in soups. This seaweed is long and thin, and bunches are made up of several strips.

Bonito flakes

Bonito *(katsuobushi)* is a type of fish that's often sold filleted, boiled, and dried. This version appears very much like a wooden block that happens to look like a fish! Japanese cooks slice bonito using a unique tool called a *katsuobushi kezuri,* or a *katsuobushibako,* which is a wooden box with a blade, like a carpenter's plane. Cooks rub the fish back and forth over the plane, and transparently thin shavings result.

I use bonito that already comes in the flake form, called *kezuribushi,* which look like rosy colored, fluffy wood shavings, so you won't need any special tools. They are so fluffy that they're hard to measure by volume. I do suggest that you have a scale because this is a much more accurate way to measure them. One ounce of bonito flakes equals approximately 3 cups.

The flaked version is used often in Japan nowadays, so don't think you're cheating!

Book VII

Japanese Cooking

Sake: Sock it to me

Sake is rice wine, although rice liquor is a more appropriate description, and the Japanese word *nihonshu* is translated as such. Japan has many different brewing companies and small regional breweries, and the Japanese never seem to tire of this delicate beverage.

Sake types

Sake is served warm and cold, depending on the variety. There are many different types, and the quality varies. Here's what you need to know before you try sake:

- ✔ Traditionally sake was served warm; now that the quality has increased dramatically, many are better chilled. Chilled means just slightly cooled, not ice cold. Warm means about 100 to 104 degrees, slightly above body temperature.

- ✔ Ginjoshu sake begins with very highly polished rice and is considered the most refined and the best. It's produced in very limited quantities and hard to find in the United States. If you do find it, serve it chilled. In general, the higher the quality, the cooler it should be served.

✔ Junmaishu is pure rice sake with no added alcohol and has a fairly heavy body. Try it warm, chilled, or at room temperature — your choice.

✔ Honjozukuri is rich in flavor while still being mild (ginjoshu is the highest quality of this sort of sake)

✔ Nigorizake is filtered but not through very fine filters; it still retains a cloudy appearance. It is frequently unpasteurized. (Actually, any type of sake can be left unpasteurized, in which case it must be kept chilled or it will spoil).

✔ The other designations to be aware of are karakuchi, which means dry, and amakuchi, which means sweet.

So which do you buy? You gotta try them all! As with wine, if you like it, it's a good sake for you.

Although the alcohol content is the same in warm and cold sake, the warm type seems to hit some people harder — especially the next morning, if you know what I mean. Always drink in moderation, and if you should feel a little sluggish in the morning, try a bowl of miso soup and noodles, a traditional Japanese hangover cure.

Serving sake

Sake is never served from the bottle as wine sometimes is. First, you decant it into a *tokkuri,* a heat-resistant container usually made of ceramic or glass. Although you can find ones made out of bamboo, these are often lined so that the sake doesn't absorb the "wood" flavors.

To warm sake, pour it into a tokkuri and place the tokkuri into a bowl of hot water until it comes up to the correct temperature. To tell whether it's warm enough, dab a bit on the inside of your wrist — like when you test a baby's bottle. If it feels slightly warm, that means it's just above body temperature, which is what you want.

Two basic kinds of cups are available for serving sake: ochoko, which are broader and very open at the top, and guinomi, which are slightly larger and have straight sides. Either is appropriate. Ochoko cups send the aromas flying up to your nose, which is pleasant, but these cups are often very tiny. Guinomi are more typical for everyday use. You may come across square masu sake cups, which are cedar boxes. These were often used years ago, but they can impart an undesirable taste to the sake. Modern ones may be lined with glass.

Rice: Short and sweet

More than 300 varieties of rice *(kome)* are grown in Japan, but in general, Japanese cuisine highlights short-grain types that, when cooked, are faintly sweet and slightly sticky, making it easy to pick up with chopsticks *(hashi).*

Rice is an extremely important ingredient that's served at every meal, including breakfast. For this reason, learning how to make rice properly is important, so turn to Chapter 6 of Book VII for instructions for rice to eat every day and Chapter 5 of Book VII for sushi rice.

Automatic rice cookers (discussed in the equipment section, later in this chapter) are very popular both here and in Japan. They cook rice perfectly for you every time.

Three major kinds of rice are used in Japanese cuisine:

- **Genmai:** Unpolished brown rice
- **Haigamai:** Partially polished white rice
- **Seihakumai:** Highly polished white rice that is the most common type and the one I use in the recipes in this book.

The wonders of soy

Soybeans *(edamame)* are eaten straight out of the pod and made into countless ingredients in the Japanese kitchen.

Edamame

Soybeans, which come two or three to a pod, are sold right in the pod. You can find them fresh in the exotic produce section of your supermarket or frozen in any Asian grocery store and some natural foods stores. See Chapter 4 for an easy appetizer recipe that serves edamame straight from the pod.

Soy sauce

Three types of soy sauce are used in Japanese cooking — a dark, a light, and a wheat-free version. But more important than the type is the way it is made or, more specifically, brewed. I love well-brewed soy sauce but abhor "bad" soy sauce.

I can't stress strongly enough that chemically processed soy sauce doesn't belong anywhere near your deliciously prepared homemade Japanese food. Please take the time to read labels and buy only soy sauce that's labeled "naturally brewed." I like Eden and San-J brands, which are easy to find in natural foods markets. These are of the "dark" variety and fine for the recipes in this book.

Soy sauce labeled "tamari" is a dark Japanese soy sauce brewed without wheat. "Shoyu" is a term used for Japanese soy sauce made with wheat. The two flavors are different, and tamari is traditionally used as a condiment after cooking, such as when it's served with sashimi and sushi. Chinese soy sauces are usually saltier than Japanese, and I don't like them as much. So what do

Book VII

Japanese Cooking

you do? If you go to a specialty food store, Asian food store, or an online Asian resource, you can have your choice. Go for one of the Japanese soy sauces if you can but, most importantly, use a naturally brewed one!

Miso

Miso is a fermented soybean paste with a texture of soft peanut butter or, more accurately, apple butter. It's made by steaming a grain, such as rice, barley, or millet, to which koji, a mold, is added to start the fermentation process. Soybeans are steamed as well and added to the mixture, which is allowed to age for a period of time, often as long as a year or more. This is a simplified explanation, of course, and the end result is a very complex, delicious, nutritious paste that belies its humble ingredients.

Miso is used in a variety of ways in Japanese cuisine. The most basic way is in soup, but it also flavors marinades for soups and stews and is spread on fish to add flavor before cooking.

Lighter miso, which can vary from a creamy white to a yellow and is made from ingredients such as sweet rice, barley, and millet, is the mellowest tasting type of miso. It's aged for shorter periods of time. Darker, richer miso, like brown rice miso, has a stronger flavor and is aged longer; these types of miso can be a very dark black-brown or reddish brown.

You may come across these terms when reading miso labels:

- **Kuro miso** is a dark, almost black miso that's strong tasting and usually aged the longest.

- **Hatcho miso** is an all-soybean, dark brown miso that is a type of kuro miso.

- **Aka miso** is reddish in color and often very salty.

- **Mugi miso** is all barley, with no soybeans, and usually a medium brown color.

- **Shinsu miso** is yellow miso and often the easiest to find.

- **Shiro miso** is a lightly aged, pale-colored miso that can actually be quite sweet.

All miso is nutrient dense and high in protein and contains live enzymes that aid in digestion, particularly unpasteurized brands. You can find miso in Asian grocery stores as well as natural food stores. Refrigerate it after opening or, if you purchase it already refrigerated, chill it immediately.

You can order a traditional, unpasteurized, domestically produced miso from South River Miso at www.southrivermiso.com. The company uses certified organic ingredients and makes, hands down, my favorite miso, regardless of the variety. Ask for a sampler pack and tell them I sent you!

Tofu

Tofu is a processed soybean product that is healthy, delicious, and widely used in Japan. Did I lose you there when I said it was delicious? It really is! You need to give it a chance. Served properly, tofu can be a sublime experience. You can find tofu in almost any supermarket nowadays, and it comes in packages ranging from about 12 to 16 ounces each. Here are descriptions of the varieties that I use in my recipes:

- ✔ **Silk tofu:** This silky tofu is very light and creamy. It's perfect when serving tofu chilled with condiments (see Chapter 4 of Book VII).

- ✔ **Regular tofu:** This is a denser tofu, sometimes referred to as cotton tofu because its texture is somewhat cottony. It's labeled "firm" or "extra firm." To enhance its compact, meaty texture, it's often pressed and drained to make it even firmer when used in stews or pan-fried.

  To store either of these types of fresh tofu, use soon after purchasing. If you have some left over, store it in an airtight container filled with fresh water and change the water daily. Heed the "use by" date on the package. Old tofu has a sour taste.

  Many supermarkets carry flavored tofu, which has spices added. Although this tofu may be a convenience product when making stir-fries, buy fresh, plain tofu for the Japanese recipes in this book.

- ✔ **Aburage:** You can find cans of aburage, which are fried, seasoned tofu pouches, from any Asian grocery store. Think of them as little pita-bread pockets! You just stuff them and eat them, as in the Inarizushi recipe in Chapter 5 of Book VII, where the aburage are filled with sushi rice and sesame seeds.

Noodles galore

The Japanese, like food lovers worldwide, adore noodles. In Japanese cuisine, you find soba, udon, somen, and ramen noodles. You can read more about noodles in Chapter 6.

- ✔ **Soba:** Soba are linguine-sized buckwheat noodles that are hearty, healthy, and served both hot and cold. They're sold dried in Asian grocery stores. Some versions have green tea added, which yields a green colored noodle.

- ✔ **Udon:** These cream-colored, wheat-based noodles are slightly fatter than udon and often featured in soups. These are also easy to find, right next to the soba.

- ✔ **Somen:** These wheat-based noodles are as fine as a hair. I don't provide any recipes for them, but you can try cooking somen and adding them to your favorite soup.

Book VII

Japanese Cooking

✔ **Ramen:** Every supermarket has instant ramen, usually in a large variety of flavors. This instant soup, comprised of dried noodles and a flavor packet, is as popular in Japan as it is here. It is famously popular with the cash-poor college crowd, and Web sites highlight the hundreds of recipes you can make with these easy-to-find and even easier-to-cook noodles. I, however, give you a recipe for a thick noodle soup (see Chapter 6) using fresh ramen. You can substitute Chinese-style egg noodles, which are essentially the same thing as ramen. You can find them in the refrigerator section of Asian grocery stores. They are long, with a rich yellow color and about the same thickness as linguine.

Fish, fish, fish!

Fish is the most popular and common protein to be found in the island nation of Japan. The Japanese are famous for eating every part of a fish. The head appears in soup, the liver may be minced and featured in a dish, and the skin may be fried and served on its own. And don't overlook their fondness for certain fish intestines! But the recipes offered in this book use only the fish (and fish parts) that are most popular with Western diners of Japanese food. For a full treatise on these fish, see Chapter 5.

One fish product that I do want to mention here is kamaboko. You can find this semicircular processed fish cake frozen in Asian grocery stores. Each one is about 5 inches long by 2 inches wide, white in the center, and often tinted red on the outside for visual appeal. If you've ever had a Japanese soup or stew with a slice of something that looks like this but had no idea what it was — ta da! Now you know. Because it's only faintly fishy, you may not have even identified it as a fish product. Keep some on hand in the freezer to use as a quick and filling addition to soups and stews.

Green tea: Not just for leprechauns

Green tea, like all tea, comes from the *Camellia sinensis* plant. What makes it "green" is that the plant's leaves are picked, steamed, and dried, but not fermented. (Black teas have had their leaves fermented to various degrees).

Discovering the varieties of green tea

Japanese cuisine features several different kinds of green tea:

✔ **Gyokuro:** This is the premium variety of green tea and is translated as "jewel dew." It's made from very young leaves and harvested in the spring when the plants are most tender. Make this fragrant, mellow, and expensive tea with hot, but not boiling, water. It's not unusual for tea masters to use water at a temperature of 125 degrees; hotter water spoils the delicate nuances of this tea. I have also enjoyed gyokuro iced, both at home and at esteemed teahouses, such as Ito En in New York City, a tea emporium and restaurant specializing in green tea. So if this respected teahouse ices this green tea, even though doing so strays somewhat from tradition, you can ice it, too, and feel perfectly comfortable about making it that way.

✔ **Sencha:** This is the most commonly used green tea. The flavors can vary widely, from fresh and haylike to very green and grassy tasting. The color could be a pale gold or a light green. Brew this tea with water at a temperature of about 170 degrees.

✔ **Bancha:** This tea is comprised of stems as well as leaves and can look very "twiggy." You can use boiling water to brew this type.

✔ **Hojicha:** This is roasted bancha and makes a very smoky-tasting brown tea. You can use boiling water.

✔ **Genmaicha:** This tea is a mixture of bancha and roasted grains of rice.

✔ **Matcha:** Entire books have been written about matcha, the powdered vivid green tea principally used in the Japanese tea ceremony, where it is whipped into a frothy, creamy beverage. It is fairly bitter, and the tea is prepared differently than when making leaf tea. Matcha is a revered beverage that you should treat with respect when brewing. I use it in an ice-cream recipe in Chapter 8. Please consult books devoted to this beverage in order to find out more about it. I recommend *The Tea Ceremony,* by Sen'o Tanaka (Kodansha International, New York, 1998) and *The Japanese Way of Tea* by V. Dixon Morris (University of Hawaii Press, Honolulu, 1998).

Brewing green tea

I am a tea lover and brew a pot of black tea every morning and green tea every afternoon. Green tea does contain caffeine, although less than black tea and even less than coffee. For black tea, use boiling water. For green tea, the water temperature can vary from about 125 to 170 degrees. In general, the higher the quality of the green tea, the lower the water temperature should be.

To brew a good pot of tea, you must start with good water. Use bottled spring water if necessary.

Follow these steps for making tea:

1. **Rinse a teapot with hot water to warm it.**

2. **Place a teaspoon of green tea in the pot for every 6-ounce cup of tea you need.**

   Measuring dry tea leaves is tricky. The larger and fluffier the leaves, the greater volume you have to use per serving. If the leaves are very small, or even crushed, use less, as it will be more concentrated. You have to experiment with this process, using the tea at hand. You may need a few tries before you brew a pot that you like.

3. **Using fresh, cold (or room-temperature bottled) water, measure out 6 ounces of water for every teaspoon of tea in the pot.**

4. **Bring the water to a boil and then let it sit off the heat for a few moments.**

   Or, alternatively, watch the water as it heats, and as soon as very tiny bubbles appear around the edges of the pot, the water is hot enough. Of course, if you have a thermometer, use it to bring water to proper temperature. Pour the correct temperature water over the leaves in the pot.

5. **Allow to brew for 2 to 3 minutes and then immediately strain and serve. Allowing the tea to steep too long makes it bitter.**

Green tea is traditionally enjoyed without sweetener, milk, or lemon.

If you don't like the flavor of the pot you brewed, determining the cause of the problem can be difficult. But usually you have over- or undermeasured the leaves, or over- or understeeped the tea. If the tea is very strong or very weak, you probably used too much or too little tea. If it's bitter, you probably steeped it for too long. These are subtle differences (between strong and bitter), but the more you drink and taste, the more familiar you'll become with the brewing process.

Azuki beans

These tiny, reddish purplish dried beans, referred to as azuki, aduki, or adzuki, are often used in Japanese sweets. They're cooked into a sweetened paste and used in a variety of ways, including as a filling for pastries.

They're also sometimes cooked with rice — and they tint the rice pink! This festive-looking dish is used for celebrations such as birthdays.

You can also buy azuki bean paste as well as sweetened azuki bean paste.

Condiments, seasonings, and more

Condiments, certain seasonings, and ingredients are used frequently in Japanese cooking. In order to make the recipes in this book, have these items on hand.

Japanese breadcrumbs

Often labeled *panko,* Japanese breadcrumbs are extremely crunchy and absolutely perfect for *tonkatsu,* a breaded, fried pork cutlet (see the recipe in Chapter 7 of Book VII). Regular American breadcrumbs just won't cut it — make the extra trip to the Asian grocery store to find the Japanese variety.

And, by the way, I've never figured out a way to mimic their texture in a homemade version.

Mirin

This sweet wine is used for cooking, not for drinking. The alcohol content is very low, so you can find it in grocery stores, not liquor stores, probably on a shelf near the soy sauce.

Pickled ginger

This pink, tangy condiment, called *gari,* is great for digestion and served with sushi. It's thinly sliced ginger that is pickled and sometimes tinted a pale pink. The light red color comes from red shiso leaves (see the section "Shiso," later in this chapter). Sometimes it is very bright red and labeled beni shoga. You can find these products in Asian grocery stores refrigerated, vacuum packed, or in jars.

Rice vinegar

Sometimes labeled *komezu,* this very mild, golden vinegar is made from fermented rice. It's easy to find, even in Asian sections of regular supermarkets.

Sesame seeds, sesame oil

Sesame seeds *(goma)* come in both white and black, and I specify the type you needed in each recipe. They're often toasted before using: Simply place the desired amount in a heavy-bottomed saucepan (I use cast-iron), place over medium heat, and cook, stirring frequently, until toasted to a light golden brown. If toasting the black seeds, just watch them carefully and remove them from the heat the moment they begin to give off a toasty fragrance.

Sesame oil comes both toasted and untoasted. The untoasted is fairly mild and similar to other vegetable oils that you might use every day, like for salad dressing. The toasted, however, is a deep amber color and incredibly fragrant. Just a little will add loads of flavor to a dish, such as in the Seaweed Salad in Chapter 4.

Shichimi

Shichimi is a dry, granular seven-spice powder made of dried red chiles, orange peel, sansho (a pepperlike berry), poppy seeds, sesame seeds, hemp seeds, and crushed nori. Some Japanese cooks make their own at home, but you can purchase it ready-made. It usually comes in a shaker-top container so that it's easy to add to food. Shake some on a bowl of rice to taste it to see whether you like it.

Shiso

This commonly used Japanese herb is similar to basil. You can use it to garnish sashimi, and it is sometimes used to flavor and color pickled ginger and

Book VII

Japanese Cooking

pickled plums (the red version). Occasionally shiso is fried in tempura batter. It has a basil-like, almost minty flavor, and I've even eaten it in a sweet iced dessert, which was most refreshing.

Umeboshi

These pickled green (as in unripe) plums are actually pinkish red in color. Just to make it even more confusing, even though they're referred to as plums, they're actually more of an apricot! Although some Japanese cooks pickle their own, many good ones are on the market and easy to find. Look for them in Asian grocery stores as well as natural food stores. They're tart and tangy and often used in makizushi (sushi rolls). Some people say they're an aid for digestion.

Wasabi

Ahhh, this is my favorite Japanese condiment. It's often called Japanese horseradish because its pungent flavor is similar to Western horseradish. You very occasionally find fresh wasabi, but it's very difficult to find, so I assume that you'll use prepared products.

Some prepared wasabi comes in tubes and is creamy, but the kind I prefer is a dry powder and comes in a can or jar. It has a longer shelf life and therefore is handier to have around in your kitchen.

To reconstitute wasabi powder, use equal amounts of powder and water and stir to combine. Allow to sit a few moments for the flavor to develop. You want the texture to be creamy but thick enough to form into a tiny ball, cone, or mound to serve along with your sushi.

Wasabi is the green paste that is served with sashimi and sushi. It is a delicious accompaniment but can also overpower the delicate nature of raw fish, so use it sparingly. You'll know if you use too much because your sinuses will be instantly cleared and you'll begin to cry!

Choosing Equipment for the Japanese Kitchen

You need basic kitchen tools, such as sharp knives, pots and pans, and cutting boards, for Japanese cooking, but you should also have a few pieces of additional equipment that is specific to Japanese cooking.

Japanese kitchens don't usually have an oven. Although microwave ovens have become popular, as has Western-style food, the Japanese do most cooking on top of the stove. A typical Japanese kitchen has a stovetop with just two burners.

Electric rice cookers (suihanki)

The Japanese eat rice three times a day, so a lot of rice cooking is going on. An electric rice cooker is very common in Japan as it makes the cook's job easier. Because many Japanese kitchens have few burners on their stoves, one way to maximize the kitchen's efficiency is to use an electric rice cooker because it frees an extra burner for your other cooking. Automatic rice cookers are just that — automatic! You simply add rice and water and press a button, and it cooks your rice perfectly. Be sure to follow the individual manufacturer's instructions. To make rice on top of the stove, see Chapter 6 of Book VII, or turn to Chapter 5 of Book VII for sushi rice.

Bamboo skewers

Thin bamboo skewers, about 12 inches long, are available in most supermarkets, either in the kitchenware section or the fish department. In Japanese cuisine, they're used when making yakitori (see Chapter 7) or to straighten out shrimp before dipping them in tempura batter.

Ginger grater

Fresh ginger is quite stringy. Although you can grate it on a Western-style box grater, specific graters are available for grating ginger. One is shown in Figure 2-2. They are made from porcelain, metal, or wood and have very small, sharp spikes. When you rub the ginger over it, it grates to an extremely fine texture. If you grate over a small dish, any ginger juice that exudes may be collected and added to your recipe. You can also use these gadgets to grate fresh wasabi root and daikon radish.

Book VII

Japanese Cooking

Figure 2-2: A Japanese ginger grater.

Knives and cleavers

Sharp knives are a necessity for most styles of cooking, and Japanese cuisine is no exception. Japanese knives and cleavers are available, but you can use regular knives.

Some Japanese knives, such as the very long, thin ones used for sushi, have very specific uses. They allow a degree of control (due to their balance of construction) that helps make cutting raw fish easier than it might be otherwise. Here's a description of the most common Japanese knives:

✔ **Debabocho** are basic kitchen knives and are most similar to the more familiar chef's knives sold in the United States.

✔ **Takobiki** (shown in Figure 2-3) are very long and thin and used for slicing sashimi and fish for sushi.

✔ **Usubabocho or Nakiribocho** (also shown in Figure 2-3) look like the basic cleavers you may already have in your kitchen, but these have a slightly rounded end.

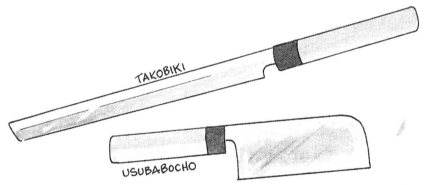

Figure 2-3:
Japanese
knives.

Mortar and pestle

The Japanese version of this tool is called a *suribachi* (the bowl part) and *surikogi* (the grinder part), but it's commonly referred to simply as a suribachi, as in "hand me the suribachi, please." They are made of clay with sharp ridges in the inside of the bowl. This rough texture encourages the grinding process. Sesame seeds, for instance, can be ground very easily in a suribachi.

Chopsticks — for eating and cooking

Chopsticks are the eating utensils of choice in Japan. Some are bamboo, and others are made of lacquered wood or even ivory (if they are very old). Chopsticks are used for more than eating. Longer chopsticks are joined at the top by a thread and used in cooking. The cooking chopsticks are always made from wood. Ones for personal use, which are shorter, are called *hashi;* the longer ones used in the kitchen are called *saibashi.* Disposable chopsticks that come presented in paper envelopes in restaurants are called *waribashi.* One estimate claims that 8 billion disposable wooden chopsticks are used every year! There's a lot of people using chopsticks out there!

If a chopstick rest *(hashioki)* is provided (see Figure 2-4), then by all means lay your chopsticks on it when you aren't using them. The rest should be vertical to the edge of the table so that the chopsticks lay horizontal. If you need help using your chopsticks to eat, see Figure 2-5.

Figure 2-4:
Using a
chopstick
rest.

Book VII

**Japanese
Cooking**

If a chopstick rest isn't provided and you want to put your chopsticks down, place them parallel to the table, right in front of you near the table's edge.

Never stick chopsticks upright in your rice or food; it's considered very impolite. (For more on etiquette, see Chapter 1.)

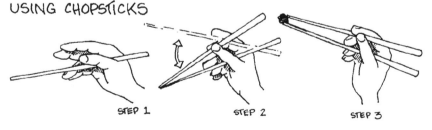

USING CHOPSTICKS

Figure 2-5:
Using
chopsticks
is easy.

STEP 1   STEP 2   STEP 3

Dipping dishes

Diners at sushi restaurants receive a small shallow dish in which to pour soy or other sauces (see Figure 2-6). Then they can dip their own sushi and sashimi into it before eating.

These tiny dishes come in handy at many other times. For instance, if you're eating chilled tofu, it's nice to have individual dishes for any accompanying sauce or condiment.

Figure 2-6:
Dipping
dishes hold
sauces and
condiments.

Japanese pots and pans

Here are a few of the various types of Japanese pots that are useful to have:

- **Donabe:** This earthenware casserole is often used for dishes such as sukiyaki, oden, and shabu shabu. You can place it directly over a flame, but you shouldn't use it in an oven.

- **Shabu shabu pot:** *Shabu shabu,* or pot-cooked beef, is cooked in this pot, which is made of metal or earthenware and often has a center core so that the portion that holds food forms a ring around the core. It too can go directly on a burner.

- **Tetsunabe:** These cast-iron pots are used to make *nabemono,* or one-pot meals, such as sukiyaki.

Portable gas stoves

Small, portable, gas-powered burners are often used to heat the pots mentioned in the section "Japanese pots and pans." Because the Japanese kitchen offers few burners, this appliance is a way to extend the cooking facilities in the household. It's not necessary, but it is convenient to have. It enables you to cook communally at the table.

Steamers

Both bamboo and metal steamers are used throughout Japan, but they're made essentially the same way. Each type of steamer is shaped like a basket — with perforations on which to place food, and a cover. The unit is placed over a pot with boiling water, and the food inside is steamed. Although bamboo steamers are very attractive and I like the tactile sense they provide, the collapsible metal type are just fine. Another aspect to consider, if you are shopping for one or the other, is that the metal ones are quite small and store easily — a boon to those with little storage space.

Bamboo steamers have a flat steamer area, which enables a lot of food to be steamed on the given surface area, and it all steams evenly. Any steamer works better if the steamer area (the perforated part) is large and relatively flat.

Tools for making sushi

Making certain kinds of sushi at home does require a few different implements. Here's what you need:

- **Wooden sushi tub:** Called *hangiri,* these wooden tubs, usually made of cypress wood, are the perfect receptacle in which to make sushi rice. The large surface area cools the rice quickly, and the wood has the perfect level of porosity to absorb excess moisture. You don't need one, but it's nice to have if you make a lot of sushi.

- **Wooden paddle:** The *shamoji,* or wooden paddle, is used to stir sushi rice as it cools and while the sweetened vinegar is added. Think of this useful tool as a Japanese spatula.

- **Bamboo rolling mats:** Called *makisu,* these mats, made from thin pieces of bamboo tied together with string, enable you to make sushi rolls *(makizushi)* fairly easily. They're inexpensive, and you can find them in any Asian grocery store and some natural food stores.

- **Wooden sushi molds:** Some sushi, such as *oshizushi,* or pressed sushi, is made by using a mold, often made of wood. The rice and toppings go into the mold, and the top is put into place and pressed downward. The resulting pressed "cake" is removed and cut into bite-size pieces.

Book VII

Japanese
Cooking

Chapter 3

Mastering a Few Simple Techniques

Good technique in the kitchen is the foundation of any cuisine. After first becoming familiar with your ingredients, you then must find out how to bring their best characteristics out in the dishes that you prepare. This chapter explains the basic techniques used in Japanese cooking.

Working with Vegetables

You may know how to mince and dice already, but the Japanese take cutting veggies to a whole new level of food as art. Although the basics of cutting and slicing veggies will suffice, if you have the time to make some of the following fancier cuts, your dishes will be more visually pleasing. Some Japanese cooks believe that the techniques enhance flavor as well. For example, a roll-cut carrot has many cut surfaces, allowing more flavor to be absorbed from seasonings, sauces, and soups.

- **Rounds (*wagiri*):** You probably already know this technique. Simply slice cylindrical veggies, such as carrots, crosswise into rounds.

- **Half moons (*hangetsugiri*):** Cut cylindrical veggies in half lengthwise and then slice them crosswise into half-rounds.

- **Quarter rounds:** Cut cylindrical veggies into quarters lengthwise and then slice them crosswise into quarter-rounds.

- **Rolling cut (*rangiri*):** Cut cylindrical veggies on the diagonal, roll and cut, roll and cut, always on the diagonal. This technique creates a multi-faceted cut.

- **Chunks (*butsugiri*):** Cut cylindrical vegetables into lengths of desired size.

- **Diagonal cuts (*nanamegiri*):** Cut cylindrical vegetables into lengths of desired size on the diagonal.

- **Slanting cuts (*sogigiri*):** Thick vegetables, such as mushrooms, can be sliced on a slight slant, which elongates their shape, thus increasing their surface area — all the better to soak up flavors.

- **Wedge cuts (*kushigatagiri*):** Cut a round vegetable, such as a lemon, into wedges.

- **Rectangle cuts (*tanzakugiri*):** Cut small, very thin rectangles, about ½ inch × 1 inch, from root vegetables. With a daikon, for instance, you can square off the cylinder and then cut it into thin slices.

- **Sticks (*hyoshigigiri*):** Square off the vegetable as described for the rectangle cuts and then cut into ⅛- to ¼-inch square sticks, like thin French fries.

- **Dice (*sainomegiri*):** Cut sticks as described for the sticks (hyoshigigiri) technique and then cut into ¼-inch square dice.

- **Julienne sticks (*sengiri*):** Cut into thin rectangles as described for the rectangle cuts (tanzakugiri) technique, stack several of them on top of one another, and then cut into very thin julienne strips.

Steaming and Simmering

Steaming, called *mushimono,* is a very popular Japanese cooking technique for a variety of reasons: It takes place on top of the stove or on a portable burner, which benefits the many Japanese households that don't have ovens. Steaming is easy to do and a healthy method of cooking that helps retain foods' natural shape, flavor, and nutritional content. Dishes such as the Egg Custard Soup in Chapter 4 of Book VII are examples of steamed dishes.

You can use a traditional bamboo steamer, but any steaming setup you have in your kitchen works just fine, as long as there is a large, relatively flat steaming area.

Nimono is the term used for simmered dishes, such as Simmered Mackerel in Miso (see Chapter 7 of Book VII). Simmering ingredients in liquid creates a rich, nutritious, delicious broth. Simmering is an easy technique, as all the cooking occurs in one pot and you use minimal, if any, added fat.

For simmering, any wide, deep, covered pot will work. The heavier the pot, the more even the heat and the easier it is to retain a slow, gentle simmer.

One-Pot Cooking

Japanese cuisine includes a specific style of cooking called one-pot cooking, or *nabemono.* All the ingredients are added in succession to a pot to cook and are then served from the same pot. You can find examples of this style of cooking in the Beef Sukiyaki and Oden Stew recipes in Chapter 7 of Book VII. Any deep, wide pot that can go on top of the stove works well for this technique. If the pot is attractive enough to bring to the table, all the better! This way, you can show off your pretty arrangement of ingredients.

Donabe, which are earthenware casseroles, and *tetsunabe,* which are made of cast iron, are traditionally used for dishes such as *sukiyaki.*

Grilling, Broiling, and Pan-Frying

Grilling or broiling can take place over an outdoor grill or under a broiler, as with the Chicken Yakitori in Chapter 7 of Book VII. These dishes are referred to as *yakimono.*

Pan-frying takes place in a shallow heavy pan on top of the stove with a little bit of fat in the bottom. The Teriyaki Salmon in Chapter 7 and the Rolled Omelet used in sushi in Chapter 5 both use the pan-frying technique.

Book VII

Japanese Cooking

Deep-Frying

Tempura is a classic example of Japanese style deep-frying, *agemono* in Japanese. Unlike the heavy, sodden batters that coat the onion rings or fish sticks at your local greasy spoon, tempura is light and crispy and oh so delectable.

Seafood and vegetables of all kinds are deep-fried in tempura batter and served with a subtle dipping sauce. Turn to Chapter 7 of Book VII for a recipe for Japanese Shrimp and Veggie Tempura.

Deep-fried pork may seem like a dish you would find in a restaurant in the southeastern United States, but *tonkatsu* is quite popular in Japan. Turn to Chapter 7 of Book VII for my recipe, which uses tender slices of pork covered in extra-crispy breadcrumbs before being fried. You'll love it; in fact, this is a good place to start when introducing Japanese foods to the less adventurous. You serve it with an easy-to-make tangy sauce.

Deep-fat frying the right way

To keep deep-fat fried foods as light and crisp as possible, follow these tips:

- ✔ Use a light vegetable oil, such as canola, sunflower, safflower, or grape-seed. You can also use peanut oil if you're sure that none of your guests have peanut allergies. These are great frying oils because they have a high smoking point.

- ✔ Always use enough oil. The foods should have plenty of room to move around. Never crowd the pot.

- ✔ Make sure that the oil is hot enough (temperatures are given in individual recipes, but a range of 365 to 375 degrees is typical).

- ✔ Make sure that the oil comes back up to temperature with subsequent batches.

- ✔ Oil can combust. Don't let it get so hot that it begins to smoke. If it does begin smoking, immediately cover with a lid and turn off the heat source.

- ✔ As you fry batches of food, skim out any bits of food or batter floating around in the oil. Keep the oil clean and clear.

- ✔ Always drain your fried foods on paper towels to absorb any excess oil.

- ✔ All deep-fat fried foods are best if eaten soon after frying time.

Managing oil temperature

A discussion of deep-fat frying isn't complete unless I talk about hot oil. Some people don't like deep-fried foods because the foods they've eaten have been improperly fried. If you fry at a temperature that is too low, the foods become soggy and absorb the oil. If the oil is hot enough, it seals and browns the outside, and you get light, crispy fried food.

If you don't have a deep-fat fryer, then using a thermometer is the way to go. But if you don't have a deep-fat fryer or a thermometer and simply must fry up a batch of tempura right away, here's what to do. Fill up your receptacle with oil and heat it up. When you think it's hot enough, drop a 1-inch cube of bread in the oil and set the timer for 1 minute. After the allotted time, the bread should be evenly golden brown. This means that the oil is about 365 degrees, which is a good frying temperature for the tempura recipe in Chapter 7 of Book VII.

Chapter 4

Soups, Salads, and Pickles

In This Chapter

▶ Discovering dashi, the basic Japanese stock

▶ Making soup with miso

▶ Turning to salads

▶ Fixing pickles in a jiffy

*T*he world of Japanese soups and salads is quite varied. Soups *(shirumono)* come both thick, as in an egg custard, and clear, as in miso soup. Clear soups are called *suimono,* which means "something to drink."

The most frequently encountered Japanese soup is some variation of miso, of which there are many. All are very simple and quick to prepare and make a perfect start to a meal.

Salads are of two varieties: *sunomono,* which are "vinegary things," and *aemono,* which are often cooked and always coated with a dressing. In this chapter, a simple cucumber salad serves as an example of sunomono, and a chilled tofu dish, a seaweed salad, and a spinach salad with a miso dressing are examples of aemono.

Pickled vegetables, called *tsukemono,* are a common addition to the Japanese meal; they're very easy to make and really just salted veggies. I give you a quick pickle recipe in this chapter.

Starting with Dashi: The First Step in Soup Making

To make almost any Japanese soup, you need to start with a good basic stock. In European and American cooking, that basic is beef bouillon or chicken stock. In Japanese cooking, you need to make *dashi,* which is made with water and a two ingredients you may not be familiar with: *konbu,* a seaweed of the kelp variety, and *katsuobushi,* dried bonito, a type of mackerel. This fish product is available as dried fillets as well as flakes that look like dried wood shavings. These flakes, *kezuribushi,* are easy to use and are what I use in my recipes. (You can read more about these ingredients in Chapter 2 of Book VII.)

Although any stock tastes best if freshly made, it's an extra step that many cooks, especially home cooks (both Japanese and American), simply don't want to bother with. Although making homemade dashi takes less than 10 minutes, if you really don't want to bother, see the sidebar "Instant dashi."

Dashi — Easy Japanese Stock

Three ingredients give you a basic of Japanese cuisine — dashi — which is used as a base for many soups and sauces.

Special tools: *Cheesecloth*

Preparation time: *Less than 5 minutes*

Cooking time: *Less than 5 minutes*

Yield: *1 quart*

4 cups water

1 ounce (approximately 15 inches long x 4 inches wide) konbu, wiped clean

1 ounce (approximately 3 cups) dried bonito flakes

1 Place the water and konbu in a medium-sized saucepan over medium heat. Heat to just under a boil and immediately remove the konbu. You can save the konbu to use in other recipes. (Refrigerate until needed.)

2 Turn the heat up to high and bring the water to a boil. Remove from the heat and quickly stir in the bonito flakes. Let the pot sit for about 1 minute, or just until the flakes settle to the bottom. Strain the stock through a cheesecloth-lined strainer into a storage container.

3 Store the dashi in the refrigerator in an airtight container for up to 4 days. Or pour it into ice cube trays, freeze, and store the cubes in resealable plastic bags for up to a month.

Tip: *Don't let the konbu boil. The stock will become quite strong — stronger than you want! Similarly, after the stock does boil, remove it from the heat before adding the bonito flakes, as these shouldn't be boiled either. Dashi is all about subtlety and nuance of flavor.*

Instant dashi

If you don't want to make your own dashi, you can use an easy-to-find product called *dashinomoto*, a premade stock. Two kinds are available: One type comes in mesh bags, like tea bags, which can be immersed in water. The other kind, which I prefer, comes in a jar or a box of packets and is granular in texture. You just measure it out when you're ready and dissolve it in boiling water. Each brand gives you the proper ratio of its product to water. Although I want you

to feel free to use this instant type, and many Japanese home cooks do, I do provide a recipe for dashi from scratch in this chapter.

Always follow the instructions on the container of instant dashi that you're using, but, in general, stir 1 teaspoon instant dashi granules into 4 cups of simmering water and use immediately. Don't store this type of dashi; just make it as you need it.

Vegetarian Konbu Dashi

Although traditional dashi is made with konbu and fish flakes, strict vegetarians can use an alternative recipe, also used in Japan. This version is a simple konbu stock.

Preparation time: *35 minutes*

Cooking time: *Less than 5 minutes*

Yield: *1 quart*

4 cups water

1½ ounces konbu, wiped clean

1 Place the water and konbu in a medium-sized saucepan and allow to sit for 30 minutes. Place over medium heat and bring to just under a boil; immediately remove the konbu. You can use the konbu in other recipes. (Refrigerate until needed.)

2 Store the dashi in the refrigerator in an airtight container for up to 4 days. Or pour it into ice cube trays, freeze, and store the cubes in resealable plastic bags for up to a month.

Book VII

Japanese
Cooking

Tapping the best water for your dashi

How does your tap water taste? Whether your water comes from a private well or a town or city water facility, it may have off flavors that affect your cooking. If you drink bottled or filtered

water, use it for your dashi for best results. Particularly with delicate broths such as dashi, better-tasting water makes all the difference.

Weights and measures

Some items are easy to measure, such as a tablespoon of miso or a cup of water, but some ingredients are best weighed, so I do expect you to have a scale when making some of these recipes. The seaweed and fish flakes used to make dashi, for example, are difficult to measure but easy to weigh. Also, weight always gives you an exact measurement, ensuring excellent results. (I give you both volume and weight, where appropriate throughout the book.)

Weight is always more accurate. For instance, the weight to volume ratio of bonito flakes may vary due to the differing densities of various brands. Some are cut more thickly than others. This is why a cup of your bonito flakes might be a different weight than my cup of bonito flakes.

Adding Flavor and Nutrition with Miso

Miso is fermented soybean paste. I know that sounds horrible, but it's truly a wondrous ingredient, packed with both flavor and nutrition. Depending on the ingredients and the preparation, the color ranges from a creamy white to a rich nutty brown color, with ranges of yellow and red in between. For more information, turn to Chapter 2 of Book VII.

Many Japanese households develop their own blends of two or even three kinds of miso to create a flavor profile in their soup that is unique and that they particularly like. In this way, this very simple soup recipe can take on myriad flavors and characteristics. Consider the Miso Soup recipe in this chapter a starting point.

In Japan, miso soup is often served for breakfast. You might try that, but many non-Japanese prefer to serve it as a starter to a daytime or evening meal.

Although making miso soup is very quick and easy, you need to follow specific techniques for the best results. In particular, never boil miso. Boiling spoils the flavor and diminishes the nutrition.

Miso Soup

You can use any kind of miso that you like, but I suggest trying a rich red miso for starters. If you're a bit timid in the taste-testing department, try a light yellow miso.

Preparation time: *Less than 5 minutes*

Cooking time: *Less than 5 minutes*

Yield: *4 servings*

3 tablespoons miso

4 cups dashi (see the recipes earlier in this chapter)

1 Place the miso in a small bowl; set aside.

2 Place the dashi in a medium-sized saucepan over medium heat and bring to just under a boil. Immediately ladle out about ½ cup of dashi and pour over the miso. Mash the miso with the back of a spoon or fork and stir to combine with stock; it will be thick and creamy, but still liquid. Return the miso mixture to the dashi in the saucepan to heat; do not allow to boil.

3 Remove the pan from the heat, divide the soup among bowls, and serve immediately.

Tip: Miso soup separates after a few minutes of sitting. A cloudy portion sinks to the bottom, while the top becomes clear. The soup is still okay to eat and actually becomes quite beautiful. It looks like clouds suspended in your soup! If you like, you can stir the soup with a chopstick to re-combine it before you drink it.

Vary It! To make miso soup with tofu and scallions, follow the recipe, but in Step 2, add ⅓ pound soft diced tofu to the hot broth. Finish the recipe as directed and then sprinkle the soup with ¼ cup thinly sliced scallions before serving. Many Japanese restaurants in the United States serve miso soup this way.

Book VII

Japanese Cooking

Steaming Foods in Serving Cups

Many foods in Japan are steamed right in the cup in which they're served. These are referred to as *chawanmushi,* which means "steamed in a cup." You can buy special chawanmushi cups in stores that carry Asian utensils, but you can also use ceramic custard cups that hold about two-thirds to three-quarters cup of liquid.

Egg Custard Soup

This soup is actually a steamed egg-based custard, although it's still often referred to as soup. When offered at the beginning of a meal, it can take the place of soup. In cold months, you can serve it hot. During hot weather, try it chilled.

Special tools: *Six 6-ounce custard cups, pot with cover, and flat steamer insert*

Preparation time: *15 minutes*

Cooking time: *22 minutes*

Yield: *6 servings*

¼ of a whole skinless, boneless chicken breast, cut into ½-inch cubes (about ½ cup of cubes)

2 fresh medium shiitake mushrooms, wiped clean, stems removed, and cut into ¼-inch slices

2 teaspoons sake

2 teaspoons soy sauce

3 chives (about 12-inches long)

6 large shrimp, shelled and deveined

1 medium carrot, peeled and cut into ⅛-inch slices

Custard:

4 eggs

2½ cups dashi (see the recipes earlier in this chapter)

1 tablespoon soy sauce

1 Place the chicken and mushrooms in a small bowl and sprinkle with the sake and soy sauce. Allow to marinate while you prepare the chives, shrimp, and carrots.

2 Cut the chives in half crosswise and tie a knot in the center of each one; set aside. If all you find are chives that are 6-inches or less, do not cut them in half; simply tie them in a knot.

3 Bring a small pot of water to a simmer over medium heat, add the cleaned shrimp, and cook just until they turn opaque, about 1 minute. Remove the shrimp with a slotted spoon and set aside.

4 Drop the carrot slices into the same simmering pot of water and cook until just tender, about 2 minutes. Drain and set aside.

5 Make the custard by combining the eggs, dashi, and soy sauce in a small bowl and whisking until the eggs are frothy. Strain the custard through a fine-meshed sieve into a large measuring cup with a pouring spout.

6 Divide the chicken and mushrooms (along with any marinating liquid not absorbed), shrimp, and carrots among 6 custard cups. Pour the egg mixture into the custard cups, dividing evenly. Place a knotted chive on top. Cover each cup with foil and place the cups on top of a steamer insert set above simmering water. Cover the pot and steam for about 22 minutes. Remove the foil and insert a bamboo skewer into the custard; if it comes out clean without any wet custard sticking to it and a clear liquid is left behind around the edges, it's ready. Take care not to overcook or the chicken and custard will be tough. Serve immediately.

Tip: *The custard cups take up a lot of room, and chances are, your steamer setup holds only 3 or 4 cups. Check beforehand to see whether you need an additional steamer. Alternatively, use a roasting pan with a flat roasting rack set inside. Cover each individual custard cup with foil, pour water in the bottom of the pan, and cover the entire pan with aluminum foil in lieu of a lid. Make sure that the aluminum foil fits tightly so that the custard steams. If cooking the custard cups in a roasting pan, you bring the water to a simmer with the custard cups already in place, so the total cooking time is slightly longer — check after 25 minutes total cooking time.*

Tip: *To add a decorative touch that you would commonly find in a dish such as this in Japan, cut the carrots into little flower shapes. Simply wash and peel a carrot and then cut a shallow triangular notch down the length of the carrot in four places, evenly spaced around the vegetable. Then, when you make slices, each piece will look like a little flower. You can also cut the mushrooms on a slant to increase their surface area for maximum flavor absorption and to give them a more decorative look.*

Vary It! *To convert this custard into a vegetarian version, leave out the chicken and shrimp and add extra mushrooms. You also can try other kinds of mushrooms, such as oyster mushrooms or enoki. When making the custard, use the vegetarian dashi.*

Book VII

**Japanese
Cooking**

Assembling Salads: Sunomono and Aemono

No wedges of iceberg lettuce with blue cheese dressing here! Japanese salads are usually very light and refreshing and very easy to make. You can use them as accompaniments to a complete Japanese meal, or try one on the side with your own roast chicken or meat loaf!

Wakame is a sea vegetable that is very popular in Japan and is used in a variety of ways, including in soups and in salads. Almost every Japanese restaurant I go into these days in the United States offers a cold seaweed salad as an appetizer. I've re-created a similar one, the Seaweed Salad, for you to make at home.

Cucumbers with Sweet Vinegar Dressing

This refreshing salad is a good accompaniment to almost any Japanese meal. The dressing, which is sweetened with sugar, is very typical of dressings used for many vegetables in Japan. If you can find the English hothouse cucumbers, which are thin skinned and very meaty with few seeds, by all means use those.

Preparation time: *25 minutes*

Yield: *4 servings*

2 medium regular cucumbers or 1 English hothouse cucumber

Salt

1 cup dashi (see the recipes earlier in this chapter)

1 cup rice vinegar

¼ cup soy sauce

1½ tablespoons sugar

1 Peel the cucumbers, leaving a few thin strips of peel. Slice in half lengthwise and scoop out the seeds with a teaspoon. Slice the cucumbers into very thin slices and place in a shallow mixing bowl. Sprinkle with salt, toss to coat, and let sit 15 minutes. Drain well (the cucumbers will become moisture-laden); place in a clean, absorbent cloth towel; and squeeze dry with your hands. Taste a slice; if it's very salty, rinse with water, drain, and squeeze dry again. Place in a mixing bowl.

2 Whisk together the dashi, vinegar, soy sauce, and sugar in a mixing bowl until the sugar is dissolved. Pour about half of the sauce over the cucumbers, toss to coat, and drain; squeeze dry, again using a clean towel, and return to bowl.

3 Pour the remaining sauce over the cucumbers, toss, divide into small serving dishes, and serve.

Enjoying soybeans straight from the shell

Miso, tofu, and soy sauce are all made from soybeans. But what about eating the soybean (edamame) itself? The Japanese quickly boil soybeans still in the pod and then eat them straight from the pod. They're easy to prepare and delicious to eat, and you can find them frozen in 1-pound bags in most Asian supply stores and in the freezer section of some natural foods stores. Some supermarkets have them fresh in the exotic produce section.

Simply bring a large pot of salted water to a boil and add the fresh or frozen soybeans. Bring the water back to a boil and boil for 2 to 3 minutes for fresh and 4 to 5 minutes for frozen. Drain. Place in a bowl and sprinkle with salt. Serve immediately; and don't forget to set out a bowl for discarded pods. Invite guests to pick up a pod, open with their fingers, and pop the soybeans directly in their mouths. These are healthy, lowfat, and delicious — and quite the conversation starter, too.

Chilled Tofu

Use silky soft tofu in this recipe for best results. Check the expiration date on the tofu package and make sure that it's very fresh. This recipe is all about the pure, fresh flavor of the tofu, so you need to start with the highest quality raw ingredients. Most packages come in a 12- to 16-ounce size, and any of those sizes works for this recipe.

Preparation time: *1 hour (prepare any toppings while the tofu sits)*

Yield: *4 servings*

12 to 16 ounces soft tofu

Lemon Garlic Sauce with Ginger:

¼ cup soy sauce

2 tablespoons dashi (see the recipes earlier in this chapter)

2 tablespoons lemon juice

1 teaspoon minced garlic

1 teaspoon grated ginger

Optional toppings:

Bonito flakes

Wasabi

Grated ginger

Minced garlic

Thinly sliced nori seaweed

Thinly sliced scallions

Minced chives

Book VII

Japanese Cooking

1 Place a colander in the sink and line the bottom with a double layer of paper towels. Remove the tofu from the container and place on paper towels to drain for 1 hour; this step allows excess moisture to drain away. Take care when handling soft tofu as it is very delicate.

2 Meanwhile, make the sauce: Combine all the sauce ingredients in a small bowl and whisk together; set aside.

3 Prepare the toppings, if using, and place in individual dishes.

4 When ready to serve, cut the tofu into large cubes, about 1 inch square. Place on a serving dish and drizzle with some sauce (more or less, depending on the size of the tofu cake).

5 Invite diners to take some tofu onto their own plates and add toppings as they like.

Going All Out: *If you have enough individual dipping dishes for each guest, pour sauce into the dishes and provide one for each place setting. Invite guests to pick up cubes of tofu with their chopsticks and dip them in the sauce.*

Spinach Salad with Sesame Dressing

Simply cooked spinach is dressed with a sesame sauce that comes together very quickly.

Preparation time: *10 minutes*

Cooking time: *5 minutes*

Yield: *4 servings*

1 tablespoon white or black sesame seeds	*2 teaspoons soy sauce*
1 pound fresh spinach, preferably baby spinach	*2 teaspoons sugar*
2 teaspoons sake	

1 Toast the sesame seeds by placing them in a heavy skillet or cast-iron pan. Place over medium heat and watch carefully, stirring frequently. Continue cooking until they turn very light golden brown, if using white. Watch black sesame seeds carefully and remove from heat as soon as you smell a fragrance. Immediately remove from the pan so that they don't continue to cook and possibly overbrown because of the residual heat in the pan.

2 Prepare the spinach. If the spinach is large leafed, remove the thick stems and submerge in cold water to release any dirt. Drain well but do not pat dry. If you're using baby spinach, simply trim off any stems that extend beyond the leaf. Wash and drain.

3 To cook the spinach, place the damp spinach in a large pot, cover, and place over medium heat. The water droplets clinging to the spinach will steam it. Cook until the spinach leaves have wilted. Drain the spinach and squeeze dry with your hands (yes, your hands — or use a clean absorbent towel to wrap them in and then squeeze dry). Place on a cutting board, coarsely chop, and place in a mixing bowl.

4 Prepare the dressing by whisking together the sake, soy sauce, and sugar; pour over the spinach and toss to coat. Divide among the serving dishes, sprinkle with sesame seeds, and serve immediately. Serve this dish slightly warm or at room temperature.

Going All Out: If you have a coffee grinder or spice grinder, you can grind the sesame seeds, which is often done in Japan. For this version, whisk the ground sesame seeds into the dressing and pour that mixture over the spinach, toss, and serve. If you have a traditional suribachi (Japanese mortar and pestle), use it to grind sesame seeds.

Seaweed Salad

In this recipe, refrigerated or frozen wakame seaweed is cooked and simply dressed with a sesame-soy dressing. Make sure you rid the wakame of excess salt before proceeding with the rest of the recipe.

Preparation time: *10 minutes*

Cooking time: *10 minutes*

Yield: *4 servings*

10 ounces refrigerated or frozen and defrosted salted wakame (about 1½ cups)

½ regular or ¼ English hothouse cucumber

1 teaspoon white or black toasted sesame seeds (or a combination of both colors)

2 tablespoons soy sauce

1 tablespoon mirin

1 tablespoon rice vinegar

1 tablespoon sesame oil

1 Place the wakame in a mixing bowl and fill with water. Swish it around, drain, and repeat until the water no longer has a salty taste (just dip your finger in to try it).

2 Place the wakame in a saucepan and cover with fresh water. Cover pot, bring to a boil over medium-high heat, turn the heat down, and simmer for 10 minutes.

3 Meanwhile, peel the cucumbers, slice in half lengthwise, and scoop out the seeds with a teaspoon. Cut the cucumbers into matchstick-sized pieces and place in a mixing bowl; set aside.

4 Drain the wakame in a colander and shake dry with your hands or squeeze dry in a clean, absorbent towel. Add to the cucumber and sprinkle the sesame seeds over the vegetables.

5 Whisk together the soy sauce, mirin, rice vinegar, and sesame oil in a small bowl and pour over the salad. Toss to coat and serve. (You may refrigerate the salad overnight in an airtight container.)

Tip: *Wakame is available in dried form, but for this recipe, you need the refrigerated or frozen kind. It often comes salted and refrigerated or frozen in plastic pouches, and the instructions in the recipe explain how to deal with this — after all, the wakame is quite high in sodium as it is and you need to get rid of the excess salt! Sometimes I find packages in Asian grocery stores that simply say "seaweed" on the front. You have to hunt all over the package to find the words "wakame." Ask if you're not sure.*

Book VII

Japanese Cooking

Pickling Vegetables: Tsukemono

Quickly salted vegetables, called *tsukemono*, are a type of Japanese pickle that are eaten every day. Serve a little to accompany a bowl of rice and whatever else you're eating. Not only does the fresh, salty, pickled vegetable complement the rice and main dish, but pickles are also said to aid in digestion.

Carrot and Turnip Quick Pickles

You can make these Japanese-style pickles in a little over an hour, and they'll last all week in the refrigerator.

Preparation time: *15 minutes*

Sitting time: *1 hour, 5 minutes*

Yield: *6 servings*

5 large carrots, peeled and trimmed of stem and root end

5 medium turnips, peeled and trimmed of stem and root end

5 tablespoons salt

4-inch-square piece of konbu

1-inch square of lemon zest

1 Cut the carrots and turnips into thin sticks *(hyoshigigiri)* and place in a bowl; the vegetables should be about ⅛-inch thick and about 2 inches long . Sprinkle with salt and toss thoroughly. I use my hands to toss because I can feel when all the pieces have been evenly coated. Allow to sit at room temperature for 5 minutes; the carrots and turnips will give off water.

2 Drain the vegetables and return to the bowl. Add piece of konbu and lemon zest and cover with plastic wrap, pressing down onto the vegetables. Place a small plate on top of the plastic. It must be smaller than the bowl so that it can press the veggies down. Place a heavy canned good on the plate or something else to weigh it down. Allow to sit for 1 hour at room temperature.

3 Drain the vegetables, remove the konbu and lemon zest, toss well, and pack into an airtight container. The pickles are now ready to use and will keep for almost a week in the refrigerator. To serve, present a small dish at the table; guests can add a small amount to their own plate of food.

Tip: *You can use almost any kind of vegetable. Try daikon or cucumbers, for instance, or any combination you like.*

Chapter 5

Sushi and Sashimi: They're Not Just Raw Fish

I hope the title of this chapter got your attention. Although raw fish is certainly the focal point of some sushi — and all sashimi — it's not the whole story. Sushi can take the form of fingers of rice topped with raw or cooked fish, or even sweetened omelet, or it can be cone shaped rolls of nori seaweed filled with jewel-toned fish eggs and veggies. It can be cylindrical rolls filled with rice, nori, and avocado, either thin or wide. It can even take the form of a bowl of rice with fish and other flavorful ingredients scattered on top. There is huge variety!

Serving sashimi is an art form and can be as simple as a few slices of tuna on a plate, to a rainbow selection of fish with grated daikon, wasabi, and dipping sauce on the side.

By the end of this chapter, you will discover how to prepare all of these dishes, and more! But first, let's start with some definitions.

Fishing for the Details about Sushi

Sushi is not just raw fish, as you may have believed. The word actually refers to the "fingers" (finger shapes, that is) of vinegared rice that support choice morsels of raw fish, or sometimes other items such as cooked shrimp or a bit of rolled omelet. This kind of sushi is referred to as *nigirizushi*. Here are descriptions of the different kinds of sushi:

- **Nigirizushi:** Fingers of vinegared rice topped with raw fish or other items, such as cooked shrimp or sweet omelet.

- **Makizushi:** Sushi rolls made with a makisu, a mat made from thin pieces of bamboo that facilitates the rolling process. They usually consist of a sheet of nori seaweed filled with sushi rice and some sort of filling in the center. You also can find inside-out rolls, which have the rice on the outside and the nori and fillings on the inside.

- **Temaki:** These are also called "hand rolls" as they're made by simply stuffing sheets of nori with rice and fillings and rolling by hand into a cone shape. You eat these out of hand rather than with chopsticks.

- **Oshizushi:** This sushi is a specialty of Osaka, and you need a special mold to make it. You press sushi rice into a wooden (or sometimes metal) mold and then top it with fish or other toppings. The top of the mold is put into place and presses down on the whole shebang. When you remove the top, you have a large cake of sushi, which is then cut into bite-sized pieces.

  If you have the mold, you can see how this is an easy way to make many pieces of sushi at once — great for a party. You can find the molds at some Asian grocery stores.

- **Inarizushi:** This is a simple-to-make vegetarian option for sushi lovers. You purchase *aburage,* which are fried pouches of tofu, so much of the work is already done. You simply stuff the pouches with sushi rice and some seasonings. These are great for picnics and lunch boxes.

- **Chirashizushi:** Literally translated as "scattered" sushi, which is exactly what it is. This is the easiest sushi to make: You take a bowl of sushi rice and "scatter," quite artfully, a selection of fish and vegetables. As with the oshizushi mentioned earlier in this list, this is a great party dish. You can make one big bowl and let guests serve themselves, or you can take a little more time to arrange individual bowls for a dinner party.

Following Etiquette When Eating Sushi and Sashimi

When you sit down to eat sushi in better restaurants, you're presented with a warm, wet washcloth with which to wipe your hands. Not only is this a gracious way to start, but if you're eating the sushi with your fingers, which is perfectly okay, it's sanitary as well.

Every place setting should have a small dipping dish (for soy sauce) and a pair of chopsticks. Every table should have a small bottle of soy sauce. Many restaurants make a house sauce by combining soy sauce, mirin, sake, and bonito flakes; but if you're serving sushi at home, you can just use soy sauce or try the recipe for my Sushi Dipping Sauce later in this chapter.

Here are some rules of etiquette to remember:

- ✔ Pour some soy sauce or dipping sauce into your own dipping dish.

- ✔ Pick up each piece of nigirizushi with chopsticks or your fingers and dip the topping in soy sauce in your little dish. If you dip the side with the rice, it will fall apart.

- ✔ It's most proper to eat your nigirizushi in one bite — two at the most.

- ✔ When eating sushi rolls, you can use chopsticks or your fingers. Hand rolls are always eaten out of hand.

- ✔ Wasabi and pickled ginger are offered with your sushi and sashimi. Add a dab of wasabi to your sushi and sashimi to taste, and eat pickled ginger between bites of sushi to cleanse the palate.

- ✔ Sashimi is often presented with a mound of finely shredded daikon; eat it between pieces of fish to refresh your palate.

  The pickled ginger and daikon cleanse the palate between bites so that your taste buds can more fully appreciate the next type of fish.

- ✔ If you are presented with some sushi made from sweetened rolled omelet, eat it last; it's kind of looked upon as a mini-dessert because it is sweet.

- ✔ When it's time to take a break, or you are finished, place your chopsticks horizontally in front of you, parallel to the edge of the table that's closest to you.

Book VII

Japanese Cooking

Selecting Fish and Seafood for Sushi and Sashimi

When it comes to sushi, certain kinds of fish are always offered, such as types of tuna, which are very popular both in the United States and Japan. Other types of fish, such as giant clam, may be desirable but not as easy to find. I want to introduce you to some seafood to consider using in your own kitchen when making sushi and sashimi. And remember that the seafood should be impeccably fresh. Shop for it at a fish store, not the supermarket, and tell the fishmonger that you plan to eat it raw so that they can help you make the freshest selections. Ask the fishmonger what days the store's deliveries arrive and buy fish on that day only. Consider the following types of seafood for your sushi:

- **Tuna:** You can enjoy three main types of tuna raw:
  - **Maguro:** This is the most basic tuna and is a rich, dark red. It has been compared to eating a fine, rare steak.
  - **Chutoro:** One step up in desirability from maguro, this is a fattier tuna with a paler pink color and subtler flavor than maguro.
  - **Toro:** This is a prime tuna, with a very pale gold pink color, high fat content, and luxurious texture and sublime, subtle flavor.
- **Hamachi:** Yellowtail, another popular fish at sushi bars.
- **Ebi:** Cooked shrimp.
- **Odori:** Raw shrimp, often called raw or dancing shrimp.
- **Ika:** Squid — usually raw.
- **Tako:** Octopus, usually cooked.
- **Ikura:** Salmon roe. These large, glowing orange crunchy fish eggs provide a wonderful textural experience in your mouth — they burst between your teeth!
- **Tobiko:** Bright orange-red flying fish roe; these are very tiny fish eggs.
- **Tamago:** Sweetened omelet, often served with a strip of nori. This is traditionally eaten last.
- **Uni:** Sea-urchin roe; this is a delicacy, and often considered an acquired taste.
- **Unagi:** Broiled sea eel. I know it sounds yucky, but it's delicious. It is brushed with a thick, sweet sauce before and after being cooked and is absolutely delectable.
- **Hirame:** Flounder.
- **Saba:** Mackerel.
- **Hotategai:** Scallops.
- **Suzuki:** Sea bass.
- **Tai:** Sea bream.

Preparing Fish for Sushi and Sashimi

Most sushi, such as types of *nigirizushi,* feature raw fish. To make it, you must know a few things about handling and cutting the fish properly. The same goes for sashimi; the fish must be carefully prepared.

Speaking the language of sushi

Here are some common terms you may see on a menu and can use when talking about sushi and sashimi, whether in a restaurant or at home:

- **Omakasezushi:** The chef's choice. When you say this at a sushi bar, it means that you're putting your order in the chef's capable hands. You'll get what is freshest and, quite possibly, most expensive.

- **Tekkamaki:** Tuna roll.

- **Kappamaki:** Cucumber roll.

- **Tekkappamaki:** Selection of both tuna and cucumber rolls.

- **Futomaki:** Thick rolled sushi, about 2 to 3 inches across.

- **Hosomaki:** Thin rolled sushi, about 1 inch across.

- **Inarizushi:** Fried tofu pockets filled with sushi rice and seasonings.

- **Kore o kudasai:** "I'll have some of this, please."

- **Oaiso o onegai shimasu:** "Check, please."

You may be saying to yourself, "It's just a slice of fish. What's there to know?" Well, you can take the same piece of tuna, cut it thin, cut it thick, dice it in tiny cubes, cut it with the grain or against, and each bite gives you a very different sensation in the mouth. Even different condiments work better with some cuts than others. Japanese chefs study for years how to best present various types of fish. Here, I simply give you some basics so that you can serve sushi and sashimi at home.

I assume that your fish is already filleted and, in some cases, also skinned. Again, just make sure that it's as fresh as possible, and even ask the fishmonger for a bag of crushed ice to keep your fish cool on the way home. Refrigerate it right away and use it as soon as possible. Then prepare it as close to serving time as possible.

Always use fresh fish; never use fish that has been previously frozen.

Here are some directions for slicing fish fillets such as mackerel, sea bass, and sea bream:

- Look for a solid piece of fish that is free of veins. Remove any tiny bones by using a pair of pliers (yes, pliers!).

- Place the fillet on your work surface, skin side up (if there is any), with the narrow end of the fillet near you and the thicker end toward the top of your surface.

- Use a very sharp, thin-bladed knife. Angle the top of the knife blade away from you so that the top of the blade is tilted toward the back of your work surface and the sharp edge is near you. Make sweeping, arcing cuts, from the base of the blade toward the tip, slicing crosswise across the fillet, making the pieces about ⅜ inch thick.

- ✔ Sometimes, with white-flesh fish such as the sea bass, it's nice to cut it even thinner for sashimi. Then you can lay it slightly overlapping on a plate, and the fish will literally be translucent. You also can roll up very thinly sliced fish and form little "roses" out of the fish.

For tuna and salmon, proceed as follows:

- ✔ **For sushi,** have a hunk of fish about 1 inch thick and 2 to 2½ inches wide. Cut ¼-inch thin pieces crosswise, against the grain, slightly angling your knife blade.

- ✔ **For sashimi,** you may cut even a tad thicker, again cutting crosswise.

Getting the Rice Right

Making rice for your sushi dishes is the place to start; rice is the cornerstone in sushi recipes and should be prepared and cooled to room temperature before proceeding. The ingredients are simple enough: short-grain rice, water, rice vinegar, sugar, and salt. The technique, however, is very different from techniques for making other kinds of rice. It's not difficult, just a specific technique, which I describe in the next recipe.

Once your sushi rice is cooked, never refrigerate it or the texture will become hard and quite unpleasant. For this reason, make only as much rice as you need.

Sushi Rice

Sushi rice *(su-meshi)* is sweetened vinegared rice; it's the first recipe you need to know how to cook when making sushi. This recipe is based on the version in the book *Japanese Cooking, A Simple Art* by Shizuo Tsuji (Kodansha International, Tokyo, 1980), which is a fantastic resource. Purchase rice that's suitable for sushi, which is short-grained polished white rice. The bag should specify that it's for sushi, or ask your grocer for guidance.

Preparation time: *20 minutes*

Cooking time: *20 minutes*

Yield: *8 cups*

3⅓ cups short-grain sushi rice	*5 tablespoons rice vinegar*
4 cups water	*3 tablespoons sugar*
4-inch-square piece konbu	*1 teaspoon salt*

1 Place the rice in a large bowl, cover with cold water (not the 4 cups listed above, just some water from the tap), and rub between your fingers and palms; drain and repeat several times or until the water is clear. After the final draining, allow the rice to air-dry in a colander for 30 minutes, tossing once or twice for even air circulation.

2 Place the 4 cups water and rice in a heavy-bottomed pot, place the piece of konbu on top, cover, and place over medium-high heat until it comes to a boil. Remove the konbu immediately, cover again, reduce the heat, and simmer gently for about 15 minutes, or until all the liquid is just absorbed.

3 Remove the pot from the heat. Do not lift the lid. Allow the rice to sit for 15 minutes. This resting period is very important and yields perfectly textured rice. While the rice is resting, prepare the vinegar dressing.

4 Stir the vinegar, sugar, and salt together in a small saucepan and heat over medium heat until the sugar and salt are dissolved, about 1 minute. Remove from the heat; pour into a small bowl and stir frequently to cool it down quickly. (Do not allow to vigorously boil or the flavor of the vinegar will be compromised.)

5 Spread the rice in a thin layer in a wide, shallow bowl, preferably wooden, as shown in Figure 5-1. Use a traditional *hangiri* (wooden sushi rice tub) if you have one. Use a wide, flat wooden spoon or classic *shamoji* (wooden paddle) and make wide back-and-forth motions through the rice. By cutting horizontally through the rice, you cool it down, which you want to do, but the gentle motion minimizes the crushing of any rice grains.

6 Sprinkle some of the vinegar dressing over the rice while you move your paddle back and forth. Here's the tricky part: You need to also fan it at the same time to cool it quickly. You may use a paper fan, or just a magazine. Fan back and forth over the bowl with one hand and "stir" with the other. Better yet, get a friend to fan while you work on the rice.

7 Keep fanning, stirring, and adding vinegar dressing until the rice is at room temperature. Taste as you go along; the rice should be well flavored — you should be able to taste the vinegar, sugar, and salt — but you may not need all the dressing, The rice grains should remain separate and not become mushy or too wet. The entire process takes about 10 minutes.

8 The sushi rice is now ready to use and should be used the same day. You may place a clean, damp cloth over the rice and cover that with plastic wrap. Leave at room temperature; never refrigerate sushi rice.

Tip: *When you handle cooked sushi rice, it sticks to your hands. But to keep your fingers relatively rice free, do as the Japanese do and use tezu, which is "hand-vinegar," when forming nigirizushi or sushi rolls. It's simply a combination of water and vinegar that you can dip your fingers into while making your sushi.*

Book VII

**Japanese
Cooking**

SUSHI RICE

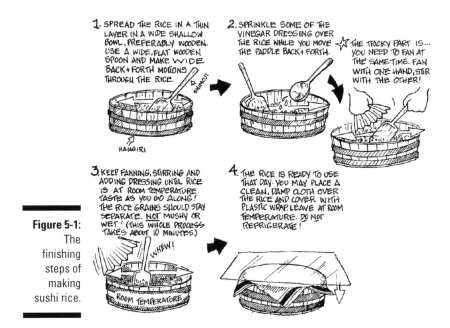

1. SPREAD THE RICE IN A THIN LAYER IN A WIDE SHALLOW BOWL, PREFERABLY WOODEN. USE A WIDE, FLAT WOODEN SPOON AND MAKE WIDE BACK + FORTH MOTIONS THROUGH THE RICE.

HANGIRI

2. SPRINKLE SOME OF THE VINEGAR DRESSING OVER THE RICE WHILE YOU MOVE THE PADDLE BACK + FORTH.

THE TRICKY PART IS.... YOU NEED TO FAN AT THE SAME TIME. FAN WITH ONE HAND, STIR WITH THE OTHER!

3. KEEP FANNING, STIRRING AND ADDING DRESSING UNTIL RICE IS AT ROOM TEMPERATURE. TASTE AS YOU GO ALONG! THE RICE GRAINS SHOULD STAY SEPARATE. NOT MUSHY OR WET! (THIS WHOLE PROCESS TAKES ABOUT 10 MINUTES.)

WHEW!

ROOM TEMPERATURE

4. THE RICE IS READY TO USE THAT DAY. YOU MAY PLACE A CLEAN, DAMP CLOTH OVER THE RICE AND COVER WITH PLASTIC WRAP. LEAVE AT ROOM TEMPERATURE. DO NOT REFRIGERATE!

Figure 5-1:
The finishing steps of making sushi rice.

Offering Dipping Ingredients for Sushi

Whether you're serving nigirizushi, sushi rolls, or inarizushi, you should offer soy sauce or a dipping sauce (see the Sushi and Sashimi Dipping Sauce recipe), wasabi, and pickled ginger. You dip these kinds of sushi in the sauce, add some extra wasabi, if you like, and eat pickled ginger between bites to cleanse your palate.

I use wasabi powder: To reconstitute wasabi powder, use equal amounts of powder and warm water and stir to combine. Allow to sit a few moments for the flavor to develop.

Always have wasabi, soy sauce, and pickled ginger on hand when making sushi and sashimi. I assume you do, so I don't list these ingredients individually in every recipe. When you serve your sushi, place a small mound of wasabi and a larger mound of the pickled ginger on the serving platter, and offer the sauce in a pitcher for guests to pour into their own dipping dishes.

When serving sashimi, offering a mound of finely shredded daikon is also a nice gesture. Simply peel the daikon and shred it on a box grater on the small holes. Squeeze gently to remove excess water, if necessary, and then mound it on the serving platter along with your sashimi. For more information about daikon, see Chapter 2 of Book VII.

Sushi and Sashimi Dipping Sauce

This sauce comes together in a flash and is tastier than straight soy sauce for your dipped sushi.

Preparation time: *1 minute*

Yield: *1¼ cups*

1 cup soy sauce   ¼ cup mirin

Stir together the soy sauce and mirin in a small bowl to combine. Pour into a small pitcher for serving with your sushi and sashimi. (You may store the sauce at room temperature in an airtight container indefinitely.)

Tip: *Mirin tempers the saltiness of the soy sauce and adds a bit of sweetness. You can experiment with the proportions of the two ingredients to adjust them to your taste.*

Exploring the World of Nigirizushi

When you think of sushi, this is probably what comes to mind — individual fingers of sweetened rice flavored with vinegar and topped with a piece of raw fish. Basically, that is what *nigirizushi* is, but there's so much more! You can top it with egg or cooked shrimp or wrap it with a piece of nori, and then top it with items such as fish eggs or sea urchin.

Getting prepped

Making *nigirizushi* at home is easy if you follow a few rules. That said, Japanese sushi chefs study for years to hone their art. An expert sushi chef supposedly can coax all the rice grains into the same direction! We won't be that picky here, however, so don't worry.

Here's how to get ready to make nigirizushi:

- ✔ The number one rule is to make raw-fish sushi only if you can get impeccably fresh fish. If you can't, limit yourself to cooked toppings such as sweet omelet and cooked shrimp — or even a bit of cooked salmon.

- ✔ Have sushi rice cooked and at room temperature; if it's warm, it could spoil your raw fish.

- ✔ Have all your ingredients ready to go before you start preparing your *nigirizushi,* and read the recipe thoroughly so that you can proceed smoothly. (Read the section "Preparing Fish for Sushi and Sashimi," earlier in this chapter.)

Nori is best if served lightly toasted. See Chapter 2 of Book VII for more information about toasting nori.

✔ Make *tezu,* or "hand vinegar" (see the recipe for Nigirizushi later in this chapter). You dip your fingers in this vinegared water to keep the rice from sticking.

✔ Make your *nigirizushi* right before serving time.

Serving nigirizushi

If you want to serve *nigirizushi* in the classic Japanese style, you need to have a few special items and follow some simple guidelines.

Among the items you need to serve nigirizushi is a pretty platter on which to serve the sushi. Japanese restaurants use wooden platforms that look like thick, blond, wooden trays on thick wooden strips that act as feet to raise them above the table. You can buy a special nigirizushi presentation piece, but you certainly don't have to. Choose a flat platter, in a color that will show off and enhance — not compete with — the sushi. A solid color is usually best. The size is important, too. You want to spread your *nigirizushi* about the tray, so that they're not crowded; you want to see and appreciate each one. You also need room for a tiny marble-sized mound of wasabi, a large golf-ball-sized mound of pickled ginger, and a similar-sized mound of finely shredded daikon.

Make sure that each guest has a set of chopsticks, a small dipping dish for the soy sauce, and a small plate in front of the place setting. The soy sauce should be in a decorative pitcher.

You can offer straight soy sauce or use my Sushi and Sashimi Dipping Sauce recipe in this chapter.

Invite your guests to pour some soy sauce (or the sauce you made) into their own dipping dish. They can take a little bit of wasabi and pickled ginger and place it on their own plate, if they like. Then guests choose a piece of sushi, and pick it up with their chopsticks (fingers are okay, too), and dip it — fish side down — into the soy sauce to season to taste. (If you dip the rice side in the soy sauce, it will fall apart.) Then pop it in your mouth, preferably in one bite. If you must take multiple bites, try to make it two at the most. If the piece of sushi begins to fall apart, just place it on your dish and begin again by getting a better grip with your chopsticks.

If you like the hotness of the wasabi, you can add a smear of it to the pieces of sushi before you eat them. Some people like to dissolve some wasabi in their soy sauce. Take bites of pickled ginger and daikon between bites of fish to cleanse your palate.

Rolled omelet is a somewhat sweet egg dish used as a classic topping for nigirizushi and should be included in your assortment. To make sweet Japanese-style omelets, the Japanese use a square pan. Actually, they can be square or rectangular, and the best-quality ones are tin-lined copper. If you have one, great! But I certainly don't expect you to; the recipe I present uses a standard round pan.

Rolled Omelet

This somewhat sweet egg dish is used as a classic topping for nigirizushi and should be included in your assortment of toppings.

Special tools: *8-inch nonstick saute pan (measured across the bottom of the inside), bamboo rolling mat, plastic wrap*

Preparation time: *5 minutes*

Cooking time: *8 minutes*

Yield: *2 omelets (24 pieces for nigirizushi)*

2 tablespoons dashi (see Chapter 4 of Book VII)	2 teaspoons sugar
1 tablespoon mirin	5 eggs
2 teaspoons soy sauce	Vegetable oil

1 Place the dashi, mirin, soy sauce, and sugar in a mixing bowl and whisk to combine until the sugar dissolves. Add the eggs and mix, using chopsticks. By using chopsticks, you can blend the mixture but not incorporate too much air; you don't want the eggs to become frothy. If the mixture has clumps of egg white or yolk, that's okay.

2 Lightly moisten a wadded-up paper towel with vegetable oil and use it to wipe the inside of a nonstick sauté pan to create a very thin layer of oil. Place a bamboo rolling mat on a work surface and cover with a piece of plastic wrap; set aside.

3 Heat the pan over medium-high heat until very hot. Add one-fourth of the egg mixture and tilt the pan in all directions to create a very thin layer of egg. Cook until just set but not dry. Use a spatula or chopsticks to lift the edge and roll the omelet over itself; leave in the pan. Wipe the rest of the pan again with the oiled towel. Add another one-fourth of the eggs; lift up the rolled omelet to allow wet eggs to flow underneath. Cook this omelet as you did the first. Roll it up using the first omelet as the core so that the second omelet is wrapped around it.

4 Roll the omelet out onto the plastic-lined rolling mat. Cover with the plastic and use the mat to roll it up and compress gently to form a round shape. The roll should be about 1½ inches in diameter. Slip the plastic, with the rolled omelet inside, off the mat and set aside. Cover the mat with another piece of plastic wrap.

5 Cook and roll the second omelet the same way as the first (see Step 3). Now you have two omelets. To use for *nigirizushi,* please refer to that recipe.

Tip: *Sometimes it helps to flatten out the omelet before slicing it; just press down on it gently with your fingers to make the shape a bit more squat.*

Book VII

Japanese Cooking

Nigirizushi

This is a basic recipe for individual fingers of rice with various toppings. After you master this recipe, you can make any kind of *nigirizushi* that you like.

Preparation time: *15 minutes*

Yield: *24 pieces*

Tezu	*2 cups cooked sushi rice (see the recipe earlier in this chapter)*
⅔ cup water	
4 teaspoons rice vinegar	*24 assorted pieces of raw fish cut for sushi (see the section "Selecting Fish and Seafood for Sushi and Sashimi," earlier in this chapter)*
1 tablespoon powdered wasabi	
1 tablespoon warm water	

1 Make the tezu (hand vinegar) by stirring together the water and rice vinegar in a small bowl. Combine the wasabi and water in a small bowl, stir well, and allow to sit for a few minutes for the texture and flavor to develop.

2 Dip your fingers in the tezu and clasp your hands together to dampen your palms. Take about 1½ tablespoons of rice in your fingers and gently compress the rice into a finger shape, about ¾ inches wide and 1½ inches long (it will be about ¾ inch high).

3 Take a piece of fish and place a dab of wasabi in the center of one of the flat sides. (Alternatively, smear a little wasabi on top of the rice finger.) Place the fish, wasabi side down, on the rice finger and gently press together; transfer this *nigirizushi* to your serving platter.

4 Repeat with the remaining rice and fish. Take the remaining wasabi and place in a small mound on the platter. Serve immediately with soy sauce or dipping sauce and wasabi and pickled ginger on the side.

Vary It! Instead of fish, you may top the rice with a bit of rolled omelet (see the following recipe). Place a strip of omelet on top of the rice (no wasabi is used with the egg), cut a tiny strip of nori, about ¼ inch wide by 4 inches long, and wrap it around the sushi crosswise. Dampen the edges with water and press to adhere. Place this seam on the bottom. Place the omelet so that the layers of rolled egg are facing up and you can see them; the nori adds flavor and decoration and helps the egg stay on top of the rice.

Tip: Another way to use nori is to cut a strip about 1 inch thick by 6 inches long. Wrap it around the sides of the rice finger; it acts as a collar going all the way around the rice. Use water to seal the edges. The top edge will be higher than the top of the rice. Fill the space on top of the rice with salmon egg, red caviar, or sea urchin roe. These are called boat-shaped sushi.

Tip: For shrimp nigirizushi, you can cook the shrimp if you like. Start with cleaned and deveined medium-sized shrimp (about 30 to the pound) and thread a skewer through the shrimp, head to tail, to straighten it out. Bring a pot of water to a simmer, submerge the shrimp, and cook very briefly, just until it has lost its translucence, about 1 minute. Pick them up by the skewers and quickly allow cool water to run over them to stop the cooking. Allow to cool completely to room temperature, remove the skewers, and you're ready to place them on your rice fingers.

Going Casual with Sushi: Chirashizushi

Chirashizushi is very easy to make, and it's as versatile and variable as the ingredients you happen to have on hand. Basically, it's a bowl of sushi rice, sometimes with some cooked veggies or other flavorings mixed in, that is then topped with whatever you like: raw fish, strips of kamaboko, egg, pieces of vegetables in various guises, and so on.

Oshizushi: Molded sushi

Oshizushi is very easy sushi to make — if you have the proper mold. Oshizushi molds are usually made of wood, though some modern ones are made of metal. They consist of a rectangular base with a lid that fits inside. I like to use plastic wrap to help the process, although doing so isn't part of the classic technique. Here's my method of making oshizushi:

1. **Line the bottom and sides of the mold with a large piece of plastic wrap and add a layer of raw fish, omelet, or even cooked shrimp or chicken.**

2. **On top of that, smear some seasonings, if you like, such as wasabi or umeboshi plum, and top with a layer of sushi rice.**

3. **Place a piece of plastic wrap on top of the rice, set the top of the mold into place, and press down on it to compress the layers of food.**

You can even weigh down the top for a bit to make sure that everything is compressed nicely.

4. **Remove the lid, peel away the plastic, and invert the entire cake of sushi onto a cutting board.**

5. **Remove all the plastic, cut the sushi into bite-sized pieces, and serve as you would nigirizushi. The number of pieces you get depends on the size of the mold.**

You can try this at home with a springform pan and a flat dish that fits inside the pan.

1. **Set up your springform pan with the sides in place.**

2. **Press a layer of rice on the bottom, followed by seasonings and fish or other toppings.**

3. **Press the plastic wrap right onto the toppings, place a plate on top, and weigh it down for a while until the ingredients are compressed.**

4. **Remove the plate and plastic. Remove the sides of the pan and cut the sushi into bite-sized pieces.**

Book VII

Japanese Cooking

Because you make it in one big bowl (or you can make individual portions) with a variety of ingredients, it can take on different looks, textures, and tastes depending on what you use. This is casual sushi! So, in that vein, the following recipe is just a guide. Use your imagination, and what you have on hand, when making chirashizushi.

Chirashizushi

Chirashizushi is great party sushi because you simply fill one big bowl (or smaller individual bowls) with sushi rice and then decoratively assemble all sorts of flavorful and colorful toppings over the rice — you're done! Let's eat!

Preparation time: 15 minutes, plus 30 minutes for mushrooms to soak

Cooking time: 10 minutes

Yield: 4 servings

6 dried shiitake mushrooms, stemmed	5 cups cooked sushi rice, at room temperature (see the recipe earlier in this chapter)
¼ cup dashi (see Chapter 4 in Book VII)	
2 tablespoons mirin	1 square nori, toasted and finely shredded
2 tablespoons soy sauce	5 medium or large cooked shrimp
2 teaspoons sake	1 rolled omelet (half the recipe), cut crosswise into ¼-inch-wide strips (see the recipe earlier in this chapter)
12 snow peas	
4 slices cooked, canned lotus root, cut crosswise into half-moons	
¼ pound squid, body only, cut into 3-inch-square pieces	12 pieces raw fish sliced for sushi (see the section "Preparing Fish for Sushi and Sashimi," earlier in this chapter)

1 Place the shiitake mushrooms in a bowl of warm water and place a drop lid on top to keep them submerged. (See Chapter 7 of Book VII for a description of a drop lid.) Allow to soak for 30 minutes and then drain. Combine the dashi, mirin, soy sauce, and sake in a small pot and add the mushrooms. Place a drop lid on top of mushrooms and bring to a boil over high heat, turn the heat down, and simmer for 15 minutes, or until the mushrooms are completely tender. Drain and allow to cool to room temperature. Finely chop three of the mushrooms and set aside. Thinly slice the remaining three mushrooms; set aside.

2 Prepare the snow peas by cutting off the stem end and removing the string. Bring a small pot of water to a boil over high heat, drop the snow peas in, and boil for 30 seconds or until crisp-tender. Remove from the water, place in a colander, and run under cold water to stop the cooking; set aside.

3 Bring the same pot of water to a boil and drop in the lotus root. Boil for 3 minutes, remove from the water, place in a colander, and run under cold water to stop the cooking; set aside.

4 Prepare the squid: Take each piece of squid and cut a ¼-inch crosshatch design on the diagonal, going about halfway through the squid. Do not cut all the way through.

5 Bring the same pot of water to a simmer over medium heat (add some more water if it has evaporated) and add the squid. Simmer for 30 seconds; the squid will curl up and form a pine-cone shape (this is called *matsukasa*). Drain in a colander and run under cold water to stop the cooking; set aside.

6 You can prepare all the ingredients in the preceding steps up to a day ahead and refrigerate them in individual airtight containers. Bring the ingredients back to room temperature before proceeding.

7 Assemble your chirashizushi right before serving. Place the sushi rice, chopped mushrooms, and shredded nori in a mixing bowl and stir to combine. Scrape the rice mixture into your serving bowl. Arrange the sliced mushrooms, snow peas, lotus root, squid, shrimp, omelet, and raw fish artistically on top of the rice. Serve with soy sauce or dipping sauce, wasabi, and pickled ginger. Serve immediately by dolling out portions to each diner; make sure everyone gets a little bit of every ingredient.

Makizushi: Let's Get Rolling!

Sushi rolls, called *makizushi,* can take many different guises: nori on the outside with rice and fillings within, nori and fillings on the inside and rice on the outside for "inside-out" rolls, and small cones of nori stuffed with rice and fillings to be eaten out of hand. Here are some Japanese words and definitions on the topic of sushi rolls:

✔ **Futomaki (large rolls):** These are large rolls with nori on the outside.

✔ **Hosomaki (thin rolls):** These are similar to futomaki but about half the size in diameter.

✔ **Uramaki (inside-out rolls):** Here the rice is on the outside with the nori and fillings inside.

✔ **Temaki (hand rolls):** These are sheets of nori that are rolled up into a cone and filled. These are always eaten by hand (and made by hand) hence the term "hand-rolls."

Hand rolls are picked up and eaten with your hands. All the other sorts of rolls may be eaten with chopsticks or your fingers; either is perfectly OK.

For all but the hand rolls, you need a bamboo rolling mat, which facilitates the rolling procedure. They're inexpensive and easy to find, either in Asian grocery stores or even some supermarkets; my supermarket has them in the seafood department, right next to containers of wasabi powder and bottles of rice vinegar.

I know that sushi rolls look fancy and intimidating, but once you've made them, they're actually very easy. The instructions are a bit long, but they're necessary so that you get all the nuances of the technique. After you assemble all your ingredients, making them goes quite quickly.

Filling your sushi rolls

Making sushi rolls is assembly-line cooking. You must have all your ingredients ready to go before you start rolling: You should have your sushi rice made and cooled to room temperature, your wasabi prepared, and all other ingredients cooked, sliced, peeled, or otherwise prepared. Here's a list of ingredients to get you started. Just pick and choose from the following:

- **Raw fish:** Cut into ¼-inch diameter strips

- **Cooked or raw scallops:** Cut into thin pieces

- **Cooked or raw squid:** Cut into thin pieces

- **Cooked shrimp:** Cooked on a skewer so that they're straight

- **Cooked tempura shrimp:** Cooked on a skewer so that they're straight

- **Cooked crab:** Cut into long, thin pieces

- **Rolled omelet:** Cut into ¼-inch diameter strips

- **Simmered shiitake** (see the Chirashizushi recipe earlier in this chapter): Cut into strips

- **Cooked eel (anago):** Cut into ¼-inch diameter strips

- **Pickled daikon:** Cut into ¼-inch diameter strips (you purchase this ready-made at Asian grocery stores)

- **Cucumber:** Peeled, seeded, and cut into ¼-inch diameter strips

- **Crisp-cooked asparagus:** Preferably thin asparagus

- **Crisp-cooked carrots:** Cut into ¼-inch diameter strips

- ✔ **Umeboshi plums:** Minced

- ✔ **Wasabi**

- ✔ **Flying fish roe**

Here are some tried-and-true combinations:

- ✔ **Tekkamaki:** Nori filled with rice and tuna

- ✔ **Kappamaki:** Nori filled with rice and cucumber

- ✔ **Sakemaki:** Nori filled with rice and salmon

- ✔ **California roll:** Nori filled with rice, crab, avocado, and cucumber

- ✔ **Ebi tempura maki:** Nori filled with rice and tempura cooked shrimp

- ✔ **Vegetarian roll:** Nori filled with rice, umeboshi plum, pickled daikon, cucumber, and avocado

Troubleshooting sushi rolls

Okay, even if you follow my directions in the following recipe to the letter, maybe your sushi rolls doesn't turn out as expected. Here are some potential problems and my troubleshooting tips:

- ✔ **The rice sticks to your fingers.** Always use your tezu, or hand vinegar. Without it, the rice will definitely stick. Also, if you cook the rice with too much water and/or if you add too much seasoned vinegar to the rice after cooking it, you can make it too wet and sticky.

- ✔ **The fillings fall out while rolling.** You may have used too much filling, or you may just need to make that ridge of rice at the top as described in Step 4 of the Futomaki recipe.

- ✔ **The roll is bursting!** You used too many fillings or too much of the fillings you chose. I know you probably want to pack the roll with all your favorites, but the rolls are about the sushi rice, too! Try again with less filling.

- ✔ **The rolls are uneven — fat on one end, skinny on the other.** You didn't place the fillings evenly. For instance, if you use cucumber, the piece or pieces of cucumber must make one even line all the way across before beginning to roll it up.

- ✔ **The rounds fall apart after slicing.** You didn't compress the roll as you were making it. Follow Step 8, a vital part of sushi roll making, in the Futomaki recipe.

✔ **You just can't get the hang of rolling:** Make sure that your nori is placed squarely on the mat and that it's flush with the bottom edge — then re-read the instructions and try, try again! Even your mistakes are edible, so go for it!

One way to use your "mistakes" is to just collect them in a bowl and eat them as an extremely random version of chirashizushi!

Futomaki

These are the larger of the sushi rolls — the ones with the nori on the outside — and the easiest to make of the rolled kind, so start with these. Figure 5-2 should provide some assistance, and be sure to follow the cutting instructions for neatly sliced rolls.

Special tool: *Bamboo rolling mat*

Preparation time: *8 minutes*

Yield: *8 pieces*

⅔ *cup water*

4 teaspoons rice vinegar

1 full sheet nori, toasted

1½ cups cooked sushi rice, at room temperature (see the recipe earlier in this chapter)

Fillings of choice (see the section "Filling your sushi rolls," earlier in the chapter)

1 Make the tezu (hand vinegar) by stirring together the water and rice vinegar in a small bowl.

2 Place the rolling mat in front of you so that the bamboo pieces are horizontal.

3 Place the nori shiny side down (textured side up) on top of the mat with the shorter edge near you; align the edge of the nori with the edge of the rolling mat so that the nori is squared off.

4 Dip your fingers in the hand vinegar and use them to spread the rice over the nori, covering the surface from edge to edge but leaving a 1-inch portion of nori bare at the top. The rice should be about ¼ inch thick. (If you're using several fillings in one roll, add an additional ridge of rice at the far edge of the rice. Doing so keeps the fillings from falling out of the center when you begin the rolling process.)

5 Use your finger to make a shallow indentation in the center of the rice that runs horizontally across.

6 Smear some wasabi or umeboshi in the indentation, if included, and add your fillings: Begin by making an even row of one ingredient, such as cucumber, for example. Place the pieces of cucumber end to end so that one even line runs across the rice in the indentation. Then add a line of tuna right above the cucumber and other ingredients, if you're using multiple fillings.

7 Now comes the rolling part. Place your fingers on top of the fillings to help keep them in place, and use your thumbs to lift the bamboo mat up and over, rolling it forward. Bring the bottom edge of the nori and rice up and over the filling to meet the end of the rice (where the ridge is, if you have made one).

8 Your fingers should now be on top of the mat and around the roll; squeeze your fingers back toward you, tucking under the bottom and far side of the roll. Doing so compresses the filling(s) and rice to make a nice tight roll.

9 Pull up on the top edge of the mat (or it will get tucked into the roll) and, with the roll still inside and under the mat, continue to press the roll forward onto the exposed strip of nori at the top of the roll. This completes the roll. Gently squeeze the roll to firm it up and round out its shape. Slide the edges of the roll to the edges of the mat, one at a time, with the bamboo mat still over it. Use your fingers to press the rice and filling firmly into the nori roll, as some of the fillings may be loose along the ends and/or have been squeezed out a tiny bit.

10 Using a thin, sharp knife, cut the roll in half crosswise and then cut each half into quarters. Wipe the blade with a clean, warm cloth in between slices for the cleanest cuts.

11 Arrange on a serving dish and serve with soy sauce or dipping sauce and wasabi and pickled ginger on the side. Serve immediately.

Book VII

Japanese Cooking

Tip: *If you are having difficulty making the rolls nice and neat, play around with a little less rice or filling; chances are you might be overstuffing the roll and less filling is easier to work with.*

Vary It! *For hosomaki, or thin rolls, the technique is the same as for futomaki, but you use fewer ingredients: Cut the nori in half crosswise and then proceed, using proportionately less ingredients but following the same techniques. These smaller rolls are best with few fillings, such as just wasabi and tuna or umeboshi and pickled daikon. Cut these rolls into 6 pieces.*

Tip: *The larger rolls are best cut straight across, but the smaller rolls can be cut on the diagonal for a decorative effect. Cut so that one edge is straight and the other angles. Stand them up on the serving platter on their flat side; the diagonal side will be on top.*

MAKING ROLLED SUSHI

1. MAKE THE TEZU BY STIRRING THE WATER AND RICE VINEGAR IN A SMALL BOWL.

2. PLACE THE ROLLING MAT IN FRONT OF YOU SO THE BAMBOO PIECES ARE HORIZONTAL.

☆ YOU ARE HERE!

3. PLACE THE NORI SHINY SIDE DOWN ON TOP OF THE MAT WITH THE SHORTER END NEAR YOU. ALIGN EDGE OF NORI WITH EDGE OF ROLLING MAT.

SHINY SIDE DOWN!

4. DIP YOUR FINGERS IN THE HAND-VINEGAR AND USE THEM TO SPREAD THE RICE OVER THE NORI COVERING THE SURFACE FROM EDGE TO EDGE. LEAVE A 1" PORTION OF NORI BARE AT THE TOP. RICE SHOULD BE ABOUT ¼" THICK.

☆ TIP: IF YOU ARE USING MORE THAN 1 FILLING, ADD AN EXTRA RIDGE OF RICE AT THE FAR END TO KEEP THE FILLINGS FROM FALLING OUT OF THE CENTER WHEN YOU BEGIN TO ROLL.

EXTRA RIDGE

NORI

RICE

5. USE YOUR FINGER TO MAKE A SHALLOW INDENTATION IN THE CENTER OF THE RICE RUNNING HORIZONTALLY ACROSS.

6. SMEAR SOME WASABI (OPTIONAL) IN THE INDENTATION. THEN ADD FILLINGS. BEGIN BY MAKING AN EVEN ROW OF ONE INGREDIENT PLACE PIECES END TO END SO THERE IS ONE EVEN LINE RUNNING ACROSS THE RICE INDENTATION.

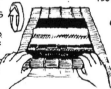

THEN ADD ADDITIONAL LINES OF INGREDIENTS RIGHT ABOVE THE FIRST ONE.

7. ROLL! PLACE FINGERS ON TOP OF FILLINGS KEEPING THEM IN PLACE. USE THUMBS TO LIFT THE MAT UP AND OVER, ROLLING IT FORWARD. BRING THE BOTTOM EDGE OF THE NORI AND RICE UP AND OVER THE FILLING TO MEET THE END OF THE RICE.

8. YOUR FINGERS SHOULD BE ON TOP OF THE MAT AND AROUND THE ROLL. SQUEEZE YOUR FINGERS BACK TOWARDS YOU AND TUCK UNDER THE BOTTOM AND FAR SIDE OF THE ROLL TO COMPRESS RICE & FILLING INTO A NICE TIGHT ROLL.

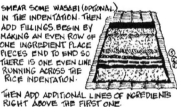

9. PULL UP ON TOP EDGE OF MAT AND, WITH THE ROLL INSIDE + UNDER, CONTINUE TO PRESS FORWARD ONTO THE EXPOSED NORI AT THE TOP. THIS COMPLETES THE ROLL. GENTLY SQUEEZE TO FIRM IT UP AND ROUND OUT IT'S SHAPE. SLIDE THE EDGES OF THE ROLL TO THE EDGES OF THE MAT, WITH THE BAMBOO STILL OVER IT. USE YOUR FINGER TO PRESS THE RICE AND FILLING INTO THE NORI.

10. USE A THIN, SHARP KNIFE. CUT THE ROLL IN HALF CROSSWISE. THEN CUT EACH HALF INTO QUARTERS. WIPE THE BLADE CLEAN, WARM CLOTH IN BETWEEN SLICES FOR THE CLEANEST CUTS.

11. ARRANGE ON A SERVING DISH. SERVE WITH SOY SAUCE OR DIPPING SAUCE, WASABI AND PICKLED GINGER ON THE SIDE. SERVE IMMEDIATELY!

LARGE ROLLS: CUT STRAIGHT ACROSS. SMALLER ROLLS: CUT ON A DIAGONAL.

Figure 5-2: Rolling sushi takes practice but is worth the effort.

Temaki

These are easy to make and easy to eat. They're also great for make-your-own sushi parties. Have all the prepped ingredients set out, and show your guests how to roll them up. (Practice on your own first. Your guests will be amazed.) Then let them try assembling the temaki themselves. Your guests can pick and choose whatever fillings they like. Tradition calls for making the rolls with your hands and in your hands, but I give you directions for making them on your countertop, as that method may be easier at first (see Figure 5-3). Once you get the hang of it, pick up the ingredients and roll away!

Preparation time: *10 minutes*

Yield: *4 pieces*

⅓ cup water

2 teaspoons rice vinegar

¼ cup sushi rice (see the recipe earlier in this chapter)

1 full sheet nori, quartered (use scissors)

Fillings of choice

1 Make the tezu (hand vinegar) by stirring together the water and rice vinegar in a small bowl.

2 Dip your fingers in the tezu and clasp your hands together to dampen your palms. Take 1 tablespoon of rice in your fingers and gently compress the rice into a finger shape, about 3 inches long and 1 inch wide; set aside. Repeat with the remaining rice.

3 Make your hand rolls: Place one piece of nori horizontally in front of you on your work surface. Place a finger of sushi rice diagonally from the bottom center angling up toward the left. It should be about ½ inch above the bottom edge. Arrange any fillings you are using alongside the rice.

4 It's time to roll! Take the bottom left corner and fold it, on the diagonal, up and over the fillings, tucking the point underneath the far side of the fillings. Angle it so that the bottom of the roll is tight and closed — you're forming a cone. Continue rolling up until the cone is complete. Repeat with the remaining ingredients. Serve with soy sauce or dipping sauce and wasabi and pickled ginger on the side. Serve immediately.

Tip: With temaki, which are more loosely constructed than futomaki or hosomaki, you want the bottom to be a tight point so that the fillings don't fall out. However, on the open end, it is expected, and even attractive, to have all the fillings exposed.

Book VII

Japanese Cooking

MAKING TEMAKI SUSHI

1. MAKE THE TEZU BY STIRRING TOGETHER THE WATER AND RICE VINEGAR IN A SMALL BOWL.

2. DIP YOUR FINGERS IN THE TEZU. CLASP HANDS TOGETHER TO DAMPEN PALMS. TAKE 1 TABLE-SPOON OF RICE IN YOUR FINGERS AND COMPRESS A SHAPE, 3" LONG AND 1" WIDE. SET ASIDE. REPEAT WITH THE REMAINING RICE.

3. TO MAKE HAND ROLLS, PLACE 1 PIECE OF NORI HORIZONTALLY IN FRONT OF YOU ON YOUR WORK SURFACE. PLACE FINGER OF SUSHI RICE DIAGONALLY FROM THE BOTTOM CENTER ANGLING UP TOWARDS THE LEFT. IT SHOULD BE ABOUT ½" ABOVE THE BOTTOM EDGE. ARRANGE ANY FILLING YOU ARE USING ALONGSIDE THE RICE.

4. IT'S TIME TO ROLL! TAKE THE BOTTOM LEFTHAND CORNER AND FOLD IT, ON THE DIAGONAL, UP AND OVER THE FILLINGS. TUCK THE POINT UNDER-NEATH THE FAR SIDE OF THE FILLINGS. ANGLE IT SO THE BOTTOM OF THE ROLL IS TIGHT AND CLOSED (YOU ARE FORMING A CONE!)

☆ WITH TEMAKI, WHICH ARE MORE LOOSELY CONSTRUCTED, YOU WANT THE BOTTOM TO BE A TIGHT POINT SO THAT THE FILLINGS DON'T FALL OUT. ON THE OPEN END IT IS EXPECTED AND ATTRACTIVE TO HAVE THE FILLINGS EXPOSED!

SERVE IMMEDIATELY WITH SOY SAUCE, DIPPING SAUCE AND WASABI. AND PICKLED GINGER ON THE SIDE...

Figure 5-3:
An easy way to make and serve sushi.

Inarizushi

For this recipe you need to buy *aburage,* which are fried, seasoned, rectangular tofu pouches that you open and fill. You want the ones that come in a can, which probably has the word *inarizushi* somewhere on the label. After you prepare your sushi rice, this recipe is very easy to make.

Preparation time: *10 minutes*

Cooking time: *5 minutes*

Yield: *8 pieces*

⅓ *cup water*

2 teaspoons rice vinegar

8 pieces canned aburage

1½ cups cooked sushi rice, warm or room temperature (see the recipe earlier in this chapter)

1 tablespoon white or black toasted sesame seeds (or a combination of both colors)

1 Make the tezu (hand vinegar) by stirring together the water and rice vinegar in a small bowl; set aside.

2 Bring a medium pot of water to a boil over high heat, add the aburage, turn the heat down, and simmer for 30 seconds, just enough to warm them through. Drain; set aside.

3 Meanwhile, stir together the rice and sesame seeds in a small bowl.

4 Carefully pry open the aburage, using your fingers. Take care not to tear the pouches.

5 Dip your fingers in the tezu and clasp your hands together to dampen your palms. Scoop up a generous tablespoon of rice with your fingers and stuff it inside, pushing it all the way to the bottom. The rice should come within ½ inch of the open sides. Pinch the open sides together to close, or fold one over the other and place the inarizushi, seam side down, on a serving platter. Repeat with the remaining ingredients. These are ready to serve immediately, although you can cover them with plastic wrap and let them sit at room temperature for a few hours. Serve with soy sauce or dipping sauce and wasabi and pickled ginger on the side.

Tip: *The aburage that I buy comes ready to stuff; the pieces already have an open cut side and measure about 2 inches by 3 inches. If yours are larger, chances are that they haven't been cut in half yet. Simply cut in half crosswise before filling.*

Vary It! *You can easily make this dish more elaborate. Have some minced pickled daikon on hand, or some minced pickled vegetables, umeboshi plums, or wasabi. Stuff the aburage with rice as described in the preceding recipe, make a small pocket inside the rice — just press your fingers inside to make a space — and fill the space with a little bit of minced veggies or a smear of umeboshi or wasabi, or both! Seal up the rice and finish the recipe. Now you have stuffed inarizushi!*

Getting the Raw Facts about Sashimi

Sashimi is raw fish and shellfish. It's a delicacy that you can enjoy in restaurants or make yourself at home.

Actually, in Japan, chicken, beef, and horse meat are sometimes sliced and served raw, but I talk only about the fishies in this book.

For sushi or sashimi it is helpful to know about what kinds of fish and shellfish are popular, easy to find, and delicious to eat. See the sections "Selecting Fish and Seafood for Sushi and Sashimi" and "Preparing Fish for Sushi and Sashimi," earlier in this chapter, for more information.

It should go without saying, but I will say it anyway, IN LOUD WORDS, that freshness is of the utmost importance, no matter what kind of seafood you use. Freshness is important for health reasons and for flavor as well. Simply said, the fresher the better. In Japan, some connoisseurs even restrict their sashimi eating to early in the day because that's closer to the time when the fish was caught.

Sashimi

You can slice and serve practically any fresh — very fresh — fish raw. I suggest that you try tuna, as it's the most popular with American palates. In fact, it is often described as meaty and is similar to eating a very rare steak. Sashimi is usually served with shredded daikon, in addition to soy sauce or dipping sauce, wasabi, and pickled ginger, so make sure to have all of them on hand. Judging serving portions of fish can be difficult, but a slice or two of one type of fish per person should suffice when served among other offerings, such as nigirizushi and makizushi.

This recipe calls for tuna, but use your best judgment in selecting which type of fish to use. For example, if you live in the Pacific Northwest and some impeccably fresh salmon is available, use that instead. Freshness should prevail.

Preparation time: *8 minutes*

Yield: *8 slices*

6 ounces fresh tuna, about 1 inch thick and
2½ inches wide

1 Cut about ⅓-inch-thick pieces of the tuna crosswise, against the grain, slightly angling your knife blade. (Each piece will be about ¾ ounce.)

2 Arrange slices of the tuna on a serving platter. Serve with soy sauce or dipping sauce, wasabi, pickled ginger, and shredded daikon on the side. Serve immediately.

Tip: *I like my tuna a bit thick for sashimi. For white-fleshed fish like yellow tail, try it sliced thinly enough to see through.*

Tip: *This recipe is so simple that you can, and should, take the time to present it as artfully as possible. Choose a platter or serving dish that will show off the fish. Solid colors work best, as a busy design detracts from the jewel colors of the fish. You can fan the fish slices out, overlap them in a line, or arrange small groupings of each kind of fish. There is really no wrong way to present them. That said, leave the plate somewhat bare: Place the fish slices, a mound of daikon, a mound of pickled ginger, and a bit of wasabi on the plate, but use plate that's large enough for you to spread out the items. You want to be able to take in all the textures and colors of the ingredients so that you can tempt your eyes as well as your taste buds.*

Tip: *With thinly sliced fish, you can roll the pieces up to look like little flowers. Just roll up from a short end, slightly pinch one side, and spread open the other end slightly to look like an open flower.*

Don't let fugu be the death of you

Fugu, a type of blowfish, can kill you if it's not prepared properly. Yes, that's right, kill you. You're dead. No more sushi for you! So I want to make one thing perfectly clear: You are not, I repeat, not going to prepare fugu at home. The fish contains a powerful toxin inside its internal organs, and if it's not prepared properly, the toxins will contaminate the flesh, and you will die or get very sick.

So why do the Japanese eat fugu? Because its flesh is said to be a delicacy unlike any other, and because chefs attend school to study how to prepare the fish safely. Hey, they want you to come back and buy more sushi and sashimi, right? Killing you off wouldn't be good for business. Special restaurants in Japan specialize in fugu preparation. The fish is best enjoyed during the winter months, when the fish is at its peak and the toxin is at its lowest level.

Fugu dishes are usually quite expensive, and the chefs take great care in the artistic presentation of the fish. A meal of fugu is reserved for special occasions, and the whole experience is expected to be one of luxury, with beautiful dishes used and the skills of the chef shown off to their best advantage.

Here are some terms you may see in a restaurant featuring fugu:

- **Fugu teishoku:** This is an entire meal made from various dishes featuring fugu.

- **Fugu sashi:** This is fugu served as sashimi (raw); it is always very thinly sliced and almost translucent and usually begins the meal, along with a special sauce for dipping.

- **Fugu chiri:** This is the main part of the meal and consists of a cooked fugu and vegetable stew.

- **Fugu zosui:** The meal might end with this rice porridge made with fugu.

Book VII

Japanese Cooking

Chapter 6

Rice and Noodles

The Japanese eat rice at almost every meal, so you can be sure that every Japanese cook knows how to make a perfect pot of rice — and you should, too! As I mention in several places in this section, automatic rice cookers are one way to go; many Japanese home cooks have one in their kitchen. If you own one, by all means use it, following the manufacturer's instructions. For everyone else, I include a simple recipe for rice in this chapter.

Take time to master the rice recipe because so many Japanese meals depend on it. If you can make a pot of rice and a bowl of miso soup, you'll always be able to make a meal.

As far as noodles and pasta are concerned, I love linguine with clam sauce, spaghetti with marinara, and a good carbonara sauce, but Japanese noodle dishes hold a special place in my heart. Whether I eat them hot or cold, be they buckwheat soba or wheaty udon, they not only satisfy my appetite but also always make me feel nourished and cared for. The aromas wafting up from the table, their attractive tangle on a bamboo tray, and their languid twisting in a bowl enhance their appeal. They smell and look as good as they taste. And you get to make noise! Not only is it most appropriate for you to slurp your soba, but if you don't, your host will think that you're not enjoying the meal. So slurp away!

Making the Perfect Pot of Rice

I'm not talking brown rice or wild rice or converted white rice here — I'm talking basic white rice — *kome* — Japanese style. The most common Japanese rice is a short-grain polished rice called *seihakumai*. Rice is cultivated all over Japan, and different locales produce different rice, to a degree. All of it is of the short-grain variety, which is a bit sticky, but that makes eating with chopsticks easy — well, at least easier!

Figure on about ½ cup uncooked rice per person. Japanese short-grain rice expands about 75 percent after cooking.

The size of pot you use is important; it depends on the amount of rice being cooked. Ideally, you want the rice and water to come about halfway up the sides of the pot. If the pot is too large and the level of rice very low, it's more prone to scorching. If the pot is narrow and deep, the cooked rice will be overly sticky. Always use a pot with a heavy bottom and a tight-fitting lid.

The ratio of water to rice is also somewhat variable. Different brands cook differently. The age of the rice and its dryness or moisture level, among other factors, all affect the amount of cooking water needed. The following recipe should work with your short-grain white rice, but consider it as more of a guide.

Once you have mastered the basic rice recipe, there are many options. You can serve it as is as a side dish along with some pickled vegetables to some simply cooked fish, or, try the upcoming recipe for rice balls stuffed with pickled daikon and flavored with vinegar.

For a recipe for sushi rice, turn to Chapter 5 of Book VII.

Basic White Rice

Simple white rice is easy to prepare and is a foundation in Japanese cuisine.

Preparation time: *35 minutes*

Cooking time: *15 minutes*

Yield: *4 servings*

2¼ cups water   2 cups rice

1 Place the rice in a large bowl, cover with cold water, and rub between your fingers and palms; drain and repeat several times or until the water is clear. After the final draining, allow the rice to air-dry in a colander for 30 minutes, tossing once or twice for even air circulation.

2 Place the water and rice in a heavy-bottomed covered pot over medium-high heat until it comes to a boil. Reduce the heat to low and simmer gently, the lid still in place, for about 15 minutes, or until all the liquid is just absorbed.

3 Remove the covered pot from the heat. Do not lift the lid. Allow the rice to sit for 15 minutes. This resting period is very important and yields perfectly textured rice. After it rests, fluff the rice gently with a fork, and it's ready to serve.

Tip: *A few brands of Japanese-style short-grain rice that are available in the United States are Nishiki, Kokuho, and Maruyu. Look for them in Asian food stores.*

Stuffed Rice Balls

Rice balls are called *onigiri* in Japan. These easy-to-make balls use cooked rice, so make sure that you have finished that step before starting this recipe. These balls make a great lunch or snack, and they even pack well for picnics. I like to serve them with a little dipping dish of soy sauce with some wasabi on the side.

Special tool: *Teacup with rounded bottom*

Preparation time: *20 minutes*

Yield *8 rice balls (2 per person)*

1 cup water	⅓ cup minced pickled daikon
1 tablespoon rice vinegar	2 tablespoons toasted sesame seeds, white or black or a combination (optional)
1 recipe Basic White Rice, still warm (see the recipe earlier in this chapter)	
3 umeboshi plums, pitted and chopped	4 sheets nori, toasted (see Chapter 2 of Book VII)

1 Combine the water and rice vinegar in a small bowl and place on your work surface; you dip your fingers into this mixture (called *tezu*) to keep them from sticking to the rice. Rinse a teacup with warm water and set aside. (Most teacups hold about ⅔ cup; if your teacups are larger, the rice will not fill them, but that is just fine. The molding technique will still work.)

2 Divide the warm, cooked rice into 8 portions. Place half of one portion in the bottom of the teacup and press firmly along the bottom and up the sides, creating a depression in the middle. Add a little bit of umeboshi plum and a sprinkling of daikon. Add the remaining half of this portion of rice and press firmly on top of the filling, encasing it completely.

3 Unmold the rice from the teacup, dip your fingers into the warm water, and form the rice into a ball with your hands, compressing it gently. Coat the ball with some sesame seeds, if desired. (I like to coat half the balls with sesame seeds and leave the others plain.) Set aside and repeat with the remaining rice and filling ingredients.

4 Use scissors to cut the nori sheets into 1-inch-wide strips. Wrap a strip, shiny side facing out, around each ball, using more than one strip if necessary. The nori adds flavor and visual interest and makes it easy to pick up the balls in your fingers. Serve immediately.

Vary It! *You can vary the fillings as you like: Use minced pickled vegetables, some wasabi, or even some minced cooked fish. You can incorporate the sesame seeds into the rice itself before molding or add shredded nori to the rice for a confetti effect. Experiment!*

Tip: *If you don't have a teacup, don't worry. Just use your hands to mold the balls from the get-go. Take a quantity of rice into your moistened palms; squeeze gently to make a ball. Use your fingers to create a hole in the ball and fill with the chosen fillings. Add more rice if necessary to cover the fillings, or just close up the hole and form into a ball with your moist hands. That's it!*

Cooking Noodles the Japanese Way

To cook Japanese noodles, you begin with a large pot of boiling water, just like you do when cooking spaghetti and macaroni. Unlike cooking pasta for Italian cuisine, however, you do not salt the water. Then, using the desired amount of noodles, you add them slowly to the water (to keep the water boiling). As with all pasta, keep the heat high to encourage a rapid boil. Stir the noodles as soon as you add them to the water to separate them and discourage sticking. Continue boiling until the noodles reach the al dente stage, or are just cooked. The best way to check is to bite into a noodle. You should feel a slight resistance against your teeth, but the noodles should be cooked and not crunchy.

Cooking times are roughly 5 minutes for soba, 8 minutes for ramen, and 12 minutes for udon, but obviously the cooking time all depends on how rapidly your water is boiling, how many noodles you're cooking, whether the noodles are fresh or dried, and so on. Always taste-test. If one trap is easy to fall into here, it's overcooking the noodles, so take care when approaching the end of the suggested cooking time.

Follow the preceding suggestions if you're cooking noodles to serve cold. If you plan to serve them hot, slightly undercook them, as they'll cook further when added to a hot broth or stew.

Traditionally, noodles, particularly soba, were added to boiling water and then cold water was added to lower the temperature. When the water returned to a boil, cold water was added again. This process was repeated three or four times until the noodles were cooked to the proper texture. In this way, the noodles were cooked very gently; the technique helped preserve their chewy texture. Although connoisseurs still cook them in this way, it's a little more time-consuming, and I don't want the exactitude of this technique to keep you from eating noodles. If you want to try it, go ahead, and know that you're following in the footsteps of many traditional Japanese cooks.

Book VII

Japanese Cooking

Savoring soba noodles

Nutty brown soba noodles are made from buckwheat and are common to Tokyo and the northern part of Japan. Eating this hearty noodle, which is served both cold and hot, tames the colder climate of the north. Soba noodles are often eaten on New Year's Eve as a way of saying goodbye to the old year and ringing in the new. Friendly neighbors also bring soba noodles to new neighbors as a way of saying welcome.

Soba noodles are not made from 100 percent buckwheat; they can be light, with 20 percent buckwheat, or quite hearty, with about 80 percent buckwheat. The remaining percentage is made up of wheat flour. Occasionally, green tea is added to the dough, giving the noodles a greenish color; these noodles are called *chasoba*.

Whether served cold or hot, soba noodle dishes are very easy to make. Cold soba noodles are perfect in the summertime, while hot soba noodles make a great family meal on a cold day. An added bonus is that soba noodles are considered quite healthy; they're high in protein and low in fat and have an abundance of B vitamins, iron, and calcium.

When dining on chilled soba in a restaurant, you're presented with the cold noodles on a bamboo tray (or other dish), as well as dipping sauce and condiments. The sauce, which is based on dashi, is subtle but flavorful. The condiments can be as simple as grated daikon or also include scallions, wasabi, or other additions. Add some daikon or any other condiments to your own bowl of dipping sauce and then pick up the soba with your chopsticks, dip them in the sauce, and slip them into your mouth — enjoy!

 If you like, you can do what the Japanese do and, at the end of the meal, serve the water in which the soba was cooked. The soba water cleanses the palate and provides nutritious benefits, as it contains protein and vitamins from the cooked soba. Pour some into the last few bits and slurps of dipping sauce in your bowl, and your broth takes on a whole new dimension. Take it into your mouth slowly to appreciate the nuances of this newly created liquid. You can serve the soba water with both cold and hot soba.

Chilled Soba

Take care to start with a good dashi (see Chapter 4 of Book VII) because it truly enhances the dipping sauce. You can prepare the sauce ahead of time to make the recipe go quickly. You don't have to use all the condiments, but at least provide the grated daikon.

Preparation time: *10 minutes*

Cooking time: *15 minutes*

Yield: *6 servings*

Dipping sauce:

3 cups dashi

½ cup soy sauce

¼ cup mirin

1 ounce bonito flakes

Noodles:

¾ pound dry soba noodles

Condiments:

¼ cup finely shredded toasted nori (optional)

¼ cup finely grated daikon (white radish)

¼ cup thinly sliced scallion

1 tablespoon prepared wasabi

1 Make the dipping sauce: Place the dashi, soy sauce, and mirin in a saucepan and bring just to a boil over medium heat. Stir in the bonito flakes and immediately remove from the heat. Allow to sit while the bonito flakes sink to the bottom; they may not all sink. Just let the dipping sauce sit for about 5 minutes. Strain the sauce and allow it to come to room temperature before using. (You may refrigerate the dipping sauce in an airtight container for up to 4 days; always bring back to room temperature before using.) Pour the dipping sauce into individual bowls; set aside.

2 Cook the soba, drain well, and plunge into ice-cold water to chill and remove the surface starch. Drain again and pile on individual bamboo trays or the serving dishes of your choice. Sprinkle the nori over each serving, if desired.

3 Place the daikon, scallion, and wasabi in separate serving dishes. Give each person his own serving of soba and dipping sauce. To eat, invite each diner to mix condiments into his dipping sauce. Pick up strands of soba with chopsticks, dip in the sauce, and enjoy!

Going All Out: *To increase the heartiness factor, add some cubed firm tofu to the soba for dipping and eating.*

Book VII

Japanese Cooking

Preparing noodle broth

The following broth can be used with both the soba and the udon recipes later in this chapter. A good broth is a huge part of a good soup. Without a tasty broth, the rest of the soup will suffer. That said, the broths used for the soups in this section are very simple to make and use few ingredients. Because of this, make sure to use the highest quality ingredients and take care while making the soup by following the directions carefully. Also, Japanese noodle broths are subtle, but they are delicious. Keep an open mind when tasting your broth: It will not knock you out like a hearty chicken stock. Rather, the flavors will slowly develop in your mouth.

Noodle Broth

You can use this multipurpose broth for serving both soba and udon. Take advantage of the fact that you can make it several days ahead.

Preparation time: *5 minutes*

Cooking time: *5 minutes*

Yield: *4 servings*

10 cups dashi (see Chapter 4 of Book VII)   ¼ cup plus 1 tablespoon mirin

½ cup plus 2 tablespoons soy sauce

Place the dashi, soy sauce, and mirin in a large saucepan and bring to a boil over medium-high heat. Use immediately or cool to room temperature. (You may refrigerate the broth in an airtight container for up to 4 days.)

Tip: *I use San-J or Eden brand soy sauces and Kikkoman Mirin. With these products, the amounts in the recipe balance quite nicely. Your soy sauces may have a different degree of saltiness, and your mirin may be more or less sweet. Start with my suggested amounts and adjust to taste, if necessary.*

Soba in Broth

Here, soba is served hot in a nourishing, tasty broth.

Preparation time: *5 minutes*

Cooking time: *15 minutes*

Yield: *6 servings*

1 pound dried soba   ½ cup thinly sliced scallion

1 recipe Noodle Broth (see the preceding recipe)

1 Cook the soba until al dente, drain well, and rinse to remove the surface starch.

2 Bring the prepared broth to a simmer in a large pot. Quickly stir the cooked noodles into the simmering broth and heat them through, about 1 minute. Ladle the broth and noodles into individual bowls, dividing evenly, sprinkle with scallion, and serve immediately.

Tip: *Serving the noodles can be tricky. The easiest way is to use tongs to remove the noodles, place them in serving bowls, and then ladle broth over top.*

Vary It! *You can embellish this soup to your heart's content, Here are some ingredients that work well; just add them to hot broth before adding noodles:*

- *Rehydrated dried mushrooms*
- *Fresh mushrooms*
- *Slices of fish cake (kamaboko)*
- *Slivers of cooked chicken or duck*
- *Cooked shrimp*
- *Hard-cooked eggs, halved*

A classic addition is one splendid tempura cooked shrimp. Try it! (See Chapter 7 of Book VII for a tempura recipe.)

About that slurp . . .

When you're eating hot soba noodles, it's perfectly acceptable, even desirable, to make noise. The idea is to eat them quickly, which really can't be done quietly, so that you enjoy them while they're at their peak. Slurping allows cool air to enter your mouth at the same time as the noodles, thereby cooling them down and allowing you to eat them while they're quite hot.

Slurping your noodles also tells your host that you love the food. Therefore, the sound is a sign of appreciation and considered proper etiquette.

Eating oodles of udon noodles

Udon noodles are wheat-based noodles with a very pale, creamy-white color. They're excellent served in a nourishing broth; for a simple presentation, you may substitute them for the soba in the preceding recipe for Soba in Broth.

I decided to bring you a slightly more elaborate version, Moon Udon, in which the "moon" is represented by an egg yolk. If you look down into the bowl, the yolk truly looks like a golden moon floating in a warm liquid sky. You can always count on the Japanese to be poetic, even with their food.

Moon Udon

This delicious dish highlights tender udon noodles swimming in broth, embellished with a golden egg yolk.

Preparation time: *10 minutes*

Cooking time: *15 minutes*

Yield: *6 servings*

1 recipe Noodle Broth (see the recipe earlier in this chapter)

1 pound dried udon

5-x-2-inch fish cake (kamaboko), cut into ¼-inch slices

½ cup thinly sliced scallion

7-spice mixture (shichimi)

6 egg yolks

1 Cook the udon until al dente, drain well, and rinse to remove the surface starch.

2 Bring the prepared broth to a simmer in a large pot. Quickly stir the cooked noodles and fish cake slices into the simmering broth and heat them through, about 2 minutes. Ladle the broth, noodles, and fish cake into individual bowls, dividing evenly. Sprinkle with scallion and shichimi to taste.

3 Make a depression in the middle of each bowl by pressing a ladle down into the noodles. Slip the egg yolks into each depression. Allow to sit for 1 minute to briefly cook the
egg, and then serve immediately. (The egg should still be soft, like a poached egg. If you
have health concerns, pre-cook the egg until at least part of the yolk is opaque. This will
change the dish dramatically, however, and not for the better. Skip this recipe if this is a
real concern.)

4 Invite your guests to use chopsticks as well as a spoon to eat. Pierce the "moons" (egg
yolks) with chopsticks, stir into the broth, and enjoy!

Tip: *The easiest way to handle egg yolks is to separate the yolks from the whites one at a
time. Discard the white, or save for another use, and save the egg yolk in a small, shallow
saucer. Then just pick up the saucer, tilt it over a bowl filled with soup, and the yolk will
slip right in. Repeat with the remaining egg yolks and bowls of soup.*

Enjoying rich ramen noodles

Ramen noodles are another type of wheat-based noodle often made with
eggs, making it a rich noodle. Although they're classically Chinese, they have
made their way into Japanese cuisine in a big way. They're usually served
with some sort of meat and vegetables in a broth, served hot. Sometimes I
can't find dried ramen packaged without other ingredients, in which case I
use fresh Chinese-style egg noodles. You can find these in the refrigerated
sections of Asian food stores.

Chinese egg noodles are not like the typical egg noodles you find in the
pasta section of the supermarket. Those are broad, flat, and ribbonlike.
The Chinese style is more like a long, thin, round, curly spaghetti.

You may be familiar with instant ramen, which you can find in almost any
supermarket. It comes in a single-serving size with a flavor packet to make
the broth. Web sites are devoted to the many, many ways (thousands!) that
you can serve these instant noodles. They're considered a staple food for
underfunded college students everywhere. These ramen noodles are called
instant because making them takes just minutes, but with a little more time
and effort, you can have a truly delicious and nourishing meal.

Book VII

**Japanese
Cooking**

Ramen with Pork and Vegetables

Ramen and pork have a natural affinity for one another. For lunch or dinner, this is a very popular dish. The fresh, crunchy cabbage is a nice addition to the dish. If you can't find *hakusai* (Chinese cabbage) in your supermarket or Asian grocery store, use bok choy instead.

Preparation time: *15 minutes*

Cooking time: *1 hour*

Yield: *6 servings*

1 tablespoon oil

2 pounds boneless pork loin, cut into 1-inch cubes

8 scallions, cut into 1-inch pieces, ¼ cup reserved

1-inch knob of fresh ginger, peeled and cut into 4 slices

1 large garlic clove, sliced in half lengthwise

10 cups chicken broth (homemade or canned is fine; try to use low-sodium)

¾ cup mirin

¼ cup soy sauce

1½ pounds fresh Chinese-style egg noodles

1½ pounds Chinese cabbage (hakusai) or bok choy, rinsed, ends trimmed, and chopped into bite-size pieces

Sesame oil

Chili oil

1 Place the oil in a large pot and add the cubed pork. Cook over high heat, stirring occasionally, until the pork is seared on all sides, about 4 minutes.

2 Add the larger portion of scallions, the ginger, and the garlic and cook for a minute or two, stirring frequently. Add the chicken broth, mirin, and soy sauce. Bring to a boil, reduce the heat to a simmer, cover, and cook over low-medium heat for about 45 minutes or until the pork is very tender. Remove all 4 pieces of ginger and 2 pieces of the garlic and discard. (You can make this soup up to 2 days ahead and refrigerate it in an airtight container; skim any fat off when it's chilled if you follow this step. Reheat when you're ready to finish the recipe.)

3 Cook the egg noodles until al dente, drain well, and rinse to remove the surface starch.

4 Skim any fat or foam off the surface of the soup. Make sure that the broth is simmering and add the cabbage. Cook until the cabbage is tender, about 8 minutes.

5 Quickly stir the cooked noodles into the simmering broth and heat them through, about 2 minutes. Ladle into bowls, dividing the pork and greens evenly. Sprinkle with the remaining scallions and serve immediately. Add a few drops of sesame oil or chili oil.

Vary It! *If you like, you can add 3 hard-cooked eggs to this recipe. Peel them, cut them in half crosswise, and add 1 egg half to each bowl. Sometimes I also add some slices of fish cake (kamaboko) along with the cabbage for a more complex version.*

Chapter 7

The Main Event

In This Chapter

- Simmering your meals
- Broiling and pan-frying foods
- Getting the hang of tempura
- Making one-pot dishes

*W*hen you go to a Japanese restaurant, you may have it in your head that you're going to limit your dining to sushi and sashimi. But this cuisine includes so much more, and many of these other sorts of dishes are very easy to re-create at home.

Nimono are simmered dishes, which are simply made on top of the stove. *Yakimono* are broiled and pan-fried dishes, which again are easy to cook in almost any kitchen, using the equipment you have on hand. *Agemono* are deep-fried dishes. *Tempura* is a classic example that you may be familiar with. Possibly simplest of all are *nabemono* — one-pot dishes. Here, you assemble all your ingredients in an artful way in one pot, simmer them on top of the stove, and serve out of the same pot. These are fun to make and easy to serve, and they look great presented at the table.

You may be a sushi lover and have never thought of eating anything else when considering Japanese cuisine. I intend to change your mind with this chapter! It includes fish, chicken, beef, shellfish, and veggies — something for everyone — so read on and head for the kitchen.

Nimono: Simmered Dishes

Many cuisines feature simmered dishes. The French *pot-au-feu* is a chicken simmered in a pot with vegetables. In the United States, you can find good ole American beef stew and Texan chili. The Italians have their hearty osso buco, and India has its curries. You get the idea.

Submerging food with a drop lid

In some Japanese simmered dishes, the recipe requires something called a drop lid. These are often made of wood and are smaller in diameter than the pot they're used with so that they can literally be dropped down inside to sit right on top of the food. They keep the food submerged in the liquid while it cooks. To rig up a facsimile, simply form a round of aluminum foil with thick crumpled edges, to give it some weight and structure, and place that right on top of the food. Or, if you have a lid from a small pot, it just may fit inside the large pot you're using.

Japanese cooks have been simmering foods for a long, long time. I read one statistic that said a Japanese pot was carbon-dated to 10,000 B.C.! Can't you picture someone stirring food in a rustic pot over an open fire? Simmering is quite easy to do. You simply combine ingredients with water or flavored liquid, such as a broth or sake, and simmer them gently until cooked.

The term *simmer* is occasionally misunderstood. Simmering means that the liquid is bubbling very gently with tiny bubbles. A raucous boil, one in which the bubbling is fast and furious, is a much harsher approach and can toughen food and evaporate the liquid. Think low-medium heat and a gentle ripple through the liquid — that's a simmer!

Along with meats, fish, and vegetables, Japanese simmered foods feature certain flavorings, including sake for flavor and tenderizing, mirin and sugar for sweetness, and soy sauce and miso for a deep, rich flavor and color. I provide a fish and miso dish for you in this section.

Simmered Mackerel in Miso

Mackerel is a hearty fish that is complemented by the assertive flavor of the miso; you can substitute bluefish, if you like. Use whatever is freshest.

Preparation time: *8 minutes*

Cooking time: *12 minutes*

Yield: *4 servings*

½ teaspoon vegetable oil	3 tablespoons sugar
6 scallions, trimmed and cut into 1-inch lengths	2 pounds mackerel fillets, cut crosswise into 3-inch-wide pieces
¾ cup dashi (see Chapter 4 of Book VII)	
1-inch knob fresh ginger, peeled and cut crosswise into 6 rounds	3 tablespoons mirin
	1½ tablespoons soy sauce
3 tablespoons sake	3 tablespoons dark miso

1 Heat the oil in a wide, deep, straight-sided heavy-bottomed saucepan (at least 3-quart) over high heat. Add the scallions and sauté until the scallions have softened and lightly browned, about 3 minutes.

2 Add the dashi, ginger, sake, and sugar and stir to combine. Bring to a boil for a minute or two until the sugar is dissolved. Turn down the heat to a simmer.

3 Add the pieces of fish, skin side up, to the pan. Cover the bottom of the pan first, and then make another layer if you have to. Place a drop lid right on top of the fish and simmer over medium heat for about 3 minutes.

4 Add the mirin and soy sauce, replace the lid, and cook for another 3 minutes. Meanwhile, place the miso in a small bowl; ladle out some of the broth (about ⅓ cup) from the saucepan and stir it into the miso to make a smooth, fluid paste. Add the miso paste to the pot; do not replace the lid. The fish and sauce should be starting to look rich and brown. Continue to cook gently for another minute or two, shaking the pot back and forth to keep the miso from scorching or boiling. You can also just move the fish around a little bit by using a wooden spatula. The fish should just be cooked through; you can check by cutting into one of the pieces — it should flake apart. Now the fish is ready to serve. Serve with rice and some pickled vegetables.

Tip: Make sure not to serve the large pieces of ginger. Remember, 6 pieces went in, so take 6 pieces out!

Tip: If you aren't partial to fish skin, simply slip it off each piece before serving. It will come right off — try using a teaspoon, butter knife, or even your fingers to help peel it off.

Yakimono: Broiled and Pan-Fried Dishes

The category of yakimono includes both broiled and grilled dishes, such as the Chicken Yakitori and the Salmon Teriyaki in this chapter and pan-fried dishes such as the sweet Rolled Omelet from Chapter 5 of Book VII.

Yakitori, or broiled dishes, start with a special sauce, called *tare*. It is always a combination of sake, mirin, and soy sauce; and the more complex, traditional versions also include roasted chicken bones. The chicken bones give the sauce a depth of flavor that can't be duplicated. Although restaurants often have easy access to chicken bones from all the chickens they debone, I have devised a recipe for you to try at home that uses chicken wings, which are easy to find and inexpensive to purchase.

Japan has restaurants called *yakitori-ya*, which specialize in yakitori dishes. Yakitori is popular and a great technique to try at home. With the ingredients and tools on hand, you can make the recipe quite quickly, so stock up on the ingredients that you need — and don't forget to buy some bamboo skewers. You can find them in supermarkets in the housewares aisle, or sometimes in the fish department.

Chicken Yakitori

This recipe includes a recipe for yakitori sauce, which you can brush over other foods, such as meat, fish, or vegetables, if you like. After you finish making the sauce, don't throw out the chicken wings — you can eat them as appetizers. This classic recipe calls for serving the sauce with chicken, but I have added bell peppers for flavor, color, and crunch.

Special tools: *15 bamboo skewers, 8 to 12 inches long*

Preparation time: *15 minutes, plus 1 hour for soaking the skewers, which can soak while you prepare the sauce*

Cooking time: *1 hour and 10 minutes*

Yield: *15 skewers, about 4 servings*

8 chicken wings	4 boneless chicken thighs, cut into 1½-inch square pieces, skin attached
2½ cups mirin	
1½ cups sake	2 bell peppers, green, red, yellow or orange, cored, seeded, cut into 1½-inch squares
⅓ cup sugar	
2½ cups soy sauce	

1 Place the bamboo skewers in a pan and cover with hot water; allow to soak for 1 hour. Doing so keeps them from burning when you cook the chicken.

2 Make the yakitori sauce: Preheat the broiler. Place the chicken wings on a rack set over the broiler pan and place about 3 inches from the broiler source. Broil until just starting to char, and then flip over and char the other side. This step takes about 5 minutes total; set aside.

3 Place the mirin, sake, sugar, and soy sauce in a medium saucepan, stir to combine, and bring to a boil over high heat; allow to boil for about 1 minute, stirring once or twice, or until the sugar is dissolved. Add the chicken wings, cover, reduce the heat slightly, and simmer for about 25 minutes, stirring occasionally. Uncover and continue to simmer for about 25 minutes more or until the sauce has reduced slightly. Remove the chicken wings and skim off any excess fat from the surface. The sauce is now ready to use. You may refrigerate it for up to 1 week in an airtight container before proceeding. Bring it back to a boil before using.

4 Meanwhile, prepare the skewers: Take a skewer and thread a piece of pepper onto it, followed by a chunk of chicken, pepper, chicken, pepper, chicken, and ending with pepper. (You should have three pieces of chicken and four pieces of pepper on each skewer.)

5 Preheat the broiler. Pour about three-fourths of the yakitori sauce into a shallow pan. Place the skewers on a rack set over a roasting pan and set about 2 inches from the broiler source. Broil until you just begin to see juices coming to the surface of the chicken, about 3 minutes; flip the skewers over and cook 3 minutes more. Remove the pan from oven; one by one roll each skewer around in the sauce and replace on the pan. Broil for an additional 3 minutes, dip again, replace with the other side up, and continue to cook until done. You can cut into a piece of chicken to check. It should be cooked through with no pink left in the meat, and the juices should run clear. Be careful not to overcook, however, or the meat will be very dry.

6 Brush the chicken and peppers with some of the reserved sauce and serve immediately. Place the skewers on a platter to pass around. Encourage guests to nibble directly off of the skewers, or you may slide the meat and peppers off onto plates.

Book VII

Japanese Cooking

Tip: *If you want to use skinless thighs, go right ahead. The chicken will be a little drier, but you do have the choice.*

Tip: *If you have a charcoal or gas grill, you can cook the yakitori in that fashion as well.*

Tip: *You may have sauce left over. You can refrigerate it in an airtight container for up to a week. Boil it for a full 5 minutes before using, which will render it safe, even though it was used to marinate the chicken.*

Salmon Teriyaki

Salmon is a popular fish these days not only because it's delicious but also because it contains heart-healthy omega-3 fatty acids. Here, it's simply broiled with a sweet, tangy teriyaki sauce.

Preparation time: *35 minutes*

Cooking time: *12 minutes*

Yield: *4 servings*

3 tablespoons mirin	*2 tablespoons sugar*
3 tablespoons sake	*1⅓ pounds salmon fillets, cut crosswise into 4 pieces*
3 tablespoons soy sauce	

1 To make the teriyaki marinade, place the mirin, sake, soy sauce, and sugar in a small saucepan, stir to combine, and bring to a boil over medium-high heat. Boil for a minute to dissolve the sugar. Remove from the heat, pour into a shallow dish, and cool to room temperature.

2 Place the salmon fillets in a dish with the teriyaki marinade. Let sit for 15 minutes, turn the salmon pieces over, and marinate for 15 minutes more.

3 Preheat the broiler. Set a broiler rack over a broiler pan; coat the rack with nonstick spray. Place the fillets skin side up on the rack so that they aren't touching each other. Broil about 2 inches from the broiler for about 3 minutes. Carefully flip the fillets over, brush with some teriyaki sauce, and broil for about 4 minutes more or until just cooked through. You can tell the fish is done when it flakes easily and has just lost its translucency. Serve immediately with rice and pickled vegetables (see Chapter 4 of Book VII).

Tip: During the last blast under the broiler, you can pour the extra marinade in a small saucepan and boil it over high heat. In a couple minutes, it will reduce to a thick, glossy glaze. Brush this over the fish right before serving.

Agemono: Deep-Fried Dishes

Deep-fried dishes seem to have a universal appeal, whether it is Southern fried chicken, fried belly clams from Cape Cod, or everybody's favorite — French fries! Japanese cuisine has a few specialties of its own in this arena, and you can make them at home. Tempura, which features a light batter that coats vegetables and fish, is one favorite. Tonkatsu, which is deep-fried pork, is also wildly popular in Japan and appeals to American tastes.

See Chapter 3 of Book VII for more information on deep-frying Japanese food.

Preparing tempura

Tempura is a Japanese deep-fried dish, but the batter is light and lacy. So if you're thinking of heavy fried chicken batter, stop right there. The coating is very simply made from flour, water, and egg yolks; and the items to be dipped are always vegetables or fish, never chicken or meat. It is deep-fried, however, so the dish does have some substance, but the Japanese skillfully pair the tempura with a thin but flavorful dipping sauce that flavors the food and cuts some of the fattiness.

You must make this dish right before serving. All fried foods are best served soon after frying, and this dish is no exception. My version of tempura includes shrimp and veggies. The recipe uses 2 pounds of ingredients to be dipped into batter; you can mix and match whatever you like. Love shrimp? Add more in proportion to veggies. If you use shrimp, or pieces of fish, cook those pieces together (shrimp with shrimp, fish with fish). Similarly, cook like vegetables together so that they cook evenly.

This deep-fried dish was actually introduced to the Japanese by the Spanish and Portuguese missionaries as early as the 16th century.

Here are my favorite ingredients to cook as tempura (all ingredients are raw before dipping them in the batter):

- ✔ Broccoli florets
- ✔ Carrots (peeled) cut thinly on the diagonal
- ✔ Sweet potatoes (peeled) cut thinly on the diagonal
- ✔ Kabocha or butternut or buttercup winter squash, peeled and seeded and cut into thin pieces
- ✔ Whole or halved mushrooms, including white button mushrooms and exotic varieties
- ✔ Green beans
- ✔ Sugar snap beans
- ✔ Onion rings (about ½ inch wide)

Book VII

Japanese Cooking

- ✔ Scallions cut into 2-inch lengths

- ✔ Daikon radish cut thinly on the diagonal

- ✔ Lotus root, cut into ¼-inch-thick slices, dropped in lemon/vinegar water

- ✔ Whole shelled and deveined shrimp

- ✔ Hunks of firm white fish, such as monkfish

After washing and/or peeling your vegetables, make sure that they're dry. Shrimp and fish should also be dry. The drier the items to be fried, the better the batter will stick and the more effective the hot oil will be at producing a crisp piece of food.

If you have a deep-fat fryer, use it for the tempura and tonkatsu recipes; however, if you don't, you can still make these dishes.

Japanese Shrimp and Veggie Tempura

This lightly battered deep-fried dish is a classic Japanese recipe. Don't be scared by the seaweed in the sauce. It just provides a subtle background flavor that, although important, doesn't scream seaweed at you.

Special tools: *Deep-fat fryer, electric fryer, or deep, heavy pot; thermometer with range up to 400 degrees*

Preparation time: *20 minutes*

Cooking time: *3 minutes per batch*

Yield: *6 servings*

1 cup dashi (see Chapter 4 of Book VII)

⅓ cup mirin

⅓ cup soy sauce

½ cup finely grated daikon

2 teaspoons minced fresh ginger

2 pounds prepared vegetables and shrimp (all vegetable pieces should be similar in size;

see the section "Preparing tempura," earlier in this chapter)

Vegetable oil for deep-fat frying

2 egg yolks

2 cups ice water

1¾ cups all-purpose flour, sifted

1 To make the dipping sauce, place the dashi, mirin, and soy sauce in a small pot and whisk to combine. Heat gently and then stir in the daikon and ginger; set aside but keep warm.

2 Have all your veggie, shrimp, and fish ingredients ready to fry. Fill a fryer or heavy pot with oil to at least a 3-inch depth. Use a thermometer if the unit isn't equipped with one and heat the oil to 375 degrees. Also at this time, preheat the oven to 175 degrees and place a heatproof serving platter inside on a rack to keep the fried pieces warm while you fry the rest.

3 While the oil is preheating, make the batter. Place the egg yolks in a large bowl and whisk until smooth. Add the ice water and combine lightly. Swirls of egg will be suspended in the water; that's how it should be. Add the flour all at once and stir it around a few times but leave it lumpy. The lumpy texture is important! Do not stir it until smooth. The lumpier the batter, the lacier the final effect, which is what you want. The small pockets of flour that you see scattered throughout the batter are okay. Many Japanese chefs use chopsticks to stir in the flour because doing so is a very gentle way of incorporating it into the egg and water mixture.

4 Coat the vegetables and shrimp/fish with the batter right before frying. Cook similar ingredients together — shrimp with shrimp, broccoli with broccoli — for the most even cooking. Dip the items one by one in the batter (I like to use chopsticks, but you can also use two forks), letting any excess drip back into the batter bowl. Fry the pieces in small batches until golden brown, turning them frequently with clean chopsticks or a slotted spoon. The pieces should move freely around the pot and have room to be evenly bathed in the fat. The frying takes about 3 minutes; the ingredients should be light golden brown. Remove them with a slotted spoon and drain on paper towels. Transfer them to a platter in the oven to keep them warm while you fry the remaining items.

5 Serve mounded on a warm platter with the warm dipping sauce alongside.

Tip: *Make sure to bring the oil back up to 375 degrees between batches and to not crowd the pot. Depending on the size of the pieces of food, you probably don't want to fry more than 5 or 6 pieces at a time.*

Tip: *If you have some bamboo skewers around, thread one through each shrimp from head to tail to straighten it out before you dip it in tempura batter. Cook the shrimp right on the skewer; this classic Japanese technique keeps the shrimp stick-straight.*

Book VII

Japanese Cooking

Using panko (extra-crunchy Japanese breadcrumbs) when deep-frying

The following recipe calls for breadcrumbs — a special kind called *panko* that you can find in Asian grocery stores. They're extra-crunchy, white-bread-based breadcrumbs that are very different from regular grocery store breadcrumbs, so do not substitute. Also, you can't duplicate them at home, so just make the extra trip to the Asian grocery to make this dish as authentic as possible.

Tonkatsu

This dish features deep-fried pork coated with crunchy Japanese-style breadcrumbs. It's traditionally served with a sweet, thick sauce that you can easily duplicate by combining easy-to-find ketchup and Worcestershire sauce. Some Asian stores may stock prepared tonkatsu sauce, which you can try as well.

Special tools: *Deep-fat fryer, electric fryer, or deep, heavy pot; thermometer with range up to 400 degrees.*

Preparation time: *20 minutes*

Cooking time: *3 minutes per batch*

Yield: *2 to 3 servings*

⅔ cup ketchup	Salt
5 tablespoons Worcestershire sauce	Pepper
1 pound boneless pork loin chops, cut crosswise into 1-inch-wide strips	2 eggs
	1 cup Japanese-style breadcrumbs
⅓ cup all-purpose flour	Vegetable oil

1 Make the sauce: Place the ketchup and Worcestershire sauce in a small bowl and whisk to combine; set aside. (You may make the sauce 1 week ahead and store refrigerated in an airtight container.)

2 Prepare a deep-fat fryer or place at least 3 inches of oil in a heavy-bottomed pot. Bring the oil to 350 degrees. Also at this time, preheat the oven to 175 degrees and place a heatproof serving platter inside on a rack to keep fried pieces warm while you fry the rest.

3 Place the flour in a small bowl and season well with salt and pepper. Place the eggs and breadcrumbs in separate small bowls; whisk the eggs until frothy. Dip pieces of pork into the flour and toss to coat. Follow by a dip in the egg, and then finally roll the pork around in the breadcrumbs to coat completely.

4 Fry the pieces in small batches until golden brown, turning them frequently with clean chopsticks or a slotted spoon. The pieces should move freely around the pot and have room to be evenly bathed in the fat. The frying takes about 2 minutes; the pieces should be light golden brown. Remove with a slotted spoon and drain on paper towels. Transfer the pork pieces to a platter in the oven to keep them warm while you fry the remaining items.

5 Serve immediately with sauce alongside.

Tip: *For best results, pat the pork dry before dipping it in the flour, egg, and breadcrumbs.*

Tip: *A traditional accompaniment to tonkatsu is finely shredded cabbage. Place the cabbage on a plate, top with some pieces of pork, and serve with pickled vegetables on the side. Pass the sauce separately for guests to add to taste.*

Remember: *Always bring the oil back up to the desired temperature between batches for best results – and don't crowd the pot!*

Nabemono: One-Pot Dishes

What could be easier than assembling all your food in one pot for cooking and then bringing that pot to the table to serve? This is what nabemono, or one-pot dishes, are all about. All you need are the ingredients for your recipe and a pot, such as a cast-iron pot, that is wide and about 4 inches deep and has a cover. These are great meals to bring to the table, so use a pot that will look good in the dining room.

If you have a portable gas burner, place it on the table and do the cooking at the table, which is actually the traditional way. If you don't have a portable burner but you have a warming tray, use that to keep the food warm at the table. You also can use a chafing dish to keep your food hot. If you have none of the above, you can still serve this dish. Just make sure that it's very hot, right off the stove, and place it on a heatproof trivet on the table.

Beef Sukiyaki

Every Japanese cook has his or her variation of sukiyaki, but they all include well-marbled tender beef, vegetables, often tofu, and a clear noodle, called shirataki. These noodles are somewhat gelatinous and are used more for texture than flavor. This dish is traditionally cooked right at the table, using a portable gas stove, but you can make it in a large pot on your kitchen stove and serve it to your guests as soon as it's done, if you like. The instructions are for making it in two batches, right at the table on a portable burner. If you want to make it in the kitchen, you can do it all at once in a very large pot.

Special tool: *Portable gas stove*

Preparation time: *70 minutes*

Cooking time: *15 minutes*

Yield: *4 servings*

¾ cup soy sauce

⅔ cup mirin

½ cup sake

2 tablespoons sugar

1¼ pounds well-marbled boneless beef sirloin, placed in freezer for 1 hour for easy slicing

21 to 24 ounces shirataki noodles, cooked, packed in water (the packages come in 7- or 8-ounce sizes)

1 pound enoki mushrooms, stems removed

12 medium fresh shiitake mushrooms, stems removed

12 scallions, trimmed and cut into 2-inch lengths on the diagonal, using all the white part and just some of the firm green part

8 ounces firm tofu, drained, pressed, and cut into 1-inch cubes

2 bunches watercress, bottom stems removed and chopped into 2-inch lengths

4 eggs

1 ounce beef suet (fat), divided in half

1 Make the sauce: Place the soy sauce, mirin, sake, and sugar in a small saucepan and stir to combine. Heat over medium heat and bring to a boil for 1 minute or until the sugar is dissolved. Pour into a liquid measuring cup and set aside.

2 Prepare the semi-frozen beef by slicing across the grain into ⅛-inch-thick pieces about 1 × 2 inches; they should be easy to pick up with chopsticks. Place them in an overlapping fashion on a plate, cover with plastic wrap, and refrigerate until needed.

3 Open the noodle packages and drain. Bring a large pot of water to a boil, add the noodles, and cook for 2 to 3 minutes or until heated through; drain, rinse with cold water and cut into 6-inch lengths. Take a large platter, one that's pretty enough to bring to the table, and place the drained noodles in a mound in a corner of the platter. Place the enoki and shiitake mushrooms in separate mounds on the platter, along with a mound of the scallions, tofu, and watercress. All of the ingredients should be separate and attractively arranged.

4 When you're ready to cook, call everyone to the table and give them individual bowls with one egg broken into each bowl. They should also have a set of chopsticks.

5 Have your burner ready at the table. Place the platter of beef and the platter with noodles, mushrooms, scallions, tofu, and watercress on the table. If you have a pair of long chopsticks (saibashi), place them at the table as well. Otherwise, use tongs. Place a heavy tetsunabe or wide cast-iron pot on the burner. Place 1 piece of beef suet in the pot.

6 You're going to cook the sukiyaki in two batches, so the remaining instructions are for half of all the ingredients. Melt 1 piece of suet over high heat and use your chopsticks or tongs to move the suet around; you want to coat the bottom of the pot with an even layer of fat. Add half the scallions to the pot and cook for a few minutes, moving them around with the chopsticks occasionally, until they begin to soften. While you begin cooking, invite your guests to mix their egg with their chopsticks.

7 Add half the meat to the pan and cook for about a minute or just until the pieces begin to brown on the bottom and are partially cooked (you want it to be partially pink). Add a quarter of the sauce and bring to a simmer. Add half of the noodles, mushrooms, scallions, and tofu, one ingredient at a time, placing them in groups in the pot: the enoki to one side, the shiitake to another, the cubed tofu to another, and so on. Allow to cook and soften for a few minutes. Add another quarter of the sauce, bring to a simmer, and add half the greens in a small mound to one side and cook briefly until they're wilted.

8 Now you're ready to eat. Invite guests to take bits of meat and other ingredients, dipping them into their raw beaten egg and then right into their mouths. (I have served this many times to guests who prefer not to use the raw egg, and the dish still tastes great.)

9 When the pot is empty, repeat the process with the remaining ingredients and make another batch.

Tip: *Although guests traditionally take food directly from the cooking pot, I find it easier to actually serve the guests portions of all the ingredients in individual bowls. That way, they can dip pieces into their own egg dish as they eat, if they like.*

Vary It! *If you can't find the shirataki, you can use udon noodles instead.*

Remember: *Saying "beef" sukiyaki is somewhat redundant as the most popular version of the dish always features beef, but I included the word in the title anyway because I thought it would help you find the recipe more easily if you were in the mood for red meat.*

Book VII

Japanese Cooking

Oden Stew

Oden stew, which features many different kinds of prepared fish and occasionally tofu, is even better if made the day before, so plan accordingly. Also, please note that some of the ingredients, such as the fried tofu cutlets and fried fish cutlets are purchased already fried. They are easy to find in Asian specialty stores.

Preparation time: *15 minutes*

Cooking time: *1 hour and 30 minutes*

Yield: *6 servings*

½ pound daikon, trimmed, peeled, cut length-wise, and sliced into 1-inch-thick half-moons

4 medium yellow or red-skinned potatoes, peeled and quartered

4 fried tofu cutlets (atsuage), cut into 1-inch-wide strips

11-ounce fried fish cutlet, cut into ½-inch lengths

8 satsuma (fried fish balls)

8 cups dashi (see Chapter 4 of Book VII)

½ cup mirin

¼ cup soy sauce

Two 6- to 8-inch-long chikuwa (grilled fish cakes), cut into 2-inch lengths

5-inch kamaboko, cut into ¼-inch slices

8-ounce konnyaku loaf, cut into 1-inch triangles

4 hard-cooked eggs, shelled

¼ cup dry mustard

Warm water

1 Bring a medium-sized pot of water to a boil, add the daikon, and boil until tender when pierced with a knife, about 12 minutes. Remove from the pot and set aside.

2 Using the same pot of water, bring it back to a boil, add the potatoes, and cook until tender when pierced with a knife, about 10 minutes. Drain and set aside.

3 Place the tofu, fish cutlet, and fish balls in a colander in the sink. Bring a large pot of water to a boil and pour a steady stream of boiling water over them to rinse away surface oil.

4 Place the dashi, mirin, and soy sauce in a large pot. Add the tofu, fish cutlets, fish balls, fish cake, kamaboko, and konnyaku and bring to a boil over high heat. Turn the heat down and simmer, covered, for 45 minutes. Add the daikon and potatoes and simmer for 10 minutes more. Add the hard-cooked eggs and cook for 5 minutes to heat them through.

5 Meanwhile, combine the mustard with enough warm water to form a soft consistency and allow to sit for 10 minutes for the flavor and texture to develop.

6 You may serve immediately with a small condiment dish filled with mustard and a communal bowl of rice. Guests serve themselves rice and stew from the pot and add mustard to taste to their own dish. Alternatively, refrigerate the stew overnight for flavors to develop, and reheat before serving.

Chapter 8

Sweet Endings

I was a pastry chef for years, and I have to say that Japanese desserts and dessert trends didn't figure heavily in my repertoire. That is, they didn't until I discovered green tea ice cream, which is delicious, even to the Western palate, which usually demands much sweeter desserts. I provide you with a from-scratch recipe for this exotically flavored ice cream for which you do need an ice-cream maker. I include a simplified version, however, which gives you a taste of this treat without the use of a machine.

A classic Japanese dessert is some form of fresh fruit, but don't picture an apple passed off to you to eat out of hand. The fruits that the Japanese serve for dessert are perfect in ripeness. The aroma is enticing, the color vibrant, and the flesh yielding and juicy; whatever qualities are desired in that fruit are in evidence. In this chapter, I present some serving suggestions for fruit.

Your idea of Jell-O is probably a shimmering, sweet, jellylike dessert. The colors are day-glow, and the flavors intense but not entirely natural. Now, don't get me wrong — I happen to love Jell-O at the right place and time, but after a Japanese meal, I prefer something a bit subtler. Apparently, the Japanese agree; they have their version (actually theirs came first), which is called *kanten*. Kanten, or agar-agar, is a seaweed-based ingredient that jells liquids, such as sweetened water or fruit juice. It also holds sweetened bean paste *(an)* together to make a host of desserts based on bean paste.

Fruity Finishes

Perfectly ripe, fresh fruit is a welcome ending to a Japanese meal. It is sweet and soothing, slips down your throat easily, and satisfies the Japanese cook's desire for something colorful, pretty, and seasonal. Consider dried fruit as well, as it too is a favored treat in Japan.

Use whatever fruit is in season. Here are some fruits that have been enjoyed in Japan for many years:

- ✔ Apples
- ✔ Apricots
- ✔ Grapes
- ✔ Peaches
- ✔ Pears
- ✔ Persimmons
- ✔ Strawberries

To serve, choose your dish, bowl, or plate appropriately — one that will show off the fruit to its best advantage in terms of color and shape. Serve berries and grapes whole and slice larger fruit attractively.

I recently ordered a fruit assortment at an upscale Japanese restaurant and was served an attractively arranged plate of pineapple, cantaloupe, papaya, and mango, so you can see that you can expand on the list of suggestions that I provide.

Mochi: Sweet Glutinous Rice

The Japanese love rice, so you shouldn't be surprised to find out that they figured out how to transform it into a chewy, sweet ingredient unlike anything you've ever tasted.

Mochi refers to a rice product that's made from sweet glutinous rice that has been steamed and pounded. The resulting creamy white sticky mass is formed into small rounds or squares and dried. The resulting pieces look like shiny soap!

You can buy mochi at most Asian grocery stores. They're convenient to have on hand because they have a long shelf life and are used in savory as well as dessert preparations.

To try mochi as a dessert, cut mochi into 1-inch pieces and place them on a baking sheet. Bake in a 400-degree oven until lightly golden and puffed, about 8 minutes. Split the pieces open, fill with a dollop of fruit preserves, sprinkle with powdered sugar, and enjoy.

Sweet Red Bean Paste

Book VII

Japanese Cooking

Azuki (also spelled *aduki* and *adzuki*) beans are small, burgundy-red beans beloved by the Japanese. They're used in savory preparations in addition to being sweetened and made into a paste, which is referred to as *an.* I know it sounds odd. A somewhat similar ingredient that everyone is familiar with is peanut butter. After all, on its own it's savory, but it's often combined with something sweet, such as jelly or chocolate.

Anyway, you have to give *an* a try because there's really nothing like it. If you don't want to take the trouble to cook the beans yourself for your first taste, you can buy dehydrated bean powder, called *sarashian,* from an Asian supply store. You can combine sarashian with boiling water and sugar for a quick-to-prepare version; just follow the directions on the package.

I suggest that you scoop out some vanilla ice cream and top it with a dollop of sweet bean paste and a sprinkle of sesame seed brittle (see the following recipes). This dessert combines American tastes — ice cream — with Japanese favorites — sweet bean paste and sesame seeds.

Vanilla Ice Cream with Sweet Bean Paste and Sesame Seed Brittle

Start with purchased vanilla ice cream; you don't need an ice cream maker for this recipe. The sesame candy can be made 2 weeks ahead; the sweetened bean puree can be made up to 4 days ahead and refrigerated in an airtight container. To serve, simply scoop out some ice cream and top with a dollop of sweet bean paste and a sprinkling of sesame candy. Don't be put off by the long cooking time; this recipe has several components, which you can spread over a couple of weeks.

Preparation time: *15 minutes*

Cooking time: *1 hour and 25 minutes*

Yield: *6 servings*

½ cup sugar	5 cups water, divided
2 tablespoons water	½ cup sugar
Pinch of cream of tartar	Pinch of salt
¼ cup sesame seeds	1½ pints vanilla ice cream
½ cup dried azuki beans	

1 Make the sesame candy: Line a baking sheet with aluminum foil and coat with nonstick spray; set aside.

2 Place the sugar, water, and cream of tartar in a heavy-bottomed saucepan and stir to combine. Place over medium-high heat and bring to a boil without stirring. Brush down the sides of the pot once or twice with a pastry brush dipped in cold water and boil until the mixture turns light golden brown. This will take about 2 minutes, but the time is less important than the golden brown color.

3 Remove from the heat and quickly stir in the sesame seeds. Immediately pour the mixture onto the baking sheet lined with aluminum foil. Spread it out to get it as thin as possible.

4 Allow to sit at room temperature for about 30 minutes or until hardened and crisp. Break it into pieces and store in an airtight container at room temperature for up to 2 weeks.

5 Make the sweetened bean paste: Place the beans in a colander, remove any small stones or debris, and rinse. Place in a large pot and add 2½ cups of the water. Bring to a boil over high heat, drain, and return the beans to the pot.

6 Add the remaining 2½ cups water and again bring to a boil over high heat. Reduce the heat, cover, and simmer until the beans are tender, about 1 hour. Some unabsorbed water will probably remain in that pot; that's okay.

7 Drain the beans, reserving the cooking liquid. Place the beans in the bowl of a food processor fitted with a metal blade. Turn the machine on and process until the beans become a smooth puree, about 2 minutes. Add the cooking liquid if necessary to make a thick but smooth paste. It should be thick but still flow from a spoon. You may have to scrape down the sides of the bowl once or twice.

8 To create an ultrasmooth texture, scrape the puree into a fine-meshed strainer set over a bowl and press the puree through the strainer by using a wooden spoon or a rubber spatula.

9 Add the paste back to the pot and add the sugar and the pinch of salt. Cook over low heat, bringing the mixture to a simmer; stir frequently with a back-and-forth motion, using a wooden paddle or spoon. Cook until it becomes as thick as miso or apple butter. Cool to room temperature. You can use the paste immediately or pack it into an airtight container and refrigerate for up to 4 days.

10 To serve, divide the ice cream in serving dishes and top each with a dollop of room-temperature sweet bean paste and a sprinkling of sesame candy crumbled into bite-size pieces. Serve immediately.

Tip: *The back-and-forth motion used to stir the bean paste is said to retain its satiny texture. Supposedly, using the classic stirring motion of going round and round the pot dulls the luster of the paste.*

Agar-agar and Kuzu

Book VII

Japanese
Cooking

The next two recipes are for fruit juice kanten. Kanten is made with agar-agar, a seaweed that has gelatinous thickening properties. Traditional kanten dishes don't always appeal to Western palates. Picture clear, somewhat mildly flavored, jellied seaweed cubes combined with fruit and a dark syrup. Or squares of red bean paste suspended inside unflavored kanten. These aren't exactly ice-cream sundaes! I have some less adventurous, but still somewhat classic, recipes for you in this chapter. The great thing about cooking is that you can get the basic technique and ingredients for any given cuisine and then go from there with your own inventive recipes. So more than anywhere else in this Japanese book, I have exercised some license with the interpretation of these recipes.

To make the following kanten desserts, you need *agar-agar,* a seaweed thickener, and *kuzu,* a thickener made from the root of a vine (the kuzu vine, as a matter of fact). You can find both in Asian grocery stores and some natural food stores. Natural food stores often stock products made by the Eden Company, which makes and packages many Asian ingredients, including both of these ingredients.

Agar-agar comes in a variety of forms. Long "bars" of it, which are made up of long threads of the agar-agar, are less expensive, but harder to work with and take a bit more simmering before they dissolve. Flaked agar-agar, which Eden packages, is pricey but easy to measure out and use, as the flakes dissolve easily.

My recipes use the agar-agar flakes. If you can find only the bars, cut a hunk off with a sharp serrated knife (pieces of the clear, brittle seaweed will fly everywhere) and firmly pack the shreds into a ⅓ cup measuring cup. The measurement will not be as exact, but it will probably work.

Kuzu is a white chalky thickener that comes in small packages. Again, Eden markets it. It's easy to measure out and use. For authenticity and best results, don't substitute any other thickener.

By now, you may be thinking that you just don't want to eat a dessert thickened with seaweed, and you may be about to skip this dessert chapter. Well, did you know that some of your favorite ice-cream treats contain *carrageenan,* another kind of seaweed? The agar-agar is very mild and lets the fruit and fruit juice in the recipes shine through, so give it a try.

Just to clarify, I tend to call the raw ingredient agar-agar and the finished dish kanten.

Fruited Summer Kanten

This light, refreshing dessert is comprised of a cooling kanten jelly made from fruit juice. Serve it in individual dishes with fresh warm-weather fruit.

Preparation time: *10 minutes, plus 3½ hours cooling time*

Cooking time: *8 minutes*

Yield: *6 servings*

3¾ cups apricot nectar	1 cup fresh blueberries
⅓ cup (⅛ ounce) agar-agar	1 cup fresh raspberries
¼ cup water	1 cup fresh blackberries
1 tablespoon kuzu	

1 Place the apricot nectar and agar-agar in a large pot and stir to combine. Heat over medium heat, bring to a simmer, and cook, whisking frequently, until the agar-agar dissolves, about 3 minutes.

2 Meanwhile, place the water and kuzu in a small bowl and whisk until the kuzu dissolves. With the nectar mixture simmering, add the kuzu mixture and whisk it in well.

3 Keep the mixture simmering and cook until the mixture thickens slightly, about 2 minutes. Gently stir in half of the blueberries, raspberries, and blackberries, cook for 30 more seconds, and then remove the pot from the heat.

4 Pour into a shallow glass dish and allow to cool to room temperature; then refrigerate for 3 hours or until chilled through.

5 To serve, scoop out a bit of the kanten into each bowl, scatter the remaining fresh berries over the kanten, and serve.

Tip: *The cooling stage at room temperature in Step 4 is important. Unlike animal-based gelatins, kanten firms up at room temperature, so don't rush this step.*

Fruited Winter Kanten

This version of jellied kanten dessert is comprised of cranberry juice and cider and fruits found in the cooler months.

Preparation time: *15 minutes, plus 3½ hours cooling time*

Cooking time: *8 minutes*

Yield: *6 servings*

1 apple, peeled, cored, and diced

1 ripe pear, peeled, cored, and diced

1 cup seedless grapes (red, green, or black), halved vertically

1 teaspoon fresh lemon juice

1 teaspoon sugar

2 cups cranberry juice

1¾ cups cider or apple juice

⅓ cup agar-agar

¼ cup water

1 tablespoon kuzu

1 Place the apple, pear, and grapes in a mixing bowl and toss to mix evenly. Sprinkle the lemon juice and sugar over the fruit and toss to coat; set aside.

2 Place the cranberry juice, cider, and agar-agar in a large pot; stir to combine. Heat over medium heat, bring to a simmer, and cook, whisking frequently, until the agar-agar dissolves, about 3 minutes.

3 Meanwhile, place the water and kuzu in a small bowl and whisk until the kuzu dissolves. With the juice simmering, add the kuzu mixture and whisk it in well.

4 Keep the mixture simmering and cook until the mixture thickens slightly, about 2 minutes. Gently stir in the fruit mixture, including any juice left in the bowl, and cook for 1 more minute; remove the pot from the heat.

5 Pour into a shallow glass dish, allow to cool to room temperature, and then refrigerate for 3 hours or until chilled through.

6 To serve, scoop out a bit of the kanten into each bowl and serve.

Frozen Green Tea Sounds Good to Me

Many Japanese restaurants in the United States offer ice cream and sorbet as dessert. The cool, light nature of these desserts complement Japanese cuisine beautifully. Believe it or not, green tea ice cream is common, as are flavors such as ginger, chestnut, and vanilla.

Powdered green tea — *matcha* — is used in the classic and traditional Japanese tea ceremony. Nothing could be more strictly Japanese. But green tea ice cream? Okay, maybe Japanese emperors haven't been enjoying it for hundreds of years, but it is delicious and now available in many Japanese restaurants.

You can find the green tea used in the next recipe at select tea emporiums or order it from Upton Tea Imports.

Upton Tea Imports
34-A Hayden Rowe Street
Hopkinton, MA 01748
800-234-8327
Fax: 508-435-9955
E-mail: cservice@uptontea.com
www.uptontea.com

I order most of my tea from this company, which offers a great selection as well as personalized service. You can order matcha tea to make your green tea ice cream, but also take some time to talk with them about green teas to drink. They can help steer you toward a purchase that you will be very happy with and can also provide specific measuring and steeping instructions for your chosen tea.

I was once offered an intermezzo, or palate cleanser, at the end of the meal at a Japanese restaurant — it was shiso ice! It had a grainy, watery texture with flecks of shiso leaf, which is somewhat minty but similar to basil at the same time. It was sweetened, and as odd as it sounds, boy, was it good!

Green Tea Ice Cream

You use powdered green tea called *matcha* to make this ice cream. Don't be put off by the long preparation time; much of it is spent in the refrigerator.

Special tool: *Ice-cream maker*

Preparation time: *10 minutes, plus 6 hours and 15 minutes for sitting and cooling*

Cooking time: *10 minutes*

Yield: *4½ cups*

2 cups whole milk	*6 egg yolks*
2 cups heavy cream	*1 cup granulated sugar*
2 tablespoons matcha (green tea powder)	

1 Place the milk and cream in a saucepan and bring to a boil over medium heat. Immediately remove from the heat and whisk in the tea powder. Allow to sit for 15 minutes.

2 Whisk together the egg yolks and sugar in a medium-sized, heatproof bowl.

3 Reheat the cream/tea mixture over low-medium heat. Slowly add a little bit to the egg mixture, whisking all the while, to temper the eggs. Add the remaining liquid, whisking gently until smooth and combined.

4 Return the mixture to the saucepan and cook over medium heat, stirring constantly, until the custard has thickened slightly and coats the back of a spoon, about 5 minutes. Do not let it boil.

5 Strain through a fine-meshed strainer. Cool to room temperature, stirring occasionally to release heat. Transfer to an airtight container and refrigerate for 6 hours or overnight. Pour into an ice-cream maker and follow the manufacturer's instructions. Freeze in an airtight container and eat within 3 days.

Tip: *This ice cream is lovely served with a crisp butter cookie, such as shortbread. This isn't a traditional Japanese pairing, but it's delicious nonetheless.*

Tip: *If you are short on time or don't have an ice-cream maker, you can still approximate this dessert. Purchase a premium vanilla ice cream and some matcha tea. Soften the ice cream and place in a bowl. Stir the matcha into the ice cream to combine thoroughly. Pack back into the ice cream container and freeze solid before serving. For every pint of ice cream, try 1 to 2 tablespoons of matcha. Start with 1 tablespoon and add more to taste.*

Book VII

Japanese Cooking

Book VIII
Thai Cooking

The 5th Wave   By Rich Tennant

"Do you want your papaya salad shaken, throttled or just tossed?"

In this book . . .

Thai cuisine is a relative newcomer to most American diners, but its popularity seems to grow by the hour. It's easy to see why: Thai food entices with exotic spices, delectable sauces, and unusual preparations. If you want to prepare Thai at home, this book guides you through the surprisingly easy process. After some background information on Thai ingredients and preparation methods, you find out how to prepare a number of traditional dishes from Chicken Satay to Red Curry Beef.

Contents at a glance

Chapter 1

A Taste of Thailand

*I*magine having a hunger for chicken stir-fried with bright pieces of basil, or for shiny rice noodles tossed with beef and fiery flecks of chile pepper, or for shrimp so fresh it seems to still be sparkling with seawater. Picture yourself eating such a meal in a small country restaurant or on a busy city street, with the passing cars and motorbikes creating urban background music.

If you can envision yourself dining on such food in such a setting, you must be thinking of Thailand.

In Thailand, you don't have to rely on your imagination for very long because good food is at hand seemingly everywhere, all the time. Thailand is known as "The Land of Smiles," but it surely didn't get that title because of mere friendliness. You'd be grinning too if dining — in or out — were such a pleasure.

Yet often the true greatness of the cuisine is lost when it gets translated outside of the country's borders. In America, for instance, Thai food has enjoyed enormous popularity among diners, but it also has suffered as a result of its wide acceptance. So many restaurants have sprung up in cities and towns across the United States that the authentic Thai experience gets diluted. Customers expect inexpensive curry, noodle, and stir-fry dishes in a restaurant that gets most of its personality from a travel poster hanging on the wall. Chinese and Italian restaurants went through the same phase early in their American citizenships, but as customers became more sophisticated, they began to demand more than chow mein and spaghetti and meatballs.

Thai food is slowly getting a little more respect too, as diners have more restaurants to choose and compare from, and as cooks gain more confidence in the kitchen and easier access to foreign ingredients. Because you're reading this book of recipes from around the world, you're probably one of those cooks who do feel comfortable in the kitchen and know where to get some hard-to-find ingredients. You're probably ready to get cooking right now, thinking about serving a plate of real pad Thai, or a bowlful of that hot and sour lemongrass soup that soothed you through some dreary winter days.

Well, Thai food has that effect.

Earth, Sea, and Sky: A Bountiful Culinary Experience

Thailand is blessed with some magnificent resources when it comes to food. The lengthy coastline that wraps around much of the country means that fresh fish and shellfish are never far away. A tropical climate and rich land guarantee a well-filled fruit basket and a vegetable bin brimming with fine produce. Chicken, duck, beef, lamb, and pork all are welcome on the Thai table — okay, provided the diners aren't vegetarians! — and that makes for an interesting variety of ingredients in every dish.

The food markets in Thailand are increasingly of the Western supermarket variety, but Thailand's bounty is most evident in the outdoor markets, packed to the very limits with inviting stalls piled with fresh ingredients. Another shopping option is the floating markets, where long, canoelike boats drift up and down the canals of a central market area, offering raw produce and cooked snacks to interested buyers.

With all the variety available to them, Thai people have no patience for bland food, always opting for plenty of herbs and spices — not to mention an undertone, at the minimum, of hot chili peppers. Your mouth will always find something interesting to savor.

What appeals to the Thai palate is not just excitement, however, but balance, harmony, and beauty. Take a look at any piece of Thai artwork, and you'll find an appreciation for color, a fondness for elaborate detail, and an evident willingness to bring happiness to the beholder. Thai food is no different from the artwork, really. From an elegantly presented dish served at an expensive restaurant to the short-order serving style of a street vendor, Thai food is consistently offered with a harmonious blend of aroma, color, texture, and flavor. This attention to all aspects of food applies no matter what type of dish is being served. For example, a humble dish of stir-fried tofu and vegetables gets a special touch when ginger, green onions, spinach, and peanuts are added to the composition. And at a formal meal, carrots, radishes, whole watermelons, and mangoes all may be meticulously carved into flower or animal shapes, just for the purpose of adding visual appeal to the plate.

Eating on the Go or in Royal Thai Style

If you ever have the chance to visit Thailand, the whole range of dining experiences is worth exploring.

Dining casually — in the street

If you want to dine inexpensively and casually, try something from the cart of a street vendor. Don't get pale at the suggestion, remembering all the travel warnings about eating in a foreign country. The food here is made fresh and cooked to order, and any visitor who is careful to choose a clean, busy stand can find a hot, filling meal for just a few dollars.

Many Thais regularly eat from the street vendors. Every day, the streets of big cities such as Bangkok and even the little villages are lined with rows of metal food carts. The food vendors have a steady business, but the big rush starts in the early evening as work lets out and business remains steady through the night. Hungry commuters, late-evening shoppers, and nightlife revelers all find their way to a favorite stand for a quick dish of curry or noodles.

If a visitor must buy one thing from a street vendor, it's a cool sip of coconut juice. Look for the man or woman standing next to a pile of trimmed coconuts, shorn of their familiar bark. Upon request, the salesperson will grab one of the heavy shells, whack the top off with a machete, and pop a straw into the middle of the coconut, which now serves as its own cup. At the end of the straw is a clear, sweet juice, as sugary and refreshing on a hot day as a cup of lemonade.

Having a seat and minding your manners

If a sit-down meal on something other than a metal chair on the sidewalk is in order, you'll want to experience what is known as "royal" Thai cuisine. You'll find this in upscale restaurants that follow the more delicate, elaborate style of the palace traditions. The kingdom, which reaches back more than 700 years, has a proud history that learned to incorporate outside influences while remaining mostly independent; it is the only Southeast Asian nation to never have been colonized by any European country.

What evolved in Thailand's culinary identity was an insistence on balance in every dish, with the repeated use of salty ingredients such as fish sauce; sour components from acidic fruits such as lime and tamarind; the heat of some fiery chili peppers; and a touch of sweetness, usually from palm sugar. You'll find similar combinations in a meal in Vietnam, to the east of Thailand, and in the neighboring countries of Myanmar, Laos, and Cambodia.

Book VIII

Thai Cooking

A formal Thai meal follows a certain serving etiquette, with small dishes, such as appetizers and salads, being served one at a time, followed by soup and noodle dishes, all of which are admired and enjoyed individually. But the main dishes — the curries, stir-fries, and eye-catching displays such as a whole fried or grilled fish — come out family style. Rice and entrées are passed around, while the host makes sure that everyone has plenty to eat.

You'll find that, as with many Asian cuisines, the ingredients are cut in small enough portions that a knife isn't necessary. That doesn't mean, however, that chopsticks are the utensil of choice at a Thai meal; those come into play only when you're eating noodles. For the most part, you get that good food into your mouth with the aid of a fork and spoon. And even here, pay attention: The fork, or the back of it, anyway, is used mainly to push food into the bowl of the spoon.

This reliance on the spoon makes even more sense when you think about the lovely sauces that envelope so many good Thai recipes. What better implement for getting every last drop, and holding onto a bite of rice as well, than a good, serviceable spoon?

As you can see, the rules are minor and easy to learn when the time comes for a Thai meal. What is most important, both to the cook and the guest, is that both come to appreciate how wonderful a good meal can be, however it is served, and in whatever language.

Master that bit of Thai culture, and you'll find a smile on your face, too!

Chapter 2

Ingredients for Thai Cooking

In This Chapter

▷ Shopping for herbs, fruits, and vegetables

▷ Browsing the supermarket shelves and refrigerator section

Asian ingredients that once were almost impossible to find are now available in many well-stocked American grocery stores. And you can find the more unusual items in Thai and Chinese markets.

One big difference between food shopping in the United States and in Thailand is that daily trips to the market for fresh local ingredients are necessary in Thailand because many Thai homes lack the large refrigerators found in most U.S. homes. While shopping, Thais choose the day's main meal based on what's available rather than on specific ingredients called for in a recipe. So take a cue from Thai cooks and cook with what's seasonally fresh, gathering colorful peppers, vibrant greens, and sparkling fresh fish from their display cases. But keep in mind, as with any ethnic cuisine, that every good kitchen must have certain indispensable staples. Coconut milk and fish sauce are as common in the Thai pantry as canned soup and ketchup are in the American home.

After you have become familiar with common Thai ingredients, you can vary recipes to suit your taste. Begin experimenting with different herbs, such as basil, and discover the subtle or not-so-subtle nuances between the different varieties. Try several types of the multitude of chile sauces available. A whole new world of tantalizing flavors awaits you!

Fresh Herbs and Aromatics

Thai cuisine uses all kinds of interesting herbs and aromatics. The following sections give you an overview.

Basil (bai horapa)

A member of the mint family, basil is one of the most popular herbs used in Thai cooking. A number of species of basil are native to southern Asia, ranging from overtones of anise licorice-like flavor to cinnamon or citrus scents.

In many cultures, basil holds symbolic meaning. It is considered sacred and is said to provide strength and to represent love, hate, and royalty. Basil also has many medicinal uses, such as aiding in circulation; relieving fever, headaches, and dog bites; and even treating bad breath. We stick to the culinary use, explaining how common or sweet basil, holy *(bai kapao)*, lemon *(bai mangluk)*, and Thai *(bai horapa)* rule in the Thai kitchen (see Table 2-1).

No matter whether you decide to tear or chop basil leaves, you should wait until the last minute to add fresh basil to a cooked dish to prevent the basil from turning brownish-green too quickly.

Table 2-1	Favorite Basils in Thai Cooking	
Herb	*Thai Name*	*Description*
Common or sweet basil	Bai horapa (used to denote sweet or Thai basil)	Green leaves, licoricelike and clovelike flavor. The most common of all basils, this variety can be used as a substitute when other specific varieties called for in a recipe are unavailable.
Holy basil	Bai kapao	Small green leaves with notes of mint and clove and a slight bitterness. Occasionally, a variety can be found with red leaves.
Lemon basil	Bai mangluk	With a definite, clean, lemon aroma and taste, lemon basil has fine leaves which are lighter green than common basil. Use in salads or with fish.
Thai basil	Bai horapa	Used interchangeably with common basil, Thai basil has narrow, pointed, dark green leaves with purple stems and dark purple flower tips. The *bai,* or leaves, have a slightly peppery taste with a hint of licorice (anise).

Cilantro *(pak chee)*

Fresh cilantro, or Chinese parsley, is the fragrant herbal leaf of the coriander plant and is used to flavor many savory Thai dishes. The flowering dried coriander seed is considered a spice and is used as an ingredient in some curry pastes. Medical and culinary use of the coriander plant dates back over 3,000 years.

Galangal (khaa)

Two main species, lesser *(krachi)* and greater *(khaa)* galangal, are members of the ginger family. The fresh rhizome of the greater galangal, known also as Siamese ginger, is the one mostly used by Thai cooks because of its rich lemony, peppery flavor. It's an essential component in freshly made Thai curry pastes, so choose firm, nonshriveled rhizomes, avoiding pieces that look dry and have a low moisture content. If you can't find fresh, look for packages of dried, sliced galangal, labeled as *kha* or *khaa*.

Ginger (khing)

The ginger family contains more than 1,300 species. Cultivated in Southeast Asia over 3,000 years ago, ginger is one of the oldest tropical spices used in both sweet and savory cooking. Fresh ginger is sold in small, knobby, branch-like pieces. These peeled rhizomes are added to vegetable dishes and stir-fries, and they can be substituted for galangal in curry pastes. (When you substitute ginger for galangal, the dish won't be as aromatic, and the flavor of the ginger won't be as intense as fresh galangal.)

Lime leaves (bai makrut)

Although the kaffir lime tree produces a fruit similar to limes, only the rind and leaves of this fruit are used because they are where you find the aroma and flavor. The fruit, although in the same citrus family as limes and lemons is actually quite bitter. The fragrant leaf is pulverized for curries and finely cut into thin strips to impart a unique citrus flavor when added to soups or used as a garnish. It's common practice not to eat the leaf when used whole or in large pieces. Think of it as an aromatic enhancement like bay leaf, but leave it in the bottom of the bowl! You can find lime leaves packaged in plastic bags in the produce sections of Asian markets.

Lemon grass (takrai)

Lemon grass is a tall perennial grass in which the lower tender part of the long, thin stalk is used to give a lemony flavor and a light floral aroma to sauces, marinades, soups, stews, curry pastes, and beverages. Even after cooking, it remains fibrous, so unless you pound it to a paste or finely mince it, you don't want to eat it — leave it on the plate.

Fresh Fruits and Vegetables

Your mother always told you to eat your fruits and vegetables, and Thai moms are no different. What follows are the fruits and vegetables often featured in Thai cooking.

Bananas (kluay)

Thai cooks enjoy bananas both raw and cooked and in both savory and sweet dishes. Why shouldn't they, when they have more varieties to choose from than we do? A favorite variety is baby bananas, also called dwarf or finger bananas, which are sweeter than their relative, the Cavendish banana, the fruit that most Americans are familiar with. Plantains, a much larger variety, have a milder flavor and are frequently cooked while still green. Thais also eat salads made from raw banana blossoms and steam food in banana leaves.

Daikons (hua chai po)

This large Asian radish ranges from 6 to 15 inches in length and from 2 to 3 inches in diameter. The creamy beige to black skin is peeled away to reveal a crisp, white flesh that can be shredded raw for salads, cut as a garnish, or cut up and cooked in stir-fry. In Thai markets, you also may find daikon radishes under the name *mooli*.

Garlic (kratiem)

Thai cooks love garlic, a member of the lily family, and use the fresh cloves liberally in much of their cooking. Another favorite use is to deep-fry thin slices and use as a garnish for added flavor.

Limes (manao)

Freshly squeezed juice from the small green citrus fruit contrasts and balances the spiciness of chiles and red pepper flakes or the sweetness of sugar and coconut milk when used in soup, salads, or main dishes.

Long beans (tua fak yao)

Also known as yard-long beans, these thin legumes related to the black-eyed pea family look like green beans on steroids. The long, stringless pods hang in pairs, which can grow 3 feet long, but they're usually picked at around 18 inches in length. Light to dark green, the many varieties are generally identified by the color of their mature seeds. Long beans stir-fry quickly yet hold up well in recipes that require longer cooking times.

Lychees; litchis (linchee)

This small fruit comes packaged in its own shell. Fresh fruits are available from June through mid-July. Peel the brightly colored skin to reveal the sweet, juicy, creamy white flesh. Eat it plain or add it to a dessert. Canned and dried lychees, sometimes called lychee nuts, are eaten as a snack similar to the way people in the United States eat candy and nuts. They're available year-round.

Mangoes (mamuang)

With more than 100 varieties, mangoes are one of the most popular fruits in the world. Unripe green mangoes are very tart and used in fresh vegetable dishes. As the fruit ripens, the skin becomes yellow with a trace of red, while the inner, bright orange flesh becomes sweet and fragrant. Mangoes are frequently used in salads and desserts — a favorite use is mango slices paired up with sweet sticky rice (see Sweet Sticky Rice with Mango Slices in Chapter 8 of Book VIII).

Papayas (green) (malako)

The unripe green papaya is usually shredded raw and is the basis for SomTum, a piquant salad from the northeastern region of Issan that's now served throughout Thailand.

Shallots (hom daeng)

Shallots are a member of the onion family, but are shaped more like a bulb of garlic with fewer cloves. The flavor is milder and more subtle than the common large onions used in U.S. homes. Separate sections of the shallot and remove the fine paper skin prior to slicing.

Thai eggplants (ma keua pro)

This small round to oval eggplant is generally 1 to 2 inches in diameter. Colors range from pale green or creamy white to green with cream-colored stripes. Eat raw or add to cooked curry dishes.

The Pantry

Who could have imagined finding exotic Thai ingredients in the cupboard 30, 20, or even 10 years ago? Now a vast assortment of once foreign products are readily available and waiting for you to experience. This is not your mother's pantry — or maybe it is, and you're just becoming familiar with it!

Shelf-stable staples

Keeping some of these "easy to have on hand" items around helps in preparing a quick Thai meal.

Book VIII

**Thai
Cooking**

Bamboo shoots (normai)

Tender ivory-colored shoots are harvested from a particular species of bamboo before the shoot has time to harden into the cane. Rarely seen fresh, they're available packed in brine in cans or jars at most grocery stores.

Bean sauces (tow jiew)

Made from fermented black or yellow soybeans, bean sauces are found in thin, pourable consistencies, as well as thicker pastes. Black bean sauce has a salty, intense, earthy flavor and is sometimes combined with garlic or star anise. Brown bean sauce has a thicker consistency and is made from fermented yellow soybeans.

Chile sauces and chile oils (sod prik, nam prik pao)

One of the largest sections of shelving in Thai grocery stores seems to be devoted to chile sauces and chile oils. Here are a few varieties that are available:

- **Chile sauce** is prepared with dried red chiles, vinegar, and salt. This spicy, condiment has a thin, pourable consistency.

- **Chile-garlic sauce** gets a hit of flavor from garlic and shallots added to the sauce. Thais tend to use this sauce sparingly.

- **Sweet chile sauce** (often spelled sweet "chilli" sauce) gets its sweetness from sugar combined with water, pickled red chiles, vinegar, garlic, salt, and stabilizers.

- **Chile oil,** which is fiery hot, is made with vegetable oil, usually soybean oil, which takes on the deep red color of the chiles that are used.

- **Sesame-chile oil** gets a different aroma and flavor from the sesame oil used in place of the standard vegetable oil.

- **Chile pastes** are made with fermented beans and are more commonly used in Chinese cooking.

Degrees of mildness or hotness abound in chile sauces and oils because of the compound capsaicin that's found in the seeds and membranes of the fresh or dried chile used in the manufacturing process. For greater shelf life, store opened chile sauces and oils in the refrigerator.

The many varieties of chile sauces, oils, and pastes aren't necessarily inter-changeable. Take care when substituting — an oil-based chile flavor isn't the same as a tart vinegary one.

Coconut milk and cream (ka-ti)

Making coconut milk at home is a lengthy process, so purchase processed coconut milk, which is readily available in cans at most grocery stores. The contents separate into a thin, watery liquid and a top layer of thick coconut cream inside the can. For recipes that call for coconut milk, shake the can well (before removing the lid!) and use the combined mixture. When a recipe calls for coconut cream, use the thick layer on top.

Dried shrimp (kung haeng)

Tiny sun-dried shrimp are used as a flavoring ingredient. Used whole, chopped, or ground, they impart a salty shrimp flavor to soups, salads, stir-fries, and noodles. Asian markets sell them in small cellophane packages. Look for light-orangey pink shrimp that are plump and resilient.

Fish sauces (nam pla)

Perhaps the most vital ingredient in Thai cooking, fish sauce is the by-product of dried, fermented fish, usually anchovies or shrimp. Quality varies. The best sauce is pale amber in color and has a light, refreshing, salty taste. *Nam pla,* also known as *nuoc nam* in Vietnam, has a pungent smell, but when used in cooking, the sauce mellows, blending well into each dish it's prepared with. Strict vegetarians can replace fish sauce with light soy sauce when called for in a recipe. Adjust the amount of saltiness by adding or decreasing the quantity of soy sauce to taste.

Fried garlic and fried shallots (kratiem jiow, hom jiow)

You know that green bean casserole with crunchy french-fried onion pieces on top? Well, Thais have their own version of this fragrant, crunchy condiment. Dried, fried slivers of garlic or shallots are used to garnish soups, noodles, and curry dishes. Although you can fry these tasty morsels at home, you can easily find jars of fried garlic and shallots in Asian markets. Once opened, store them tightly sealed at room temperature.

Oils

With the vast assortment of cooking oils available, deciding which oil is the best to use for a particular cooking application can sometimes be confusing. The stage at which any fat, whether vegetable or animal in origin, begins to smoke when heated is called the *smoke point.* The higher this temperature is, the better the oil is for stir-frying or deep-frying. Some oils impart a flavor, while others remain neutral to the food being cooked. You can choose from some of the following oils, letting personal taste be your guide.

- **Peanut oil,** which is extracted from pressed peanuts, is a great choice for frying because of its high smoke point of 450 degrees. American peanut oil has a mild flavor, whereas the ones produced in Asian countries are more distinct.

- ✔ **Soybean oil,** made from soybeans, and **safflower oil,** a flavorless oil made from the seeds of the flowering safflower plant, are other oils that take equally well to high heat.

- ✔ **Canola oil,** from the rape seed, is very low in saturated fat and gets its name from the Canadian seed-oil industry. Although it has a slightly lower smoke point of 435 degrees, it's a good choice for most cooking purposes.

- ✔ **Corn oil,** the popular oil made from corn kernels, has a smoke point of 410 degrees and is another good choice. The generic term *vegetable oil* is generally a blend of vegetable oils.

- ✔ **Sesame oil,** on the other hand, is not a wise choice for frying. It's used more as a flavoring ingredient on its own or combined with other oils in small amounts, giving a nutty taste to foods.

Palm sugar (nam tan peep)

Palm sugar, also called coconut-palm sugar, comes from the sap of young coconut palm trees. Lightly caramel in flavor, it's sold as semisoft, light brown compressed cakes or found in a firmer consistency in jars or cans. If unavailable, substitute with light brown sugar or turbinado sugar (a coarse-crystal raw sugar with a delicate molasses flavor), but the flavor will not be the same.

Preserved vegetables

You find endless varieties of cans or jars of preserved vegetables in Asian markets. Everything from cabbages, radishes (usually daikon), lettuces, mustard greens, and broccoli is available in preserved form. Used sparingly, these ingredients add tang when cooked in a dish.

Shrimp paste (kapee)

A blend of salt and ground fermented shrimp, shrimp paste is among the most intense flavoring ingredients in Thai cooking. The soft paste is used sparingly and is added to curry pastes. Store in a tightly closed jar because the odor can permeate other foods it's stored with.

Tamarind (makham)

The tall, shade tamarind tree bears a podlike fruit. This fruit is used to produce the unique sweet-sour flavoring ingredient of tamarind that's added to Thai, Indian, and Middle Eastern foods. It's available as a dark raisin-colored concentrated pulp in jars, as whole pods that are dried into bricklike shapes, and as a ground powder. The sweet syrup concentrate is used to flavor soft drinks. You may be surprised to find that tamarind is also an integral component in Worcestershire sauce. You can easily find good varieties of the liquid concentrate in Thai, Asian, and Indian markets.

In the refrigerator and freezer

If you're serious about Thai cooking, you need to stock up on the following perishable items.

Banana leaves (bai klouy)

The long, broad leaves of the banana plant are used for wrapping food that is to be steamed or baked. Fresh leaves are not as readily available, so look for them in the freezer section in Asian (or Latin) markets. Rinse before using and dip into boiling water to make the leaves more pliable.

Spring roll wrappers (poh pia), egg roll wrappers

Spring roll wrappers and egg roll wrappers are made primarily of wheat flour, water, and a little salt. The larger of the two, spring roll wrappers are 8-inch sheets of dough and are thinner and more transparent than the slightly smaller egg roll wrappers. Egg roll wrappers and wonton skins, which are either square or round, and about 3½ inches across, have a yellow color from the eggs added to the dough. Thickness varies among them because of the intended use — deep-frying, baking, or steaming. The thin rice paper wrappers used in making uncooked spring rolls are moistened with a tiny bit of water, wrapped up around vegetables, tofu, and cooked meat or shrimp, and served cold. You'll find packages of assorted wrappers in the freezer section of Asian markets or sometimes on a refrigerated shelf set up in the produce department of larger grocery stores.

Tofu (tao hoo)

High in protein and cholesterol-free, tofu has been eaten all over Asia for 2,000 years. The amazing tofu grade soybean is put through a process similar to that of making cheese from milk. The mashed soybeans and boiling water produce a slurry. During various stages, the liquid is drawn off to create soymilk, while the remaining pulp is used for animal feed. To create tofu, coagulants are added to the soymilk, whereby the curds separate from the whey and float to the top. They're then scooped up into a forming container lined with cheesecloth and allowed to drain.

As versatile as the potato in its many preparations, tofu has the ability to take on the flavor of the food with which it's cooked. Purchase firm or extra-firm tofu, which is generally packaged in water (or more recently available packaged in the innovative "juice box" container), not the softer, "silken" variety to use in stir-fry, salads, soups, and vegetarian dishes. Drain and press out excess liquid before using (see the following tip). Place unused tofu in a container with fresh water, cover it, and refrigerate it for up to a week. You need to change the water daily.

To extract excess liquid from tofu, wrap the compressed cake in a clean kitchen towel and gently weight it down with a plate, as shown in Figure 2-1. Allow to drain for 10 to 20 minutes, depending on how firm you want the tofu to be. Pat dry and then slice or dice according to the recipe directions.

PRESSING TOFU

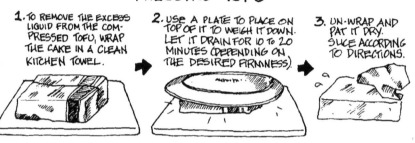

Figure 2-1:
Pressing
tofu to
extract
excess
liquid.

1. TO REMOVE THE EXCESS LIQUID FROM THE COMPRESSED TOFU, WRAP THE CAKE IN A CLEAN KITCHEN TOWEL.

2. USE A PLATE TO PLACE ON TOP OF IT TO WEIGH IT DOWN. LET IT DRAIN FOR 10 TO 20 MINUTES (DEPENDING ON THE DESIRED FIRMNESS).

3. UN-WRAP AND PAT IT DRY. SLICE ACCORDING TO DIRECTIONS.

Chapter 3

Mastering a Few Simple Techniques

In This Chapter

▷ Discovering the ancient ritual of grinding with a mortar and pestle

▷ Cooking in a wok

▷ Understanding the basics of stir-frying and deep-frying

▷ Garnishing the Thai plate

You don't need a lot of experience in the kitchen to prepare authentic Thai recipes. Fancy gizmos and gadgets aren't necessary either. A few musts are a good heat source to cook on, a sharp knife, and a decent pan in which to prepare meals. Those are the basics; you can add to your repertoire of cooking equipment as your interest increases and your budget permits.

Grinding with a Mortar and Pestle

Long before people became completely reliant on modern conveniences such as the food processor, the rhythmic motion of the pestle gently rocking against the concave base of the mortar was the most effective way to grind together the fragrant herbs and spices that enhance the foods of many cultures. Thai cuisine is no exception. Small amounts of ingredients can be easily crushed to release their flavorful oils or essence. Most Thai cooks would agree that there's no substitute for a stone mortar and pestle when pounding spices to make a curry paste or for crushing peanuts.

You can purchase relatively inexpensive equipment at many Asian markets. Look for a stone mortar at least 6 to 8 inches in diameter. Using a pestle with a little weight to it helps pulverize the ingredients more quickly. Sometimes the "gentle rocking" analysis isn't quite accurate; perhaps it's more like a good upper-arm aerobic workout. For small quantities, all the ingredients can go into the mortar at the same time. For larger quantities, begin by crushing the dried spices first and then add fibrous ingredients such as chiles, lime peel, lemon grass, or ginger. Continue on with garlic, shallots, and shrimp paste. Keep mashing until you achieve a thick paste or consistency.

Now back to modern conveniences. Even if you acknowledge that the mortar and pestle is an indispensable tool in the Thai kitchen, it's unrealistic to think that you'll put away the food processor for life. So when a recipe in this book calls for the use of a mortar and pestle, I also include instructions for using a food processor. You choose which method you prefer. It depends on whether you're in a hurry or whether you'd rather work out a few of the day's aggressions!

Discovering How to Wok

You don't need a wok to make great-tasting Thai meals, but once you gain confidence using this ingeniously shaped piece of equipment, you'll wonder why you hadn't figured out how to use it before. It's really an all-purpose pan that can be used for stir-frying, deep-frying, steaming, and even preparing a simple sauté.

Woks come in a variety of materials and sizes. Originally round-bottomed and made of iron, most are now made from carbon steel (which most traditional Asian cooks prefer), stainless steel, aluminum, and even copper. Some have nonstick surfaces. The handles on woks traditionally were two metal handles, but the more contemporary versions now have one long wooden handle. Bottom surfaces are either rounded, usually with a "collar" to help balance the wok on the heating source, or flat-bottomed, which generally work better on an electric range. Although restaurants may have woks that can be several feet across, a 12- to 14-inch-diameter wok works well for home cooks.

Stovetops vary in output of heat, not only between gas and electric ranges but even among the various burners on the same stove. One burner can have a higher or lower Btu rating than the others. ("Btu" stands for British thermal unit, a measurement of the quantity of heat that's required to raise the temperature of one pound of water by one degree Fahrenheit.) Start with a medium-high heat under your wok and adjust the temperature by increasing or decreasing the intensity of the burner as needed. Allow the oil to get hot, but not to the point where it's smoking.

If using a wok to deep-fry, never overfill it with oil because as food is added, the oil will rise and bubble up. You should allow several inches of clearance at the top of the wok for this bubbling to occur.

Seasoning and cleaning your carbon steel wok

If you have a carbon steel wok, first and foremost, read the manufacturer's instructions about the use and care of your wok. If instructions are not provided, following these suggestions will help you care for your wok for many years to come.

✔ The manufacturer places a protective coating on the wok that needs to be washed off. Using a nonabrasive pad, first wash the wok with hot water and a small amount of dish detergent. It's okay to scrub the outside more vigorously, but be gentler on the interior. Rinse and dry the wok thoroughly.

✔ Place the wok on the stove over medium-low heat. Pour in 1 tablespoon of vegetable oil. Fold up one or two paper towels and rub the oil all over the inside surface of the wok. (If you're concerned about burning your fingers, you may want to use a pair of tongs to move the paper towel around in the oil.)

Allow the wok to heat up for 10 to 15 minutes, occasionally rubbing the interior with the oil-coated paper towel. Add a little more oil to the paper towel if necessary. Do not add it directly in the pan.

✔ Wipe the wok with a few clean paper towels, which will be filled with a black residue when you're done. Let the wok cool completely, gently rinse again in warm water, and allow it to dry thoroughly. The wok is now ready to use.

✔ After each use, gently wash the wok by rinsing it with hot water, rubbing with a plastic scouring pad if necessary. Dry thoroughly. This is about the most care you will need to give the wok. An occasional reseasoning may be necessary if the wok shows any signs of rust or if by chance someone gets overzealous with a scouring pad.

You can use higher temperatures with carbon steel woks. If you have a nonstick wok, decrease the temperature to protect the nonstick coating.

Helpful Hints for Successful Stir-Frying and Deep-Frying

The following tips not only help you organize the preparation for cooking a Thai meal, but they are useful for all general cooking practices. Having ingredients prepared and assembled before you begin the cooking process is one of the most important ways to ensure you'll master the challenge of a new culinary experience.

✔ Have all your ingredients prepped before you begin cooking. In French it's called "mise en place," meaning "everything in its place."

✔ Cut vegetables in uniform pieces. Add thicker-cut or longer-cooking vegetables to the pan before quicker-cooking ones.

✔ Washed greens need adequate time to drain, so make sure that they're dry before stir-frying or adding them to the deep-fryer.

✔ Cut meats such as beef across the grain. Marinate meat if called for in the recipe.

✔ Have sauces and seasonings at your reach.

✔ Assemble ingredients on a cookie sheet or jelly roll pan in the order in which you will add them to the wok or frying pan.

✔ Prepare rice and noodles before you begin cooking the main dish.

✔ Make sure that the oil is hot enough before adding food to the pan. If the oil temperature drops after adding ingredients, allow it to get hot again before adding additional items.

Stir-frying

This efficient way to cook dinner allows you to whip up a nutritious and colorful meal in almost no time. Yes, preparing the ingredients before cooking takes a little time, but once the oil is hot, within literally a few minutes, you're serving up a great meal. The wok is the best piece of equipment for stir-frying, but you may substitute a large frying pan.

With all your ingredients at hand, heat the wok or frying pan over medium-high heat for a minute or two. Pour a tablespoon or two of oil along the inside wall of the wok and allow it to heat up. Add the flavoring ingredients, such as garlic, and cook briefly to flavor the oil. Add the meat or longest-cooking food item, stirring and tossing the food rapidly. As a general rule, transfer the meat to a bowl if other ingredients will take a longer time to cook, and continue cooking the vegetables, starting with the ones needing the longest cooking times first. Briefly cook greens to retain their crispness and color. You can add the previously stir-fried meat back to the pan, along with any sauces or liquid called for in the recipe. Add aromatic herbs at the end and serve immediately.

Deep-frying

You can use a wok for deep-frying, but a tall-sided 3- or 4-quart saucepan works well also. The amount of oil and its temperature vary depending on what's being cooked. Generally, 2 to 4 cups of oil is adequate.

A deep-fry thermometer is an indispensable tool when monitoring the temperature of the oil. Most foods cook best between 350 and 375 degrees. Keeping the oil at a steady temperature is important, so don't overcrowd the wok or pan by adding all the food at once. Fry in small batches, transferring the food in and out with a slotted spoon or skimmer. As you cook, the added ingredients force the oil temperature to drop, so allow the oil to come back up to the proper temperature before you continue cooking. Drain the cooked food on paper towels or, if using a wok with a tempura rack, drain the fried food on the rack first and then transfer to a platter lined with paper towels.

If you don't own a deep-fry thermometer, try this simple trick. Place a wooden chopstick or long strand of uncooked spaghetti in the hot oil, standing it straight up. When tiny bubbles form all around the chopstick or spaghetti, the oil should be hot enough to fry in.

Cleaning up spattered oil on the kitchen floor can be the worst part of deep-frying. Place several unfolded newspapers on the floor in front of the area where you'll be cooking — this way, all you have to do is refold the paper and throw it away!

Making Simple Garnishes for the Thai Plate

The constant Thai quest for harmony within a dish doesn't end with the cooking; it also carries over to the presentation. Almost all food is served with some form of garnish. In Thailand, skilled artisans prepare elaborately carved fruits and vegetables to be served along with the royal family meals.

You don't need to train for years to prepare decorative accompaniments to the serving bowl or platter. Following a few of the guidelines that follow not only adds color or flavor to a finished dish but also shows that you prepared the food with great care.

Chile flowers

Select unblemished, brightly colored fresh chiles with the stems attached. Thin chiles 2 to 3 inches in length work best — if using longer ones, simply cut off a portion at the pointed end. Wearing protective gloves, cut the chili lengthwise with scissors from the narrow tip to about ½ inch from the top, near the stem. Continue cutting thin sections, or petals, around the chile. Remove some of the seeds if desired, and place the chile in a bowl of ice water until the petals begin to curl outward, as shown in Figure 3-1. Use chile flowers as a garnish to show that the prepared dish is hot or spicy.

Book VIII

Thai Cooking

Figure 3-1:
Making
chile
flowers.

Carrot blossoms

Peel a large carrot with a vegetable peeler, trim off the ends, and cut it into two pieces with a knife. Working with a citrus stripping tool, peel away sections of the carrot lengthwise from end to end. Leave a small space and continue peeling another section until you have alternating ¼-inch-deep cuts all around the carrot. With a knife, cut ⅛-inch-thick slices vertically across each piece. Place in a bowl of cold water and refrigerate. You can prepare cucumber slices in the same way, but don't store them in water — wrap them in plastic wrap and refrigerate until needed.

Scallion brushes

Trim the root end of a green onion and cut it into 3 or 4 pieces. Lay each piece flat. Starting in the middle of each piece and cutting through to one of the ends, cut the onion lengthwise with a sharp knife. Continue to make as many thin cuts as possible, rotating the scallion piece as needed to make multiple thin strands. Place in a bowl of ice water, allowing the ends to curl up, as shown in Figure 3-2. This method also works for thin pieces of celery. Use the brushes simply as a garnish or as a "brush" to baste sauces or condiments on the prepared food.

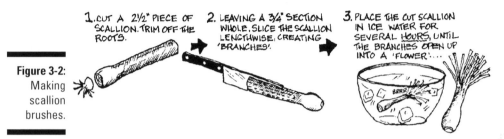

MAKING A SCALLION BRUSH

1. CUT A 2½" PIECE OF SCALLION. TRIM OFF THE ROOTS.

2. LEAVING A ¾" SECTION WHOLE, SLICE THE SCALLION LENGTHWISE, CREATING 'BRANCHES'.

3. PLACE THE CUT SCALLION IN ICE WATER FOR SEVERAL HOURS, UNTIL THE BRANCHES OPEN UP INTO A 'FLOWER'....

Figure 3-2:
Making
scallion
brushes.

Lime twists

Small squeezes of fresh lime juice add a burst of citrus flavor to soups, salads, and main dishes. Slice the lime horizontally into thin ⅛-inch slices. Lay each slice flat and make a cut from the center, out toward the rind. Pick the slice up and twist the ends out in opposite directions.

Fresh herbs and chopped nuts

Simple additions to the serving plate can give a finished look to a dish. For a garnish, choose an herb that is used in the prepared recipe. For example, pick a small cluster of basil leaves still attached to the stem and place it alongside the food. Or mince cilantro and other herbs or chop additional peanuts and sprinkle them on the top of a dish just before serving.

Book VIII

**Thai
Cooking**

Chapter 4

First Impressions

*O*ne of the delights of a traditional Thai meal is the procession of courses leading up to the entrée. It is common to serve a refreshing cool salad, followed by various fried or steamed nibbles and a flavorful soup. Beer and wine are appropriate; for the latter, choose a spicy, full-bodied wine that can stand up to all those Asian flavors.

Small Bites

Thai cooks are champions at creating meals out of mini-courses. Sometimes a simple plate of fresh or fried spring rolls dipped into a sweetened chile sauce, or a few skewers of chicken, pork, or beef satay swirled with peanut sauce, is just the thing to tide you over.

Fried Spring Rolls (Po Pia Krob) with Sweet Chile Dipping Sauce (Nam Prik Wan)

It's nearly impossible to visit a Thai, Chinese, or Vietnamese restaurant without beginning a meal with some style of spring roll or egg roll. You can easily make these appetizers at home with minimal preparation. The hot spiciness of the sauce contrasts nicely with the extra crunch you get from using two layers of spring roll wrappers.

Preparation time: *50 minutes*

Cooking time: *7 to 8 minutes*

Yield: *12 spring rolls*

3¾-ounce package bean thread vermicelli	*2 to 3 cloves garlic, minced*
6 ounces small shrimp, peeled and deveined	*1 tablespoon minced ginger*
6 ounces pork or chicken, cut into ½-inch dice	*3 tablespoons soy sauce*
2½ cups finely shredded Chinese cabbage (napa cabbage)	*2 teaspoons sugar*
1 cup bamboo shoots, rinsed and drained	*½ teaspoon salt*
4 green onions, thinly sliced	*½ teaspoon white pepper*
1 medium carrot, shredded	*24 spring roll wrappers*
¼ cup finely chopped Thai basil or cilantro	*3 cups peanut or vegetable oil*

1 Soak the vermicelli for 10 minutes in water. Drain well and cut the noodles into 2-inch lengths.

2 Transfer the noodles to a large bowl. Add the shrimp, pork or chicken, cabbage, bamboo shoots, green onions, carrot, Thai basil or cilantro, garlic, ginger, soy sauce, sugar, salt, and pepper, and mix well.

3 Place two layers of spring roll wrappers together on a flat work surface. With the wrappers positioned in a diamond shape, scoop ½ cup of the prepared filling onto the upper third of the wrapper, as shown in Figure 4-1. Begin to tightly roll up the upper edge over the filling. Midway through, turn the sides in over the roll to keep the ingredients from spilling out. Moisten the remaining corner with water and continue rolling up, pressing to seal the wrapper closed.

4 Heat the oil in a wok or deep-sided saucepan to 360 degrees. With a pair of tongs, add 2 or 3 spring rolls to the oil and fry for 2 to 2½ minutes, until golden brown. Turn the spring rolls once or twice to ensure even browning.

5 Transfer to a platter lined with paper towels. Continue frying the remaining rolls. Serve immediately with the dipping sauce.

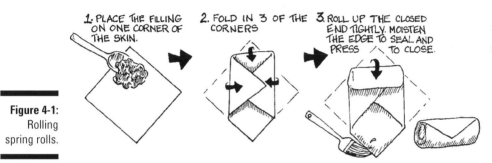

SPRING ROLLS

1. PLACE THE FILLING ON ONE CORNER OF THE SKIN.

2. FOLD IN 3 OF THE CORNERS

3. ROLL UP THE CLOSED END TIGHTLY. MOISTEN THE EDGE TO SEAL AND PRESS TO CLOSE.

Figure 4-1:
Rolling
spring rolls.

Sweet Chile Dipping Sauce (Nam Prik Wan)

Yield: *1 cup*

1⅓ cups sugar

1⅓ cups rice vinegar or white wine vinegar

½ teaspoon salt

3 small fresh Thai red chiles, finely chopped

2 cloves garlic, finely minced (optional)

Combine the sugar and vinegar in a small saucepan and bring to a low boil over medium-high heat. Reduce the heat to medium and stir in the salt. Simmer until slightly thickened, 5 to 6 minutes, stirring occasionally. Turn off the heat and mix in the chiles and garlic, if desired. Cool and serve at room temperature. Covered and refrigerated, the sauce will keep for several weeks.

Tip: *If you want sauce with less heat, substitute larger red, less-hot chiles and remove most of the seeds before adding to the sauce. Or try seeded minced jalapeño pepper.*

Book VIII

**Thai
Cooking**

Chicken Satays (Satay Kai) with Peanut Sauce (Nam Satay)

Chicken satay is one of Thailand's most popular street foods and a well-liked snack. Originally a one-bite morsel, chicken satay is now available in larger versions and endless adaptations.

Special tools: *20 bamboo skewers, soaked in water for at least 30 minutes*

Preparation time: *25 minutes*

Cooking time: *5 to 6 minutes*

Yield: *6 to 8 servings (approximately 20 skewers)*

½ cup coconut milk	*½ teaspoon salt*
2 tablespoons fish sauce	*⅛ teaspoon ground turmeric*
2 tablespoons vegetable oil	*1¼ pounds boneless, skinless chicken breast, cut into ½-inch-thin strips across the grain*
2 tablespoons brown sugar	
1½ teaspoons Red Curry Paste (see Chapter 6 of Book VIII)	*Peanut Sauce (see the following recipe)*

1 Make the marinade by combining the coconut milk, fish sauce, vegetable oil, brown sugar, Red Curry Paste, salt, and ground turmeric in a small bowl. Place the chicken in a heavy-duty resealable plastic bag and pour in the marinade. Close the bag and move the contents around, ensuring that the marinade coats all the chicken strips. Marinate at least 2 hours.

2 Light a grill on high heat. Thread the chicken onto the skewers and grill for 5 to 6 minutes, rotating the skewers 2 or 3 times during cooking. You can also grill them on the stovetop.

3 Serve with room-temperature Peanut Sauce.

Tip: *You can marinate the chicken overnight if you want to prepare this recipe in advance.*

Peanut Sauce

1¼ cups coconut milk	*2 teaspoons finely minced lemon grass*
4 to 5 tablespoons brown sugar	*½ cup chunky peanut butter*
1 to 1½ teaspoons Red Curry Paste (see Chapter 6 of Book VIII)	*½ to 1 teaspoon fish sauce*

1 Combine the coconut milk, brown sugar, curry paste, and lemon grass in a medium saucepan. Bring to a boil over medium heat and cook, simmering for 1 minute.

2 Place the peanut butter and fish sauce in a blender, and pour in the warm coconut milk mixture. Blend until smooth. Refrigerate if preparing in advance but bring to room temperature before serving.

Salads

Considering the wealth of fresh vegetables available at the Thai market, as well as the need for refreshing dishes in such a hot climate, it's no wonder that salads are a Thai trademark. They can be simple creations of cucumbers drenched in a puckery vinegar dressing or more substantial fare of green papaya with sliced beef. Either way, the salads are as loaded with fresh herbs and seasonings as any main dish.

Thai Cucumber Salad (Nam Thaeng Kwa)

This dish, a favorite condiment served on the side, can also hold its own as a refreshing first course. Use a food processor fitted with a thin slicing attachment to cut ultrathin slices of cucumber. If you don't have a food processor, slice the cucumbers about $\frac{1}{16}$-inch thin with a knife.

Preparation time: *15 minutes*

Yield: *4 servings*

$2\frac{1}{2}$ *tablespoons fresh lime juice*

2 tablespoons distilled white vinegar

2 tablespoons sugar

¾ teaspoon salt

½ to 1 teaspoon fish sauce

2 large cucumbers, peeled, cut in half lengthwise, seeded, and thinly sliced (see Figure 4-2)

2 small Thai green chiles, minced

2 tablespoons chopped cilantro

1 Place the lime juice, vinegar, sugar, salt, and fish sauce in a medium bowl and whisk until the sugar is dissolved.

2 Add the cucumbers and chiles to the bowl and toss to coat. Cover and refrigerate.

3 Stir in the chopped cilantro before serving.

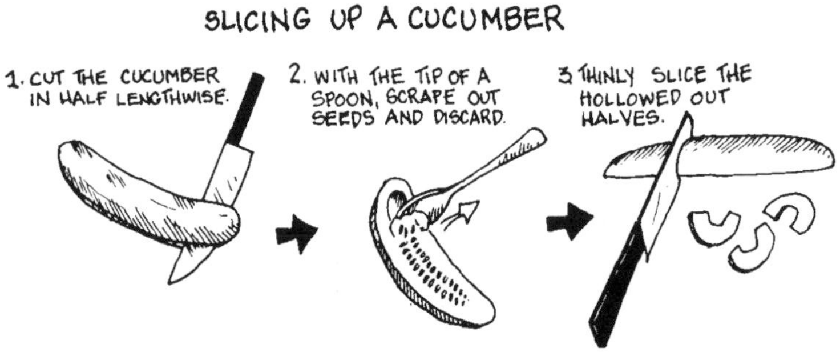

SLICING UP A CUCUMBER

1. CUT THE CUCUMBER IN HALF LENGTHWISE.

2. WITH THE TIP OF A SPOON, SCRAPE OUT SEEDS AND DISCARD.

3. THINLY SLICE THE HOLLOWED OUT HALVES.

Figure 4-2:
Seeding and slicing a cucumber.

Green Papaya Salad with Chopped Peanuts (Som Tum)

There truly is something special about *The Scent of Green Papaya* — both the 1993 movie set in Vietnam and also the vegetable with the fresh green aroma and crisp, refreshing flesh. The green papaya helps to tame the fiery heat of the chiles. But don't be fooled. This salad, although pared down for the U.S. palate, still packs a punch!

Preparation time: *15 minutes*

Yield: *4 servings*

1¼ pounds unripe green papaya, peeled, seeded, and cut into 2-inch-long julienne strips

2 long beans or 8 green beans, trimmed and cut into thin 2-inch-long julienne strips

2 fresh red Thai chiles, chopped

2 cloves garlic

3 tablespoons lime juice

2 tablespoons fish sauce

2 teaspoons sugar

1 medium tomato, cut into wedges

¼ to ½ cup chopped unsalted peanuts

Cabbage leaves or iceberg lettuce for serving

1 Place the papaya and long beans in a medium bowl.

2 Put the chiles, garlic, lime juice, fish sauce, and sugar in the bowl of a food processor and process until the sugar dissolves, about 1 minute. (Alternatively, pound the ingredients in a mortar and pestle.) Add the tomato wedges and pulse on and off 2 or 3 times. Pour over the papaya and beans, mixing well.

3 Before serving, mix in the peanuts. Serve alongside the cabbage or lettuce leaves. To eat, spoon a small mound of the salad onto a cabbage or lettuce leaf, roll it up, and eat it with your hands.

Spicy Chicken Salad (Laab)

Americans may take ground meat and turn it into a burger, but Thais season ground meat with chiles and lime and spoon it into crisp fresh lettuce cups. This recipe makes for a refreshing first course or snack on a hot day.

Preparation time: *15 minutes*

Cooking time: *4 to 6 minutes*

Yield: *6 servings*

1 tablespoon vegetable oil

1 tablespoon minced ginger

1 pound ground chicken or pork

¼ cup lime juice

3 shallots, chopped

2 scallions, chopped

1 small, fresh, red Thai chile, seeds removed, finely chopped

2 teaspoons chopped lime zest

1 teaspoon fish sauce

6 large, sturdy lettuce leaves

Chopped cilantro for garnish

1 Heat the oil in a large skillet or wok over medium-high heat. Stir in the ginger and cook for 1 minute. Add the ground chicken or pork and cook, stirring, until the pink color disappears and the meat is cooked through, 3 to 5 minutes. Remove the meat and ginger from the pan with a slotted spoon and set aside on a plate to cool slightly.

2 Combine the lime juice, shallots, scallions, chile, lime zest, and fish sauce in a mixing bowl. Stir in the cooked meat.

3 Divide the lettuce leaves among the serving plates and spoon the laab onto the leaves. Garnish with cilantro to serve.

Tip: The zest of citrus fruits, such as limes, lemons, and oranges, is the colored part of the skin and contains lots of juicy oils and fragrance. Remove the zest with a vegetable peeler, being careful not to include the pith, or white underside, of the skin, as the pith can be very bitter.

Thai Soups

Few dishes capture the essence of Thai cuisine like a bowl of hot soup. Aromatic and nourishing, tasty one-bowl meals can be prepared with a few vegetables, small amounts of protein, and noodles or rice, and enhanced by adding fresh herbs to a rich broth.

Basic Chicken Stock

There's no comparison between homemade chicken stock and store-bought canned broth. Preparing it is easier than you might think. This basic stock can be used in any of your soup, sauce, or gravy recipes already in your recipe files.

Preparation time: *20 minutes*

Cooking time: *2½ to 3 hours*

Yield: *2 quarts*

3½ pounds chicken bones (backs, necks, or wings), rinsed

1 onion, peeled and coarsely chopped

1 stalk celery, coarsely chopped

1 carrot, peeled and coarsely chopped

3 sprigs of parsley

3 sprigs of fresh thyme

1 bay leaf

6 whole peppercorns

3 quarts water

1 Place the bones, onion, celery, carrot, parsley, thyme, bay leaf, and peppercorns in a large pot. Cover with the water and bring to a boil over high heat.

2 Reduce the heat to medium-low and simmer, partially covered, for 2½ to 3 hours, until the bones give off a rich flavor. During the first 15 minutes of simmering, skim away any foam or impurities that rise to the surface. Occasionally check to ensure that the bones are covered with water. Add water if necessary.

3 Carefully strain the stock through a mesh strainer into a container. Cool to room temperature, cover, and refrigerate.

4 Remove the fat that congeals on the top before adding the stock to recipes. The stock will keep for several days in the refrigerator. For greater shelf life, label containers with the date and contents and place in the freezer for up to 3 months.

Vary It! *Give that basic stock a Thai flair. If you're making stock for a specific recipe that requires a more aromatic chicken broth base, add 3 garlic cloves, peeled, and 6 stems of cilantro to the basic recipe.*

Shrimp Soup with Lemon Grass (Tom Yum Kung)

Chicken noodle soup gets a lot of credit in the West for soothing a head cold, but few things have the power to blast through the dreary effects of winter like this comforting recipe. Your taste buds will perk up in only seconds from the appealing combination of sour lime juice, spicy chiles, sweet shrimp, and mild chicken broth.

Preparation time: *20 minutes*

Cooking time: *8 minutes*

Yield: *4 servings*

8 cups Basic Chicken Stock (see the preceding recipe) or low-sodium chicken broth

⅓ cup lime juice

¼ cup fish sauce

1 tablespoon red chile paste

½ stalk lemon grass, trimmed and cut into 2-inch pieces

4 dried red chiles

3 lime leaves

2 large button mushrooms, thinly sliced

¼ pound large shrimp, peeled and deveined

¼ cup cilantro leaves

1 Bring the chicken stock to a boil in a large saucepan over medium-high heat. Add the lime juice, fish sauce, chile paste, lemon grass, dried chiles, and lime leaves. Reduce the heat to medium and simmer for 5 minutes.

2 Add the mushrooms to the pan and cook for 1 minute. Stir in the whole shrimp. Cook until the shrimp turn opaque, 1 to 2 minutes. Stir in the cilantro before dividing the soup among 4 bowls.

Tip: *A lot of seasonings go into this flavorful soup, but not all are best consumed. Either spoon around or remove altogether the lemon grass and whole red chiles, unless you crave a mouthful of fire.*

Book VIII

Thai Cooking

Chicken and Coconut Milk Soup
(Tom Kha Kai)

Think of this as a sort of Thai cream of chicken soup, but with a lot more personality. Toss in some cooked rice if you want to make this recipe substantial enough for a whole meal.

Preparation time: *20 minutes*

Cooking time: *9 to 12 minutes*

Yield: *4 servings*

1 teaspoon vegetable oil

2 shallots, roughly chopped

2 teaspoons minced ginger or galangal

2 dried small Thai red chiles, seeded

½ pound boneless, skinless chicken breast, sliced into ½-inch pieces

4 cups Basic Chicken Stock (see the recipe earlier in this chapter) or low-sodium chicken broth

2 cups coconut milk

¼ cup lime juice

3 tablespoons fish sauce

3 lime leaves

¼ cup cilantro leaves

1 Heat the oil in a large soup pot over medium-high heat. Add the shallots, ginger, and chiles. Cook, stirring, until the shallots and chiles are softened, 3 minutes. Add the chicken; cook for 1 minute.

2 Pour in the chicken stock, coconut milk, lime juice, and fish sauce. Stir in the lime leaves and simmer the soup for 5 to 8 minutes.

3 Divide the soup among serving bowls and garnish with cilantro leaves.

Tip: A lot of seasonings go into this flavorful soup, but not all are best consumed. Either spoon around the lime leaves or remove them altogether.

Curry Noodle Soup (Kaow Soi Kai)

This specialty of northern Thailand, particularly the city of Chiang Mai, is loaded with texture, from the combination of fried and boiled noodles to the crunchy fresh garnishes that top it all off. If deep-frying isn't your favorite kitchen activity, use chow mein or ramen noodles from the store; then start with Step 2.

Preparation time: *20 minutes*

Cooking time: *10 minutes*

Yield: *4 servings*

3 to 4 cups vegetable oil for deep frying

1 pound egg noodles

2 tablespoons vegetable oil

1 tablespoon Red Curry Paste (see Chapter 6 of Book VIII)

1 tablespoon curry powder

1 teaspoon turmeric

½ pound boneless, skinless chicken breast, cut into ½-inch slices

4 cups coconut milk

2 cups Basic Chicken Stock (see the recipe earlier in this chapter) or low-sodium broth

2 tablespoons fish sauce

1 tablespoon sugar

Garnishes:

½ cup Chinese pickled cabbage, chopped

1 large lime, quartered

1 bunch green onions, chopped

2 shallots, chopped

1 Heat the 3 to 4 cups of oil in a deep-fry pan or wok over high heat until bubbling. (For more on deep-frying, see Chapter 3 of Book VIII.) Take half the noodles and drop them into the hot oil. Fry them, stirring, until the noodles just turn a golden brown color, about 2 minutes. Remove noodles from the oil with a strainer and let dry on a plate layered with paper towels. Discard the oil after it cools.

2 To make the soup, heat the 2 tablespoons oil in a large soup pot over medium-high heat. Add the curry paste, curry powder, and turmeric. Cook the spices, stirring until they're fragrant, about 1 minute. Add the chicken breast; cook, stirring, until the chicken loses its pink color, about 2 minutes. Stir in the coconut milk, chicken stock, fish sauce, and sugar and stir to blend. Add the remaining egg noodles.

3 Bring the soup to a simmer and cook for about 5 minutes to soften the noodles and allow the flavors to come together. Serve in individual bowls, garnished with fried noodles, pickled cabbage, lime quarters, green onions, and shallots.

Book VIII

Thai Cooking

Chapter 5

Noodles

*T*hailand's most famous culinary export is a dish of noodles tossed with meat and seafood and called *Pad Thai*. While this dish of slippery strands may not be the official dish of the country, it certainly is beloved. But the Thai enthusiasm for noodles does not stop with Pad Thai. Every food establishment, from fine restaurants all the way to street food stalls, makes its own specialty of Asian-style pasta, colored with vegetables, lacquered with soy sauce and hot chili oils, and plumped up with slivers of poultry and pork, rings of squid, and curls of pink shrimp.

Dried and Fresh Noodles

Here are some of the that are available to you find at Thai markets:

✔ **Rice noodles (send chan):** Made from rice flour, these noodles can be found in bundles of long and short strands, wide enough for saucy stir fries and skinny enough to be part of a spring roll filling. The dried noodles should be cooked before using, but fresh noodles also are available, sold in folded sheets. (Although called fresh because they are tender enough to be used without boiling first, the "fresh" noodles are most likely to be found in a freezer at the Thai grocery store.)

✔ **Egg noodles (ba mee):** These spaghetti-like, long, curly strands have a yellow color from the egg (or, sometimes, food coloring). Chewy and resilient, egg noodles are a good match for chewy meats such as duck or barbecued pork.

✏ **Bean thread noodles (woon sen):** Also known as cellophane or glass noodles, these dried noodles made from mung beans look almost transparent. They are very thin and shouldn't be teamed with ingredients cut into large pieces, or with heavy sauces such as curry. Before cooking, soak the noodles in warm water to soften.

Thai Noodles with Shrimp and Chicken (Pad Thai)

If there's one dish that everybody has sampled at a Thai restaurant, this is it. Although each cook in Thailand prepares Thai noodles with shrimp and chicken her own way — for example, by varying the sweetness or adjusting the number of peanuts — this recipe always keeps its essential identity as a jumble of tender rice noodles, seafood, chicken, tofu, and crunchy bean sprouts in a sweet-tangy tamarind sauce. Serve this recipe hot and steaming out of the pan, like the street vendors do in Thailand.

Preparation time: 20 minutes, plus 20 minutes for soaking the noodles

Cooking time: 8 minutes

Yield: 4 servings

8 ounces rice noodles

2 tablespoons lime juice

1 tablespoon tamarind paste

1 tablespoon sugar

1 tablespoon fish sauce

2 tablespoons skinless peanuts, ground

2 tablespoons vegetable oil

4 ounces skinless, boneless chicken breast, cut into 1-inch pieces

4 ounces medium shrimp, peeled and deveined

2 large shallots, finely chopped

1 cup fresh bean sprouts

2 ounces firm tofu, cut into 1/4-inch cubes

1/4 cup dried tiny shrimp (optional)

2 eggs, beaten

Garnishes:

1 cup fresh bean sprouts

2 bunches green onions, trimmed to 4-inch lengths

1/3 cup cilantro leaves

1 lime, cut into quarters

1 Soak the noodles in a bowl of warm water for 20 minutes. Drain and set aside. Mix the lime juice, tamarind paste, sugar, and fish sauce together in a small bowl. Stir in the ground peanuts.

2 Heat a skillet or wok over high heat and add 1 tablespoon of the oil. Stir in the chicken and cook until it loses its pink color and is cooked through, about 2 to 3 minutes, stirring frequently. Remove the chicken with a slotted spoon and set aside on a plate. Add the shrimp, cooking until they're cooked through, about 2 minutes, stirring frequently. Set aside with the chicken.

3 Add the remaining 1 tablespoon of oil to the pan. Stir in the shallots and cook for 1 minute. Stir in the bean sprouts and cook for 1 minute. Add the tofu and the dried shrimp, if desired, to the pan and cook, stirring, for 1 minute.

4 Add the drained noodles to the pan, along with the chicken and shrimp. Make a space at the side of the pan and pour in the eggs. Let them cook briefly and then stir into the rest of the ingredients. Add the lime juice and tamarind mixture and stir all the ingredients together well.

5 Place the noodle mixture on a large serving platter. Place the fresh bean sprouts and green onions on the side to be mixed as desired. Scatter the cilantro over the noodles and garnish with lime wedges before serving.

Finding Thai noodles

When searching the market for noodles, feel free to go to most any Asian market, not just the Thai ones. Chinese, Vietnamese, and Thai pastas may have different names, but they are virtually the same. And if you can't find exactly what you're looking for, consider experimenting a little — just as you may use spaghetti when linguine isn't available. What's important is just having something to swirl around your fork — or chopstick.

Wide Rice Noodles with Beef and Broccoli (Pad See Iew Nua)

This dish of tender, wide rice noodles and broccoli in a mild sauce is almost as classic a dish as the famous Pad Thai. Look for leafy Asian broccoli, if available; its slightly bitter edge adds dimension to the sauce's sweetness.

Preparation time: *20 minutes*

Cooking time: *6 minutes*

Yield: *4 servings*

2 tablespoons vegetable oil

1 pound flank steak or boneless beef round, sliced into ¼-inch-thick slices, 3 inches in length

3 eggs, beaten

1 clove garlic, minced

1 pound broccoli, cut into florets

¾ pound fresh wide rice noodles

¼ cup oyster sauce

¼ cup sweet yellow bean sauce

1 tablespoon soy sauce

1 Heat 1 tablespoon of the oil in a wok or large skillet over medium-high heat. Add the beef and cook, turning, for 1 minute. Pour in the eggs and cook with the beef, stirring lightly to break up the eggs into small pieces without scrambling them. Remove the beef and eggs from the pan with a slotted spoon and set aside on a plate.

2 Add the remaining 1 tablespoon of oil to the pan and stir in the garlic. Cook for 30 seconds and then stir in the broccoli. Cook until the broccoli turns dark and glossy and has softened somewhat, about 1 minute. Remove from the pan and set aside with the beef.

3 Cut the rice noodles into 3-inch lengths and add to the pan. Cook until the noodles are slightly golden, about 2 minutes. Return the beef, eggs, garlic, and broccoli to the pan and toss to combine.

4 Stir together the oyster sauce, bean sauce, and soy sauce. Add to the pan and toss well. Cook for 1 minute before serving.

Thin Rice Noodles with Seafood (Lad Na Talay)

Here is another use for those comfy rice noodles. Choose the slender fresh noodles for this dish, which is designed to appeal to seafood lovers.

Preparation time: *20 minutes*

Cooking time: *6 minutes*

Yield: *4 servings*

2 tablespoons vegetable oil

½ pound medium shrimp, peeled and deveined

½ pound scallops

½ pound squid, cut into rings (optional)

2 cloves garlic, minced

2 cups snow peas

¾ pound fresh thin rice noodles

¼ cup sweet yellow bean sauce

¼ cup Basic Chicken Stock (see Chapter 4 of Book VIII) or low-sodium broth

1 tablespoon soy sauce

1 tablespoon fish sauce

1 teaspoon chile oil

1 Heat 1 tablespoon of the vegetable oil in a wok or large skillet over medium-high heat. Add the shrimp, scallops, and, if desired, the squid and cook, turning, for 1 minute. Remove the seafood from the pan with a slotted spoon and set aside on a plate.

2 Add the remaining 1 tablespoon vegetable oil to the pan and stir in the garlic. Cook for 30 seconds and then stir in the snow peas. Cook until the peas have softened, about 1 minute. Remove from the pan and set aside with the seafood.

3 Add the noodles to the pan. Cook until the noodles are slightly golden, about 2 minutes. Add the seafood and snow peas to the pan and toss to combine.

4 Stir together the bean sauce, chicken stock, soy sauce, fish sauce, and chile oil. Add to the pan and toss until the ingredients are well-coated. Cook for 1 minute before serving.

Egg Noodles with Barbecued Pork (Mu Ba Mee)

The sweet and tangy flavor of the barbecue needs a sturdy noodle like this bed of chewy egg noodles. This dish resembles something that you may find in a Chinese restaurant, and a Chinese restaurant or market is where you should look for the pork called for here. If neither of those retail sources is located nearby, any cooked, sliced, or shredded barbecued pork tenderloin is a fine substitute.

Preparation time: *15 minutes*

Cooking time: *8 minutes*

Yield: *4 servings*

10 ounces thin egg noodles	*¼ cup Basic Chicken Stock (see Chapter 4 of Book VIII) or low-sodium broth*
1 tablespoon sesame oil	*3 tablespoons soy sauce*
1 tablespoon vegetable oil	*2 tablespoons lime juice*
4 green onions, chopped	*1 teaspoon fish sauce*
2 cloves garlic, minced	*1 teaspoon sugar*
2 tablespoons shallots, minced	*¾ pound sliced Chinese barbecued pork, at room temperature*
1 tablespoon minced ginger	

1 Fill a large soup pot with water and bring to a boil. Drop in the egg noodles and cook until al dente, about 5 minutes. Drain, toss with the sesame oil, and set aside.

2 Heat the vegetable oil in a wok or large skillet over medium-high heat. Stir in the onions, garlic, shallots, and ginger. Cook until the vegetables are soft, about 1 minute. Stir in the chicken stock, soy sauce, lime juice, fish sauce, and sugar and blend well.

3 Add the noodles and cook, tossing, for 2 minutes. Divide the noodles among serving bowls and top with slices of pork.

Tip: The literal translation for the Italian phrase "al dente," is "to the tooth." This means that the noodles should be cooked until they still give a little resistance when bitten into. Adding overly cooked noodles to a dish that needs further cooking will make the noodles soft and mushy.

Bean Thread Noodles with Chicken (Pad Woon Sen Gai)

These delicate noodles seem almost to disappear into this dish, but once they're in your mouth, you'll find that they add a nice, gentle chewiness. Feel free to substitute pork or shrimp for the chicken, but because the noodles are so fine, cut the pieces small to keep things in proportion.

Preparation time: *25 minutes, plus 15 to 20 minutes for soaking the noodles*

Cooking time: *7 minutes*

Yield: *4 servings*

12 ounces bean thread noodles

2 tablespoons vegetable oil

2 cloves garlic, minced

½ pound boneless, skinless chicken breast, cut into ½-inch pieces

2 green onions, chopped

4 ounces firm tofu, diced

2 cups bean sprouts

1 cup shredded Chinese or savoy cabbage

½ cup tamarind juice

2 tablespoons sugar

2 tablespoons fish sauce

½ cup skinless salted peanuts, chopped

1 Place the noodles in a large bowl and cover with lukewarm water. Allow the noodles to soak for 15 to 20 minutes, or until they're thoroughly soft. Drain thoroughly and set aside.

2 Heat 1 tablespoon of the oil in a wok or large skillet over medium-high heat. Add the garlic and chicken and cook, stirring, for 2 minutes. Remove from the pan with a slotted spoon and set aside on a plate.

3 Add the remaining 1 tablespoon of oil to the pan. Add the green onions and cook for 30 seconds. Stir in the tofu, bean sprouts, and cabbage and cook, stirring, for 2 minutes.

4 Combine the tamarind juice, sugar, and fish sauce and add to the pan, tossing well to combine.

5 Return the garlic and chicken to the pan and toss with the vegetables and sauce. Add the noodles and stir with the other ingredients until the noodles are warmed through, about 2 minutes. Serve hot, topped with the chopped peanuts.

Book VIII

Thai Cooking

Chapter 6

Curries

The term *curry* has become so identified with Indian cooking that many people are surprised to find the fiery food an essential part of Thai cooking as well. Even though milder dishes such as Pad Thai (see the recipe in Chapter 5 of Book VIII) and fresh spring rolls are more-famous exports of the country, Thai people also like their food hot, hot, hot.

So along with a meal of grilled meats and stir-fried vegetables and wok-tossed noodles, Thai cooks regularly prepare a pot full of curry, thick with meat or fish, glistening with oil, and winking with specks of hot chile pepper.

In Thai cooking, curry, the meal, always starts with curry, the paste. It's possible to purchase a dried curry blend, but the preferred way to start a curry is with a freshly made paste. Right away, you can see the difference between Thai and Indian curry. Indian cooks create their curry base from a combination of fragrant dried spices, such as cinnamon, cumin, black pepper, and cloves. A Thai curry may use one or more of these dried goods, but it gets more of its aromatic dazzle from fresh herbs and chile peppers.

Basil, lime leaves, lemongrass, garlic, ginger, and shallots offer a whole garden of delights! These ingredients give Thai curries a fresh, lively flavor that comes through even in the most tongue-searing blend.

But the combination and proportion of flavorings that go into a curry are as unique to each Thai cook as a barbecue rub is to a Texas grill master. To complicate matters further, the curries can differ depending on what part of the country you're dining in; some Thai food experts even separate city-style curry from country-style curry. This chapter gives you some basic principles to help sort out the curry confusion.

Looking at All the Pretty Colors of Curry

The Thai love of the visual accounts for some of the reason that their curries don't just come in one color — say, muddy brown. The result is three basic types: red, green, and yellow. (Don't let the colors fool you, however; they aren't always reliable indicators of which is hottest.)

You find red curry all over Thailand, but regional preferences are evident. Green curry is favored in the central part of the country, and yellow finds much favor in the south. Green curry often is milder on the chile scale but more aromatically charged with the use of herbs and spices, while yellow curry can outsear one made with even the most ferocious-looking red chile paste. Looking for rules? You may be out of luck. Curries can be soupy and thin, or thick and creamy. When tamarind or lime juice is added, it becomes known as a "sour curry."

 What's most important is to provide a balanced blend of flavors. Setting your mouth on fire isn't the point — it goes against the Thai culinary concept of harmony. Heat is great, sure, but also give your recipe an undertone of sweetness and saltiness and enough chewy textures from a combination of vegetables, meat, and fish. Here are a few tips when preparing curries:

- ✔ For the vegetables, choose such ingredients as eggplant, mushrooms, string beans, and bamboo shoots, which will retain their texture.

- ✔ Curry is most often made with meat, everything from beef and pork to chicken and mutton. But fish curries are wonderful, too. Just choose a firm-textured fish or shellfish that won't turn to mush while cooking.

- ✔ Like a good stew, Thai curry is what you make of it. Get started with your own experiments from the recipes provided here for red and green curry pastes. You can make yellow curry by adding 1 tablespoon or two of turmeric to the red curry paste.

Try to use plastic kitchen gloves, if available, when working with fresh or dried chiles, and wash your cutting board thoroughly with hot, soapy water afterward. The oil from a chile has a sneaky way of creeping onto your fingers and burning you later. *Never* touch your eyes after handling chiles directly.

Choosing Your Chiles

The fiery chile pepper, a gift to Thailand from the Americas, has become an essential part of Thai cooking. It must have been refreshing — not to mention eye-popping — to be introduced to an ingredient that had the power to offer both heat and chills to every meal.

What Thai cooks use is a combination of fresh and dried hot peppers:

- **Fresh chiles *(prik sodd)*:** These are best to use in fresh, uncooked, or minimally cooked recipes, naturally. Think of appetizers, salads, and dipping sauces. Feel free to use poblano, jalapeño, and serrano peppers — at least one kind of which should be readily available in the supermarket — when fresh, hot green peppers are called for.

  Small red chiles, also known as Thai or bird chiles *(prik kee nu)*, with a slightly wrinkled skin, should be in many supermarket produce departments.

- **Dried chiles *(prik haeng)*:** Here's what you use for long-cooking recipes, curries, soups, and anything that may need an extra depth of flavor. Dried chiles can be toasted by shaking in a dry skillet over medium-high heat until they start to give off a slightly smoky, hot aroma. If the recipe doesn't call for an extended cooking time, soak the dried chiles in hot water to soften before using. Large dried red Thai or bird chiles are one option, but you may also substitute New Mexico Anaheim chiles if you need to.

A general rule is that the smaller the chile, the hotter it is.

To lessen the heat index, split fresh or dried chiles open and remove and discard the seeds.

Concocting Curry Pastes

A good curry stew starts with a good curry paste. The following recipes give you that foundation and are the basis for upcoming recipes.

Book VIII

Thai
Cooking

Red Curry Paste (Krung Kaeng Ped)

Double this recipe if you want to store some for later. You can pack the curry paste in an airtight storage container and freeze it for up to 6 months.

Preparation time: *30 minutes*

Yield: *1 cup*

1 cup dried red Thai chile peppers, seeds removed

6 cloves garlic

4 large shallots

1 stalk lemon grass, trimmed and chopped

¼ cup lime juice

1 tablespoon ground coriander

1 tablespoon ground cumin

1 tablespoon shrimp paste

2 teaspoons salt

1 Place the seeded chile peppers in a bowl of hot water; let them soak until softened, 20 to 30 minutes. Drain well.

2 Place the chile peppers, garlic, shallots, lemon grass, lime juice, coriander, cumin, shrimp paste, and salt in a food processor. Puree until the mixture is quite smooth. (Alternatively, follow the guidelines for grinding with a mortar and pestle in Chapter 3 of Book VIII.)

Green Curry Paste (Krung Kaeng Kiew Wan)

Double this recipe if you want to store some for later. You can pack the curry paste in an airtight storage container and freeze it for up to 6 months.

Preparation time: *10 minutes*

Yield: *1 cup*

2 poblano peppers, seeded

⅔ cup fresh, small green chile peppers

6 cloves garlic

4 shallots

1 stalk lemon grass, trimmed and chopped

¼ cup chopped cilantro

¼ cup lime juice

1 tablespoon black peppercorns

1 tablespoon ground coriander

1 tablespoon salt

1 tablespoon shrimp paste

2 teaspoons salt

Place all the ingredients in a food processor. Puree until the mixture is quite smooth. (Alternatively, follow the guidelines for grinding with a mortar and pestle in Chapter 3 of Book VIII.)

Creating Curried Main Dishes

After making your own curry pastes, whose recipes are in the previous section, you're ready to tackle some main dishes.

Green Curry Chicken with Thai Eggplant (Kaeng Kiew Wan Kai Makua)

Everyone will ask, "Where's the eggplant?" when you serve this curry. That's because Thai eggplant looks more like a green tomato than the purple vegetable Americans find at the grocery (see Chapter 2 of Book VIII). Moderate the heat as you wish by adding more coconut milk or broth to the recipe — or turn the volume up with even more curry paste!

Preparation time: *20 minutes*

Cooking time: *13 minutes*

Yield: *4 servings*

2 tablespoons vegetable oil

¼ cup Green Curry Paste (see the recipe earlier in this chapter)

1 jalapeño pepper, seeded and minced

1 tablespoon minced ginger or galangal

1½ pounds boneless, skinless chicken breast, sliced into ½-inch pieces

2 cups coconut milk

1½ cups Basic Chicken Stock (see Chapter 4 of Book VIII) or low-sodium broth

1 tablespoon palm sugar

1 tablespoon fish sauce

1 teaspoon ground black pepper

½ teaspoon salt

2 lime leaves, finely sliced

3 baby eggplants, quartered

½ cup basil leaves

1 Heat the oil in a large saucepan over medium-high heat. Add the curry paste, jalapeño pepper, and ginger; cook, stirring, for 2 minutes. Add the chicken and cook for 1 minute, stirring.

2 Stir in the coconut milk, chicken stock, palm sugar, fish sauce, black pepper, and salt until blended. Add the lime leaves and eggplants. Cook, simmering, until the eggplant is soft and the flavors are well blended, about 8 to 10 minutes. Garnish with the basil leaves before serving with steamed rice.

Book VIII

Thai Cooking

Red Curry Beef (Kaeng Ped Nua)

This spicy preparation using rich slices of beef tenderloin is less a stew than a stir-fry. The mild flavor of the beef gets a fiery lift — and a rosy dose of color — from the curried sauce.

Preparation time: *15 minutes*

Cooking time: *5 minutes*

Yield: *4 servings*

2 tablespoons vegetable oil

1½ pounds beef tenderloin, cut into 1½-inch strips

½ cup Red Curry Paste (see the recipe earlier in this chapter)

2 cups coconut milk

2 tablespoons fish sauce

2 tablespoons sugar

¼ teaspoon salt

¼ teaspoon ground black pepper

2 lime leaves, finely sliced

1 Heat the oil in a large skillet or wok over medium-high heat. Add the tenderloin and cook, stirring, until it loses its pink color, about 2 minutes. Remove with a slotted spoon and set aside.

2 Place the curry paste in the skillet and cook for 1 minute. Stir in the coconut milk, fish sauce, sugar, salt, and pepper. Return the meat to the pan and toss well. Simmer until all the sauce is heated and thickened, about 3 minutes. Garnish with the lime leaves and serve with steamed rice.

Tip: *Tougher cuts of beef have to be marinated, braised, or stewed before they become tender enough for the relatively short cooking time in this recipe. Instead, consider using leftover cooked meat, such as flank steak, roast beef, pot roast, or even pork and stirring it into the hot sauce to heat through.*

Muslim Curry (Kaeng Masaman)

Although the majority of Thai people are practicing Buddhists, the country includes a minority of other religions, including Christians, Hindus, and Muslims. The latter give their name to this generously spiced curry, borrowing from the culinary traditions of the Muslims in Malaysia, to the south of Thailand.

Preparation time: *20 minutes*

Cooking time: *14 minutes*

Yield: *4 servings*

2 tablespoons vegetable oil

⅓ cup Red Curry Paste (see the recipe earlier in this chapter)

1 teaspoon ground cardamom

1 teaspoon ground cumin

1 teaspoon ground cinnamon

1 teaspoon ground white pepper

1 teaspoon coriander

½ teaspoon salt

½ teaspoon ground nutmeg

¼ teaspoon ground cloves

1½ pounds boneless, skinless chicken breast, cut into 1-inch slices

2 shallots, sliced

1½ cups coconut milk

1½ cups Basic Chicken Stock (see Chapter 4 of Book VIII) or low-sodium broth

2 tablespoons tamarind paste

2 tablespoons fish sauce

2 tablespoons sugar

2 ripe avocados, cut into ½-inch cubes

1 cup skinless, unsalted peanuts

1 Heat the oil in a large saucepan over medium-high heat. Add the curry paste, cardamom, coriander, cumin, cinnamon, white pepper, salt, nutmeg, and cloves. Cook, stirring, for 1 minute. Add the chicken and shallots and cook for 1 minute.

2 Add the coconut milk, chicken stock, tamarind paste, fish sauce, and sugar, stirring well to blend. Cook, simmering, for 10 minutes. Stir in the avocados and peanuts and cook for an additional 2 minutes before serving with steamed rice.

Book VIII

Thai Cooking

Chapter 7

The Main Event

Rice is an essential part of the Thai meal, as it is in most Asian countries. Even when a noodle dish is offered as a separate course, main dishes of meat, seafood, or vegetables always are served with a bowl of steaming hot rice. And it would be unthinkable to set a bowl of curry on the table without offering rice alongside to help soak up the liquid and tame the pepper's fire at the same time!

The Importance of Rice

Without a doubt, rice is one of the most important foods that people eat: More than half the world's population depend on rice for daily survival. Although ancient varieties of the grains are still cultivated, modern rice varieties have helped double the supply of rice over the last 25 years, to between 500 and 600 million tons annually. Talk about a great way to mop up all those delectable sauces!

In Thailand, rice is the most important crop grown in the country, occupying half the amount of cultivated land. The average person, regardless of income level, eats about 280 pounds of milled rice per year. That's around three-quarters of a pound a day! Not only does this miracle food help to sustain the domestic population, but 4 million tons of rice are exported annually. The demand for high-quality, lower-yielding rice crops from Thailand has been one of the major reasons that the planting of more modern, high-yielding rice varieties has been slow to catch on with rice farmers.

Looking at three favorite U.S. rices

U.S. consumption of rice can't come close to Thailand's, but annual per capita consumption of rice in the United States has tripled over the last 35 years and now weighs in at around 26 pounds per person. But although the people of Thailand eat numerous varieties of rice, the types of rice most commonly consumed with Thai food in the United States are jasmine, sticky, and basic long-grain white rice:

- ✔ **Jasmine rice:** The official name of jasmine rice, sometimes called fragrant, scented, or aromatic rice, is *Thai hom mali* rice. Consumed mostly in a local area surrounding Bang Klar, a village in central Thailand, traditional jasmine rice was dark in color and cooked to a soft texture. In the early 1970s, the Thai government sought alternative jasmine rice varieties for export and looked to the northeastern region of the country for high-quality, long-grain, pure white rice that continued to cook up soft, yet hold on to its fragrant aroma. Slightly chewy and denser in texture, jasmine rice is now one of the best known of the aromatic rice varieties grown. (See "Cooking jasmine rice the Thai way," later in this chapter.)

- ✔ **Sticky rice:** The beauty of this rice, also known as glutinous rice, is that, when cooked, the short grains clump together and can be easily scooped up. You'll find that most rice dessert dishes are made with the small, sweet grain of sticky rice, as it loves to meld with the richness of coconut milk.

- ✔ **Long-grain white rice:** With dozens of brands, long-grain white rice is the common standard found in every grocery store in America. It's a favorite because of its ability to cook up dry and fluffy. Converted white rice is parboiled before being milled, resulting in a less sticky rice when cooked. Although long-grain white rice is enjoyable to eat, for a true Thai meal, reward your efforts with jasmine or sticky rice, which is the preferred accompaniment.

Cooking jasmine rice the Thai way

Before measuring cups and rice cookers were available, the old method of cooking rice required adding a generous amount of rice to a large quantity of water. The water was brought to a boil, the rice was tested for doneness, and the excess water was poured off (or more likely was saved and drunk at another time). Then over moderate heat, the rice was tossed, flipped, and moved about the pan in order to dry it out. That was it! If this method appears too challenging and a rice cooker is unavailable, try the method in the following recipe.

Jasmine Rice Thai Style

This recipe presents an easy way to cook jasmine rice on your stovetop. If you don't have a rice cooker, this is the way to go.

Preparation time: *2 minutes*

Cooking time: *50 minutes*

Yield: *12 servings*

3 cups jasmine rice   3½ cups water

1 Place the rice in a mesh strainer and rinse under water until the water runs clear. Or add it to a pot and swirl the rice around in several batches of fresh water until the water pours off clear. Drain the rice well and add it to a heavy-bottomed 3- or 4-quart pot.

2 Pour in enough water to cover the rice by ¾ inch or so, about 3½ cups. The traditional method of testing for adequate water is performed by placing the tip of your index finger on top of the rice. The water should just barely come up to the first joint of the finger.

3 Bring the water to a boil over medium-high heat and simmer the rice for 20 seconds, stirring once or twice.

4 Cover with a tight-fitting lid, reduce the heat to medium-low, and simmer for 15 minutes.

5 Remove from the heat and allow to stand for 10 minutes without lifting the lid. At this point, check the rice for doneness. Flip the rice on top around with the rice on the bottom of the pot. (If you're lucky, a little bit of lightly crusted-brown rice may form on the bottom of the pan, making a thin, nutty-flavored "rice pancake" — Thais love it!)

6 Cover again and allow to sit for several minutes. The rice is best eaten within an hour of cooking.

Adding Protein: Poultry, Meat, and Seafood

From the beautiful sight of a fried whole catfish to the tiniest mince of a chicken breast, the Thai table is host to almost every kind of protein. Beef, pork, chicken, and duck take turns appearing in main dishes with every kind of fish and shellfish, and it isn't uncommon to see food from the land and food from the sea all mixed together.

What you should take into consideration, though, is that meat and fish are rarely the sole focus of a dish. Instead, they add body to a colorful creation of vegetables and herbs, or they give texture to a saucy curry or slurpable soup. Always cut meat or fish into bite-sized pieces, as knives are rarely found on the table.

Chicken with Holy Basil (Kai Pad Kapraow)

This popular recipe is one that you can quickly fix for a weeknight dinner. It contains a cup of basil, a popular ingredient in Thai cooking that adds fresh green color and a crisp herb flavor. (See Chapter 2 of Book VIII for more about basil.) Serve with jasmine or steamed white rice.

Preparation time: *20 minutes*

Cooking time: *5 minutes*

Yield: *4 servings*

1 tablespoon fish sauce

1 tablespoon granulated sugar

1 teaspoon soy sauce

2 tablespoons vegetable oil

1 tablespoon minced garlic

1 red Thai chile pepper, minced

1½ pounds boneless, skinless chicken breast, cut into 1-inch pieces

1 cup loosely packed, roughly chopped fresh holy basil or common basil leaves

Sprigs of fresh basil for garnish

1 Combine the fish sauce, sugar, and soy sauce in a small bowl and set aside.

2 Heat the oil in a skillet or wok over medium-high heat. Add the garlic and chile and cook for 1 minute. Add the chicken and cook, stirring, until the chicken is golden brown and cooked through, 3 minutes. Stir in the sauce mixture and basil leaves and cook for 1 minute. Scatter with sprigs of fresh basil to serve.

Stir-Fried Tofu with Vegetables
(Tao Hoo Phat)

Tofu is a beloved ingredient in Thai cooking, not only because of its usefulness as a protein but because it adapts to any sauce or seasoning added to it. You may make this an all-vegetarian recipe or add any meat or seafood you desire.

Preparation time: *20 minutes*

Cooking time: *6 minutes*

Yield: *4 servings*

12 ounces firm tofu	*½ cup sliced white mushrooms*
2 tablespoons vegetable oil	*½ cup canned straw mushrooms, rinsed and drained*
2 shallots, chopped	
1 clove garlic, chopped	*¾ cup Basic Chicken Stock (see Chapter 4 of Book VIII) or low-sodium broth*
1 cup broccoli florets	
1 cup cauliflower florets	*2 tablespoons soy sauce*
1 cup baby sweet corn	*1 teaspoon fish sauce*
1 cup snow peas	*1 teaspoon chile oil*

1 Press the tofu firmly to extract as much moisture as possible. (For more information about tofu, see Chapter 2 of Book VIII.) Pat dry with paper towels. Cut the tofu into ½-inch cubes — or any size you desire — and set aside.

2 Heat the oil in a large wok or skillet over medium-high heat. When the oil is sizzling, add the shallots and garlic and cook, stirring, for 1 minute. Add the broccoli and cauliflower and cook to soften, about 2 minutes. Stir in the sweet corn, snow peas, mushrooms, and tofu and cook for 1 minute.

3 Turn the heat to high and add the chicken stock, soy sauce, fish sauce, and chile oil. Cook, stirring, for 2 minutes, until the chicken stock reduces slightly. Serve hot with rice.

Vary It! *Add about a pound of shrimp, chicken, beef, or pork as desired.*

Book VIII

Thai Cooking

Chile Pepper Beef (Nua)

Thin slices of beef stand up to the robust flavor of hot chiles in this easy stir-fry.

Preparation time: *20 minutes, plus 1 hour for marinating*

Cooking time: *10 minutes*

Yield: *4 servings*

1½ pounds flank steak

2 tablespoons soy sauce

1 tablespoon fish sauce

2 tablespoons vegetable oil

3 shallots, sliced

2 small red Thai chiles, seeded and sliced

2 tablespoons lime juice

1 tablespoon granulated sugar

¼ cup chopped cilantro

1 Slice the beef across the grain into 1½-inch strips and place in a mixing bowl. Sprinkle with the soy sauce and fish sauce and toss well. Set aside to marinate for 1 hour.

2 Heat the vegetable oil in a skillet or wok over medium-high heat. Add the shallots and chiles and cook, stirring, for 2 minutes. Add the beef and cook, stirring, for 1 minute. Stir in the lime juice and sugar and cook for 1 minute.

3 Turn the beef out onto a serving platter and garnish with the cilantro before serving.

Tip: Beef is easier to slice if it's firm. Place the meat, wrapped well in plastic, in the freezer for 20 to 30 minutes before slicing.

Shrimp with Sweet Chile Sauce (Kung Phat Nam Prik)

Thailand is one of the world's major producers of farm-raised shrimp, and the United States is Thailand's biggest market. But although much of what people in the United States buy is relatively small, frozen shrimp, Thai cooks are used to purchasing large, head-on, shell-on prawns, which have tiny claws like a lobster. The meat is sweet and firm-textured, but large or jumbo shrimp from a good fish market are a fine substitute.

Preparation time: *15 minutes*

Cooking time: *6 minutes*

Yield: *4 servings*

16 large shrimp

3 tablespoons vegetable oil

1 clove garlic, minced

¼ cup palm or brown sugar

2 tablespoons fish sauce

2 tablespoons red chile paste

1 tablespoon Basic Chicken Stock (see Chapter 4 of Book VIII) or low-sodium broth

1 tablespoon lime juice

1 Peel the shrimp and use a sharp knife to slice along the back of the shrimp, exposing the black intestinal vein. Remove the vein, rinse the shrimp, and pat dry well with paper towels.

2 Heat 2 tablespoons of the oil in a large skillet over medium-high heat. Place the shrimp in the pan and cook on one side until they begin to turn golden brown, about 1 minute. Turn the shrimp over and cook until they're turning pink and are just cooked through, about 1 minute more. Remove from the pan with a slotted spoon and set aside on a plate. Cover the shrimp with aluminum foil to keep warm.

3 Add the remaining 1 tablespoon of oil to the pan and let heat for 30 seconds. Add the garlic and cook, stirring, 1 minute. Stir in the sugar, fish sauce, chile paste, chicken stock, and lime juice, cooking until all the ingredients are well blended and cooked through, about 3 minutes.

4 Divide the shrimp among serving plates. Spoon the sweet chile sauce over the top of the shrimp and serve with hot rice.

Tip: To get shrimp with a nice, slightly crisp texture, cook in the pan in batches to avoid overcrowding. When pieces of fish or meat touch each other while cooking, they give off moisture, which just steams the ingredients.

Book VIII

Thai Cooking

Fried Catfish in Garlic Sauce (Pla Duk Tod Krob Phat)

Whole catfish, deep-fried from head to tail, is a classic presentation in Thai restaurants. Preparing it takes a bit of skill to master, however, and home cooks may find that wrangling a large, bone-in fish in hot oil is a little messy for their kitchens! Instead, try this recipe, which uses catfish fillets.

Preparation time: *15 minutes*

Cooking time: *11 to 12 minutes*

Yield: *4 servings*

1½-pound catfish fillet, cut into 4 serving pieces

Salt

Freshly ground black pepper

5 tablespoons vegetable oil

5 cloves garlic, minced

¼ cup sweet chile sauce

1 tablespoon soy sauce

1 teaspoon granulated sugar

1 teaspoon fish sauce

¼ cup chopped cilantro for garnish

Fried shallots for garnish (see Chapter 2 of Book VIII for more about fried shallots)

1 Rinse the catfish fillets and pat dry. Season with salt and pepper.

2 Heat 3 tablespoons of the oil in a large skillet over high heat. When the oil is sizzling, place the fillets in the pan, 2 at a time if necessary to avoid overcrowding. Cook on one side until golden brown, about 2 minutes. Turn and fry until the fish are cooked through and flaky, about 3 minutes. Set aside on a plate lined with paper towels and repeat with the remaining fish.

3 Add the remaining 2 tablespoons oil to the skillet and allow to heat for 30 seconds. Stir in the garlic and cook until golden, about 1 minute. Add the chile sauce, soy sauce, sugar, and fish sauce and stir until blended.

4 Return the fish to the pan and gently spoon the sauce over, taking care not to break up the fish. Place the catfish and sauce on a serving platter and garnish with the cilantro and fried shallots before serving.

Chapter 8

Sweet Beginnings and Endings

The dessert course is where different cultures often show their strongest differences. The English may have adopted Indian curries as a part of their national cuisine, and the Japanese have learned to embrace American-style hamburgers, but the sugary finish to a meal is more difficult to translate from one country to another.

For instance, Americans adore pastries, ice cream, and anything with chocolate. The staple dessert ingredients in the United States are dairy products, sugar, and refined white flour.

Thailand's rich array of desserts, on the other hand, comes from a variety of bean flours, tapioca, rice, fruit, and, of course, the ubiquitous coconut. Instead of using floury confections to create doughs and batters, Thais prefer recipes fashioned from or thickened with starchy tubers or other vegetables, such as pumpkin and taro, and they also tend to make their desserts less sweet.

Ice cold or steeping hot, Thais love their tea and coffee sweet. Not only is sugar added to the cup, but the whole beverage is topped off with sweetened condensed milk. Rare is the person who drinks a cup of black Thai coffee.

Saving the Best Bite for Last

One of the easiest desserts to find favor in Thai cooking is the classic mango with sticky rice. The sweetened rice is reminiscent of Western rice pudding, although without spices or raisins; instead, the best possible flavor for this dessert comes from beautifully ripe mangoes.

Fruit is a refreshing and popular meal-ender in such a hot climate, and if you're lucky enough to be in Thailand, there is no end to the natural treats to choose from. If the idea of fruit for dessert sounds a little too plain, a little too much like that apple for dessert while you're on a diet, then you haven't tried the fruits of Thailand!

There is something purely luxurious about reaching into a platter of sliced, reddish-fleshed papayas, circles of sugary pineapple, buttery baby bananas, ebony-seeded watermelon, and juicy lychees. Even the infamous durian, a fruit banned from Thai Airways flights because it smells somewhat like gym socks, offers a velvety texture and delicate flavor to those adventurous enough to try it.

More sugary options are the colorful gelatin desserts fashioned into tiny molds, and the refreshing bowls full of crushed ice, sugar syrup, and chopped fruit.

But true Thai craftsmanship comes into play with the miniature candies called *luk chup*. Made of mung bean paste, egg, sugar, and gelatin, the dough is turned into tiny, expertly carved fruit shapes and "painted" with food coloring. Think of it as Thai-style marzipan!

Coconut Custard with Glazed Bananas (Sangkaya)

In case you haven't had enough coconut milk throughout your Thai meal, here is a dessert that should do the trick! The traditional Thai method has been altered for the Western palate by using both coconut milk and heavy cream for the base. This combination gives the custard a creamier texture while retaining the coconut flavor. The bananas and sauce are a luscious addition.

Special tools: *Six 4-ounce heatproof custard cups*

Preparation time: *15 minutes*

Cooking time: *55 minutes*

Yield: *6 servings*

1½ cups coconut milk

1 cup heavy cream

⅔ cup palm sugar or light brown sugar

⅛ teaspoon salt

5 egg yolks

½ cup brown sugar

2 tablespoons coconut milk

1½ tablespoons water

1 tablespoon unsalted butter

2 medium bananas or 4 baby bananas, ripe but still firm, sliced into ¼-inch rounds

1 Heat the oven to 350 degrees. Combine the coconut milk, heavy cream, the ⅔ cup palm sugar, and salt together in a saucepan over medium-high heat, stirring until the sugar is dissolved. Do not boil. Place the egg yolks in a bowl and whisk in 1 to 2 tablespoons of the warm coconut milk mixture as shown in Figure 8-1. Continue whisking and slowly pouring in the warm liquid until completely blended with the eggs.

2 Divide the mixture evenly between the custard cups. Place the cups in a roasting pan and add enough hot water in the pan to come halfway up the sides of the cups. Bake until the custard is set, about 50 minutes.

3 Remove from the oven and allow to cool to room temperature before placing in the refrigerator. Chill for at least 3 hours.

4 Place the ½ cup brown sugar in a medium skillet and combine with 2 tablespoons coconut milk, water, and butter. Turn the heat to medium and stir for 1 minute, until the sugar and butter begin to melt. Continue cooking without stirring for 2 to 3 minutes, mix in the banana slices, and toss to coat, cooking 1 minute more. Serve the custards with warm banana slices and sauce on top.

Tip: *To ensure that the custard is done, insert the tip of a knife into the center of one custard. If the knife comes out clean, it's done. If not, continue baking for an additional 5 minutes. But don't overbake. The custard should still slightly jiggle when hot, but it will firm up once refrigerated.*

TEMPERING THE HOT LIQUID INTO THE EGG YOLKS

1. COMBINE THE COCONUT MILK, HEAVY CREAM, ⅔ CUP OF THE PALM SUGAR AND SALT TOGETHER IN A SAUCEPAN OVER MEDIUM-HIGH HEAT STIRRING UNTIL SUGAR IS DISSOLVED.

2. PLACE THE EGG YOLKS IN A BOWL AND WHISK IN 1 TO 2 TABLESPOONS OF THE WARM COCONUT MILK MIXTURE.

3 CONTINUE WHISKING AND SLOWLY POURING IN THE WARM LIQUID UNTIL COMPLETELY BLENDED WITH THE EGGS.

Figure 8-1:
Tempering
egg yolks.

Book VIII

Thai
Cooking

Sweet Sticky Rice with Mango Slices
(Koaw Niew Mamuang)

When mangoes are in season and at their most beautifully ripe, Thais love to pair them with sweetened sticky rice. Think of it as an Asian version of rice pudding. Cut bite-sized pieces of mango and eat it together with spoonfuls of the rice.

Preparation time: *15 minutes, plus 1 hour for soaking the rice and 30 minutes standing time for the rice*

Cooking time: *12 minutes*

Yield: *6 servings*

1½ cups sticky rice (glutinous)	¼ teaspoon salt
3 cups water	3 ripe mangoes
1 cup coconut milk	6 tablespoons coconut cream
3 to 4 tablespoons granulated sugar	

1 Soak the rice in an ample amount of water for 1 hour. To cook the rice, place it in a fine mesh strainer and rinse it under cold running water. When the water looks mostly clear, place the rice in a saucepan with the 3 cups water. Bring it to a boil, cover, and reduce the heat to medium-low. Cook the rice until the grains are fluffy and tender and the water has evaporated, about 10 minutes.

2 While the rice is cooking, combine the coconut milk, sugar, and salt together in a small saucepan. Stir over medium-low heat until the sugar dissolves. Do not boil. Pour the mixture over the warm rice and toss thoroughly until the rice is well coated. Put the cover back on the rice and allow it to sit for 30 minutes.

3 Meanwhile, peel and cut the mangoes into slices. Divide the mangoes among 6 serving plates. Place a large serving-size scoop of the rice in a mound next to the fruit. Drizzle coconut cream over the rice before serving.

Vary It! *Mangoes are a favorite choice for this dish, but creamy slices of ripe papaya make a nice variation.*

Coo-Coo for Condensed Milk

Just as canned coconut milk runs in a river throughout the Thai menu, canned condensed sweet milk also has a role to play. Condensed milk's most essential appearance is in two specialty drinks: Thai iced coffee and tea. Both coffee and tea are grown in Thailand, giving the beverages an even more local flavor.

Thai Iced Tea (Cha Thai)

The tea used for this beverage comes from tea leaves grown and processed in Thailand. The country's soil and climate seem to impart its own flavor into leaves that turn somewhat orange when brewed. In the packaged instant Thai teas you find in the grocery stores, the tea is combined sugar, non-dairy creamer, vanilla, spices, and artificial coloring. These teas do not require brewing or additional sugar.

Preparation time: *5 minutes, plus 5 minutes for steeping*

Yield: *4 servings*

4 cups water	*¼ cup sugar*
⅔ cup Thai tea leaves	*½ to ¾ cup sweetened condensed milk*

1 Bring the water to a boil in a medium saucepan. Stir in the tea leaves, remove from the heat, and allow to steep for 5 minutes.

2 Using a mesh strainer or coffee filter, strain the tea into a tall pitcher, mix in the sugar, and cool to room temperature. Cover and refrigerate until chilled.

3 Fill 4 tall glasses with ice. Pour the tea over the ice and float 2 to 3 tablespoons condensed milk on top. Serve with long iced tea spoons to allow your guests to stir their own tea.

Book VIII

Thai Cooking

Thai Iced Coffee (Oliang Thai)

As with the tea leaves, the coffee beans that come from Thailand are pre-packaged as a coarsely ground powder and blended with ground corn, soy, and sesame seeds, which give it its unique taste.

Preparation time: *5 minutes, plus 10 minutes for steeping*

Yield: *4 servings*

4 cups water	⅓ cup granulated sugar
½ cup Thai coffee powder	½ to ¾ cup sweetened condensed milk

1 Bring the water to a boil in a medium saucepan. Stir in the coffee powder, blending well. Remove from the heat, and allow to steep for 10 minutes.

2 Using the mesh strainer or coffee filter, strain the coffee into a tall pitcher, mix in the sugar, and cool to room temperature. Cover and refrigerate until chilled.

3 Fill 4 tall glasses with ice. Pour the coffee over the ice and float 2 to 3 tablespoons condensed milk on top. Serve with long iced tea spoons to allow your guests to stir their own coffee.

Index

Notes

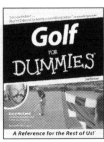

FOR DUMMIES®

A world of resources to help you grow

TRAVEL

0-7645-5453-0

0-7645-5438-7

0-7645-5444-1

Also available:

America's National Parks For Dummies
(0-7645-6204-5)

Caribbean For Dummies
(0-7645-5445-X)

Cruise Vacations For Dummies 2003
(0-7645-5459-X)

Europe For Dummies
(0-7645-5456-5)

Ireland For Dummies
(0-7645-6199-5)

France For Dummies
(0-7645-6292-4)

Las Vegas For Dummies
(0-7645-5448-4)

London For Dummies
(0-7645-5416-6)

Mexico's Beach Resorts For Dummies
(0-7645-6262-2)

Paris For Dummies
(0-7645-5494-8)

RV Vacations For Dummie
(0-7645-5443-3)

EDUCATION & TEST PREPARATION

0-7645-5194-9

0-7645-5325-9

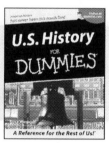

0-7645-5249-X

Also available:

The ACT For Dummies
(0-7645-5210-4)

Chemistry For Dummies
(0-7645-5430-1)

English Grammar For Dummies
(0-7645-5322-4)

French For Dummies
(0-7645-5193-0)

GMAT For Dummies
(0-7645-5251-1)

Inglés Para Dummies
(0-7645-5427-1)

Italian For Dummies
(0-7645-5196-5)

Research Papers For Dumr
(0-7645-5426-3)

SAT I For Dummies
(0-7645-5472-7)

U.S. History For Dummies
(0-7645-5249-X)

World History For Dummi
(0-7645-5242-2)

HEALTH, SELF-HELP & SPIRITUALITY

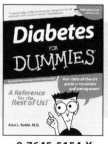

0-7645-5154-X

0-7645-5302-X

0-7645-5418-2

Also available:

The Bible For Dummies
(0-7645-5296-1)

Controlling Cholesterol For Dummies
(0-7645-5440-9)

Dating For Dummies
(0-7645-5072-1)

Dieting For Dummies
(0-7645-5126-4)

High Blood Pressure For Dummies
(0-7645-5424-7)

Judaism For Dummies
(0-7645-5299-6)

Menopause For Dummies
(0-7645-5458-1)

Nutrition For Dummies
(0-7645-5180-9)

Potty Training For Dummi
(0-7645-5417-4)

Pregnancy For Dummies
(0-7645-5074-8)

Rekindling Romance For Dummies
(0-7645-5303-8)

Religion For Dummies
(0-7645-5264-3)

Available wherever books are sold. Go to www.dummies.com or call 1-877-762-2974 to order direct

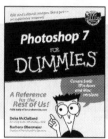

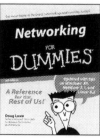